TECHNOLOGY IN ACTION

PREMIUM MEDIA SITE

Improve your grade with hands-on tools and resources!

- Master key terms and vocabulary
- Assess your knowledge with fun Crossword Puzzles and Jeopardy games
- Prepare for exams by taking practice quizzes

And for even more tools, you can access the following Premium Resources using your Access Code. Register now to get the most out of *Technology in Action!*

- Practice what you learn with interactive Active Helpdesk Calls*
- Use the Sound Byte lessons to practice your skills*
- Experience real-world computer situations with Simulations*
- *Check Your Understanding* section
- *Replay* videos from the authors provide a video review of each chapter Part in an easy-to-use format you can use on your phones, tablets, or computers!*

*Access code required for these premium resources

P9-AOO-435

Your Access Code is:

TIATEN-MUSIL-KULAK-BLIGH-DOLBY-ADOWA

Note: If there is no silver foil covering the access code, it may already have been redeemed, and therefore may no longer be valid. In that case, you can purchase online access using a major credit card or PayPal account. To do so, go to **www.pearsonhighered.com/techinaction**, select your book cover, click on "Buy Access" and follow the on-screen instructions.

To Register:

- To Start you will need a valid email address and this access code.
- Go to **www.pearsonhighered.com/techinaction** and scroll to find your text book.
- Once you've selected your text, on the Home Page, click the link to access the Student Premium Content.
- Click the Register button and follow the on-screen instructions.
- After you register, you can sign in any time via the log-in area on the same screen.

System Requirements

Windows 7 Ultimate Edition; IE 8
Windows Vista Ultimate Edition SP1; IE 8
Windows XP Professional SP3; IE 7
Windows XP Professional SP3; Firefox 3.6.4
Mac OS 10.5.7; Firefox 3.6.4
  Mac OS 10.6; Safari 5

Technical Support

http://247pearsoned.custhelp.com

Alan Evans • Kendall Martin • Mary Anne Poatsy

Technology in Action
Complete

Custom Edition for Western Illinois University

Taken from:
Technology in Action, Complete, Tenth Edition
by Alan Evans, Kendall Martin, Mary Anne Poatsy

Cover Art: Courtesy of Pearson Learning Solutions.

Taken from:

Technology in Action, Complete, Tenth Edition
by Alan Evans, Kendall Martin, Mary Anne Poatsy
Copyright © 2014, 2013, 2012 by Pearson Education, Inc.
Published by Prentice Hall
Upper Saddle River, New Jersey 07458

This special edition published in cooperation with Pearson Learning Solutions.

Pearson Learning Solutions, 501 Boylston Street, Suite 900, Boston, MA 02116
A Pearson Education Company
www.pearsoned.com

Printed in the United States of America

2 3 4 5 6 7 8 9 10 VOZN 18 17 16 15 14 13

000200010271771496

SR

ISBN 10: 1-269-34419-6
ISBN 13: 978-1-269-34419-7

Contents at a Glance

Contents

Chapter 1

Chapter 2

Chapter 4

Application Software: Programs That Let You
Work and Play 124

Chapter 5

System Software: The Operating System, Utility Programs, and File Management........................... 162

TECHNOLOGY IN FOCUS
Information Technology Ethics 206

Chapter 6

Understanding and Assessing Hardware: Evaluating Your System 226

Chapter 7

Networking: Connecting Computing Devices 262

Chapter 9

Securing Your System: Protecting Your Digital Data and Devices

TECHNOLOGY IN FOCUS

Chapter 11

Behind the Scenes: Databases and Information Systems

Dedication

For my wife, Patricia, whose patience, understanding, and support continue to make this work possible . . . especially when I stay up past midnight writing! And to my parents, Jackie and Dean, who taught me the best way to achieve your goals is to constantly strive to improve yourself through education.

Alan Evans

For all the teachers, mentors, and gurus who have popped in and out of my life.

Kendall Martin

For my husband, Ted, who unselfishly continues to take on more than his fair share to support me throughout this process, and for my children, Laura, Carolyn, and Teddy, whose encouragement and love have been inspiring.

Mary Anne Poatsy

What's New
Technology in Action, 10th Edition

We are delighted for you to explore the Tenth Edition of *Technology in Action*! This is an extensive revision that brings the content fully in line with 21st-century technology and students. All content has been updated and revised, the structure has been finely tuned, Part breaks have been added at logical stopping points in each chapter, and Windows 8 coverage has been included.

Additionally, we made the following enhancements:

- NEW *visual design* draws students in to the book and keeps them engaged by providing content in more consumable sections and by integrating images more effectively to illustrate difficult concepts visually and enhance the interest of charts and tables

- NEW *Chapter Parts* provide easier navigation and give students a mid-point review opportunity using the *Check Your Understanding* section

- NEW *Try This* section lets students try what they've been learning in a hands-on, step-by-step activity

- Enhanced visual chapter table of contents includes images that are repeated in the major chapter headings *and* in the Chapter Summary, providing a visual mnemonic for students

- Chapter objectives are now numbered and tied to the numbered objectives outlined in the Chapter Summary, providing a more integrated learning tool

And We Have New Media Offerings!

- All new *Interactive Game—Tech Town—*that can be used as homework, in-class activity, a lecture, assessment, supplemental activities, and more. The game is designed to engage students in learning about computer concepts by completing various missions and playing a variety of roles in technology scenarios. It's fun, assessable, and brings technology to life!

- NEW *Replay* videos from the authors provide a video review of each Chapter Part in an easy-to-use format students can view with their phones, tablets, or computers

- *Fully interactive eBook* available through MyITLab allows you to provide a completely digital solution for your students! The eBook is engaging, interactive, and provides an immersive learning experience where

students are using the technology they are learning about!

- And of course, the *HelpDesks* and *SoundBytes* continue to offer the hands-on, interactive lessons that let students take on the role of a helpdesk staffer, or get a quick lesson on a complex topic with a Sound Byte.

In addition to these changes, all chapters have been thoroughly updated with new images, current topics, and state-of-the art technology coverage. Some of the major chapter changes are listed here:

Chapter 1: Using Technology to Change the World

- Throughout the chapter, text has been updated and condensed, and figures and photos have been updated.

- NEW "Try This: Skyping Around the World" activity has been added.

Chapter 2: Looking at Computers: Understanding the Parts

- Throughout the chapter, text has been updated and condensed, and figures and photos have been updated.

- A Learning Objective related to power controls has been added in both the chapter table of contents and summary.

- Smartphones are now mentioned as types of computers.

- "Input Devices" section has been condensed and updated to reflect student knowledge of topics.

- "Dig Deeper: How Touch Screens Work" has been moved to earlier in the chapter, closer to the touch screen discussion.

- NEW "Try This: What's Inside My Computer?" activity has been added.

- Expanded discussion on input devices available for people with disabilities.

Chapter 3: Using the Internet: Making the Most of the Web's Resources

- Throughout the chapter, text has been updated and condensed, and figures and photos have been updated.

- NEW "How Cool Is This?" feature has been added on Google Goggles.
- A new timeline (How the Internet Began, Figure 3.1) has been added.
- NEW Bits & Bytes, "What's Your Pinterest?" (replaces one on Twitter)
- "Conducting Business Over the Internet: E-Commerce" has been revised to make the distinctions between types of e-commerce clearer, and a discussion of social commerce has been added.
- NEW "Try This: Create a SkyDrive Account and Store and Share Your Files in the Cloud" activity has been added.
- "Dig Deeper: The Semantic Web" has been condensed and moved earlier in the chapter.

Technology in Focus: The History of the PC (replaces Tech in Focus: Ethics in IT – moved to after Chapter 5).

- This Tech in Focus has been updated and condensed throughout. It is now placed later in the book, following Chapter 3.
- A new timeline (Timeline of Early Personal Computer Development, Figure 1) has been added.
- A number of new images have been added including images of a transistor, the Univac, and processor.

Chapter 4: Application Software: Programs That Let You Work and Play

- Throughout the chapter, text has been updated and condensed, and figures and photos have been updated.
- A Learning Objective has been revised to address ways in which students can access and use software.
- The previous edition Learning Objective related to drawing software is now part of the Learning Objective encompassing multimedia and entertainment software.
- The Learning Objectives on buying/installing/uninstalling software have been revised.
- NEW "Trends in IT: Mobile Commerce: What Have You Bought with Your Phone Lately?" replaces the previous edition Trends in IT on apps.

- NEW "Bits & Bytes: Alternatives to PowerPoint" has been added, with material taken from the deleted Tech in Focus Computing Alternatives feature.
- NEW "Bits & Bytes: Need to Work on Files Together? Try These Real-Time Collaboration Tools" has been added, replacing a PDF Bits & Bytes from the previous edition.
- NEW "Try This: Citing Website Sources" activity has been added.
- NEW "Bits & Bytes: Video File Formats for Portable Media Players" has been added.
- "Getting Help with Software" has been removed, with important pieces of the information mentioned in other places in the chapter.

Chapter 5: System Software: The Operating System, Utility Programs, and File Management

- Throughout the chapter, text has been updated and condensed, and figures and photos have been updated.
- Content throughout has been updated to include coverage of Windows 8.
- NEW "How Cool Is This?" feature has been added on iPhone custom vibration patterns.
- A new figure (Figure 5.12) has been added that illustrates how preemptive multitasking works.
- NEW "Try This: Adding Icons to the Start Screen in Windows 8" activity has been added.
- "The Windows Interface" section has been revised and updated to include coverage of Windows 8.
- NEW "Bits & Bytes: Touch Language for Windows 8" has been added.
- Bits & Bytes content on recovering a deleted file from the previous edition is now part of the regular text.

Technology in Focus: Information Technology Ethics (formerly after Chapter 3)

- This Tech in Focus has been updated and condensed throughout.
- The "Using Computers to Support Ethical Conduct" section is now at the end of the Tech in Focus.
- The Social Justice topic has been changed to "Brain Technology: Creating Cyborgs?"
- The Privacy topic has been changed to "Can Employers Peer into Your Personal Life?"

- The "Geolocation" section has been rewritten to focus on Foursquare and other technologies.

Chapter 6: Understanding and Assessing Hardware: Evaluating Your System

- Throughout the chapter, text has been updated and condensed, and figures and photos have been updated. The previous edition worksheets have been replaced with more visual summary figures.

- NEW "How Cool Is This?" feature has been added on the Nikisi ultrabook.

- NEW "Bits & Bytes: Not Much Power at All" has been added, replacing the "Taking Your System Out of the Box" and "Moving to a New Computer Doesn't Have to Be Painful" Bits & Bytes from the previous edition.

- NEW "Bits & Bytes: Where's the Free TV?" has been added, replacing the "HDTV on Your Notebook" Bits & Bytes from the previous edition.

- NEW "Try This: Measure Your System Performance" activity has been added.

- The "Ethics in IT" has changed titles, from "Free (as in Speech, not Beer)" to "Free Hardware for All" to better reflect content.

Chapter 7: Networking: Connecting Computing Devices

- Throughout the chapter, text has been updated and condensed, and figures and photos have been updated.

- The "Connecting to the Internet" section has been updated and revised substantially, with major emphasis shifting to wired and wireless connections.

- Revised "Bits & Bytes: How Do You Find Your Wi FI?" has been moved to this chapter from Chapter 8.

- NEW "Try This: Testing Your Wired and Wireless Internet Connection Speeds" activity has been added.

- The "Installing and Configuring Home Networks" section has been updated and revised substantially.

- A new "Bits & Bytes: Want to Use Your Phone as a Remote Control?" has been added.

- "Securing Wireless Networks" section now comes last in the chapter and has been updated thoroughly.

Technology in Focus: Under the Hood

- This Tech in Focus has been updated throughout, with many new photos.

- The "Number Systems" section has been revised to provide more headings to make the material easier for students to process.

- A new boxed feature on cache memory ("Using a Little Hideaway") has been added, replacing material in the regular text in the previous edition.

Chapter 8: Digital Devices and Media: Managing a Digital Lifestyle

- Throughout the chapter, text has been updated and condensed, and figures and photos have been updated.

- Learning Objectives have been revised to match revised chapter content.

- NEW "How Cool Is This?" feature has been added on the Pebble e-paper watch.

- Chapter has been reorganized to begin with a discussion of digital convergence and devices. Material explaining digital vs. analog formats has been moved to later in the chapter.

- NEW "Bits & Bytes: How Smart Is Your Phone?" has been added, replacing "Make Your Cell/Smartphone Deliver."

- NEW "Bits & Bytes: Texting for Change" has been added, replacing "411 for Answers."

- NEW "Bits & Bytes: Looking for the Perfect Cell Phone Plan? Try Bill Shrink" has been added.

- GPS section has moved and is now covered within the context of smartphones.

- The Trends in IT has been retitled from "Near Field Communication" to "NFC Chips: Do You Have a Digital Wallet?" to better reflect content and has been moved earlier in the chapter.

- NEW section "Tablets, Netbooks, and Ultrabooks" has been added, including some content from various locations in the previous edition chapter.

- NEW "Try This: Creating and Publishing a Movie" activity has been added.

- NEW "Dig Deeper: The Shift to Digital Music: A Bumpy Ride" has been added, including some content that was in the previous edition.

- NEW "Bits & Bytes: Need Money for Your Band? Try Indiegogo" has been added, replacing "Trick Out Your iTouch/iPhone."
- The "Digital Convergence" section from the previous edition has been revised and has been placed earlier in the chapter.

Chapter 9: Securing Your System: Protecting Your Digital Data and Devices

- Throughout the chapter, text has been updated and condensed, and figures and photos have been updated.
- Screenshots throughout have been updated to reflect Windows 8.
- The Learning Objective on social engineering has been revised to reflect reduced coverage of phishing.
- The firewall figure (Figure 9.14) has been clarified with callouts to increase student comprehension.
- NEW "Try This: Testing Your Network Security" activity has been added.

Technology in Focus: Careers in IT

- This Tech in Focus has been updated and condensed throughout.
- NEW box feature "Certifications: How Important Are They?" has been added using content from the previous edition.

Chapter 11: Behind the Scenes: Databases and Information Systems

- Throughout the chapter, text has been revised, updated, and condensed, and figures, screenshots, and photos have been updated.
- Learning Objectives have been revised in terms of their order to reflect chapter flow.
- NEW "How Cool Is This?" feature has been added on the Taps Form Database.
- "Database Types" section has been revised considerably to improve sequencing, with information on relational databases being moved here from other parts in the chapter.
- The "Relational Database Operations" section from the previous edition has now been worked into other sections.
- NEW "Try This: Using Excel's Database Functions" feature has been added.
- "Bits & Bytes: CRM Tools Go Online" has been deleted.

About the Authors

Alan Evans, MS, CPA
aevans@mc3.edu

Alan is currently a faculty member at Moore College of Art and Design and Montgomery County Community College, teaching a variety of computer science and business courses. He holds a BS in accounting from Rider University and an MS in information systems from Drexel University, and he is a certified public accountant. After a successful career in business, Alan finally realized that his true calling is education. He has been teaching at the college level since 2000. Alan enjoys giving presentations at technical conferences and meets regularly with computer science faculty and administrators from other colleges to discuss curriculum development and new methods of engaging students.

Kendall Martin, PhD
kmartin@mc3.edu

Kendall is an Associate Professor at Montgomery County Community College with teaching experience at both the undergraduate and graduate levels at a number of institutions, including Villanova University, DeSales University, Ursinus College, and Arcadia University.

Kendall's education includes a BS in electrical engineering from the University of Rochester and an MS and a PhD in engineering from the University of Pennsylvania. She has industrial experience in research and development environments (AT&T Bell Laboratories), as well as experience with several start-up technology firms.

Mary Anne Poatsy, MBA
mpoatsy@mc3.edu

Mary Anne is a senior faculty member at Montgomery County Community College, teaching various computer application and concepts courses in face-to-face and online environments. She enjoys speaking at various professional conferences about innovative classroom strategies. She holds a BA in psychology and education from Mount Holyoke College and an MBA in finance from Northwestern University's Kellogg Graduate School of Management.

Mary Anne has been in teaching since 1997, ranging from elementary and secondary education to Montgomery County Community College, Gwynedd-Mercy College, Muhlenberg College, and Bucks County Community College, as well as training in the professional environment. Before teaching, she was a vice president at Shearson Lehman Hutton in the Municipal Bond Investment Banking Department.

Acknowledgments

First, we would like to thank our students. We constantly learn from them while teaching, and they are a continual source of inspiration and new ideas.

We could not have written this book without the loving support of our families. Our spouses and children made sacrifices (mostly in time not spent with us) to permit us to make this dream into a reality.

Although working with the entire team at Pearson has been a truly enjoyable experience, a few individuals deserve special mention. The constant support and encouragement we receive from Jenifer Niles, Executive Acquisitions Editor, and Michael Payne, Editor in Chief, continually make this book grow and change. Our heartfelt thanks go to Shannon LeMay-Finn, our Developmental Editor. Shannon, who returns to the *Technology in Action* project this edition, was our original DE on the first three editions. Her creativity, drive, and management skills helped make this book a reality. And given the changes we made this edition, having her return to the project was a critical component in continuing to deliver this innovative product! In addition, Keri Rand, our Editorial Project Manager, did a fantastic job of coordinating all details of the project, and was especially helpful as we rolled out a new interior design. We also would like to extend our appreciation to Rhonda Aversa, our Production Project Manager, who works tirelessly to ensure that our book is published on time and looks fabulous. The timelines are always short, the art is complex, and there are many people with whom she has to coordinate tasks. But she makes it look easy! We'd like to extend our thanks to the media and myITlab team: Eric Hakanson, Taylor Ragan, Jaimie Noy, and Jessica Brandi for all of their hard work and dedication.

There are many people whom we do not meet in person at Pearson and elsewhere who make significant contributions by designing the book, illustrating, composing the pages, producing multimedia, and securing permissions. We thank them all. We would also like to thank the supplement authors for this edition: Wanda Gibson, Julie Boyles, Lisa Hawkins, Terry Holly, Abigail Miller, Stephanie Emrich, Doug Courter, Lori Damanti, Susan Fry, Tony Nowakowski, Sara Buscaino, Sharon Behrens, Diane Coyle, and Stacy Everly.

And finally, we would like to thank the reviewers and the many others who contribute their time, ideas, and talents to this project. We appreciate their time and energy, as their comments help us turn out a better product each edition.

10th Edition Reviewers

Pearson and the authors would like to thank the following people for their help and time in making this book what it is. We couldn't publish this book without their contributions.

Alexis Stull	Fairmont State University
Amy Roche	Northampton Community College
Amy Rutledge	Oakland University
Ann Taff	Tulsa Community College
Barbara Garrell	Delaware County Community College
Benjamin Marrero	Ivy Tech
Brian Powell	West Virginia University
Carolyn Barren	Macomb Community College
Casey Wilhelm	North Idaho College
Charles R. Whealton	Delaware Technical and Community College
ChongWoo Park	Georgia Gwinnett College
Christie Jahn Hovey	Lincoln Land Community College
Cliff Sherrill	Yavapai College
David Kerven	Georgia Gwinnett College
David R. Surma	Indiana University South Bend
Deidre Grafel	Chandler-Gilbert Community College
Denise Sullivan	Westchester Community College
Donald Riggs	Schenectady County Community College
Dr. Kate LeGrand	Broward College
Eric Cameron	Passaic County Community College
Faye Tippey	Ivy Tech
Gene Carbonaro	Long Beach City College
Gina Bowers-Miller	Harrisburg Area Community College
Holly Gould	Ivy Tech
James R. Anthos	South University
James Taggart	Atlantic Cape Community College
Janet Gelb	Grossmont College
Jessica Helberg	Northern Virginia Community College
Jill Canine	Ivy Tech
Joyce Thompson	Lehigh Carbon Community College
Juliana Cypert	Tarrant County College
Karen Allen	Community College of Rhode Island
Kari Walters	Louisiana State University
Kate LeGrand	Broward College

Kemit Grafton	Oklahoma State University-Oklahoma City
Laurie Wallmark	Raritan Valley Community College
Linda Arnold	Harrisburg Area Community College
Lisa A. Hawkins	Frederick Community College
Lisa Jackson	Phoenix College
Lynne Lyon	Durham College
Mark Connell	State University of New York at Cortland
Mary Zegarski	Northampton Community College
Michele Smolik	Columbia College
Mike Puopolo	Bunker Hill Community College
Nancy Evans	Indiana University-Purdue University Indianapolis
Natalia Grigoriants	Pierce College
Neal Stenlund	Northern Virginia Community College
Paul Koester	Tarrant County College, Northwest
Phil Whitney	Bakersfield College
Rebecca Giorcelli	Fairmont State University
Rick Barnes	Catawba Valley Community College
Roger Young	Ivy Tech
Scott Rosen	Santa Rosa Junior College
Stacia Dutton	SUNY Canton
Stacy Ward	Grafton High School
Steve St. John	Tulsa Community College - Northeast Campus
Susan Fry	Boise State University
Susan LaBrie	Northampton Community College
Sylvia Emerson	Rock Valley College
Terri Helfand	Chaffey College
Terry Rigsby	Hill College
Thomas Yip	Passaic County Community College
Tiffany Johnson	Tulsa Community College
Tom Foston	Chandler-Gilbert Community College
Valerie Golay	Ivy Tech
Vicki Brooks	Columbia College
Kae Cooper	BCTC/KCTCS

Letter from the Authors
Our 10th Edition—A Letter from the Authors

Why We Wrote This Book

The past 10 years have been an incredible time for those of us who love technology. It's hard to believe that when we began to write the first edition of *Technology in Action*, Apple was struggling to make a profit and the world had not heard of Skype, Firefox, and Gmail, not to mention the iPhone, iPad, and Angry Birds.

Even the most agile of learners and educators need support in keeping up with this pace of change. As was the case from the very first edition, with this, our 10th edition, we have strived to make *Technology in Action* a learning system that pushes the envelope of what is possible in technology, and what is helpful in teaching. In short: we have worked hard to build a text that fits the way students are learning now.

Our combined almost 50 years of teaching computer concepts have coincided with sweeping innovations in computing technology that have affected every facet of society. From iPads to Web 2.0, computers are more than ever a fixture of our daily lives—and the lives of our students. But although today's students have a much greater comfort level with their digital environment than previous generations, their knowledge of the machines they use every day is still limited.

Part of the student-centered focus of our book has to do with making the material truly engaging to students. From the beginning, we have written *Technology in Action* to focus on what matters most to today's student. Instead of a history lesson on the microchip, we focus on tasks students can accomplish with their computing devices and skills they can apply immediately in the workplace, the classroom, and at home.

We strive to keep the text as current as publishing timelines allow, and we are constantly looking for the next technology trend or gadget. We have augmented the text with weekly technology updates to help you keep your classroom on top of the latest breaking developments and continue to include a number of multimedia components to enrich the classroom and student learning experience. The result is a learning system that sparks student interest by focusing on the material they want to learn (such as how to integrate computing devices into a home network) while teaching the material they need to learn (such as how networks work). The sequence of topics is carefully set up to mirror the typical student learning experience.

As they read through this text, your students will progress through stages of increasing difficulty:

1. Thinking about how technology offers them the power to change their society and their world
2. Examining why it's important to be computer fluent
3. Understanding the basic components of computing devices
4. Connecting to and exploring the Internet
5. Exploring software
6. Learning the operating system and personalizing their computer

7. Evaluating and upgrading computing devices

8. Understanding home networking options and keeping computing devices safe from hackers

9. Going mobile with smartphones, netbooks, tablets, and laptops

10. Going behind the scenes, looking at technology in greater detail

We continue to structure the book in a "spiraling" manner, intentionally introducing on a basic level in the earlier chapters concepts that students traditionally have trouble with and then later expanding on those concepts in more detail when students have become more comfortable with them. Thus, the focus of the early chapters is on practical uses for the computer, with real-world examples to help the students place computing in a familiar context.

For example, we introduce basic hardware components in Chapter 2, and then we go into increasingly greater detail on some hardware components in Chapter 6 and in the "Under the Hood" Technology in Focus feature. The Behind the Scenes chapters venture deeper into the realm of computing through in-depth explanations of how programming, networks, the Internet, and databases work. They are specifically designed to keep more experienced students engaged and to challenge them with interesting research assignments.

For the 10th edition, we've made a number of exciting changes in response to student and instructor feedback. Major enhancements include:

- A **new and fresh design** that captures the excitement of the material in a more visual format and that encourages students to read the book and makes it more visually interesting when they do.

- A **two-part structure in each chapter** to make learning and digesting the content even more manageable for students.

- A Check Your Understanding **mini-quiz** at the end of each part that lets students easily see if they've mastered the main concepts they just read.

- A new **Try This section** in the middle of each chapter that provides a hands-on, step-by-step activity for students to try.

- A **more visual, more concise text** that includes visual elements to relay and review concepts while replacing (or reducing) large blocks of text. We've also improved the visual table of contents so that it ties into the chapter heads and summary to help learners find material more quickly and associate it more easily.

- **New Replay Videos** that let students visually review concepts they've learned in each part of a chapter. Students can even view Replay Videos on their phones, a feature that students demanded.

- An **improved and enhanced electronic version** of *Technology in Action* that delivers a truly interactive electronic product to students on their tablets, phones, and computers.

Throughout the years we have also developed a comprehensive multimedia program to reinforce the material taught in the text and to support both classroom lectures and distance learning:

- The **Helpdesk training content**, created specifically for *Technology in Action*, enables students to take on the role of a helpdesk operator and work through common questions asked by computer users.

- Exciting **Sound Byte multimedia**—fully integrated with the text—expand student mastery of complex topics.

- The **Tech Bytes Weekly updates** deliver the latest technology news stories to you for use in your classroom. Each is accompanied by specific discussion topics and activities to expand on what is within the textbook materials.

This book is designed to reach the students of the 21st century and prepare them for the role they can take in their own community and the world. It has been an honor to work with you over the past 10 years to present and explain new technologies to students, and to show them the rapidly growing importance of technology in our world.

Visual Walk-Through

Topic Sequence

Concepts are covered in a spiraling manner between chapters to mirror the typical student learning experience.

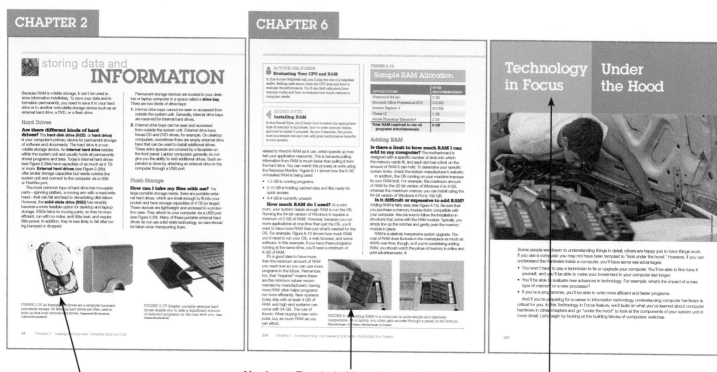

Hardware First Introduced
Chapter 2 is the first time students read about introductory hardware. It's covered at the beginning level because this is students' experience level at this point of the book.

Hardware Taught in More Depth in Additional Chapters
In later chapters, students read about hardware in greater depth because they're more experienced and comfortable working with their computers.

Technology in Focus
Four special features that teach key uses of technology today.

Multimedia Cues
Visual integration of multimedia.

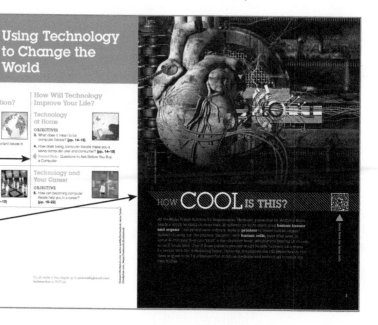

How Cool Is This?
Highlights the latest and greatest websites, gadgets, and multimedia.

Student Textbook

ethics in IT
The Digital Divide and the Mobile Bridge

FIGURE 1.5 Can we bridge the digital divide through mobile devices? Should we?

trends in IT
Innovations in Printing

FIGURE 2.46 Cloud-ready printers only need an Internet connection to be accessed from any mobile device.

DIG DEEPER
Making Reality Even More Real

Ethics in IT
Boxes examine the ethical dilemmas involved with technology.

Trends in IT
Boxes explore hot topics in computing.

Dig Deeper
Boxes cover technical topics in depth to challenge advanced students.

BITS&BYTES
Putting Your Computer to Work…While You Sleep

Bits & Bytes
Help make the topics immediately relevant to students' lives.

Check Your Understanding
Multiple Choice, True-False, and Critical Thinking

Try This
Activity found between Parts 1 and 2 of each chapter.

check your understanding//

TRY THIS
What's Inside My Computer?

The Multimedia

Companion Website
Includes an interactive study guide, online end-of-chapter material, additional Internet exercises, and much more.

pearsonhighered.com/techinaction

Transcript button
Used to turn transcript on or off

Sound Bytes
Multimedia lessons with video, audio, or animation and corresponding labs featuring multiple-choice quizzing.

Also available as podcasts.

Navigational tool

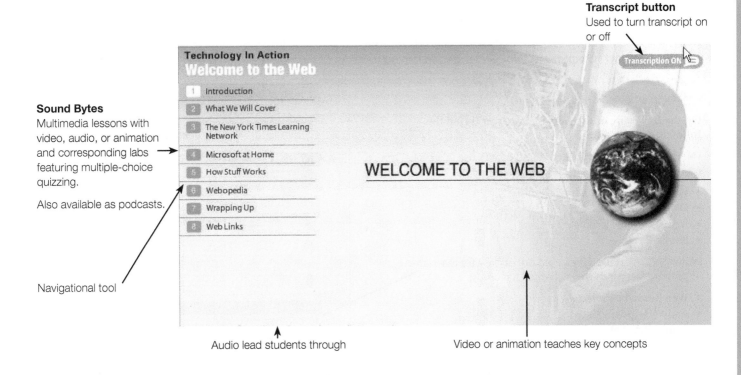

Audio lead students through

Video or animation teaches key concepts

Active Helpdesk
Interactive training that puts the student in the role of a helpdesk staffer fielding questions from callers.

Supervisor available to assist students.

Features textbook page references within each call and assessment at the end of each call.

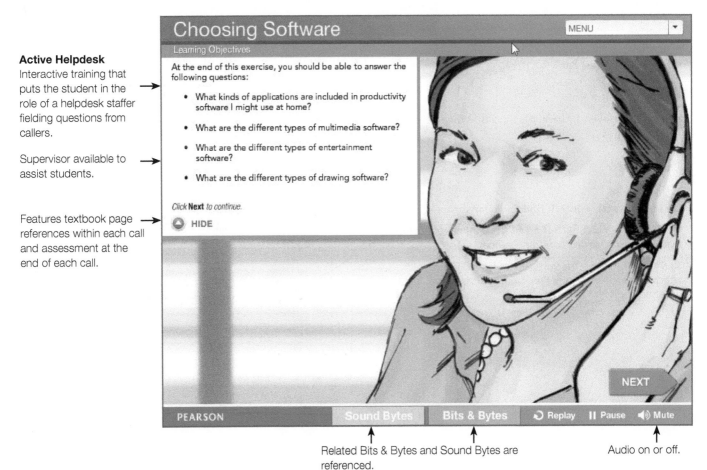

Related Bits & Bytes and Sound Bytes are referenced.

Audio on or off.

Annotated Instructor Edition

Provided with each chapter are two divider pages like the ones outlined below.

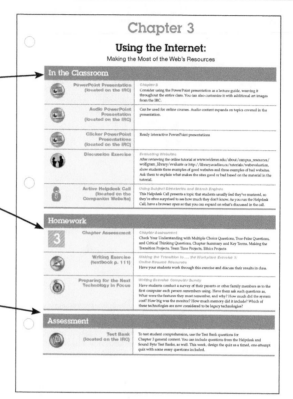

FRONT OF CHAPTER TAB

On the front side of each chapter tab, you'll find the following categories:

IN THE CLASSROOM: Activities you can use in a classroom or in online classes, including:

- **PowerPoint Presentations**
- **Discussion Exercises**
- **Active Helpdesk Calls**
- **Sound Bytes**

HOMEWORK: Activities used out of class for assessment or preparation for the next chapter, including:

- **Web Resource Projects**
- **Active Helpdesk Calls**
- **Sound Byte Labs**

ASSESSMENT:

- **Blackboard**
- **WebCT**
- **TestGen**
- **myitlab**
- **Student Text Test Bank**
- **Sound Byte Test Bank**
- **Help Desk Test Bank**

The back side of each chapter tab includes the relevant Try This exercise.

ETHICS TAB

On the Ethics tab, you will find the following:

OPPOSING VIEWPOINTS TABLE: Outlines ethics topics that you can use to debate in the classroom.

KEYWORDS: Provides you with additional words with which to search the Internet for more information related to the ethics topic.

Instructor Resources

Instructor Resources

Online Instructor Resources Include:

- PowerPoint Presentations
- Clicker PowerPoint Presentations
- Student Text Test Bank
- Sound Byte Test Bank
- Help Desk Test Bank
- End of Chapter Answer Keys
- Rubrics

- Web Resources
- Image Library
- Sample Syllabi
- Additional Web Projects
- What's New in 10e
- Transition Guide
- TestGen

**Technology In Action
Complete, 10/E**
Alan Evans
Kendall Martin
Mary Anne Poatsy

ISBN-10: 0133056228
ISBN-13: 9780133056228

Contact your local Pearson sales rep to learn more about the
Technology in Action instructional system.

1 Using Technology to Change the World

How Will You Put Technology in Action?

Technology on the World Stage

OBJECTIVE

1. How can becoming proficient with technology help you understand and participate in important issues in the world at large? **(pp. 4–6)**

Technology and Our Society

OBJECTIVE

2. How can knowledge of technology help you influence the direction our society takes? **(pp. 8–10)**

How Will Technology Improve Your Life?

Technology at Home

OBJECTIVES

3. What does it mean to be computer literate? **(pp. 14–15)**

4. How does being computer literate make you a savvy computer user and consumer? **(pp. 14–15)**

🔊 **Sound Byte:** Questions to Ask Before You Buy a Computer

Technology and Your Career

OBJECTIVE

5. How can becoming computer literate help you in a career? **(pp. 16–22)**

For all media in this chapter go to **pearsonhighered.com/techinaction** or MyITLab.

(iconeer/iStockphoto; carlos castilla/Shutterstock; Jesus Conde/iStockphoto; Sergej Khakimullin/Shutterstock)

(Science Photo Library/Alamy)

HOW COOL IS THIS?

Scan here for more info

At the Wake Forest Institute for Regenerative Medicine, researcher Dr. Anthony Atala heads a group working on more than 30 different projects developing **human tissues and organs**. One project uses ordinary desktop **printers** to create human organs! Instead of using ink, the printers "bioprint" with **human cells,** layer after layer. In about 40 minutes they can "print" a two-chamber heart, which starts beating on its own about 5 hours later. One of these portable printers would be able to create skin onsite for people with life-threatening burns. Currently, the printers are still experimental, but there is great hope for advances that combine medicine and technology to repair our own bodies.

How Will You Put Technology in Action?

Ask yourself: Why are you in this class? Maybe it's a requirement for your degree, or maybe you want to improve your computer skills. But let's step back and look at the bigger picture.

Technology today is not just a means for career advancement or merely a skill set needed to survive in society. It's a tool that enables us all to make an impact beyond our own lives. We've all seen the movies that dangle the dream in front of us of being the girl or guy who saves the world—and gets to drive a nice car while doing it! Whether it's *Transformers* or *Spider-Man,* we are drawn to heroes because we want our work and our lives to mean something and to benefit others.

Technology can be your ticket to doing just that, to influencing and participating in projects that will change the world. We'd like to ask you to think about how your talents and skills in technology will let you contribute on a larger scale, beyond the benefits they will bring to you personally.

 technology on the
WORLD STAGE

Recent political and global issues are showing that technology is accelerating change around the world and galvanizing groups of people in new ways. Let's look at a few examples.

Political Issues

Egypt. At the end of 2010, a series of revolutions took place across the Arab and North African regions fueled by social networking tools like Facebook and Twitter. These **social networking** tools enable the gathering together of groups of people to connect and exchange ideas, and they brought together people facing repression and censorship in many countries in this region.

The powerful uprising in Egypt is one example of the impact an individual armed with an understanding of modern technology can have. The reigning government in Egypt had been in power for over 30 years. In June 2010, after Egyptian businessman Khaled Said was killed by authorities, Wael Ghonim, a Google marketing manager in Egypt, anonymously launched the Facebook page "We Are All Khaled Said." The Facebook page became a tool that made people aware there were others who were dissatisfied with the direction of the country. By January 2011, the government responded to the increasing unrest online by "turning off" Egypt's Internet. The government told the four largest Internet providers to shut down and thus closed access to 93 percent of Egyptian networks. Protests against this shutdown turned violent, and Egyptian Internet providers began to restore service a few days later.

Back in the virtual world of Facebook and Twitter, thousands offered ideas on how they could protest meaningfully. Finally, a silent gathering near the sea in Alexandria, Egypt, was chosen. This movement from "virtual community" to physical community (see Figure 1.1)

FIGURE 1.1 How much of a role did social media play in the transfer of power in Egypt in 2011? *(AP Photo/Muhammed Abu Zaid)*

was a turning point, and in February 2011, President Hosni Mubarak of Egypt resigned.

Social networking tools are providing a level of instant connection and information distribution that is reshaping the world. For Wael Ghonim, it led to an opportunity to recast the future of his country. What can you do with social networking tools that will change the future of your community?

Kenya. Another example of technology influencing society recently occurred in Kenya. In December 2007, the closest election in Kenya's history ended with the current president declaring victory despite allegations of electoral fraud. Nairobi lawyer Ory Okolloh began to get messages describing acts of violence occurring all over the country. She tried to post the messages on her blog, *KenyanPundit,* but was quickly overwhelmed. She put out a request for help through the blog.

Within 72 hours, two programmers, Erik Hersman and Juliana Rotich, had created Ushahidi (Swahili for "testimony"). It is a **crisis-mapping tool** that collects

FIGURE 1.2 The Ushahidi crisis-mapping tool saved lives during the Kenyan elections, but now it is also used for many other purposes, like finding the nearest Fair Trade store at **ftrn.org/ispotfairtrade**.

information from e-mails, text messages, blog posts, and Twitter tweets and then maps them, instantly making the information publicly available. The developers then made Ushahidi a free platform anyone in the world can use. To date, it has been used during the earthquakes and tsunami in Japan, to battle election violence in the Democratic Republic of Congo, to help people in Somalia have a voice, and to make it easier to locate the nearest store that supports Fair Trade practices (see Figure 1.2). In what other ways could technology help us face times of crisis?

Other Global Issues

Political crises are not the only arena in which technology is enabling global change.

Health Care. Infectious diseases account for about one-fifth of all deaths worldwide. Researchers say the odds of a flu pandemic occurring in the next century are nearly 100 percent. Could technology help us develop and deliver vaccines in a way that saves lives? With newer scientific visualization tools, scientists are developing antibodies for flu viruses and even HIV, viruses that are difficult to target because they continually change shape. Computationally intense modeling software is helping researchers increase the pace of vaccine production, saving lives.

Retinal prosthetics are another example of global health concerns being addressed with technology. Macular degeneration and retinitis pigmentosa are two diseases that destroy the retina; they account for the majority of blindness in developing nations. Sheila Nirenberg of Cornell University is working on a microchip that can replace the function of the retina, translating incoming light into the electrical pulses the brain needs for vision. These biomedical chips could restore quality vision to the blind.

The Environment. What if every cell phone in the world had built-in atmospheric sensors? Then millions of points of air and water quality data from around the world could be constantly acquired. Tagged with geographical information, the data could alert scientists to new trends in our environment. And what if phone sensors could monitor for flu viruses? We could protect ourselves from pandemics by identifying outbreaks very early. Ideas like these are being explored by University of California, Los Angeles researcher Dr. Deborah Estrin, the director at the Center for Embedded Networked Sensing. Can you think of other ways you could use your cell phone to improve society?

The Digital Divide. There is a great gap between the levels of Internet access and the availability of technical tools in different regions of the world. The term coined for this difference in ease of access to technology is the **digital divide**. One danger of a digital divide is that it prevents us from using all the minds on the planet to solve the planet's problems. But this challenge created by technology is also being answered by technology.

The Next Einstein Initiative (NEI) is a plan to focus resources on the talented mathematical minds of Africa (see Figure 1.3). By expanding the African Institute for Mathematical Sciences (AIMS) across the continent, the future of Africa can be profoundly changed. Cambridge professor Neil Turok founded AIMS to bring together the brightest young minds across Africa with the best lecturers in the world. The NEI has won funding from Google's Project 10^{100}, an initiative to award $10 million to a set of five projects, selected by open public voting. By capturing the enthusiasm of the world with presentations distributed through TED (**ted.com**) and Project 10^{100}, there is now a push to create 15 additional AIMS centers across Africa.

Figure 1.4 shows additional examples of people putting technology into action to impact the world. How will you join them? ◼

FIGURE 1.3 The Next Einstein Initiative is rallying the support of the world to identify mathematical genius.
(The Next Einstein Initiative)

FIGURE 1.4

Technology in Action: Taking on Global Problems

PERSON/ ORGANIZATION		GLOBAL PROBLEM	TECHNOLOGY USED	ACTION	FIND OUT MORE . . .
Peter Gabriel/ The Witness Project		Human rights abuses	Video cameras	Provide video documentation of human rights abuses; the project contributed to the arrest of warlords in the Democratic Republic of Congo for the recruitment of child soldiers	The Witness Project: **witness. org**
Johnny Lee/Google		The digital divide prevents many from taking advantage of modern learning devices like smartboards	Nintendo Wii remote and open source software	Enables users to create a smartboard for $50; the smartboard can record and store lecture content and is touch sensitive	Johnny Lee's blog: **procrastineering. blogspot.com**
United Nations World Food Programme (WFP)		One in seven people in the world do not get enough food to eat	GIS (geographical information systems) and mobile devices	The WFP can analyze the location and need for food, positioning food where it will help the most	World Food Programme: **wfp.org**
Hod Lipson and Evan Malone/The Fab@Home Project		Cost and access barriers prevent people from having basic devices, gears, and parts	3-D printers and open source software	Printers enable users to fabricate 3-D objects such as electrical parts	Fab@Home: **fabathome.org**
Massachusetts Institute of Technology (MIT) Center for Future Civic Media		Disposal of so many display devices into landfills	Software that allows multiple displays to connect and be reused	The software enables users to create one huge display device from a set of smaller units, thereby keeping monitors out of landfills	Junkyard Jumbotron: **jumbotron.media. mit.edu**

ethics in IT

FIGURE 1.5 Can we bridge the digital divide through mobile devices? Should we? *(EIGHTFISH/Alamy)*

The digital divide, the gap between those with easy access to technology and those with little to no access (see Figure 1.5), is a problem that leads to complex social issues. For those who lack access to the Internet and computers, it is difficult to develop computer skills, which are very often critical to future success. Less familiarity with the Internet can also lead to a lower level of active, engaged citizenship. So how should we attack the problem of the digital divide in the United States?

Recent studies from the University of Michigan show that without Internet access at home, teens from low-income households (family income under $30,000 a year) are more likely than their wealthier counterparts to use their cell phones to go online. So the widening penetration of cell phones might be the answer to ending the digital divide. Or is it?

Going online using a cell phone plan is the most expensive of all options, and data transfer speeds are often slow. So teens with the least money are likely paying the most to get the slowest online experience. And they are more likely paying for it themselves, as opposed to teens from wealthier households in which, according to the same University of Michigan study, the teens are more likely to be on family plans paid for by someone else.

In addition, teen cell phone usage is limited to managing online social networks, playing games, or listening to music. Computer tasks and skills that could lead to economic advancement, like filling out job applications or running a business, are not yet handled easily on mobile devices. So by not having free Internet access available, is our society placing those groups least able to afford access at an unfair disadvantage?

Will the increasing penetration of smartphones and faster cellular Internet access eliminate the digital divide in the United States? Should our government intervene and make sure there is sufficient free Internet access for all? Is it ethical to deprive the poorer segment of our society of a needed commodity? Answering challenging questions like these is part of being an informed citizen.

technology and
OUR SOCIETY

Technology is also allowing us to redefine very fundamental parts of our social makeup—how we think, how we connect with each other, and how we purchase and consume products.

Technology Impacts How We Think

What We Think About. What do you think about in your free time? In the late twentieth century, a common trend was to think about what to buy next—or perhaps what to watch or listen to next. Information and products were being served up at an amazing rate, and a pattern of consumption became habit. As more and more web applications began to appear that allowed each individual to become a "creator" of the web, a new kind of Internet came into being. It was nicknamed **Web 2.0**, and it had a set of new features and functionality that allowed users to contribute content easily and to be easily connected to each other. Now everyone could collaborate internationally at the click of a mouse.

Web 2.0 has fostered a dramatic shift across the world from simply consuming to having the ability to volunteer and collaborate on projects. In his book *Cognitive Surplus: Creativity and Generosity in a Connected Age,* author Clay Shirky created the term **cognitive surplus** to mean the combination of leisure time and the tools to be creative. The world's population has an estimated one trillion hours a year of free time. When coupled with the available media tools and the easy connectivity of Web 2.0, and with generosity and a need to share, projects like Ushahidi and the Witness Project (see Figure 1.4) emerge.

But why would anyone bother to work on projects like these in their free time? Modern theories of motivation show that what pushes people to apply their free time in altruistic causes, for no money, is the excitement of autonomy, mastery, and purpose (see Figure 1.6):

- **Autonomy:** the freedom to work without constant direction and control.
- **Mastery:** the feeling of confidence and excitement from seeing your own skills progress.
- **Purpose:** the understanding that you are working for something larger than yourself.

Together, these three factors play into how we are fundamentally wired and can produce incredibly motivated behavior. The combination of motivation, technology, and a cognitive surplus is leading to powerful projects that are changing the world.

Technology Impacts How We Connect

Connecting Through Music. In many societies, people connect intimately in gatherings and local celebrations through shared experiences. Technology like classical composer and conductor Eric Whitacre's Virtual Choir has added breadth to this aspect of our lives. Whitacre began the idea of a virtual choir by posting to YouTube a video of himself conducting one of his works, "Lux Aurumque." The idea was that listeners would follow his lead and, as they heard the piano track, each would record their part of the piece as either a soprano, an alto,

FIGURE 1.6 Our understanding of human motivation can play a role in our use of technology to impact society.

a tenor, or a bass. The submitted videos were edited together, the audio was aligned, and the first piece from the Virtual Choir was released, with 50 recorded voices. A blog connects the members of the choir and builds a real sense of community between members. A glance at the Virtual Choir Map (**ericwhitacre.com/the-virtual-choir/map**) shows the physical location of each voice (see Figure 1.7).

Connecting Through Business. One of the most profound ways we can connect with each other is to support other people's dreams. Kickstarter (**kickstarter.com**) helps us connect in this way by allowing people to post their ideas for community projects, games, and inventions and to ask for funding directly. Donors are given rewards for different levels of pledges, such as a signed edition of a book or a special color of a product. This style of generating capital to start a business is known as **crowdfunding**, asking for small donations from a large number of people, often using the Internet.

Technology Impacts How We Consume

Technology is changing all aspects of how we purchase and consume goods—from strategies for convincing you to purchase a certain product to the mechanics of how you buy and own things.

Marketing. New strategies in marketing are counting on the fact that most people have a cell phone with a camera and Internet access. A technology called **QR (quick response) codes** lets any piece of print host a link to online information and video content. From your smartphone, simply run your QR app and hold the phone near the QR image anywhere you see it—like the one you see here and on page 3 of this chapter. Your phone scans the QR image and then takes you to a website, video, schedule, or Facebook page for more information about the product.

Studies show 82 percent of shoppers go to the Internet on their cell phone before they make a purchase. They are often using so-called location-aware price comparison tools. Apps like ShopSavvy and RedLaser scan the bar code of the item and then compare prices with those of nearby stores and with the best prices available online. Techy shoppers can then get "mobile coupons" (or *mobicoupons*) delivered to their cell phones thanks to sites like Zavers and Cellfire. The future promises specialized coupons created just for you based on your location and past buying preferences.

FIGURE 1.7 The Virtual Choir 3 performance of "Water Night" included over 3,700 singers from 73 countries.

Marketers also have to be aware of the phenomenon of **crowdsourcing**—checking in with the voice of the crowd. Consumers are using apps like MobileVoice to check people's verdicts on the quality of items. Forward-thinking companies are using this input to improve their products and services. AT&T, for example, has an app that lets customers report locations of coverage gaps.

Access Versus Ownership.   Even the idea of ownership is evolving thanks to new technologies. Items like cars and bikes can become "subscriptions" instead of large one-time purchases. For example, ZipCar allows hundreds of thousands of people to use shared cars, and Call a Bike is a popular bike-renting program in Germany. With ZipCar, a phone call or online reservation activates your personal ZipCard. This card allows you to automatically open the door of the car you have reserved, and away you drive. GPS technology is used to track where the car is, whether it has been dropped off at the right location, and how far it has been driven. In Germany, racks of Call a Bikes are located at major street corners in large cities (see Figure 1.8). Simply call the phone number printed on the bike and it texts you a code to unlock the bike. When you're done riding the bike, simply relock it and you're billed automatically.

These subscription-style business models are spreading now to smaller goods. Swap.com helps people trade books, video games, and DVDs with one another, using the power of peer-to-peer connections, for example, to find the best set of matches for a used Portal game in exchange for a season of *Curb Your Enthusiasm*.

Rachel Botsman and Roo Rogers make the case in their book *What's Mine Is Yours: The Rise of Collaborative Consumption* that the real fuel beneath these services is a shift in our acceptance of sharing. **Collaborative consumption** implies that we are joining together as a group to use a specific product more efficiently. We are so constantly connected with each other that we have again found the power of community. There are increasing opportunities to redistribute the things we have purchased and to share the services a product provides instead of owning it outright. Add in the pressure of mounting environmental concerns and a global financial crisis, and we are migrating toward collaborative consumption. ■

Before moving on to Part 2:
• Watch Replay Video 1.1 ▶.
• Then check your understanding of what you've learned so far.

FIGURE 1.8 Call a Bike uses digital technology to change our lifestyle from one of ownership to one of subscription. *(Ernst Klinker/Alamy)*

For a quick review to see what you've learned so far, answer the following questions. Visit **pearsonhighered.com/techinaction** to check your answers.

multiple choice

1. Which is NOT a technology that has been used to deliver assistance during times of crisis?

    a. Ushahidi   **c.** social networking

    b. QR codes   **d.** e-mail

2. Cognitive surplus means that we now find many people with

    a. more money than free time.

    b. limited access to the Internet.

    c. excess time and free tools for collaboration.

    d. mobile devices.

3. Collaborative consumption is when people get together to

    a. find the best prices on products.

    b. exchange reviews on services and goods they have purchased.

    c. fight diseases of the respiratory tract.

    d. increase the use of a single product by sharing access to it.

4. Social networking tools

    a. played a part in the revolution in Egypt.

    b. are limited to social dating.

    c. have encouraged increased censorship in the United States.

    d. include software like Microsoft Office and Adobe Illustrator.

5. The crisis of a growing digital divide is being addressed by

    a. Ushahidi.

    b. the Next Einstein Initiative project.

    c. the Freecycle program.

    d. building faster computers

true–false

_____ **1.** The move toward access versus ownership is a sign of collaborative consumption.

_____ **2.** Projects like Virtual Choir show that technology has forced us into increased isolation.

critical thinking

1. **The World Stage**

    How might access to (or denial of) electronic information affect the education of a country's citizens? Could that affect who the world's next technology power will be? Could it eliminate third-world status? Examine the ideas behind the Next Einstein Initiative project at **nexteinstein.org** to explore this further. What consequence might developments in Africa have on you, your family, and your experiences?

2. *Ushahidi* **Means "Witness"**

    We saw that the Ushahidi software has been used for a wide range of applications. What kind of events in your world would benefit from this mapping software? Think of a few ways that having real-time collection and mapping of information would make life easier at your school, safer in your town, or just more fun.

Continue ➡

TRY **THIS**

Skyping Around the World

Understanding what your computer can do to improve your life is one of the benefits of being computer literate. In this exercise, we'll show you how to make a free phone call over the Internet using Skype, a popular Voice over Internet Protocol (VoIP) service.

What You Need

Wired Internet Connection or WiFi Signal	A Device (computer, smartphone, tablet, Skype-ready television)	A Friend

Step 1 **Set Up an Account.** Go to Skype (**skype.com**) and click on the **Get Skype** tab. Download the proper version for your device and install. Fill out the information required to set up a free account. You'll be able to call anyone with Skype and talk with just audio, with audio and video, or with free instant messaging.

(gst/Shutterstock; Dvougao/iStockphoto; Brandon Laufenberg/iStockphoto; Andrea Zanchi/iStockphoto)

Step 2 **Build Your Contact List.** To build your list of contacts, you can add friends one at a time by clicking **Contacts**, then **Add Contact** (as shown below left). (You need to add a phone number only if you plan on using Skype to call people on their *phone*, which, unlike computer-to-computer calls, is not a free service.)

Or, you can blast in a whole group of contacts at one time (as shown below right). To do so, click **Contacts**, then **Import Contacts**. Give Skype your Facebook or Gmail login info, and it will automatically bring in all your contacts and add them to your Skype contact list.

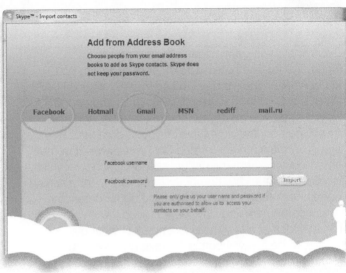

Step 3 **Make a Call.** Now we're ready to call someone! Let's start by calling the people at Skype and making sure everything is hooked up properly. Under your Contacts list, click the **Echo/Sound Test Service**. Then call in by clicking the green **Call** button. The Skype service will answer your call, record a short message from you, and play it back to you. You'll know everything is set to go, and you can begin calling the world for free!

How Will Technology Improve Your Life?

Technology is creating huge changes in the world as well as in how we behave socially, but it is also important to you on a more personal level. Being **computer literate** means being familiar enough with computers that you understand their capabilities and limitations and that you know how to use them safely and efficiently. As we discuss here, the more you understand technology, the more productive and protected you'll be at home, and the better prepared you'll be for any career.

 technology at HOME

Everywhere you go, you see ads like the one in Figure 1.9 for computers and other devices. Do you know what all the words in the ad mean? What is RAM? What is a CPU? What are MB, GB, GHz, and cache? How fast do you need your computer to be, and how much memory should it have? If you're computer literate, you'll be a more informed consumer when it comes time to buy computers, peripherals, and technology services. Understanding computer terminology and keeping current with technology will help you better determine which computers and devices you need.

Let's look at a few more examples of what else it means to be a savvy computer user and consumer, in other words, computer literate (see Figure 1.10). If you're not a savvy user now, don't worry—the following topics and more are covered in detail in the remaining chapters.

- **Avoiding hackers and viruses.** Do you know what hackers and viruses are? Both can threaten a computer's security. Being aware of how hackers and viruses operate and knowing the damage they can do to your computer can help you avoid falling prey to them.

- **Protecting your privacy.** You've probably heard of identity theft—you see and hear news stories all the time about people whose "identities" are stolen and whose credit ratings are ruined by "identity thieves." But do you know how to protect yourself from identity theft when you're online?

- **Understanding the real risks.** Part of being computer literate means being able to separate the real privacy and security risks from things you don't have to worry about. For example, do you know what a *cookie* is? Do you know whether it poses a privacy risk for you when you're on the Internet? What about a *firewall*? Do you know what one is? Do you really need a firewall to protect your computer?

- **Using the web wisely.** Anyone who has ever searched the web can attest that finding information and finding *good* information are two different things. People who are computer literate know how to find the information they want effectively. How effective are your searches?

- **Avoiding online annoyances.** If you have an e-mail account, chances are you've received electronic

FIGURE 1.9 Do you know what all the words in a computer ad mean? Can you tell whether the ad includes all the information necessary to make a purchasing decision? *(Akova/ Fotolia; Dmytro Shevchenko/Fotolia; Norman Chan/Fotolia)*

Processor:	Intel i7-965 Extreme, Factory O'Cd to 3.73 GHz
RAM:	16 GB *Tri Channel* Corsair DDR3 (1066 MHz)
Video:	ATI Radeon HD 5870 X2 with 1 GB *DDR5*
Audio:	Creative Labs X-Fi Elite Pro; HDA 7.1 surround channel sound
Network:	Native *Gigabit* Ethernet
Optical Drive:	Blu-ray burner
Storage Drive:	1 TB Serial ATA hard drive with support for up to 5 additional drives with *RAID options*
Ports:	8 USB and 2 USB 3.0 2 DVI and 1 S-Video 2 IEEE 1394 1 *S/PDIF* out
Cooling:	Two-stage *liquid cooling* system
Portable Storage:	Bluetooth wireless 19-in-1 media hub with *VoIP* stereo headset

NEW!

junk mail, or **spam**. How can you avoid spam? What about adware and spyware—do you know what they are? Do you know the difference between those and viruses, worms, and Trojan horses? Do you know which **software** programs, the instructions that tell the computer what to do, you should install on your computer to avoid online annoyances?

- **Being able to maintain, upgrade, and trouble-shoot your computer.** Learning how to care for and maintain your computer and knowing how to diagnose and fix certain problems can save you a lot of time and hassle. Do you know how to upgrade your computer if you want more memory, for example? Do you know which software and computer settings can keep your computer in top shape?

Finally, becoming computer literate means knowing which technologies are on the horizon and how to integrate them into your own life. Can you connect your television to your wireless network? What is Bluetooth, and does your computer need it? Can a USB 3.0 flash drive be plugged into an old USB 1.0 port? Knowing the answers to these and other questions will help you make better purchasing decisions.

This book and course will help you become computer literate. In Chapter 3, you'll find out how to get the most from the web while staying free from the spam and clutter Internet surfing can leave behind on your computer. Chapter 6 shows you how to determine if your hardware is limiting your computer's performance and how to upgrade or shop for a new system. Chapter 9 covers how to keep your computer and your digital life secure. You'll be able to save money, time, and endless frustration by understanding the basics of how computers and computer systems operate. ■

> **SOUND BYTE**
> **Questions to Ask Before You Buy a Computer**
>
> This Sound Byte will help you consider important questions to ask before you buy a computer, such as whether you should buy a new computer or a used or refurbished one.

FIGURE 1.10

What Does It Mean to Be Computer Literate?

You can **avoid falling prey to hackers and viruses** because you are aware of how they operate.

You know how to **protect yoursef from identity theft.**

You can **separate the real privacy and security risks from things you don't have to worry about.**

You know how to find information and **use the web effectively.**

You can **avoid being overwhelmed by spam, adware, and spyware.**

You know how to **diagnose and fix problems** with your hardware and software.

technology and
YOUR CAREER

Information technology (IT) is a field of study focused on the management and processing of information and the automatic retrieval of information. IT careers include working with computers, telecommunications, and software deployment. Career opportunities in IT are on the rise, but no matter what career you choose, new technology in the workplace is creating a demand for new skill levels in technology from employees. A study from the National Research Council concludes that by the year 2030, computers will displace humans in 60 percent of current occupations. Having advanced skills is becoming more critical every year.

One of the benefits of being computer literate is that you will undoubtedly be able to perform your job more effectively. It also will make you more desirable as an employee and more likely to earn more and to advance in your career. In fact, your understanding of key concepts in technology can "future-proof" you, letting you easily and quickly react to the next round of new technologies.

Before we begin looking at a computer's parts and how a computer operates in Chapter 2, let's look at a whole range of industries and examine how computers are a part of getting work done.

Retail: Working in a Data Mine

Businesses accumulate a lot of data, but how do employees make sense of it all? They use a technique known as **data mining**, the process of searching huge amounts of data with the hope of finding a pattern (see Figure 1.11). For example, retailers often study the data gathered from register terminals to determine which products are selling on a given day and in a specific location. In addition to inventory control systems, which help managers figure out how much merchandise they need to order to replace stock that is sold, managers can use mined data to determine that if they want a certain product to sell well, they must lower its price—especially if they cut the price at one store and see sales increase, for example. Data mining thus allows retailers to respond to consumer buying patterns.

Have you ever wondered how Amazon or Netflix suggests items that fit your taste? Or how such websites automatically display lists of items people bought after they ordered the camera you just picked out? Data mining can keep track of the purchases customers make, along with their geographic data, past buying history, and lists of items they looked at but did not purchase. This data can be translated into marketing that is customized to your shopping. This is the motivation behind the discount cards grocery stores and drugstores offer. In exchange for tracking your buying habits, they offer you special pricing. In the age of data mining, you may be using its capabilities in a number of careers.

FIGURE 1.11 Data mining is the art of translating huge volumes of raw data into presentations like charts and graphs that provide managers with information, such as buying trends, that enable them to make better decisions. *(McIek/Shutterstock; Richard Peterson/Shutterstock; Dmitriy Shironosov/Shutterstock; Simon Krzic/Shutterstock; Saleeee/Shutterstock; yuyangc/Shutterstock; Shutterstock)*

Arts: Ink, Paints, and a Laptop?

Some design students think that because they're studying art, there's no reason for them to study computers. Of course, not all artwork is created using traditional materials such as paint and canvas. Many artists today work exclusively with computers. Mastery of software such as Adobe Illustrator, Adobe Photoshop, and Corel Painter is essential to creating digital art. Eventually you'll want to sell your work, and you'll need to showcase your designs and artistic creations to employers and customers. Wouldn't it be helpful if you knew how to create and manage a website?

Using computers in the arts and entertainment fields goes far beyond just producing web pages, though. Dance and music programs like the ones at the Atlanta Ballet and The Juilliard School use computers to create new performances for audiences. A live dancer can be wired with sensors connected to a computer that captures the dancer's movements. Based on the data it collects, the computer generates a virtual dancer on a screen. The computer operator can easily manipulate this virtual dancer, as well as change the dancer's costume and other aspects of the dancer's appearance, with the click of a mouse. This allows artists to create new experiences for the audience.

And what if you see yourself working in an art museum? Today, museums are using technology to

BITS&BYTES

NASA Wants You . . . to Learn

As you read this chapter, hundreds of satellites are orbiting the globe and taking detailed pictures of Earth. Until recently, these photos weren't available to the public. However, thanks to NASA and some savvy software developers, an application called World Wind is making some 10 trillion bytes of imagery available to you. Need a picture of Mount Fuji for your science project or an aerial picture of your house for your PowerPoint presentation? Just download the software from **nasa.gov/offices/education/programs/national/ltp/opportunities**, and you're ready to go. You'll find several learning applications at this site as well. For example, Virtual Lab lets you pretend you have your own scanning electron microscope, and Moonbase Alpha is a game that simulates life on a space settlement, complete with 3-D graphics, team play, and chatting features. With a few clicks, you can have interactive learning resources that open the world to you.

FIGURE 1.12 Multimedia tours using mobile devices and wireless technology are commonplace in museums and galleries. *(AP Photo/Danny Johnston)*

enhance visitors' experiences (see Figure 1.12). New York's Museum of Modern Art (MoMA), for example, offers a full range of options for tech-savvy visitors: old-fashioned museum audio guides, podcasts that visitors can listen to with their smartphones, and multimedia tours that visitors download through MoMA WiFi (**moma.org**) to their own MP3 device. These multimedia guides even enable visitors to listen to music the artist listened to when he or she was creating a particular work or to look at other works that reflect similar techniques or themes as those they're viewing. Developing these solutions for museums is a great career for someone with an artistic education and knowledge of technology.

Education: Teaching and Learning

The education industry uses computer technology in numerous ways. Courses are designed around course management software such as Blackboard or Moodle so that students can communicate outside of class, take quizzes online, and find their class materials easily. The Internet has obvious advantages in the classroom as a research tool for students, and effective use of the Internet allows teachers to expose students to places students otherwise couldn't access. There are simulations and instructional software programs on the web that are incredible learning tools. For example, teachers can employ these products to give students a taste of running a global business (see Figure 1.13) or the experience of the Interactive Body (**bbc.co.uk/science/humanbody**).

Want to take your students to a museum in another state or country? There's no need to board a plane—many museums offer virtual tours on their websites that allow students to examine the museum collections. Another resource, the Art Project, is a collaboration of several museums that allows online visitors to explore over a thousand pieces of art using the same technology employed in Google Street View. A custom viewer allows visitors to zoom in on the artwork itself at incredibly high resolution (see Figure 1.14). The information panel takes you to related videos and other related websites. So, even if you teach in Topeka, Kansas, you can take your students on a virtual tour of the Tate Britain in London.

Computerized education in the classroom may prove to be the tool that helps teachers reach greater success, despite increasing class sizes and tightening financial constraints. The Khan Academy (**khanacademy.org**) is a terrific example of a technological tool for education. Salman Khan was an investment analyst in Boston in 2006 when he began to post videos to YouTube so that he could teach algebra to his young cousins in New Orleans. Today, his nonprofit Khan Academy contains over 3,000 videos, and several million students a month use the site.

FIGURE 1.13 Internet applications have become sophisticated learning resources. For example, IndustryMasters (**industrymasters.com**) allows students to compete online for domination of a global market while giving instructors the chance to introduce many business concepts.

FIGURE 1.14 The Art Project presents an interactive tour through several museums. Thousands of works of art are displayed in high resolution with a pullout information panel (**googleartproject.com**). *(REUTERS/Stefan Wermuth)*

A classroom teacher can also follow what is happening in the classroom by using the *dashboard,* a screen that shows which topics each student has mastered, which they are making progress with, and which have them spinning their wheels. Now a teacher can approach a student already knowing exactly what is frustrating them and can avoid the dreaded question, "Oh, what don't you understand?"

As an educator, being computer literate will help you constructively integrate computer technologies like those discussed here into lesson plans and interactions for your students.

Law Enforcement: Put Down That Mouse—You're Under Arrest!

Today, wearing out shoe leather to solve crimes is far from the only method available to you if you want to pursue a career in law enforcement. Computers are being used in police cars and crime labs to solve an increasing number of crimes. For example, facial reconstruction systems like the one shown in Figure 1.15 can turn a skull into a finished digital image of a face, allowing investigators to proceed far more quickly with identification than before.

One technique used by modern detectives to solve crimes uses computers to search the vast number of databases on the Internet. Proprietary law enforcement databases such as the National Center for the Analysis of Violent Crime database enable detectives to analyze a wealth of information for similarities between crimes in an attempt to detect patterns that may reveal serial crimes. In fact, a law enforcement specialty called computer forensics is growing in importance in order to fight modern crime. **Computer forensics** analyzes computer systems with specific techniques to gather potential legal evidence. For example, Steven Zirko was recently convicted for two Chicago-area murders based on computer forensics work. Computer forensics examiners

trained by the FBI scoured Zirko's computer and located searches for terms like *hire a hitman* and *GHB,* the date-rape drug. Zirko had also used his computer to find the daily schedule for his victim's two school-aged children and to get directions to her home. In many cases, files, videos, and conversations conducted using a computer can be recovered by forensics specialists and can be used as evidence of criminal activity.

Medicine: The Chip Within

A career in medicine will connect you to new ways of using technology to better people's lives. Earlier we mentioned how biomedical chips may one day restore sight to the blind. Indeed, the goals of modern biomedical chip research are to provide technological solutions to physical problems and a means for identifying individuals.

One type of chip is already being implanted in humans as a means of verifying a person's identity. Called VeriMed, this personal identification chip is about the size of a grain of rice and is implanted under the skin. When exposed to radio waves from a scanning device, the chip transmits its serial number to the scanner. The scanner then connects to a database that contains the name, address, and medical conditions of the person in whom the chip has been implanted. In the course of a nursing career, you may be using VeriMed to help keep Alzheimer's patients safe, for example.

Currently, nonimplant versions of identity chips are used in hospitals. When chips are attached with bands to newborn infants, the hospital staff can instantly

FIGURE 1.15 Tissue-rendering programs add layers of muscles, fat, and skin to recovered skulls to create faces that can be used to identify victims. *(Digital Art/Corbis)*

DIG DEEPER

We're familiar with digital data—comfortable with carrying around music, some files, contact lists, and calendars. But what about combining what you see with additional digital information, as you see it?

Augmented reality combines our normal sense of the world around us with an overlay of digital information, all displayed on a screen. For example, a number of smartphone apps are currently available that use the integrated compass and camera of your phone to add information to your environment. As shown in Figure 1.16, the image seen through the camera's lens provides a baseline, and additional information can be displayed over the image. New York Nearest Subway is another popular app that augments reality by indicating in an overlay the location of the nearest subway.

There are also devices being created that will augment reality even more intelligently. One of the most promising of these new tools is called SixthSense. This wearable device, which hangs around your neck and consists of a camera, a projector, and a mirror, can communicate with the Internet wirelessly via your cell phone. SixthSense augments your experience of reality by adding the information you need as you need it.

For example, say you're in a bookstore and select the title *Ambient Findability* (see Figure 1.17). As you hold the book, its Amazon rating appears on the cover. You open to the inside sleeve, and the comments from readers at Amazon begin to scroll over the page. Then you can tap any of those comments for more detail.

SixthSense also responds to gestures, so that when you make a rectangle with your fingers, it takes a photograph. Any flat surface—a wall, table, whatever—can be used to "dump" your photos

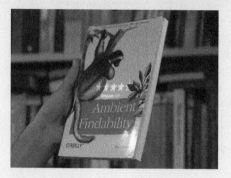

FIGURE 1.17 SixthSense recognizes what information you might want added to your environment and displays it automatically. *(Pranav Mistry)*

into a "pile." Using your hands, you can shuffle the images or resize or rotate an image. You can even draw a watch-sized circle on your wrist and SixthSense will display an analog watch face on your arm.

In fact, your hand is as good a flat surface as any to SixthSense. Need to make a phone call? SixthSense will display a keypad, like the one shown in Figure 1.18, on your palm. Tap out the numbers on the virtual keypad, and one touch of a red CALL button that appears on your palm places your call.

The shirt of the person walking toward you will also work as a projection surface. As a person approaches a SixthSense wearer, it recognizes their face, heads off to their Facebook page or blog, and scans the most recent entries. It then projects the keywords that describe the person and their interests on their clothing as you watch them approach.

Currently, SixthSense is small but not very stylish. The product is constructed from off-the-shelf components costing about $350. Within a few years, its inventors believe it can be produced as a button-sized device, costing less than a cell phone costs now. In fact, you can read directions for building the hardware yourself and can download the software for free at **code.google.com/p/sixthsense**.

Augmented reality combines the digital information we have accumulated in an immediate and spontaneous manner. This kind of direct integration of digital information with the physical world around us is a hallmark of our digital future. So where will your new reality take you?

FIGURE 1.16 Augmented reality apps let you look through your phone's camera to see your environment with extra information superimposed. *(Kyodo/AP Images)*

FIGURE 1.18 Any surface can become an input device using SixthSense. *(Pranav Mistry)*

FIGURE 1.19 No bigger than the period at the end of this sentence, Hitachi's µ-chip can hold digital information, which can then be read when it passes a detector. *(ERIKO SUGITA/Reuters/Landov)*

monitor the location of any baby. Elevators and doors are designed to allow only certain people to enter with a specific baby, even if hospital power is interrupted. Although the use of implantable tags is becoming more commonplace, it remains to be seen whether people will decide that the advantages of having their medical data quickly available justifies having chips implanted in their bodies. As a doctor, would you advise your patients to use an implantable chip?

Hitachi makes a similar device, called the *µ-chip* ("mu chip"), which is smaller than the period at the end of this sentence (see Figure 1.19). Those concerned with privacy issues worry because the µ-chip could be easily attached to, or ingested by, a person without his or her knowledge. On the other hand, researchers are excited by the possibility of using the µ-chip to confirm that the correct drugs and dosages have been given. If your career takes you into the medical field, how will you evaluate the risks and benefits of biomedical chips?

Science: Simulating Reality

Thanks to a partnership between the National Severe Storms Lab and the National Center for Supercomputing Applications, tornado forecasting is becoming increasingly accurate (see Figure 1.20). Scientists have been able to create a model so detailed that it takes nine days for a supercomputer to generate it, even though the computer is executing 4 trillion operations a second.

Simulations also can model the structure of solar magnetic flares, which can interfere with broadcasts on Earth. With a career in meteorology, you will be studying the data produced by these simulations, hoping to improve predictions about weather phenomena.

Other technological applications in the sciences are being used on some of the oldest sites on Earth. The ancient site of Pompeii has been under the scrutiny of tourists and archaeologists for decades. Sadly, decades of foot traffic and hundreds of years of exposure to the elements have eroded portions of the ruins. Today, scientists are using 3-D scanners and imaging software to capture a detailed record of the ruins' current condition. This virtual re-creation is so lifelike that archaeologists can study the ruins on-screen instead of at the actual site. Using the scans as well as satellite imagery, aerial photography, and other data, scientists will eventually be able to re-create missing portions of the ruins in a virtual model. Will you be using these tools someday to make records of other decaying sites?

FIGURE 1.20 Software that combines radar information in new ways increases the accuracy of tornado predictions and allows for earlier warning of threatened towns. *(Steve Bloom Images/Alamy; National Oceanic and Atmospheric Administration NOAA)*

Psychology: You Should Smile . . . Now

Science fiction has always been populated with robots that emulate humans, seemingly effortlessly. So, when will we have personal robots laughing at our jokes or bringing us our favorite snack when they recognize we're sad? A career as a psychologist may take you into an exciting exploration of the boundaries between the nature of being human and the nature of machines.

Psychologists and computer scientists are jointly conducting research to develop computer systems that respond to human affect and emotional expression, as well as to enable computer systems to develop social and emotional skills. **Affective computing** is computing that relates to emotion or that deliberately tries to influence emotion. Most computers you are familiar with can perform calculations and do the tasks they are programmed for much faster than humans can, but they fail miserably at telling a good joke or modifying their behavior based on your frustration. This wide gap in the computing abilities of computers versus their emotional abilities is the target of research in affective computing.

One project to emerge in the affective computing field is the emotional-social prosthesis (ESP) device developed by a group at the MIT Media Lab. The ESP system is targeted at helping people who have autism. Individuals with autism can be extremely intelligent, but they do not easily sense nonverbal cues such as facial expressions and tone of voice. The ESP is a wearable system that isolates the movements and facial expressions of people, interprets what their mood and intentions probably are, and communicates this information back to the user.

While engineers work to create computers that can understand us emotionally, psychologists and computer scientists are also working to evolve systems toward a more human appearance (see Figure 1.21). With a career in robotics or psychology, you could find yourself at the heart of developing a new kind of relationship between man and machine. ■

> **Before moving on to the Chapter Review:**
> - Watch Replay Video 1.2 ▶.
> - Then check your understanding of what you've learned so far.

FIGURE 1.21 Robots with articulated joints that mimic human limbs can balance, stand, walk, and even hug. *(Press Association/AP Images)*

check your understanding //

For a quick review to see what you've learned so far, answer the following questions. Visit **pearsonhighered.com/techinaction** to check your answers.

multiple choice

1. Artists interface with technology often, but cannot yet
   a. use computers to generate images that respond to the environment.
   b. use computers to create a virtual storefront.
   c. use software to suggest plot endings.
   d. use software to create and enhance virtual performances.

2. People who do not read emotion easily in others hope for new progress in the field of
   a. affective computing.
   b. data mining.
   c. bioprinting.
   d. forensic science.

3. Which of the following allows retailers to respond to consumer buying patterns?
   a. outsourcing
   b. data mining
   c. smart labels
   d. Bluetooth technology

4. Computer forensics uses computer systems and technology to
   a. simulate a person's anatomical system.
   b. train law enforcement officers to be more effective.
   c. create a crisis map.
   d. gather potential legal evidence.

5. IT is the abbreviation for
   a. information training.
   b. Internet training.
   c. Internet technology.
   d. information technology.

true–false

_____ 1. QR codes let companies track your past purchases and customize offers for you.

_____ 2. Criminal investigators may find evidence on a computer, but that evidence cannot be used in court.

critical thinking

1. **Working 9 to 5**

   This chapter lists many ways in which becoming computer literate is beneficial. Think about what your life will be like once you're started in your career. What areas of computing will be most important for you to understand? How would an understanding of computer hardware and software help you in working from home, working with groups in other countries, and contributing your talents?

2. **Computerized Assessment**

   As more and more computer-based training and testing is available, there is pressure to move toward a different educational model. Should introductory courses be run in a new style, heavily based on computer training modules to develop and assess skills? What is the role of the instructor in this model? What key factors need to be available to you to succeed in learning?

Continue

1 Chapter Review

summary //

Technology on the World Stage

1. How can becoming proficient with technology help you understand and participate in important issues in the world at large?

- Whether it's political issues, environmental issues, or questions addressing the global digital divide, it's important that you become proficient with technology to be able to participate.
- Technology can be the means by which you find your voice in the world and impact others in meaningful ways.

Technology and Our Society

2. How can knowledge of technology help you influence the direction our society takes?

- Technology is changing how we think, how we connect with each other, and how we purchase and consume products and services.
- By using current technology, you can become a creator of new pieces of music, connect with people from around the world, and collaborate to create or consume.

Technology at Home

3. What does it mean to be computer literate?

- Computer literacy goes beyond knowing how to use a mouse and send e-mail. If you're computer literate, you understand the capabilities and limitations of computers and know how to use them wisely.

- Being computer literate also enables you to make informed purchasing decisions, use computers in your career, and understand the many ethical, legal, and societal implications of technology today. Anyone can become computer literate.

4. How does being computer literate make you a savvy computer user and consumer?

- By understanding how a computer is constructed and how its various parts function, you'll be able to get the most out of your computer.
- Among other things, you'll be able to avoid hackers, viruses, and Internet headaches; protect your privacy; and separate the real risks of privacy and security from those you don't have to worry about.
- You'll also be better able to maintain, upgrade, and troubleshoot your computer; make good purchasing decisions; and incorporate the latest technologies into your existing equipment.

Technology and Your Career

5. How can becoming computer literate help you in a career?

- As computers increasingly become part of our daily lives, it is difficult to imagine any career that does not use computers in some fashion.
- Understanding how to use computers effectively will help you be a more productive and valuable employee, no matter which profession you choose.

> Be sure to check out the companion website for additional materials to help you review and learn, including a Tech Bytes Weekly newsletter—**pearsonhighered.com/techinaction**. And don't forget the Replay Videos ▶.

key terms //

making the transition to . . . next semester //

1. **Computer Literacy**

   In your academic career, you'll be spending time understanding the requirements of the degree program you choose. At many schools, computer literacy requirements exist either as incoming requirements (skills students must have before they're admitted) or as outgoing requirements (skills students must prove they have before graduating). Does your program require specific computer skills? Which skills are they? Should they be required? How can students efficiently prove that they have these skills? How often does the set of skills need to be reviewed and updated?

2. **The Mind of the Mob**

   Crowdsourcing is the gathering of data in real time, as an event happens, from a growing crowd of people. Because of the large number of students who now own phones with Internet access, crowdsourcing on campus could start to be useful. In what settings would making decisions based on information from a gathering crowd on campus be valuable? How would you react to your professor using a form of crowdsourcing to determine your grade on an essay?

3. **Recycle, Repair, Redistribute**

   The Microsoft-authorized refurbisher program and TechSoup both help provide resources to people in need to reduce the barrier of the digital divide. These organizations recycle hardware and supply software inexpensively to needy families. How could a program be set up at your school to make people aware of these options? Could students donate materials or retrofit systems as part of their coursework? As part of a club activity? How could you make these programs work for your community?

making the transition to . . . the workplace //

1. **Patients and Medical Computing**

   As more hospitals and doctors' offices begin to use electronic medical records (EMRs), the flow of information among the doctors and care facilities a patient uses could become much more reliable. In their training and work, doctors and nurses rely on computers. What about patients? Examine Microsoft Health Vault at **microsoft.com/en-us/healthvault** for an example of an electronic medical history. How does this migration from a traditional paper records system impact the skills required for medical office workers? New ethical questions also often arise when technology changes. How would a medical facility now protect and verify its data records? What risks are there with a product like the Microsoft Health Vault?

2. **Social Media Careers**

   With the explosion of users on social media sites, businesses need to establish their presence on social media sites. Just search for "Vans" or "Starbucks" on Facebook for examples of company sites. To manage their interaction with customers (and fans), companies need to hire social media managers. Using a job site such as Monster.com, search for "social media manager" and review the job postings. What are the educational requirements for social media managers? What technical skills do these jobs require? Given your major, what companies would you do well for as a social media manager? What steps should you take while in school to prepare yourself for a career as a social media manager?

3. **Portfolio of Electronic Skills**

   Job seekers want to highlight their skills for prospective employers—show employers both what they can do right now and provide evidence that they can learn quickly and grow into new technologies and new responsibilities. What skills could you place in a portfolio to demonstrate your current mastery of computer concepts and computer applications? How would you document for your employer your ability to learn, adapt quickly to changes in technology, and acquire new skills?

A Culture of Sharing

Problem

As more and more peer-to-peer music-sharing services appeared, like BitTorrent and LimeWire, many felt a culture of theft was developing. Some argued there was a mindset that property rights for intellectual works need not be respected and that people should be able to download, for free, any music, movies, or other digital content they wanted.

But there is another view of the phenomenon. Some are suggesting that the amount of constant access to other people—through texting, e-mail, blogging, and the easy exchange of digital content—has created a culture of trust and sharing. This Team Time will explore both sides of this debate as it affects three different parts of our lives—finance, travel, and consumerism.

Task

Each of three groups will select a different area to examine—finance, travel, or consumerism. The groups will find evidence to support or refute the idea that a culture of sharing is developing. The finance group will want to explore projects like Kickstarter (**kickstarter.com**) and Kiva (**kiva.org**). The travel group should examine what is happening with CouchSurfing (**couchsurfing.org**) to start their research. The team investigating consumerism will want to look at goods-exchange programs like Freecycle (**freecycle.org**).

Process

1. Divide the class into three teams.

2. Discuss the different views of a "culture of sharing." With the other members of your team, use the Internet to research up-and-coming technologies and projects that would support your position. People use social media tools to connect into groups to exchange ideas. Does that promote trust? Does easy access to digital content promote theft, or has the value of content changed? Are there other forces like the economy and the environmental state of the world that play a role in promoting a culture of sharing? What evidence can you find to support your ideas?

3. Present your group's findings to the class for debate and discussion.

4. Write a strategy paper that summarizes your position and outlines your predictions for the future. Will the pace of technology promote a change in the future from the position you are describing?

Conclusion

The future of technology is unknown, but we do know that it will impact the way our society progresses. To be part of the developments that technology will bring will take good planning and attention, no matter what area of the culture you're examining. Begin now—learn how to stay on top of technology.

Should Information Be Free?

In this exercise, you'll research and role-play a complicated ethical situation. The role you play might not match your personal beliefs; regardless, your research and use of logic should enable you to represent the view assigned. An arbitrator will watch and comment on both sides of the arguments, and together, team members will agree on an ethical solution.

Problem

The crisis-mapping tool Ushahidi has been used to collect and present information in times of unrest. This allows everyone to be involved in gathering the actual facts about what is happening and to help address the needs of people who are lost and hurt.

WikiLeaks is another example of a tool that gathers information and "frees" it by presenting it to the public. Whistleblowers and secret and classified media have been exposed to the world community through publication via WikiLeaks. However, some people feel that WikiLeaks has endangered people by revealing information that should have been kept confidential.

What is the nature of information? Should it be "free"—available without censure or government controls? Is there a limit—should only certain information be free, whereas other information should be kept away from the public for the greater good?

Research Topics to Consider

- Electronic Frontier Foundation
- Government 2.0

Process

1. Divide the class into teams. Each team will select a web-based tool that allows us access to information.
2. Team members should each think of a situation where a person would benefit from the easy access to information and a situation where it might be undesirable
3. Team members should arrange a mutually convenient time to meet and exchange ideas, using either the chat room feature of MyITLab or the discussion board feature of your course management software or by meeting in person. Select the most-powerful and best-constructed arguments and develop a summary conclusion.
4. Team members should present their findings to the class or submit a PowerPoint presentation for review by the rest of the class, along with the summary conclusion they developed.

Conclusion

As technology becomes ever more prevalent and integrated into our lives, ethical dilemmas will present themselves to an increasing extent. Being able to understand and evaluate both sides of the argument, while responding in a personally or socially ethical manner, will be an important skill.

2 Looking at Computers: Understanding the Parts

Understanding Digital Components

Understanding Your Computer

OBJECTIVES

1. What exactly is a computer, and what are its four main functions? **(p. 30)**

2. What is the difference between data and information? **(p. 30)**

3. What are bits and bytes, and how are they measured? **(pp. 30–34)**

Sound Byte: Binary Numbers Interactive

Active Helpdesk: Understanding Bits and Bytes

Input Devices and Output Devices

OBJECTIVES

4. What devices can I use to get data into the computer? **(pp. 35–41)**

5. What devices can I use to get information out of the computer? **(pp. 42–48)**

Sound Byte: Tablet and Notebook Tour

Active Helpdesk: Using Output Devices

Processing, Storage, and Connectivity

Processing, Memory, and Storage

OBJECTIVES

6. What's on the motherboard? **(pp. 52–53)**

7. Where are information and programs stored? **(pp. 54–56)**

Sound Byte: Virtual Computer Tour

Active Helpdesk: Exploring Storage Devices and Ports

Sound Byte: Port Tour: How Do I Hook It Up?

Ports and Power Controls

OBJECTIVES

8. How are devices connected to the computer? **(pp. 57–59)**

9. What's the best way to turn my computer on and off, and when should it be done? **(pp. 60–61)**

Setting It All Up

OBJECTIVE

10. How do I set up my computer to avoid strain and injury? **(pp. 62–64)**

Sound Byte: Healthy Computing

For all media in this chapter go to **pearsonhighered.com/techinaction** or MyITLab.

(Login/Shutterstock; Wildcat123/Dreamstime; Iofoto/Dreamstime; Lola & Bek/ImageZoo/Alamy)

COOL IS THIS?

...rience is pretty common at the movies, and even on many TVs, but ...your laptop? Computer manufacturers, such as Sony, Asus, and Toshiba, ...**high-end laptops** that have 3-D viewing capabilities. That means ...**s, movies, and websites** can be experienced in 3-D. These machines ...ward **gamers and 3-D movie enthusiasts** and require high-end ...onents, such as the 3-D kit by NVIDIA that includes a combination of ...d graphics processor unit and monitor, software, and **specialized 3-D** ...hieve the 3-D effects. The first no-glasses 3-D laptop was introduced ...ate 2011. It uses the laptop's web camera and eye-tracking technology ...-D effects. Although this laptop's **high price and weight** (9 lbs.) are ...o some users, 3-D in an affordable, portable format that doesn't require

After reading Chapter 1, you can see why becoming computer literate is important. But where do you start? You've no doubt gleaned some knowledge about computers just from being a member of society. However, even if you have used a computer before, do you really understand how it works, what all its parts are, and what those parts do?

understanding your

COMPUTER

Let's start our look at computers by discussing what a computer does and how its functions make it such a useful machine.

Computers Are Data Processing Devices

Strictly defined, a **computer** is a data processing device that performs four major functions:

1. **Input:** It gathers data, or allows users to enter data.
2. **Process:** It manipulates, calculates, or organizes that data into information.
3. **Output:** It displays data and information in a form suitable for the user.
4. **Storage:** It saves data and information for later use.

What is the difference between data and information? People often use the terms *data* and *information* interchangeably. Although they may mean the same thing in a simple conversation, the distinction between data and information is an important one.

In computer terms, **data** is a representation of a fact, a figure, or an idea. Data can be a number, a word, a picture, or even a recording of sound. For example, the

number 7135553297 and the names Zoe and Richardson are pieces of data. Alone, these pieces of data probably mean little to you. **Information** is data that has been organized or presented in a meaningful fashion. When your computer provides you with a contact listing that indicates Zoe Richardson can be reached at (713) 555-3297, the data becomes useful—that is, it becomes information.

How do computers interact with data and information? Computers are excellent at **processing** (manipulating, calculating, or organizing) data into information. When you first arrived on campus, you probably were directed to a place where you could get an ID card. You most likely provided a clerk with personal data that was entered into a computer. The clerk then took your picture with a digital camera (collecting more data). All of the data was then processed appropriately so that it could be printed on your ID card (see Figure 2.1). This organized output of data on your ID card is useful information.

Bits and Bytes: The Language of Computers

How do computers process data into information? Unlike humans, computers work exclusively with numbers (not words). To process data into

FIGURE 2.1 Computers process data into information. *(Michaeljung/Shutterstock)*

information, computers need to work in a language they understand. This language, called **binary language**, consists of just two digits: 0 and 1. Everything a computer does, such as processing data, printing a report, or editing a photo, is broken down into a series of 0s and 1s. Each 0 and 1 is a **binary digit**, or **bit** for short. Eight binary digits (or bits) combine to create one **byte**. In computers, each letter of the alphabet, each number, and each special character (such as @, pronounced "at") consists of a unique combination of eight bits, or a string of eight 0s and 1s. So, for example, in binary language, the letter *K* is represented as 01001011. This is eight bits, or one byte.

What else can bits and bytes be used for? Bits and bytes not only are used as the language that tells the computer what to do, they are also used to represent the *quantity* of data and information that the computer inputs and outputs. Word processing files, digital pictures, and even software are represented inside a computer as a series of bits and bytes. These files and applications can be quite large, containing thousands or millions of bytes.

To make it easier to measure the size of such files, we need units of measure larger than a byte. Kilobytes, megabytes, and gigabytes are therefore simply larger amounts of bytes. As shown in Figure 2.2 (p. 32), a **kilobyte (KB)** is approximately 1,000 bytes, a **megabyte (MB)** is about 1 million bytes, and a **gigabyte (GB)** is around 1 billion bytes. Today, personal computers are capable of storing **terabytes (TB)** of data (around 1 trillion bytes), and many business computers can store up to a petabyte (PB) (1,000 terabytes) of data. The Google search engine processes more than 1 PB of user-generated data per *hour*!

How does your computer process bits and bytes? Your computer uses hardware and software to process data into information that lets you complete tasks such as writing a letter or playing a game. **Hardware** is any part of the computer you can physically touch. However, a computer needs more than just hardware to work. **Software** is the set of computer programs that enables the hardware to perform different tasks.

There are two broad categories of software: *application software* and *system software*. **Application software** is the set of programs you use on a computer to help you carry out tasks such as writing a research paper. If

you've ever typed a document, created a spreadsheet, or edited a digital photo, for example, you've used application software.

System software is the set of programs that enables your computer's hardware devices and application software to work together. The most common type of system software is the **operating system (OS)**—the program that controls how your computer system functions. It manages the hardware, such as the monitor and printer, and provides a means by which users can interact with the computer. Most likely, the computer you own or use at school runs a version of Windows, probably Windows 7 or 8, as the system software. However, if you're working on an Apple computer, you're probably running OS X.

Types of Computers

What types of computers are popular for personal use? There are two basic designs of computers: portable and stationary. For portable computers, a number of options exist:

- A **laptop (or notebook) computer** is a portable computer that has a keyboard, monitor, and other devices integrated into a single compact case.

- A **netbook** is a small, lightweight laptop computer that is generally 7 to 10 inches wide and has a longer battery life than a laptop.

- A **tablet PC** is similar to a laptop computer, but the monitor swivels and folds flat (see Figure 2.3a). You can then input data and commands primarily by using a special pen called a *stylus* across the touch screen, and you can input text by pressing keys on the virtual keyboard.

- In 2010, Apple introduced the iPad, which created a new class of portable computers. A **tablet computer**, such as the iPad or Samsung Galaxy Tab, is a portable computer integrated into a flat multitouch-sensitive screen. It uses an onscreen virtual keyboard, but you can connect separate keyboards to it via Bluetooth or wires.

- An **ultrabook** is a full-featured but lightweight laptop computer designed to compete with the MacBook Air. Ultrabooks feature low-power processors and solid state drives and try to reduce their size and weight to extend battery life without sacrificing performance.

FIGURE 2.2

How Much Is a Byte?

NAME	NUMBER OF BYTES	RELATIVE SIZE
Byte (B)	1 byte	One character of data (8 bits, or binary digits)
Kilobyte (KB)	1,024 bytes (2^{10} bytes)	1,024 characters, or about 1 page of plain text
Megabyte (MB)	1,048,576 bytes (2^{20} bytes)	About 4 books (200 pages, 240,000 characters)
Gigabyte (GB)	1,073,741,824 bytes (2^{30} bytes)	About 4,500 books, or over twice the size of Sir Isaac Newton's library (considered very large for the time)
Terabyte (TB)	1,099,511,627,776 bytes (2^{40} bytes)	About 4.6 million books, or about the number of volumes in the Rutgers University Library
Petabyte (PB)	1,125,899,906,842,624 bytes (2^{50} bytes)	About 4.7 billion books, which would fill the Library of Congress (the United States' largest library) 140 times!
Exabyte (EB)	1,152,921,504,606,846,976 bytes (2^{60} bytes)	About 4.8 trillion books, which, if housed as if in the Library of Congress, would occupy about 11,000 square miles, or an area almost the size of the state of Maryland
Zettabyte (ZB)	1,180,591,620,717,411,303,424 bytes (2^{70} bytes)	The library required to house the 4.9 quadrillion books equal to a ZB of data would occupy about 11.3 million square miles, or an area about 1 million square miles larger than all of North America

(Ninice64/Fotolia; Georgios Kollidas/Fotolia; D aniel/Fotolia; Flavijus Piliponis/Fotolia)

FIGURE 2.3 (a) A tablet PC has a monitor that swivels to become a touch-sensitive input device; (b) an all-in-one computer does not need a separate tower. *(PRNewsFoto/Mindjet LLC/AP Images; PRNewsFoto/Apple/AP Images)*

A **desktop computer** is intended for use at a single location, so it is stationary. Most desktop computers consist of a separate case or tower (called the **system unit**) that houses the main components of the computer plus peripheral devices. A **peripheral device** is a component, such as a monitor or keyboard, that connects to the computer. An **all-in-one computer**, such as the Apple iMac (Figure 2.3b) or HP TouchSmart, eliminates the need for a separate tower because these computers house the computer's processor and memory in the monitor. Many all-in-one models, such as the TouchSmart, also incorporate touch-screen technology.

Are there other types of computers?
Although you may never come into direct contact with the following types of computers, they are still very important and do a lot of work behind the scenes of daily life:

- A **mainframe** is a large, expensive computer that supports many users simultaneously. Mainframes are often used in businesses that manage large amounts of data, such as insurance companies, where many people are working at the same time on similar operations, such as claims processing. Mainframes excel at executing many computer programs at the same time.

- A **supercomputer** is a specially designed computer that can perform complex calculations extremely rapidly. Supercomputers are used when complex models requiring intensive mathematical calculations are needed (such as weather forecasting or atomic energy research). Supercomputers are designed to execute a few programs as quickly as possible, whereas mainframes are designed to handle

many programs running at the same time but at a slower pace.

- An **embedded computer** is a specially designed computer chip that resides in another device, such as your car or the electronic thermostat in your home (see Figure 2.4). Embedded computers are

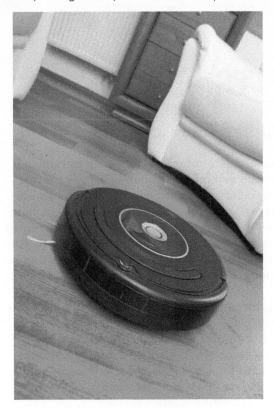

FIGURE 2.4 This robot vacuum includes an embedded computer. *(Jirsak/Shutterstock)*

self-contained computer devices that have their own programming and that typically don't receive input from you or interact with other systems.

Even your smartphone is a computer. A **smartphone** does more than let you make and answer phone calls. It also has productivity (application software), media player, and camera features, as well as web connectivity. And just like your laptop computer, your smartphone has a CPU, memory, and storage. Examples of smartphones include the iPhone and the HTC Thunderbolt.

Each part of your computer has a specific purpose that coordinates with one of the functions of the computer—input, processing, output, or storage (see Figure 2.5). Additional devices, such as modems and routers, help a computer communicate with the Internet and other computers to facilitate the sharing of documents and other resources. Let's begin our exploration of hardware by looking at your computer's input devices. ■

Input

Processing

Storage

Output

FIGURE 2.5 Each part of the computer serves a special function.

BITS&BYTES

Putting Your Computer to Work...While You Sleep

Complex scientific research, such as human genome exploration, requires vast computing power. Software has been developed to tie individual computers in a grid to enable them to work together. This effectively creates a cheap supercomputer that many not-for-profit research organizations use to research problems that will benefit the greater good...and your computer can help. Visit the World Community Grid (**worldcommunitygrid.org**) and download its software. Once installed on your computer, it allows your computer to work on research during the many times when your CPU is idle (or at least not working to its full potential). Your computer can participate in exciting research projects on muscular dystrophy, sustainable water, and cancer. So tell your computer to get to work!

(adimas/Fotolia)

input
DEVICES

An **input device** lets you enter data (text, images, and sounds) and instructions (user responses and commands) into your computer. A **keyboard** is an input device you use to enter typed data and commands, and a **mouse** is used to enter user responses and commands.

There are other input devices as well. Microphones input sounds, scanners input nondigital data (such as magazine articles and old photographs) by turning it into a digital form, and digital cameras input digital images. A **stylus** is an input device that looks like a pen, which you use to tap commands or draw on a screen. We'll explore these and other input devices next.

Keyboards

Aren't all keyboards the same? Most computers come with a standard **QWERTY keyboard**. This keyboard layout gets its name from the first six letters in the top-left row of alphabetic keys and is the standard English-language keyboard layout. The QWERTY layout was originally designed for typewriters and was meant to slow typists down and prevent typewriter keys from jamming. Although the QWERTY layout is considered inefficient because it slows typing speeds, efforts to change to more efficient layouts, such as that of the Dvorak keyboard (see the Bits and Bytes on the next page), have not been met with much public interest.

What's special about laptop keyboards? To save space and weight, netbook and smaller laptop keyboards (14 inches and under) are more compact than standard desktop keyboards and, therefore, often have fewer keys. To retain the same functionality as a standard keyboard, some laptop keys may have alternative functions.

How do wireless keyboards work? Wireless keyboards are powered by batteries, so you're not tied to the computer by wires. These keyboards send data to the computer using a form of wireless technology that uses *radio frequency (RF)*. A radio transmitter in the keyboard sends out signals that are received either by a receiving device plugged into a USB port or by a Bluetooth receiving device located in the system unit. You've probably heard of **Bluetooth technology** if you use a headset or earpiece with your cell phone. Bluetooth is a wireless transmission standard that lets you connect devices such as cell phones, smartphones, and computers to peripheral devices such as keyboards and headsets.

If you use a wireless keyboard with your home computer, you can be as far as 6 to 30 feet from your computer, depending on the quality of the keyboard. Wireless keyboards used in conference rooms or auditoriums can be as far away as 100 feet from the computer.

What are some other alternative keyboards? The size of laptop keyboards and other portable computer devices have become quite compact. *Flexible keyboards* are a terrific alternative if you want a full-sized keyboard for your laptop, netbook, or tablet. You can roll one up, fit it in your backpack, and plug it into a USB port when you need it. Another compact keyboard alternative is the *virtual laser keyboard* (see Figure 2.6), which is about the size of a cell phone. It projects an image of a keyboard onto any flat surface, and sensors detect the motion of your fingers as you "type." Data is transmitted to the device via Bluetooth.

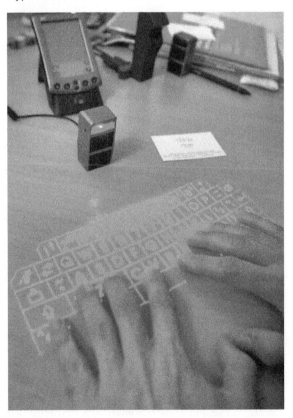

FIGURE 2.6 The virtual laser keyboard projects the image of a QWERTY keyboard on any surface. Sensors detect typing motions, and data is transmitted to a computing device via Bluetooth technology. *(Martin Meissner/AP Images)*

BITS&BYTES

Switching Your Keyboard Layout

The Dvorak keyboard is an alternative keyboard layout that puts the most commonly used letters in the English language on "home keys"—the keys in the middle row of the keyboard. The Dvorak keyboard's design reduces the distance your fingers travel for most keystrokes, increasing typing speed.

But did you know that you can change your keyboard from the QWERTY layout to the Dvorak layout without buying a new keyboard? You can use the Windows operating system to customize the keyboard by changing the keyboard layout. The keyboard layout then controls which characters appear on the screen when you press the keys on your keyboard. If you suffer from a repetitive strain injury such as carpal tunnel syndrome, you may find it useful to switch to the Dvorak keyboard layout. You can also switch layouts to conform to different foreign languages. Instructions for changing keyboard layouts are shown in Figure 2.7.

You might also find it useful to cover the keys on the keyboard with stickers of the corresponding characters of the newly configured layout so that the characters on your keyboard match up to the new layout.

FIGURE 2.7 You can customize the layout of your keyboard using the Windows operating system.
>*To change the keyboard layout in Windows 8, open Control Panel, click* **Change input methods** *in the Clock, Language, and Region section. Click the* **Options** *link. Click the* **Add an input method** *link. Scroll to find the appropriate keyboard and click the* **Preview** *link to view it. Then left-click the keyboard, and click* **Add***.*

Toggle keys: keys whose function changes between two options. (Example: Caps Lock key)

Internet controls

Multimedia controls

Function keys (F keys): shortcut keys you press to perform special tasks in software programs.

Numeric keypad: lets you enter numbers quickly.

Cursor control keys

Alt key: works with other keys to execute shortcuts and special tasks.

Control (Ctrl) key: used with other keys to perform shortcuts. (Example: Ctrl + B makes text bold)

Windows key: used alone, it toggles between the Start screen and the foremost running app. Used with other keys, it performs shortcuts. (Example: Windows key + C displays charms)

FIGURE 2.8 Keyboards have a variety of keys that help you work more efficiently. (Note that on Macs, function keys are slightly different, the Control function is the Apple key or Command key, and the Alt function is the Option key.) *(Artur Synenko/Shutterstock)*

How can I use my keyboard most efficiently? All keyboards have the standard set of alphabetic and numeric keys that you regularly use when typing. As shown in Figure 2.8, many keyboards for laptop and desktop computers have additional keys that perform special functions. Knowing how to use the special keys shown in Figure 2.8 will help you improve your efficiency.

Mice and Other Pointing Devices

What kinds of mice are there? The mouse type you're probably most familiar with is the **optical mouse**. An optical mouse uses an internal sensor or laser to detect the mouse's movement. The sensor sends signals to the computer, telling it where to move the pointer on the screen. Optical mice don't require a mouse pad, though you can use one to enhance the movement of the mouse on an uneven surface or to protect your work surface from being scratched.

If you have special ergonomic needs or want to customize the functionality of your mouse, there are plenty of options. Most mice have two or three buttons that let you execute commands and open shortcut menus. (Mice for Macs sometimes have only one button.) As shown in Figure 2.9, many mice, such

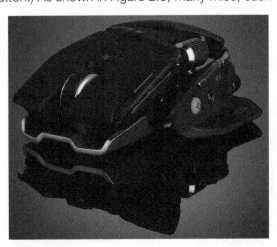

FIGURE 2.9 Customizable mice offer programmable buttons and adjustable fittings to meet most any need. *(R.A.T.)*

BITS&BYTES

Keystroke Shortcuts

Did you know that you can combine certain keystrokes to take shortcuts within an application, such as Microsoft Word, or within the operating system itself? The following are a few of the most helpful Windows-based shortcuts. For more Windows-based shortcuts, visit **support.microsoft.com**. For a list of shortcuts for Macs, see **apple.com/support**.

TEXT FORMATTING	FILE MANAGEMENT	CUT/COPY/ PASTE	WINDOWS CONTROLS
Ctrl+B applies (or removes) **bold** formatting to/from selected text.	**Ctrl+O** opens the Open dialog box.	**Ctrl+X** cuts (removes) selected text and stores it in Clipboard.	**Alt+F4** closes the current window.
Ctrl+I applies (or removes) *italic* formatting to/from selected text.	**Ctrl+N** opens a new document.	**Ctrl+C** copies selected text to Clipboard.	**Windows Key+Tab** displays open Windows 8 apps.
Ctrl+U applies (or removes) <u>underlining</u> to/from selected text.	**Ctrl+S** saves a document.	**Ctrl+V** pastes selected text (previously cut or copied) from Clipboard.	**Windows Key+L** locks the computer.
	Ctrl+P opens the Print dialog box.		**Windows Key+F** opens the Search bar in Files mode.

have their own receivers that often clip into the bottom of the mouse for easy storage when not in use.

Apple has developed the Magic Mouse, the first multitouch wireless mouse (see Figure 2.10). The top surface of the mouse is the button. Use your finger to scroll in any direction, swipe your finger across the mouse to move through web pages and photos, and tap on the mouse to click and double-click.

Are touch pads considered mice? Most laptops have an integrated pointing device such as a **touch pad** (or **trackpad**), a small, touch-sensitive area at the base of the keyboard (see Figure 2.11). Mac laptops include multitouch trackpads, which do not have buttons but are controlled by various one-, two-, three-, and four-finger actions. For example, scrolling is controlled by brushing two fingers along the trackpad in any direction. Most touch pads are sensitive to taps, interpreting them as mouse clicks. Most laptops also have buttons under or near the pads to record mouse clicks. Some laptops incorporate a **trackpoint device**, a small, joystick-like nub that allows you to move the cursor with the tip of your finger (see Figure 2.11).

What input devices are used with games? Game controllers such as joysticks, game pads, and steering wheels are also considered input devices because they send data to the computer. Game controllers, which are similar to the devices used on gaming consoles such as the Xbox 360 and the PlayStation, are also available for use with computers. They have buttons and miniature pointing devices that provide input to the

as the Cyborg R.A.T. 9 Gaming Mouse, have additional programmable buttons and wheels that let you quickly maneuver through web pages or games. In addition, the R.A.T. 9 is customizable to fit any size hand and grip style by allowing for length and width adjustments. Aside from gamers, many people use customizable mice to reduce susceptibility to repetitive strain injuries.

How do wireless mice work? Wireless mice are similar to wireless keyboards in that they use batteries and send data to the computer by RF or Bluetooth technologies. If you have an RF wireless keyboard, then your RF wireless mouse and keyboard usually can share the same RF receiver. Wireless mice for laptops

FIGURE 2.10 The Magic Mouse by Apple has multitouch technology. *(Marcio Jose Sanchez/AP Images)*

Trackpoint device

Touch pad

FIGURE 2.11 Touch pads and trackpoint devices take the place of a mouse on laptop computers. *(Borislav Dopudja/Alamy)*

computer. Most game controllers, such as those for Rock Band and the Wii system, are wireless to provide extra mobility.

Touch Screens

How else can I input data and commands? You've all heard about the iPad—the greatest new gadget since the cell phone. And you've seen and used touch-sensitive screens in fast-food restaurants, airport check-in kiosks, and ATM machines. These **touch screens** are display screens that respond to commands initiated by touching them with your finger or a stylus. Touch screens are becoming

the norm on many computing devices, especially smartphones such as the Droid and iPhone and tablet computers such as the iPad and Samsung Galaxy Tab. Tablets and other touch-screen devices use a virtual keyboard (see Figure 2.12) that displays on screen when input of text is required. These keyboards show basic keyboard configurations and use special keys to switch to numeric, punctuation, and other special keys. You can also connect a wireless keyboard to your tablet if you prefer.

Image Input

What are popular input devices for images? Digital cameras, camcorders, and cell phones are common devices for capturing pictures and video, and all of them are considered input devices. These devices can connect to your computer with a cable, transmit data wirelessly, or transfer data automatically through the Internet. **Scanners** can also input images. They work similarly to a photocopy machine, but instead of generating the image on paper, they create a digital image, which you can then print, save, or e-mail.

How do I capture live video from my computing device? A **webcam** is a small camera that sits on top of your computer monitor (connected to your computer by a cable) or is built into a laptop or tablet computer. Although webcams are able to capture still images, they're used mostly for capturing and transmitting live video. Videoconferencing technology lets a person using a computer equipped with a webcam and a microphone transmit video and audio across the Internet. Video call sites such as Skype (see the Try This in Chapter 1, pages 12–13) and ooVoo (see Figure 2.13) make it easy to videoconference with as many as

FIGURE 2.12 Virtual keyboards are found on tablets and other touch-screen devices. *(PhotoNonStop/Glow Images)*

FIGURE 2.13 Videoconferencing is simplified with software from **ooVoo.com**.

DIG DEEPER

How Touch Screens Work

Touch-screen technology was developed in 1971 and was used primarily with ATMs and fast-food order displays. The technology for monitors and other displays was made popular by the iPod Touch in 2007 and is now in many smartphones, tablet computers, and laptop and desktop monitors. Windows 8 brought the touch-screen interface to Windows users. But how do touch-screen monitors know where you're touching? How do they know what you want them to do?

The basic idea behind touch screens is pretty straightforward—when you place your finger or stylus on a screen, it changes the physical state of the screen and registers your touch. The location of your touch is then translated into a command. Three basic systems are used to recognize a person's touch: *resistive, capacitive,* and *surface acoustic wave.* All of these systems require the basic components of a touch-responsive glass panel, controller, and software driver, combined with a display and computer processor.

The *resistive system* maps the exact location of the pressure point created when a user touches the screen. The *capacitive system* (see Figure 2.14) uses the change in the electrical charge on the glass panel of the monitor, which is created by the user's touch, to generate a location. The third technology, *surface acoustic wave system,* uses two transducers (electrical devices that convert energy from one form to another) that are placed along the x and y axes of the monitor's glass plate. Reflectors, which are also placed on the glass, are used to reflect an electric signal sent from the sending transducer to the receiving transducer. The receiving transducer determines whether the signal has been disturbed by a touch event and locates the touch instantly. With all three systems, the display's software driver then translates the touch into something the operating system can understand, similar to how a mouse driver translates a mouse's movements into a click or drag.

Because the resistive system uses pressure to register a touch, it doesn't matter if the touch is created by a finger or another device. On the other hand, a capacitive system must have conductive input, so generally a finger is required. The surface acoustic wave system allows touches by any object.

The iPhone introduced another complexity to the touch-screen system—a multitouch user interface. In addition to just pressing the screen in one location, multitouch technology can process multiple simultaneous touches on the screen. For example, pinching or spreading out your thumb and finger together makes the display zoom out and in, respectively. The features of each touch, such as size, shape, and location, are also determined.

A touch-sensitive screen, like the one used with the iPhone and iPad and with many other smartphones and tablet computers, arranges the capacitors in a coordinate system so the circuitry can sense changes at each point along the grid (see Figure 2.15). Consequently, every point on the grid

FIGURE 2.14 Some basic touch screens use a capacitive system to detect touches and translate them into meaningful commands that are understood by the computer's operating system.

FIGURE 2.15 Multitouch screens use a coordinate-based grid to arrange the capacitors so the circuitry can detect and respond to multiple touches occurring at the same time.

generates its own signal when touched, and can do so even as another signal is being generated simultaneously. The signals are then relayed to the device's processor. This allows the device to determine the location and movement of simultaneous touches in multiple locations.

After detecting the position and type of touch occurring on the display, the device's processor combines this information with the information it has about the application in use and what was being done in the application when the touch occurred. The processor relays that information to the program in use, and the command is executed. All this happens seemingly instantaneously.

12 people. You can also exchange files, swap control of computers, and text message during the call. There is also a mobile application to make it easy to conference on the go.

Sound Input

Why would I want to input sound to my computer? In addition to letting others hear you in a videoconference, equipping your computer to accept sound input opens up a variety of possibilities. You can conduct audio conferences with work colleagues, chat with friends or family over the Internet, record podcasts, and more. Inputting sound to your computer requires using a **microphone** (or **mic**), a device that lets you capture sound waves (such as your voice) and transfer them to digital format on your computer. Most laptop and tablet computers come with built-in microphones.

What types of add-on microphones are available? For specialized situations, built-in microphones don't always provide the best performance. You may want to consider adding other types of microphones, such as those shown in Figure 2.16, to your system for the best results. ■

FIGURE 2.16

Types of Microphones

MICROPHONE TYPE	ATTRIBUTES	BEST USED FOR
Close Talk	• Attached to a headset (allows for listening) • Leaves hands free	• Video conferencing • Phone calls • Speech recognition software
Omnidirectional	• Picks up sounds equally well from all directions	• Conference calls in meeting rooms
Unidirectional	• Picks up sounds from only one direction	• Recordings with one voice (podcasts)
Clip-on (Lavalier)	• Clips to clothing • Available as wireless	• Presentations requiring freedom of movement • Leaves hands free for writing on whiteboards

(Yuri Arcurs/Fotolia; Blue Microphones; Sumnersgraphicsinc/Fotolia; Feliks Gurevich/Shutterstock)

ethics in IT

What Is Ethical Computing?

You've probably heard news stories about people using computers to unleash viruses or commit identity theft. You may also have read about students who were prosecuted for illegally sharing copyrighted material such as songs and videos. These are both examples of *unethical* behavior while using a computer. However, what constitutes *ethical* behavior while using a computer?

Loosely defined, *ethics* is a system of moral principles, rules, and accepted standards of conduct (see Figure 2.17). So what are the accepted standards of conduct when using computers? The Computer Ethics Institute has developed the Ten Commandments of Computer Ethics, which is widely cited as a benchmark for companies developing computer usage and compliance policies for employees. These guidelines are applicable for schools and students, as well. The ethical computing guidelines listed below are based on the Computer Ethics Institute's work:

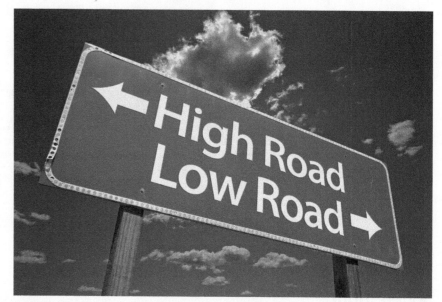

FIGURE 2.17 Strive to take the "high road" and behave ethically by not claiming others' work as your own intellectual output. *(Andy Dean Photography/Shutterstock)*

Ethical Computing Guidelines

1. Avoid causing harm to others when using computers.
2. Do not interfere with other people's efforts at accomplishing work with computers.
3. Resist the temptation to snoop in other people's computer files.
4. Do not use computers to commit theft.
5. Agree not to use computers to promote lies.
6. Do not use software (or make illegal copies for others) without paying the creator for it.
7. Avoid using other people's computer resources without appropriate authorization or proper compensation.
8. Do not claim other people's intellectual output as your own.
9. Consider the social consequences of the products of your computer labor.
10. Only use computers in ways that show consideration and respect for others.

The United States has enacted laws that support some of these guidelines, such as Guideline 6, the breaking of which would violate copyright laws, and Guideline 4, which is enforceable under numerous federal and state larceny laws. Other guidelines, however, require more subtle interpretation as to what behavior is unethical because there are no laws designed to enforce them.

Consider Guideline 7, which covers unauthorized use of resources. The school you attend probably provides computer resources for you to use for coursework. But if your school gives you access to computers and the Internet, is it ethical for you to use those resources to run an eBay business on the weekends? Although it might not be technically illegal, you're tying up computer resources that other students could use for their intended purpose: learning and completing coursework. (This behavior also violates Guidelines 2 and 10.)

Throughout the chapters in this book, we touch on many topics related to these guidelines. So keep them in mind as you study, and think about how they relate to the actions you take as you use computers in your life.

output
DEVICES

An **output device** lets you send processed data out of your computer in the form of text, pictures (graphics), sounds (audio), or video. The most common output device is a **monitor** (sometimes referred to as a **display screen**), which displays text, graphics, and video as soft copies (copies you can see only on screen). Another common output device is the **printer**, which creates hard copies (copies you can touch) of text and graphics. Speakers and earphones (or earbuds) are the output devices for sound.

Monitors

What are the different types of monitors? The most common type of monitor is a **liquid crystal display (LCD)**. An LCD monitor, also called a flat-panel monitor, is light and energy efficient. Some newer monitors use **light-emitting diode (LED)** technology, which is more energy efficient and may have better color accuracy and thinner panels than LCD monitors. LCD flat-panel monitors have replaced cathode ray tube (CRT) monitors. CRT monitors are considered **legacy technology**, or computing devices that use techniques, parts, and methods that are no longer popular. Although legacy technology may still be functional, it has been replaced by newer technological advances.

Organic light-emitting diode (OLED) displays use organic compounds that produce light when exposed to an electric current. Unlike LCDs and LEDs, OLEDs do not require a backlight to function and therefore draw less power and have a much thinner display, sometimes as thin as 3 mm (see Figure 2.18). They are also brighter and more environmentally friendly than LCDs. Because of their lower power needs, OLED displays run longer on a single battery charge than do LEDs, which is why OLED technology is probably the technology used in your cell phone, iPod, and digital camera.

How do LCD monitors work? Monitor screens are grids made up of millions of tiny dots, called **pixels**. When these pixels are illuminated by

FIGURE 2.18 Because they don't need a backlight, OLED displays are much thinner than traditional screens, making LCD and LED screens seem bulky. *(Jae C. Hong, file/AP Images)*

the light waves generated by a fluorescent panel at the back of your screen, they create the images you see on the screen or monitor. Each pixel is actually made up of three red, blue, and green subpixels; some newer LCD TVs on the market have even added a fourth color: yellow. LCD monitors are made of two or more sheets of material filled with a liquid crystal solution (see Figure 2.19). A fluorescent panel at the back of the LCD monitor generates light waves. When electric current passes through the liquid crystal solution, the crystals move around and either block the fluorescent light or let the light shine through. This blocking or passing of light by the crystals causes images to form on the screen. The various combinations of red, blue, and green make up the components of color we see on our monitors.

What factors affect the quality of an LCD monitor? When choosing an LCD monitor, the most important factors to consider are aspect ratio and resolution. The **aspect ratio** is the width-to-height proportion of a monitor. Traditionally, aspect ratios have been 4:3, but newer monitors are available with an aspect ratio of 16:9 to accommodate HD format video. The screen **resolution**, or the clearness or sharpness of the image, reflects the number of pixels on the screen. An LCD monitor may have a native (or maximum) resolution of 1600 × 1200, meaning it contains 1,600 vertical columns with 1,200 pixels in each column. The higher the resolution, the sharper and clearer the image will be, but generally, the resolution of an LCD monitor is dictated by the screen size and aspect ratio. Although you can change the resolution of an LCD monitor beyond its native resolution, the images will become distorted. Generally, you should buy a monitor with the highest resolution available for the screen size (measured in inches). Figure 2.20 lists these and other factors to consider when judging the quality of an LCD monitor.

Is a bigger screen size always better? The bigger the monitor, the more you can display, and depending on what you want to display, size may matter. In general, the larger the panel, the larger number of pixels it can display. For example, a 27-inch monitor can display 2560 × 1440 pixels, whereas a 21.5-inch monitor may only be able to display 1680 × 1050 pixels. However, most new monitors have at least the 1920 × 1080 resolution required to display Blu-ray movies.

Larger screens can also allow you to view multiple documents or web pages at the same time, creating the effect of using two separate monitors side by side. Buying two smaller monitors might be cheaper than buying one large monitor. For either option—a big screen or two separate screens—check that your computer has the appropriate video hardware to support these display devices.

What other features should I look for in an LCD monitor? Some monitors, especially those on laptop computers, come with built-in features

such as speakers, webcams, and microphones. A built-in multiformat memory card reader is convenient for displaying images directly on the monitor or for downloading pictures quickly from a camera memory card to your PC. Another nice feature to look for in a desktop LCD

FIGURE 2.19 A magnification of a single pixel in an LCD monitor.

FIGURE 2.20

Factors to Consider When Shopping for a Monitor

FACTOR	POSSIBLE PROBLEMS	LOOK FOR
Aspect ratio: Width-to-height proportion of a screen	• An odd aspect ratio may make images look distorted	• Ratios of 4:3 or 16:9 (HDTV)
Screen resolution: Number of pixels displayed on the screen	• Low screen resolution = unclear image • High resolution on a small size monitor results in image being too small	• Highest resolution monitor is capable of displaying (make sure you are comfortable viewing that size image)
Contrast ratio: Difference in light intensity between brightest white and darkest black a monitor can produce	• Ratio too low results in colors fading when adjusting brightness	• Ratios between 400:1 and 1,000:1
Viewing angle: Distance in degrees from which you can move to the side of (or above or below) a monitor before the image degrades	• Angle too low means people not sitting directly in front of the monitor will see a poor image	• 150 degrees or more is preferable
Brightness: Greatest amount of light showing when the monitor is displaying pure white (measured in candelas per square meter [cd/m^2] or *nits*)	• Image will be hard to see in bright rooms if brightness level is too low	• 300 cd/m^2 or greater
Response time: Time it takes for a pixel to change color (in milliseconds)	• High response time results in images appearing jerky	• Seek lowest possible response time if viewing live action sports

BITS&BYTES

Testing and Calibrating Your PC Monitor

Most new PC monitors don't need color or tint adjustments, but some can benefit from a few tweaks that will ultimately enhance your video experience. This might be especially important if you're a web designer, digital photographer, or graphics professional. In those professions especially, you want to make sure the colors are displayed on the monitor as accurately as possible. Before you start the calibration process, check that your monitor is set to the "native" resolution (usually the recommended setting). Some monitors have their own calibration program; otherwise, you can work through the adjustments manually or use the display utility in your operating system.

If you're running Windows 7 or 8, you can use the Display Color Calibration utility found by displaying the Control Panel and then clicking Appearance and Personalization. Click Display, and then in the Navigation Pane, click Calibrate color. The Display Color Calibration utility will check the gamma, brightness, contrast, and color balance settings. Gamma describes the relationship between the varying levels of brightness a monitor can display. Brightness determines how dark colors appear on your display. When brightness is set too high, dark colors appear washed out. Contrast determines how white and light colors display. (Note that most laptop computers don't have controls to adjust contrast.) Color balance makes adjustments to the red, blue, and green controls.

---

monitor is a built-in USB port. This feature lets you connect extra peripherals easily without reaching around the back of the PC.

How do I show output to a large group of people? A **projector** lets you project images from your computer onto a wall or viewing screen. Projectors are commonly used in business and education settings such as conference rooms and classrooms. Many projectors are small and lightweight, and some, such as the 3M MPro 150 (see Figure 2.21), are small enough to fit in the palm of your hand. These portable projectors are ideal for businesspeople who have to make presentations at client locations. *Entertainment projectors,* such as the Wonderwall, include stereo speakers and an array of multimedia connectors, making them a good option for use in the home to display TV programs, DVDs, digital images, or video games in a large format. If your computer is equipped with an HDMI port, you can

also choose to connect your computer directly to an HDTV.

Printers

What are the different types of printers? There are two primary categories of printers: inkjet and laser, both of which are considered nonimpact printers. A **nonimpact printer** such as an inkjet printer sprays ink or uses laser beams to transfer marks onto the paper. An **impact printer** has tiny hammer-like

FIGURE 2.21 Inexpensive projectors are showing up more frequently in business and the home to provide large images for movie viewing and gaming. *(3M)*

keys that strike the paper through an inked ribbon to make marks on the paper. For most users, impact printers are legacy technology.

What are the advantages of inkjet printers? An **inkjet printer** (see Figure 2.22) is the type of printer found in most homes. These printers are popular because they're affordable and produce high-quality printouts quickly and quietly. Inkjet printers work by spraying tiny drops of ink onto paper and are great for printing black-and-white text as well as color images. In fact, when loaded with the right paper, higher-end inkjet printers can print images that look like professional-quality photos. One thing to consider when buying an inkjet printer is the type and cost of the ink cartridges the printer needs. Some printers use two cartridges: black and color. Others use four or more cartridges: typically, black, magenta, cyan, and yellow.

Why would I want a laser printer? A **laser printer** uses laser beams and static electricity to deliver toner (similar to ink) onto the correct areas of the page (see Figure 2.23). Heat is used to fuse the toner to the page, making the image permanent. Laser printers are often used in office or classroom settings because they print faster than inkjet printers and produce higher-quality printouts. Black-and-white laser printers have also been common in homes for

FIGURE 2.23 Laser printers print quickly and offer high-quality printouts. *(Xerox Corporation)*

a decade. Over the past few years, the price of color laser printers has fallen dramatically, making them price competitive with high-end inkjet printers. Thus, color laser printers are a viable option for the home. If you print a high volume of pages, consider a laser printer. When you include the price of ink or toner in the overall cost, color laser printers can be more economical than inkjets.

Why should I consider a wireless printer? One reason you may have bought a laptop was to use a computer without the restriction of wires. Wireless printing offers you the same freedom. In addition, wireless printers let several people print to the same printer from different places. There are two types of wireless printers: WiFi and Bluetooth. Both WiFi and Bluetooth printers have a range of up to approximately 300 feet. WiFi, however, sends data more quickly than Bluetooth.

Wireless printers are also great for printing from portable devices. If you're using a device running Apple's iOS (such as an iPhone), AirPrint makes printing easy. AirPrint is a feature of iOS that facilitates printing to AirPrint-compatible wireless printers, and many printers produced today are AirPrint compatible.

Can I carry my printer with me? Although some inkjet printers are small enough to be considered portable, you may want to consider a printer designed for portability. These compact printers can

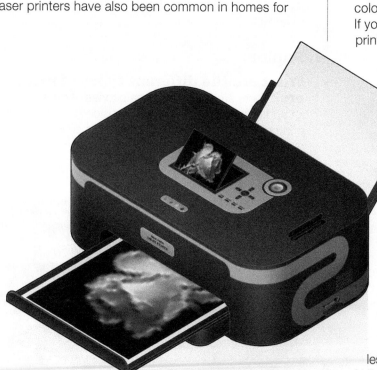

FIGURE 2.22 Inkjet printers are popular among home users, especially with the rise of digital photography. Many inkjet printers are optimized for printing photos from digital cameras. *(TheVectorminator/Shutterstock)*

FIGURE 2.24 Specialty printers: (a) all-in-one printer, (b) plotter, (c) thermal printer. *(Adisa/Fotolia; Provided Courtesy of Xerox Corporation; Zebra Technologies)*

connect to your computer, camera, or smartphone via Bluetooth technology or through a USB port. Portable printers are often compact enough to fit in a briefcase or backpack, are lightweight, and can run on batteries as well as AC power.

Are there any other types of specialty printers? Although you'll probably use laser or inkjet printers most often, you might also encounter several other types of printers:

- An **all-in-one printer** (see Figure 2.24a) combines the functions of a printer, scanner, copier, and fax into one machine. Popular for their space-saving convenience, all-in-one printers may use either inkjet or laser technology.

- A **plotter** (see Figure 2.24b) prints oversize pictures that require the drawing of precise and continuous lines, such as maps and architectural plans. Plotters use a computer-controlled pen that provides a greater level of precision than the series of dots that laser or inkjet printers make.

- A **thermal printer** (see Figure 2.24c) works either by melting wax-based ink onto ordinary paper (a process

called *thermal wax transfer printing*) or by burning dots onto specially coated paper (a process called *direct thermal printing*). Thermal printers are used in stores to print receipts and in airports for electronic ticketing, and many models feature wireless technology. Thermal printers are also popular for mobile printing in conjunction with smartphones and similar devices.

How do I choose the best printer? Your first step is to decide what your primary printing need is. If you're planning to print color photos and graphics, an inkjet printer or color laser printer is a must, even though the cost per page will be higher. If you'll be printing mostly black-and-white, text-based documents or will be sharing your printer with others, a black-and-white laser printer is best because of its speed and overall economy for volume printing. It's also important to determine whether you want just a printer or a device that prints and scans, copies, or faxes (an all-in-one). In addition, you should decide whether you want to print wirelessly.

Once you have narrowed down the *type* of printer you want, you can use the criteria listed in Figure 2.25 to help you determine the best model to meet your needs.

Sound Output

What are the output devices for sound?
Most computers include inexpensive **speakers**, which are the output devices for sound. These speakers are sufficient to play the standard audio clips you find on the web and usually for letting you participate in videoconferencing or phone calls over the Internet. However, if you plan to digitally edit audio files or are particular about how

BITS&BYTES

Does It Matter What Paper I Print On?

The quality of your printer is only part of what controls the quality of a printed image. The paper you use and the printer settings that control the amount of ink used are equally important.

- If you're printing text-only documents for personal use, using low-cost paper is fine. You also may want to consider selecting draft mode in your printer settings to conserve ink. However, if you're printing more formal documents, such as business correspondence, you may want to choose a higher-quality paper (determined by the paper's weight, whiteness, and brightness) and adjust your print setting to "normal" or "best."
- The weight of paper is measured in pounds, with 20 pounds being standard. A heavier paper may be best for projects such as brochures, but be sure to check that your printer can handle the added thickness of the paper.
- The degree of paper whiteness is a matter of personal preference. Generally, the whiter the paper, the brighter the printed color. However, for more-formal documents, you may want to use a creamier color.
- The brightness of paper usually varies from 85 to 94. The higher the number, the brighter the paper, and the easier it is to read printed text.
- Opacity, or the "show through" of ink from one side of the paper to the other, is especially important if you're printing on both sides of the paper.

If you're printing photos, paper quality can have a big impact on your results. Photo paper is more expensive than regular paper and comes in a variety of textures ranging from matte to high gloss. For a photo-lab look, high-gloss paper is the best choice. Semigloss (often referred to as satin) is good for formal portraits, while a matte surface is often used for black-and-white photo printing.

your music sounds, you may want a more sophisticated speaker system, such as one that includes subwoofers (special speakers that produce only low bass sounds) and surround-sound speakers. A **surround-sound speaker** is a system of speakers and audio processing that envelops the listener in a 360-degree field of sound. In addition, wireless speaker systems are available to help you avoid cluttering up your rooms with speaker wires.

FIGURE 2.25

Major Printer Attributes

ATTRIBUTE	CONSIDERATIONS
Speed	• Print speed is measured in *pages per minute (PPM)*. • Black-and-white documents print faster than color documents. • Laser printers often print faster than inkjets.

Resolution	• Resolution refers to a printer's image clarity.
	• Resolution is measured in *dots per inch (dpi)*.
	• Higher dpi = greater level of detail and clarity.
	• Recommended dpi:
	  ○ Black-and-white text: 300
	  ○ General purpose images: 1200
	  ○ Photos: 4800

Color Output	• Printers with separate cartridges for each color produce the best quality output. • Inkjet and laser color printers generally have four colors (black, cyan, magenta, and yellow). • Higher-quality printers have six cartridges (the four above plus light cyan and light magenta). • With separate cartridges, you only need to replace the empty one.
Cost of Consumables	• Consumables are printer cartridges and paper. • Printer cartridges can exceed the cost of some printers. • Consumer magazines such as *Consumer Reports* can help you research costs.

(Freshidea/Fotolia; Michael Nivelet/Fotolia; ThomasAmby/Fotolia; Tomislav Forgo/Fotolia)

If you work in close proximity to other employees or travel with a laptop, you may need to use headphones or earbuds to avoid distracting other people. Both devices plug into the same jack on the computer to which speakers connect. Studies of users of portable media players have shown that hearing might be damaged by excessive volume, especially when using earbuds because they fit into the ear canals. Exercise caution when using these devices. ■

Before moving on to Part 2:
- Watch Replay Video 2.1 ▶.
- **Then check your understanding of what you've learned so far.**

check your understanding//

For a quick review to see what you've learned so far, answer the following questions. Visit **pearsonhighered.com/techinaction** to check your answers.

multiple choice

1. What is a terabyte?

   a. one million bytes   **c.** one billion bits

   b. one trillion bytes   **d.** one trillion bits

2. The type of computer that you might find in your automobile is

   a. a mainframe computer.   **c.** an embedded computer.

   b. a supercomputer.   **d.** none of the above.

3. Which of the following is not an input device?

   a. a touch-screen monitor   **c.** a keyboard

   b. an optical mouse   **d.** a laser printer

4. Which is TRUE about supercomputers?

   a. They perform complex calculations rapidly.

   b. They support hundreds of users simultaneously.

   c. They execute many programs at the same time.

   d. They are specially designed computing devices that reside in other devices.

5. Which is NOT important to consider when buying a monitor?

   a. screen resolution   **c.** color depth

   b. viewing angle   **d.** aspect ratio

true–false

_____ **1.** Data and information are NOT interchangeable terms.

_____ **2.** Inkjet printers are considered legacy technology.

critical thinking

1. Computer of the Future

Think about how mobile our computing devices have become and the convergence of different devices such as cameras, phones, and computers. What do you think the computer of the future will be like? What capabilities will it have that computers currently don't have? Do you see desktop computers becoming obsolete in the near future?

2. Table Monitors and PixelSense Monitors

Table monitors and PixelSense monitors are monitor-like devices built into tabletops and work surfaces. Users "grab" and manipulate objects on the display using touch commands. Like an iPod Touch or iPhone, the display is multi-touch and can accept simultaneous input from multiple users, so the table monitor can be helpful with games or other products that require interactivity. Microsoft launched a product called PixelSense in 2007, and although it never really took off, you see similar devices featured on some TV crime-fighting shows as detectives manipulate crime evidence and photos. Why do you think this device never really captured the interest of the public? Would this be a useful object to have in your home, classroom, or office? Why or why not?

3. Ethics Violations

Review the Ethics in IT section in this chapter. Which of the 10 Ethical Computing Guidelines do you think students violate most often? Why do you think these violations occur, and what do you think could be done to reduce or eliminate such unethical behaviors?

Continue ➡

TRY THIS

What's Inside My Computer?

Understanding what capabilities your current computer has is one of the first steps toward computer literacy. In this exercise, you'll learn how to explore the components of your Windows computer.

Step 1 To gather information about the storage devices on your computer, on the Start screen, click **File Explorer** (previously called Windows Explorer) to switch to the Desktop and display File Explorer. In the navigation pane, click **Computer** to display information about your computer's drives.

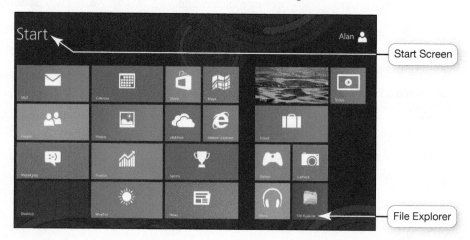

Step 2 The File Explorer Computer screen displays information about internal storage devices (such as internal hard drives), optical storage devices (such as DVD drives), and portable storage devices (such as external hard drives). The total amount of usable storage space, as well as the amount of space actually free (unused), on the devices is shown.

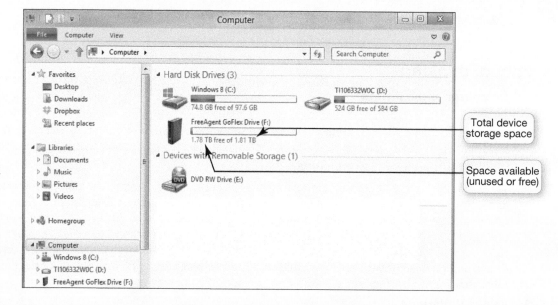

Step 3 To display the System screen, click the **Computer** tab on the File Explorer Ribbon, and then click the **Properties** button.

Step 4 You can gather quite a bit of information from the System screen, such as:

- Version of Windows
- Type of processor
- Speed of the processor
- Amount of RAM installed
- System type (32-bit or 64-bit)

Step 5 On the System screen, click the **Windows Experience Index** link to display the Windows Experience Index screen. This lets you compare the Windows performance of your computer to other computers on a scale developed by Microsoft. Base scores can be interpreted as follows:

- 3.0 to 3.9: sufficient to run most of the cool features of Windows 8 or 7
- 4.0 to 5.9: preferable if you will be running a lot of programs simultaneously (multitasking)
- Above 5.9: indicates a computer that is preferable for optimal 3-D gaming and HDTV viewing experiences

If your base score is not in the range you prefer, looking at the subscores can provide you with guidance as to which components you might want to upgrade to improve performance. For example, installing a higher-end video card and a faster hard drive for the computer shown here would help improve the base score.

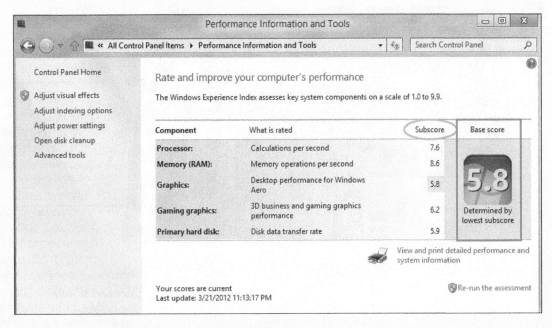

Processing, Storage, and Connectivity

So far, we have explored the components of your computer that you use to input and output data. But where does the processing take place, and where is the data stored? And how does your computer connect with peripherals and other computers?

 ## processing and memory on the
MOTHERBOARD

The **motherboard** is the main circuit board that contains the central electronic components of the computer, including the computer's processor (CPU), its memory, and the many circuit boards that help the computer function (see Figure 2.26). On a desktop, the motherboard is located inside the system unit, the metal or plastic case that also houses the power source and all the storage devices (CD/DVD drive and hard drive). In a laptop computer, the system unit is combined with the monitor and the keyboard into a single package.

What's on the motherboard besides the CPU and memory? The motherboard also includes slots for **expansion cards** (or **adapter cards**), which are circuit boards that provide additional functionality. Typical expansion cards found in the system unit are sound and video cards. A **sound card**

provides a connection for the speakers and microphone, whereas a **video card** provides a connection for the monitor. Laptops have video and sound capabilities integrated into their motherboards. High-end desktops use expansion cards to provide video and sound capabilities.

Other expansion cards provide a means for network and Internet connections. These include the *modem card,* which provides the computer with a connection to the Internet via a traditional phone line. Modem cards are rapidly becoming legacy technology. A **network interface card (NIC)**, which enables your computer to connect with other computers or to a cable modem to facilitate a high-speed Internet connection, is now the most common connectivity port. Lastly, some expansion cards provide additional USB and FireWire ports.

Memory

What exactly is RAM? **Random access memory (RAM)** is the place in a computer where the programs and data the computer is currently using are stored. RAM is much faster to read from and write to than the hard drive and other forms of storage. The processor can request the RAM's contents, which can be located, opened, and delivered to the CPU for processing in a few nanoseconds (billionths of a second). If you look at a motherboard, you'll see RAM as a series of small cards (called *memory cards* or *memory modules*) plugged into slots on the motherboard (see Figure 2.26).

Expansion slots

Memory (RAM) slots

CPU

Ports

FIGURE 2.26 A motherboard contains the computer's processor (CPU), the memory (RAM) modules, ports, and slots for expansion cards. *(S.Dashkevych/Shutterstock)*

Because the entire contents of RAM are erased when you turn off the computer, RAM is a temporary or **volatile storage** location. To save data permanently, you need to save it to your hard drive or to another permanent storage device such as a CD or flash drive.

Does the motherboard contain any other kinds of memory besides RAM? In addition to RAM, the motherboard contains a form of memory called **read-only memory (ROM)**. ROM holds all the instructions the computer needs to start up when it is powered on. Unlike data stored in RAM, which is volatile storage, the instructions stored in ROM are permanent, making ROM a **nonvolatile storage** location, which means the data isn't erased when the power is turned off.

Processing

What is the CPU? The **central processing unit** (**CPU**, or **processor**) is sometimes referred to as the "brains" of the computer because it controls all the functions performed by the computer's other components and processes all the commands issued to it by software instructions. Modern CPUs can perform as many as tens of billions of tasks per second without error, making them extremely powerful components.

How is processor speed measured? Processor speed is measured in units of hertz (Hz). Hertz is a measurement of machine cycles per second. A machine cycle is the process of the CPU getting the data or instructions from RAM and decoding the instructions into something the computer can understand. Once the CPU has decoded the instructions, it executes them and stores the result back in system memory. Current systems run at speeds measured in **gigahertz (GHz)**, or billions of machine cycles per second. Therefore, a 3.8 GHz processor performs work at a rate of 3.8 billion machine cycles per second. It's important to realize, however, that CPU processor speed alone doesn't determine the performance of the CPU.

What else determines processor performance? Although speed is an important consideration when determining processor performance, CPU performance is also affected by other factors. One factor is the number of *cores,* or processing paths, a processor has. Initially, processors could handle only one instruction at a time. Now,

processors have been designed so that they can have two, four, or even eight different paths, allowing them to process more than one instruction at a time (see Figure 2.27). Applications such as virus protection software and the operating system, which are always running behind the scenes, can have their own processor paths, freeing up the other paths to run other applications such as a web browser, Word, or iTunes more efficiently.

Besides the number of cores, what other factors determine processing power? The "best" processor will depend on your particular needs and is not always the processor with the highest processor speed and the greatest number of cores. Intel, one of the leading manufacturers of computer processor chips, has created a pictorial rating system for CPU chips. Intel uses one to five stars to illustrate the relative computing power of each type of CPU within the Intel line of processors. ■

FIGURE 2.27 With multi-core processors, CPUs can work in parallel, processing two or more separate programs at the same time instead of switching back and forth between them.

storing data and INFORMATION

Because RAM is volatile storage, it can't be used to store information indefinitely. To save your data and information permanently, you need to save it to your hard drive or to another nonvolatile storage device such as an external hard drive, a DVD, or a flash drive.

Hard Drives

Are there different kinds of hard drives? The **hard disk drive (HDD**, or **hard drive)** is your computer's primary device for permanent storage of software and documents. The hard drive is a nonvolatile storage device. An **internal hard drive** resides within the system unit and usually holds all permanently stored programs and data. Today's internal hard drives (see Figure 2.28a) have capacities of as much as 6 TB or more. **External hard drives** (see Figure 2.28b) offer similar storage capacities but reside outside the system unit and connect to the computer via a USB or FireWire port.

The most common type of hard drive has moveable parts—spinning platters, a moving arm with a read/write head—that can fail and lead to devastating disk failure. However, the **solid-state drive (SSD)** has recently become a more feasible option for desktop and laptop storage. SSDs have no moving parts, so they're more efficient, run with no noise, emit little heat, and require little power. In addition, they're less likely to fail after being bumped or dropped.

Permanent storage devices are located in your desktop or laptop computer in a space called a **drive bay**. There are two kinds of drive bays:

1. *Internal drive bays* cannot be seen or accessed from outside the system unit. Generally, internal drive bays are reserved for internal hard drives.

2. *External drive bays* can be seen and accessed from outside the system unit. External drive bays house CD and DVD drives, for example. On desktop computers, sometimes there are empty external drive bays that can be used to install additional drives. These extra spaces are covered by a faceplate on the front panel. Laptop computers generally do not give you the ability to add additional drives. Such expansion is done by attaching an external drive to the computer through a USB port.

Flash Storage

How can I take my files with me? For large portable storage needs, there are portable external hard drives, which are small enough to fit into your pocket and have storage capacities of 4 TB (or larger). These devices are lightweight and enclosed in a protective case. They attach to your computer via a USB port (see Figure 2.29). Many of these portable external hard drives do not use solid-state technology, so care should be taken when transporting them.

FIGURE 2.28 (a) Internal hard drives are a computer's primary nonvolatile storage. (b) External hard drives are often used to back up data from internal hard drives. *(Ragnarock/Shutterstock; Utflytter/Shutterstock)*

FIGURE 2.29 Smaller, portable external hard drives enable you to take a significant amount of data and programs on the road with you. *(Inga Nielsen/Shutterstock)*

BITS&BYTES

Taking Care of Flash Drives

Although they're fairly rugged and can withstand much abuse, flash drives can fail. Therefore, it's important to know how to care for your flash drive to extend its life and keep your data safe.

1. Don't expose your flash drive to moisture or extreme temperatures.

2. Keep the end covered or closed when not in use. This prevents dust and other particles from interfering with the connections.

3. Never "defragment" a flash drive, as doing so can reduce its life expectancy.

4. A flash drive has a limited amount of writes in its lifetime. Depending on the device, it could be 10,000 or 100,000, which seems like a lot. However, over years of extensive use, the number of writes will add up. It's best to make edits to documents on the computer and then transfer the finished document to your flash drive.

5. Remove the flash drive correctly. All files and folders must be closed, with no active documents running, before the device is removed. To properly eject the device, use the "Safely remove hardware" feature in the taskbar, or select Eject from Windows Explorer (called File Explorer in Windows 8). (Mac users should select Eject from the Finder menu.) If you find that you can't eject the flash drive using these methods, power down the computer before removing the drive.

FIGURE 2.30 Flash drives are a convenient means of portable storage and come in many different shapes and sizes. *(Rafael Angel Irusta Machin/Alamy; Handout/KRT/Newscom)*

A **flash drive** (sometimes referred to as a **jump drive**, **USB drive**, or **thumb drive**) uses solid-state flash memory, storing information on an internal memory chip. When you plug a flash drive into your computer's USB port, it appears in the operating system as another disk drive. You can write data to it or read data from it as you would a hard drive. Because a flash drive contains no moving parts, it's quite durable. It's also tiny enough to fit in your pocket. Despite their size, flash drives can have significant storage capacity—currently as much as 256 GB. Often, flash drives are combined with other de-

vices such as pens or pocketknives (see Figure 2.30) for added convenience.

Another convenient means of portable storage is a **flash memory card** such as a CompactFlash card. Like the flash drive, memory cards use solid-state flash memory. Most desktops and laptops include slots for flash memory cards, but if your computer is not equipped, there are memory card readers that you can plug into a USB port. Flash memory cards let you transfer digital data between your computer and devices such as digital cameras, smartphones, video cameras, and printers. Although incredibly small—some are even smaller than the size of a postage stamp—these memory cards have capacities that exceed the capacity of a DVD. Figure 2.31 compares the storage capacities of hard drives and flash drives.

Optical Storage

What other kinds of storage devices are available? Most desktop and laptop computers come with at least one **optical drive** that can read from and maybe even write to CDs, DVDs, or Blu-ray discs. Data is saved to such discs as tiny pits that are burned

FIGURE 2.31

Hard Drive and Flash Drive Storage Capacity

DRIVE TYPE	IMAGE	TYPICAL CAPACITY
Solid-state drive (SSD)		5 TB or more
External portable hard drive		4 TB or more
Mechanical internal hard drive		As much as 6 TB or more
Flash drive		256 GB or more
Flash memory card		128 GB

(Oleksiy Mark/iStockphoto; Joel-t/iStockphoto; D. Hurst/Alamy; Cphoto/Fotolia; ZUMA Wire Service/Alamy)

FIGURE 2.32

Optical Storage Media Capacities

MEDIUM TYPE	IMAGE	TYPICAL CAPACITY
Blu-ray (dual layer)		50 GB
Blu-ray		25 GB
DVD DL (dual layer)		8.5 GB
DVD		4.7 GB
CD		700 MB

(PRNewsFoto/Sony Electronics Inc/AP Images; Coyote-Photography.co.uk/Alamy; dimedrol68/Fotolia; Niels Poulsen/Alamy; Studio 101/Alamy)

into the disc by a high-speed laser. **Compact discs (CDs)** were initially created to store audio files. **Digital video (or versatile) discs (DVDs)** are the same size and shape as CDs but can store up to 14 times more data than CDs.

What if you want even more storage capacity? Blu-ray is the latest incarnation of optical storage to hit the market. **Blu-ray discs (BDs)**, which are similar in size and shape to CDs and DVDs, can hold as much as 50 GB of data—enough to hold approximately 4.5 hours of movies in high-definition (HD) digital format. Many systems are now available with BD-ROM drives and even Blu-ray burners. External BD drives are another inexpensive way to add HD storage capacity to your system. Figure 2.32 shows the storage capacities of the various optical storage media. ■

connecting peripherals to the
COMPUTER

Throughout this chapter, we have discussed peripheral devices that input, store, and output data and information. A **port** is a place through which a peripheral device attaches to the computer so that data can be exchanged between it and the operating system (see Figure 2.33). Although many ports are located on the back of computers, some commonly used ports are found on the front and sides for easier access when connecting devices such as flash drives or digital and video cameras.

High-Speed and Data Transfer Ports

What is the most common way to connect devices to a computer? A **universal serial bus (USB) port** (see Figure 2.34) is the port type most commonly used to connect input and output devices to the computer. This is mainly because of a USB port's ability to transfer data quickly. USB ports can connect a wide variety of peripherals, including keyboards, printers, mice, smartphones, external hard drives, flash drives, and digital cameras, to the computer. USB 2.0 ports are the current standard and transfer data at 480 megabits per second (Mbps). The new USB 3.0 standard provides transfer speeds of 4.8 Gbps and charges devices faster than its predecessor. USB 3.0 is quickly becoming the port of choice.

What other types of data transfer ports are there? You may also see other ports, such as **FireWire 400** and **FireWire 800**. The FireWire 400 interface moves data at 400 Mbps, whereas the FireWire 800 doubles the rate to 800 Mbps. Devices such as external hard drives, digital video cameras, portable music players, and digital media players all benefit from the speedy data transfer capabilities of FireWire. FireWire 400 ports have two different configurations, as shown in Figure 2.34. FireWire 400 ports on computers generally have six pins, whereas FireWire 400 ports on digital cameras have four pins.

a

b

Ethernet port

Memory card slots

Audio/video ports

FireWire ports

S-video

USB ports

FIGURE 2.33 Many of the same ports appear on both (a) desktop and (b) laptop computers. *(Restyler/Fotolia; Alexkar08/Shutterstock)*

USB ports

6-pin FireWire port

4-pin FireWire port

Port icons

Ethernet port

Modem port

FIGURE 2.34 Common data transfer and connectivity ports. Each port is represented by a standard icon. *(jStock/Fotolia)*

To transfer data between two devices, a special cable that has an appropriate connector at each end is needed. The faster FireWire 800 requires a nine-pin connection and is found on storage devices such as external and portable hard drives. The FireWire 3200 standard, with data transfer rates of 3.2 Gbps, has been ratified but has yet to reach the market.

Connectivity and Multimedia Ports

Which ports help me connect with other computers and the Internet?
Another set of ports on your computer helps you communicate with other computers. A **connectivity port** can give you access to networks and the Internet. To find a connectivity port, look for a port that resembles a standard phone jack but is slightly larger. This port is called an **Ethernet port** (see Figure 2.34). Ethernet ports transfer data at speeds up to 10,000 Mbps. You can use an Ethernet port to connect your computer to a digital subscriber line (DSL) or cable modem, or to a network. Some computers still feature a second connectivity port that will accept a standard phone line connector. This jack is the **modem port** (see Figure 2.34). It uses a traditional telephone signal to connect the computer to the Internet over a phone line. Modem ports are quickly becoming legacy technology.

How do I connect monitors and multimedia devices?
Other ports on the back and sides of the computer include audio and video ports (see Figure 2.35). Audio ports are where you connect headphones, microphones, and

speakers to the computer. Whether you're attaching a monitor to a desktop computer, or adding a second, larger display to a laptop computer, you'll use a video port. The **video graphics array (VGA) port** is the port to which older LCD monitors connect (see Figure 2.35).

Newer LCD monitors, as well as other multimedia devices such as televisions, DVD players, and projectors, connect to **digital video interface (DVI) ports** (see Figure 2.36).

How can I connect my computer to TVs and gaming consoles? The latest digital connector designed for use in HD home theater environments is a **high-definition multimedia interface (HDMI)**, a compact audio–video interface that carries

FIGURE 2.35 Video ports (VGA ports) connect monitors and multimedia devices to the computer; audio ports are used to connect speakers, headphones, and microphones.

FIGURE 2.36 VGA (left) and DVI (right) cables are used to connect LCD monitors to computers. *(Marek Kosmal/Fotolia)*

FIGURE 2.37 HDMI is the latest digital connector type for HD home theater equipment. *(DSGPro/iStockphoto)*

both HD video and uncompressed digital audio on one cable. (DVI can only carry video signals.) Because HDMI can transmit uncompressed audio and video, there's no need to convert the signal, which could ultimately reduce the quality of the sound or picture. Most DVD players, televisions, and game consoles have at least one HDMI port (see Figure 2.37).

Adding Ports: Expansion Cards and Hubs

What if I don't have all the ports I need?

If you're looking to add the newest ports to an older desktop computer or to expand the number of ports on it, you can install special expansion cards into an open expansion slot on the motherboard to provide additional ports. If your laptop computer requires additional ports, you can add them with an express card adapter, which fits into a slot on the side of your laptop. Figure 2.38 shows an example of both of these scenarios.

Another alternative is adding an expansion hub (shown in Figure 2.39). An expansion hub is a device that connects to one port, such as a USB port, to provide additional ports. It works like the multiplug extension cords used with electrical appliances. ■

 SOUND BYTE
Port Tour: How Do I Hook It Up?

In this Sound Byte, you'll take a tour of both a desktop system and a laptop system to compare the number and variety of available ports. You'll also learn about the different types of ports and compare their speed and expandability.

a

b

FIGURE 2.38 Expansion cards can (a) fit on the motherboard in a desktop computer or (b) in a card slot on your laptop to provide your computer with additional ports. *(Andrew Kitching/Alamy; Editorial Image, LLC/Alamy)*

FIGURE 2.39 If you don't have enough USB ports to support your USB devices, consider getting an expansion hub, which can add four or more USB ports to your system. *(Norman Chan/Fotolia)*

power

CONTROLS

What's the best way to turn my computer on and off? The **power supply**, which is housed inside the system unit, transforms the wall voltage to the voltages required by computer chips. Powering on your computer from a completely turned off state, such as when you start your computer in the morning, is called a **cold boot**. In Windows 8, you can turn your computer off by pressing the computer's power button or by using the Shut Down option from the power icon found under Settings on the Charms bar.

Should I turn off my computer every time I'm done using it? Some people say you should leave your computer on at all times. They argue that turning your computer on and off throughout the day subjects its components to stress because the heating and cooling process forces the components to expand and contract repeatedly. Other people say you should shut down your computer when you're not using it. They claim that it's not as environmentally friendly and that you'll end up wasting money on electricity from the computer running all the time.

Modern operating systems include power-management settings that allow the most power-hungry components of the system (the hard drive and monitor) to shut down after a short idle period. With the power-management options of Windows 8, for example, you only need to shut down your computer completely when you need to repair or install hardware in the system unit or move it to another location. However, if you use your computer only for a little while each day, it would be best to power it off completely after each daily use.

Can I "rest" my computer without turning it off completely? In Windows 8, the main method of power management is Sleep. When your computer enters **Sleep mode**, all of the documents, applications, and data you were using remain in RAM (memory), where they're quickly accessible when you restart your computer.

In Sleep mode, the computer enters a state of greatly reduced power consumption, which saves energy. To put your computer into Sleep mode in Windows 8,

FIGURE 2.40 You can determine what happens when you click the power button on your computer or close the lid through the Power Options System Settings screen.

>*To access Power Options System Settings, display the Control Panel, click* **Hardware and Sound,** *and then select* **Change what the power buttons do** *under Power Options.*

FIGURE 2.41 The Settings panel in Windows 8 presents several power options. For a warm boot, choose **Restart**. To power down the computer completely, choose **Shut down**. To put your computer into a lower power mode, select **Sleep**.

>*To select a particular power option, display the Charms bar, click **Settings**, then click the **Power** button.*

display the Charms bar, click (or touch) the Setting option, then click Power option and select the Sleep option. To wake up your computer, press a key or the power button. In a few seconds, the computer will resume with exactly the same programs running and documents displayed as when you put it to sleep.

If you don't ever want to completely turn off your computer, you can change what happens when you press the power button or close the lid on your laptop. By accessing the Power Options System Settings window (see Figure 2.40), you can decide if you want your computer to Sleep, Hibernate, or Shut Down when you press the power button. The **Hibernate** option is similar to Sleep except that your data is stored on your hard drive instead of in RAM and your computer is powered off. This uses much less battery power than Sleep and is a good choice if you won't be using your laptop for a

long time and won't have the opportunity to charge it. However, Sleep is still a good option to choose if you just won't be using your computer for a short time. You may want to set your computer so it sleeps when you close the lid but hibernates when you press the power button, giving you quick access to either option.

What's the restart option in Windows for? If you're using Windows 8, you have the option to restart the computer when you display the Charms bar, click (or touch) Settings, then click the Power button (see Figure 2.41). Restarting the system while it's powered on is called a **warm boot**. You might need to perform a warm boot if the operating system or other software application stops responding or if you've installed new programs. It takes less time to perform a warm boot than to power down completely and then restart all your hardware. ■

setting it
ALL UP

It's important that you understand not only your computer's components and how they work together but also how to set up these components safely. **Ergonomics** is the science that deals with the design and location of machines and furniture so that the people using them aren't subjected to an uncomfortable or unsafe experience. In terms of computing, ergonomics refers to how you set up your computer and other equipment to minimize your risk of injury or discomfort.

Why is ergonomics important? Studies suggest that teenagers, on average, spend 31 hours online each week. When you factor in other computer uses such as typing school reports and playing video games, there is great potential for injury. The repetitive nature of long-term computer activities can place too much stress on joints and pull at the tendons and muscles, causing repetitive stress injuries such as carpal tunnel syndrome and tendonitis. These injuries can take months or years to develop to a point where they become painful, and by the time you notice the symptoms, the damage has already taken place. If you take precautionary measures now, you may prevent years of unnecessary pain later.

How can I avoid injuries when I'm working at my computer? As Figure 2.42 illustrates, it's important to arrange your monitor, chair, body, and keyboard in ways that will help you avoid injury, discomfort, and eyestrain. The following additional guidelines can help keep you comfortable and productive:

- **Position your monitor correctly**. Studies suggest it's best to place your monitor at least 25 inches from your eyes. Experts recommend that you position your monitor either at eye level or at an angle 15 to 20 degrees below your line of sight.
- **Purchase an adjustable chair.** Adjust the height of your chair so that your feet touch the floor (or use a footrest to get the right position). The back support needs to be adjustable so that you can position it to support your lumbar (lower back) region. You should also be able to move the seat or adjust the back so that you can sit without exerting pressure on your knees. If your chair doesn't adjust, place a pillow behind your back to provide support.
- **Assume a proper position while typing.** Improperly positioned keyboards are one of the leading causes of repetitive stress injuries in computer users. Your wrists

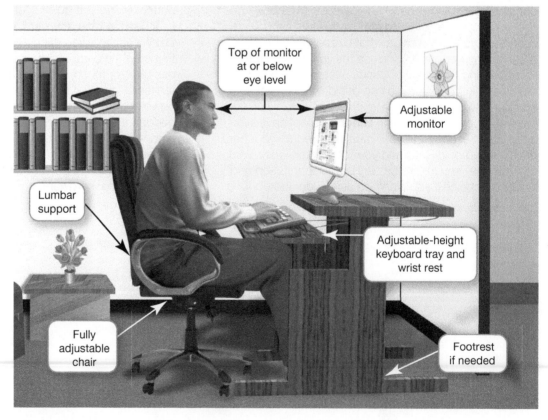

FIGURE 2.42 Using proper equipment that is adjusted correctly helps prevent repetitive strain injuries while working at a computer.

should be flat (not bent) with respect to the keyboard, and your forearms should be parallel to the floor. Additionally, your wrists should not be resting on the keyboard while typing. You can adjust the height of your chair or install a height-adjustable keyboard tray to ensure a proper position. Specially designed ergonomic keyboards such as the one shown in Figure 2.43 can help you achieve the proper wrist position.

- **Take breaks.** Remaining in the same position for long periods of time increases stress on your body. Shift your position in your chair and stretch your hands and fingers periodically. Likewise, staring at the screen for long periods can lead

FIGURE 2.43 Ergonomic keyboards that curve and contain built-in wrist rests help maintain proper hand position and minimize wrist strain. *(Dmitry Melnikov/Shutterstock)*

FIGURE 2.44

Preventing Injuries While on the Go

	PDA/SMARTPHONE REPETITIVE STRAIN INJURIES	PORTABLE MEDIA PLAYER HEARING DAMAGE	SMALL-SCREEN VISION ISSUES	LAP INJURIES	TABLET REPETITIVE STRAIN INJURIES
Malady	Repetitive strain injuries (such as DeQuervain's tendonitis) from constant typing of instant messages	Hearing loss from high-decibel sound levels in earbuds	Blurriness and dryness caused by squinting to view tiny screens on mobile devices	Burns on legs from heat generated by laptop	Pain caused from using tablets for prolonged periods in uncomfortable positions
Preventative measures	Restrict length and frequency of messages, take breaks, and perform other motions with your thumbs and fingers during breaks to relieve tension.	Turn down volume (you should be able to hear external noises, such as people talking), use software that limits sound levels (not to exceed 60 decibels), and use external, over-ear style headphones instead of earbuds.	Blink frequently or use eye drops to maintain moisture in eyes, after 10 minutes take a break and focus on something at least 8 feet away for 5 minutes, use adequate amount of light, and increase the size of fonts.	Place a book, magazine, or laptop cooling pad between your legs and laptop.	Restrict the length of time you work at a tablet, especially typing or gaming. Use the same ergonomic position you would use for a laptop when using a tablet.

to eyestrain, so rest your eyes by periodically taking them off the screen and focusing them on an object at least 8 feet away.

- **Ensure the lighting is adequate.** Ensuring that you have proper lighting in your work area minimizes eyestrain. Eliminate sources of direct glare (light shining directly into your eyes) or reflected glare (light shining off the computer screen) and ensure there is enough light to read comfortably. If you still can't eliminate glare from your computer screen, you can buy an antiglare screen to place over your monitor.

Is ergonomics important when using mobile devices?

Working with mobile computing devices presents interesting challenges when it comes to injury prevention. For example, many users work with laptops resting on their laps, placing the monitor outside of the optimal line of sight and thereby increasing neck strain. Figure 2.44 provides guidelines on preventing injuries when computing on the go.

So, whether you're computing at your desk or on the road, consider the ergonomics of your work environment. Doing so will help you avoid injury and discomfort.

What devices are available for people with disabilities?

People who have physical challenges sometimes need special devices to access computers. For visually impaired users, voice recognition is an input option. For those users whose visual limitations are less severe, keyboards with larger keys are available. Keyboards that display on a touch screen or specialized input consoles (see Figure 2.45a) can make input easier for individuals who can't type with their hands: The user presses the keys with a pointing device. There are also keyboards, such as those made by Maltron, designed for individuals who can use only one hand (see Figure 2.45b).

People with motor control issues may have difficulty with pointing devices. To aid such users, special trackballs are available that can be easily manipulated with one finger and can be attached to almost any surface, including a wheelchair. When arm motion is severely restrained, head-mounted pointing devices can be used. Generally, these involve a camera mounted on the computer monitor and a device attached to the head (often installed in a hat). When the user moves his or her head, the camera detects the movement and moves the cursor. In this case, mouse clicks are controlled by a switch that can be manipulated by the user's hands or feet or even by using an instrument that fits into the mouth and senses the user blowing into it. ■

Before moving on to the Chapter Review:
- Watch Replay Video 2.2 ▶.
- Then check your understanding of what you've learned so far.

a

b

FIGURE 2.45 (a) Input consoles for people who can't type with their hands and (b) keyboards designed for one-handed use make computer interaction easier for individuals with disabilities. *(www.maltron.com; www.maltron.com)*

With the advent of the computer, many speculated that ours would become a paperless society. Instead of saving printed documents and other output as was done prior to the PC, information would be saved in a digital state: hard drives replacing filing cabinets, online photo buckets replacing photo albums and scrapbooks, and e-books replacing our favorite texts. Hard drive capacities do enable us to save more content, and online storage systems enable us to save pictures and other files to the "cloud." Additionally, e-book readers have increased in popularity. But has this push toward digital content begun to make the printer obsolete? Surprisingly, no. People still have a deep-rooted need to see, feel, mark, share, or use their digital images or information in a physical form. New technologies that push the boundaries of printing, such as printing from the cloud and 3-D printing, are being developed and refined.

Cloud Printing

To print a document from a desktop or laptop computer, you must have a printer associated with your computer. Usually this is not a problem because at home, at school, or in the office, there is generally one printer, and all the PCs connected to it have the software and cables or wireless capabilities needed to use it. But what happens if you want to print something from your smartphone or tablet? Common solutions have been to e-mail the document to yourself or transfer the document to a web-based storage service such as Dropbox so that a printer-connected computer could access it. Another solution is Google Cloud Print, a service that lets you configure your printers so you can access them from mobile devices.

Google Cloud Print uses cloud-ready printers (see Figure 2.46) that are now available from manufacturers such as HP, Kodak, and Epson. These printers connect directly to the Internet and register themselves with Google Cloud Print without needing to be connected to a computer. Once a printer is registered with Cloud Print, printing jobs can be sent to it from mobile devices (such as tablets and smartphones) using the Internet. Conventional printers that you already own can also be registered with Cloud Print, although they require connection to the Internet through a computer.

FIGURE 2.46 Cloud-ready printers only need an Internet connection to be accessed from any mobile device.

3-D Printing

Printing a 3-D model of a proposed building or new prototype is common for architects and engineers. The process builds a model one layer at a time from the bottom up. The procedure begins by spreading a layer of powder on a platform. Then, depending on the technology, the printer uses nozzles similar to those in an inkjet printer to spray tiny drops of glue at specific places to solidify the powder, or the powder is solidified through a melting process. The printer repeats solidifying layers of powder until the model is built to specifications. This technology has spurred the manufacturing of a variety of consumer goods, from toys to clothing. Shapeways (**shapeways.com**) uses 3-D printing to enable anyone to turn his or her 3-D designs into real physical models. Then, those models can be personalized, bought, or sold through Shapeways's online community.

3-D printing is being used in the medical community as well. Bespoke Innovations (**bespokeinnovations.com**) is using 3-D printing to create prosthetic limbs with more life-like form and textures, as well as to give the recipient the ability to further personalize the prosthetic to include tattoos! As mentioned in Chapter 1, researchers at Wake Forest Institute for Regenerative Medicine have developed a way to use similar inkjet technologies to build heart, bone, and blood vessel tissues in the lab. They have also developed a way to "print" restorative cells directly into a soldier's wound at the site where the injury occurred, thus significantly improving the soldier's chances of survival.

Taking traditional technologies, such as inkjet printing, and applying them to solve current human struggles is a long and tedious process, but without these pioneers experimenting with different applications, society would advance a lot more slowly.

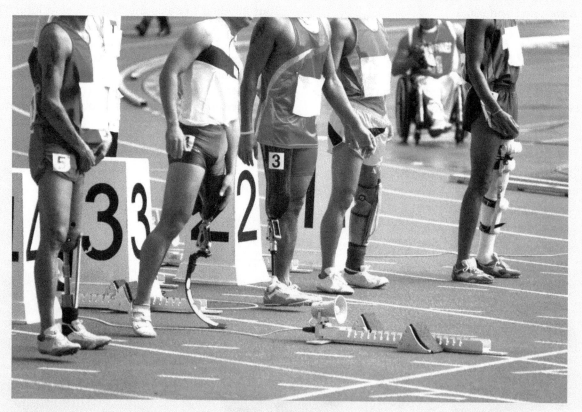

3D printing is being used to produce more realistic artificial limbs that can even contain tattoos! *(Shariff Che'Lah/Fotolia)*

check your understanding //

For a quick review to see what you've learned so far, answer the following questions. Visit **pearsonhighered.com/techinaction** to check your answers.

multiple choice

1. Which port enables your computer to communicate with networks and other computers?
   a. USB
   b. connectivity
   c. DVI
   d. VGA

2. To add ports to your computer, what do you need?
   a. a digital media card reader
   b. an external hard drive
   c. an expansion hub
   d. a flash memory card

3. Which of these are NOT located on the motherboard?
   a. CPU
   b. ROM
   c. RAM
   d. hard drive

4. Which of these is NOT an optical storage device?
   a. flash drive
   b. CD drive
   c. DVD drive
   d. Blu-ray drive

5. Ergonomics is an important consideration
   a. only for desktop computers.
   b. only for laptop computers.
   c. only for laptop and desktop computers, but never for mobile devices.
   d. for all computing devices.

true–false

_____ **1.** The hard drive is an example of a volatile storage device.

_____ **2.** The processor speed of the CPU is not the only measure of a processor's expected performance.

critical thinking

1. **External Storage**

   Hard drives are great for storing data on your computer, but there are many reasons why you might want to have alternative storage devices. List various external and mobile storage devices discussed in this chapter, and describe the purposes and uses of each. Which device types do you currently use, and for what purposes? What device(s) might you have a need to use in the next year or so?

2. **iPad**

   The Apple iPad has been enthusiastically accepted because of its multitouch screen, useful apps, two cameras, and small, light frame. If the CEO of Apple were to ask you for your advice as to what to include in the next version of the iPad, what would you suggest? What features would make tablets even more appealing to students?

Continue

Understanding Your Computer

1. What exactly is a computer, and what are its four main functions?

- Computers are devices that process data. They help organize, sort, and categorize data to turn it into information.

- The computer's four major functions are: (1) input: gather data, or allow users to enter data; (2) process: manipulate, calculate, or organize that data; (3) output: display data and information in a form suitable for the user; and (4) storage: save data and information for later use.

2. What is the difference between data and information?

- Data is a representation of a fact or idea. The number 3 and the words *televisions* and *Sony* are pieces of data.

- Information is data that has been organized or presented in a meaningful fashion. An inventory list that indicates that "three Sony televisions" are in stock is processed information. It allows a retail clerk to answer a customer query about the availability of merchandise. Information is more powerful than raw data.

3. What are bits and bytes, and how are they measured?

- To process data into information, computers need to work in a language they understand. This language, called *binary language*, consists of two numbers: 0 and 1.

- Each 0 and each 1 is a binary digit, or bit. Eight bits create one byte.

- In computers, each letter of the alphabet, each number, and each special character consists of a unique combination of eight bits (one byte)—a string of eight 0s and 1s.

- For describing large amounts of storage capacity, the terms *megabyte* (approximately 1 million bytes), *gigabyte* (approximately 1 billion bytes), and *terabyte* (approximately 1 trillion bytes) are used.

Input Devices and Output Devices

4. What devices can I use to get data into the computer?

- An input device enables you to enter data (text, images, and sounds) and instructions (user responses and commands) into a computer.

- You use keyboards to enter typed data and commands, whereas you use the mouse to enter user responses and commands.

- Touch screens are display screens that respond to commands initiated by a touch with a finger or a stylus.

- Images are input into the computer with scanners, digital cameras, camcorders, and smartphones.

- Live video is captured with webcams and digital video recorders.

- Microphones capture sounds. There are many different types of microphones, including desktop, headset, and clip-on models.

5. What devices can I use to get information out of the computer?

- Output devices enable you to send processed data out of your computer. It can take the form of text, pictures, sounds, or video.

- Monitors display soft copies of text, graphics, and video, whereas printers create hard copies of text and graphics.

- There are two primary categories of printers: inkjet and laser. Specialty printers are also available. These include all-in-one printers, plotters, and thermal printers. When choosing a printer, you should be aware of factors such as speed, resolution, color output, and cost.

- Speakers are the output devices for sound. Most computers include speakers; more-sophisticated systems include subwoofers and surround sound.

Processing, Memory, and Storage

6. What's on the motherboard?

- The motherboard, the main circuit board of the system, contains a computer's CPU, which coordinates the functions of all other devices on the computer. The performance of a CPU is affected by the speed of the processor (measured in GHz), the amount of cache memory, and the number of processing cores.

- RAM, the computer's volatile memory, is also located on the motherboard. RAM is where all the data and instructions are held while the computer is running.

- ROM, a permanent type of memory, is responsible for housing instructions to help start up a computer.

- The motherboard also houses slots for expansion cards, which have specific functions that augment the computer's basic functions. Typical expansion cards are sound and video cards.

7. Where are information and programs stored?

- To save programs and information permanently, you need to save them to the hard drive or to another permanent storage device such as a CD, DVD, or flash drive.

- The hard drive is your computer's primary device for permanent storage of software and files. The hard drive is a nonvolatile storage device, meaning it holds the data and instructions your computer needs permanently, even after the computer is turned off.

- Mechanical hard drives have spinning platters on which data is saved, whereas newer solid-state drives (SSDs) use solid-state memory, similar to that used with flash drives.

- External hard drives are essentially internal hard drives that have been made portable by enclosing them in a protective case and making them small and lightweight.

- Optical drives that can read from and write to CD, DVD, or Blu-ray discs are another means of permanent, portable storage. Data is saved to CDs, DVDs, and Blu-ray discs as pits that are burned into the disc by a laser.

- Flash drives are another portable means of storing data. Flash drives plug into USB ports.

- Flash memory cards let you transfer digital data between your computer and devices such as digital cameras, smartphones, video cameras, and printers.

Ports and Power Controls

8. How are devices connected to the computer?

- There is a wide variety of ports that allow you to hook up peripheral devices (such as your monitor and keyboard) to your system.

- The most common type of port used to connect devices to a computer is the USB port. USB 2.0 is the current standard but is quickly being replaced by the newer, faster USB 3.0 standard.

- FireWire ports provide additional options for data transfer.

- Connectivity ports, including Ethernet ports and modem ports, give you access to networks and the Internet and enable your computer to function as a fax machine.

- Multimedia ports include VGA and DVI ports. They connect the computer to monitors and other multimedia devices.

- Audio ports are where you connect headphones, microphones, and speakers to the computer.

- HDMI ports are used as a connection between monitors, TVs, and gaming consoles and work with both audio and video content.

9. What's the best way to turn my computer on and off, and when should it be done?

- Powering on your computer from a completely turned off state. In Windows 8, you can turn your computer off by pressing the computer's power button or by using the Shut Down option from the power icon found under Settings on the Charms bar.

- With the power-management options of Windows 8, for example, you only need to shut down your computer completely when you need to repair or install hardware in the system unit or move it to another location. However, if you use your computer only for a little while each day, it would be best to power it off completely after each daily use.

Setting It All Up

10. How do I set up my computer to avoid strain and injury?

- *Ergonomics* refers to how you arrange your computer and equipment to minimize your risk of injury or discomfort.

- Ergonomics includes positioning your monitor correctly, buying an adjustable chair, assuming a proper position while typing, making sure the lighting is adequate, and not looking at the screen for long periods. Other good practices include taking frequent breaks and using specially designed equipment such as ergonomic keyboards.

- Ergonomics is also important to consider when using mobile devices.

Be sure to check out the companion website for additional materials to help you review and learn, including a Tech Bytes Weekly newsletter—
pearsonhighered.com/techinaction
And don't forget the Replay Videos ▶.

key terms//

making the transition to . . . next semester //

1. **Watching Device Demos**

   YouTube is a great resource for product demonstrations. Open your browser, navigate to YouTube (**youtube.com**), and search on any type of computer peripheral discussed in this chapter to see if you can find a demonstration of a cool product.

   How helpful are these demonstrations? Make a video demonstration of a computing device you have and post it to your course management system or present it to your classmates (as specified by your instructor).

2. **Communicating with the Computer**

   You're involved in many group projects at school. Between your work, your classes, and other outside responsibilities, you're finding it difficult to meet in person. Investigate the devices you would need to be able to have virtual group meetings.

3. **Turn Your Monitor into a TV**

   You've heard how easy it is to convert an LCD monitor into a TV. Your parents just bought a new computer and are giving you their old PC monitor. You need a new TV for your dorm room, so you decide to give the conversion a try.

   a. What does your monitor need to retrofit it into a TV? What other devices do you need?

   b. How much will it cost? How much do new LCD TVs cost?

   c. Is this something you would consider doing? Why or why not?

   d. What would you do if your parents gave you their old LCD TV? Could you turn it into a monitor? If so, what would you need to do that?

making the transition to . . . the workplace //

1. **Backing Up Your Work**

   You've embarked on a position as a freelance editor. You'll be using your own computer. Until now, you haven't worried too much about backing up your data. Now, however, it's extremely important that you back up all your work frequently. Research the various backup options available, including online backup services, external hard drives, and portable flash storage. What are the size limitations of each? What are the initial and ongoing costs of each? How frequently do the options allow you to perform backups? Which option would you would choose, and why?

2. **What Hardware Will You Use?**

   When you arrive at a new position for a company, your employer will most likely provide you with a computer. Based on the career you're in now or are planning to pursue, answer the following questions:

   a. What kind of computer system would the company mostly likely provide to you—desktop, laptop, tablet PC, or something else? How does that compare with the type of system with which you prefer to work?

   b. If you were required to use a type of computer you'd never used before (such as a Mac instead of a PC), how would you go about learning to use the new computer?

   c. What other devices might your employer provide? Consider such items as smartphones or printers. How important is it for these devices to conform to the latest trends?

   d. Should you be able to use employer-provided equipment, such as a smartphone, for personal benefit? Does your answer differ if you have to pay for part or all of the device?

Which Mobile Device Is the Best?

Problem

You've joined a small business that's beginning to evaluate its technology setup. Because of the addition of several new sales representatives and other administrative employees, many new computers need to be purchased. You're trying to decide which mobile devices would be better to purchase—laptop computers, tablet PCs, tablet computers (iPads), or a combination of these devices.

Task

Split your class into teams of three and assign the following tasks:

- Member A explores the benefits and downfalls of laptop computers.
- Member B explores the benefits and downfalls of tablet PCs.
- Member C explores the benefits and downfalls of tablet computers.

Process

1. Think about what the technology goals are for the company and what information and resources you will need to tackle this project.

2. Research and then discuss the components of each system you're recommending. Are any components better suited for the particular needs of certain types of employees (sales representatives versus administrative staff)? Consider all the input, output, processing, and storage devices. Are any special devices or peripherals required?

3. Consider the different types of employees in the company. Would a combination of devices be better than a single solution? If so, what kinds of employees would get which type of computer?

4. As a team, write a summary position paper. Support your system recommendation for the company. Each team member should include why his or her type of computer will be part of the solution or not.

Conclusion

Laptops, tablet PCs, and tablet computers have their own merits as computing systems. Being aware of the options in the marketplace, knowing how to analyze the trade-offs of different designs, and recognizing the different needs each type of computer fulfills allows you to become a better consumer as well as a better computer user.

Green Computing

Ethical conduct is a stream of decisions you make all day long. In this exercise, you'll research and then role-play a complicated ethical situation. The role you play may or may not match your own personal beliefs, but your research and use of logic will enable you to represent whichever view is assigned. An arbitrator will watch and comment on both sides of the arguments, and together, the team will agree on an ethical solution.

Background

Green computing—conducting computing needs with the least possible amount of power and impact on the environment—is on everyone's minds. Although it's hard to argue with an environmentally conscious agenda, the pinch to our pocketbooks and the loss of some comforts sometimes makes green computing difficult. Businesses, including colleges, need to consider a variety of issues and concerns before jumping into a complete green overhaul.

Research Areas to Consider

- End-of-life management: e-waste and recycling
- Energy-efficient devices
- Renewable resources used in computer manufacturing
- Costs of green computing
- Government funding and incentives

Process

1. Divide the class into teams.
2. Research the areas cited above and devise a scenario in which your college is considering modifying its current technology setup to a more green information technology (IT) strategy.
3. Team members should write a summary that provides background information for their character—for example, environmentalist, college IT administrator, or arbitrator—and that details their character's behaviors to set the stage for the role-playing event. Then, team members should create an outline to use during the role-playing event.
4. Team members should arrange a mutually convenient time to meet for the exchange, using either the collaboration feature of MyITLab or the discussion board feature of your course management software or by meeting in person.
5. Team members should present their case to the class or submit a PowerPoint presentation for review by the rest of the class, along with the summary and resolution they developed.

Conclusion

As technology becomes ever more prevalent and integrated into our lives, more and more ethical dilemmas will present themselves. Being able to understand and evaluate both sides of the argument, while responding in a personally or socially ethical manner, will be an important skill.

Working and Playing on the Web

The Internet and How It Works

OBJECTIVES

1. What is the origin of the Internet? **(pp. 76–77)**

2. How does data travel on the Internet? **(pp. 77–78)**

Communicating and Collaborating on the Web

OBJECTIVES

3. How can I communicate and collaborate with others using Web 2.0 technologies? **(pp. 79–85)**

4. How can I communicate with others using e-mail and instant messaging? **(pp. 80–82)**

◀ **Sound Byte:** Blogging

Web Entertainment

OBJECTIVE

5. What multimedia files are found on the web, and what software is needed to access those files? **(pp. 86–87)**

Conducting Business over the Internet: E-Commerce

OBJECTIVE

6. What is e-commerce, and what online safeguards are available? **(pp. 88–90)**

🛂 **Active Helpdesk:** Doing Business Online

Using the Web Effectively

Accessing and Moving Around the Web

OBJECTIVES

7. What is a web browser, and what are a URL and its parts? **(pp. 94–96)**

8. How can I use hyperlinks and other tools to get around the web? **(pp. 96–100)**

◀ **Sound Byte:** Welcome to the Web

Searching the Web Effectively

OBJECTIVE

9. How do I search the Internet effectively, and how can I evaluate websites? **(pp. 101–106)**

🛂 **Active Helpdesk:** Using Subject Directories and Search Engines

🛂 **Active Helpdesk:** Getting Around the Web

◀ **Sound Byte:** Finding Information on the Web

For all media in this chapter go to **pearsonhighered.com/techinaction** or MyITLab.

(Dny3d/Fotolia; Marish/Shutterstock; Angela Waye/Shutterstock; Maxx-Studio/Shutterstock; Adimas/Fotolia; HaywireMedia/Fotolia)

REUTERS/Andrew Winning

Scan here for more info

HOW **COOL** IS THIS?

Have you ever seen something and wanted to know what it is or know more about it, but you didn't know how to find out? **Google Goggles** is an app you install on your smartphone. It's a **visual search engine** that uses pictures you've taken in order to search the web. Just **snap a picture** with your phone's camera, upload the picture into Google Goggles, and wait for the search results. Goggles will analyze the image and **highlight the objects** it recognizes; you can then click on the objects to **find out more**. For example, you can use Google Goggles to learn more about a book or DVD by taking a picture of the cover. Or you can get more information about a product by snapping a photo of the **label or bar code**. You can even **capture a landmark** or building and submit it to Goggles for more information.

Because visual search is relatively new, Goggles doesn't work on things such as plants, animals, apparel, cars, and furniture, but it works well with many other items. So, get out your Goggles and find out more about the world around you by taking a few pictures!

Working and Playing on the Web

You most likely know at least a little bit about how to use the web's resources to communicate and collaborate with others, how to work with multimedia files, and how business is conducted over the web. In this section, we'll explore these and other topics. But first, let's start with a brief lesson on the history of the Internet.

the internet and how

IT WORKS

It's hard to imagine life without the **Internet**, the largest computer network in the world. The Internet is actually a network of networks that connects billions of computer users globally, but its beginnings were much more modest.

The Origin of the Internet

Why was the Internet created? The concept of the Internet was developed in the late 1950s while the United States was in the midst of the Cold War with the Soviet Union (see Figure 3.1). At that time, the U.S. Department of Defense needed a computer network that wouldn't be disrupted easily in the event of an attack.

At the same time, researchers for the Department of Defense were trying to get different computers to communicate with each other using a common communications method that all computers could use. The Internet was created to respond to these two concerns: establishing a *secure* form of communications and creating a means by which *all* computers could communicate.

FIGURE 3.1 How the Internet Began

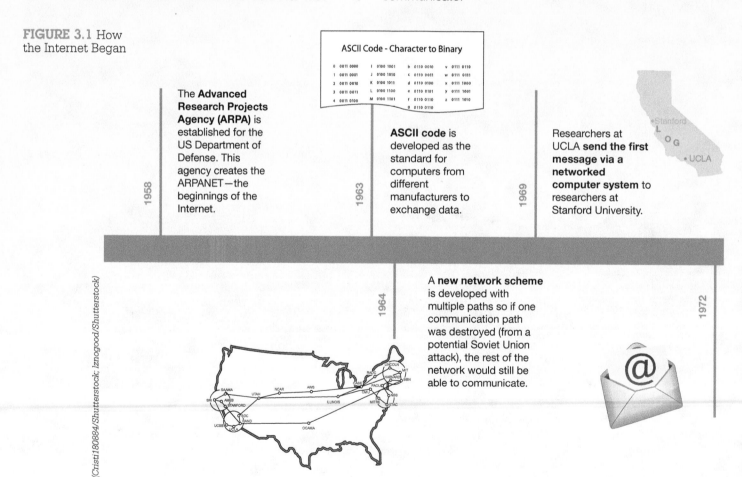

ASCII Code - Character to Binary

0	0011 0000	I	0100 1001	b	0110 0010	v	0111 0110
1	0011 0001	J	0100 1010	c	0110 0011	w	0111 0111
2	0011 0010	K	0100 1011	d	0110 0100	x	0111 1000
3	0011 0011	L	0100 1100	e	0110 0101	y	0111 1001
4	0011 0100	M	0100 1101	f	0110 0110	z	0111 1010
				g	0110 0110		

1958 — The **Advanced Research Projects Agency (ARPA)** is established for the US Department of Defense. This agency creates the ARPANET—the beginnings of the Internet.

1963 — **ASCII code** is developed as the standard for computers from different manufacturers to exchange data.

1969 — Researchers at UCLA **send the first message via a networked computer system** to researchers at Stanford University.

1964 — A **new network scheme** is developed with multiple paths so if one communication path was destroyed (from a potential Soviet Union attack), the rest of the network would still be able to communicate.

1972

(Cristi180884/Shutterstock; Iznogood/Shutterstock)

Who invented the Internet? The modern Internet evolved from an early U.S. government-funded "internetworking" project called the Advanced Research Projects Agency Network (ARPANET). ARPANET began as a four-node network involving UCLA, Stanford Research Institute, the University of California at Santa Barbara, and the University of Utah in Salt Lake City. The first real communication occurred in 1969 between the computer at Stanford and the computer at UCLA. Although the system crashed after the third letter was transmitted, it was the beginning of a revolution. Many people participated in the creation of the ARPANET, but two men, Vinton Cerf and Robert Kahn, are generally acknowledged as the "fathers" of the Internet. They earned this honor because in the 1970s they were primarily responsible for developing the communications protocols (standards) still in use on the Internet today.

So are the web and the Internet the same thing? Because the **World Wide Web** (**WWW** or the **web**) is what we use the most, we sometimes think of the Internet and the web as being interchangeable. However, the web is only a subset of the Internet, dedicated to broadcasting HTML pages and the means by which we access information over the Internet. The web is based on the Hypertext Transfer Protocol (HTTP), which is why you see an *http://* at the beginning of web addresses. What distinguishes the web from the rest of the Internet is its use of the following:

- Common communications protocols that enable computers to talk to each other and display information in compatible formats
- Special links that enable users to navigate from one place to another on the web

Did the same people who created the Internet also create the web? The web began in 1991, based on a protocol developed by Tim Berners-Lee, a physicist at the European Organization for Nuclear Research (CERN), who wanted a method for linking his research documents so that other researchers could access them. In conjunction with Robert Cailliau, Berners-Lee developed the basic architecture of the web and created the first **web browser**, software that lets you display and interact with text and other media on the web. The original browser could handle only text. Then, in 1993, the Mosaic browser, which could display graphics as well as text, was released. The once-popular Netscape Navigator browser evolved from Mosaic and heralded the beginning of the web's monumental growth.

How the Internet Works

How does the Internet work? All computers and other devices such as smartphones that are connected to the Internet create a network of networks. These Internet-connected devices communicate with

1973
Vincent Cerf and Bob Kahn develop a set of communication rules—the **TCP/IP protocol**—that allow different types of computers to communicate.

1991
Tim Berners-Lee developed and made public **HTTP protocol and the World Wide Web**. WWW is a subset of the Internet that is connected via hypertext (text containing hyperlinks to other documents and media).

Ray Tomlinson writes a program to send **e-mail** over the ARPANET and develops the "user@host" convention.

1978
By 1978, there were 111 hosts on ARPANET.

1992
By 1992, there were 1 million hosts on ARPANET.

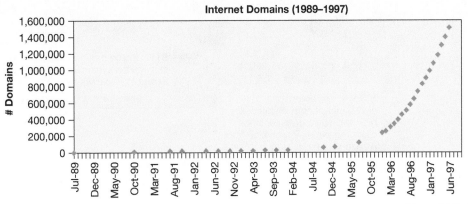

Internet Domains (1989–1997)

(Matthias Pahl/Shutterstock; Alphaspirit/Shutterstock)

BITS&BYTES

Ever Heard of the Internet2?

Although the Internet2 may sound like a new and separate network meant to replace the Internet, this is not the case. The Internet2 is actually a consortium of U.S. leaders in education, research, industry, and government that seeks to expand the possibilities of the existing Internet by developing new technologies and applications and then quickly deploying them to the public. These experimental technologies require a faster and more efficient Internet, so the researchers use separate data lines that support extremely high-speed communications—up to 8.8 terabits per second (Tbit/s). In fact, many of the Internet's current technologies are possible because of the research done by the Internet2 consortium.

each other in turns, just as we do when we ask a question and get an answer. Thus, a computer (or other device) connected to the Internet acts in one of two ways: Either it's a **client**, a computer that asks for data, or it's a **server**, a computer that receives the request and returns the data to the client. Because the Internet uses clients and servers, it's referred to as a **client/server network**.

When a client computer puts out a request for information from the server computer, the request travels along transmission lines. These transmission lines are similar to our highway system of roads, with some roads having different speed limits. The transmission lines with the fastest speeds are referred to as **Internet backbones**.

How do computers talk to each other? Suppose you want to order something from Amazon.com. Figure 3.2 illustrates what happens when you type **www.amazon.com** into your web browser and when Amazon's home page displays on your computer monitor.

How does the data get sent to the correct computer? Each time you connect to the Internet, your computer is assigned a unique identification number. This number, called an **Internet Protocol (IP) address**, is a set of four numbers separated by periods, such as 123.45.245.91, and is commonly referred to as a *dotted quad* or *dotted decimal*. IP addresses are the means by which computers connected to the Internet identify each other. Similarly, each website is assigned a unique IP address. However, because the numbers that make up IP addresses are difficult for people to remember, websites are given text versions of their IP addresses. So, Amazon's website has an IP address of 72.21.211.176 and a name of **www.amazon.com**. When you type "www.amazon.com" into your browser, your computer (with its unique IP address) looks for Amazon's IP address (72.21.211.176). Data is exchanged between Amazon's server computer and your computer using these unique IP addresses. ■

STEP 4: The server returns the requested data to your computer using the fastest pathway, which may be different from the one the request took.

Amazon.com's server

STEP 3: Your data flows along the backbone and on to smaller pathways until it reaches its destination, which is the server computer for Amazon's website.

STEP 5: The web browser interprets the data and displays it on your monitor.

HTML

Client

STEP 1: You enter www.amazon.com in your web browser. Your computer is the client requesting information from Amazon.com's website.

URL

STEP 2: The request is sent to the server via a system of data pathways, similar to a roadway system.

FIGURE 3.2 How the Internet's Client/Server Model Works *(Leo Lintang/ Fotolia; Edhar/Shutterstock)*

communicating and collaborating
ON THE WEB

Over time, our use of the web has evolved from passively browsing web pages that were created for us (now referred to as *Web 1.0*) to actively creating our own web content and sharing and collaborating on it with others (referred to as *Web 2.0*). **Web 2.0** can be classified as the *social web,* in which the user is also a participant. Before Web 2.0 technologies were in place, we were unable to collaborate with others through web applications such as Google Docs, to rate and recommend products or services with Yelp, to tag a friend on social networks such as Facebook, or to share a video on YouTube or a favorite image on Pinterest. These new means of Web 2.0 communication are collectively called *social media* and also include blogs, wikis, podcasts, and webcasts. Although e-mail still remains the most widely used form of communication on the Internet, social media has truly changed how we communicate.

Social Networking

Who hasn't heard of Facebook or social networking? As you probably know, **social networking** refers to using the web to communicate and share information among your friends and others. Social networking services such as Facebook and Twitter have become widely popular because they provide fun ways for users to communicate with their friends through Wall posts, chats, and tagged images. Other social networking sites, such as YouTube and Flickr, provide ways for users to show their friends favorite videos and images they have taken themselves or have found on the web.

How is social networking used in business? In the business community, professionals often engage in in-person networking to locate and fill open job positions as well as to find clients. Today, networking also happens online. Professional, business-oriented online networks such as LinkedIn are helpful for members seeking potential clients, business opportunities, jobs, or job candidates. Like a true business network, these sites can help you meet other professionals through the people you already know. In addition, businesses use social networking for marketing and communicating directly with their customers. For example, companies may post special deals and offers on their Facebook page or solicit responses from

followers that may help with product development or future marketing campaigns.

Figure 3.3 shows the various sites that are considered Web 2.0 social networking sites. As you can see, there is more to social networking than just Facebook and Twitter.

What are some dos and don'ts of social networking? When social networking sites first became popular, there was concern over privacy issues, especially for school-aged children who put personal information on their pages without considering the possibility of that information being misused by a stalker or identity thief. Although those concerns still exist, many of the most popular social networking sites have improved their privacy policies, thereby reducing, but not eliminating, such concerns. Still, users must be cautious about the type of content they post on these sites. Consider these precautions as you use social networking sites:

- Keep your personal information personal. The year you were born, your physical address, and the routines of your life (sports games, practices, work schedules) should not be broadcast to the general public.
- Know who your friends are, and know who can see the information you post. Review your privacy settings periodically, as sites change and update their privacy practices frequently.
- Do not post information such as your favorite teacher or your first pet's name because these are often used as security questions to verify your identity.
- Use caution when posting images, and know what images others are posting of you. Although privacy settings may offer some comfort, some images may be available for view through search engines and may not require site registration to be seen. Online images may become public property and subject to reproduction, and you might not want some—or any—of those images to be distributed.

Many employers and colleges use social networks as a means of gaining information about potential applicants before granting an interview or extending a job offer. In fact, there have been instances of people being fired from their jobs and being expelled from school for using social media, such as Facebook, Twitter, and blogs, in a questionable way. Generally, questionable

(Kevin Britland/Alamy; M4OS Photos/Alamy; Günay Mutlu/iStockphoto; Mixxt; Kristoffer Tripplaar/Alamy; PhotoEdit/Alamy; Günay Mutlu/gmutlu/iStockphoto; M4OS Photos/Alamy; Web Pix/Alamy; PhotoEdit/Alamy; www.slideshare.net; M4OS Photos/Alamy; NetPics/Alamy; StumbleUpon)

FIGURE 3.3

Types of Social Networking Sites

	DESCRIPTION	SUGGESTED URLS
Social Exchange Networks	Allow users to connect with others, provide status updates	facebook.com facebook twitter.com twitter
Create Your Own Social Networks	Allow users to create their own social network around a common topic; groups can be public or private	ning.com NING mixxt.net mixxt
Business-Related Social Networks	Allow users to seek potential clients, business opportunities, jobs, or job candidates	linkedin.com Linked in
Media Sharing Networks	Allow users to share pictures and videos	youtube.com You Tube flickr.com flickr from YAHOO! picasa.google.com Picasa
Information Sharing Networks	Allow users to share information	delicious.com delicious wikipedia.org WIKIPEDIA The Free Encyclopedia slideshare.net slideshare Present Yourself
Information Recommendations and Filtering (Bookmarking) Networks	Allow users to post their opinion of a product, service, news, or web item for others to see and use	reddit.com reddit digg.com digg stumbleupon.com StumbleUpon

content on social media includes negative discussion about the poster's job, employer, or colleagues, or inappropriate content about the poster. The responsibility for your content rests with you. Even though you may have strong privacy settings, you can't control what those who you allow to see your content do with it. Therefore, treat all information posted on the web as public, and avoid posting damaging words and pictures. Bottom line: Make sure your profile, images, and site content project an image that accurately represents you.

E-Mail

Why do I need e-mail? Despite the increasing popularity of social networking, e-mail is still the primary means of communication over the Internet. **E-mail** (short for **electronic mail**) is a written message sent or received over the Internet. E-mail is the primary method of electronic communication worldwide because it's fast and convenient. And because it's *asynchronous*, users do not need to be communicating at the same time. They can send and respond to messages at their own convenience. E-mail is also convenient for exchanging and collaborating on documents via attachments.

How private is e-mail? Although e-mail is a more private exchange of information than public social networking sites, e-mails really are not private. Consider the following:

- Because e-mails can be printed or forwarded to others, you never know who may read your e-mail.
- Most e-mail content is not protected, so you should never use e-mail to send personal or sensitive information such as bank account or Social Security numbers. Doing so could lead to identity theft.
- Employers have access to e-mail sent from the workplace, so use caution when putting negative or controversial content in e-mail.
- Even after you've deleted a message, it doesn't really vanish. Many Internet service providers and companies archive e-mail, which can be accessed or subpoenaed in the event of a lawsuit or investigation.

What are some tips on e-mail etiquette? When you write a casual e-mail to friends, you obviously don't need to follow any specific e-mail guidelines (except to remember that your e-mail may be forwarded). But when you send e-mail for professional reasons, you should use proper e-mail etiquette. The following are a few guidelines (also see Figure 3.4):

- Be concise and to the point.
- Use the spell-checker and proofread your e-mail before sending it.
- Avoid using abbreviations such as *u*, *r*, *LOL*, and *BRB*.

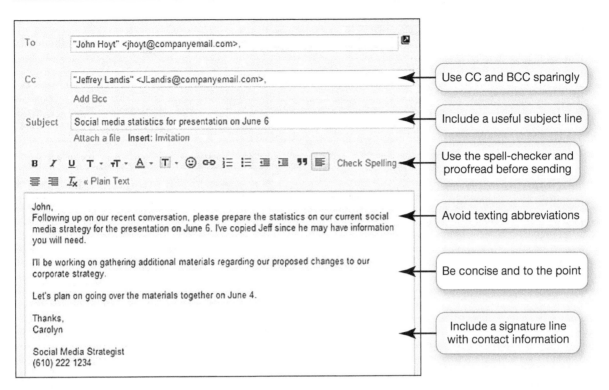

FIGURE 3.4 Using simple guidelines of e-mail etiquette can promote a professional image and make your message more effective.

- Include a meaningful subject line to help recipients prioritize and organize e-mails.
- Add a signature line that includes your contact information.
- Include only those people on the e-mail who truly need to receive it.

Following such guidelines maintains professionalism, increases efficiency, and might even help protect a company from lawsuits.

Are there different types of e-mail systems? There are two different types of e-mail systems:

1. **Web-based e-mail**, such as Yahoo! mail or Gmail, is managed with your web browser and allows you to access your e-mail from the web.

2. An **e-mail client** requires a program, such as Microsoft Outlook, to be installed on your computer. When you open the program, your e-mail is downloaded to your computer.

The primary difference between the two is access. Web-based e-mail allows you to access e-mail from any Internet-connected device, but you can't see your e-mail when you're offline. With an e-mail client, you view your e-mail on the computer on which the e-mail client software has been installed, but you can then view and manage your e-mail while you're

offline. Both systems can be used together for the "best of both worlds." You can have a Gmail account, for example, so that you can read your e-mail from any computer connected to the Internet, and you can also have Outlook installed on your primary computer and set up the program to display your Gmail account (see Figure 3.5).

Instant Messaging

Is instant messaging just for friends?

You've most likely used **instant messaging (IM)** services—programs that let you communicate in real time over the Internet. Although IM is most often used for conversations between friends, many businesses use IM as a means of instant communication between co-workers. Some IM systems provide mechanisms to hold conversations with more than one person, either through simultaneous individual conversations or with group chats. And some programs even let you conduct video chats using a webcam.

AIM, Google Chat, Windows Messenger, and Yahoo! Messenger are proprietary IM services, meaning you can IM or chat only with those who share the same IM service and are on your contact or buddy list. Another option is to chat with those you've "friended" on Facebook through Facebook's chat option. There

FIGURE 3.5 (a) Client-Based and (b) Web-Based E-mail Systems

are also universal chat services such as Trillian and Digsby that you install on your computer and that allow you to chat with users of all popular IMs, regardless of the service they use.

Wikis

What are wikis? You've no doubt heard of Wikipedia (**wikipedia.org**), the popular collaborative online encyclopedia. Wikipedia is one example of a **wiki**, a website that allows users to add, remove, or edit its content. Wiki content such as that found on Wikipedia is created collaboratively by multiple users, resulting in an emergent "common" opinion rather than the opinion of an individual writer. Because of wiki technology, Wikipedia's content can be updated continually.

What else are wikis used for? Wikis are not just used to create Wikipedia; they're also useful tools for business collaboration. Rather than needing to pass documents back and forth via e-mail and possibly losing track of which version is the most recent, wikis allow all who have access to the wiki page to post their ideas and modify the content of just one document (see Figure 3.6). Wikis provide the extra benefit of users

being able to access, review, and even revert back to past versions at any time.

Some web-based document products, such as Google Docs (**docs.google.com**), have wiki-like features to promote similar online collaboration, and specific wiki software, such as Wikispaces (**wikispaces.com**) and MediaWiki (**mediawiki. org**), is available that you can download for free. The Wikimedia Foundation, which hosts Wikipedia, also hosts other collaborative projects, such as Wikibooks (textbooks), Wikiversity (learning tools), and Wikisource (a document library). These wiki-type collaborative efforts apply to a variety of other useful applications. For example, wikiHow (**wikihow.org**) is an online project that uses both wikis and the collaborative process to build a large, online how-to manual.

Why isn't Wikipedia good to use as a source for a research paper? The idea behind content that is managed and edited by many users, such as that found in Wikipedia and other large public wikis, is that the group will keep the content valid. However, because wikis are publicly editable, they can't be trusted completely. If a user adds erroneous

Elijah provides initial text
(in black)

Project Home
Week 7: *Publicity Law*
9/17/12 – 9/23/12

9/18/12
Mackenzie-Jordan Law Associates has a significant number of celebrity clients. One of the most important aspects of our legal counsel to these individuals is to help protect the use of their images and likenesses.
Sometimes this is referred to as the right of publicity. This right is a valuable asset because there are endless licensing opportunities that can be quite lucrative.
Some states have a publicity law that protects a celebrity's image and likeness for 100 years, but as yet that law has not been enacted in the state of Texas.

9/19/12
The merchandising of celebrity images has become a huge source of income for many celebrities as well as others.
In recent years, legal disputes have resulted from artists and illustrators manipulating celebrity images.
In the past, courts have typically protected the First Amendment rights of artists in these cases. But recently there have been a few cases where celebrities have been allowed to sue creators of fictional works for the violation of the right of publicity.
~~The right of publicity is intended to prevent others from capitalizing on a celebrity's fame.~~ Many people in the entertainment industry are fearful that unauthorized biographies, docudramas, and celebrity spoofs and satires will no longer be protected. Many entertainment lawyers say a celebrity's right to publicity is intended solely for ads and merchandise, not for literary works.

Stephanie removes text
(shaded with green and
shown with strikethrough)

FIGURE 3.6 Rather than collaborating by exchanging e-mails and attachments—and potentially losing track of the most recent version of a document—different users can collaborate on a wiki page. *(Orange Line Media/Shutterstock; Christopher Halloran/Shutterstock; Kzenon/Shutterstock)*

content, the community of users can quickly catch and correct it, but if you used Wikipedia as a source, you may have referenced erroneous content before it was corrected. To help address these concerns, Wikipedia has implemented tighter access controls, requiring users who want editing privileges to register with the site. Citizendium (**citizendium.org**), another open wiki encyclopedia, requires contributors to provide real names and sign an ethics pledge, and all postings are monitored.

Blogs

Why do people write blogs? A **blog** (short for **weblog**) is a personal log or journal posted on the web. Anyone can create a blog, and there are millions of blogs available to read, follow, and comment on. Blogs are generally written by a single author and are arranged as a listing of entries on a single page, with the most recent blog entry appearing at the top of the list. In addition, blogs are public. Blogs have searchable and organized content, making them user friendly. They're accessible from anywhere using a web browser.

Jordan includes
additional text
(shaded yellow)

Many people use blogs as a sort of personal scrapbook. Whenever the urge strikes, they report on their daily activities. Many other blogs focus on a particular topic. For example, the Movie Blog (**themovie blog.com**) contains reviews and opinions about movies, and engadget (**engadget.com**) is a blog devoted to discussing technogadgets. Many corporations, such as Walmart and Best Buy, have blogs written by employees. Technorati (**technorati.com**) and Blogcatalog (**blogcatalog.com**) are two of many blog directories that can help you find blogs that fit your interests.

Are all blogs text-based? The traditional form of a blog is primarily text-based but may also include images and audio. A **video log** (**vlog** or **video blog**) is a blog that uses video as the primary content (although it can also contain text, images, and audio). Vlogs are quickly becoming a popular means of personal expression, and many can be found by searching YouTube (**youtube.com**) and Tout (**tout.com**).

How do I create a blog? Many websites provide the tools you need to create your own blog. Two sites that offer free blog hosting are Blogger (**blogger.com**) and WordPress (**wordpress.com**). Such tools also let you add features like pictures or subpages to your blog. You can also choose to host your blog yourself so that the URL reflects your name or the name of your business. If you choose this option, you'll need your own website and a URL so people can access it.

Are there any problems with blogs? The popularity of blogs has brought about a new problem: *spam blogs* (*splogs*), which are

---

🔊 SOUND BYTE
Blogging

In this Sound Byte, you'll see why blogs are one of today's most popular publishing mediums. You'll also learn how to create and publish your own blog.

artificially created blog sites filled with fake articles or stolen text (a tactic known as *blog scraping*). Splogs, which contain links to other sites associated with the splog's creator, have the intention of either increasing traffic to, or increasing search engine rankings for, these usually disreputable or useless websites. Although not really harmful, splogs are another unwanted form of content that continues to grow like weeds on the web.

Podcasts and Webcasts

What is a podcast? A **podcast** consists of a series of audio or video files that are distributed over the Internet. There are podcasts for radio shows, audiobooks, magazines, and even educational programs, which you can download to your computer, iPod, or other music player. What makes podcasts different from other audio

BITS&BYTES

What's Your Pinterest?

Pinterest (**pinterest.com**) is one of the newest crazes to hit the social media scene. The site describes itself as a "virtual pinboard," or scrapbook, on which users create collections of images of things they love. It's like going through a magazine, cutting out pictures you like, and tacking them up on a bulletin board—only better! You can "pin" virtually any image on the web to a Pinterest collection. Like other social networking sites, users share their collections as well as follow others' collections. Pinterest collections range in topic from wedding inspirations, home decorating, fashion, and cooking to DJ equipment, sports, and politics.

Launched in 2010, the site has quickly grown in popularity, and it was recognized by *Time* magazine as one of the 50 best websites in 2011. Women are the predominant users of the site, which has engaged many companies and non-profits to market their brands on Pinterest. If you haven't yet, check out Pinterest, but be careful—the act of looking through collections of great images can be addicting!

files found on the web is that podcasts deliver their content using **Really Simple Syndication (RSS)**. RSS is a format that sends the latest content of the podcast series automatically to an **aggregator** such as iTunes or Google Reader. An aggregator locates all the RSS series to which you've subscribed and automatically downloads only the new content to your computer or media player. If you have several favorite websites or podcasts, rather than needing to check each site for updated content, aggregators collect all the site updates in one place. These updates or changes to the content are then delivered automatically if you subscribe to the podcast, instead of you having to search for the latest content and download it yourself.

Where can I find podcasts? Most newspapers, television news organizations, and radio sites offer podcasts of their programs. Although many podcasts are news related, others offer entertaining and educational content. For example, you can access lessons on yoga, foreign language classes, or DIY tips. Many schools are beginning to supply students with course content updates through podcasts, and instructors sometimes create podcasts of their lectures. Figure 3.7 lists some places you can find podcasts.

Can I create my own podcast? It's simple to create a podcast. Although high-end equipment will produce more-sophisticated output, to record the audio content all you need is a computer with a microphone. If you want to make a video podcast, you also need a webcam or video camera. You may also need additional software to edit the audio and video content, depending on how professional you wish the podcast to be. After you've recorded and edited the podcast content, you need to export it to MP3 format. The free program Audacity (**audacity.sourceforge.net**) lets you both edit audio files and export them to MP3 format. All that's left is for you to create an RSS feed (tricky, but doable) and then upload the content to a site that hosts podcasts, such as iTunes, Podcast.com, or Podcast Pickle.

FIGURE 3.7

Podcast Directories and Aggregators

iTunes (itunes.com)
- Software makes it easy to play, manage, and share your favorite podcasts

Podcast.com (podcast.com)
- Broad collection of podcasts

Podcast Pickle (podcastpickle.com)
- Includes discussion forums and reviews

YouTube (youtube.com)
- Good source for video blogs (vlogs)

What's a webcast? A **webcast** is the (usually live) broadcast of audio or video content over the Internet. Unlike podcasts, which are prerecorded and made available for download, most webcasts are distributed in "real time," meaning that they're live or one-time events. Some webcasts are archived so they can be viewed at a later date. Webcasts are not updated automatically like podcasts, but some, such as Microsoft's On-Demand Webcasts, are RSS feeds.

Webcasts use continuous audio and video feeds, which let you view and download large audio and video files. Webcasts can include noninteractive content such as a simultaneous broadcast of a radio or television program, but more recent webcasts invite interactive responses from the viewing or listening audience. For example, ORLive (**orlive.com**) provides surgical webcasts that demonstrate the latest surgical innovations and techniques. Webcasts also are used in the corporate world to broadcast annual meetings and in the educational arena to transmit seminars.

Figure 3.8 lists the popular methods of online communication that we've discussed. ■

FIGURE 3.8

Methods of Online Communication

SOCIAL NETWORKING

- Web 2.0 technology
- Lets you build an online network of friends
- Lets you share media content

E-MAIL

- Most common form of online communication
- Asynchronous (not having to be done at the same time)

INSTANT MESSAGING

- Real-time exchange
- Can be used with multiple persons simultaneously
- Video/audio chats available

WIKIS

- Great collaborative tool
- Content updated by many users
- Historical content kept, so you can revert to past versions

BLOGS

- Written by a single author
- Chronologic entries
- Searchable content
- May include images, audio, and video

PODCASTS

- Audio/video files delivered via RSS
- New RSS content collected with aggregator
- Can download and view content on portable music player

WEBCASTS

- Most often live, streamed broadcasts

(Ben Legend/Fotolia; Beboy/Fotolia; LiveStock/Shutterstock; Kheng Guan Toh/Shutterstock; ayzek/Shutterstock; 3drenderedlogos com/Shutterstock; On-Air/iStockphoto)

web ENTERTAINMENT

When you think of how you use the Internet for entertainment purposes, what comes to mind? Streaming audio and video, Internet radio, MP3s, interactive gaming, and smart TV are all favorite responses. What makes all these forms of web entertainment so popular is their multimedia content. **Multimedia** is anything that involves one or more forms of media in addition to text. It includes the following:

- *Graphics* such as drawings, charts, and photos (the most basic form of multimedia)
- *Audio files* such as the clips you hear when you visit websites, MP3 files you download, podcasts and webcasts, and live broadcasts you can listen to through Internet radio
- *Video files* ranging from simple, short video clips on sites such as YouTube (**youtube.com**) to movies and television shows on sites such as Hulu (**hulu.com**)

What are streaming audio and video? Streaming audio continuously feeds an audio file to your browser so you avoid having to wait for the entire file to download completely before listening to it. Likewise, **streaming video** continuously feeds a video file to your browser so that you can watch large files as they download instead of first having to download the files completely. Without streaming audio and video, you wouldn't be able to watch movies on Netflix or on demand from your cable provider, listen to live audio broadcasting, or even play some online games.

Do I need anything besides a browser to view or hear multimedia on the web? Most graphics on the web will appear in your browser without any additional software. However, to view and hear some multimedia files—for example, podcasts, YouTube videos, and audio files—you might need a special software program called a **plug-in** (or **player**). Figure 3.9 lists the most popular plug-ins.

How do I get players and plug-ins? If you purchased your computer within the past several years, many plug-ins

FIGURE 3.9

Popular Plug-Ins and Players and Their Uses

PLUG-IN OR PLAYER NAME	WHERE YOU CAN GET IT	WHAT IT DOES
Adobe Reader	**adobe.com**	Views and prints portable document format (PDF) files
Flash Player	**adobe.com**	Plays animation and movies through web browsers
QuickTime Player	**apple.com**	Plays MP3 animation, music, musical instrument digital interface (MIDI), audio, and video files
Shockwave Player	**adobe.com**	Plays interactive games, multimedia, graphics, and streaming audio and video on the web
Silverlight	**microsoft.com**	Similar to Flash; plays web-based animations and videos
Windows Media Player	**microsoft.com**	Plays MP3, WAV, and music files; movies; and live audio and video broadcasts on the web

BITS&BYTES

Why Can't I Run Flash-Based Multimedia on My iPad or iPhone?

Your friend showed you a great video clip on her new Android tablet. You try to go to the same web page on your iPhone, but the video won't run. Why not? Apple devices don't support Flash! Apple's website gives a complete explanation of Apple's "Thoughts on Flash" (**apple.com/hotnews/thoughts-on-flash**); succinctly, Apple's main problem with Flash is that it's not "open" software, but rather 100% proprietary. Apple also says that there are reliability, security, and performance issues with Flash, so it would rather use open standard products such as HTML5, CSS, and JavaScript. Flash is also tough on battery consumption and doesn't work well on devices using touch commands rather than mice commands.

What to do if you have an iPad, iPod Touch, or iPhone and want to view a Flash video content? One work-around is to download the Skyfire web browser, which converts Flash video content into iOS-friendly HTML5. Another way is to check whether the content site you're using has a native iOS application, which often provides access to the video. For example, YouTube and Dailymotion have applications available. Unfortunately, though, you have to find and hunt for the clip that your friend shared with you on a web page.

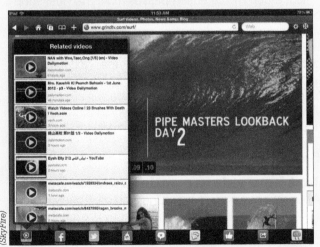

(SkyFire)

probably came preinstalled on your computer. If a website requires a plug-in you don't have, it usually displays a message on the screen that includes links to a site where you can download the plug-in free of charge. For example, to use streaming video, your browser might send you to the Adobe website, where you can download Flash Player.

Do I need to update players and plug-ins? Improvements and updates are often made available for players and plug-ins, and most will alert you to check for and download updates when they're available. It's best to keep the players and plug-ins as current as possible so that you get the full effects of the multimedia running with them.

Are there any risks with using plug-ins? When a browser requires a plug-in to display particular content, it usually automatically accesses the plug-in. Depending on your settings, this access happens without asking you for consent to start the plug-in. Such automatic access can present security risks. To minimize such risks, update your plug-ins and browser software frequently so that you'll have the most up-to-date remedies against identified security flaws.

Is there any way to get multimedia web content to load faster? When you're on the Internet, your browser keeps track of the sites you've visited so that it can load them faster the next time you visit them. This *cache* (temporary storage place) of the text pages, images, and video files from recently visited websites can make your web surfing more efficient, but it can also slow down your hard drive. Additionally, if you don't have your cache settings configured to check for updates to the web page, your browser may not load the most recent content. To keep your system running efficiently, consider doing the following:

- Delete your temporary Internet cache every month or so, depending on your usage.
- To ensure the most recent website content is displayed, click Refresh or press the F5 key if you revisit a site in the same browsing session.
- Clear your Internet cache manually or adjust the setting in your web browser so that it clears the cache automatically every time you exit the browser. ■

conducting business over the internet:
E-COMMERCE

It's hard to believe that only a few years ago, many people were scared to buy things online. Today, there is little hesitation, and you can buy nearly anything on the web, including big-ticket items such as homes and cars.

E-commerce—short for **electronic commerce**—is the process of conducting business online, such as through advertising and selling products. Figure 3.10 shows the most common items purchased through e-commerce transactions.

Are there different types of e-commerce? There are three types of e-commerce business models:

1. **Business-to-consumer (B2C)** transactions take place between businesses and consumers. Such transactions include those between customers and completely online businesses (such as Amazon.com) and those between customers and stores that have both an online and a physical presence, such as Target (**target.com**). Such businesses are referred to as *click-and-brick* businesses. Some click-and-bricks allow online purchases and in-store pickups and returns.

2. **Business-to-business (B2B)** transactions occur when businesses buy and sell goods and services to other businesses. An example is Omaha Paper Company (**omahapaper.com**), which distributes paper products to other companies.

3. **Consumer-to-consumer (C2C)** transactions occur when consumers sell to each other through auction sites such as eBay (**ebay.com**) and exchange sites such as Craigslist (**craigslist.org**).

Social commerce is a subset of e-commerce that uses social networks to assist in marketing and purchasing products. If you're on Facebook, you've no doubt noticed the many businesses that have Facebook pages asking you to "Like" them. Consumers are voicing their opinions on Facebook and other sites about products and services by providing ratings and reviews, and studies show that such peer recommendations have a major influence on buying behavior. When you see your friend on Facebook recommend a product or service, you're more likely to click through to that retailer and check out the product.

For example, after implementing the Facebook "Like" button, American Eagle noticed that Facebook-referred visitors spent 57% more than other online shoppers. Other peer-influenced e-commerce trends include group buying and individual customization. Groupon and Living-Social are two examples of deal-of-the-day group purchase websites that require a certain number of people to buy the discounted deal before the deal can go through. CafePress and Threadless sell T-shirts and other items that are customized with your own graphic designs.

But e-commerce encompasses more than just shopping opportunities. Today, anything you can do inside your bank you can do online, and more than 50% of U.S. households do some form of online banking. Many people use online services to check their account balances, pay bills online, and check stock and mutual fund performance. Credit card companies allow you to view, schedule, and pay your credit card bill; brokerage houses allow you to conduct investment activities online.

E-commerce Safeguards

Just how safe are online transactions?
When you buy something online, you most likely use a credit or debit card; therefore, money is exchanged

FIGURE 3.10 Top Five Online Consumer Purchases
(urfin/Shutterstock; RusN/iStockphoto)

 ACTIVE HELPDESK
Doing Business Online

In this Active Helpdesk call, you'll learn about e-commerce and what e-commerce safeguards protect you when you're doing business online.

FIGURE 3.11

Online Shopping Precautions

When shopping at home, use a firewall and antivirus software for general computer protection.

Don't shop on public WiFi networks, as they may contain spyware.

Check for visual indicators such as https:// in the URL, a closed padlock icon, and a green address bar.

Look for third-party verification from TRUSTe or the Better Business Bureau symbol.

Use a credit card, not a debit card, to protect transactions, or use a third-party payer such as PayPal or Google Wallet.

Create a strong password for all online accounts (one that includes numbers and other symbols such as @).

Deals that are too good to be true are usually just that.

Read and understand the fine print on warranties, return policies, and the retailer's privacy statements.

(beboy/Shutterstock; Godfried Edelman/iStockphoto, photoinnovation/Shutterstock; HANDOUT/ KRT/Newscom; Maxx-Studio/Shutterstock; isak55/Shutterstock; Alhovik/Shutterstock; iQoncept/ Shutterstock)

directly between your credit card company and the online merchant's bank. Because online shopping eliminates a salesclerk or other human intermediary from the transaction, it can actually be safer than traditional retail shopping.

What precautions should I take when shopping online? In addition to using some basic common computing sense such as having a firewall and up-to-date antivirus software on your computer and using strong passwords for all your online accounts, there are several important guidelines to follow to ensure your online shopping experience is a safe one (see Figure 3.11):

- **Look for visual indicators that the website is secure.** Check that the beginning of the URL changes from "http://" to "https://"—with the s standing for **secure socket layer**. Also, look for a small icon of a closed padlock in the toolbar (in both Internet Explorer and Firefox) and a green-colored address bar, indications that the site may be secure. (However, note that even if a site has these indicators, it

still might not be safe. Consider the validity of the site before making a purchase.)

- **Shop at well-known, reputable sites.** If you aren't familiar with a site, investigate it with the Better Business Bureau (**bbb.org**) or at bizrate (**bizrate.com**). Make sure the company has a phone number and street address in addition to a website. You can also look for third-party verification such as that from TRUSTe or the Better Business Bureau. But let common sense prevail. Online deals that seem too good to be true are generally just that—and may be pirated or illegal distributions.

- **Pay by credit card, not debit card.** Federal laws protect credit card users, but debit card users don't have the same level of protection. If possible, reserve one credit card for Internet purchases only; even better, use a prepaid credit card that has a small credit limit. For an extra layer of security, find out if your credit card company has a service that confirms your identity with an extra password or code that only you know to use when making an online transaction or that offers a one-time-use credit card number. Also, consider using a third-party payment processor such as PayPal or Google Wallet. PayPal also offers a security key that provides additional security to your PayPal account.

- **When you place an order, check the return policy, save a copy of the order, and make sure you receive a confirmation number.** Make sure you read and understand the fine print on warranties, return policies, and the retailer's privacy statements. If the site disappears overnight, this information may help you in filing a dispute or reporting a problem to a site such as the Better Business Bureau.
- **Avoid making online transactions when using public computers.** Public computers may have *spyware* installed, programs that track and log

your keystrokes and can retrieve your private information. Similarly, unless you have specific protection on your own notebook computer, avoid making wireless transactions in public hotspots.

Whether you're doing business, playing games, or communicating with friends or colleagues, the Internet makes these activities more accessible. The Internet can potentially make these experiences and activities more enriched as well, although you must take precautions for the safest of experiences. ■

Before moving on to Part 2:
- Watch Replay Video 3.1 ▶.
- Then check your understanding of what you've learned so far.

BITS&BYTES

Making Safe Online Payments Using PayPal and Google Wallet

When people first began making online purchases, many were not comfortable buying from sites like eBay because the sites required them to give personal financial information such as credit card numbers to strangers. PayPal (**paypal.com**) resolved that issue by serving as a payment intermediary that allows anyone to pay with credit cards and bank accounts without sharing their financial information. PayPal is now a standard means of payment for many online merchants and offers buyer protection and dispute resolution services. Figure 3.12 shows how PayPal works.

Google Wallet (**google.com/ wallet**) offers similar services to PayPal, although there are some subtle differences. For example, you can't pay directly from your bank account with Google Wallet, and you can only make purchases within

the United States. In addition, Google Wallet only provides customer support through forums and e-mail, whereas PayPal has increased its customer service considerably, so that you can now chat live with PayPal representatives.

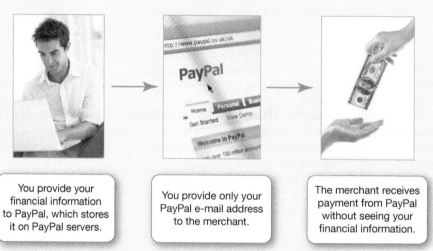

You provide your financial information to PayPal, which stores it on PayPal servers.

You provide only your PayPal e-mail address to the merchant.

The merchant receives payment from PayPal without seeing your financial information.

FIGURE 3.12 How PayPal Works *(Yuri Arcurs/Shutterstock; AKP Photos/Alamy; happydancing/ Shutterstock)*

For a quick review to see what you've learned so far, answer the following questions. Visit **pearsonhighered.com/techinaction** to check your answers.

multiple choice

1. Which is NOT true about the Internet?

    a. It is the largest computer network in the world.

    b. It was created to establish a secure form of military communications.

    c. It was developed as an additional means of commerce.

    d. It was designed as a means for all computers to communicate with each other.

2. What do you need if you want to read, send, and organize e-mail from *any* computer connected to the Internet?

    a. an e-mail client program

    b. an e-mail server

    c. an e-mail aggregator

    d. a web-based e-mail account

3. Which is NOT an example of Web 2.0 technology?

    a. e-mail

    b. social networking

    c. blogging

    d. wiki

4. Which of the following is NOT a characteristic of a blog?

    a. Blogs are used to express opinions.

    b. Blogs are generally written by a single author.

    c. Blogs are private and require password access.

    d. Blogs are arranged as a listing of entries.

5. Which of the following is true about plug-ins?

    a. Plugs-ins rarely require updating.

    b. Plug-ins track the websites you've visited.

    c. Plug-ins are necessary for viewing most web graphics.

    d. Plug-ins cannot present security risks.

true–false

_____ **1.** Deleted e-mails can be recovered—they don't really vanish.

_____ **2.** A yellow shaded address bar on a website indicates that the website is secure.

critical thinking

1. **Social Networking and Society**

    Social networking seems to have taken over our lives! Almost everyone is on Facebook and Twitter. But is this a good thing?

    a. What advantages and disadvantages does social networking bring to your life and to society?

    b. How are businesses using social networking?

2. **Apple and Adobe Flash**

    Apple has made a corporate decision not to support Flash-based files on its devices. Apple contends that working with other content written in open standard products is better for it as a company, and that consumers have reasonable "alternatives" to Flash. What do you think of Apple's position? What would you recommend it do?

Continue

TRY THIS

Create a SkyDrive Account and Store and Share Your Files in the Cloud

You probably have your favorite ways of moving your files around. Perhaps you have a USB drive or you e-mail files to yourself, or maybe you have a portable external hard drive. With any of these solutions, there can be confusion as to which is the most current version of the file if you have worked on it on multiple devices at different times. You also run the risk of losing your USB drive or deleting the e-mail attachment by mistake. These methods also make exchanging files difficult if you want to share your files or collaborate with a group.

A simpler solution is to use a web-based or cloud storage and sharing service such as SkyDrive or Dropbox. SkyDrive is part of Microsoft's Office 365 suite of web apps. With 25 GB of free storage space, you can store thousands of files and get to them anytime you're online.

Step 1 Sign in to SkyDrive: Go to **skydrive.com**. Sign in to your Microsoft account. If you don't have a Microsoft account, creating one is easy. A Microsoft account will give you access to services such as SkyDrive, Xbox LIVE, or **Outlook.com**.

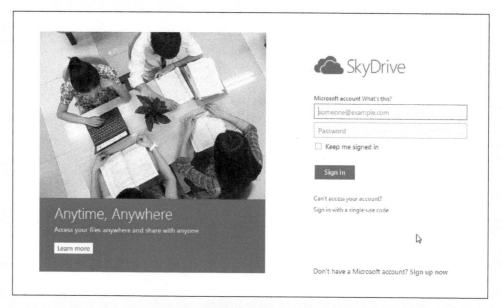

Step 2 Create a Folder and Add Files: Once you're in SkyDrive, you can create a folder and then begin to add files.

- To create a folder: Click **Create** at the top of the page, click **Folder**, and then give your new folder a name. Click the new folder to open it.
- To add a file: Click **Upload** at the top of the page, then locate the file, and click **Open**. To upload more than one file, hold the **Ctrl key** while you select each file.

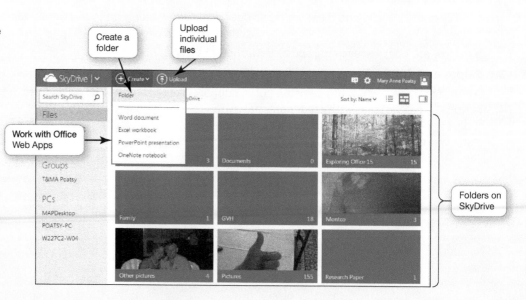

Step 3 Share a File or Folder: To share a file or folder, do the following:

- Right-click the file or folder that you want to share, and click **Share**.
- Fill in the e-mail form.
- Establish editing privileges by checking the **Recipients can edit** box, if desired, then click **Share**.

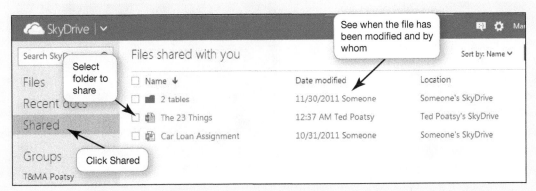

- To see what files that have been shared with you, click **Shared** in the left menu.

Step 4 Sync with Your Smartphone: If you have an iPhone or Windows Phone, you can access your documents wherever you go. You can download the SkyDrive app, or you can always access SkyDrive through your phone's browser at **skydrive.com**.

Using the Web Effectively

You no doubt know how to use the web—to buy products, send e-mail, visit Facebook, and use Google—but do you know how to use it effectively? In this section, we'll look at ways to make your online experience more enjoyable, more productive, and even more efficient.

accessing and moving
AROUND THE WEB

None of the activities for which we use the web could happen without an important software application: a web browser. Recall that a browser is software that lets you locate, view, and navigate the web. Most browsers today are *graphical* browsers, meaning they can display pictures (graphics) in addition to text and other forms of multimedia such as sound and video. The most common browsers are displayed in Figure 3.13.

Web Browsers

What features do browsers offer? Most popular browsers share similar features that make the user experience more efficient (as shown in Figure 3.14). For example, most browsers include a built-in search box in which you can designate your preferred default search engine and tools for printing, page formatting, and security settings. Other features include the following:

- *Tabbed browsing:* Web pages are loaded in "tabs" within the same browser window. Rather than having to switch among web pages in several open windows, you can flip between the tabs in one window.

You may also save a group of tabs as a Favorites group if there are several tabs you often open at the same time.

- *Pinned tabs:* You can "dock" tabs to the taskbar (in Internet Explorer 9) or minimize and save them permanently (Google Chrome and Firefox) for easier navigation of your favorite sites.

- *Tear-off tabs:* An opened tab can be dragged away from its current window so it's then opened in a new window.

- *Thumbnail previews:* Another convenient navigation tool that most browsers share is providing thumbnail previews of all open web pages in open tabs.

- *Tab isolation:* With this feature, tabs are independent of each other, so if one crashes, it does not affect the other tabs.

- *Combined search and address bar:* With this feature, you can both type a website URL or search the web from the address bar.

FIGURE 3.13 Common Web Browsers *(Pablo Fonseca Q./ La Nacion de Costa Rica/Newscom; Lucia Lanpur/Alamy; Tommy (Louth)/ Alamy; 2020WEB/Alamy)*

Internet Explorer
Most widely used browser

Firefox
Open source
Has strong following

Google Chrome
Newest browser
Quickly gaining popularity

Safari
Developed by Apple for Macs
Has a Windows version for PCs

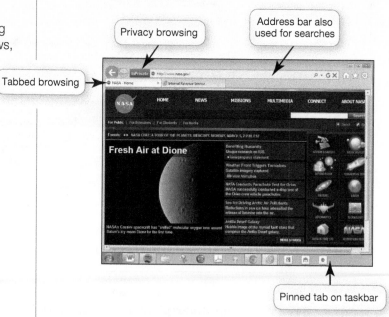

Privacy browsing

Address bar also used for searches

Tabbed browsing

Pinned tab on taskbar

FIGURE 3.14 Like most of the popular web browsers, Internet Explorer includes tabbed and privacy browsing. Pinned tabs on the taskbar make accessing your favorite sites even easier.

- *SmartScreen filter:* Most browsers offer built-in protection against phishing, malware, and other web-based threats.
- *Privacy browsing:* Privacy features (such as InPrivate Browsing in Internet Explorer) let you browse the web without retaining a history trail, temporary Internet files, cookies, or usernames and passwords. These features are especially helpful when you use public computers at college or the public library, for example.
- *Add-ons:* Add-ons are small programs that customize and increase the functionality of the browser. Examples include Video DownloadHelper that converts web videos, like those found on YouTube, to files you can save, as well as a Facebook toolbar that integrates Facebook functionality into your browser.
- *Session Restore:* Brings back all your active web pages if the browser or system shuts down unexpectedly.

URLs, Protocols, and Domain Names

What do all the parts of a URL mean? You gain initial access to a particular **website** by typing its unique address, or **Uniform Resource Locator** (**URL**, pronounced "you-are-ell"), in your browser. A website is composed of many different web pages, each of which is a separate document with its own unique URL. Like

BITS&BYTES

Why You Should Keep Your Browser Software up to Date

When new file formats are developed for the web, browsers need new plug-ins to display content properly. Constantly downloading and installing plug-ins can be tedious. Although many websites provide links to other sites where you can download plug-ins, not all do, resulting in frustration when you can't display the content you want. When new versions of browsers are released, they normally include the latest versions of popular plug-ins. Corrections of security breaches are typically included in these versions of browser software, as well. Therefore, upgrading to the latest version of your browser software provides for safer, more convenient web surfing. Fortunately, updates are free, and you can set most of the popular web browsers to notify you when updates are available or to download the updates automatically.

a regular street address, a URL is composed of several parts that help identify the web document it stands for (see Figure 3.15):

- the *protocol* (set of rules) used to retrieve the document;
- the **domain name;** and
- the *path* or subdirectory

Although every part of a URL is important information that ensures the web page you requested actually displays in your browser, you don't have to type in every part in the location or address bar of the browser. Most current browsers no longer require you to enter the protocol or the "www," and most don't even require the domain if it's a .com—the browser will enter those in automatically.

What's the protocol? You're probably most familiar with URLs that begin with *http*, which is short for **Hypertext Transfer Protocol (HTTP)**. HTTP is the protocol that allows files to be transferred from a **web server**—a computer that hosts the website you're requesting—so that you can see it on your computer. The HTTP protocol is what the web is based on.

Is HTTP the only protocol I need to use? HTTP is the most common protocol, but it's not the only one. HTTP is part of the Internet protocol suite, a group of protocols that govern how information is exchanged on a network. Another protocol in that group is the **File Transfer Protocol (FTP)**. As its name implies, FTP was originally designed, before the HTTP protocol was developed, to transfer files from your computer to a web server. Today, FTP is often used when you have large files to upload or download. To connect to most FTP servers, you need a user ID and password. To upload and download files from FTP sites, you can use a browser or file transfer software such as WS_FTP, Fetch, or FileZilla.

BitTorrent, like FTP, is a protocol used to transfer files, though it's not part of the Internet protocol suite. To use BitTorrent, you install a software client program. It uses a *peer-to-peer networking system,* so that sharing occurs

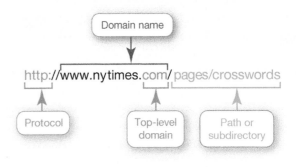

FIGURE 3.15 The Parts of a URL

between connected computers that also have the Bit-Torrent client installed. BitTorrent was developed in 2001 and has been gaining popularity, especially among users who want to share music, movies, and games. Use caution, however, when accessing BitTorrent content. Because it is a peer-to-peer system, it's possible for copyrighted material to be shared illegally.

What's in a domain name? The domain name identifies the site's **host**, the location that maintains the computers that store the website files. For example, **www.berkeley.edu** is the domain name for the University of California at Berkeley. The suffix in the domain name after the dot (such as "com" or "edu") is called the **top-level domain**. This suffix indicates the kind of organization to which the host belongs. Figure 3.16 lists the most frequently used top-level domains.

Each country has its own top-level domain. These are two-letter designations such as .za for South Africa and .us for the United States. A sampling of country codes is shown in Figure 3.17. Within a country-specific domain, further subdivisions can be made for regions or states. For instance, the .us domain contains subdomains for each state, using the two-letter abbreviation of the state. For example, the URL for Pennsylvania's website is **www.state.pa.us**.

What's the information after the domain name that I sometimes see? When the URL is only the domain name, such as **www.nytimes.com**, you're requesting a site's home page. However, sometimes a forward slash and additional text follow the domain name, such as in **www.nytimes.com/pages/crosswords**. The information after each slash indicates a particular file or **path**

FIGURE 3.16

Common Top-Level Domains and Their Authorized Users

DOMAIN NAME	WHO CAN USE IT
.biz	Businesses
.com	Originally for commercial sites, but now can be used by anyone
.edu	Degree-granting institutions
.gov	Local, state, and federal U.S. governments
.info	Information service providers
.mil	U.S. military
.net	Originally for networking organizations, but no longer restricted
.org	Organizations (often not-for-profits)

FIGURE 3.17

Examples of Country Codes

COUNTRY CODE	COUNTRY
.au	Australia
.ca	Canada
.jp	Japan
.uk	United Kingdom

Note: For a full listing of country codes, refer to **iana.org/domains/root/db/**.

(or **subdirectory**) within the website. In Figure 3.15, you would connect to the crossword page on the *New York Times* site.

Hyperlinks and Beyond

What's the best way to get around in a website? As its name implies, the web is a series of interconnected paths, or links. You've no doubt moved around the web by clicking on **hyperlinks**, specially coded elements that let you jump from one web page to another within the same website or to another site altogether (see Figure 3.18). Generally, text that operates as a hyperlink appears in a different color (often blue) and is usually underlined, but sometimes images also act as hyperlinks. When you hover your cursor over a hyperlink, the cursor changes to a hand with a finger pointing upward.

What other tools can I use to navigate a website? To move back or forward one page at a time, you can use the browser's Back and Forward buttons (see Figure 3.18).

To help navigate more quickly through a website, some sites provide a **breadcrumb trail**—a navigation aid that shows users the path they have taken to get to a web page, or where the page is located within the website. It usually appears at the top of a page. Figure 3.18 shows an example of a breadcrumb trail. "Breadcrumbs" get their name from the fairy tale "Hansel and Gretel," in which the characters drop breadcrumbs on the trail to find their way out of a forest. By clicking on earlier links in a breadcrumb trail, you can go directly to

 SOUND BYTE
Welcome to the Web

In this Sound Byte, you'll visit the web in a series of guided tours of useful websites. This tour serves as an introductory guide for web newcomers but is also a great resource for more experienced users.

FIGURE 3.18 Navigating a Web Page

a previously visited web page without having to use the Back button to navigate back through the website.

The History list on your browser's toolbar is also a handy feature. The History list shows all the websites and pages you've visited over a certain period of time. These sites are organized according to date and can go back as far as three weeks, depending on your browsing activity. To access the History list in Internet Explorer, click the star in the upper right hand corner of the browser window and then click the History tab.

Favorites, Live Bookmarks, and Tagging

What's the best way to mark a site so I can return to it later? If you want an easy way to return to a specific web page, you can use your browser's **Bookmarks** feature (Internet Explorer calls this feature **Favorites**). This feature places a marker of the site's URL in an easily retrievable list in your browser's toolbar. To organize the sites into categories, most browsers offer tools to create folders.

Favorites and Bookmarks are great for quickly locating those sites you use most, but they're accessible to you only when you're on your own computer. Although most browsers provide features that let you export the list of bookmarks to a file you can import to another computer or another browser, another way to access your Bookmarks and Favorites from any computer is to use MyBookmarks (**mybookmarks.com**), a free Internet service that stores your Bookmarks and Favorites online.

What are live bookmarks? Live bookmark is a feature in Firefox that adds the technology of RSS feeds to bookmarking. Safari and Internet Explorer also have built-in RSS readers, while Chrome requires that you add on an extension. Because the web is constantly changing, the site you bookmarked last week may subsequently change and add new content. Traditionally, you would notice the change only the next time you visited the site. Live bookmarks deliver content updates to you as soon as they become available using RSS, the same technology that updates blogs and podcasts that we described earlier in the chapter. Live bookmarks and RSS feeds are useful if you're interested in the most up-to-date news stories, sports scores, or stock prices.

What is tagging? Tagging, also known as **social bookmarking**, is like bookmarking your favorite website, but instead of saving it to your browser for only you to see, you're saving it to a social bookmarking site so that you can share it with others. A social bookmark or tag is a **keyword** or term that you assign to a web page, digital image, or video. A tag can be something you create to describe the digital content, or it can be a suggested term provided by the website. For example, as you were surfing the web you came across a web page with a great article on inexpensive places to go for spring break. You might tag the article with the term *vacations*. Others on the same social bookmarking site who are looking for websites about vacations may use *vacations* as the search term and find the article you tagged.

Delicious (**delicious.com**) is one of the original social bookmarking sites (see Figure 3.19). Delicious lets you group related links and organize them into themed "stacks." So if you've collected several links to websites about different places to go to over spring break, you can collect all those links into one stack about vacations. Or if you want to see what links others may have found about interesting vacations, you could search Delicious with the term *vacations* to see other vacation-related stacks.

Most social bookmarking sites, such as Digg (**digg.com**) and Reddit (**reddit.com**), prominently feature those articles that have been tagged the most. Some sites, like Newsvine (**newsvine.com**), just center around newsworthy articles that have been tagged, whereas others, such as TechnoratiMedia (**technoratimedia.com**), just feature blogs that readers have tagged. Diigo (**diigo.com**) allows you not only to tag and bookmark websites, but also to annotate the pages with highlights and sticky notes. Through Diigo, you can archive web pages so they are always available. StumbleUpon (**stumbleupon.com**) recommends websites based on your personal interests and preferences as well as the recommendations of people you know or the general surfing public. ∎

FIGURE 3.19 Delicious is a social bookmarking website that allows you to organize and share your favorite websites.

Think about all the types of data on the web that you access manually, such as appointment times, transportation and entertainment schedules, and store locations and hours. It would seem that computers would be helpful in plugging through all this web data, but oddly, that is not the case. Web pages are designed for people to read, not for computers to manipulate. As yet, no reliable way exists for computers to process the meaning of data on a web page so that it can be used to see relationships or make decisions.

The **semantic web** (or **Web 3.0**) is an evolving extension of the web in which data is defined in such a way to make it more easily processed by computers. Right now, search engines function by recognizing keywords such as *office hours* and *dentist*, but they can't determine, for example, in which office and on what days Dr. Smith works and what his available appointment times are. By using a so-called "agent," the semantic web would enable computers to find that type of information, coordinate it with your other schedules and preferences, and then make the appointment for you.

The semantic web would also assist you in comparing products, prices, and shipping options by finding the best product option based on specified criteria and then placing the order for you. Additionally, the agent would record the financial transaction into your personal bookkeeping software and arrange for a technician to help install the software, if needed.

For the semantic web to work, businesses, services, and software would all use the same categorization structures so that similar information would share the same attributes, ensuring consistency of metadata throughout the web. The semantic web would build on this type of capability so that each website would have text and pictures (for people to read) and metadata (for computers to read) describing the information on the web (see Figure 3.20).

Although some of the semantic web's functionalities are beginning to emerge in technologies such as Siri in the iPhone 4S, the majority of its functionality and implementation are still in development. The greatest challenge is recoding all the information currently available on the web into the type of metadata that computers can recognize. The very grandeur of that task means that we will not see a fully functional semantic web until sometime in the distant future. In the meantime, we can continue to benefit from each small step toward that goal.

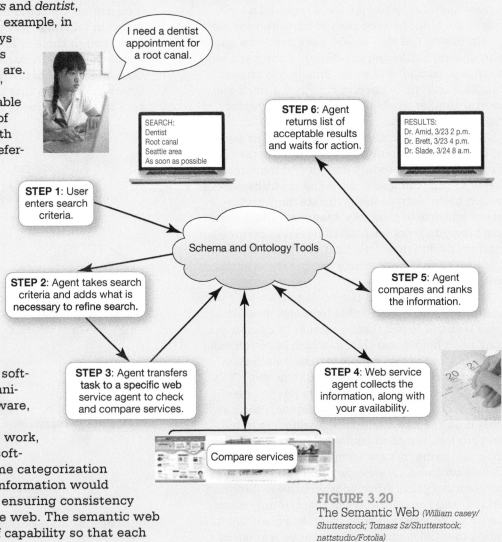

I need a dentist appointment for a root canal.

SEARCH:
Dentist
Root canal
Seattle area
As soon as possible

STEP 6: Agent returns list of acceptable results and waits for action.

RESULTS:
Dr. Amid, 3/23 2 p.m.
Dr. Brett, 3/23 4 p.m.
Dr. Slade, 3/24 8 a.m.

STEP 1: User enters search criteria.

Schema and Ontology Tools

STEP 2: Agent takes search criteria and adds what is necessary to refine search.

STEP 5: Agent compares and ranks the information.

STEP 3: Agent transfers task to a specific web service agent to check and compare services.

STEP 4: Web service agent collects the information, along with your availability.

Compare services

FIGURE 3.20
The Semantic Web *(William casey/ Shutterstock; Tomasz Sz/Shutterstock; nattstudio/Fotolia)*

Let's say you think that flip-flops in school colors would be a popular product. Your school's bookstore carries everything else with the school's colors and logo, but not flip-flops. You've asked your friends and several classmates, and most of them say they would buy flip-flops in the school's colors. So what do you do next? How do you move from product concept to selling a physical product?

Before the Internet, it would have been much more difficult and expensive to get your product produced and distributed. First, you would have had to find someone to design your flip-flops. Then, to make the flip-flops, you would have had to find a manufacturer, who may have required a high minimum order (maybe tens of thousands of pairs of flip-flops). You also would have needed a package design, marketing brochures, a company logo, a storage facility, and more. Finally, the largest hurdle would have been to convince a brick-and-mortar retailer, such as your campus bookstore, to carry your product.

Today, however, the Internet brings the power of the global economy right to your door (see Figure 3.21). For product design and manufacturing, you can visit a site like Alibaba (**Alibaba.com**), which helps entrepreneurs locate manufacturers of all sorts of products. Many manufacturers are happy to work with small business owners to custom-design products. So if you find a flip-flop style you like, you probably can get it customized with your school colors.

But what happens if the bookstore doesn't want to sell your flip-flops? If this happens, you can set up a website to sell them yourself. Of course, you may need help doing this, in which case you can locate skilled professionals by using sites such as Guru (**guru.com**) or Elance (**elance.com**). You simply create a description of the job you need done (such as logo design for a flip-flop company), post it on the site, and invite freelancers to bid on your job. You then contact the freelancers who look promising, review samples of their work, and decide on someone who can help you—and at a competitive price. After your website is designed and up and running, you can place your business on social networking sites, such as Facebook, to help potential customers discover your product

and spread the word about your great flip-flops. You probably already have lots of friends on Facebook who attend your school and would be good potential customers.

Another hurdle is determining where you'll store your product and who will package and ship it to customers. If your parents' basement isn't large enough, you can outsource warehousing and order fulfillment to Amazon.com. Amazon will (for a fee) warehouse your inventory and then package and ship it when customer orders are received. Orders don't have to come through Amazon's site (although that is an option); you can provide ordering information collected on your site to Amazon, and Amazon will take care of the rest.

Although there is always a cost to starting up a business, up-front costs are much lower when you take advantage of the global marketplace and the Internet. So, take that brilliant idea you have and turn it into a business today!

Find product design and manufacturing companies

Hire freelance website designers

Create a company Facebook page

Use Amazon to warehouse and distribute flip-flops

FIGURE 3.21 By using the services of only a few websites, you can create and distribute products, such as your own line of custom flip-flops. *(M4OS Photos/Alamy; Elance, Inc.; Kevin Britland/Alamy; Anatolii Babii/Alamy; nito/Shutterstock)*

searching the web
EFFECTIVELY

You've most likely "Googled" something today, and if you did, your search is one of over eight billion searches today. Google is the world's most popular **search engine**—a set of programs that searches the web for **keywords** (specific words you wish to look for or *query*) and then returns a list of the sites on which those keywords are found. In fact, Google has become so popular that its name is synonymous with looking for information on the web. Other popular search engines include Yahoo!, Bing, and Ask.com. But there are even more options for searching the web.

For some web searches, it might be better to use a **subject directory**, which is a structured outline of websites organized by topics and subtopics. By drilling down through the topics and subtopics, you can narrow down to a list of meaningful websites to look through. For example, if you wanted to know about exhibits of 3-D photography, you might click Arts>Visual Arts>Photography> 3-D> Exhibits in a subject directory. In Yahoo's subject directory (**dir.yahoo.com**), the result would be a list of relevant websites about 3-D photography exhibits. The website ipl2 (**ipl2.org**) is a subject directory that combines resources from the Internet Public Library and the Librarians' Internet Index websites (see Figure 3.22).

If you can't decide which search engine is best, you may want to try a metasearch engine. **Metasearch**

engines, such as Dogpile (**dogpile.com**; see Figure 3.22), search other search engines rather than individual websites. Figure 3.23 lists search engines and subject directories that are alternatives to Google, Yahoo!, and Bing.

Using Search Engines Effectively

How do search engines work? Search engines have three components:

1. The first component is a program called a *spider,* which constantly collects data on the web, following links in websites and reading web pages. Spiders get their name because they crawl over the web using multiple "legs" to visit many sites simultaneously.

2. As the spider collects data, the second component of the search engine, an *indexer program*, organizes the data into a large database.

3. When you use a search engine, you interact with the third component: the *search engine software*. This software searches the indexed data, pulling out relevant information according to your search.

The resulting list appears in your web browser as a list of hits—sites that match your search.

FIGURE 3.22 ipl2 and Dogpile are alternatives to Google. ipl2 (**ipl2.org**) is a subject directory that lists resources by subject, and Dogpile (**dogpile.com**) is a metasearch engine that searches Google, Yahoo!, and Bing.

FIGURE 3.23

Beyond Google: 10 Alternative Search Engines and Subject Directories

ChaCha **chacha.com**	Uses live people who help you search; free of charge. Also available by texting your questions to 242242.
CompletePlanet **aip.completeplanet.com**	"Deep web" directory that searches databases not normally searched by typical search engines.
Dogpile **dogpile.com**	Metasearch engine that searches Google, Yahoo!, and Bing.
Excite **excite.com**	Website that in addition to having keyword search capabilities includes links to information on a wide variety of topics including travel, weather, concert tickets, and top news items.
Info.com **info.com**	Metasearch engine that searches Google, Yahoo!, and Bing.
InfoMine **infomine.com**	Subject directory of academic resources with keyword search engine capabilities.
ipl2 **ipl2.org**	Subject directory that combines resources from the Internet Public Library and the Librarians' Internet Index websites.
Open Directory Project **dmoz.org**	Human-edited subject directory with keyword search capabilities. Maintained by a global community of volunteer editors.
Yippy **yippy.com**	Metasearch engine that groups similar results into topics called clusters (for example, NBA, College Basketball, Photo Gallery, and Articles would be some resulting clusters if you use the search term *basketball*). Clicking on any of these clusters results in listing those sites specific to that subset of basketball.

Note: For a complete list of search engines, go to **searchengineguide.com**.

Why don't I get the same results from all search engines? Each search engine uses a unique formula, or *algorithm*, to formulate the search and create the resulting index of related sites. In addition, search engines differ in how they rank the search results. Most search engines rank their results based on the frequency of the appearance of your queried keywords in websites as well as the location of those words in the sites. This means that sites that include the keywords in their URL or site name most likely appear at the top of the hit list. An important part of a company's marketing strategy is designing the corporate website to ensure it appears near the top of a Google search.

Search engines also differ as to which sites they search. For instance, Google and Bing search nearly the entire web, whereas specialty search engines search only sites that are relevant to a particular topic or industry. Specialty search engines exist for almost every industry or interest. DailyStocks (**dailystocks.com**) is a search engine used primarily by investors that searches for corporate information. Search Engine Watch (**searchenginewatch.com**) has a list of many specialty search engines, organized by industry.

 ACTIVE HELPDESK
Using Subject Directories and Search Engines

In this Active Helpdesk call, you'll play the role of a helpdesk staffer, fielding calls about how to search the Internet using search engines and subject directories, as well as how to use advanced search options to search the web more effectively.

Can I use a search engine to search just for images and videos? With the increasing popularity of multimedia, search engines such as Google, Bing, and Yahoo! let you search the web for digital images and audio and video files. After putting in your search term, select Video from Google's left menu to display only the search results that are videos. You can further narrow down the video selection by using the filtering tools. Blinkx (**blinkx.com**) is a video search engine that helps you sift through all the video posted on the web (see Figure 3.24).

How can I refine my searches for better results? You've probably searched for something on Google and gotten back a list of hits that includes thousands—even millions—of web pages that have no relevance to the topic you're interested in. Initially, Boolean operators were needed to help refine a search. **Boolean operators** are words such as *AND, NOT,* and *OR* that describe the relationships between keywords in a search. Today, most search engines offer an advanced search page that provides the same types of strategies in a well-organized form (see Figure 3.25). Using the advanced search form can make your Internet research a lot more efficient. With the simple addition of a few words

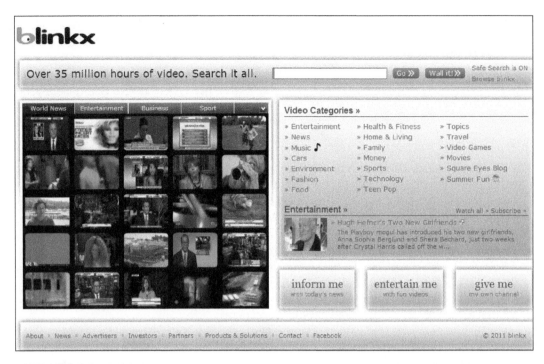

FIGURE 3.24 Blinkx is a video search engine that helps you sift through the increasing number of videos on the web. *(blinkx)*

BITS&BYTES

Searching to Do Good

Wouldn't it be great to benefit others just by searching the web? Now there's an easy way to "do good" with every search. GoodSearch (**goodsearch.com**) is a Yahoo!-powered search engine that donates half of its revenues (approximately a penny per search) to approved U.S. charities and schools that users designate. The money GoodSearch donates comes from the site's advertisers. More than 100,000 charitable organizations are being helped by GoodSearch, but if the organization you're interested in isn't on the list, as long as it's a registered U.S. not-for-profit organization, you can apply to have it added.

You can also contribute to your favorite charity by shopping online through GoodShop (**goodshop.com**). Instead of going directly to your favorite online store, go to GoodShop first, find and click through to the store of your choice, and start shopping. Participating stores donate up to 30% of the purchased amount. So, search and shop away—and do some good!

or constraints, you can narrow your search results to a more manageable and more meaningful list.

Are there other helpful search strategies? Instead of using the advanced search form, you can use other strategies to help refine your searches when entering your search phrases:

- **Search for a phrase.** To search for an exact phrase, place quotation marks around your keywords. The search engine will look for only those websites that contain the words in *that exact order*. For example, if you want information on the movie *The Green Hornet* and you type these words without quotation marks,

FIGURE 3.25 Most search engines, including Google, have an advanced search form to help you refine your searches.

your search results will contain pages that include either of the words *Green* and *Hornet*, although not necessarily in that order. Typing *"The Green Hornet"* in quotation marks guarantees that search results will include this exact phrase.

- **Search within a specific website.** To search just a specific website, you can use the search keyword, then *site:* followed by the website's URL. For example, searching with *processor site:* www.wired.com returns results about processors from the Wired.com website. The same method works for entire classes of sites in a given top-level domain or country code.

- **Use a wild card.** The asterisk ("*") is a wild card, or placeholder, feature that is helpful when you need to search with unknown terms. Another way to think about the wild card search feature is as a "fill in the blank." For example, searching with *Congress voted * on the * bill* might bring up an article about the members of Congress who voted *no* on the *healthcare* bill or a different article about the members of Congress who voted *yes* on the *energy* bill.

How else can I customize my searches? Many other specialty search strategies and services are available. Try clicking on the "More" hyperlink in Google's menu at the top of Google's website, then click the "Even More" option for a listing of all the specialized search products Google offers, including the following (see Figure 3.26):

- *Scholar* searches scholarly literature such as peer-reviewed papers, theses, and publications from academic organizations. Each search result contains bibliographic information, as well.

- *Custom Search* lets you create a customized search engine to search only a selected set of sites tailored to your needs. You can add this specialized search engine to a website or blog or design it for a specific organization.

- *Product Search* lets you search by product rather than by company. So, if you're interested in buying a digital camera, Product Search lists cameras by the most popular and provides information on the stores that carry the cameras, along with the average price.

- *Alerts* let you know by e-mail when content that you specify has been updated, so you can monitor a developing news story or be aware of breaking news about your favorite sports team, for example.

Evaluating Websites

How can I make sure a website is appropriate to use for research? When you're using the Internet for research, you shouldn't assume that everything you find is accurate and appropriate to use. The following is a list of questions to consider before you use an Internet resource; the answers to these questions will help you decide whether you should consider a website to be a good source of information:

- *Authority:* Who is the author of the article or the sponsor of the site? If the author is well known or the site is published by a reputable news source (such as the *New York Times*), then you can feel more confident using it as a source than if you are unable to locate such information. *Note:* Some sites include a page with information about the author or the site's sponsor.

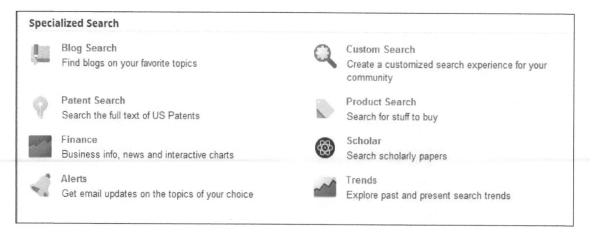

Specialized Search

Blog Search Find blogs on your favorite topics	**Custom Search** Create a customized search experience for your community
Patent Search Search the full text of US Patents	**Product Search** Search for stuff to buy
Finance Business info, news and interactive charts	**Scholar** Search scholarly papers
Alerts Get email updates on the topics of your choice	**Trends** Explore past and present search trends

FIGURE 3.26 Google's Specialized Search Tools

- *Bias:* Is the site biased? The purpose of many websites is to sell products or services or to persuade rather than inform. These sites, though useful in some situations, present a biased point of view. Look for sites that offer several sets of facts or consider opinions from several sources.
- *Relevance:* Is the information on the site current? Material can last a long time on the web. Some research projects (such as historical accounts) depend on older records. However, if you're writing about cutting-edge technologies, you need to look for the most recent sources. Therefore, look for a date on information to make sure it is current.
- *Audience:* For what audience is the site intended? Ensure that the content, tone, and style of the site match your needs. You probably wouldn't want to use information from a site geared toward teens if you're writing for adults, nor would you use a site that has a casual style and tone for serious research.
- *Links:* Are the links available and appropriate? Check out the links provided on the site to determine whether

 SOUND BYTE
Finding Information on the Web

In this Sound Byte, you'll learn how and when to use search engines and subject directories. Through guided tours, you'll learn effective search techniques, including how to use Boolean operators and metasearch engines.

they're still working and appropriate for your needs. Don't assume that the links provided are the only additional sources of information. Investigate other sites on your topic, as well. You should also be able to find the same information on at least three different websites to help verify the information is accurate. ■

Before moving on to the Chapter Review:
- Watch Replay Video 3.2 ▶.
- Then check your understanding of what you've learned so far.

ethics in IT

Plagiarism and Copyright Violation: What Can You Borrow from the Internet?

With so much information easily available on the web, the temptation to use it without receiving proper permissions is not only wrong but can also be illegal. So what can you borrow from the web and what must you seek permission to use? Consider these scenarios:

1. You find a political cartoon that would be terrific in a PowerPoint presentation you're creating for your civics class. You copy it into your presentation.
2. Your hobby is writing children's books, which you later sell online. Most of what you create is your content, but sometimes you borrow story ideas from other children's books and just change a few characters or situations. You do not obtain permission from the originators of the story ideas you borrow.
3. You're pressed for time and need to do research for a paper due tomorrow. You find

information on an obscure website and copy it into your paper without documenting the source.
4. You download a song from the Internet and incorporate it into a PowerPoint presentation for a school project. Because you assume everyone knows the song, you don't credit it in your sources.

Which of the preceding scenarios represent copyright violations? Which represent plagiarism? The distinctions between these scenarios are narrow in some cases, but it's important to understand the differences.

Plagiarism occurs when you use someone else's ideas or words and represent them as your own. In today's computer society, it's easy to copy information from the Internet and paste it into a Word document, change a few words, and call it your own. To avoid plagiarism, properly crediting

(Continued)

all information you obtain from the Internet by using quotation marks around all words you borrow directly, and credit your sources for any ideas you paraphrase or borrow.

WriteCheck (**writecheck.com**) is a website specifically for students to help check for plagiarism violations (see Figure 3.27). The site compares your document to a database of publications, books, and web content and identifies possible plagiarism violations. Although some common phrasing may be truly coincidental, real and purposeful plagiarism is reasonably easy to identify. Students can use WriteCheck before submitting an assignment to ensure their papers are free from plagiarism and avoid the serious consequences of this offense.

Copyright violation is more serious because it, unlike plagiarism, is punishable by law. Copyright law assumes that all original work is copyrighted even if the work does not display the copyright symbol (©). Copyright violation occurs when you use another person's material for your own personal economic benefit or when you take away from the economic benefit of the originator. In most cases, citing the source is not sufficient; you need to seek and receive written permission from the copyright holder.

There are exceptions to this rule. There is no copyright on government documents, so you can download and reproduce material from any government website. The British Broadcasting Corporation (BBC) is also beginning to digitize and make available its archives of material to the public without copyright restrictions. Teachers and students receive special consideration that falls under a provision called *academic fair use*. As long as the material is being used for educational purposes only, limited copying and distribution is allowed.

One standard applied to academic fair use is the effect the use has on the potential market. For example, a student can include a cartoon in a PowerPoint presentation without seeking permission from the artist. However, to avoid plagiarism, you still must credit your sources of information.

So, do you now know which of the four scenarios above are plagiarism or copyright violations? Let's review them.

1. You are not in violation because the use of the cartoon is for educational purposes and falls

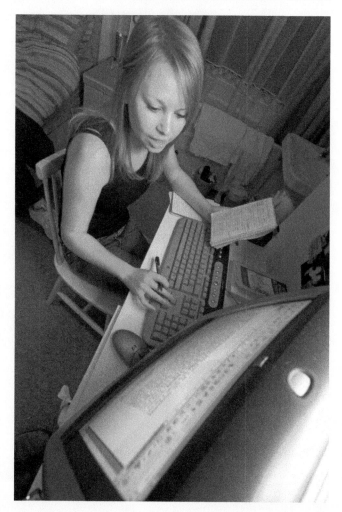

FIGURE 3.27 Students can compare their work to a database of publications in sites such as WriteCheck to check for unintended plagiarism. *(Keith morris/Alamy)*

under the academic fair use provision. You must still credit the source, however.

2. You are in violation of copyright laws because you are presenting others' ideas for children's stories as your own and receiving personal economic benefit from them.

3. You are guilty of plagiarism because you copied content from another source and implied it was your own work.

4. Again, because your copying is for a school project, you are not in violation of copyright laws because of the academic fair use provision. However, it's always important to document your sources.

check your understanding //

For a quick review to see what you've learned so far, answer the following questions. Visit **pearsonhighered.com/techinaction** to check your answers.

multiple choice

1. What is the name for a list of links you've visited within a website?

   a. favorites   **c.** bookmarks

   b. breadcrumb trail   **d.** history

2. Which is NOT a component of a search engine?

   a. spider   **c.** subject directory

   b. indexer program   **d.** search engine software

3. When using the Internet for research, you

   a. can assume that everything you find is accurate and appropriate.

   b. should evaluate sites for bias and relevance.

   c. can assume the author is an authority on the subject matter.

   d. can assume that the links provided on the site are the only additional sources of information.

4. Which of the following is not an Internet protocol?

   a. ARPANET   **c.** FTP

   b. HTTP   **d.** BitTorrent

5. eBay and Craigslist are examples of what kind of electronic commerce?

   a. C2C   **c.** B2C

   b. B2B   **d.** C2B

true–false

_____ **1.** A search engine that searches other search engines is called a SuperSearch engine.

_____ **2.** In the web address **www.facebook.com**, "facebook" is the top-level domain.

critical thinking

1. File-Swapping Ethics

Downloading free music, movies, and other electronic media from the Internet, although illegal, still occurs on sites such as BitTorrent.

   a. Do you think you should have the ability to download free music files of your choice? Do you think the musicians who oppose online music sharing have made valid points?

   b. Discuss the differences you see between sharing music files online and sharing CDs with your friends.

   c. The current price to buy a song online is about $1. Is this a fair price? If not, what price would you consider fair?

2. The Power of Google

Google is the largest and most popular search engine on the Internet today. Because of its size and popularity, some people claim that Google has enormous power to influence a web user's search experience solely by its website-ranking processes. What do you think about this potential power? How could it be used in negative or harmful ways?

   a. Some websites pay search engines to list them near the top of the results pages. These sponsors therefore get priority placement. What do you think of this policy?

   b. What effect (if any) do you think that Google has on website development? For example, do you think website developers intentionally include frequently searched words in their pages so that they will appear in more hits lists?

Continue ➤

3 Chapter Review

summary //

The Internet and How It Works

1. What is the origin of the Internet?

- The Internet is the largest computer network in the world, connecting millions of computers.
- Government and military officials developed the early Internet as a reliable way to communicate in the event of war. Eventually, scientists and educators used the Internet to exchange research.
- Today, we use the Internet and the web (which is a part of the Internet) to shop, research, communicate, and entertain ourselves.

2. How does data travel on the Internet?

- A computer (or other device) connected to the Internet acts as either a client (a computer that asks for information) or a server (a computer that receives the request and returns the information to the client).
- Data travels between clients and servers along a system of communication lines or pathways. The largest and fastest of these pathways is the Internet backbone.
- To ensure that data is sent to the correct computer along the pathways, IP addresses (unique ID numbers) are assigned to all computers connected to the Internet.

Communicating and Collaborating on the Web

3. How can I communicate and collaborate with others using Web 2.0 technologies?

- Web 2.0 can be described as the social web, in which the user is also a participant. Before Web 2.0 technologies were in place, we were only able to be passive users of the web.
- Examples of Web 2.0 technologies include social networking sites, blogs, wikis, podcasts, and webcasts. Social networking sites enable you to communicate and share information with friends as well as meet and connect with others.
- Blogs are journal entries posted to the web that are generally organized by a topic or area of interest and are publicly available. Generally, one person writes the blog, and others can comment on the journal entries.

- Video logs are personal journals that use video as the primary content in addition to text, images, and audio.
- Wikis are a type of website that allows users to collaborate on content—adding, removing, or editing it.
- Podcasts are audio or video content that is available over the Internet. Users subscribe to receive updates to podcasts.
- Webcasts are broadcasts of audio or video content over the Internet. Most webcasts are distributed in "real time," unlike podcasts that are usually prerecorded and made available for download.

4. How can I communicate with others using e-mail and instant messaging?

- Communication was one of the reasons the Internet was developed and is one of the primary uses of the Internet today.
- E-mail allows users to communicate electronically without the parties involved being available at the same time, whereas instant-messaging services are programs that enable you to communicate in real time with others who are online.

Web Entertainment

5. What multimedia files are found on the web, and what software is needed to access those files?

- Multimedia is anything that involves one or more forms of media in addition to text, such as graphics, audio, and video clips.
- Sometimes you need a special software program called a *plug-in* (or *player*) to view and hear multimedia files. Plug-ins are often installed in new computers or are offered free of charge at manufacturers' websites.

Conducting Business over the Internet: E-Commerce

6. What is e-commerce, and what online safeguards are available?

- E-commerce is the business of conducting business online.
- E-commerce includes transactions between businesses (B2B), between consumers (C2C), and between businesses and consumers (B2C).

- Because more business than ever before is conducted online, numerous safeguards have been put in place to ensure that transactions are protected. Some important safeguards to keep in mind include looking for indicators that the website is secure, shopping at well-known, reputable sites, and avoiding making online transactions on public computers.

Accessing and Moving Around the Web

7. What is a web browser, and what are a URL and its parts?

- Once you're connected to the Internet, in order to locate, navigate to, and view web pages, you need to install special software called a web browser on your system.
- The most common web browsers are Internet Explorer, Firefox, Google Chrome, and Safari.
- You gain access to a website by typing in its address, called a Uniform Resource Locator (URL).
- A URL is composed of several parts, including the protocol, the domain, the top-level domain, and paths (or subdirectories).

8. How can I use hyperlinks and other tools to get around the web?

- One unique aspect of the web is that you can jump from place to place by clicking on specially formatted pieces of text or images called *hyperlinks*.
- You can also use the Back and Forward buttons, History lists, breadcrumb trails, and Favorites or Bookmarks to navigate the web.
- Favorites, live bookmarks, and social bookmarking help you return to specific web pages without having to type in the URL and help you organize the web content that is most important to you.

Searching the Web Effectively

9. How do I search the Internet effectively, and how can I evaluate websites?

- A search engine is a set of programs that searches the web using specific keywords you wish to query and then returns a list of the websites on which those keywords are found.
- Search engines can be used to search for images, podcasts, and videos in addition to traditional text-based web content.
- A subject directory is a structured outline of websites organized by topic and subtopic. Metasearch engines search other search engines.
- Not all websites are equal, and some are better sources for research than others. To evaluate whether it is appropriate to use a website as a resource, determine whether the author of the site is reputable and whether the site is intended for your particular needs. In addition, make sure that the site content is not biased, the information on the site is current, and all the links on the site are available and appropriate. If multiple sites offer the same content, this is another indication that the information is accurate.

Be sure to check out the companion website for additional materials to help you review and learn, including a Tech Bytes Weekly newsletter— **pearsonhighered.com/techinaction**. And don't forget the Replay Videos ▶.

key terms //

making the transition to . . . next semester//

1. **Plagiarism Policies**

   Does your school have a plagiarism policy?

   a. Search your school's website to find the school's plagiarism policy. What does it say?

   b. How well do you paraphrase? Find some websites that help test or evaluate your paraphrasing skills.

   c. Create an account at WriteCheck. This website checks your written work against content on the web and produces an originality report. Submit at least three different drafts of your work to WriteCheck to check for any intended or unintended cases of plagiarism before submitting your final work for a grade. What were the results?

2. **Searching Beyond Google**

   While Google is probably your first choice among search engines, there are many other very good search engines that are worth knowing about. Conduct searches for inexpensive travel deals for spring break by using the search engines in the following list. Record your results and a summary of the differences among search engines. Would you choose to use any of these search engines again? Why or why not?

   a. Yippy.com

   b. Dogpile.com

   c. Chacha.com

making the transition to . . . the workplace//

1. **Online Résumé Resources**

   Using a search engine, locate several web resources that offer assistance in writing a résumé. For example, the University of Minnesota (**umn.edu/ohr/careerdev/resources/resume**) has a résumé tutor that guides you as you write your résumé.

   a. What other websites can you find that help you write a résumé?

   b. Do these sites all offer the same services and have the same features?

2. **Evaluating Web 2.0 Content**

   You are aware of the guidelines you should use to evaluate the quality of content on a website, but you find yourself using other kinds of web content such as blogs, wikis, social networking sites, and social bookmarks. Visit **library.albany.edu/usered/eval/evalweb** and review the new guidelines for evaluating web content in the Web 2.0 environment. After reviewing the guidelines, describe the guidelines for evaluating web content at the following sites:

   a. Free research sites such as Google Scholar (**scholar.google.com**)

   b. Document repositories such as California Digital Library (**cdlib.org**)

   c. Blogs and wikis such as TechCrunch (**techcrunch.com**)

   d. Social networking sites such as Twitter (**twitter.com**)

   e. Social bookmarking sites such as Delicious (**delicious.com**)

   f. Multimedia sites such as YouTube (**youtube.com**)

3. **Facebook Privacy and Security**

   Your aunt contacted you last night. Your cousin, who is 14, wants a Facebook account. Your aunt has heard lots of stories of how difficult it is to protect your privacy on Facebook, and she wants your advice. Research the privacy and security settings on Facebook and create a "User's Guide" for your aunt to work through with your cousin. Make sure you include information on how to remove your cousin from Facebook search results, make contact information private, keep friendships private, adjust Wall posting visibility, set up photo album privacy, and customize photo tagging, and explain what personal information should and should not be included on your cousin's profile.

Comparing Internet Search Methods

Problem

With millions of sites on the Internet, finding useful information can be a daunting—and, at times, an impossible—task. However, there are methods to make searching easier, some of which have been discussed in this chapter. In this Team Time, each team will search for specific items or pieces of information on the Internet and compare search methodologies.

Process

Split your group into three or more teams, depending on class size. Each group will create a team wiki using free wiki software such as that found at **pbworks.com**. To appreciate fully the benefits of wiki collaboration, each team should have at least five or six members.

1. Each team should come up with a theme for its wiki. Suggestions include the following:
   - Best computer technology websites
   - Coolest new technology gadgets
   - All-time greatest musicians
   - All-time greatest athletes
   - Best places to visit in the United States
   - Best beaches in the United States
   - Best skiing areas around the world

2. Each student should pick one example to research and then design a wiki page highlight-ing that subject. For example, if the team chose all-time greatest musicians, one student could select Bruce Springsteen and create a wiki page on Bruce Springsteen. The wiki page should contain links to other websites and, if possible, images and videos.

3. After the team wikis are created, teams should make their wikis available to the other teams for comments.

Conclusion

After all the team wikis have been completed and shared, discuss the following with your class: What is the benefit of using wiki technology to create team pages? How did wikis help or hinder the team process? What other conclusions can the class draw about using wiki technology?

ethics project //

Plagiarism

In this exercise, you'll research and then role-play a complicated ethical situation. The role you play may or may not match your own personal beliefs, but your research and use of logic will enable you to represent whichever view is assigned. An arbitrator will watch and comment on both sides of the arguments, and together the team will agree on an ethical solution.

Problem

Plagiarism, or portraying another's work as your own, has been around for a long time and extends well beyond the classroom. For example, Nick Simmons, the son of Gene Simmons (from KISS) and a member of A&E's *Family Jewels* reality series, created a comic book series, *Incarnate*. Radical Publishing picked up the series but quickly stopped publication when Internet messages accused the author of copying from other similar series. Similarly, the Australian band Men at Work was cited for copying a melody from "Kookaburra Sits in the Old Gum Tree" for its 1980s hit "Down Under" and owes the owner years of royalties.

Research Areas to Consider

- Plagiarism violations
- Comic book series *Incarnate*
- Australian band Men at Work
- Plagiarism consequences

Process

1. Divide the class into teams.
2. Research the areas cited above and devise a scenario in which someone has violated plagiarism rules.
3. Team members should write a summary that provides background information for their character—for example, author, publisher, or arbitrator—and that details their character's behaviors to set the stage for the role-playing event. Then, team members should create an outline to use during the role-playing event.
4. Team members should arrange a mutually convenient time to meet for the exchange, using either the collaboration feature of MyITLab or the discussion board feature of your course management software or by meeting in person.
5. Team members should present their case to the class or submit a PowerPoint presentation for review by the rest of the class, along with the summary and resolution they developed.

Conclusion

As technology becomes ever more prevalent and integrated into our lives, more and more ethical dilemmas will present themselves. Being able to understand and evaluate both sides of an argument, while responding in a personally or socially ethical manner, will be an important skill.

Technology in Focus

The History of the Personal Computer

Ever wonder how big the first personal computer was or how much the first laptop weighed? Computers are such an integral part of our lives that we don't often stop to think about how far they've come or where they got their start. In just 40 years, computers have evolved from expensive, huge machines that only corporations could own to small, powerful devices that almost anyone can have. In this Technology in Focus feature, we look at the history of the personal computer.

FIGURE 1 Timeline of Early Personal Computer Development

The Altair 8800

- Only 256 bytes of memory
- No keyboard or monitor
- Switches on front used to enter data in machine code (1s and 0s)
- Lights on front indicated results of a program

1975

Commodore PET

- Featured in *Popular Science* magazine
- Popular in business settings in Europe

October 1977

1976

June 1977

Apple I

Steve Jobs and Steve Wozniak form Apple Computer

Apple II

- Featured color monitor, sound, and game paddles
- 4 KB of RAM
- Operating system stored in ROM
- Optional floppy disk to load programs (mostly games)

The First Personal Computer: The Altair

Our journey through the history of the personal computer starts in 1975. At that time, most people weren't familiar with the mainframes and supercomputers that large corporations and the government owned. With price tags exceeding the cost of buildings, and with few if any practical home uses, these monster machines weren't appealing to or attainable by average Americans.

However, in 1975, the first personal computer, the **Altair 8800** (see Figure 1), was born. At $395 for a do-it-yourself kit or $498 for a fully assembled unit (about $2,100 in today's dollars), the price was reasonable enough that computer fanatics could finally own their own computers.

The Altair was primitive by today's standards—no keyboard, no monitor, and completely not user friendly. Despite its limitations, computer enthusiasts flocked to the machine. Many who bought it had been taught to program, but until that point, they had access only to big, clumsy computers at their jobs. With the Altair, they could create their own programs. Within three months, 4,000 orders were placed for the machine.

The release of the Altair marked the start of the personal computer boom. In fact, two men whose names you might have heard were among the first Altair owners: Bill Gates and Paul Allen were so enamored by the "minicomputer" that they wrote a compiling program (a program that translates user commands into commands the computer can understand) for it. The two later convinced the Altair's developer to buy their program, marking the start of a company called Microsoft. We'll get to that story later. First, let's see what their rivals were up to.

The Apple I and II

Around the time the Altair was released, **Steve Wozniak**, an employee at Hewlett-Packard, was dabbling with his own computer design. **Steve Jobs**,

TRS-80

- Introduced by Radio Shack
- Monochrome display
- 4 KB of RAM
- Circuitry hidden under keyboard
- Wildly popular with consumers—sold 10,000 units in the first month

November 1977

IBM PC (5150)

- Marketed to businesses and consumers
- 64 KB to 256 KB of RAM
- Floppy disk drives optional
- Hard disks not supported in early models

August 1981

April 1981

- First "portable" computer
- Weighed 24.5 pounds
- 5-inch screen
- 64 kilobytes of RAM
- Two floppy disk drives
- Preinstalled with spreadsheet and word processing software

Osbourne

(Interfoto/Alamy; Interfoto/Alamy; Science & Society Picture Library/Contributor/Getty Images)

who was working for computer game manufacturer Atari at the time, liked Wozniak's prototypes and made a few suggestions. Together, the two built a personal computer, the **Apple I**, in Wozniak's garage (see Figure 1) and formed the Apple Computer Company in 1976.

A year later, in 1977, the **Apple II** was born (see Figure 1). The Apple II included a color monitor, sound, and game paddles. Priced around $1,300 (about $4,900 in today's dollars), one of its biggest innovations was that the operating system was stored in read-only memory (ROM). Previously, the operating system had to be rewritten every time the computer was turned on. The friendly features of the Apple II operating system encouraged less technically oriented computer enthusiasts to write their own programs.

An instant success, the Apple II would eventually include a spreadsheet program, a word processor, and desktop publishing software. These programs gave personal computers like the Apple functions beyond gaming and special programming and led to their popularity.

Enter the Competition

Around the time Apple was experiencing success with its computers, a number of competitors entered the market. The largest among them were Commodore, Radio Shack, Osborne, and IBM. The **Commodore PET** (see Figure 1) was aimed at the business market and did well in Europe, while Radio Shack's **TRS-80** (see Figure 1) was clearly aimed at the U.S. consumer market. Just one month after its release in 1977, it had sold about 10,000 units.

The Osborne: The Birth of Portable Computing

The Osborne Company introduced the first portable computer, the **Osborne**, in 1981 (see Figure 1). Although portable, the $1,795 (about $4,500 in today's dollars) computer weighed 24.5 pounds and featured a miniscule 5-inch screen. The Osborne was an overnight success,

and its sales quickly reached 10,000 units per month. However, despite the Osborne's popularity, the Osborne Company eventually closed. Compaq bought the Osborne design and in 1983 produced its own portable computer.

IBM PCs

By 1980, IBM primarily made mainframe computers, which it sold to large corporations, and hadn't taken the personal computer seriously. In 1981, however, IBM released its first personal computer, the **IBM PC** (see Figure 1). Because many companies were familiar with IBM mainframes, they adopted the IBM PC. The term *PC* soon became the term used to describe all personal computers.

IBM marketed its PC through retail outlets such as Sears to reach the home market, and it quickly dominated the market. In January 1983, *Time* magazine, playing on its annual person of the year issue, named the computer "1982 Machine of the Year."

Other Important Advancements

It wasn't just the hardware of the personal computer that was developing. At the same time, advances in programming languages and operating systems and the influx of application software were leading to more useful and powerful machines.

The Importance of BASIC

The software industry began in the 1950s with programming languages such as FORTRAN, ALGOL, and COBOL. These languages were used mainly by businesses to create financial, statistical, and engineering programs. However, the 1964 introduction of **Beginners All-Purpose Symbolic Instruction Code (BASIC)** revolutionized the software industry. BASIC was a language that beginning programming students could easily learn. It thus became enormously popular—and the key language of the PC. In fact, **Bill Gates** and **Paul Allen** (see Figure 2) used BASIC to write their program for the Altair. As we noted earlier, this program led to the creation of **Microsoft**, a company that produced computer software.

The Advent of Operating Systems

Because data on the earliest personal computers was stored on audiocassettes, many programs weren't saved or reused. This meant that programs had to be rewritten whenever they were needed. In 1978, Steve Wozniak designed a 5.25-inch floppy disk drive so that programs could be saved easily and operating systems developed.

Operating systems are written to coordinate with the specific processor chip that controls the computer. At that time, Apples ran on a Motorola chip, whereas PCs (IBMs and so on) ran on an Intel chip. **Disk Operating System (DOS)**, developed by Wozniak and introduced in 1977, was the OS that controlled the first Apple computers. The **Control Program for Microcomputers (CP/M)**, developed by Gary Kildall, was the OS designed for the Intel 8080 chip (the processor for PCs).

In 1980, when IBM was entering the personal computer market, it approached Bill Gates at Microsoft to write an OS program for the IBM PC. Gates recommended that IBM investigate the CP/M OS, but IBM couldn't arrange a meeting with the founder, Gary Kildall. Microsoft reconsidered the opportunity and developed **MS-DOS** for IBM computers. Eventually, virtually all PCs running on the Intel chip used MS-DOS as their OS. Microsoft's reign as one of the dominant players in the personal computer landscape had begun.

The Software Application Explosion: VisiCalc and Beyond

Because the floppy disk was a convenient way to distribute software, its inclusion in personal computers set off an application software explosion. In 1978, Harvard Business School student Dan Bricklin recognized the potential for a personal computer spreadsheet program. He and his friend Bob Frankston (see Figure 3) created the program **VisiCalc**, which became an instant success. Finally, ordinary home users could see how owning a personal computer could benefit them. More than 100,000 copies of VisiCalc were sold in its first year.

After VisiCalc, other electronic spreadsheet programs entered the market. **Lotus 1-2-3** came on the market in 1983, and **Microsoft Excel** entered the

FIGURE 2 Bill Gates and Paul Allen are the founders of Microsoft. *(Doug Wilson/CORBIS)*

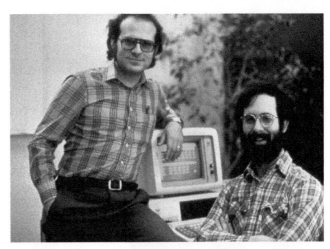

FIGURE 3 Bob Frankston and Dan Bricklin created VisiCalc, the first business application developed for the personal computer. *(© www.jimraycroft.com 1982/Daniel Bricklin http://www.bricklin.com/pressinfo.htm)*

scene in 1985. These products became so popular that they eventually put VisiCalc out of business.

Meanwhile, word processing software was gaining a foothold in the industry. Until then, there were separate, dedicated word processing machines; personal computers, it was believed, were for computation and data management only. However, once **WordStar**, the first word processing application, became available for personal computers in 1979, word processing became another important use for the personal computer. Competitors such as **Word for MS-DOS** (the precursor to Microsoft Word) and **WordPerfect** soon entered the market. Figure 4 lists some of the important dates in application software development.

FIGURE 4

Application Software Development

YEAR	APPLICATION
1978	**VisiCalc:** First electronic spreadsheet application **WordStar:** First word processing application
1980	**WordPerfect:** Best DOS–based word processor, was eventually sold to Novell and was later acquired by Corel
1983	**Lotus 1-2-3:** Added integrated charting, plotting, and database capabilities to spreadsheet software **Word for MS-DOS:** Introduced in the pages of *PC World* magazine on the first magazine-inserted demo disk
1985	**Excel:** One of the first spreadsheets to use a graphical user interface **PageMaker:** The first desktop publishing software

FIGURE 5 The Alto was the first computer to use a GUI, and it provided the basis for the GUI that Apple used. However, because of marketing problems, the Alto never was sold. *(Josie Lepe/MCT/Newscom)*

FIGURE 6 The Lisa was the first computer to introduce a GUI to the market. Priced too high, it never gained the popularity it deserved. *(SSPL/The Image Works)*

The Graphical User Interface

Another important advancement in personal computers was the introduction of the **graphical user interface (GUI)**, which allowed users to interact with the computer more easily. Until that time, users had to use complicated command- or menu-driven interfaces to interact with the computer. Apple was the first company to take full commercial advantage of the GUI, but the GUI was not invented by a computer company.

Xerox: Birth of the GUI

In 1972, a few years before Apple launched its first personal computer, photocopier manufacturer **Xerox** was designing a personal computer of its own. Named the **Alto** (see Figure 5), the computer included a word processor, based on the What You See Is What You Get (WYSIWYG) principle, that incorporated a file management system with directories and folders. It also had a mouse and could connect to a network. None of the other personal computers of the time had these features. For a variety of reasons, Xerox never sold the Alto commercially. Several years later, it developed the Star Office System, which was based on the Alto. Despite its convenient features, the Star never became popular because no one was willing to pay the $17,000 asking price.

The Lisa and the Macintosh

Xerox's ideas were ahead of their time, but many of the ideas of the Alto and Star would soon catch on. In 1983, Apple introduced the **Lisa**, the first

successful personal computer brought to market that used a GUI (see Figure 6). Legend has it that Jobs had seen the Alto during a visit to Xerox in 1979 and had been influenced by its GUI. He therefore incorporated a similar user interface into the Lisa, providing features such as windows, drop-down menus, icons, a file system with folders and files, and a point-and-click device called a mouse. The only problem with the Lisa was its price. At $9,995 (about $23,000 in today's dollars), few buyers were willing to take the plunge.

A year later, in 1984, Apple introduced the **Macintosh**, shown in Figure 7. The Macintosh was everything the Lisa was and then some, and at about

FIGURE 7 The Macintosh became one of Apple's best-selling computers, incorporating a GUI along with other innovations such as the 3.5-inch floppy disk drive. *(Ed Kashi/CORBIS)*

a third of the cost. The Macintosh was also the first personal computer to utilize 3.5-inch floppy disks with a hard cover, which were smaller and sturdier than the previous 5.25-inch floppies.

The Internet Boom

The GUI made it easier for users to work on the computer. The Internet provided another reason for people to buy computers. Now people could conduct research and communicate in a new way. In 1993, the web browser **Mosaic** was introduced. This browser allowed users to view multimedia on the web, causing Internet traffic to increase by nearly 350%.

Meanwhile, companies discovered the Internet as a means to do business, and computer sales took off. IBM–compatible PCs became the computer system of choice when, in 1995, Microsoft introduced **Internet Explorer**, a browser that integrated web functionality into Microsoft Office applications, and **Windows 95**, the first Microsoft OS designed to be principally a GUI OS.

About a year earlier, in 1994, a team of developers launched the **Netscape** web browser, which soon became a predominant player in browser software. However, pressures from Microsoft became too strong, and in 1998, Netscape announced it would no longer charge for the product and would make the code available to the public.

Making the Personal Computer Possible: Early Computers

Billions of personal computers have been sold over the past three decades. But the computer is a compilation of parts, each of which is the result of individual inventions. Let's look at some early machines that helped to create the personal computer we know today.

The Pascalene Calculator and the Jacquard Loom

From the earliest days of humankind, we have been looking for a more systematic way to count and calculate. Thus, the evolution of counting machines led to the development of the computer we know today. The **Pascalene** was the first accurate mechanical calculator. This machine, created by the French mathematician **Blaise Pascal** in 1642, used revolutions of gears, like odometers in cars, to count by tens. The Pascalene could be used to add, subtract, multiply, and divide. The basic design of the Pascalene was so sound that it lived on in mechanical calculators for more than 300 years.

Nearly 200 years later, **Joseph Jacquard** revolutionized the fabric industry by creating a machine that

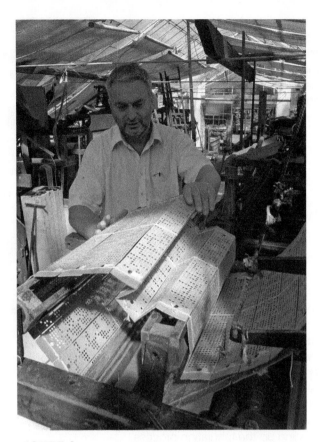

FIGURE 8 The Jacquard loom used holes punched in stiff cards to make complex designs. This technique would later be used in punch cards that controlled the input and output of data in computers. *(JANEK SKARZYNSKI/AFP/Getty Images/Newscom)*

automated the weaving of complex patterns. Although not a counting or calculating machine, the **Jacquard loom** (shown in Figure 8) was significant because it relied on stiff cards with punched holes to automate the weaving process. Much later, this punch-card process would be adopted as a means for computers to record and read data.

Babbage's Engines

In 1834, **Charles Babbage** designed the first automatic calculator, called the **Analytical Engine** (see Figure 9). The machine was actually based on another machine called the **Difference Engine**, which was a huge steam-powered mechanical calculator that Babbage designed to print astronomical tables. Although the Analytical Engine was never developed, Babbage's detailed drawings and descriptions of the machine include components similar to those found in today's computers, including the store (akin to RAM) and the mill (a central processing unit), as well as input and output devices. This invention gave Charles Babbage the title of "father of computing."

Meanwhile, Ada Lovelace, who was the daughter of poet Lord Byron and was a student of mathematics (which was unusual for women of the time), was fascinated with Babbage's Engines. She translated an Italian paper on Babbage's machine and, at the request of Babbage, added her own extensive notes. Her efforts are thought to be the best description of Babbage's Engines.

The Hollerith Tabulating Machine

In 1890, **Herman Hollerith**, while working for the U.S. Census Bureau, was the first to take Jacquard's punch-card concept and apply it to computing with his **Hollerith Tabulating Machine**. Until that time, census data had been tabulated manually in a long, laborious process. Hollerith's tabulating machine automatically read data that had been punched onto small punch cards, speeding up the tabulation process. Hollerith's machine became so successful that he left the Census Bureau in 1896 to start the Tabulating Machine Company. His company later changed its name to International Business Machines, or IBM.

FIGURE 9 The Analytical Engine, designed by Charles Babbage, was never fully developed but included components similar to those found in today's computers. *(Chris Howes/Wild Places Photography/Alamy)*

The Z1 and the Atanasoff–Berry Computer

German inventor **Konrad Zuse** is credited with a number of computing inventions. His first, in 1936, was a mechanical calculator called the **Z1**. The Z1 is thought to be the first computer to include certain features integral to today's systems, such as a control unit and separate memory functions.

In 1939, John Atanasoff, a professor at Iowa State University, and his student Clifford Berry built the first electrically powered digital computer, called the **Atanasoff–Berry Computer (ABC)**, shown in Figure 10. The computer was the first to use vacuum tubes, instead of the mechanical switches used in older computers, to store data. Although revolutionary at the time, the machine weighed 700 pounds, contained a mile of wire, and took about 15 seconds for each calculation. (In comparison, today's personal computers can perform billions of calculations in 15 seconds.) Most importantly, the ABC was the first computer to use the binary system

and to have memory that repowered itself upon booting. The design of the ABC would be central to that of future computers.

The Harvard Mark I

From the late 1930s to the early 1950s, **Howard Aiken** and **Grace Hopper** designed the Mark series of computers used by the U.S. Navy for ballistic and gunnery calculations. Aiken, an electrical engineer and physicist, designed the computer, while Hopper did the programming. The **Harvard Mark I**, finished in 1944, could add, subtract, multiply, and divide.

However, many believe Hopper's greatest contribution to computing was the invention of the **compiler**, a program that translates English-language instructions into computer language. The team was also responsible for a common computer-related expression. Hopper was the first to "debug" a computer when she removed a moth that had flown into the Harvard Mark I that had caused the computer to break down (see Figure 11). After

FIGURE 10 The Atanasoff–Berry Computer laid the design groundwork for many computers to come. *(Ames Laboratory)*

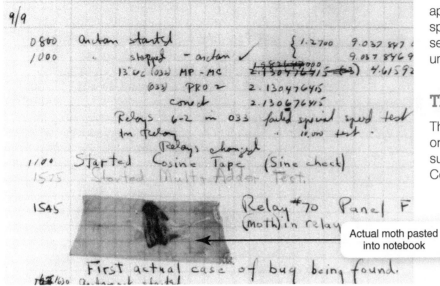

FIGURE 11 Grace Hopper coined the term *computer bug* when a moth flew into the Harvard Mark I, causing it to break down. *(Naval Historical Center)*

that, problems that caused a computer not to run were called *bugs*.

The Turing Machine

Meanwhile, in 1936, British mathematician **Alan Turing** created an abstract computer model that could perform logical operations. The **Turing Machine** was not a real machine but rather a hypothetical model that mathematically defined a mechanical procedure (or algorithm). Additionally, Turing's concept described a process by which the machine could read, write, or erase symbols written on squares of an infinite paper tape. This concept of an infinite tape that could be read, written to, and erased was the precursor to today's RAM.

The ENIAC

The **Electronic Numerical Integrator and Computer (ENIAC)**, shown in Figure 12, was another U.S. government–sponsored machine developed to calculate the settings used for weapons. Created by **John W. Mauchly** and **J. Presper Eckert** at the University of Pennsylvania, it was placed in operation in 1944. Although the ENIAC is generally thought of as the first successful high-speed electronic digital computer, it was big and clumsy. The ENIAC used nearly 18,000 vacuum tubes and filled

approximately 1,800 square feet of floor space. Although inconvenient, the ENIAC served its purpose and remained in use until 1955.

The UNIVAC

The **Universal Automatic Computer**, or **UNIVAC**, was the first commercially successful electronic digital computer. Completed in 1951, the UNIVAC operated on magnetic tape (see Figure 13), which set it apart from its competitors, which ran on punch cards. The UNIVAC gained notoriety when, in a 1951 publicity stunt, it was used to predict the outcome of the Stevenson–Eisenhower presidential race. After analyzing only 5% of the popular vote, the UNIVAC correctly identified Dwight D. Eisenhower as the victor. After that, UNIVAC soon became a household word. The UNIVAC and computers like it were considered **first-generation computers** and were the last to use vacuum tubes to store data.

Transistors and Beyond

Only a year after the ENIAC was completed, scientists at the Bell Telephone Laboratories in New Jersey invented the **transistor**, another means to store data (see Figure 14). The transistor replaced the bulky vacuum tubes of earlier computers and was smaller

FIGURE 12 The ENIAC took up an entire room and required several people to manipulate it. *(University of Pennsylvania/AP Images)*

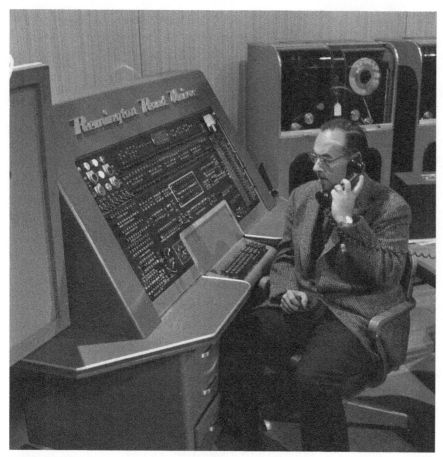

FIGURE 13 UNIVACs were the first computers to use magnetic tape for data storage. *(CBS/Landov)*

A few years later, in 1958, **Jack Kilby**, while working at Texas Instruments, invented the world's first **integrated circuit**, a small chip capable of containing thousands of transistors. This consolidation in design enabled computers to become smaller and lighter. The computers in this early integrated-circuit generation were considered **third-generation computers**.

Other innovations in the computer industry further refined the computer's speed, accuracy, and efficiency. However, none was as significant as the 1971 introduction by the Intel Corporation of the **microprocessor chip**, a small chip containing millions of transistors (see Figure 15). The microprocessor functions as the central processing unit (CPU), or brains, of the computer. Computers that use a microprocessor chip are called **fourth-generation computers**. Over time, Intel and Motorola became the leading manufacturers of microprocessors. Today, the Intel Core i7 is one of Intel's most powerful processors.

As you can see, personal computers have come a long way since the Altair and have a number of inventions and people to thank for their amazing popularity. What will the future bring? ■

and more powerful than tubes. It was used in almost everything, from radios to phones. Computers that used transistors were referred to as **second-generation computers**. Still, transistors were limited as to how small they could be made.

FIGURE 14 Transistors were 1/10 the size of vacuum tubes, faster, and produced much less heat. *(borissos/Fotolia)*

FIGURE 15 Today's microprocessors can contain billions of transistors. *(Tudor Voinea/Shutterstock)*

check your understanding //

For a quick review of what you've learned, answer the following questions. Visit **pearsonhighered.com/techinaction** to check your answers.

multiple choice

1. What was the name of the first web browser?

    a. Mosaic

    b. Internet Explorer

    c. Netscape

    d. Firefox

2. Which programming language revolutionized the software industry?

    a. ALGOL

    b. BASIC

    c. COBOL

    d. FORTRAN

3. Which invention enabled computers to be made smaller and lighter?

    a. the integrated circuit

    b. RAM

    c. ROM

    d. magnetic tape

4. Which computer was touted as the first portable computer?

    a. Altair

    b. Commodore PET

    c. Lisa

    d. Osborne

5. What was the importance of the Turing machine to today's computers?

    a. It described a system that was a precursor to today's notebook computer.

    b. It was the first electronic calculator and a precursor to the computer.

    c. It was the first computer to have a monitor.

    d. It described a process to read, write, and erase symbols on a tape and was the precursor to today's RAM.

6. Which computer first stored its operating system in ROM?

    a. Apple I

    b. Apple II

    c. Lisa

    d. Macintosh

7. What was the first spreadsheet application?

    a. Lotus 1-2-3

    b. Excel

    c. WordStar

    d. VisiCalc

8. Which components are a characteristic of third-generation computers?

    a. Transistors

    b. Vacuum tubes

    c. Integrated circuits

    d. Microprocessor chips

9. For what is the UNIVAC computer best known?

    a. It was the first computer used to tabulate U.S. census data.

    b. It was the first computer to use the binary system.

    c. It was the first computer to incorporate a magnetic tape system.

    d. It was the first computer used as a mechanical calculator.

10. Who are the founders of Apple?

    a. Paul Allen and Bill Gates

    b. Steve Jobs and Steve Wozniak

    c. Steve Jobs and Bill Gates

    d. Bill Gates and Steve Wozniak

4

Application Software: Programs That Let You Work and Play

Programs That Let You Work

The Nuts and Bolts of Software

OBJECTIVES

1. What's the difference between application software and system software? **(p. 126)**

2. What are the different ways I can access and use software? **(pp. 126–127)**

Productivity and Business Software

OBJECTIVES

3. What kinds of applications are included in productivity software? **(pp. 128–137)**

4. What kinds of software do small and large businesses use? **(pp. 137–138)**

 Sound Byte: Creating Web Queries in Excel 2010

Programs That Let You Play

Multimedia and Entertainment Software

OBJECTIVE

5. What different types of multi-media and entertainment software are available? **(pp. 142–148)**

Sound Byte: Enhancing Photos with Image-Editing Software

Active Helpdesk: Choosing Software

Managing Your Software

OBJECTIVES

6. What's important to know when buying software? **(pp. 149–152)**

7. How do I install and uninstall software? **(pp. 152–154)**

Active Helpdesk: Buying and Installing Software

For all media in this chapter go to **pearsonhighered.com/ techinaction** or MyITLab.

(Norebbo/Shutterstock; mmaxer/Shutterstock; IKO/Shutterstock; Timo Darco/Fotolia)

AT&T 3G   **2:43 PM**

stitching panorama

28% complete

INTERACTIVE SHARING

Sharing an interactive panorama on Facebook lets your friends step inside and explore it.

(AP Photo/Microsoft)

HOW COOL IS THIS?

You've just returned from a great **vacation** and want to relive your wonderful experience. Looking at traditional digital images is nice, but wouldn't it be fun if you could create a **3-D walkthrough** of your favorite places? Upload your pictures to the 20 GB of free storage space on Microsoft's **Photosynth** and relive your experience in 3-D. Photosynth takes a selection of photos, examines them for similarities to estimate the shape of the subject, and determines the vantage point from which each photo was taken. Using this information, Photosynth then **stitches** the images together to create a 3-D effect. Check out some 3-D images that others have created at **photosynth.net**, and then go make one from your own photos!

Scan here for more info

Programs That Let You Work

A computer without software is like a sandwich without filling. Although a computer's hardware is critical, a computer system does nothing without software. In this section, we'll look at programs created to help you work more effectively and efficiently. First, let's check out some software basics.

the nuts and bolts of
SOFTWARE

Technically speaking, the term **software** refers to a set of instructions that tells the computer what to do. An instruction set, also called a **program**, provides a means for us to interact with and use the computer, even if we lack specialized programming skills. Your computer has two main types of software:

1. **Application software** is the software you use to do tasks at home, school, and work. Figure 4.1 shows the various types of application software we'll discuss in this chapter.

2. **System software** includes software that helps run the computer and coordinate instructions between application software and the computer's hardware devices. System software includes the operating system (such as Windows and OS X) and utility programs (programs in the operating system that help manage system resources). We discuss system software in detail in Chapter 5.

Other types of software, such as web browsers, virus protection, and backup and recovery software, are used every day. We'll discuss these types of software elsewhere in this book.

What software do I need to install on my computer? Virtually every new computer comes with software preinstalled, including an operating system and some application software, depending on which computer you buy. If you need to add other software to your system, you'll need either to install the software yourself or to access it from the web. There are two types of software you can install on your computer:

1. **Proprietary (or commercial) software** is software you buy, such as

the Microsoft Office applications you're probably familiar with. You can download proprietary software directly from the Internet or you can buy it on a CD or DVD.

2. **Open source software** is free software that is available with few licensing and copyright restrictions. One advantage of open source software is that a community of users continues to make changes to the software, keeping it current without needing to wait for periodic updates. However,

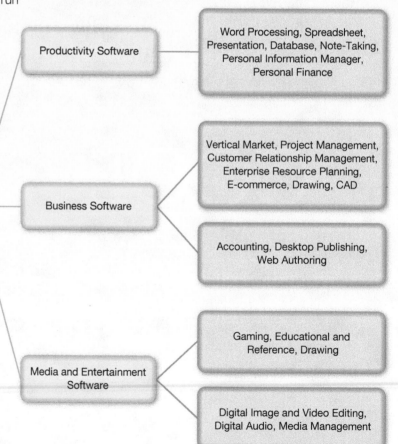

FIGURE 4.1 Application software lets you perform a variety of tasks.

trends in IT

Mobile Commerce: What Have You Bought with Your Phone Lately?

Most people own a mobile phone, so it's no surprise that companies regard *mobile commerce*—using applications on smartphones and tablets to buy and sell products—as a trend that shouldn't be ignored.

Making purchases from a mobile device is on the rise, but mobile commerce hasn't taken over traditional methods of e-commerce just yet. Why? Many say most mobile applications aren't yet as user-friendly as traditional websites accessed via a browser. Over time, that will change, especially as the functionality of mobile devices and their software continue to adapt. Consider two trends some predict will gain more acceptance in the near future in the mobile commerce market:

1. *Mobile payments:* Instead of using your credit card or debit card to buy something, consider using your smartphone (see Figure 4.2). Google Wallet stores credit card information so that you can use the app on your smartphone to make a payment in retail locations that have a special reader. Starbucks and Target have also joined the mobile payment bandwagon, letting you use their mobile apps to pay for your super macchiato or Jason Wu dress.

2. *Mobile coupons and barcodes:* Many consumers use mobile device apps to look up information by scanning special quick response (QR) codes (such as the one shown on page 125) on products. Many stores also have virtual store loyalty cards on their apps that let you access coupons, product information, and store discount programs.

Although many mobile device owners feel it's not as safe to use their mobile devices to make purchases, it's just as safe as making purchases with your computer on the web. Time and education will help to relieve those fears.

FIGURE 4.2 Have you made a payment using your smartphone instead of a credit card yet? (*Dai Sugano/MCT/Newscom*)

unlike Microsoft Office and other proprietary applications, open source applications offer little or no formal support. Instead, they're supported from their community of users across websites and newsgroups.

Can I use software directly from the web? Another way to obtain software is through **Software as a Service (SaaS)**, in which the vendor hosts the software online and you access and use the software over the Internet without having to install it on your computer. With these **web-based applications**, you can collaborate online with others, avoiding the coordination mess that often occurs when transferring documents via e-mail. Although many web-based applications are not as fully featured as their installable counterparts, most work with files from other applications. ■

productivity and business
SOFTWARE

One reason computers are invaluable is that they make it easier to complete our daily tasks. **Productivity software** includes programs that let you perform various tasks required at home, school, and business and includes word processing, spreadsheet, presentation, database, and personal information manager programs.

Buying Productivity Software

Is it better to buy software individually or in a bundled package? For proprietary software, it's cheaper to buy a **software suite** than to buy each program individually. Software suites are available for all types of software—productivity, graphics, virus protection, and others:

- Microsoft Office is the standard proprietary software suite for Windows. A version is also available for Apple computers.
- Apache OpenOffice is an open source productivity suite that provides functionality similar to that of Microsoft Office. You can download the installation file you'll need to run OpenOffice at **openoffice.org**.
- Apple iWork is a productivity suite made especially for Apple computers.

Microsoft Office Web Apps and Google Docs are examples of web-based productivity suites. Microsoft Office Web Apps are part of Microsoft Office 365 and are online versions of Word, Excel, PowerPoint, and OneNote, but with less functionality than the installed versions. Google Docs (**docs.google.com**) includes word processing, spreadsheet, and presentation functionality, as well as forms and drawing applications. If you're looking for basic productivity software that you can access from any computer, Google Docs is sufficient. Figure 4.3 lists more examples of productivity suites, along with the individual applications each suite offers.

The individual programs within a suite work well together because they share common features, toolbars, and menus. For example, when using applications in the Microsoft Office suite, you can seamlessly create a spreadsheet in Excel, import it into Access, and then link a query created in Access to a Word document. It would be much harder to do the same thing using different applications from a variety of software developers.

Word Processing Software

What are the most common word processing applications? You've probably used **word processing software** to create and edit documents such as research papers, class notes, and résumés. Microsoft Word is the most popular word processing program that you can buy and install on your computer. If you're looking for a more affordable alternative, you might want to try an open source alternative such as Writer, a word processing program from the Apache OpenOffice suite (**openoffice.org**). Writer is similar to Microsoft Word. When saving a document in Writer, the default file format has an OpenDocument file (.odt) extension. However, by using the Save As command, you can save files in other formats, such as .doc for Word.

What special tools do word processing programs have that I might not know about? You're probably familiar with the basic tools of word processing software, such as the spelling and grammar checking tools, the thesaurus, and the find-and-replace tool. But did you know you can translate words or phrases into another language or automatically correct your spelling as you type? You also can automatically summarize key points in a text document, add bibliographical references, and include illustrations with different picture styles.

BITS&BYTES

Finding the Right Software

There are millions of applications, and new ones are developed and released every day. How can you find the right ones to meet your needs? What are the cool new applications or the ones that just don't work? The editors and analysts at *PC Magazine* have put together AppScout (**appscout.com**), a site that provides reviews of the best software, websites, and web applications. Next time you're looking for a new application, check out AppScout.

FIGURE 4.3

Productivity Software Suites

PRODUCTIVITY SUITE	WORD PROCESSING	SPREADSHEET	PRESENTATION	DATABASE	NOTE-TAKING	PIM/E-MAIL
Installed: Proprietary						
Microsoft Office	Word	Excel	PowerPoint	Access	OneNote	Outlook
Apple iWork	Pages	Numbers	Keynote			
Installed: Open Source						
Apache OpenOffice	Writer	Calc	Impress	Base		
Web-Based						
Microsoft Office 365	Word	Excel	PowerPoint		OneNote	Outlook
Google Docs	Documents	Spreadsheets	Presentation			Gmail
Zoho	Writer	Sheet, Books	Show	Creator	Notebook	
ThinkFree	Document	Spreadsheet	Presentation		Note	

How can I make my documents look more professional? With word processing software, you can easily change fonts, font styles, and sizes; add colors to text; adjust margins; add borders to portions of text or to entire pages; insert bulleted and numbered lists; and organize your text into columns. You also can insert pictures from your own files or from a gallery of images and graphics, such as clip art and SmartArt, which are included with the software.

You also can enhance the look of your document by creating an interesting background or by adding a "theme" of coordinated colors and styles. Figure 4.4 shows what a document can look like when you apply formatting options found in many word processing applications. (Note that although many of the open source and web-based applications have great formatting capabilities, most are not as fully featured as the installed version of Microsoft Word.)

Spreadsheet Software

Why would I use spreadsheet software?
Spreadsheet software is software that lets you make calculations and perform numerical analyses. You can use it to track your expenses or create a simple budget, as shown in Figure 4.5a, for example. Microsoft Excel and Apache OpenOffice Calc are two examples of spreadsheet software. (Web-based options are available within

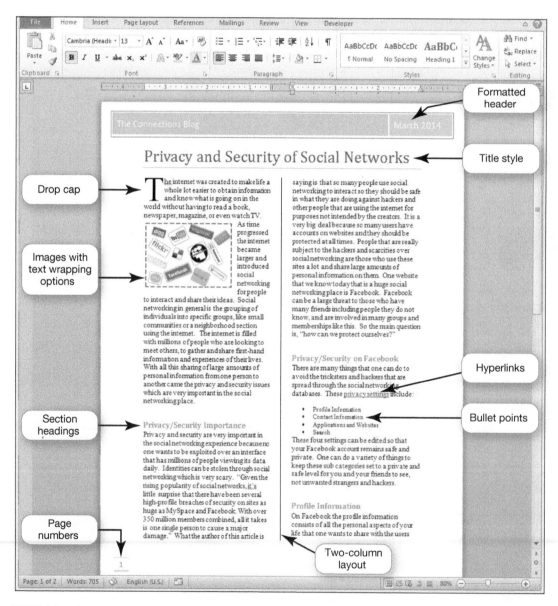

FIGURE 4.4 Nearly every word processing application has formatting features that let you give your documents a professional look.

FIGURE 4.5 Spreadsheet software lets you easily calculate and manipulate numerical data with the use of built-in formulas.

the Google Docs and Office Web Apps suites.) One benefit of spreadsheet software is that it can automatically recalculate all formulas and functions in a spreadsheet when values for some of the inputs change. For example, as shown in Figure 4.5b, you can insert an additional row in your budget ("Membership") and change a value (for September Financial aid), and the results for "Total Expenses" and "Net Income" recalculate automatically.

Because automatic recalculation lets you immediately see the effects different options have on your spreadsheet, you can quickly test different assumptions. This is called *what-if analysis*. Look again at Figure 4.5b and ask, "If I don't get as much financial aid next semester, what impact will that have on my total budget?" The recalculated cells in rows 21 and 22 help answer your question. In addition to financial analysis, many spreadsheet applications have limited database capabilities to sort, filter, and group data.

How do I use spreadsheet software?

The basic element in a spreadsheet program is the *worksheet,* which is a grid consisting of columns and rows. As shown in Figure 4.5a, the columns and rows

form individual boxes called *cells*. Each cell can be identified according to its column and row position. For example, a cell in column A, row 1 is referred to as cell A1. You can enter several types of data into a cell:

- *Text:* Any combination of letters, numbers, symbols, and spaces. Text is often used as labels to identify the contents of a worksheet or chart.
- *Values and Dates:* Numerical data that represents a quantity or a date/time and is often the basis for calculations.
- *Formulas:* Equations that use addition, subtraction, multiplication, and division operators, as well as values and cell references. For example, in Figure 4.5a, you would use the formula =D8-D20 to calculate net income for November.
- *Functions:* Formulas that are preprogrammed into the spreadsheet software. Functions help you with calculations ranging from the simple (such as adding groups of numbers) to the complex (such as determining monthly loan payments), without requiring you to know the exact formula. In

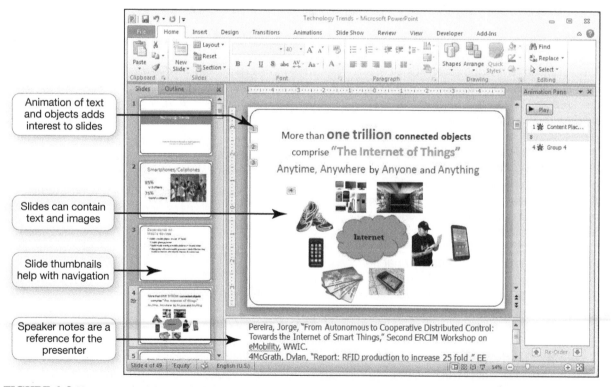

		1 Year History		
	Current	Trend	High	Low
Microsoft	$ 25.79		30.54	20.26
Apple	$ 255.96		261.09	125.83
Intel	$ 20.95		22.84	15.72
Hewlett Packard	$ 46.05		53.15	34.35
Dell	$ 13.24		16.2	11.57

Sparklines

FIGURE 4.7 Sparklines, a feature of Microsoft Excel 2010, are tiny graphs that fit into a single cell.

FIGURE 4.6 (a) Column charts show comparisons. (b) Pie charts show how parts contribute to the whole. (c) Line charts show trends over time.

Figure 4.5a, to calculate the total of all expenses for September, you could use the built-in addition function, which would look like this: =SUM(B10:B19).

What kinds of graphs and charts can I create with spreadsheet software? As shown in Figure 4.6, most spreadsheet applications let you create a variety of charts, including basic column charts,

pie charts, and line charts, with or without 3-D effects. In addition to these basic charts, you can make stock charts (for investment analysis) and scatter charts (for statistical analysis) or create custom charts. New in Excel 2010 are *sparklines*—small charts that fit into a single cell and make it easy to show data trends (see Figure 4.7).

Presentation Software

How can software help with my presentations? You've no doubt sat through presentations where the speaker used **presentation software** such as Microsoft PowerPoint (see Figure 4.8) to create a slide show. Because these applications are simple to use, you

- Animation of text and objects adds interest to slides
- Slides can contain text and images
- Slide thumbnails help with navigation
- Speaker notes are a reference for the presenter

FIGURE 4.8 You can use Microsoft PowerPoint 2010 to create dynamic presentations. *(Akhilesh Sharma/Fotolia; Scanrail/Fotolia; HaywireMedia/Fotolia; ThinkGeek, Inc.; Gladcov Vladimir/Fotolia; Maksym Dykha/Fotolia; Scanrail/Fotolia; Scanrail/Fotolia)* can produce high-quality presentations without a lot of training. With some of the new capabilities in PowerPoint 2010, you can embed online videos, add effects, and even trim video clips without the need for a separate video-editing program.

What are some tips to make a great presentation? Undoubtedly, you've seen at least one bad presentation. Don't make your audience suffer through another one! Here are some tips for designing good presentations:

- *Be careful with color:* Choose dark text on a light background or light text on a dark background. Avoid using clashing text and background colors.

- *Use bullets for key points:* Limit the number to four to six bulleted points per slide. Avoid full sentences and paragraphs.

- *Use images:* Images can convey a thought or illustrate a point. Make sure any text over an image can be read easily.

- *Consider font size and style:* Keep the font size large enough to read from the back of the room. Avoid script or fancy font styles. Use only one or two font styles per presentation.

- *Keep animation and/or background audio to a minimum:* They can be distracting.

Database Software

Why is database software useful?
Database software such as Oracle, MySQL, and Microsoft Access are powerful applications that let you store and organize data. As mentioned earlier, spreadsheet applications are easy to use for simple tasks such

BITS&BYTES

Alternatives to PowerPoint

If you're looking for an open source or web-based alternative to PowerPoint, consider using Apache OpenOffice Impress or Zoho Show (see Figure 4.9), which are similar to PowerPoint in functionality. Another cool alternative is Prezi (**prezi.com**), a web-based program that uses an innovative way to produce presentations. Rather than using a set

of slides, Prezi uses a large canvas in which you connect ideas. By using the zoom and navigation features, you can move over the canvas, focusing on individual aspects, then zoom in on the finer details and zoom out to see the bigger concept. You can add videos as well as rotate the canvas for added visual interest.

FIGURE 4.9 (a) Apache OpenOffice Impress and (b) Zoho Show are alternatives to Microsoft PowerPoint.
(Akhilesh Sharma/Fotolia; Scanrail/Fotolia; HaywireMedia/Fotolia; ThinkGeek, Inc.; Gladcov Vladimir/Fotolia; Maksym Dykha/Fotolia; Scanrail/Fotolia; Scanrail/Fotolia)

FIGURE 4.10 In databases, information is organized into fields, records, and tables.

as sorting, filtering, and organizing data. However, you need to use a more robust, fully featured database application to manage larger and more complicated groups of data that contain more than one table; to group, sort, and retrieve data; and to generate reports. Traditional databases are organized into *fields, records,* and *tables,* as shown in Figure 4.10.

How do businesses use database software? Businesses like Amazon, iTunes, Craigslist, and Pandora all rely on databases to keep track of products, clients, invoices, and personnel information. Often, some of that information is available to a home computer user. For example, at Amazon.com, you can access the history of all the purchases you've ever made on the site. FedEx, UPS, and other shipping companies also let you search their online databases for tracking numbers, allowing you to get instant information on the status of your packages.

Note-Taking Software

Is there software to help me take notes? Microsoft OneNote is a popular note-taking and organizational tool you can use for research, brainstorming, and collaboration, as well as just organizing random bits of information. Using OneNote, you can organize your notes into tabbed sections, similar to a multisubject spiral-bound notebook (see Figure 4.11). In addition, you can access your OneNote notes from other Microsoft Office applications. For example, if you're writing a research paper in Word, click the OneNote icon in the Word ribbon to open OneNote, where you can add your notes—perhaps

a reference to a website where you found some interesting research. Later, if you open OneNote and click on that reference, it will bring you to the exact spot in the Word document where you made the reference.

You can also add audio or video recordings of lectures to OneNote, and you can search for a term across all the digital notebooks you created during the semester to find common ideas such as key points that might appear on a test. There is also a OneNote app for the iPhone and iPad.

Several very good and functional free and online note-taking options are also available to help you take notes or to just jot down a quick reminder. Evernote (**evernote.com**), for example, lets you take notes via the web, your phone, or your computer and then sync your notes between your devices. You can then share your notes with other Evernote users for easy collaboration. Figure 4.12 lists some popular alternative note-taking applications.

> Tabs help organize topics within a notebook

> Individual notebooks

> Pages within a tab further organize your notes

FIGURE 4.11 Microsoft OneNote is a great way to collect and organize notes and other information. The files are readily searchable and easy to share.

FIGURE 4.12

Beyond Microsoft One-Note: Alternative Note-Taking Applications

Evernote (evernote.com)

- Web-based
- Notes can be shared for easy collaboration
- Syncs notes between all devices

Springpad (springpad.com)

- Automatically categorizes notes based on your categories
- Links with Facebook

Simplenote (simplenoteapp.com)

- Web-based, open source
- Notes organized by tags
- Mobile apps available

SoundNote (soundnote.com)

- iPad app
- Drawing feature
- Records longer audio notes

Personal Information Manager Software

How can software help me manage my e-mail, time, contact lists, and tasks? Most productivity suites contain some form of **personal information manager (PIM) software** to help you manage e-mail, contacts, calendars, and tasks in one place. Microsoft Outlook (see Figure 4.13) is the most widely used PIM program. If you share a network at home or at work and are using the same PIM software as others on a common network, a PIM program simplifies sharing calendars and scheduling meetings.

Many web-based e-mail clients, such as Yahoo! and Google, also include coordinating calendar and contacts similar to Microsoft Outlook. Yahoo! includes Notepad for jotting down notes and tasks. Google's calendar and contacts sync with Outlook so you can access your Outlook calendar information by logging into Google. This gives you access to your schedule anywhere you have access to a computer and an Internet connection.

There are a wide variety of other to-do lists and simple organizers that work with all your mobile and computing devices. For example, Toodledo (**toodledo.com**) is a free program that coordinates well with Microsoft Outlook, and OmniFocus (**omnifocus.com**) is a more full-featured option for Mac devices.

Microsoft Office Productivity Software Features

What tools can help me work more efficiently with productivity software?

Whether you're working on a word processing document, spreadsheet, database, or slide presentation, you can make use of several tools to increase your efficiency:

- A **wizard** walks you through the steps necessary to complete a complicated task. At each step, the wizard asks you questions. Based on your responses, the wizard helps you complete that portion of the task. When you install software, you're often guided by a wizard.

FIGURE 4.13 The Outlook Today feature in Microsoft Outlook includes common PIM features, such as a summary of appointments, a list of tasks, and the number of new e-mail messages.

- A **template** is a predesigned form. Templates are included in many productivity applications. They provide the basic structure for a particular kind of document, spreadsheet, or presentation. Templates can include specific page layout designs, formatting and styles relevant to that particular document, and automated tasks (macros).
- A **macro** is a small program that groups a series of commands so that they will run as a single command. Macros are best used to automate a routine task or a complex series of commands that must be run frequently. For example, a teacher may write a macro to sort the grades in her grade book in descending order and to highlight grades that add up to less than a C average. Every time she adds the results of an assignment or a test, she can set up the macro to run through this series of steps.

Personal Financial Software

How can I use software to keep track of my finances? Financial planning software helps you manage your daily finances. Financial planning programs include electronic checkbook registers and automatic bill payment tools. With these features, you can make recurring monthly payments, such as rent or student loans, with automatically scheduled online payments. The software records all transactions, including online payments, in your checkbook register. In addition, you can assign categories to each transaction and then use these categories to create budgets and analyze your spending patterns.

Intuit's installed and web-based products, Quicken and Mint (**mint.com**; see Figure 4.14), respectively, are the market leaders in financial planning software. Both are great at tracking and analyzing your spending habits and at offering advice on how to better manage your finances. With either, you also can track your investment portfolio. With Mint, you can monitor and update your finances from any computer with a private and secure setting. You can also access Mint on a smartphone and tablet, so your information is conveniently accessible. Mint also provides access to a network of other users with whom to exchange tips and advice.

What software can I use to prepare my taxes? Tax preparation software such as Intuit TurboTax and H&R Block At Home let you prepare your state and federal

FIGURE 4.14 Mint (**mint.com**) is an online financial management tool. An extensive online community provides helpful tips and discussions with other people in similar situations. *(Courtesy of Mint.com)*

taxes on your own instead of hiring a professional. Both programs offer a complete set of tax forms and instructions, as well as videos that contain expert advice on how to complete each form. Each company also offers free web-based versions of federal forms and instructions. In addition, error-checking features are built into the programs to catch mistakes. TurboTax can also run a check for audit alerts, file your return electronically, and offer financial planning guidance to help you plan and manage your financial resources effectively in the following year (see Figure 4.15).

Some financial planning applications also coordinate with tax preparation software. Both Quicken and Mint, for example, integrate seamlessly with TurboTax, so you never have to go through your debit card statements and bills to find tax deductions, tax-related income, or expenses. Many banks and credit card companies also offer online services that download a detailed monthly statement into Quicken and Mint. Remember, however, that the tax code changes annually, so you must obtain an updated version of the software each year.

Small Business Software

What kinds of software are helpful for small business owners?
If you have a small business or a hobby that produces income, you know the importance of keeping good records and tracking your expenses and income. **Accounting software** helps small business owners manage their finances more efficiently by providing tools for tracking accounts receivable and accounts payable. In addition, these applications offer inventory management, payroll, and billing tools. Examples of accounting applications are Intuit QuickBooks and Sage Peachtree. Both programs include templates for invoices, statements, and financial reports so that small business owners can create common forms and reports.

If your business requires the need for newsletters, catalogs, annual reports, or other large, complicated publications, consider using **desktop publishing (DTP) software**. Although many word processing applications include some of the features that are hallmarks of desktop publishing, specialized DTP software, such as Microsoft Publisher, QuarkXPress, and Adobe InDesign, allows professionals to design books and other publications that require complex layouts.

What software do I use to create a web page?
Web page–authoring software allows even the novice to design interesting and interactive web pages without knowing any HTML code. Web page–authoring applications often include wizards, templates, and reference materials to help novices complete most web page–authoring tasks. More experienced users can take advantage of these applications' advanced features to make the web content current, interactive, and interesting. Microsoft Expression Web and Adobe Dreamweaver are two programs that both professionals and casual web page designers use.

Note that if you need to produce only the occasional web page, you'll find that many applications include features that let you convert your document into a web page. For example, in some Microsoft Office applications, you can choose to save a file as a web page.

Software for Large and Specialized Businesses

What types of software do large businesses use?
There is an application for almost every aspect of business. There are specialized programs for project management software, customer relationship management (CRM), enterprise resource planning (ERP), e-commerce, marketing and sales, finance, point of sale, security, networking, data management, and human resources, to name just a few. Figure 4.16 lists many of the common types of business-related software. Some applications are tailored to the specific needs of a particular company or industry. Software designed for a specific industry, such as property management software for real estate professionals, is called **vertical market software**.

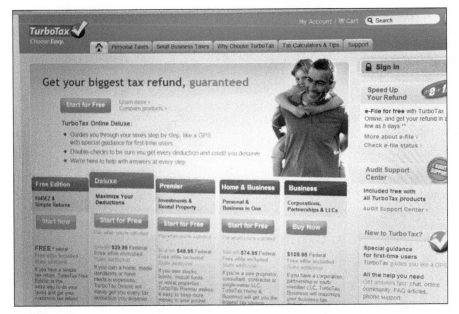

FIGURE 4.15 Tax preparation software such as Intuit TurboTax lets you prepare and file your taxes using a guided, systematic process. *(Vika Sabo/Alamy)*

FIGURE 4.16

Common Types of Large Business–Related Software

PROJECT MANAGEMENT		CUSTOMER RELATIONSHIP MANAGEMENT (CRM)		ENTERPRISE RESOURCE PLANNING (ERP)	
	Creates scheduling charts to plan and track specific tasks and to coordinate resources		Stores sales and client contact information in one central database		Controls many "back office" operations and processing functions such as billing, production, inventory management, and human resources management
E-COMMERCE		**COMPUTER-AIDED DESIGN (CAD)**		**VERTICAL MARKET**	
	Facilitates website creation and hosting services, shopping cart setup, and credit card–processing services		Creates automated designs, technical drawings, and 3-D model visualizations for architecture, automotive, aerospace, and medical engineering industries		Addresses the needs of businesses in a specific industry or market such as the real estate, banking, and automotive industries

BITS&BYTES

Need to Work on Files Together? Try These Real-Time Collaboration Tools

You're part of a group working together on a project. You could share files via e-mail, but you've found that can lead to confusion, with multiple versions of the document being revised at the same time. Consider some of these other methods to share and collaborate on files:

- Skype (**skype.com**) lets users work together through video calling and share desktops remotely with other Skype users. This lets two users view the same file at the same time, and the remote user can follow the cursor on the screen of the host user to see exactly what the host user is doing, just as if they were working together in the same room.
- Google Docs (**docs.google.com**) and wikis allow multiple users to work together in real time on the same document and to communicate with project members via live text chat.
- Scribblar (**scribblar.com**) is a multiuser whiteboard with live audio chat, which is great for holding virtual brainstorm sessions.

What software is used to make 3-D models? Engineers use **computer-aided design (CAD)** programs such as Autodesk's AutoCAD to create automated designs, technical drawings, and 3-D model visualizations. Here are some cool applications of CAD software:

- Architects use CAD software to build virtual models of their plans and readily visualize all aspects of design before actual construction.
- Engineers use CAD software to design everything from factory components to bridges. The 3-D nature of these programs lets engineers rotate their models and adjust their designs if necessary, eliminating costly building errors.
- CAD software also is used in conjunction with GPS devices for accurate placement of fiber optic networks around the country.
- The medical engineering community uses CAD software to create anatomically accurate solid models of the human body, developing medical implants quickly and accurately.

The list of CAD applications keeps growing as more and more industries realize the benefits CAD can bring to their product development and manufacturing processes. ■

> Before moving on to Part 2:
> - Watch Replay Video 4.1 ▶.
> - Then check your understanding of what you've learned so far.

check your understanding//

For a quick review to see what you've learned so far, answer the following questions. Visit **pearsonhighered.com/techinaction** to check your answers.

multiple choice

1. Software that is available on-demand via the Internet is called
   a. proprietary software.
   b. web-based software.
   c. productivity software.
   d. Internet software.

2. What type of software enables you to create dynamic slide shows?
   a. word processing   c. presentation
   b. spreadsheet   d. database

3. Which is NOT an advantage of using a software suite?
   a. The cost is cheaper than buying programs individually.
   b. The programs provide for better integration.
   c. The programs integrate easily with programs from other software suites.
   d. The programs share common features such as toolbars.

4. Which of the following is true about open source software?
   a. The program code is confidential.
   b. The program can be changed and freely distributed.
   c. The program can be freely distributed as long as the program code is not changed.
   d. The program code is subject to copyright protection.

5. Which program can you use to take notes in class?
   a. SoundNote   c. OneNote
   b. Evernote   d. all of the above

true–false

_____ 1. System software is another term for application software.

_____ 2. Only productivity software is offered bundled as a software suite.

critical thinking

1. **Living on the Cloud**

   Cloud computing is becoming more popular, and many users are working from the cloud and not even realizing it. What kinds of software applications are you using that are completely web-based? Why do you use them instead of installed software applications? Envision a time when all software is web-based and describe how being totally on the cloud might be an advantage. What disadvantages might a cloud-based environment present?

2. **What's Your App?**

   Small applications are being developed every day for smartphones. If you have a smartphone, what apps are the most useful to you? If you don't own a smartphone, what kind of app do you think would be the most useful? Describe an app not currently available that would be your "killer app."

Continue ➡

You've been assigned a research paper, and your instructor requires citations and a bibliography. In the past, you might have resorted to using websites such as Son of Citation Machine (**citationmachine.net**) or EasyBib (**easybib.com**) to create your citations and generate a bibliography. But did you know there are tools built right into Microsoft Word that do the same thing?

To Add a New Citation and Source to a Document:

Step 1   Click at the end of the sentence or phrase that you want to cite.

Step 2   On the References tab, in the Citations & Bibliography group, click **Insert Citation**.

Step 3   To add the source information, click **Add New Source**.

Note: To create a citation and fill in the source information later, click **Add New Placeholder**.

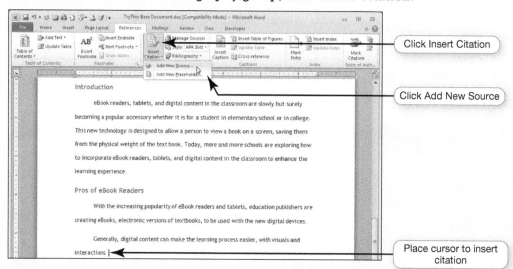

Step 4   Begin to fill in the source information by clicking the arrow next to Type of Source.

Step 5   The citation will appear in your document.

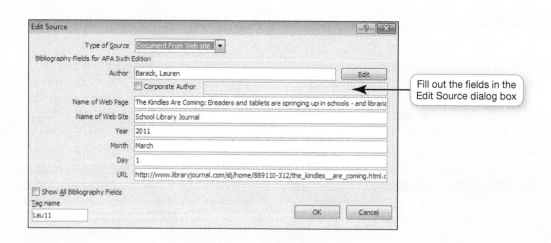

To Create a Bibliography:

You can create a bibliography at any point after you insert one or more sources in a document. Click where you want to insert a bibliography, usually at the end of the document. Then do the following:

Step 1 On the References tab, in the Citations & Bibliography group, click **Bibliography**.

Step 2 Click a predesigned bibliography format to insert the bibliography into the document.

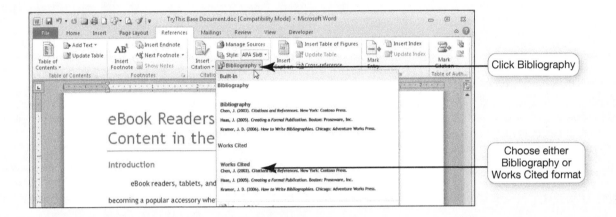

Step 3 The bibliography is automatically generated.

Step 4 You can update information in your sources and bibliography if information is added or changed by clicking on the **Bibliography** insert in the document and then clicking **Update Citations and Bibliography**.

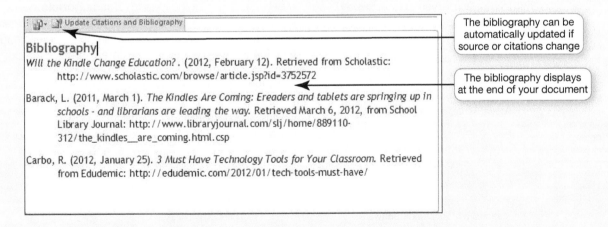

Programs That Let You Play

While many programs help you be more productive, there are also programs that entertain you with audio, video, and digital images and through games, animations, and movies. Regardless of whether the software helps you work or play, it's important to know how to work with and manage the software so that you install it correctly and use it legally. This section discusses both aspects of entertainment software.

 multimedia and entertainment
SOFTWARE

From movies and television to music and photography, the entertainment world is becoming digital. **Multimedia software** includes digital image- and video-editing software, digital audio software, and other specialty software required to produce computer games, animations, and movies. In this section, we look at several popular types of multimedia and entertainment software, as shown in Figure 4.17.

Digital Image- and Video-Editing Software

How can I edit, share, and organize digital images? One great advantage of taking digital images is that you can easily manipulate them and then share them on the web. While Facebook is a great option for sharing images, Flickr (**flickr.com**) is a website specifically for sharing photos. It lets you organize your images and then share them publicly with millions of users, or just with your closest friends and family. Discussion boards are also available so that people can leave comments about the images.

If you want to edit your photos before sharing, Adobe Photoshop Elements is **image-editing software** geared to the casual photographer. Image-editing software includes tools for basic modifications to digital photos such as removing red-eye; modifying contrast, sharpness, and color casts; or removing scratches or rips from scanned images of old photos. Many programs also include painting tools such as brushes, pens, and artistic media (such as paints, pastels, and oils) that let you create realistic-looking images. Some include templates so you can insert your favorite pictures into preformatted pages for digital scrapbooks or greeting cards. Google Picasa (**picasa.google.com**) is a popular application that not only lets you edit images but also helps to organize and share your digital images (see Figure 4.18). Picasa also stores your photos on the web.

Several other online photo-sharing and photo-storing sites, such as Snapfish (**snapfish.com**), Kodak (**kodak.com**), and Shutterfly (**shutterfly.com**), let you upload your digital images from your computer, create photo albums, and share them with friends and family. These sites offer printing

Multimedia and Entertainment Software

- Digital Image- and Video-Editing Software
- Digital Audio Software
- Media Management Software
- Gaming Software
- Educational and Reference Software
- Drawing Software

FIGURE 4.17 There are many varieties of multimedia and entertainment software.

Image editing tools

Images placed here and arranged in collage

E-mail, print, and export tools

FIGURE 4.18 You can create collages of your favorite images using Google Picasa. *(Mary Anne Poatsy)*

services as well, letting you create customized cards, stationery, books, and even iPhone cases with your images.

What image-editing programs might a professional use? Adobe Photoshop and Corel PaintShop Photo Pro are fully featured image-editing applications. GIMP (**gimpshop.com**) is a free download that has most of the features offered by the for-pay applications. Photoshop and PaintShop Photo Pro each offer sophisticated tools for tasks like layering images and masking images (hiding parts of layers to create effects such as collages). Designers use these more sophisticated tools to create the enhanced digital images used commercially in logos, in advertisements, and on book and CD covers.

What software do I need to edit digital videos? While it's easy to upload videos directly to YouTube or Facebook unedited, you can use **digital video–editing software** to help refine your videos. Although the most expensive products (such as Adobe Premiere Pro and Apple's Final Cut Pro) offer the widest range of special effects and tools, some moderately priced video-editing programs have enough features to keep the casual user happy. Windows Movie Maker

and iMovie have intuitive drag-and-drop features that make it simple to create professional-quality movies with little or no training (see Figure 4.19).

Window used to view or edit movie clips

Video clips in clips pane

Movie clips display in clip viewer

GTrans icon controls transition effects between clips

FIGURE 4.19 Video-editing programs such as Apple iMovie make it easy to create and edit movies. *(Press Association/AP Images)*

Digital Audio Software

What's the difference between all the digital audio file types on my computer? You probably have a variety of digital audio files stored on your computer, such as downloaded music files, audiobooks, or podcasts. These types of audio files have been *compressed* so they're more manageable to transfer to and from your computer and over the Internet. MP3, short for MPEG-1 Audio Layer 3, is a type of audio compression format and is the most common compressed digital format, but there are other compressed formats, such as AAC and WMA.

You may also see *uncompressed* audio files on your computer, such as WAV or AIFF files. Uncompressed files—the files found on audio CDs, for example—have not had any data removed, so the quality is a perfect representation of the audio as it was recorded. Unfortunately, the file size is much larger than that of compressed files. Compressed formats remove data such as high frequencies that the human ear does not hear in order to make the files smaller and easier to download and store. MP3 format, for example, makes it possible to transfer and play back music on iPods and other music players. A typical CD stores between 10 and 15 songs in uncompressed format, but with files in MP3 format, the same CD can store between 100 and 180 songs. The smaller file size not only lets you store and play music in less space, it also allows quick and easy distribution over the Internet. Ogg Vorbis (or just Ogg) is a free, open source audio compression format alternative to MP3. Some say that Ogg produces a better sound quality than MP3.

What do I use to create my own audio files? There are many digital audio applications that let you create and record your own audio files. With programs such as MAGIX Music Maker or Apple GarageBand, you can compose your own songs or soundtracks with virtual instruments, voice recorders, synthesizers, and special audio effects, and these will end up as uncompressed MIDI files. Other programs, such as Audacity and Cakewalk SONAR, let you record audio files.

Can I edit audio files? Audio-editing software includes tools that make editing audio files as easy as editing text files. Software such as the open source Audacity (**audacity.sourceforge.net**) and Sony Sound Forge Pro 10 (**sonycreativesoftware.com**) lets you perform such basic editing tasks as cutting dead air space from the beginning or end of a song or clipping a portion from the middle. You can also can add special sound effects, such as echo or bass boost, and remove static or hiss from MP3 files. AudioAcrobat (**marketersmojo.audioacrobat.com**), a web-based program, makes it easy to record and stream audio and video and hosts your audio files. These applications support recording sound files from a microphone or any source you can connect through the input line of a sound card.

BITS&BYTES

Video File Formats for Portable Media Players

If you're converting video files to play on your iPod or other portable media player, be aware of the video file format you choose. Video files for portable media players are either in the MP4 or H.264 video format. Both formats store digital audio and video streams as well as other files, such as text for subtitles and still images. Similar to the MP3 format, MP4 and H.264 compress the audio and video content into a more manageable file size. While MP4 files are certainly of sufficient video quality, H.264 is best for delivery of high definition video and can also be applied to a wider variety of networks and systems than MP4.

Media Management Software

How do I manage the audio, video, and image files on my system? Media management software such as Windows Media Player, Apple iTunes, and Winamp lets you organize music, video, pictures, and even recorded TV files so that you can sort, filter, and search your media collection by artist, title, or other category

 ACTIVE HELPDESK
Choosing Software

In this Active Helpdesk call, you'll play the role of a helpdesk staffer, fielding calls about the different kinds of multimedia software, educational and reference software, and entertainment software.

DIG DEEPER

How Cloud Computing Works

Have you ever done any of the following?

- Posted pictures on Facebook that your friends accessed from their iPhone
- Used Dropbox or SkyDrive to store your files instead of carrying around a flash drive
- Used Google Docs or Microsoft Office Web Apps to collaborate on a team project
- Used Carbonite to back up your data online

By doing any of these activities, you have participated in cloud computing. So what exactly is **cloud computing**?

Cloud computing refers to storing data, files, and applications on the web and being able to access and manipulate these files and applications from any Internet-connected device. Being able to work from the cloud eliminates the need to have everything stored on your own computer's drives and lets you access your pictures, music, files, and programs as long as you have access to the Internet. In addition, cloud computing makes it easier to collaborate and communicate with others, and it can cut down on administrative tasks for organizations maintaining large amounts of computer hardware and software.

There are two sides to cloud computing:

1. The *front end* is the side we see as users. It involves a web browser like Internet Explorer, Firefox, or Google Chrome.
2. The *back end* consists of various data centers and server farms that house the files and programs you access "on the cloud" (see Figure 4.20). These data centers and server farms are warehouses full of computers and servers, and they are being created all over the world, providing us with "cloud storage." The computers in the data centers or server farms are designed to work together, adjusting to the varying degrees of demand placed on them at any time.

Google is one of the first true explorers in the cloud, building applications such as Google Docs, Gmail, and the Chrome web browser in an effort to create a completely virtual operating environment. A fully functioning operating environment would enable users to sign in on any computer and have "their" computer setup (desktop configurations and images, programs, files, and other personalized settings) display. Additionally, cloud computing would reduce the need for all of us to have the fastest computers with the most memory and storage capabilities. Instead, we could all have simple front-end terminals with basic input and output devices because the computers on the back end will be providing all the computing muscle.

Chromebooks are Google's first attempts at a notebook (called a netbook) where all the applications and files are stored on the web. Nothing is installed or saved to a hard drive. All programs are accessed and all work is done through the browser, so sending e-mail, editing photos, and working on documents are all done via web-based applications. Since the Chromebooks require an Internet connection to get most tasks done, users must be near a WiFi connection or pay for a data plan.

FIGURE 4.20 There are two sides to cloud computing: the side we see as users and the banks of computers and servers that house the files and programs we access. *(Jupiterimages/Photos.com/Thinkstock; Neil Fraser/Alamy; Monashee Frantz/Alamy; zentilia/Shutterstock; PhotoEdit/Alamy; digitallife/Alamy; Google, Inc.; Anatolii Babii/Alamy; PhotoEdit/Alamy)*

There are some considerations with cloud computing of which you need to be aware:

- *Security and privacy:* Right now, the security of information stored on the web is built on trusting that the passwords we set and the security systems that the data centers put in place are able to keep our information away from unauthorized users. Caution is always warranted, as nothing is completely safe and private.

- *Backup:* Because even the devices in these large data centers and server farms inevitably will break down, the cloud computing systems have redundant systems to provide backup. However, for critical files that you must have, it might be a good idea not to completely rely on the cloud but to have your own backup files, as well.

- *Access issues:* With cloud computing, you access your files and programs only through the Internet. If you couldn't access the Internet due to a power failure or system failure with your Internet service provider, you wouldn't be able to access your files. Storing your most critical files and programs offline will help reduce the inconvenience and loss of productivity while access to the Internet is being restored.

Before relying on cloud computing, consider the above concerns against the advantages of the convenience of having your information when and where you want it and the ability to promote better collaboration.

(see Figure 4.21). Using these programs, you can manage individual tracks, generate playlists, and even export the files to a database or spreadsheet application for further manipulation. When you burn the songs to a CD, the programs can print liner notes that you can place inside the CD case.

Most digital audio management software programs, such as Apple iTunes and Windows Media Player, do the following:

- *MP3 recording* lets you record directly from streaming audio and other software or microphone sources to MP3 format.

- *CD ripping* lets you copy or extract CDs and encode to the MP3 format.

- *CD burning* lets you create your own CDs from your MP3 collection.

- *Encoding and decoding* is done by *encoders,* programs that convert files to the MP3 format at varying levels of quality. Most ripping software programs have encoders built in to convert the files directly into MP3 format.

- *Format conversion* programs let you convert MP3 files to other digital audio formats such as WAV (Waveform Audio File Format), WMA (Windows Media Audio), and AIFF (Audio Interchange File Format).

Gaming Software

Can I make video games? Now that video games represent an industry with revenue of more than $25 billion each year, designing and creating video games is emerging as a desirable career opportunity. Professionally created video games involve artistic storytelling and design, as well as sophisticated programming. Major production houses

FIGURE 4.21 Software programs such as iTunes help you manage all the music files on your computer. You can sort, filter, and search your collection by artist, album, or category, and you can create playlists.

such as Electronic Arts use applications not easily available to the casual home enthusiast. However, you can use the editors and game engines available for games such as EverQuest, Oblivion, and Unreal Tournament to create custom levels and characters to extend the game.

If you want to try your hand at creating your own video games, multimedia applications such as Unity, Adobe Flash, and RPG Maker VX provide the tools you need to explore game design and creation. The program GameMaker (**yoyogames.com**) is a free product that lets you build a game without any programming; you drag and drop key elements of the new game creation into place. Alice (**alice.org**) is another free environment to check out; it lets you easily create 3-D animations and simple games. See the Sound Byte on 3-D Programming the Easy Way in Chapter 10.

Educational and Reference Software

What fun educational and reference software should I check out? If you want to learn more about a subject, you can turn to the web for many instructional videos and documents. But sometimes, it's best to use software for more complete or detailed instructions. Educational and reference software is available to help you master, study, design, create, or plan. As shown in Figure 4.22, there are software products that teach new skills such as typing, languages, cooking, and playing the guitar.

Students who will be taking standardized tests like the SAT often use test preparation software. In addition, many computer and online brain-training games and programs are designed to improve the health and

FIGURE 4.22

Educational and Reference Software: A Sample of What's Available

Test Preparation

Designed to improve your performance on standardized tests

Simulation

Allows you to experience a real situation through a virtual environment

Instructional
HOW TO instructions "What You Need to [...]"
Designed to teach you almost anything from playing a musical instrument to learning a language or cooking

Trip Planning

Generates maps and provides driving instructions; some incorporate hotel, restaurant, and other trip information

Home Design/ Improvement

Provides 2-D or 3-D templates and images to let you better visualize indoor and outdoor remodeling projects and landscaping ideas

Course Management

Web-based software system that creates a virtual learning experience, including course materials, tests, and discussion boards

Brain Training

Features games and activities to exercise your brain to improve your memory, processing speed, attention, and multitasking capabilities

Genealogy

Helps chart the relationships between family members through multiple generations

function of your brain. Lumosity (**lumosity.com**) is one such site that has a specific "workout" program that you can play on your PC or smartphone. Brain Age[2] (**brainage.com**) has software for the Nintendo DS and is designed for players of all ages.

What types of programs are available to train people to use software or special machines? Many programs provide tutorials for popular computer applications (you may even use one in your course provided with MyITLab). These programs use illustrated systematic instructions to guide users through unfamiliar skills in an environment that acts like the actual software, without the software actually being installed.

Some training programs, known as **simulation programs**, allow you to experience or control the software as if it were the actual software or an actual event. Such simulation programs include commercial and military flight training, surgical instrument training, and machine operation training. One benefit of simulated training programs is that they safely allow you to experience potentially dangerous situations such as flying a helicopter during high winds. Consequently, users of these training programs are more likely to take risks and learn from their mistakes—something they could not afford to do in real life. Simulated training programs also help prevent costly errors. Should something go awry, the only cost of the error is restarting the simulation program.

Do I need special software to take courses online? Although some courses are run from an individually developed website, many online courses are run using **course management software** such as Blackboard, Moodle, and Angel. In addition to traditional classroom tools such as calendars and grade books, these programs provide special areas for students and instructors to exchange ideas and information through chat rooms, discussion forums, and e-mail. In addition, collaboration tools such as whiteboards and desktop sharing facilitate virtual office hour sessions. Depending on the content and course materials, you may need a password or special plug-ins to view certain videos or demos.

Drawing Software

What kind of software should I use to create illustrations? Drawing software (or **illustration software**) lets you create or edit 2-D, line-based drawings. You can use it to create technical diagrams or original nonphotographic drawings, animations, and illustrations using standard tools such as pens, pencils, and paintbrushes. You also can drag geometric objects from a toolbar onto the canvas area to create images and can use paint bucket, eyedropper, and spray can tools to add color and special effects to the drawings.

Adobe Illustrator includes tools that let you create professional-quality creative and technical illustrations such as muscle structures in the human body. Its warping tool allows you to bend, stretch, and twist portions of your image or text. Because of its many tools and features, Illustrator is the preferred drawing software programs of most graphic artists.

What kind of software can be used for home or landscape planning? There are many software packages to help plan the layout of homes and landscapes, such as those offered by Broderbund. A simple, web-based and fairly full-featured free 3-D modeling application is Trimble's SketchUp (formerly owned by Google). SketchUp lets you create a 3-D image of your dream home (see Figure 4.23). ■

FIGURE 4.23 SketchUp is a free, web-based 3-D modeling application. *(Archipoch/Shutterstock)*

managing your
SOFTWARE

It's important to know how to pick out the best software for your computer, how to get it onto your computer correctly, and how to take it off. We discuss all of these topics next.

Getting Software

Is discounted software for students available? If you're a student, you can sometimes buy substantially discounted software that is no different from regularly priced software. Campus computer stores and college bookstores offer discounted prices to students who possess a valid student ID. Online software suppliers such as Journey Education Marketing (**journeyed.com**) and Academic Superstore (**academicsuperstore.com**) also offer popular software to students at reduced prices.

Can I get software for free legally? In addition to open source software, discussed previously in the chapter, **freeware** is copyrighted software that you can use for free. Explore sites like Butterscotch (**butterscotch.com**) and Freeware Home (**freewarehome. com**) to see how many good freeware programs are available. However, while much legitimate freeware exists, some unscrupulous people use freeware to distribute viruses and malware. Be cautious when installing freeware, especially if you're unsure of the provider's legitimacy.

Can I try new software before it's released? Some software developers offer beta versions of their software free of charge. A **beta version** is an application that is still under development (see Figure 4.24). By distributing free beta versions, developers hope users will report errors, or bugs, they find in their programs. Many beta versions are available for a limited trial period and are used to help the developers correct errors before they launch the software on the market.

Are there risks associated with installing beta versions, freeware, or downloading software from the Internet? By their very nature, beta products are unlikely to be bug free, so you always run the risk of something going awry with your system by installing and using beta versions. Unless you're willing to deal with potential problems, it may be best to wait until the last beta version is released—often referred to as the *gold version*. By that time, most of the serious bugs have been worked out.

As a precaution, you should be comfortable with the reliability of the source before downloading a freeware or beta version of software. If it's a reliable

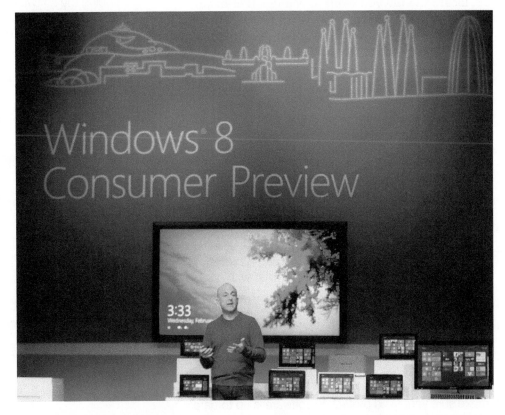

FIGURE 4.24 Windows 8 Consumer Preview, the beta for the newest version of the operating system, became available for users to try months before the final version was released. *(REUTERS/Gustau Nacarino (SPAIN - Tags: BUSINESS TELECOMS SCIENCE TECHNOLOGY))*

BITS&BYTES

How to Open Unknown File Types

Normally, when you double-click a file to open it, the program associated with the file runs automatically. For example, when you double-click a file with a .doc or.docx extension, the file opens in Microsoft Word. However, if the file has no extension or Windows has no application associated with that file type, an "Open with" dialog box appears and asks what program you want to use to open the file. In other cases, a document may open with a program other than the one you wanted to use. This is because many applications can open several file types, and the program you expected the file to open in is not currently the program associated with that file type. To assign a program to a file type or to change the program to open a particular file type, follow these instructions:

1. Use the search and navigation tools in File Explorer (previously called Windows Explorer) to locate the file you want to change. (For example, you can search for all Word files by searching for *.doc or *.docx.) Right-click on the file, and then point to **Open With**.

2. A list of programs installed on your computer appears. Click the program you want to use to open this file type. If you're sure the selected program is the one that should always be used for this file type, then instead select **Choose default program**, and make sure to check "**Use this app for all [extension] files**," and click the default program from the list.

When you double-click that file in the future, the file will open in the program you selected.

developer whose software you're familiar with, you can be more certain that a serious bug or virus isn't hiding in the software. Similarly, you should be sure that the software you're downloading is meant for your system and that your system has met all the necessary hardware and operating system requirements.

Before installing any software, it's always good to make sure your virus protection software is up to date. It's equally important that you back up your system as well as create a *restore point*. That way, if something

does go awry, you can return your system to the way it was before you started. You can create a restore point by using Windows 8 System protection tools. To access the System protection tools, click System and Security from the Control Panel, and then click System. In the left pane, click System protection to display the System Properties dialog box. On the System Protection tab, click the Create button, and type a description for the restore point (such as "Before installing [name of software]") and click Create. You will be notified when the restore point is created.

Software Licenses

Don't I own the software I buy? Most people don't understand that, unlike other items they purchase, the software they buy doesn't belong to them. The only thing they're actually purchasing is a license that gives them the right to use the software for their own purposes as the *only* user of that copy. The application is not theirs to lend.

A **software license**, also known as an **End User License Agreement (EULA)**, is an agreement between you, the user, and the software company (see Figure 4.25). You accept this agreement before installing the software on your machine. It's a legal contract that outlines the acceptable uses of the program and any actions that violate the agreement. Generally, the agreement states who the ultimate owner of the software is, under what circumstances copies of the software can be made, and whether the software can

FIGURE 4.25 You must accept the terms of the software license before using the product.

BITS&BYTES

Run versus Save When Downloading Software

When you download software from the web, often you're given the choice to run or save it (see Figure 4.26). What's the difference? When you select Run, the program is downloaded to your machine and generally stored in Temporary Internet Files. Then the file is "run," meaning that it is loaded into memory and the operating system runs it. Use the Run option when you need to use the downloaded file on a limited basis, such as a song or video that you only plan to watch once or twice. Some installation programs instead install the software on your machine in a permanent location when Run is selected.

When you select Save (or sometimes Save As) on a download, the file will be copied to your hard disk. There may be an AutoRun program associated with the file that starts the installation automatically. Otherwise, you may need to navigate to the stored location and execute (or run) the file independently. The big difference is that the saved file is not downloaded into a temporary location. Use Save when you want to keep the file for a longer period of time or when you want to control where the file or program is saved.

Do you want to run or save **ChromeSetup.exe** (722 KB) from **dl.google.com**?   Run   Save ▾   Cancel   ✕

FIGURE 4.26 When downloading software, you have the choice to Run or Save.

---

be installed on any other machine. Finally, the license agreement states what, if any, warranty comes with the software.

Does a license only cover one installation? Some software is purchased with a single license to cover one person's specific use. You can't share these licenses, and you can't "extend" the license to install the software on more than one of your computers. Many manufacturers are now offering family licensing deals to allow several computers in one household to be installed with a legal copy. The family pack rate is more than a single license version but is still a savings over purchasing multiple copies. For example, Apple offers a Family Pack Software License Agreement that permits a user to install the purchased software legally on as many as five computers in the same household, and some versions of Microsoft Office come with the ability to install the software on up to three computers in the same household.

Businesses and educational institutions often buy multiuser licenses that allow more than one person to use the software. Some multiuser licenses are per-seat and limit the number of users overall, whereas others, called *concurrent licenses,* limit the number of users accessing the software at any given time.

Does open source software require a license? As you learned earlier, anyone using open source software has access to the program's code. Therefore, open source software programs can be tweaked by another user and redistributed. A free software license, the *GNU General Public License,* is required and grants the recipients the right to modify and redistribute the software. Without such a license, the recipient would be in violation of copyright laws. This concept of redistributing modified open source software under the same terms as the original software is known as **copyleft**. Thus, all enhancements, additions, and other changes to copyleft software must also be distributed as free software.

Getting the Right Software for Your System

How do I ensure the software I buy will work on my computer? Every software program has a set of **system requirements** that specify the minimum recommended standards for the operating system, processor, primary memory (random access memory, or RAM), and hard drive capacity. Sometimes there are other specifications for the video card, monitor, optical drive, and other peripherals. These requirements are printed on the software packaging or are available at the manufacturer's website. Before installing software on your computer, ensure that your system setup meets the minimum requirements as specified by the developer.

When is it worth buying a newer version? Periodically, software developers improve the functionality of their software by releasing a software upgrade. Although software developers suggest otherwise, there's no need to rush out and buy the latest version of a software program every time one is available. Depending on the software, some upgrades may not be sufficiently different from the previous version to make it cost-effective for you to buy the newest version. Unless the upgrade adds features that are important to you, you may be better off waiting to upgrade every other release. You also should consider whether you use the software frequently enough to justify an upgrade and whether your current system can handle the new system requirements of the upgraded version. In between upgrades, developers will make available software updates (sometimes referred to as software patches). Updates are usually downloaded and provide smaller enhancements to the software or fix program bugs.

If I have an older version of software and someone sends me files from a newer version, can I still open them? Software vendors recognize that people work on different versions of the same software. Vendors, therefore, make new versions backward compatible, meaning that the new versions can recognize (open) files created with older versions. However, some software programs are not forward compatible, so these older versions are not able to recognize files created on newer versions of the same software.

Installing and Uninstalling Software

What's the difference between a custom installation and a full installation? Before you use most software, you must permanently place it, or install it, on your system. The installation process may differ slightly depending on whether you're installing the software from a DVD or downloading it from the Internet. One of the first steps in the installation wizard asks you to decide between a full installation and a custom installation. A **full installation** (often referred to as a *typical installation*) copies all the most commonly used files and programs from the distribution disc to your computer's hard drive. By selecting **custom installation**, you can decide which features you want installed on your hard drive. Installing only the features you want saves space on your hard drive.

How do I start my programs in Windows 8? Every program you install on your system is listed on Start. The simplest way to start an application is by clicking the program icon on the Start screen. Alternatively, you can work from the desktop view in Windows 8 or pin a shortcut to a program on the taskbar or to the Start screen. To place a program on the taskbar or pin it to the Start screen, right-click the program icon on your desktop or right-click the program name on the Start screen. From the options that are displayed, select Pin to Taskbar or Pin to Start Menu. Windows then places an icon for this program on the taskbar or Start screen (see Figure 4.27). To uninstall a pinned icon from Start, right-click the icon and select Unpin from Start.

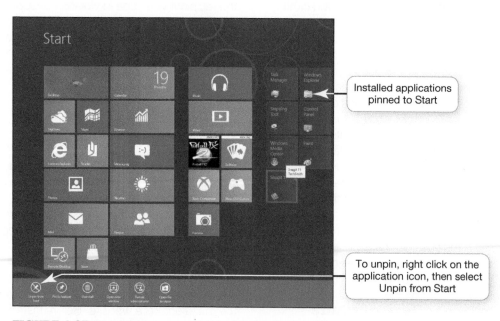

Installed applications pinned to Start

To unpin, right click on the application icon, then select Unpin from Start

FIGURE 4.27 By pinning an application to the Start screen in Windows 8, you have easy access to your most frequently used programs.

ethics in IT

Can I Borrow Software That I Don't Own?

As noted in the chapter, when you purchase software, you're purchasing a license to use it rather than purchasing the actual software. That license tells you how many times you can install the software, so it is important to read it. If you make more copies of the software than the license permits, you're participating in **software piracy** (see Figure 4.28). Historically, the most common way software has been pirated has been by borrowing installation CDs from others and installing the software on other computers. Larger-scale illegal duplication and distribution by counterfeiters are quite common as well. In addition, the Internet provides various ways to copy and distribute pirated software illegally.

Is it really a big deal to copy a program or two? As reported by the Business Software Alliance, over 40% of all software used is pirated.

Not only is pirating software unethical and illegal, the practice has financial impacts on all software consumers. The financial loss to the software industry was estimated to be over $63 billion for 2011. This loss decreases the amount of money available for further software research and development, while increasing the up-front costs to legitimate consumers.

To determine whether you have a pirated copy of software installed on your computer, conduct a software audit. The Business Software Alliance website (**bsa.org**) has several free third-party software audit tools that help you identify and track software installed on your computer and networks. These programs check the serial numbers of the software installed on your computer against software manufacturer databases of officially licensed copies and known fraudulent copies. Any suspicious software installations are flagged for your attention.

As of yet, there's no such thing as an official software police force, but if you're caught with pirated software, severe penalties do exist. A company or individual can pay up to $150,000 for each software title copied. In addition, you can be criminally prosecuted for copyright infringement, which carries a fine of up to $250,000, a five-year jail sentence, or both.

Efforts to stop groups involved with counterfeit software are in full force. Software manufacturers also are becoming more aggressive in programming mechanisms into software to prevent illegal installations. For instance, with many Microsoft products, installation requires you to activate the serial number of your software with a database maintained at Microsoft. This is different from the traditional "registration" that enrolled you voluntarily and allowed you to be notified of product updates. Failure to activate your serial number or attempting to activate a serial number used previously results in the software going into a "reduced functionality mode" after the 50th time you use it. Therefore, without activation or after activating a used serial number, you would not be able to save documents in Office.

FIGURE 4.28 Making more copies than the software license permits is pirating and is illegal. *(Igor Prole/Lepro/iStockphoto)*

How do I uninstall a program? An application contains many different files—library files, help files, and other text files—in addition to the main file you use to run the program. By deleting only the main file, you're not ridding your system of all the pieces of the program. Windows 8 makes it easy to uninstall a program: Simply right-click on the program icon on the Start screen, then from the panel that displays at the bottom, click Uninstall. To uninstall a program from the desktop view in Windows 8, right-click on the program,

BITS&BYTES

Ridding Your Computer of "Bloat"

Manufacturers often include software on new computers that you don't want or need. Called *bloatware*, this software can slow down your computer and degrade its performance. How do you get rid of it? Install an application such as PC Decrapifier (**pcdecrapifier.com**), or, if you'd rather do it yourself, consider some of these tips:

- *Uninstall preinstalled antivirus software:* If you have antivirus software on your old computer, you may be able to transfer the unexpired portion of your software license to your new computer. If this is the case, you can uninstall the preinstalled trial version on your new computer.
- *Uninstall unwanted toolbars:* Many computers come with Google, Bing, and other toolbars preinstalled. Go through Programs and Features in the Control Panel to uninstall any toolbars you don't want.
- *Remove manufacturer-specific software:* Some computer manufacturers install their own software. Some of these programs can be useful, but others are help features and update reminders that are also found in your operating system. You can remove any or all of these support applications and instead just check the manufacturer's website periodically for updates or new information.

select Programs from the Control Panel, then click Uninstall a program. Select the program you want to uninstall from the list, then click Uninstall.

If my computer crashes, can I get the preinstalled software back? Although some preinstalled software is not necessary to replace if your computer crashes, other software such as the operating system is critical to reinstall. Most manufactures use a separate partition on the hard drive to hold an image, or copy, of the preinstalled software. However, it's not always possible to reboot from the partitioned hard drive, especially when your computer crashes, so one of the first things you should do after you purchase a new computer is create a system repair disc. Generally, the manufacturer will have placed a utility on your system, or you can use the Recovery utility included in Windows to create a repair drive or disc. You can access the Recovery utility in Windows 8 from the Control Panel by typing Recovery in the search box, and then clicking Create a recovery drive under System. Then, to create the repair drive, insert a blank flash drive in a USB port (or you can choose to use a DVD) and follow the steps in the wizard. Once the copy has been made, label the flash drive or DVD and put it away in a safe place.

There is an application for almost anything you want or need to do on your computer, whether it is school or work related or just for entertainment purposes. And there are a variety of types of applications, such as proprietary, open source, web-based, and freeware. Have fun exploring all the various possibilities! ■

Before moving on to the Chapter Review:
- Watch Replay Video 4.2 ▶.
- Then check your understanding of what you've learned so far.

check your understanding//

For a quick review to see what you've learned so far, answer the following questions. Visit **pearsonhighered.com/techinaction** to check your answers.

multiple choice

1. The minimum set of recommended standards for a program is known as the
   a. operating system.
   b. system requirements.
   c. setup guide.
   d. installation specs.

2. Image-, video-, and audio-editing software belong in the category of what kind of software?
   a. gaming software
   b. multimedia software
   c. photo-enhancing software
   d. production software

3. Which of the following is considered a benefit of using simulation programs?
   a. They allow users to experience potentially dangerous situations without risk.
   b. They help to prevent costly errors.
   c. They allow users to train on software that is not installed on their systems.
   d. All of the above

4. Which of the following is NOT necessary to do before installing beta software?
   a. Creating a restore point
   b. Backing up your system
   c. Defragging the hard drive
   d. Ensuring your virus protection software is updated

5. Which software is best to use if you want to change the looks of your digital pictures?
   a. image-editing program
   b. video-editing program
   c. media management software
   d. All of the above

true–false

_____ 1. Audio files can include music you have downloaded or installed, audiobook files, or podcast files.

_____ 2. When you buy software, you then own it and can do anything you'd like with it, including giving it to friends to install on their machines.

critical thinking

1. **Media Management**

   Less than a decade ago, most home users had few media files on their computer systems. Today, many users have a library of music, a collection of digitized movies, personal photo collections, and even a large set of recorded television shows. Examine three different software packages on the market today for managing these materials. What features do they need to make the PC the primary entertainment device for a home? What would make users move their PC from the office into the living room?

2. **Software Myths and Misconceptions**

   There are several myths and misconceptions about software, such as the 24-hour rule, the 80/20 rule, and the Abandonment rule. The 24-hour rule claims a person can download software for 24 hours and then have the choice of deleting it or buying it. The 80/20 rule implies that for single-use licenses, a person can install software on both a work and home computer as long as work use is not more than 80%, and home use is not more than 20%. The Abandonment rule claims that one can use software if it is no longer supported or was created by a company that is no longer in business. Explain how you think each of these is a violation of copyright law.

3. **Can You Reuse Software?**

   Several years ago, you purchased Adobe Acrobat so you could create, edit, and mark up PDF documents. You have since changed computers, and your version of Acrobat is not compatible with the operating system on your new computer. You're required to purchase an upgrade of Adobe Acrobat to run on the new machine. Your sister wants to install the old version of Adobe Acrobat on her computer since you're not using it anymore. Do you think this will be legal to do? Why or why not?

Continue

4 Chapter Review

The Nuts and Bolts of Software

1. What's the difference between application software and system software?

- The term *software* refers to a set of instructions that tells the computer what to do.
- Application software is the software you use to do everyday tasks at home, school, and work. Application software includes the following:

  o Productivity software, such as word processing, finance, and personal information management programs
  o Business software for small and large businesses
  o Multimedia software, such as applications used for image and video editing, recording and editing digital audio, and media management; gaming software; and
  o Educational and reference software

- System software is the software that helps run the computer and coordinates instructions between application software and the computer's hardware devices. System software includes the operating system and utility programs.

2. What are the different ways I can access and use software?

- Some software comes preinstalled on your computer. You will need to add other software by installing the software or accessing the software from the web. There are two types of software that you can install on your computer:

  1. Proprietary (or commercial) software is software you buy.
  2. Open source software is program code that is free and publicly available with few licensing and copyright restrictions. The code can be copied, distributed, or changed without the stringent copyright protections of software products you purchase.

- Web-based applications are those that are hosted online by the vendor and made available to the customer over the Internet. This web-based distribution model is also referred to as Software as a Service

(SaaS). Web-based applications are accessed via an Internet connection to the site that hosts the software.

Productivity and Business Software

3. What kinds of applications are included in productivity software?

- Productivity software programs include the following:

  o Word processing: to create and edit written documents
  o Spreadsheet: to do calculations and numerical and what-if analyses easily
  o Presentation: to create slide presentations
  o Database: to store and organize data
  o Note-taking: to take notes and easily organize and search them, and
  o Personal information manager (PIM): to keep you organized by putting a calendar, address book, notepad, and to-do lists within your computer

- Individuals can also use productivity software to help with business-like tasks such as managing personal finances and preparing taxes.

4. What kinds of software do small and large businesses use?

- Businesses use software to help them with the following tasks:

  o Finances and accounting
  o Desktop publishing
  o Web page authoring
  o Project management
  o Customer relationship management (CRM)
  o Enterprise resource planning (ERP), and
  o E-commerce

- Businesses may use specialized business software (or vertical market software) that is designed for their specific industry.
- Some businesses also use specialized drawing software to create technical drawings and computer-aided design (CAD) software to create 3-D models.

Multimedia and Entertainment Software

5. What types of multimedia and entertainment software are available?

- Multimedia software is software for playing, copying, recording, editing, and organizing multimedia files. Multimedia software includes the following:

  o Digital image- and video-editing software
  o Digital audio software
  o Media management software, and
  o Specialty software to produce computer games

- Educational and reference software is available to help you master, study, design, create, or plan.

  o Simulation (training) programs let users experience or control the software as if it were the actual software or an actual event. Simulated programs safely allow users to experience potentially dangerous situations without the risks of experiencing the same situations in real life.
  o Course management software provides traditional classroom tools such as discussion areas, assignment features, and grade books over the Internet.
  o Drawing software includes a wide range of software programs that help you create and edit simple line-based drawings or create more-complex designs for both imaginative and technical illustrations.

Managing Your Software

6. What's important to know when buying software?

- You must purchase software unless it is freeware or open source. As a student, you can purchase, at a reduced price with an academic discount, the same software found online or in stores.
- When you purchase software, you're actually purchasing the license to use it and therefore must abide by the terms of the licensing agreement you accept when installing the program.

- Before installing software on your computer, ensure that your system setup meets the system requirements that specify the minimum recommended standards for the operating system, processor, primary memory (RAM), and hard drive capacity. Sometimes, there are other specifications for the video card, monitor, optical drive, and other peripherals.

7. How do I install and uninstall software?

- When installing software, you are often given the choice between a full (typical) or custom installation.

  o A full installation copies all the files and programs from the distribution disc to your computer's hard drive.
  o A custom installation lets you decide which features you want installed on your hard drive.

- When uninstalling software, it's best to use the uninstall feature that comes with the operating system.

  o In Windows 8, right-click on the program icon on the Start screen, then select Uninstall from the bottom panel that displays.
  o Using the uninstall feature of the operating system when uninstalling a program will help you ensure that all additional program files are removed from your computer.

- Your system comes with preinstalled software, such as the operating system and possibly some files from the manufacturer.
- One of the first things you should do after you purchase a new computer is create a system repair disc that you can use to reboot the computer after a system failure and return the computer to the condition it was in when you first purchased it.

Be sure to check out the companion website for additional materials to help you review and learn, including a Tech Bytes Weekly newsletter—**pearsonhighered.com/techinaction.** And don't forget the Replay Videos .

key terms //

making the transition to . . . next semester//

1. **Picture Perfect**

   You just spent the summer volunteering in a remote village in Africa, and you have tons of pictures you want to share with friends and family. For your friends, it's easy to upload them into Facebook, but you don't want to give your family access to your Facebook account. Research different websites that you would consider using to upload your pictures to show your family. Create a table that lists the different services along with the pros and cons of each site. Discuss which services you would use and explain your reasoning.

2. **Collaborating with Software**

   You've been assigned the dreaded group project. For once, you have a great group of students to work with, but none of your schedules line up so that you can meet in person. You decide to use web-based applications because they are great for collaborating online. Research different types of software you anticipate your group needing to use, including web-based productivity software, sites that enable sharing and storing files online, and sites to use for group video chats and group texting. Create a chart or list that identifies the best software for these needs.

3. **Using OneNote**

   You've been assigned a research paper, which will be very extensive. You're required to collect information for the paper throughout the semester, so you need a good system to keep your notes, readings, and data organized. You've heard OneNote is a great tool for just this type of project, but since you've never used the software, you don't know where to start. Go to **microsoft.com** and search for "Templates for OneNote." Find several good templates that will help you get started. What are the features of the templates that you chose? Discuss which template you would most likely use, and why.

making the transition to . . . the workplace//

1. **Required Software for the Job**

   Almost every profession requires some use of technology and software. Identify the field you would like to enter upon graduation, and then after doing some research, compile a list of software applications you expect to use in your job. If possible, list a proprietary application, as well as open source and web-based alternatives. Note those applications for which you will need training. If your chosen field currently does not require software, discuss why that may be the case. Do you foresee a time when software may be helpful? If so, what kind of software might that be?

2. **Tracking Your Personal Finances**

   You are finally out on your own—graduated from college and working your first job. It's time to track how much you spend versus what you're earning. You really don't want to live paycheck to paycheck, and you want to begin a savings plan to build a rainy-day fund. Investigate online financial planning sites such as Mint (**mint.com**) and Yodlee (**yodlee.com**) and then choose the one that seems best. If you can, download a version of the software for your smartphone. Track your expenses for a few weeks, and identify areas in which you can cut back on your spending. What are the features of the software that you like? Discuss how this may or may not help you in your goal of achieving financial independence.

Software for Startups

Problem

You and your friends have decided to start Recycle Technology, a not-for-profit organization that would recycle and donate used computer equipment. In the first planning session, the group recognizes the need for certain software to help them with various parts of the business such as tracking inventory, designing notices, mapping addresses for pickup and delivery, and soliciting residents by phone or e-mail about recycling events, to name a few.

Task

Split your class into as many groups of four or five as possible. Make some groups responsible for locating free or web-based software solutions and other groups responsible for finding proprietary solutions. Another group could be responsible for finding mobile app solutions. The groups will present and compare results with each other at the end of the project.

Process

1. Identify a team leader who will coordinate the project and record and present results.
2. Each team is to identify the various kinds of software that Recycle Technology needs. Consider software that will be needed for all the various tasks required to run the organization such as communication, marketing, tracking, inventory management, and finance.
3. Create a detailed and organized list of required software applications. Depending on your team, you will specify either proprietary software or open source software.

Conclusion

Most organizations require a variety of software to accomplish different tasks. Compare your results with those of other team members. Were there applications that you didn't think about, but that other members did? How expensive is it to ensure that even the smallest company has all the software required to carry out daily activities, or can the needs be met with free, open source products?

Open Source Software

Ethical conduct is a stream of decisions you make all day long. In this exercise, you'll research and then role-play a complicated ethical situation. The role you play might or might not match your own personal beliefs, but your research and use of logic will enable you to represent the view assigned. An arbitrator will watch and comment on both sides of the arguments, and together, the team will agree on an ethical solution.

Topic: Proprietary Software versus Open Source Software

Proprietary software has set restrictions on use and can be very expensive, whereas open source software is freely available for users to use as is or to change, improve, and redistribute. Open source software has become acceptable as a cost-effective alternative to proprietary software—so much so that it is reported that the increased adoption of open source software has caused a drop in revenue to the proprietary software industry. But determining which software to use involves more than just reducing the IT budget.

Research Areas to Consider

- Open source software (Linux, Apache OpenOffice suite, and Mozilla.org)
- Proprietary software (Microsoft Windows and Office, Apple Mac OS X and iWork)
- Copyright licensing
- Open source development

Process

1. Divide the class into teams.
2. Research the areas cited above and devise a scenario in which someone is a proponent for open source software but is being rebuffed by someone who feels that "you get what you pay for" and is a big proponent of using proprietary software.
3. Team members should write a summary that provides background information for their character—for example: open source proponent, proprietary developer, or arbitrator—and that details their character's behaviors to set the stage for the role-playing event. Then, team members should create an outline to use during the role-playing event.
4. Team members should arrange a mutually convenient time to meet for the exchange, using either the collaboration feature of MyITLab or the discussion board feature of your course management software or by meeting in person.
5. Team members should present their case to the class or submit a PowerPoint presentation for review by the rest of the class, along with the summary and resolution they developed.

Conclusion

As technology becomes ever more prevalent and integrated into our lives, more and more ethical dilemmas will present themselves. Being able to understand and evaluate both sides of the argument, while responding in a personally or socially ethical manner, will be an important skill.

5

System Software: The Operating System, Utility Programs, and File Management

Understanding System Software

Operating System Fundamentals

OBJECTIVES

1. What software is included in system software? **(p. 164)**

2. What are the different kinds of operating systems? **(pp. 164–166)**

3. What are the most common operating systems? **(pp. 166–169)**

🔊 **Sound Byte:** Customizing Windows

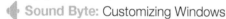

What the Operating System Does

OBJECTIVES

4. How does the operating system provide a means for users to interact with the computer? **(p. 170)**

5. How does the operating system help manage resources such as the processor, memory, storage, hardware, and peripheral devices? **(pp. 171–174)**

6. How does the operating system interact with application software? **(pp. 174–175)**

The Boot Process: Starting Your Computer

OBJECTIVE

7. How does the operating system help the computer start up? **(pp. 176–178)**

👤 **Active Helpdesk:** Starting the Computer: The Boot Process

Using System Software

The Windows Interface

OBJECTIVE

8. What are the main features of the Windows interface? **(pp. 182–186)**

Organizing Your Computer: File Management

OBJECTIVE

9. How does the operating system help me keep my computer organized? **(pp. 188–192)**

🔊 **Sound Byte:** File Management

👤 **Active Helpdesk:** Organizing Your Computer: File Management

Utility Programs

OBJECTIVE

10. What utility programs are included in system software and what do they do? **(pp. 193–199)**

👤 **Active Helpdesk:** Using Utility Programs

🔊 **Sound Byte:** File Compression

🔊 **Sound Byte:** Hard Disk Anatomy

🔊 **Sound Byte:** Letting Your Computer Clean Up After Itself

For all media in this chapter go to **pearsonhighered.com/techinaction** or MyITLab.

(Mary Anne Poatsy; Ferenc Szelepcsenyi/Shutterstock; Ivancovlad/Shutterstock; Stanislav Popov/Shutterstock; reji/Fotolia)

[Redshinestudio/Fotolia]

HOW COOL IS THIS?

Scan here for more info

Have you ever been expecting a **critical phone call** but been in a situation where you absolutely need to **silence your phone**? iPhone's iOS 5 lets you create **custom vibration patterns** that you can assign to individual contacts. This lets you **easily identify callers** in a near **stealth mode setting**. To try it out, first make sure custom vibrations are enabled in Settings. Then go to Contacts, choose a contact, and select Edit. Locate the Vibration > Create New Vibration option, and select it. You'll be presented with a screen on which you can tap out your own vibration rhythm. After saving, just listen for the appropriate **"buzz" pattern** you defined and you'll know who is calling **without drawing attention** to yourself or your phone.

Understanding System Software

As discussed in the previous chapter, your computer uses two basic types of software: application software and system software. **Application software** is the software you use to do everyday tasks at home and at work. **System software** is the set of programs that helps run the computer and coordinates instructions between application software and the computer's hardware devices. From the moment you turn on your computer to the time you shut it down, you're interacting with system software.

operating system
FUNDAMENTALS

System software consists of two primary types of programs: the *operating system* and *utility programs*. The **operating system (OS)** is a group of programs that controls how your computer functions. The OS:

- Manages the computer's hardware, including the processor, memory, and storage devices, as well as peripheral devices such as the printer;
- Provides a consistent means for application software to work with the central processing unit (CPU); and
- Is responsible for the management, scheduling, and coordination of tasks

You interact with your OS through the **user interface**—the *desktop, icons,* and *menus* that let you communicate with your computer.

A **utility program** is a small program that performs many of the general housekeeping tasks for your computer, such as system maintenance and file compression. A set of utility programs is bundled with each OS, but you can also buy standalone utility programs that often provide more features.

Do all computers have operating systems? Every computer, from the smallest laptop to the largest supercomputer, has an OS. Even cell phones, game consoles, cars, and some appliances have operating systems. The role of the OS is critical; the computer can't operate without it.

Are all operating systems alike? You're probably familiar with Microsoft Windows, Apple OS X, and perhaps the iPhone's iOS operating system, but many other operating systems exist. Laptops, tablet computers, and smartphones all need specific operating systems designed to take advantage of their unique characteristics. However, as devices begin to converge in terms of functionality, and operating systems continue to become more powerful, developers such as Microsoft and Apple are making operating systems that have similar functionality (such as OS X and iOS) or are making single operating systems (such as Windows 8) that can run on multiple devices. Figure 5.1 lists a number of common operating systems.

FIGURE 5.1

Common Operating Systems

OS NAME	DEVELOPED BY	AVAILABLE ON
Windows 8	Microsoft	Laptops, tablets, desktops, all-in-ones, cell phones
OS X Mountain Lion	Apple	Laptops, desktops, all-in-ones
iOS 5	Apple	Tablets, iPhones, iPod Touches
Android 3.0	Google	Cell phones, tablets
Linux	Open source	Laptops, desktops

(duaneups/Fotolia; Kevork Djansezian/Getty Images; Bloomberg/Getty Images; tibbbb/Fotolia)

When operating systems were originally developed, they were designed for a single user performing one task at a time (that is, they were *single-user, single-task operating systems*). However, modern operating systems allow a single user to **multitask**—to perform more than one process at a time. And operating systems such as Windows and OS X provide networking capabilities as well, essentially making them *multiuser, multitasking operating systems*.

Operating systems can be categorized by the type of device in which they're installed, such as robots and specialized equipment with built-in computers, mainframes and network computers, mobile devices, and personal computers. Next, we'll look at these different types of operating systems.

Real-Time Operating Systems

Why do machines with built-in computers need an OS? Machinery that performs a repetitive series of specific tasks in an exact amount of time requires a **real-time operating system (RTOS)**. Also referred to as *embedded systems,* RTOSs require minimal user interaction. This type of OS is a program with a specific purpose, and it must guarantee certain response times for particular computing tasks; otherwise, the machine is useless. The programs are written specifically for the needs of the devices and their functions. Therefore, there are no commercially available standard RTOS software programs. Devices that must perform regimented tasks or record precise results—such as measurement instruments found in the scientific, defense, and aerospace industries—require RTOSs. Examples include digital storage oscilloscopes and the Mars Reconnaissance Orbiter.

Where else are RTOSs used today? You also encounter RTOSs every day in devices such as fuel-injection systems in car engines, automobile "infotainment" systems, and some common appliances. RTOSs are also found in many types of robotic equipment. Television stations use robotic cameras with RTOSs that glide across a suspended cable system to record sports events from many angles (see Figure 5.2).

Operating Systems for Networks, Servers, and Mainframes

What kind of operating systems do networks use? A **multiuser operating system** (also known as a **network operating system**) lets more than one user access the computer system at a time by handling and prioritizing requests from multiple users. Networks (groups of computers connected to each other so that they can communicate and share resources) need a multiuser OS because many users simultaneously access the server (the computer that manages network resources such as printers). The latest versions of Windows and OS X can be considered network operating systems: They enable users to set up basic networks in their homes and small businesses.

In larger networks, a more robust network OS is installed on servers and manages all user requests. For example, on a network where users share a printer, the network OS ensures that the printer prints only one document at a time in the order the requests were made. Examples of network operating systems include Windows Server, Linux, and UNIX.

FIGURE 5.2 Devices such as TV sky cameras, cars, and medical equipment use RTOSs. *(John Pyle/Cal Sport Media/Newscom; The Washington Post/Getty Images; Elfstrom/David Elfstrom/iStockphoto)*

What is UNIX? UNIX is a multiuser, multitasking OS that is used as a network OS, primarily with mainframes, although it's also often found on PCs. Developed in 1969 by Ken Thompson and Dennis Ritchie of AT&T's Bell Labs, the UNIX code was initially not proprietary—in other words, no company owned it. Rather, any programmer was allowed to use the code and modify it to meet his or her needs. UNIX is now a brand that belongs to the company The Open Group, but any vendor that meets testing requirements and pays a fee can use the UNIX name. Individual vendors then modify the UNIX code to run specifically on their hardware.

What other kinds of computers require a multiuser OS? Mainframes and supercomputers also require multiuser operating systems. Mainframes routinely support hundreds or thousands of users at time, and supercomputers are often accessed by multiple people working on complex calculations. Examples of mainframe operating systems include UNIX and IBM's IBM i and z/OS, whereas the vast majority of supercomputers use Linux.

Operating Systems for Mobile Devices

What kind of OS does a smartphone use? Figure 5.3 shows the most common operating systems found on smartphones such as the iPhone. Most smartphones have at least modest multitasking capabilities, such as letting you check e-mail while you're on a phone call. More advanced smartphones provide greater multitasking, such as letting you talk and use apps at the same time.

What OS do tablets use? Popular tablet operating systems include iOS, Android, and Windows (see Figure 5.4). iPads use iOS, whereas a number of different tablets (such as the Samsung Galaxy Tab and the Motorola Xoom) use versions of Android. The Kindle Fire also runs a customized version of Android. Until the release of Windows 8 in 2012, Microsoft didn't have a popular tablet OS, but the company is hoping to reverse this trend with Windows 8, which is optimized for tablet devices.

Do gaming consoles and iPods use an OS? Gaming systems such as Microsoft's Xbox 360, the Nintendo Wii, and the Sony PlayStation, as well as personal media players such as the iPod all require system software developed specifically for the particular device. The system software controls the physical aspects of the device (such as game controllers) as well as

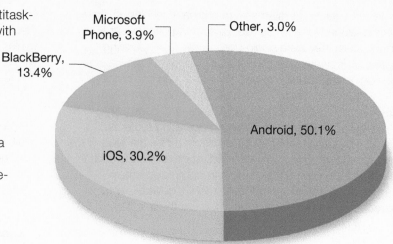

FIGURE 5.3 Popular Smartphone Operating Systems (Based on U.S. Market Share, February 2012, per comScore)

other application programs that come with the device. For example, the operating systems on gaming consoles control web browsing and file storage of media and photos as well as playing of DVDs and games.

Operating Systems for Personal Computers

What are the most popular operating systems for personal computers? Microsoft Windows, OS X, and Linux (an open source OS) are the top three operating systems for personal computers. Although they share similar features, each is unique.

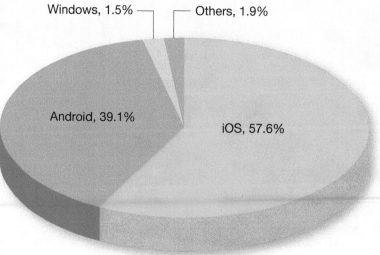

FIGURE 5.4 Popular Tablet Operating Systems (Based on Market Share, Fourth Quarter 2011, per Strategy Analytics)

What's special about Windows? Microsoft **Windows** is an operating environment that incorporates a user-friendly, visual interface like the one that was first introduced with Apple's OS. Over time, improvements in Windows have concentrated on increasing user functionality and friendliness, improving Internet capabilities, supporting home networks, and enhancing file privacy and security. The newest release of Microsoft's OS, **Windows 8**, provides a new interface optimized for touch-screen devices.

What's the difference between the various editions of Windows 8 operating systems? Windows 8 simplifies consumer choices because it's offered in only two versions: Windows 8 and Windows 8 Pro. For most users, Windows 8 is sufficient, as it now includes many features (such as remote access) that weren't included in Windows 7 Home Premium. However, Windows 8 doesn't include Media Center, which you may be used to seeing in previous versions of Windows. Media Center is now available only as an add-on package for Windows 8 Pro.

What's special about the Mac OS? In 1984, **Mac OS** became the first commercially available OS to incorporate a **graphical user interface**, or **GUI**, with user-friendly point-and-click technology. Many Mac users have switched from Windows because of the "coolness" of the Mac OS, OS X. The latest version, Mountain Lion, adds many of the popular and innovative features loved by iOS users, such as messages, reminders, notes, and a notification center. If you've been using Windows for a while, you shouldn't have any problems making the transition to OS X. You'll notice immediately that OS X uses the same desktop metaphors as Windows, including icons for folders and a Trash Can (similar to a Recycle Bin) for deleted documents. OS X also includes a window-based interface like the one in Windows.

OS X is based on the UNIX operating system, which is exceptionally stable and reliable. However, just as with any other OS, you still need to install updates as they become available and protect yourself from viruses, spyware, and other malicious software.

What is Linux? **Linux** is an open source OS designed for use on personal computers and as a network OS. Open source software is freely available for anyone to use or modify as he or she wishes. Linux began in 1991 as a part-time project

FIGURE 5.5 Developed by Google, the Android OS is based on Linux and runs easily on netbooks and tablets. *(Oleksiy Maksymenko Photography/Alamy)*

of Finnish university student Linus Torvalds. It has since been tweaked by scores of programmers as part of the Free Software Foundation GNU Project (**gnu.org**).

Linux has a reputation as a stable OS that is not subject to crashes or failures. Because the code is open and available to anyone, Linux can be modified or updated quickly by hundreds of programmers around the world.

What computers use Linux? Linux is gaining popularity among computer manufacturers, which have begun to ship it with some of their latest PCs. Android, the tablet and phone OS, is Linux based. Because the overall size of Android is much smaller than that of Windows, many netbook users choose to use it in place of the factory-installed Windows OS (see Figure 5.5). Some Linux-based operating systems have been modified to run on iPods and gaming systems.

Where can I get Linux? Linux is available for download in various packages known as **distributions**, or **distros**. Distros include the underlying Linux kernel (the code that provides Linux's basic functionality) and special modifications to the OS, and may also include additional open source software (such as OpenOffice). A good place to start researching distros is **distrowatch.com**. This site tracks Linux distros and provides helpful tips for beginners on choosing one.

Does it matter what OS is on my computer? An OS is designed to run on specific CPUs. CPUs have different designs, which can require modifying the OS software to allow it to communicate properly with each CPU. The combination of an OS and a specific processor is referred to as a computer's **platform**.

For user convenience, computers and other devices usually come with an OS already installed. However, with some PCs, you can specify which OS you'd like installed when you order your device. For example, Windows and Linux can run on most of the hardware being sold today. Your decision of an OS in this case is mostly a matter of price and personal preference. However, Apple equipment—computers, iPhones, iPads, and iPod Touches—comes with Apple operating systems preinstalled.

Note that most *application software* is OS dependent. You need to make sure you get the correct version of the application software for your OS, such as Microsoft Office 2013 for Windows and Microsoft Office 2011 for OS X.

Can I have more than one OS on my computer? Many people run more than one OS on their computers because different operating systems offer different features. For example, Windows and Linux both run well on Apple computers. A standard utility included in OS X called Boot Camp lets you boot into either Windows or OS X. And if you want to run both OS X and Windows OS at the same time, you can create "virtual drives" using virtualization software such as Parallels or VMware Fusion.

In Windows, you can create a separate section of your hard drive (called a *partition*) and install another OS on it while leaving your original Windows installation untouched. After installing the second OS, when your computer starts, you're offered a choice of which OS to use.

How do operating systems use the "cloud"? Now that broadband Internet access and providing computer resources via the Internet (so-called *cloud computing*) are becoming more commonplace, operating systems have features that are tied to cloud computing. Here are a few examples:

- Windows 8 features tighter integration with the cloud. Using your *Microsoft account,* Windows 8 stores your settings and keeps track of applications you've purchased from the Windows store online. You can easily access and store files online in your *Sky Drive account.* You can also log on to any Windows 8 machine and be able to see your familiar desktop and applications.

- Similarly, OS X Mountain Lion allows you to sign in with your *Apple ID,* which provides access to Apple's *iCloud* system. iCloud stores your content online and automatically pushes it out to all your Apple devices.

BITS&BYTES

Upgrading Your Operating System

If you've had your computer for a year or two, you may be wondering whether you should upgrade to the newest release of your OS (such as going from Windows 7 to Windows 8). Here are a few key things to consider before taking the plunge:

- **Is your current OS still supported?** When the company deploys new versions of operating systems, it may stop supporting older versions. If your current version will no longer be supported, it's best to upgrade to a newer version.

- **Are there significant features in the new version that you want?** Operating systems are often upgraded to provide extra security, better performance, and additional features intended to make your computer experience more efficient, and perhaps even more fun. But if the only features the new version offers are ones you don't need, you should reconsider upgrading.

- **Will your hardware work with the new version of the OS?** Check the minimum operating requirements (required RAM, processor speed, hard drive space, etc.) of the new version to ensure that your computer can handle the workload of the new OS. You'll also need to make sure drivers for the new OS are available for all your hardware devices and peripherals to ensure they'll work with it. Microsoft has made this easy with Windows Upgrade Advisor, which you can download from Microsoft's website. The Upgrade Advisor scans your hardware, devices, and installed programs for compatibility, advises you on how to resolve any issues, and recommends what you should do before upgrading.

- **Is your application software compatible with the new version of the OS?** Usually, application software works fine with a new version of an OS. Sometimes it doesn't. Check with software vendors regarding compatibility. Most programs that run under Windows 7 will run at least from the desktop in Windows 8. And Windows 8 has an upgrade option in its install program that lets you install Windows 8 over an existing installation of Windows 7. This alleviates you having to install all your application software after upgrading.

Before starting the upgrade, back up all your data files so you won't lose anything accidentally during the upgrading process. File Recovery and other backup features in Windows make this job less of a hassle.

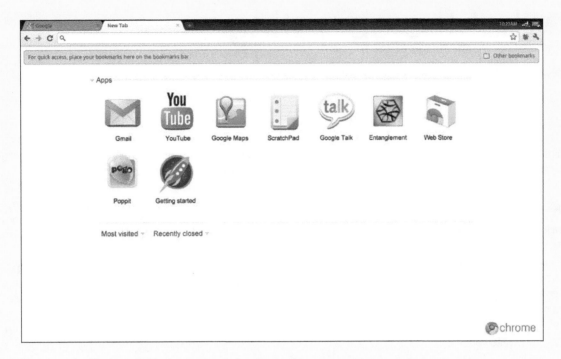

FIGURE 5.6 The Google Chrome OS has a very minimalist look.

- Google has launched the *Google Chrome OS* (see Figure 5.6), which is a web-based OS. With the Chrome OS, virtually no files are installed on your computing device. Rather, the main functionality of the OS is provided by accessing the web through a web browser. Chrome OS is only available on certain hardware from Google's manufacturing partners, and these devices are called *Chromebooks*.

Another pioneer in accessing cloud-based storage and applications with a browser is the open source product eyeOS (**eyeos.org**). eyeOS allows companies to set up private clouds containing data and applications that can be accessed by their employees, partners, or customers. Using almost any computing device with a browser, users can access their data and applications through an Internet connection. ■

BITS&BYTES

OS Market Share Battle: It's Still a Windows World

So who is winning the OS market share war? It depends on the type of device. For conventional desktop and laptop computers, hands down the winner is still Windows, with over 90% of the market (see figure here). But other operating systems have made huge inroads on portable devices such as phones and tablets. Microsoft hopes to reverse this trend with the release of Windows 8, but only time will tell how well it fares.

Mac: 7% — Linux: 1%

Windows: 92%

Desktop/Laptop Operating Systems (Based on Market Share, July 2012, per netmarketshare.com)

what the operating
SYSTEM DOES

As shown in Figure 5.7, the OS is like an orchestra's conductor. It coordinates and directs the flow of data and information through the computer system. In this section, we explore the operations of the OS in detail.

The User Interface

How does the OS control how I interact with my computer? The OS provides a user interface that lets you interact with the computer. The first personal computers used *Microsoft Disk Operating System* (*MS-DOS,* or just *DOS*), which had a command-driven interface, as shown in Figure 5.8a. A **command-driven interface** is one in which you enter commands to communicate with the computer system. The DOS commands were not always easy to understand; as a result, the interface proved to be too complicated for the average user. Therefore, PCs were used primarily in business and by professional computer operators.

The command-driven interface was later improved by incorporating a menu-driven interface, as shown in Figure 5.8b. A **menu-driven interface** is one in which you choose commands from menus displayed on the screen. Menu-driven interfaces eliminated the need for users to know every command because they could select most of the commonly used commands from a menu. However, they were still not easy enough for most people to use.

What kind of interface do operating systems use today? Current personal computer operating systems such as Microsoft Windows and OS X use a graphical user interface, or GUI (pronounced "gooey"). Unlike command- and menu-driven interfaces, GUIs display graphics and use the point-and-click technology of the mouse and cursor, making them much more user-friendly.

Linux-based operating systems do not have a single default GUI interface. Instead, users are free to choose among many commercially available and free interfaces, such as GNOME and KDE, each of which provides a different look and feel.

Manages computer hardware and peripherals

Provides a user interface

The Operating System

Provides a consistent interaction between applications and the CPU

Manages memory and storage

Manages the processor

FIGURE 5.7 The OS is the orchestra conductor of your computer, coordinating its many activities and devices. *(Lusoimages/Shutterstock; ra2 studio/Shutterstock; Yuri Arcurs/Shutterstock; aPERFECT/Shutterstock; Roman Shcherbakov/Shutterstock; Ragnarock/Shutterstock; Arno van Dulmen/Shutterstock)*

FIGURE 5.8 (a) A command-driven interface. (b) A menu-driven interface.

Processor Management

Why does the OS need to manage the processor? When you use your computer, you're usually asking the processor (also called the CPU) to perform several tasks at once. For example, you might be printing a Word document, chatting with your friends on Facebook, and watching a movie using the Blu-ray drive—all at the same time, or at least what appears to be at the same time. Although the CPU is powerful, it still needs the OS to arrange the execution of all these activities in a systematic way.

To do so, the OS assigns a slice of its time to each activity that requires the processor's attention. The OS must then switch among different processes millions of times a second to make it appear that everything is happening seamlessly. Otherwise, you wouldn't be able to watch a movie and print at the same time without experiencing delays in the process.

How exactly does the OS coordinate all the activities? When you create and print a document in Word while also watching a Blu-ray movie, for example, many different devices in the computer are involved, including your keyboard, mouse, Blu-ray drive, and printer. Every keystroke, every mouse click, and each signal to the printer and from the Blu-ray drive creates an action, or **event**, in the respective device (keyboard, mouse, Blu-ray drive, or printer) to which the OS responds.

Sometimes these events occur sequentially (such as when you type characters one at a time), but other events involve two or more devices working concurrently (such as the printer printing while you type and watch a movie). Although it looks as though all the devices are working at the same time, the OS in fact switches back and forth among processes, controlling the timing of events on which the processor works.

For example, assume you're typing and want to print a document. When you tell your computer to print your document, the printer generates a unique signal called an **interrupt** that tells the OS that it's in need of immediate attention. Every device has its own type of interrupt, which is associated with an **interrupt handler**, a special numerical code that prioritizes the requests. These requests are placed in the interrupt table in the computer's primary memory (RAM). The OS processes the task assigned a higher priority before processing a task assigned a lower priority. This is called **preemptive multitasking**.

In our example, when the OS receives the interrupt from the printer, it suspends the CPU's typing activity and Blu-ray activity, and puts a "memo" in a special location in RAM called a *stack*. The memo is a reminder of what the CPU was doing before it started to work on the printer request. The CPU then retrieves the printer request from the interrupt table and begins to process it. On completion of the printer request, the CPU goes back to the stack, retrieves the memo it placed about the keystroke or Blu-ray activity, and returns to that task until it is interrupted again, in a very quick and seamless fashion, as shown in Figure 5.9.

What happens if more than one document is waiting to be printed? The OS also coordinates multiple activities for peripheral devices such as printers. When the processor receives a request to send information to the printer, it first checks with the OS to ensure that the printer is not already in use. If it is, the OS puts the request in another temporary storage area in RAM, called the *buffer*. The request then waits in the buffer until the **spooler**, a program that helps coordinate all print jobs currently being sent to the printer, indicates the printer is available. If more than one print job is waiting, a line (or *queue*) is formed so that the printer can process the requests in order.

Memory and Storage Management

Why does the OS have to manage the computer's memory? As the OS coordinates the activities of the processor, it uses RAM as a temporary storage area for instructions and data the processor

STEP 2: CPU receives an interrupt request from the printer

CPU Processing Activity

STEP 1: CPU is playing a movie

STEP 4: CPU executes printing

STEP 6: CPU resumes playing the movie

STEP 3: Memo about movie stored in stack

Stack

STEP 5: Memo about movie retrieved from stack

RAM

FIGURE 5.9 How Preemptive Multitasking Works

needs. The processor then accesses these instructions and data from RAM when it's ready to process them. The OS is therefore responsible for coordinating the space allocations in RAM to ensure there's enough space for all the pending instructions and data. The OS then clears the items from RAM when the processor no longer needs them.

Can my OS ever run out of RAM? RAM has limited capacity. Like most users, you'll add new software and peripherals to your computer over time. Most computers sold for home use have between 4 and 16 GB of RAM. If you have an older computer system with less RAM, it might be time to consider buying a

new computer or adding more RAM. As you add and upgrade software and increase your usage of the computer system, you might find that the amount of RAM you have is no longer sufficient for your needs.

What happens if my computer runs out of RAM? When there isn't enough RAM for the OS to store the required data and instructions, the OS borrows from the more spacious hard drive. This process of optimizing RAM storage by borrowing hard drive space is called **virtual memory**. As shown in Figure 5.10, when more RAM is needed, the OS swaps out from RAM the data or instructions that haven't recently been used and moves them to a temporary storage area on the hard drive called the **swap file** (or **page file**). If the data or instructions in the swap file are needed later, the OS swaps them back into active RAM and replaces them in the hard drive's swap file with less active data or instructions. This process of swapping is known as **paging**.

Can I ever run out of virtual memory? Only a portion of the hard drive is allocated to virtual memory. You can manually change this setting to increase the amount of hard drive space allocated, but eventually your computer will become sluggish as it is forced to page more often. This condition of excessive paging is called **thrashing**. The solution to this problem is to increase the amount of RAM in your computer so that it won't be necessary for it to send data and instructions to virtual memory.

How does the OS manage storage? If it weren't for the OS, the files and applications you save to the hard drive and other storage locations would be an unorganized mess. Fortunately, the OS has a

RAM

Data and instructions not recently used

Operating System

Data and instructions needed now

Hard drive's swap file

FIGURE 5.10 Virtual memory borrows excess storage capacity from the hard drive when there isn't enough capacity in RAM. *(brontazavra/ Shutterstock; aPERFECT/Fotolia; Tim Dobbs/Shutterstock)*

ethics in IT

The Internet is a fantastic tool, but only if you can access it. In an effort to give children in developing countries a better opportunity to "learn, share, and create," the One Laptop per Child (OLPC) initiative was founded by faculty from the MIT Media Lab, in conjunction with partners such as Google, AMD, and News Corporation. The mission of OLPC (**one.laptop.org**) is to ensure that all school-aged children in lesser-developed communities receive their own personal computers so that they are no longer excluded from the benefits computers can provide. To date, the organization has distributed laptops to over 2.4 million children and teachers worldwide.

This ambitious project to develop and distribute a low-cost laptop computer (current cost: $199) is designed to provide access to electronic textbooks and other learning aids—and eventually

the Internet. The main thrust of the project is to overcome the so-called digital divide and provide computing resources to all regardless of their financial means.

Called the XO (see Figure 5.11), the laptop is small, rugged, and has a comfortable, child-sized, built-in handle. It also has a tablet-like monitor that can twist to turn the laptop into an e-book reader. The laptop is power efficient, running on less than 1/10th the power a standard laptop requires.

At the core of the XO laptop is Sugar, the OS. It is based on the Linux OS, but has a user interface that is completely different from Windows, OS X, or Linux. The key features are as follows:

- **Focus on activities and sharing rather than on applications:** Because the XO is likely to be the first computer that many children use, its user interface was designed to be intuitive. An XO-person (an O on top of an X) icon is used to represent the user and is surrounded by icons that represent home, friends, and neighborhood.

- **Focus on multimedia:** A built-in microphone, webcam, and multimedia tools are included to encourage children to create multimedia.

Continued

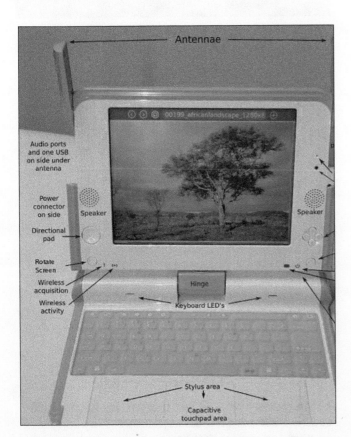

FIGURE 5.11 The XO can be easily converted from a traditional laptop to an e-book reader. *(One Laptop per Child)*

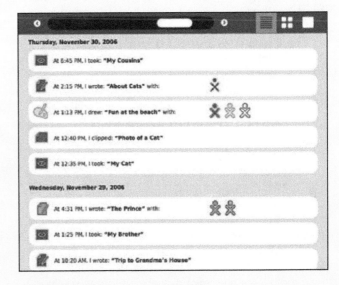

FIGURE 5.12 The journaling system chronicles what the student saves as well as the student's interaction with the machine and with others.

- **Focus on collaboration:** Each tool in the OS has the ability to collaborate, which facilitates the community learning experience.
- **Built-in networking:** A wireless mesh network connects computers in close proximity, providing the potential for every activity to be a networked activity. Browsing, for example, is no longer an isolated, individual activity; it's a collaborative group experience (see Figure 5.12).
- **Journaling:** The system records what the child has done, including interactions with others,

rather than just what the student has saved. This journal can be tagged, searched, and sorted in a variety of ways.

Another general concept behind the OS is that children learn through doing, so the software puts an emphasis on tools for exploration and expression, as well as encouraging students to learn by helping each other. Because Sugar is built on an open source platform, it also encourages students to explore how it works and to modify the code to meet their preferences.

file-management system that keeps track of the name and location of each file you save and the programs you install. We'll talk more about file management later in this chapter.

Hardware and Peripheral Device Management

How does the OS manage the hardware and peripheral devices? Each device attached to your computer comes with a special program called a **device driver** that facilitates communication between the device and the OS. Because the OS must be able to communicate with every device in the computer system, the device driver translates the device's specialized commands into commands the OS can understand, and vice versa. Devices wouldn't function without the proper device drivers because the OS wouldn't know how to communicate with them.

Do I always need to install drivers?
Today, most devices, such as flash drives, mice, keyboards, and digital cameras, come with the driver already installed in Windows. The devices whose drivers are included in Windows are called Plug and Play devices. **Plug and Play (PnP)** is a software and hardware standard designed to facilitate the installation of new hardware in PCs by including in the OS the drivers these devices need in order to run. Because the OS includes this software, incorporating a new device into your computer system seems automatic. PnP lets you plug a new device into your computer, turn it on, and immediately play (use) the device (see Figure 5.13).

What happens if the device is not PnP? Sometimes you may have a device that is so new the drivers aren't yet available automatically in Windows. You'll then be prompted to insert the driver that was provided with the device, usually on a DVD. If

FIGURE 5.13 A Windows message showing a successful driver install the first time an external hard drive was connected to the computer.

you obtain a device secondhand and don't receive the device driver, or if you're required to update the device driver, you can often download the necessary driver from the manufacturer's website. You can also go to websites such as DriverZone (**driverzone.com**) to locate drivers.

Can I damage my system by installing a device driver? Occasionally, when you install a driver your system may become unstable (that is, programs may stop responding, certain actions may cause a crash, or the device or the entire system may stop working). Although this is uncommon, it can happen. Fortunately, to remedy the problem, Windows has a Roll Back Driver feature that removes a newly installed driver and replaces it with the last one that worked (see Figure 5.14).

Software Application Coordination

How does the OS help application software run on the computer? Every computer program, no matter what its type or manufacturer, needs to interact with the CPU using computer code. For programs to work with the CPU, they must contain

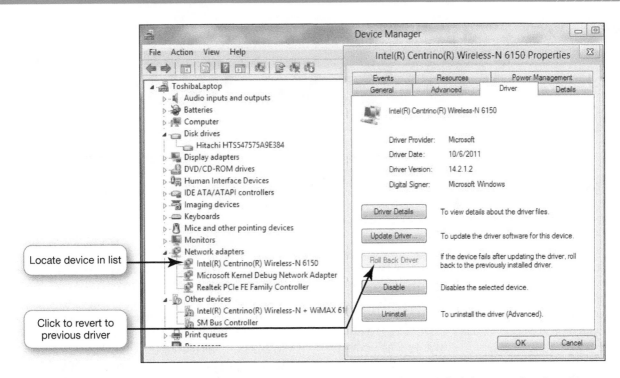

Locate device in list

Click to revert to previous driver

FIGURE 5.14 The Roll Back Driver feature in Windows removes a newly installed driver and replaces it with the last one that worked.

>*To access the Device Manager window, navigate to the desktop, display Control Panel, and click the* **Hardware and Sound** *group. Then, in the* **Devices and Printers** *group, click the* **Device Manager** *link. To display the Properties dialog box, double-click on a device. Click the* **Driver** *tab.*

code the CPU recognizes. Rather than having the same blocks of code for similar procedures in each program, the OS includes the blocks of code—each called an **application programming interface (API)**—that application software needs in order to interact with the CPU. Microsoft DirectX, for example, is a group of multimedia APIs built into the Windows OS that improves graphics and sounds when you're playing games or watching videos on your PC.

What are the advantages of using APIs? To create applications that can communicate with the OS, software programmers need only refer to the API code blocks when they write an application. They don't need to include the entire code sequence. APIs not only prevent redundancies in software code, they make it easier for software developers to respond to changes in

the OS. Software companies also take advantage of APIs to make applications in software suites (such as Microsoft Office) that have a similar interface and functionality. And since these applications share common APIs, data exchange is facilitated between two programs, such as inserting a chart from Excel into a Word document. ■

 ACTIVE HELPDESK
Managing Hardware and Peripheral Devices: The OS

In this Active Helpdesk call, you'll play the role of a helpdesk staffer, fielding calls about how the OS manages memory, storage, hardware, and peripheral devices.

the boot process: starting
YOUR COMPUTER

Many things happen quickly between the time you turn on your computer and the time it's ready for you to start using it. As we discussed earlier, all data and instructions (including the OS) are stored in RAM while your computer is on. When you turn off your computer, RAM is wiped clean of all its data (including the OS). How does the computer know what to do when you turn it on if there is nothing in RAM? It runs through a special boot process (or start-up process) to load the OS into RAM. The term *boot,* from *bootstrap loader* (a small program used to start a larger program), alludes to the straps of leather, called *bootstraps,* that people used to use to help them pull on their boots. This is the source of the expression "pull yourself up by your bootstraps."

What are the steps involved in the boot process? As illustrated in Figure 5.15, the **boot process** consists of four basic steps. Let's look at each step in detail.

Step 1: Activating BIOS

What's the first thing that happens after I turn on my computer? In the first step of the boot process, the CPU activates the **basic input/output system (BIOS)**. BIOS is a program that manages the exchange of data between the OS and all the input and output devices attached to the system. BIOS is also responsible for loading the OS into RAM from its permanent location on the hard drive. BIOS itself is stored on a read-only memory (ROM) chip on the motherboard. Unlike data stored

ROM chip

CPU

STEP 1: CPU activates BIOS
• Basic input/output system
• Stored permanently in ROM

STEP 2: Power-on self-test (POST)
• Tests components of the computer
• Compares results with configuration information in CMOS

STEP 3: Load OS to RAM
• OS loaded from hard drive
• Kernel is *memory resident*

STEP 4: Configuration and customization settings checked and Start screen displays

FIGURE 5.15 The Boot Process *(Arno van Dulmen/ Shutterstock; Ragnarock/Shutterstock)*

in RAM, data stored in ROM is permanent and is not erased when the power is turned off.

Step 2: Performing the Power-On Self-Test

How does the computer determine whether the hardware is working properly? The first job BIOS performs is to ensure that essential peripheral devices are attached and operational—a process called the **power-on self-test**, or **POST**. The BIOS compares the results of the POST with the various hardware configurations permanently stored in CMOS (pronounced "see-moss"). CMOS, which stands for *complementary metal-oxide semiconductor,* is a special kind of memory that uses almost no power. A little battery provides enough power so that the CMOS contents won't be lost after the computer is turned off. CMOS contains information about the system's memory, types of disk drives, and other essential input and output hardware components. If the results of the POST compare favorably with the hardware configurations stored in CMOS, the boot process continues.

Step 3: Loading the OS

How does the OS get loaded into RAM? Next, BIOS goes through a preconfigured list of devices in its search for the drive that contains the **system files**, the main files of the OS. When it is located, the OS loads into RAM from its permanent storage location on the hard drive.

Once the system files are loaded into RAM, the **kernel** (or **supervisor program**) is loaded. The kernel is the essential component of the OS. It's responsible for managing the processor and all other components of the computer system. Because it stays in RAM the entire time your computer is powered on, the kernel is said to be *memory resident*. Other, less critical, parts of the OS stay on the hard drive and are copied over to RAM on an as-needed basis so that RAM is managed more efficiently. These programs are referred to as *non-resident*. Once the kernel is loaded, the OS takes over control of the computer's functions.

Step 4: Checking Further Configurations and Customizations

Is that it? Finally, the OS checks the registry for the configuration of other system components. The **registry** contains all the different configurations (settings) used by the OS and by other applications. It contains the customized settings you put into place, such as mouse speed, as well as instructions as to which programs should be loaded first.

Why do I sometimes need to enter a login name and password at the end of the boot process? The verification of your login name and password is called **authentication**. The authentication process blocks unauthorized users from entering the system. You may have your home computer set up for authentication, especially if you have multiple users accessing it. All large networked environments, like your college, require user authentication for access.

On a Windows 8 computer, the default setting is to input a password to log in to your **Microsoft account** after your computer has completely booted up. Because configuration settings are stored online and associated with a particular Microsoft account, this makes it easy for multiple people to share any Windows 8 computer while maintaining access to their individual settings and preferences.

How do I know if the boot process is successful? The entire boot process takes only a few minutes to complete. If the entire system is checked out and loaded properly, the process completes by displaying the Start screen. The computer system is now ready to accept your first command.

Handling Errors in the Boot Process

What should I do if my computer doesn't boot properly? Sometimes problems occur during the boot process. Here are some suggestions for solving a boot problem:

- If you've recently installed new software or hardware, try uninstalling it. (Make sure you use the Uninstall a program feature in the Control Panel to remove the software.) If the problem no longer occurs when rebooting, you can reinstall the device or software.
- Try accessing the Windows Advanced Options Menu (accessible by pressing the F8 key during the boot process). If Windows detects a problem in the boot process, it will add Last Known Good Configuration to the Windows Advanced Options Menu. Every time your computer boots successfully, a configuration of the boot process is saved. When you choose to boot with the Last Known Good Configuration, the OS

FIGURE 5.16 The PC settings screen in Windows 8 provides access to the Refresh your PC option.

*To access the PC Settings screen, display the Charms bar on the Start screen (swipe from right, or point cursor to upper-right corner of screen), click **Settings**, then click **More PC Settings**. On the PC Settings screen, click **General**, and scroll down.*

starts your computer by using the registry information that was saved during the last shut down.

- Try refreshing your computer (new in Windows 8).

What happens when a PC is "refreshed"? Sometimes Windows does not boot properly or the system does not respond properly. You may even see messages related to "fatal exceptions." **Refresh your PC** is a new utility program in Windows 8 that attempts to diagnose and fix errors in your Windows system files that are causing your computer to behave improperly (see Figure 5.16). When a PC is refreshed, the following occurs:

- Your data files (documents, music, videos, etc.) and personalization settings are not removed or changed.
- Apps that you have downloaded from the Windows Store are kept intact.
- Apps that you have downloaded from the Internet or installed from DVDs will be removed from your PC. Therefore, you'll need to reinstall them after the refresh.

It's recommended that you back up your PC prior to refreshing it as a precautionary measure. Finally, if all other attempts to fix your computer fail, try a System Restore to roll back to a past configuration. System Restore is covered in more detail later in this chapter.

What should I do if my keyboard or another device doesn't work after I boot my computer? Sometimes during the boot process, BIOS skips a device (such as a keyboard) or improperly identifies it. Your only indication that this problem has occurred is that the device won't respond after the system has been booted. When that happens, try rebooting. If the problem persists, check the OS's website for any patches (or software fixes) that may resolve the issue. If there are no patches or the problem persists, you may want to get technical assistance. ■

Before moving on to Part 2:
- Watch Replay Video 5.1 ▶.
- Then check your understanding of what you've learned so far.

For a quick review to see what you've learned so far, answer the following questions. Visit **pearsonhighered.com/ techinaction** to check your answers.

multiple choice

1. Which is NOT an example of a smartphone OS?

   a. iOS   **c.** Android

   b. BlackBerry   **d.** Linux

2. You are most likely to find a real-time operating system (RTOS)

   a. in your automobile.   **c.** on a smartphone.

   b. on a laptop.   **d.** on an iPad.

3. All of the following are key attributes of an operating system EXCEPT

   a. it manages memory and storage

   b. it provides a user interface

   c. it manages the CPU

   d. it tracks connections to external networks

4. Modern operating systems such as Windows and OS X use a _____ interface.

   a. command-driven

   b. graphical user

   c. menu-driven

   d. text-based

5. If your computer can't store all the required OS data in RAM, it can use a temporary file on the hard drive to store data. This is known as a _____ file.

   a. Linux

   b. nonvolatile

   c. swap

   d. thrash

true–false

_____ **1.** Each device attached to your computer needs a device driver to communicate with the OS.

_____ **2.** The first step of the boot process is the power-on self-test (POST).

critical thinking

1. **Market Dominance**

   Microsoft and Apple are large corporations and have control of most of the OS market. Although there have been some innovative changes to both of their proprietary operating systems, does their size and market dominance prevent more innovation? Why or why not? Linux, as an open source environment, is poised for greater innovation. Why do you think the Linux OS doesn't have a greater market share?

2. **A Web-Based OS**

   OS interfaces have evolved from a text-based console format to the current GUI. Modern operating systems such as Windows and OS X are starting to include features that store and retrieve data from the cloud (the Internet). Many believe the OS of the future will be totally web-based and not require the installation of an OS on a specific device. Discuss the implications of this type of OS. What are the potential security issues of a totally web-based OS?

Continue ▶

Missing something that used to be on your Windows 7 desktop but isn't on the Start screen in Windows 8? Although some programs and settings that were more easily accessible in Windows 7 may not be initially visible in Windows 8, they are still available. For example, the Windows 8 Start screen doesn't feature all the old functionality of the previous Windows Start menu, but options such as Computer are still available in Windows 8—you just need to add icons for them onto the Start screen. Adding icons (creating shortcuts) for the Windows 8 Start screen is relatively easy, but it's a bit different from what you may be used to from previous versions of Windows.

Step 1 Display the Charms bar (by placing your mouse in the upper-right corner, or swiping from the right side of the screen on touch-enabled devices), and select **Search** to display the Search screen. Type **computer** in the search box to locate the Computer app.

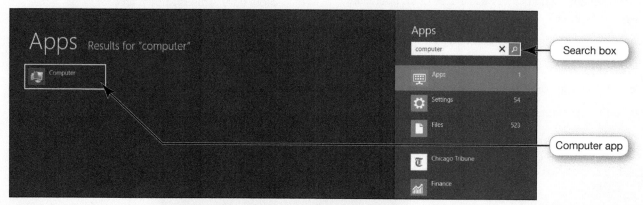

Step 2 Right-click the **Computer** app to display the options menu at the bottom of the screen. Left-click the **Pin to Start** icon to create an icon for the Computer app on the Start screen.

Step 3 Display the Start screen (press the **Windows key**), and scroll to the right to find the Computer icon you just added to the desktop. It will be at the very end of all the icons on your Start screen. Left-click and drag the icon to position it where you want it on the Start screen.

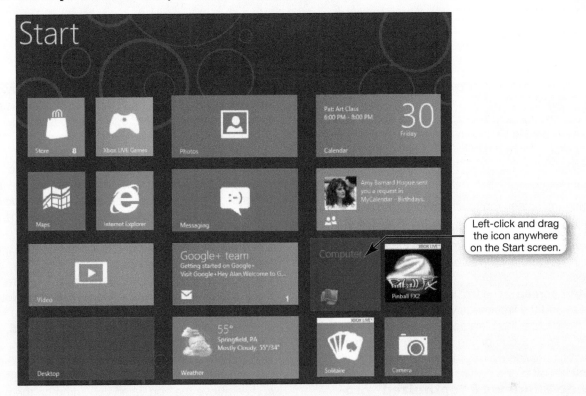

Left-click and drag the icon anywhere on the Start screen.

Using System Software

Now that you know how system software works, let's explore how specific operating systems and their tools function.

 the windows
INTERFACE

As we mentioned earlier, Windows 8 is a departure from previous versions of Windows because it's designed for a variety of devices, including laptops, desktops, and tablet PCs. To enable Windows 8 to function on all types of devices, there are often three different ways to accomplish tasks in Windows 8:

1. Using a mouse

2. Touching the screen (on touch-enabled devices)

3. Using keystrokes

Which method you use depends on the type of device you're using and, to a large extent, on your personal preferences.

The **Start screen** is the first interaction you have with the OS and the first image you see on your display. As its name implies, the Start screen is the place where you begin all of your computing activities. The Windows 8 Start screen provides you with access to your most used applications in one convenient screen.

How do Windows 8 "optimized" programs differ from older Windows apps?
Windows 8 apps are applications specifically designed to run in the interface of Windows 8. The **Windows 8 interface** features large type with clean, readable block images inspired by metropolitan service signs such as those found on bus stations and subways.

Windows 8 apps either are preinstalled with Windows 8 (such as Photos, Messaging, and Calendar) or are available for download from the Windows Store (Microsoft's apps marketplace). You can launch Windows 8 apps by clicking or tapping on their icons on the Start screen.

Windows 8 apps are displayed full screen, without the distractions of borders or controls (such as scrollbars or menus). For example, Figure 5.17 shows Internet Explorer 10, which is a Windows 8 app. Notice that unlike older versions of Internet Explorer, there are no window borders or menus visible (see Figure 5.17a), as the application fills the entire screen. Controls and settings are contained on **app bars**, such as the Tabs bar and Address bar (see Figure 5.17b), that float on screen above the app when you summon them or you need them. Right-clicking on a Windows 8 app screen usually displays the app bars.

FIGURE 5.17 (a) Internet Explorer 10, a Windows 8 app, displays full screen. (b) Right-clicking on the Internet Explorer 10 screen displays the open Tabs bar (top) and the Address bar (bottom).

What are the main features of the Windows 8 Start screen? The Start screen is based on the interface for Windows smartphones. The most useful feature of the Start screen is that it lets you customize it to meet your needs. As such, the Start screen on your computer may be different from the Start screen on your friend's computer. And because your Windows 8 settings and preferences are saved in your Microsoft account, when you log on to any Windows 8 computer, you'll see your own personal settings, preferences, and applications reflected on the Start screen (see Figure 5.18).

For performing common tasks, such as searching or sharing information, Windows 8 has created special shortcuts called **charms**. Charms are located on the *Charms bar* (see Figure 5.18), which you access by moving your cursor to the upper-right corner of the screen, swiping in from the right edge of the screen, or pressing the Windows key+C.

Why can't I see icons for certain applications on my Start screen? Not all the Windows 8 apps and programs installed on your computer are visible on the Start screen. You can choose which applications are visible on the Start screen through a process called **pinning**. Usually, when you install a Windows 8 app or any other program on your computer, it pins the program (displays it) on the Start screen by default. (For more on pinning apps, see the Try This feature on pages 180–181.) If there is an icon on the Start

screen you don't need, just right-click on it (or touch and hold) and select the Unpin from Start option that appears on the app bar at the bottom of the screen.

If you want to see all the applications installed on your computer, not just the ones pinned to your Start screen, right-click on a blank area of the Start screen and select the All apps option that appears at the bottom of the screen. This displays the Apps screen (see Figure 5.19), which shows all Windows 8 apps and other programs installed on your computer.

What happened to the Start button from Windows 7? When using Windows 8 for the first time, you might be looking for the Start button, which has been removed. There are several ways to return to the Start screen in Windows 8:

- Press the Windows key.
- Display the Charms bar and click (or touch) Start.
- Move your cursor to the lower-left corner of your screen (roughly where the Start button used to be) to display a Start screen icon. Click it to display the Start screen.

How can I quickly access useful programs and tools that were available from the Windows 7 Start button? Although the Start button is gone, right-clicking on your screen in the lower-left corner displays a menu of quick links to common administrative tasks and programs, such as Control Panel and File Explorer.

Where is the Windows desktop? If you've been using versions of Windows prior to Windows 8, you're used to the desktop being the first screen you see on your computer. The desktop from Windows 7 still exists, just in a slightly modified version. You can

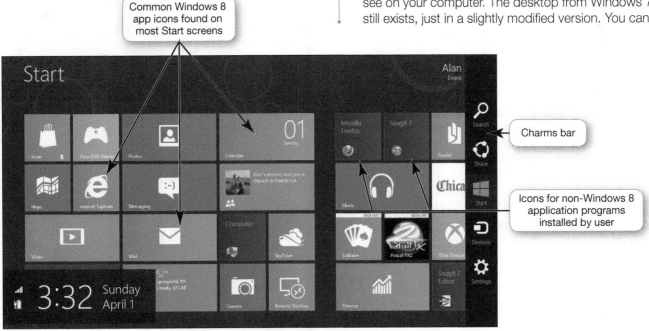

FIGURE 5.18 The Windows 8 Start screen puts the most commonly used features of the OS at your fingertips. You can easily customize it to meet your needs.

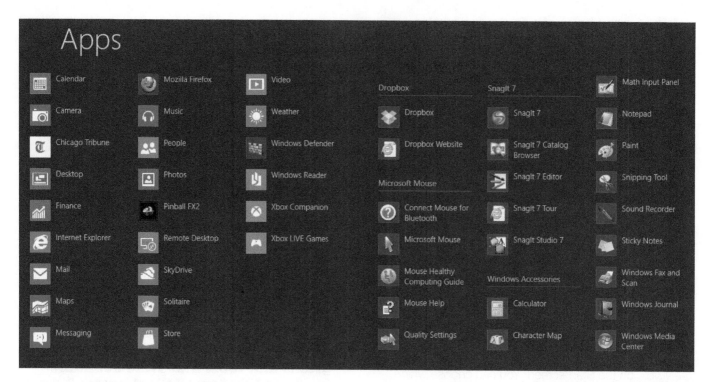

FIGURE 5.19 The Windows 8 Apps screen shows all Windows 8 apps and other programs installed on your computer.

access the Windows 8 desktop via the Desktop icon on the Start screen or by pressing the Windows key+D. Programs that have not been designed to run in the Windows 8 interface (like Microsoft Office 2010) will run on the Windows 8 desktop.

The desktop still has features like the taskbar. The **taskbar** displays open and favorite applications for easy access. You can point to an icon to preview windows of open files or programs, or move your mouse over a thumbnail to preview a full-screen image. Or, you can right-click an icon to view a Jump List—the most recently or commonly used files or commands for that application.

How can I switch between apps in Windows 8? If you want to go back to the last program you were using, just point your cursor to the upper-left corner of the screen and drag (or swipe) from the left. Drag the thumbnail image of your previous program to the middle of your screen and it will be available. Repeatedly swiping from the left will scroll backward through all your open programs.

For a list of open programs—so you can jump right to the correct one—position your cursor in the upper-left corner until the thumbnail appears, then move the cursor down (or swipe in from the left, and before you let go, swipe out again) to display a list of thumbnails of previous programs called a *switch list* (see Figure 5.20).

FIGURE 5.20 The thumbnails of open programs allow you to switch quickly between them. *(Alan Evans)*

Alternatively, pressing the Alt and Tab keys simultaneously also allows you to scroll through open apps.

How can I see more than one Windows 8 app on my screen at a time? Windows 8 apps can snap into place on either the left or right side of the screen, so you can easily display two apps at the same time. Just display the thumbnail list of running apps and click and drag the thumbnail of the second app you want to display to the left or right side of the screen. The app will snap into place while still leaving the other app you had running visible.

How do I close a Windows 8 app? When Windows 8 apps aren't displayed on the screen, Windows will suspend them temporarily so they don't use much memory or power. Therefore, theoretically, you don't ever need to shut down Windows 8 apps. However, most people prefer not to have endless apps running, and it may be inconvenient to scroll through

a huge list of running apps to find the one you want. To close a Windows 8 app from within the app, press Alt+F4. Alternatively, you can move your cursor to the top of the screen until it turns into a hand, then left-click and drag down. The app will shrink to a small window. Drag it down to the bottom of the screen and release the mouse button to close the app. Right-clicking on a thumbnail of the app on the switch list also allows you to close an app.

How does the Mac user interface compare with Windows 8? Although the OS X and the Windows operating systems aren't compatible, they're extremely similar in terms of functionality. For example, as is the case with Windows, OS X programs appear in resizable windows and use menus and icons. However, instead of the Start screen, OS X features a Dock with icons on the bottom for your most popular programs (see Figure 5.21). Mountain Lion, the latest version of

BITS&BYTES

Touch Language for Windows 8

Because the main thrust of Windows 8 is to optimize Windows for touch-screen devices, the Windows developers needed to agree on a set of touch interactions they would use when programming Windows 8. If you're using Windows 8 on a touch-screen device, you may want to learn the gestures shown here.

Press and hold **to learn**

Tap **for primary action**

Slide **to pan**

Swipe **to select**

Pinch and stretch **to zoom**

Turn **to rotate**

Swipe from edge **for app commands**

Swipe from edge **for system commands**

FIGURE 5.21 OS X Mountain Lion adds many of apps that have become so popular in iOS.

OS X, adds many applications that have become so popular in iOS.

Is a Linux user interface similar to OS X and Windows? Different distros of Linux feature different user interfaces. But most of them, like Ubuntu (see Figure 5.22), are based on familiar Windows and OS X paradigms such as using icons to launch programs and having apps run in a window environment. ■

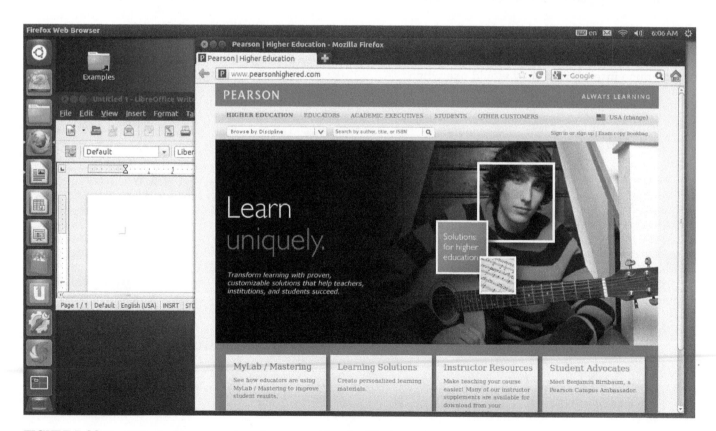

FIGURE 5.22 The Ubuntu Linux user interface resembles the Windows desktop. *(Masterfile)*

Open Source Software: Why Isn't Everyone Using Linux?

Proprietary software such as Microsoft Windows and Apple's OS X is developed by corporations and sold for profit. This means that the **source code**, the actual lines of instructional code that make the program work, is not accessible to the general public. Without being able to access the source code, it's difficult for a user to modify the software or see exactly how the program author constructed various parts of the OS.

Restricting access to the source code protects companies from having their programming ideas stolen, and it prevents customers from using modified versions of the software. However, in the late 1980s, computer specialists became concerned that large software companies (such as Microsoft) were controlling a large portion of market share and driving out competitors. They also felt that proprietary software was too expensive and contained too many bugs (errors).

These people felt that software should be developed without a profit motive and distributed with its source code free for all to see. The theory was that if many computer specialists examined, improved, and changed the source code, a more full-featured, bug-free product would result. Hence, the open source movement was born.

So, if an OS such as Linux is free and relatively bug-free, why does Windows, which users must pay for, have such a huge market share? One reason is that corporations and individuals have grown accustomed to one thing that proprietary software makers can provide: technical support. It's almost impossible to provide technical support for open source software because anyone can freely modify it; thus, there is no specific developer to take responsibility for technical support. Similarly, corporations have been reluctant to install open source software extensively because of the cost of the internal staff of programmers that must support it.

Companies such as Red Hat, Ubuntu, and Xandros have been combating this problem. Red Hat offers a free, open source OS called Fedora (see Figure 5.23). In addition, Red Hat has modified the original Linux source code and markets a version, Red Hat Enterprise Linux, as a proprietary program. Fedora is the testing ground for what eventually goes into this proprietary program. Red Hat Enterprise Linux comes in versions for servers and desktops. Purchasers of Red Hat Enterprise Linux receive a warranty and technical support. Packaging open source software in this manner has made its use much more attractive to businesses. As a result, many web servers are hosted on computers running Linux.

FIGURE 5.23 Companies like Red Hat provide free or low-cost Linux software, such as Fedora, but technical support is often not available. *(Paul Sakuma/AP Images)*

organizing your computer: file
MANAGEMENT

So far we've discussed how the OS manages the processor, memory, storage, and devices, and that it provides a way for applications and users to interact with the computer. An additional function of the OS is to enable **file management**, which provides an organizational structure to your computer's contents. In this section, we discuss how you can use this organizational structure to make your computer more organized and efficient.

Organizing Your Files

How does the OS organize files? Windows organizes the contents of your computer in a hierarchical **directory** structure composed of *drives, libraries, folders, subfolders,* and *files*. The hard drive, represented as the C: drive, is where you permanently store most of your files. Each additional storage drive (optical drive, flash drive, or external hard drive) is given a unique letter (*D, E, F,* and so on). The C: drive is like a large filing cabinet in which all files are stored. As such, the C: drive is the top of the filing structure of your computer and is referred to as the **root directory**. All other folders and files are organized within the root directory. There are areas in the root directory that the OS has filled with files and folders holding special OS files. The programs within these files help run the computer and generally shouldn't be accessed.

What exactly are files and folders? In an OS, a **file** is a collection of program instructions or data that is stored and treated as a single unit. Files can be generated from an application such as a Word document or an Excel workbook. In addition, files can represent an entire application, a web page, a set of sounds, or an image. Files can be stored on the hard drive, a flash drive, online, or on any other permanent storage medium. As the number of files you save increases, it becomes more important to keep them organized in folders and libraries. A **folder** is a collection of files.

How does the library work? In Windows, a **library** gathers categories of files from different locations and displays them as if they were all saved in a single folder, regardless of where they are physically stored. For example, you might have pictures stored all over your computer, including your external hard drive. Rather than looking through each separate location to view your pictures, you can access all of them more easily by looking in the Pictures library. There are four default libraries: Documents, Music, Pictures, and Videos.

How can I easily locate and see the contents of my computer? In Windows, **File Explorer** (previously called Windows Explorer) is the main tool for finding, viewing, and managing the contents of your computer. It shows the location and contents of every drive, folder, and file. As illustrated in Figure 5.24, File Explorer is divided into two panes, or sections:

BITS&BYTES

How to Get the Most from Windows Libraries

To get the most out of using Windows libraries, consider the following tips:

- **Add a new library:** To add a new library (such as one for your games), open File Explorer. In the Navigation Pane on the left side of the window, right-click on Libraries, click New, and then click Library. Type in a name for the new library. To add new locations to the library, open the new library, and click on Include a Folder.
- **Share or collaborate with libraries:** Say you have pictures saved on your laptop, your dad's desktop, and your mom's laptop. As long as all three computers are on the same Homegroup network, you can share each other's libraries by right-clicking the library name, pointing to Share With, and then clicking one of the two Homegroup options, depending on whether you want to allow editing privileges to those with whom you're sharing the library.
- **Create a backup library:** Do you store important data in a variety of folders on your computer? Even though it's best to back up your entire system, you might only need to back up specific folders. In that case, create a new library and call it "Backup." Add the folders you want to ensure are backed up to the library, and then point your backup software to that library.

FIGURE 5.24 File Explorer lets you see the contents of your computer.

*>Right-click the lower-left corner of the screen to display the menu, and then select **File Explorer**.*

1. The *navigation pane* on the left shows the contents of your computer. It displays commonly accessed areas, organized by Favorites and Libraries (Documents, Music, Pictures, and Videos).
2. When you select a Favorite, Library, drive, or network, the files and folders of that particular area are displayed in the *details pane* on the right.

What are some tips on how best to organize my files? Creating folders is the key to organizing files because folders keep related documents together. For example, you might create one folder called "Classes" to hold your class work. Inside the "Classes" folder, you could create subfolders for each of your classes (such as CIS 110 and BUS 336). Inside each of those subfolders, you could create further subfolders for each class's assignments, homework, and so on.

Grouping related files into folders makes it easier for you to identify and find files. Which would be easier—going to the CIS 110 folder to find a file or searching

 SOUND BYTE

File Management

In this Sound Byte, you'll examine the features of file management and maintenance. You'll learn the various methods of creating folders, how to turn a group of unorganized files into an organized system of folders with related files, and how to maintain your file system.

through the hundreds of individual files in the Documents library hoping to find the right one? Grouping files in a folder also allows you to move files more efficiently, so you can quickly transfer critical files needing frequent backup, for instance.

Viewing and Sorting Files and Folders

Are there different ways I can view and sort my files and folders? When you open any folder in File Explorer, the ribbon at the top displays a View tab. Clicking on the View tab offers you different ways to view the folders and files. In some views, the folders are displayed as *Live Icons*. Live Icons allows you to preview the actual contents of a specific file or folder without actually opening the file. Live Icons can be displayed in a variety of views. Here are the two most useful views for students:

1. **Details view:** This is the most interactive view. As shown in Figure 5.24, files and folders are displayed in list form, and the additional file information is displayed in columns alongside the name of the file. You can sort and display the contents of the folder by any of the column headings, so you can sort the contents alphabetically by name or type, or hierarchically by date last modified or file size. Right-click the column heading area to modify the display of columns.
2. **Large Icons view:** As shown in Figure 5.25, Large Icons view shows the contents of folders as small images. Large Icons view is the best view to use if your

FIGURE 5.25 The Large Icons view is a good way to display the contents of files and folders. The preview pane on the right lets you see the first page of your document without first opening it.

>*To access Large Icons view, click the* **View** *option from the ribbon in File Explorer, and then select* **Large Icons** *view. To access the Preview pane, click that icon on the View tab of the ribbon.*

folder contains picture files because you can see a few images peeking out of the folder. It's also good to use if your folder contains PowerPoint presentations because the title slide of the presentation will display, making it easier for you to distinguish among presentations. Additionally, a preview pane is available in this view. The preview pane lets you view the first page of the selected document without having to open it.

What's the best way to search for a file? In Windows 8, the Search app is the best way to search for files and the contents of folders. The Search app searches through your hard drive or other storage devices (DVD or flash drive) to locate files and folders that match the criteria you provide. Your search can be based on part of the name of the file or folder or just a word or phrase in it. You can also search for a file type by representing the file name as an asterisk (called a wildcard character) and typing the file extension (such as "*.xlsx" to search for Excel files). You access the Search app from the Charms bar or from File Explorer. OS X has a similar feature called Spotlight.

Naming Files

Are there special rules I have to follow when I name files? The first part of a file, or the **file name**, is generally the name you assign to the file

when you save it. For example, "bioreport" may be the name you assign a report you have completed for a biology class.

In a Windows application, an **extension**, or **file type**, follows the file name and a period or dot (.). Like a last name, this extension identifies what kind of family of files the file belongs to, or which application should be used to read the file. For example, if "bioreport" is a spreadsheet created in Microsoft Excel 2010, it has an .xlsx extension, and its name is "bioreport.xlsx." Figure 5.26 lists some common file extensions and the types of documents they indicate.

Why is it important to know the file extension? When you save a file created in most applications running under the Windows OS, you don't need to add the extension to the file name; it is added automatically for you. Mac and Linux operating systems don't require file extensions. This is because the information as to the type of application the computer should use to open the file is stored inside the file itself. However, if you're using the Mac or Linux OS and will be sending files to Windows users, you should add an extension to your file name so that Windows can more easily open your files.

Have you ever been sent a file by e-mail and couldn't open it? Most likely, that was because your computer didn't have the program needed to open the file. Sometimes, similar programs that you already have installed can

FIGURE 5.26

Common File Name Extensions

EXTENSION	TYPE OF DOCUMENT	APPLICATION
.docx	Word processing document	Microsoft Word 2007 and 2010
.xlsx	Workbook	Microsoft Excel 2007 and 2010
.accdb	Database	Microsoft Access 2007 and 2010
.pptx	Presentation	Microsoft PowerPoint 2007 and 2010
.pdf	Portable Document Format	Adobe Acrobat or Adobe Reader
.rtf	Text (Rich Text Format)	Any program that can read text documents
.txt	Text	Any program that can read text documents
.htm or .html	HyperText Markup Language (HTML) for a web page	Any program that can read HTML
.jpg	Joint Photographic Experts Group (JPEG) image	Most programs capable of displaying images
.zip	Compressed file	Various file compression programs

be used to open the file, so it's helpful to know what the file extension is. Sites such as FILExt (**filext.com**) can help you identify the source program.

Are there things I shouldn't do when naming my files? Each OS has its own naming conventions, or rules, which are listed in Figure 5.27. Beyond those conventions, it's important that you name your files so that you can easily identify them. Files names can have as many as 255 characters, so don't be afraid to use as many characters as you need. A file name such as "BIO 101 Research Paper First Draft.docx" makes it very clear what that file contains.

Keep in mind, however, that all files must be uniquely identified, unless you save them in different folders or in different locations. Therefore, although files may share the same file name (such as "bioreport.docx" or "bioreport.xlsx") or share the same extension ("bioreport.xlsx" or "budget.xlsx"), no two files stored on the same device and

 ACTIVE HELPDESK
Organizing Your Computer: File Management

In this Active Helpdesk call, you'll play the role of a helpdesk staffer, fielding calls about the desktop, window features, and how the OS helps keep the computer organized.

folder can share *both* the same file name and the same extension.

How can I tell where my files are saved? When you save a file for the first time, you give the file a name and designate where you want to save it. For easy reference, the OS includes libraries where files are saved unless you specify otherwise. In Windows, the default libraries are Documents for files, Music for audio files, Pictures for graphics files, and Videos for video files.

You can determine the location of a file by its **file path**. The file path starts with the drive in which the file is located and includes all folders, subfolders (if any), the file name, and the extension. For example, if you were saving a picture of Andrew Carnegie for a term paper for a U.S. History course, the file path might be C:\Documents\HIS182\Term Paper\Illustrations\ACarnegie.jpg.

As shown in Figure 5.28, "C:" is the drive on which the file is stored (in this case, the hard drive), and "Documents" is the file's primary folder. "HIS182," "Term Paper," and "Illustrations" are successive subfolders within the "Documents" main folder. Last comes the file name, "ACarnegie," separated from the file extension (in this case, "jpg") by a period. The backslash characters (\), used by Windows, are referred to as **path separators**. OS X files use a colon (:), whereas UNIX and Linux files use the forward slash (/) as the path separator.

FIGURE 5.27

File-Naming Conventions

	OS X	WINDOWS
File and folder name length	As many as 255 characters*	As many as 255 characters
Case sensitive?	Yes	No
Forbidden characters	Colon (:)	" / \ * ? <> | :
File extensions needed?	No	Yes

Note: Although OS X supports file names with as many as 255 characters, many applications running on OS X still support only file names with a maximum of 31 characters.

C:\Documents\HIS182\Term Paper\Illustrations\ACarnegie.jpg

Drive   Primary Folder   Subfolders   File Name   Extension

FIGURE 5.28 Understanding File Paths

Working with Files

How can I move and copy files? Once you've located your file with File Explorer, you can perform many other file-management actions such as opening, copying, moving, renaming, and deleting files. You open a file by double-clicking the file from its storage location. You can copy a file to another location using the Copy command. To move a file from one location to another, use the Cut command. You can access both of these commands easily by right-clicking on a file's name, which displays a shortcut menu.

Where do deleted files go? The **Recycle Bin** is a folder on the desktop, represented by an icon that looks like a recycling bin, where files deleted from the hard drive reside until you permanently purge them from your system. Unfortunately, files deleted from other drives don't go to the Recycle Bin but are deleted from the system immediately. In addition, files stored in the cloud are not cycled through the Recycle Bin. When you delete a file from a Dropbox or SkyDrive folder, consider it gone forever!

Mac systems have something similar to the Recycle Bin, called Trash, which is represented by a wastebasket icon. To delete files on a Mac, drag the files to the Trash icon.

How do I permanently delete files from my system? Files placed in the Recycle Bin or the Trash remain in the system until they're permanently deleted. To delete files from the Recycle Bin permanently, select Empty Recycle Bin after right-clicking the desktop icon. On Macs, select Empty Trash from the Finder menu in OS X.

What happens if I need to recover a deleted file? Getting a file back after the Trash has been emptied still may be possible. When the Trash is emptied, only the reference to the file is deleted permanently, so the OS has no easy way to find the file. The file data actually remains on the hard drive until it's written over by another file. You may be able to use a program such as FarStone's RestoreIT! or Norton Ghost to try to retrieve files you think you've permanently deleted. These programs reveal files that are still intact on the hard drive and help you recover them. This is how they do it on CSI! ■

BITS&BYTES

A File Type for Everyone

Say you're sending an e-mail to a bunch of people. You're not sure which word processing software each person uses. How can you be sure everyone will be able to open your attachment? Save the file in Rich Text Format (.rtf), Plain Text (.txt) format, or Portable Document Format (.pdf). Rich Text Format and Plain Text files can be read by any modern word processing program, although some formatting may be lost when you save a document in Plain Text format. Anyone can read a PDF file by downloading the free Adobe Reader program from the Adobe website (**adobe.com**). To save files as RTF, TXT, of PDF files, simply change the file type when saving your file. In Microsoft Word, for example, you can select the file type in the "Save as type" list, shown in Figure 5.29.

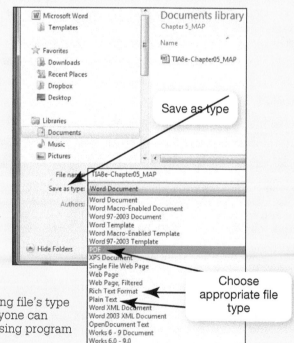

FIGURE 5.29 By changing a word processing file's type to PDF, RTF, or TXT, you can ensure that anyone can read your file, no matter which word processing program he or she uses.

utility

PROGRAMS

The main component of system software is the OS. However, *utility programs*—small applications that perform special functions on the computer—are also an essential part of system software. Utility programs come in three flavors:

1. Those that are included with the OS (such as System Restore)
2. Those sold as stand-alone programs (such as antivirus software)
3. Those offered as freeware (such as anti-malware software like Ad-Aware from Lavasoft)

Figure 5.30 lists some of the various types of utility programs available within the Windows OS as well as some alternatives available as stand-alone programs. In general, the basic utilities designed to manage and tune your computer hardware are incorporated into the OS. The stand-alone utility programs typically offer more features or an easier user interface for backup, security, diagnostic, or recovery functions. For some Windows

programs, like Task Manager and Resource Monitor, no good stand-alone alternatives exist.

In this section, we explore many of the utility programs you'll find installed on a Windows 8 OS. Unless otherwise noted, you can find Windows utilities in the Control Panel. We'll discuss antivirus and personal firewall utility programs in Chapter 9.

Display Utilities

How can I change the appearance of my Start screen and desktop? You can personalize the Start screen and the lock screen (the screen that forces you to enter a password to resume using your computer) to suit your tastes. To do so, display the Charms bar, select Settings, choose More PC settings, and then the Personalize option. This provides you with access to personalization options such as changing pictures, colors, and backgrounds. This also provides you with access to all the features you need to change the appearance of your desktop.

The Programs and Features Utility

What's the correct way to add new programs to my system? When you download Windows 8 apps from the Windows Store, they automatically

---

 ACTIVE HELPDESK
Using Utility Programs

In this Active Helpdesk call, you'll play the role of a helpdesk staffer, fielding calls about the utility programs included in system software and what these programs do.

FIGURE 5.30

Utility Programs Available Within Windows and as Stand-Alone Programs

WINDOWS UTILITY PROGRAM	STAND-ALONE ALTERNATIVES	WHAT IT DOES
File Explorer File Compression	WinZip, StuffIt	Reduces file size
Disk Cleanup	McAfee Total Protection	Removes unnecessary files from your hard drive
Error-Checking	SeaTools (free download from **seagate.com**)	Checks your hard drive for unnecessary or damaged files
Task Manager and Resource Monitor	None	Displays performance measures for processes; provides information on programs and processes running on your computer
Disk Defragmenter	Norton Utilities, iDefrag	Rearranges files on your hard drive to allow for faster access of files
System Restore	FarStone Snapshot, Acronis Backup and Security, Norton Ghost	Restores your system to a previous, stable state
File History, File Recovery	Acronis True Image, Norton Ghost	Backs up important files, makes a complete mirror image of your current computer setup

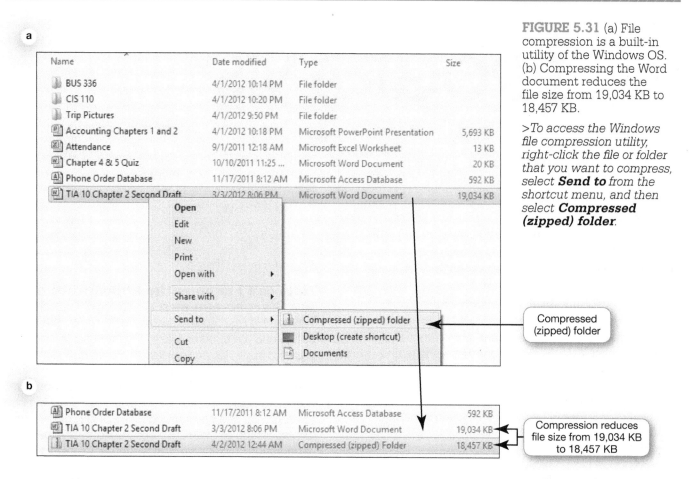

a

Name	Date modified	Type	Size
BUS 336	4/1/2012 10:14 PM	File folder	
CIS 110	4/1/2012 10:20 PM	File folder	
Trip Pictures	4/1/2012 9:50 PM	File folder	
Accounting Chapters 1 and 2	4/1/2012 10:18 PM	Microsoft PowerPoint Presentation	5,693 KB
Attendance	9/1/2011 12:18 AM	Microsoft Excel Worksheet	13 KB
Chapter 4 & 5 Quiz	10/10/2011 11:25 ...	Microsoft Word Document	20 KB
Phone Order Database	11/17/2011 8:12 AM	Microsoft Access Database	592 KB
TIA 10 Chapter 2 Second Draft	3/3/2012 8:06 PM	Microsoft Word Document	19,034 KB

Open
Edit
New
Print
Open with ▶
Share with ▶
Send to ▶
Cut
Copy

Compressed (zipped) folder
Desktop (create shortcut)
Documents

Compressed (zipped) folder

b

Phone Order Database	11/17/2011 8:12 AM	Microsoft Access Database	592 KB
TIA 10 Chapter 2 Second Draft	3/3/2012 8:06 PM	Microsoft Word Document	19,034 KB
TIA 10 Chapter 2 Second Draft	4/2/2012 12:44 AM	Compressed (zipped) Folder	18,457 KB

Compression reduces file size from 19,034 KB to 18,457 KB

FIGURE 5.31 (a) File compression is a built-in utility of the Windows OS. (b) Compressing the Word document reduces the file size from 19,034 KB to 18,457 KB.

>*To access the Windows file compression utility, right-click the file or folder that you want to compress, select* **Send to** *from the shortcut menu, and then select* **Compressed (zipped) folder***.*

install on your computer. If you install non-Windows 8 programs, the program usually automatically runs a *wizard* that walks you through the installation process. If a wizard doesn't start automatically, open the Control Panel, click Programs, then click Programs and Features. This prompts the OS to look for the setup program of the new software, and it starts the installation wizard.

What's the correct way to remove unwanted programs from my system? You can quickly uninstall Windows 8 apps by right-clicking their icon on the Start screen (or touching and holding) and selecting the Uninstall option from the app bar. For non-Windows 8 programs, you should use the Windows uninstaller utility found in Programs in the Control Panel. Using either of these methods ensures that you delete not only the main program files but also all supporting files and most registry entries.

File Compression Utilities

Why would I want to use a file compression utility? File compression makes a large file more compact, making it easier and faster for you to send large attachments by e-mail, upload them to the web, or save them onto a disc. As shown in Figure 5.31, Windows has a built-in **file compression utility**

that takes out redundancies in a file (zips it) to reduce the file size. You can also obtain several stand-alone freeware and shareware programs, such as WinZip (for Windows) and StuffIt (for Windows or Mac), to compress your files.

How does file compression work? Most compression programs look for repeated patterns of letters and replace these patterns with a shorter placeholder. The repeated patterns and the associated placeholder are cataloged and stored temporarily in a separate file called the *dictionary*. For example, in the following sentence, you can easily see the repeated patterns of letters.

The rain in Spain falls mainly on the plain.

Although this example contains obvious repeated patterns (ain and the), in a large document, the repeated patterns may be more complex. The compression

 SOUND BYTE
File Compression

In this Sound Byte, you'll learn about the advantages of file compression and how to use Windows to compress and decompress files. This Sound Byte also teaches you how to find and install file compression shareware programs.

STEP 1: Right-click zipped folder

STEP 2: Select Extract All...

STEP 3: Browse to storage location

STEP 4: Extracted file displays in selected location

FIGURE 5.32 The Extraction Wizard in Windows makes unzipping compressed folders and files easy.

program's algorithm (a set of instructions designed to complete a solution in a step-by-step manner) therefore runs through the file several times to determine the optimal repeated patterns needed to obtain the greatest compression.

How effective are file compression programs? Current compression programs can reduce text files by 50% or more, depending on the file. However, some files, such as PDF files, already contain a form of compression, so they don't need to be compressed further. Image files such as JPEG, GIF, and PNG files discard small variations in color that the human eye might not pick up. Likewise, MP3 files permanently discard sounds that the human ear can't hear. These graphic and audio files don't need further compression.

How do I decompress a file I've compressed? When you want to restore the file to its original state, you need to *decompress* the file. Generally, the program you used to compress the file can decompress the file as well (see Figure 5.32).

System Maintenance Utilities

What utilities can make my system work faster? Disk Cleanup is a Windows utility that removes unnecessary files from your hard drive. These include files that have accumulated in the Recycle Bin as well as temporary files—files created by Windows to store

data temporarily while a program is running. Windows usually deletes these temporary files when you exit the program, but sometimes it forgets to do this or doesn't have time because your system freezes or incurs a problem that prevents you from properly exiting a program.

Disk Cleanup also removes temporary Internet files (web pages stored on your hard drive for quick viewing) as well as offline web pages (pages stored on your computer so you can view them without being connected to the Internet). If not deleted periodically, these unnecessary files can slow down your computer.

How can I control which files Disk Cleanup deletes? When you run Disk Cleanup, the program scans your hard drive to determine which folders have files that can be deleted and calculates the amount of hard drive space that will be freed up by doing so. You check off which type of files you would like to delete, as shown in Figure 5.33.

How can I diagnose potential errors or damage on my hard drive? Error-checking is a Windows utility that checks for lost files and fragments as well as physical errors on your hard drive. Lost files and fragments of files occur as you save, resave, move, delete, and copy files on your hard drive. Sometimes the system becomes confused, leaving references on the **file allocation table**, or **FAT** (an index of all sector numbers in a table), to files that no longer exist or have been moved. Physical errors on the hard drive occur when the mechanism that reads the hard drive's data (which is stored as 1s or 0s) can no longer determine whether the area holds a 1 or a 0. These areas are called *bad sectors*. Sometimes Error-checking can recover the lost data, but more often, it deletes the files that are taking up space.

Error-checking also makes a note of any bad sectors so that the system won't use them again to store data. To locate Error-checking in Windows 8, display File Explorer, right-click the disk you want to diagnose, select Properties, and select the Tools tab. On Macs, you can use the Disk Utility to test and repair disks. Disk Utility is located in the Utilities subfolder in the Applications folder on your hard drive.

How can I check on a program that's stopped running? If a program has stopped working, you can use the Windows **Task Manager**

FIGURE 5.33 Using Disk Cleanup will help free space on your hard drive.

>*Disk Cleanup is accessed by displaying File Explorer, right-clicking on the disk you wish to clean, selecting* **Properties** *from the shortcut menu, and then clicking the* **Disk Cleanup** *button on the General tab.*

utility (see Figure 5.34) to check on the program or to exit the nonresponsive program. In Windows 8, the Processes tab of Task Manager lists all the programs you're using and indicates their status. "Not responding" will be shown next to a program that stopped improperly. If the status section is blank (Figure 5.34), then the program is working normally. You can terminate programs that aren't responding by right-clicking the app name and selecting End Task from the shortcut menu.

System Restore and Backup Utilities

Is there an undo command for the system?
Suppose you've just installed a new software program and your computer freezes. After rebooting the computer, when you try to start the application, the system freezes once again. You uninstall the new program, but your computer continues to freeze after rebooting. What can you do now?

 SOUND BYTE
Hard Disk Anatomy

In this Sound Byte, you'll watch a series of animations that show various aspects of a hard drive, including the anatomy of a hard drive, how a computer reads and writes data to a hard drive, and the fragmenting and defragmenting of a hard drive.

FIGURE 5.34 You can use Windows 8 Task Manager to close nonresponsive programs.

>*Task Manager is accessed by holding down* **Ctrl**, **Alt**, *and* **Del** *or by right-clicking on the taskbar at the bottom of the desktop.*

DIG DEEPER

How Disk Defragmenter Utilities Work

Disk defragmenting programs group together related pieces of files on the hard drive, allowing the OS to work more efficiently. To understand how disk defragmenter utilities work, you first need to understand the basics of how a hard disk drive stores files. A hard disk drive is composed of several platters, or round, thin plates of metal, covered with a special magnetic coating that records the data. The platters are about 3.5 inches in diameter and are stacked onto a spindle. There are usually two or three platters in any hard disk drive, with data stored on one or both sides. Data is recorded on hard disks in concentric circles called **tracks**. Each track is further broken down into pie-shaped wedges, each called a **sector** (see Figure 5.35). The data is further identified by **clusters**, which are the smallest segments within the sectors.

When you want to save (or write) a file, the bits that make up your file are recorded onto one or more clusters of the drive. To keep track of which clusters hold which files, the drive also stores an index of all sector numbers in a table. To save a file, the computer looks in the table for clusters that aren't already being used. It then records the file information on those clusters. When you open (or read) a file, the computer searches through the table for the clusters that hold the desired file and reads that file. Similarly, when you delete a file, you're actually not deleting the file itself but rather the reference in the table to the file.

So, how does a disk become fragmented? When only part of an older file is deleted, the deleted section of the file creates a gap in the sector of the disk where the data was originally stored. In the same way, when new information is added to an older file, there may not be space to save the new information sequentially near where the file was originally saved. In that case, the system writes the added part of the file to the next available location on the disk, and a reference is made in the table as to the location of this file fragment. Over time, as files are saved, deleted, and modified, the bits of information for various files fall out of order and the disk becomes fragmented.

Disk fragmentation is a problem because the OS isn't as efficient when a disk is fragmented. It takes longer to locate a whole file because more of the disk must be searched for the various pieces, slowing down your computer.

Defragmenting tools take the hard drive through a defragmentation process in which pieces of files scattered over the disk are placed together and arranged sequentially on it. Also, any unused portions of clusters that were too small to save data in before are grouped, increasing the available storage space on the disk. Figure 5.36 shows before and after shots of a fragmented disk that has gone through the defragmentation process.

The disk defragmentation utility in Windows 8 is set by default to automatically defragment the hard drive on a regular basis. Macs don't have a defragmentation utility built into the system. Those users who feel the need to defragment their Mac can use iDefrag, an external program from Coriolis Systems. For more about hard disks and defragmenting, check out the Sound Byte "Hard Disk Anatomy."

FIGURE 5.35 On a hard disk platter, data is recorded onto tracks, which are further divided into sectors and clusters.

Track

Sector

Cluster

Fragmented files on disk

Defragmented files on disk

FIGURE 5.36 Defragmenting the hard drive arranges file fragments so that they are located next to each other. This makes the hard drive run more efficiently.

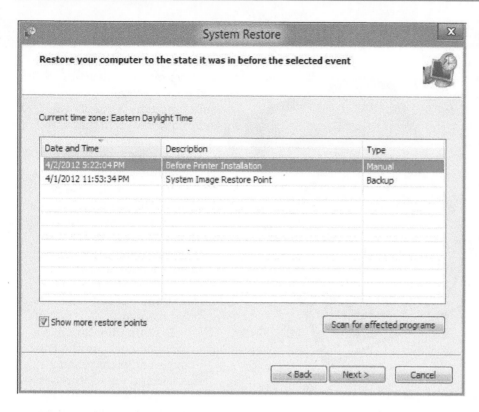

FIGURE 5.37 This System Restore Wizard shows a restore point set manually by a user and automatically by Windows before a backup was run. Setting a restore point is good practice before installing any hardware or software.

>*The System Restore Wizard is found by accessing the Control Panel, choosing **System and Security**, clicking the **System** link, selecting **System Protection**, and then clicking the **System Restore** button. The System Restore Wizard appears, with the restore points shown on the second page of the Wizard.*

Windows has a utility called **System Restore** that lets you roll your system settings back to a specific date when everything was working properly. A **system restore point**, which is a snapshot of your entire system's settings, is generated prior to certain events, such as installing or updating software, or automatically once a week if no other restore points were created in that time. You also can create a restore point manually at any time.

Should problems occur, if the computer was running just fine before you installed new software or a hardware device, you could restore your computer to the settings that were in effect before the software or hardware installation (see Figure 5.37). System Restore doesn't affect your personal data files (such as Word documents or e-mail), so you won't lose changes made to these files.

How can I protect my data in the event something malfunctions in my system? When you use the Windows 8 **File History** utility (found in the Control Panel under System and Security), you can have Windows automatically create a duplicate of your libraries, desktop, contacts, and favorites and copy it to another storage device, such as an external hard drive. A backup copy protects your data in the event your hard drive fails or files are accidentally erased. The Windows 7 File Recovery tools are still available in Windows 8 and allow you to have Windows make complete backups of your entire system that you can later restore in the event of a major hard drive crash.

OS X includes a backup utility called Time Machine that automatically backs up your files to a specified location. Apple also offers backup hardware called Time Capsules, which are hard disk drives with wireless connectivity, designed to work with Time Machine and record your backup data. Because Time Machine makes a complete image copy of your system, it can also be used to recover your system in the case of a fatal error. (For more information on backing up your files, see Chapter 9.)

SOUND BYTE

Letting Your Computer Clean Up After Itself

In this Sound Byte, you'll learn how to use the various maintenance utilities within the OS. In addition, you'll learn how to use Task Scheduler to clean up your hard drive automatically. You'll also learn the best times of the day to schedule these maintenance tasks and why they should be done on a routine basis to make your system more efficient.

FIGURE 5.38

Windows Ease of Access Tools

MAGNIFIER
- Creates a separate window that displays a magnified portion of the screen

NARRATOR
- Reads what is on screen
- Can read the contents of a window, menu options, or text you have typed

SPEECH RECOGNITION
- Allows you to dictate text and control your computer by voice

ON-SCREEN KEYBOARD
- Allows you to type with a pointing device

HIGH CONTRAST
- Color schemes invert screen colors for vision-impaired individuals

Easier to Read!

(Imagery Majestic/Fotolia; Anatoly Maslennikov/Fotolia; gilles lougassi/Fotolia)

>*The Ease of Access Center is found by accessing the Control Panel and clicking* **Ease of Access**.

Accessibility Utilities

What utilities are designed for users with special needs? Microsoft Windows includes an Ease of Access Center, which is a centralized location for assistive technology and tools to adjust accessibility settings. In the Ease of Access Center, which is accessible from the Control Panel, you can find the tools to help users with disabilities, shown in Figure 5.38. The tools shown in the figure are just a sampling of the available tools. If you're not sure where to start or what settings might help, a questionnaire asks you about routine tasks and provides a personalized recommendation for settings that will help you better use your computer.

Whether you use Windows, OS X, Linux, or another operating system, a fully featured OS is available to meet your needs. As long as you keep the operating system updated and regularly use the available utilities to fine-tune your system, you should experience little trouble from your OS. ∎

Before moving on to the Chapter Review:
- Watch Replay Video 5.2 ▶.
- **Then check your understanding of what you've learned so far.**

---

check your understanding//

For a quick review to see what you've learned so far, answer the following questions. Visit **pearsonhighered.com/ techinaction** to check your answers.

multiple choice

1. Which of the following is NOT considered an accessibility utility?

   a. System Restore
   c. Narrator

   b. Magnifier
   d. Speech Recognition

2. Windows 8 apps

   a. run on the desktop.

   b. run full screen.

   c. can't be closed down once started.

   d. use a large amount of RAM.

3. The Windows app used for file management is

   a. Disk Manager.
   c. File Explorer.

   b. Task Manager.
   d. Library Explorer.

4. The location of a file on a drive such as C:\Documents\ CIS110\Homework\Termpaper.docx is known as the

   a. document location.

   b. file path.

   c. file position.

   d. file address.

5. The _____ utility is used for detecting lost files and fragments of files on your hard drive.

   a. Disk Cleanup

   b. Disk Defragmenter

   c. Error-checking

   d. System Refresh

true–false

_____ 1. You can terminate nonresponsive programs with Task Manager.

_____ 2. System restore points can only be created by Windows automatically on a regular schedule.

critical thinking

1. **To Hackintosh or Not: That Is the Question**

   Using Mac's Boot Camp, or virtualization software such as VMware, it's easy (and legal) to install Windows on a Mac. It isn't quite as easy to install OS X on a PC, but it can be done. A PC that has been modified so that OS X can be run on it is called a *Hackintosh*. What are the benefits of tweaking a PC to run OS X? Is it okay to violate Apple's End User Licensing Agreement (EULA), which prohibits installation of OS X on non–Apple-branded equipment? If Apple changed its EULA to allow the installation of its software onto PCs, would that ultimately hurt Apple-branded computers?

2. **What App Is Best for You?**

   There are plenty of interesting apps available for Windows and Apple devices—some for fun, some to aid in productivity, some with specific utilitarian roles. Design or describe what the best app for you would be. What features must it have? Why would you need it?

5 Chapter Review

summary //

Operating System Fundamentals

1. What software is included in system software?

- System software is the set of software programs that helps run the computer and coordinates instructions between application software and hardware devices. It consists of the operating system (OS) and utility programs.
- The OS controls how your computer system functions.
- Utility programs are programs that perform general housekeeping tasks for the computer, such as system maintenance and file compression.

2. What are the different kinds of operating systems?

- There are many different kinds of operating systems.
- Real-time operating systems (RTOSs) require no user intervention. They are designed for systems with a specific purpose and response time (such as robotic machinery).
- A multiuser operating system (network operating system) provides access to a computer system by more than one user at a time.
- Smartphones have their own specific operating systems, which allow the user to multitask.
- Tablets use operating systems (such as iOS, Android, and Windows 8) that allow interaction with touch-screen interfaces.
- Gaming consoles use operating systems developed specifically for those particular devices.
- Current operating systems for desktops, laptops, and netbooks have multitasking and networking capabilities.

3. What are the most common operating systems?

- Microsoft Windows is the most popular OS. It has evolved into a powerful multiuser OS. The most recent release is Windows 8.
- Another popular OS is the Mac OS, which is designed to work on Apple computers. Apple's most recent release, Mac OS X, is based on the UNIX OS.
- There are various versions of UNIX on the market, although UNIX is most often used on networks.
- Linux is an open source OS based on UNIX and designed primarily for use on personal computers, although it is often used on servers and supercomputers.

What the Operating System Does

4. How does the operating system provide a means for users to interact with the computer?

- The OS provides a user interface that enables users to interact with the computer.
- Most OSs today use a graphical user interface (GUI). Unlike the command- and menu-driven interfaces used many years ago, GUIs display graphics and use the point-and-click technology of the mouse and cursor (or touch-sensitive screens), making the OS more user-friendly. Common features of GUIs include windows, menus, and icons.

5. How does the operating system help manage resources such as the processor, memory, storage, hardware, and peripheral devices?

- When the OS allows you to perform more than one task at a time, it is multitasking. To provide for seamless multitasking, the OS controls the timing of the events on which the processor works.
- As the OS coordinates the activities of the processor, it uses RAM as a temporary storage area for instructions and data the processor needs. The OS is therefore responsible for coordinating the space allocations in RAM to ensure that there is enough space for the waiting instructions and data. If there isn't sufficient space in RAM for all the data and instructions, then the OS allocates the least necessary files to temporary storage on the hard drive, called *virtual memory*.
- The OS manages storage by providing a file-management system that keeps track of the names and locations of files and programs.
- Programs called *device drivers* facilitate communication between devices attached to the computer and the OS. Device drivers translate the specialized commands of devices to commands that the OS can understand, and vice versa, enabling the OS to communicate with every device in the computer system. Device drivers for common devices are included in the OS software.

6. How does the operating system interact with application software?

- All software applications need to interact with the CPU. For programs to work with the CPU, they must contain code that the CPU recognizes.

- Rather than having the same blocks of code appear in each application, the OS includes the blocks of code to which software applications refer. These blocks of code are called *application programming interfaces* (APIs).

The Boot Process: Starting Your Computer

7. How does the operating system help the computer start up?

- When you start your computer, it runs through a special process called the *boot process*.
- The boot process consists of four basic steps: (1) The basic input/output system (BIOS) is activated when the user powers on the CPU. (2) In the POST check, the BIOS verifies that all attached devices are in place. (3) The OS is loaded into RAM. (4) Configuration and customization settings are checked.

The Windows Interface

8. What are the main features of the Windows interface?

- In Windows 8, the Start screen provides your first interaction with the OS and is the first image you see on your monitor once the system has booted up. It provides you with access to your computer's apps, tools, and commonly used programs.
- The Windows 8 interface is designed for touch-screen devices.
- Windows 8 apps run full screen and feature commands hidden in app bars.
- Non-Windows 8 programs run on the desktop.

Organizing Your Computer: File Management

9. How does the operating system help me keep my computer organized?

- The OS allows you to organize the contents of your computer in a hierarchical structure of directories that includes files, folders, libraries, and drives.
- File Explorer helps you manage your files and folders by showing the location and contents of every drive, folder, and file on your computer.
- Creating folders is the key to organizing files because folders keep related documents together.
- Following naming conventions and using proper file extensions are also important aspects of file management.

Utility Programs

10. What utility programs are included in system software and what do they do?

- Some utility programs are incorporated into the OS; others are sold as stand-alone off-the-shelf programs.
- Common Windows utilities include those that enable you to adjust your display, add or remove programs, compress files, clean unnecessary files off your system, check for lost files and errors, restore your system to an earlier setting, back up your files, and check on programs that have stopped running.

> Be sure to check out the companion website for additional materials to help you review and learn, including a Tech Bytes Weekly newsletter—**pearsonhighered.com/techinaction**. And don't forget the Replay Videos .

key terms//

making the transition to . . . next semester //

1. **Organizing Your Files**

   Despite all the good advice, you may not have taken the time to organize your files on your computer. On the Start screen, click File Explorer, and select Documents. Then, use the Snipping Tool to show your current file organization. If your system is well organized, explain how you set up your file-management system. If you haven't used file-management features to organize your documents, develop a plan that outlines how you'll set up libraries, folders, and subfolders for your files.

2. **Deciding on a New Computer**

   You decide it is time to buy a new computer. Decide whether you want a desktop, laptop, tablet, or netbook and then describe how the choice may affect the OS you get.

   a. Discuss the advantages and disadvantages of Windows, Mac, and Linux operating systems.

   b. Research whether you can use multiple operating systems on a single machine. Why might this be an important feature for you to consider?

   c. Research how your smartphone and personal music player might sync with your computer's OS.

   d. Explain which OS would be most useful to you and why.

3. **Creating a Backup Plan**

   Your computer just shut down unexpectedly, but fortunately, you were able to get it back up and running without any loss of data. However, this was too close of a call, so you decide to back up your precious files once and for all. Research the specific steps you'll need to take to create a backup initially and then maintain a current backup as your files change. Include in your research what stand-alone programs or OS tools you'll need to use, as well as any hardware devices or accessories you'll require. Then research the process of creating a disk image. What's the difference between creating a system backup and a disk image?

making the transition to . . . the workplace //

1. **Using a Web-Based OS**

   Your new job requires you to collaborate and visit with sales and management teams within the United States as well as globally. Discuss the benefits and disadvantages of using a web-based OS as a means to help you perform your job better.

2. **Top-Five Utility Programs**

   Create a list of the top-five utilities you feel every computer should have. For each utility, discuss whether it is included in the OS and/or if there are alternatives that can be downloaded for free or that can be purchased as stand-alone programs. Then, for each recommendation, include a review of the utility that has been written in the past year—make sure you document your sources.

3. **Accessibility Features**

   Windows offers a lot of great accessibility tools for those needing extra assistance. The vice president of human resources at the company you work for has asked you to research some stand-alone accessibility programs to determine what else, if anything, is available. List software that is available to help those who have special computing needs.

team time//

Choosing the Best OS

Problem

You're the owner of a technology consulting firm. Your current assignments include advising several startup clients on their technology requirements. The companies include a fashion design company, a small financial planning company, and an IT networking firm. The companies are holding off on buying anything until they hear from you as to the hardware and software they should purchase. Obviously, one of the critical decisions for each company is the choice of OS.

Task

Recommend the appropriate OS for each company.

Process

1. Break up into teams that represent the three primary operating systems: Windows, Mac, or Linux. (Additional teams could be assigned to consider smartphone or tablet operating systems.)

2. As a team, research the pros and cons of your OS. What features does it have that would benefit each company? What features does it not have that each company would need? Why would your OS be the appropriate (or inappropriate) choice for each company? Why is your OS better (or worse) than either of the other options?

3. Develop a presentation that states your position with regard to your OS. Your presentation should have a recommendation and include facts to back it up.

4. As a class, decide which OS would be the best choice for each company.

Conclusion

Because the OS is the most critical piece of software in the computer system, the selection should not be taken lightly. The OS that is best for a fashion design agency may not be best for a financial planning firm. An IT networking firm may have different needs altogether. It is important to make sure you consider all aspects of the work environment and the type of work being done to ensure a good fit.

Software Piracy

In this exercise, you'll research and then role-play a complicated ethical situation. The role you play may or may not match your own personal beliefs, but your research and use of logic will enable you to represent whichever view is assigned. An arbitrator will watch and comment on both sides of the arguments, and together, the team will agree on an ethical solution.

Problem

Software publishers spend millions of dollars developing new products. Illegal copies of software, including OS software, rob the developers and their shareholders of their rightful profits. In addition, some say that pervasive software piracy, especially in China, could potentially cause job loss for U.S. software companies. However, some people believe that when they buy the software, they have the right to distribute their copies as they like, thus violating the software license agreement they accepted when installing the software.

Research Areas to Consider

- Software piracy
- Software licensing agreements
- CD piracy
- China's antipiracy efforts/laws

Process

1. Divide the class into teams.
2. Research the areas cited above and devise a scenario in which an individual has been accused of software piracy.
3. Team members should write a summary that provides background information for their character—for example, representative of a software developer, public consumer of the software, or arbitrator—and that details their character's behaviors to set the stage for the role-playing event. Then, team members should create an outline to use during the role-playing event.
4. Team members should arrange a mutually convenient time to meet for the exchange, using either the collaboration feature of MyITLab or the discussion board feature of your course management software or by meeting in person.
5. Team members should present their case to the class or submit a PowerPoint presentation for review by the rest of the class, along with the summary and resolution they developed.

Conclusion

As technology becomes ever more prevalent and integrated into our lives, more and more ethical dilemmas will present themselves. Being able to understand and evaluate both sides of the argument, while responding in a personally or socially ethical manner, will be an important skill.

Technology in Focus

Information Technology Ethics

The ethical choices we make have a far-reaching impact on our lives. In this Technology in Focus feature, we examine how technology and ethics affect each other. We'll discuss several key issues related to technology and ethics, including the following:

- Intellectual property rights
- Privacy
- E-commerce
- Free speech
- Computer abuse

But first, let's get started by asking an important question: What is ethics?

What Is Ethics?

Ethics is the study of the general nature of morals and of the specific moral choices individuals make. Morals involve conforming to established or accepted ideas of right and wrong (as generally dictated by society) and are usually viewed as being black and white. Ethical issues often involve subtle distinctions, such as the difference between fairness and equity. Ethical principles are the guidelines you use to make decisions each day.

For example, say you stop to use a photocopier on campus. You discover a copy of the upcoming final exam for your psychology course that your teacher left behind in class. Do you give it back to your professor without looking at the questions? Do you share it with your friends so you can all get good grades on the final? Do you give a copy to your friend who really needs to pass the course in order to prevent losing his or her financial aid?

Doesn't everyone have the same basic ethics? There are many systems of ethical conduct. Figure 1 lists the five major ethical systems.

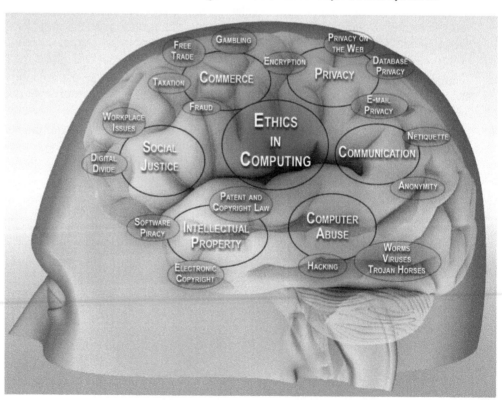

FIGURE 1

Systems of Ethics

ETHICAL SYSTEM	BASIC TENETS	EXAMPLES
Relativism	• No universal moral truth • Moral principles dictated by cultural tastes and customs	Topless bathing is prevalent in Europe but generally banned on public beaches in the United States
Divine Command Theory	• God is all-knowing and sets moral standards • Conforming to God's law is right, breaking it is wrong	Christians believe in rules such as the Ten Commandments
Utilitarianism	• Actions are judged solely by consequences • Actions that generate greater happiness are judged to be better than actions that lead to unhappiness • Individual happiness is not important—consider the greater good	Using weapons of mass destruction ends a war sooner and therefore saves lives otherwise destroyed by conventional fighting
Virtue Ethics	• Morals are internal • Strive to be a person who behaves well spontaneously	A supervisor views the person who volunteered to clean up a park as a better person than the workers who are there because of court-ordered community service
Deontology (Duty-Based)	• Focus on adherence to moral duties and rights • Morals should apply to everyone equally	Human rights (like freedom of religion) should be respected for all people because human rights should be applied universally

(Solomin Andrey/Fotolia; Sergey Galushko/Fotolia; kentoh/Fotolia; Alexmillos/Fotolia; Scanrail/Fotolia)

Aren't laws meant to guide people's ethical actions? Laws are formal, written standards designed to apply to everyone. Laws are enforced by government agencies and interpreted by the courts. However, it's impossible to pass laws that cover every possible behavior in which humans can engage. Therefore, ethics provide a general set of unwritten guidelines for people to follow.

Is unethical behavior the same as illegal behavior? Unethical behavior isn't necessarily illegal. Take the death penalty. In many U.S. states, putting convicted criminals to death for certain crimes is legal. However, many people consider it unethical to execute a human for any reason.

Not all illegal behavior is unethical, though. Civil disobedience, which is manifested by intentionally refusing to obey certain laws, is used as a form of protest to effect change. Gandhi's nonviolent resistance to the British rule of India, which led to India's establishment as an independent country, is an example of civil disobedience. Is it ever ethical for one country to control another country's people?

Note that there is also a difference between *unethical* behavior and *amoral* behavior:

- *Unethical behavior* can be defined as not conforming to a set of approved standards of behavior. For instance, using your phone to text message a test answer to your friend during an exam is unethical.
- *Amoral behavior* occurs when a person has no sense of right and wrong and no interest in the moral consequences of his or her actions, such as when a murderer shows no remorse for his or her crime.

Which system of ethics works best? There is no universal agreement on which is the best system of ethics. Most societies use a blend of different systems. Regardless of the ethical system of the society in which you live, all ethical decisions are greatly influenced by personal ethics.

Personal Ethics

What are personal ethics? Every day you say and do certain things, and each time, you're making decisions. As you choose your words and actions, you're following a set of **personal ethics**—a set of

FIGURE 2 It would be nice if there were signposts to ethical conduct, but the issues are complex. *(Iqoncept/Shutterstock)*

formal or informal ethical principles you use to make decisions in your life. Some people have a clear, well-defined set of principles they follow. Others' ethics are inconsistent or are applied differently in different situations.

It can be challenging to adhere to your own ethical principles if the consequences of your decisions might lead to an unhappy result. For example, to get the job of your dreams, should you say on your résumé that you've already finished your degree, even though you're still one credit short? Is this lying? Is such behavior justified in this setting? After all, you do intend to finish that last credit, and you would work really hard for this company if you were hired. If you tell the truth and state that you haven't finished college yet, you might be passed over for the position. Making this choice is an ethical decision (see Figure 2).

How do a person's ethics develop?
Naturally, your family plays a major role in establishing the values you cherish in your own life, and these might include a cultural bias toward certain ethical positions (see Figure 3). Your religious affiliation is another major

Family

Don't litter.

FIGURE 3 Many different forces shape your personal ethics. *(Noam Armonn/Shutterstock; AISPIX by Image Source/Shutterstock; Rachel Donahue/iStockphoto; Rob Marmion/Shutterstock)*

Religion

Don't tell lies.

Your ethical behavior

Experience

Don't speed or you'll get a ticket.

Teachers

Don't cheat on tests or you'll fail.

influence on your ethics, because most religions have established codes of ethical conduct. How these sets of ethics interact with the values of the larger culture is often challenging. Issues such as abortion, the death penalty, and war often create conflict between personal ethical systems and the larger society's established legal-ethical system.

As you mature, your life experiences also affect your personal ethics. Does the behavior you see around you make sense within the ethical principles that your family, your church, or your first-grade teacher taught you? Has your experience led you to abandon some ethical rules and adopt others? Have you modified how and when you apply these laws of conduct depending on what's at stake?

What if I'm not sure what my personal ethics are? When you have a clear idea of what values are important to you, it may be easier to handle situations in your life that demand ethical action. Follow these steps to help define a list of personal values:

1. **Describe yourself.** Write down words that describe who you are, based on how others view you. Would a friend describe you as honest, or helpful, or kind? These keywords will give you a hint as to the values and behaviors that are important to you.

2. **List the key principles you believe in.** Make a list of the key principles that influence your decisions. For example, would you be comfortable working in a lab that used animals for medical research? If not, is it because you value protecting any living being? How important is it to you that you never tell a lie? Or do you feel it is kind to lie in some situations? List the key ideas you believe to be important in conducting your life. Do you always behave this way, or are you "flexible"? Are there situations in which your answers might change (say, if the medical research was to cure cancer or the lie was to protect someone's feelings)?

3. **Identify external influences.** Where did your key principles come from—your parents? Your friends? Spiritual advisors? Television and movies? You may want to question some of your beliefs once you actually identify where they came from.

4. **Consider "why."** After writing down your beliefs, think about *why* you believe them. Have you accepted them without investigation? Do they stand up in the context of your real-world experiences?

5. **Prepare a statement of values.** Distill what you have written into a short statement. By having a well-defined statement of the values you hold most important in your own life, which you can refer to in times of challenge, it will be easier for you to make ethical decisions.

What are the benefits to ethical living? Society has established its own set of rules of conduct in the form of laws. Ignoring or being inconsistent in following these rules can have an immediate impact. And more and more research is showing the health benefits of ethical living. When your day-to-day decisions are in conflict with your ethical principles, you often develop stress and anger.

Perhaps even happiness itself is a result of living ethically (see Figure 4). **Positive psychology** is a new focus in the field of psychology. Pioneered by Dr. Martin Seligman of the University of Pennsylvania,

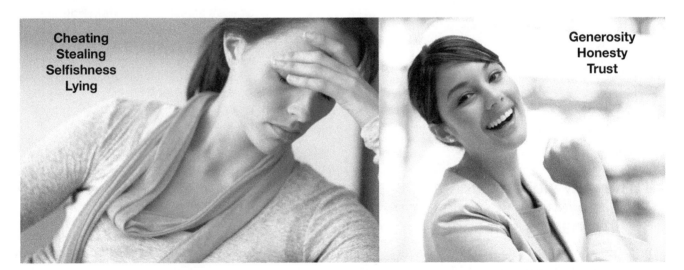

Cheating
Stealing
Selfishness
Lying

Generosity
Honesty
Trust

FIGURE 4 The field of positive psychology shows that living and working ethically affects your happiness. *(Yuri Arcurs/Shutterstock; Yuri Arcurs/Shutterstock)*

this field works to discover the *causes* of happiness instead of addressing the treatment of mental dysfunctions. Dr. Seligman's research has shown that by identifying your personal strengths and values and then aligning your life so that you can apply them every day you can be happier (and suffer less depression)—an effect equivalent to that of antidepressant medication and therapy. Thus, finding a way to identify and then apply your ethics and values to your daily life can impact your health and happiness.

Personal Ethics and Your Work Life

How do employers affect personal ethics?
You may have a set of personal ethics that guide your behavior, but do your ethics change when you go to work? Of course, your employer expects you to follow the rules of conduct established for the business. However, this doesn't mean you need to blindly follow corporate practices that you feel are unethical or detrimental to society (see Figure 5).

If you spot unethical behavior at your company, what do you do?
Whistle-blowers are people who report businesses to regulatory agencies for committing illegal acts or who expose unethical (but still legal) acts committed by their employers by publicizing unethical behavior through various media outlets. The Sarbanes–Oxley Act of 2002 requires companies to provide mechanisms for employees and third parties to report complaints, including ethics violations, anonymously. In addition, many businesses are using their websites to allow whistle-blowers to report wrongdoing anonymously, replacing previously used e-mail and telephone hotline systems, which did not shield employees from being identified. With an online system, it's easier for a company to sort and classify complaints and designate them for appropriate action.

Should your employer have control over your conduct outside of the office?
Do behavior, integrity, and honesty off the job relate to job performance? They might. But even if they don't, from your employer's perspective, your actions could reflect poorly on your employer. Consider the Transportation Security Administration (TSA) officer who was fired from his job at Chicago's O'Hare airport for making racist remarks about certain types of passengers on his Facebook page. He claimed his remarks were just an exercise of his First Amendment right to free speech. Obviously, his TSA supervisors thought his comments reflected poorly on the agency. Therefore, although your ethics might dictate one mode of behavior, you need to consider how your employer might view your actions.

How does making ethical choices in a business setting differ from making personal ethical choices?
Most personal ethical decisions involve few people. However, before making an ethical choice for a business, you need to consider the effect your choice will have on all of the business's stakeholders. **Stakeholders** are those people or entities who are affected by the operations of a business. Typical business stakeholders include customers, suppliers, employees, investors (shareholders), financial lenders, and society at large.

For instance, suppose you decide to cut costs in your restaurant by hiring workers "off the books" by paying them in cash. Although doing so might boost profits in the short term, the long-term impact on stakeholders can be severe. If you're caught avoiding paying payroll taxes by paying workers in cash, fines will be levied against your business, which may cause investors to lose money and may affect the company's

MIKE SHAPIRO

"The new hidden cameras will allow us to see if anyone is violating our privacy policy by reading someone else's email."

FIGURE 5 How should you respond if you see people in authority at work behaving unethically? *(Shapiro Mike/CSL, CartoonStock Ltd)*

ability to repay lenders. The negative publicity from being caught doing something illegal may cause a downturn in business, which, in turn, might force layoffs of employees or even closure of the business. Your simple decision on cutting costs isn't as simple as it may seem.

In summary, in a business environment, your behavior is guided by the ethical principles defined by the business owner or management, but you're ultimately guided by your own personal ethics.

Technology and Ethics: How One Affects the Other

Because technology moves faster than rules can be formulated to govern it, how technology is used is often left up to the individual and the guidance of his or her personal ethics. In the rest of this Technology in Focus feature, we explore situations in which ethics and technology affect each other: social justice (brain technology), intellectual property (international piracy), privacy (personal privacy and technology), e-commerce (geolocation), electronic communication (free speech), and computer abuse (cyberbullying).

Ethical considerations are never clear-cut. They're complex, and reasonable people can have different, yet equally valid, views. We present alternative viewpoints in each setting for you to consider and discuss. Figure 6 summarizes the issues we'll be discussing.

FIGURE 6

Ethics in Computing

TOPIC	ETHICAL DISCUSSION	DEBATE ISSUE
Social justice	Does the deployment of technology to alter the human brain blur the lines between human and machine?	Will brain technology make some humans superior to others?
Intellectual property	Do entire countries support software piracy?	Can we impose our values and intellectual property laws on the world?
Privacy	Can employers peer into your personal profiles on social media sites?	Should personal privacy be protected?
E-commerce	Do geolocation devices and applications threaten privacy?	Do the benefits of geolocation devices and applications outweigh the risks?
Electronic communication	When does big business limit free speech?	Should companies allow the Chinese government to dictate when to curtail free speech?
Computer abuse	Whose responsibility is it to monitor cyberbullying?	Should parents bear all the responsibility of monitoring cyberbullying, or should it be in the hands of public officials?

Social Justice

Brain Technology: Creating Cyborgs?

Summary of the Issue

A **cyborg**, short for "cybernetic organism," is an entity that contains both biological and artificial (e.g., electronic, mechanical, or robotic) components. How close are we to creating cyborgs in your lifetime? Perhaps closer than you think. Consider the sophisticated artificial limbs already available, the installation of which could technically classify an individual as a cyborg.

But most people aren't getting upset about prosthetic limbs. Altering the human brain raises eyebrows, though. Technological advances are being applied to the field of brain research at an increasing rate. Human brain and neurological tissue have a limited ability to regenerate and repair themselves, leading to severe handicaps after injuries or diseases that affect the brain and central nervous system, such as Parkinson's disease. Research is proceeding in three main areas:

1. **Brain-computer interfaces (BCIs):** BCIs work to establish a direct communication pathway between the brain and external devices, such as robotic limbs, computers, and wheelchairs, allowing thought to direct or control the device.

2. **Neurostimulation:** Techniques such as deep brain stimulation involve the transplantation of devices that transmit electrical impulses to the brain for treating movement disorders like Parkinson's disease as well as chronic pain. Repetitive transcranial magnetic stimulation (rTMS) is a noninvasive technique for changing brain activity by exposing it to magnetic fields and is used in treating migraines, strokes, and Parkinson's disease.

3. **Neural stem cells:** Research is underway to determine how neural stem cells respond during strokes, multiple sclerosis, and Parkinson's disease and other neurological disorders. The goal is to develop effective therapies by producing or enhancing neural stem cells to make them more effective in resisting adverse events.

Outcomes of these fields of research have been focused on the treatment of severe medical conditions. However, military organizations are interested in applying BCIs to control fighter aircraft, drones, and other weapons systems. The gaming industry is also interested in BCI technology, since it could provide the capability for thought-controlled video games. And neurostimulation and neural stem cell research hold the potential for not just treating illnesses but possibly enhancing human brain function to allow humans to progress beyond their normal brain potential.

So how should technology be allowed to affect human brain function (Figure 7)? If we can create a "smarter" or "more athletic" human, should we do so? Where do we draw the line between humans and machines? If a smart bomb (a bomb guided by computer technology) zeroes in on a military target and destroys it, a "machine" is responsible for the carnage. But if the bomb is guided by a human being connected to it through a BCI, who bears the responsibility? Where do we separate the person from the machine if we reach this point?

Questions to Think About and Research

1. Who is responsible for controlling the direction and outcomes of brain technology research?

2. If a missile controlled by a person connected to a weapons system through a BCI accidentally destroys a civilian target, who is responsible...human or machine?

3. When do the benefits of medical research outweigh the risks of the technology being used in illegal, evil, or immoral ways?

4. Does enhancing our brain capabilities with technology make us less human?

POINT

Brain Technology Research Will Provide Medical "Miracles"

Advocates of brain technology research argue that it will allow for the treatment of currently untreatable catastrophic illnesses and injuries, thus alleviating human suffering.

1. Society will dictate what the acceptable uses of brain technology are, just as they have done for other types of advancements (such as atomic energy).

2. Technology is not responsible for the actions or the consequences of the actions of people. Governments can put controls in place to limit the uses of brain technology just as the United States and Russia have done with strategic arms limitation agreements for nuclear weapons.

3. Technology has provided new tools that allow us to exercise unprecedented control over neurological systems. Ignoring these areas of research provides no relief for afflicted individuals.

COUNTERPOINT

Brain Technology Will Radically Change Society if It Is Misused

Critics maintain that the directions brain research will take cannot be adequately controlled and that creating humans with "enhanced" capabilities poses too much of a danger to society.

1. No one can ultimately prevent or control the results of brain technology research from being used for military purposes.

2. If technology is used irresponsibly, it might create strife between the groups that have access to enhanced brain technology and those who do not.

3. Integrating technology into human beings and altering their body chemistry essentially destroys what it means to be "human."

FIGURE 7 What boundaries should there be on the enhancement of the human brain using technology? *(Vladgrin/Fotolia)*

Intellectual Property

International Pirates

Summary of the Issue

Intellectual property (such as music, writing, and software) is protected by copyright law. But there have been challenges in enforcing these standards in other countries. What happens to "fair trade" if some countries refuse to enforce copyright laws? How should the trade partners of these countries respond?

NationMaster.com estimated that in 2011, 82% of China's computers ran on pirated software. For comparison, the estimated piracy levels in the United States and Sweden are 20% and 25%, respectively. This discrepancy means that businesses in China don't have to budget for operating system or productivity software, which gives them an advantage in the international marketplace. Although some companies, like Microsoft, continue to do business in China despite the high levels of piracy, smaller companies often can't survive there. For example, Tom Adams, chief executive of Rosetta Stone, pulled his company and its language training software products out of China. He describes China as a "kleptocratic society" and worries about the amount of theft of his software in that environment.

In fact, the chief executives of 12 major software companies—Microsoft, Adobe, Autodesk, Symantec, and others—have lobbied the U.S. administration and lawmakers to continue to put pressure on China to crack down on illegal copying (see Figure 8). With a potential market of more than one billion people, and an increasing number of technologically hungry purchasers, companies dread the idea of missing out on the Chinese market. In 2010, talks between the U.S. and China resulted in promises by the Chinese government of stricter enforcement of antipiracy laws and implementation of aggressive antipiracy media campaigns. But to date, software companies have failed to see any significant increases in software sales in China, indicating the Chinese government's actions have been ineffective.

It is not just China that has weakly enforced copyright laws. Countries such as Armenia, Bangladesh, Yemen, Libya, and Vietnam all have higher rates of piracy than China. The Business Software Alliance estimates the monetary losses from software piracy at more than $63 billion worldwide for 2011, although there is debate around the exact value.

Most people have had the opportunity to participate in the piracy of copyrighted materials through illegal peer-to-peer sharing and the use of torrents. This behavior is now multiplied to the level of nations, and the consequences are still being explored.

Questions to Think About and Research

1. Should a government be penalized for failing to actively enforce the laws it has enacted within its own country? If so, what should the penalties be, and how should they be enforced?
2. Does each government have the right to make its own decision on a stand against piracy?
3. How can other countries respond to international piracy?
4. Does individual piracy have any connection to the enforcement of copyright laws on an international level?

POINT

International Copyright Protections Need to Be Vigorously Enforced

Artists and software developers depend on the integrity of the protection of intellectual property, both within the United States and internationally, to make a fair profit on their work.

1. If other countries do not fight piracy, artists and developers have a disadvantage in the marketplace.

2. By allowing massive piracy, some countries are stealing from others.

3. Every country needs to have a common understanding and enforcement of intellectual property laws for trade to be fair and beneficial to everyone.

COUNTERPOINT

Global Business Demands Understanding Other Cultures

Most countries have laws on their books regarding intellectual property. It is not the job of the United States to tell a foreign government how to conduct its internal affairs.

1. The existing laws on intellectual property have worked to serve the interests of these countries. If U.S. companies do not want to sell to the billion-person market of China, then that is their choice.

2. Piracy exists within the United States, so it is hypocritical to be chastising foreign governments for software piracy.

3. Companies can pursue restitution for piracy through the foreign court systems.

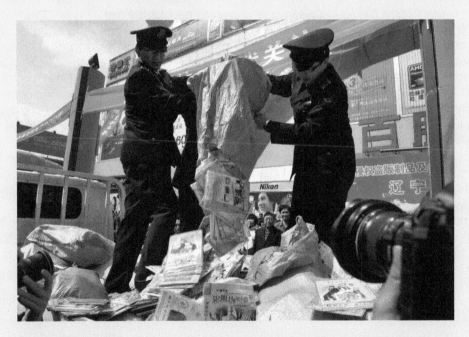

FIGURE 8 A crackdown on pirated media in China underscores that issues of intellectual property play an important role in international trade. *(MARK/epa/Corbis)*

Privacy

Can Employers Peer into Your Personal Life?

Summary of the Issue

Like respect and dignity, privacy is a basic human right. What, exactly, is privacy? Simply stated, privacy is the right to be left alone to do as one pleases. The idea of privacy is often associated with hiding something (a behavior, a relationship, or a secret). However, privacy really means not being required to explain your behavior to others. But social media sites such as Facebook are inherently about sharing information with others. Does this mean there is no such thing as personal privacy (see Figure 9) on social media sites?

Facebook and other social media allow you to set privacy filters on your personal information. You can choose to share information publically, share it with just with your friends, or keep it totally private. Employers now routinely check social media sites to gather publically shared information on prospective employees. But recently, many government agencies, such as police departments and some private employers, have been asking job seekers for access to their *private* Facebook information, as well.

Sometimes this is blatant, such as what happened to a Maryland corrections officer who was seeking reinstatement. During an interview, he was asked for his Facebook password. The interviewer then proceeded to log on to his account, purportedly to see if he had any gang affiliations.

Although this might seem like a legitimate reason for a prison system to screen candidates, the U.S. Senate disagrees. In May 2012, legislators proposed the Password Protection Act to prevent employers from demanding passwords to private sites from employees. That same month, Maryland became the first state to enact a law that prohibits employers from asking current and prospective employees for their access codes to social networking sites. Employers are currently prohibited from asking prospective employees information related to their gender, race, religion, age, and sexual orientation, but this information is often found in social media site profiles. Facebook has also warned employers against this practice, as it violates the terms-of-use agreement for the site.

Often, however, employer research is more subtle. For example, employers often encourage prospective employees to "friend" them on Facebook. Although these company profiles are set up specifically so that prospective employees can learn information about the company, once prospective employees "friend" the company, company representatives can often see more information about these would-be employees than what is visible in their public profile.

The American Civil Liberties Union (ACLU) and other privacy advocates have begun voicing opposition to these practices, citing erosion of personal privacy rights. You wouldn't give a prospective employer the keys to your house so they could poke around in your personal life. But doesn't it have almost the same effect if you let them see your private information in a social media profile?

Employers—especially small businesses—argue that hiring decisions are so critical that they need to gather as much information as possible and that people voluntarily surrendering passwords is not a violation of prospective employees' rights. But critics of these practices say that job seekers may feel powerless to refuse these invasions of their privacy for fear they'll be turned down for a job.

The control and privacy of information will continue to be a fine balancing act for the foreseeable future, with employers trying to gather intelligence while appeasing the concerns of privacy advocates. Leaving a trail of electronic breadcrumbs is to a certain extent inevitable. But cleaning up or hiding your "trail" is still important to many users, not because they're trying to hide something but because they value their basic right to privacy.

Questions to Think About and Research

1. Should you be able to decide exactly what information on a social networking site you share with others? Would you be willing to pay for this privilege?

2. Do you know what your privacy settings are on the social media sites you use? Is there any information being shared publicly that you weren't aware was being shared?

3. Should employers be allowed to ask prospective employees for their passwords to social media sites? Is this practice still legal in the United States?

4. Is there any information on sites you use that you want to restrict potential employers from seeing? Do these sites allow you to restrict the information you wish to protect?

POINT

Employers Have No Right to Job Seekers' Private Social Media Information

The advocates of protecting privacy in the United States argue that the right to privacy is a basic human right that should be afforded to everyone. Personal privacy concerns should outweigh the business needs of a corporation.

1. Social media sites have an inherent duty to protect the data of their users.

2. If employers are screening private information, they might misuse or lose control of the data or violate current employment law.

3. Default privacy settings on social media sites should all be opt-in, allowing users the ultimate control over who views their data.

COUNTERPOINT

Employers Are Entitled to Gather Personal Information Directly Related to Employment

Advocates for unrestricted sharing of information feel that business concerns outweigh privacy concerns. Businesses should have the right to screen all data in social media sites to determine the character and fitness of employment candidates.

1. Volunteering password information does not violate an individual's right to privacy.

2. Users can make their own privacy decisions and choose not to post or share sensitive information (opt out).

3. In the digital age, loss of a certain amount of privacy is inevitable.

FIGURE 9 What information are you sharing on Facebook and with whom? *(Copyright © 2011 by Facebook Inc.)*

E-Commerce

Geolocation: Who Knows Where You Are?

Summary of the Issue

"Where are you?" is the burning social-networking question these days, and your smartphone probably has the answer. The technology is called geolocation (see Figure 10), and smartphones have a GPS chip that can calculate your exact position. Services such as Foursquare, Gowalla, Brightkite, and Loopt are all hoping you'll use their geolocation services to find your friends or let your friends find you. Through the apps, you can receive recommendations of places to visit or things to do nearby. Businesses are using geolocation apps to promote their products and offer rewards for "check-ins" to help drive customers to their location.

When you sign up on Foursquare and other social media sites, you can choose what information is publically available, such as your location or your Facebook profile. Foursquare is designed to make it convenient to see where your friends are and who's in the venue where you're currently "checked in." You might be cautious and choose to make personal and location information only accessible to your friends … or it might all be public. But what if another app you know nothing about is using your information in a way never intended by the social media sites you joined?

Consider the controversy that erupted around the iPhone app "Girls Around Me." The app used data from Foursquare to create a local map that showed how many individuals logged into Foursquare were in geographic locations near you. It also allowed you to view Facebook profiles of people "around you" if they had their Facebook profiles linked to their Foursquare account. The app developer, i-Free, promoted the app as a tool to see what was happening in a wider range of locations instead of just one at a time. It viewed its tool as a way to let users identify "hot spots" of activity that had a lot of people checked in. i-Free said the app was just like looking in the window of a location to see how crowded it was, but it was also aggregating publically available information provided by other social media services.

Critics of the app decried it as a tool for stalkers that provided more information than people could gain by glancing in a window. They argued that the app violated the privacy of Foursquare users because they had no knowledge of how the Girls Around Me app was using their information. Many detractors argued that just because you agreed to make certain information public on Foursquare doesn't mean you automatically agree to the use of that same information on other apps that might function in a different (and perhaps objectionable) way. Foursquare claimed that i-Free was violating the terms of its information-sharing agreement and changed its application programming interfaces (APIs) to effectively disable the Girls Around Me app. i-Free removed the app from the App Store for retooling.

But the question remains, when you leave your home and announce your constant whereabouts through tweets and check-ins, do you lose your privacy in exchange for "fun" and "convenience"? Although you can set certain levels of privacy in the apps, there is still the potential for someone with bad intentions (stalkers, robbers) to follow your updates. And do you really know how the information you make public will be used by other app creators? In addition to opening yourself up to potential stalking or robbery, geolocation devices also can track the activities you might not want publicized, and that once documented can later be used against you.

It wasn't long ago that we were concerned about using our real names online, but now we're comfortable with sharing our exact location in a very public way. As Facebook CEO Mark Zuckerberg said, "People have really gotten comfortable not only sharing more information and different kinds, but more openly and with more people." But does such acceptance justify neglecting to maintain certain levels of privacy? Again, it seems that technology has moved more quickly than society can address the potential risks and dangers.

Questions to Think About and Research

1. Do the benefits of geolocation outweigh the risks?
2. What other devices besides cell phones track and record our movements/locations as digital records?
3. How have social networks increased the risks of geolocation?
4. What risks do geolocation pose for college students? How can users mitigate those risks?

POINT

Geolocation Devices Do Not Threaten Privacy

The advocates of using geolocation devices with minimal concern for threatened privacy are those who believe the social norm has shifted and people have become comfortable with sharing more information.

1. Businesses are adopting geolocation apps as a part of their social media strategy in order to drive customers to their business. They would lose revenue if such activities ceased.

2. As the devices and apps become better and more precise, they may become useful as public safety and news-gathering devices.

3. Society may need to reevaluate its views about how much privacy is needed in people's digital lives, as well as the degree of an individual's responsibility for making sensible decisions about sharing information through the Internet.

COUNTERPOINT

Geolocation Devices Are a Threat to Privacy

The advocates for tighter privacy controls and awareness campaigns about the potential risks of using geolocation devices suggest that the threats are too big to ignore. Society has become too complacent with privacy issues.

1. Privacy settings on apps and GPS devices should be more restrictive in order to avoid broadcasting one's location and risking personal assault.

2. Laws and regulations will need to be created as to the use and distribution of digital location information.

3. Consumers need to be educated about geolocation and the ways it can affect them so that they are able to make informed choices.

FIGURE 10 Geolocation applications help you find cool places and businesses. But who do you want to find you with geolocation? *(Cseke Timea/Fotolia)*

Electronic Communication

Does Free Speech Have a Price?

Summary of the Issue

In early 2006, when Google launched its search engine services in China, it conceded to the Chinese government's demands that it self-censor its search engine, restricting search results for sensitive information such as the details of the Tiananmen Square protests and of human rights groups. This decision prompted much discussion, with some condemning Google's decision for putting business profits over what they saw as basic human rights (see Figure 11). Google justified its actions by stating that a company must operate within the rules of the market in which it operates and that the benefits of increased access to information for people in China "outweighed our discomfort in agreeing to censor some results." And, compared with search results from Baidu.com, the leading Chinese search engine, Google was not censoring all information.

However, in 2010, Google announced that it was no longer willing to censor search results and moved the site to Hong Kong, where it hoped there would be less censorship. The departure was a reaction to a sophisticated, targeted cyberattack that Google believes was done to gather information on Chinese human rights activists. At that time, Google had about a 35% market share.

Microsoft had only a 1% share of the market, so it decided to partner with Baidu.com to provide English-language search results for China's largest search engine. Microsoft stated it would agree to abide by Chinese censorship laws (so search terms like *freedom* and *democracy* deliver filtered results), thereby respecting the laws of the countries where it operates. However, before honoring any censor requests, Microsoft insisted that Chinese authorities made legally binding requests in writing.

So how did it all work out? As of the third quarter of 2011, Google's market share has dropped to 18% in China, whereas Baidu.com has increased its market share to 78%. So far, Microsoft's decision to keep censoring its searches appears to have paid off ... at least from a monetary perspective. But is the financial result more important than the social implications of their behavior?

Questions to Think About and Research

1. Is there anything else that Google could do that would have a major impact on China's censorship laws?

2. Has Microsoft's compliance with censorship laws furthered the Chinese government's cooperation in combating software piracy in China? Are Microsoft's financial incentives even deeper than just Internet market share?

3. Can the U.S. government compel technology companies to take a firmer stance on free speech in China and elsewhere by instituting criminal charges if U.S. companies do not take reasonable steps to protect human rights?

POINT

U.S. Companies Should Comply with Local Laws in Foreign Countries

Those in favor of Microsoft's actions to remain in China feel that if a company chooses to operate in a foreign country, it knows the local laws and should be prepared to work within those laws as it does business. It is not the place of a company to try to change laws of foreign countries.

1. Microsoft conducts businesses in other countries that have censorship laws, so why not participate in China?

2. Working in China does not mean a company supports all of China's policies.

3. Microsoft's presence continues to advance the progress the Chinese government is making toward democracy. U.S. companies can ethically stay in China if they make an effort to improve human rights there. U.S. companies operating in China should agree on guidelines that respect human rights.

4. A U.S. company's presence has no impact on reform—reform must come from within.

COUNTERPOINT

U.S. Companies Should Put What Is Right Ahead of What Is Financially Expedient

Those in favor of Google's actions believe that international corporations should begin to take a firm stance against governments that do not promote basic human rights.

1. China will never change unless there are financial and political incentives to do so. Google's departure helps pressure the Chinese government.

2. Google's withdrawal from China threatens the viability of many advertising resellers in China. Will this added pressure help or hinder human rights efforts?

3. Google's decision to leave helps put pressure on China's government to play by global standards. China cannot expect to compete in the global marketplace while refusing to have a global exchange of ideas.

FIGURE 11 Is free speech possible in countries (such as China) where information availability is restricted by law? *(Kentoh/Shutterstock)*

Computer Abuse

Cyberbullying: Who Should Protect Children from Each Other?

Summary of the Issue

Cyberbullying is just like normal bullying, but it involves the use of digital technologies such as the Internet, cell phones, or video (see Figure 12). There are many types of cyberbullying, some of which might result in criminal charges depending on the type of incident:

- Bombarding a victim with harassing instant messages or text messages
- Stealing a password and then using the victim's account to embarrass the victim by sending harassing, threatening, or lewd messages while pretending to be the victim
- Spreading rumors or lies on social networking sites
- Posting embarrassing photos or videos on the web (such as candid nude shots taken in a locker room)
- Infecting the victim's computer with malware, usually to spy on the victim

The effects of cyberbullying can be devastating. Infamous cases include Alexis Pilkington, who at 17 committed suicide after being repeatedly taunted on social networking sites, and Tyler Clementi, a Rutgers freshman who committed suicide after his roommate showed fellow students videos of him having sex.

Signs that a child is a victim of cyberbullying are often the same as the signs of depression. A child may:

- Suddenly lose interest in normal activities
- Be reluctant to go to school
- Lose his or her appetite
- Have trouble sleeping
- Appear upset after using the Internet
- Experience unusual mood swings (such as bursting into tears for no apparent reason)

Signs that a child might be perpetrating cyberbullying include the following:

- Using the Internet excessively
- Sending large volumes of text messages
- Clearing the computer screen when others enter a room
- Conducting clandestine Internet activities (refusal to say what he or she is doing)

Vigilance over children's online activities is obviously key to spotting both victims and perpetrators of cyberbullying.

But who is responsible for monitoring children? Parents obviously need to protect their children, but bullying usually doesn't happen until children are exposed to other children, such as in school. So should teachers shoulder the responsibility for detecting, reporting, and mitigating cyberbullying? Children often spend more time in school during the day than under the supervision of their parents. But cyberbullying activities don't just take place in school. Most children have access to the Internet at home and can carry on campaigns of terror from their bedrooms.

There is currently no federal law prohibiting cyberbullying, but the recently passed law against cyberstalking may cover this area. According to the Cyberbullying Research Center (**cyberbullying.us**), as of April 2012, 49 states had antibullying laws on the books. However, only 40 state laws cover electronic harassment, and a mere 14 state laws cover cyberbullying. Many legislatures are reluctant to pass laws that instruct parents on how to raise their children because this tends to raise issues about personal freedom. Therefore, anti-cyberbullying laws tend to place the burden of detection on the schools. For instance, the Massachusetts law requires schools to provide age-appropriate education on bullying to students, to train school employees in detection and prevention of bullying, and to have plans developed for detecting and reporting bullying.

Questions to Think About and Research

1. What level of responsibility should school employees have for protecting children from cyberbullying?
2. Should there be federal laws that make cyberbullying a crime? If so, how would these laws be enforced?
3. What types of education for children would be beneficial in preventing cyberbullying? When should these programs begin, and how often should children be required to participate?

POINT

Parents Must Protect Their Children from Cyberbullying

Proponents of parental responsibility for detecting and preventing cyberbullying feel that it's a personal behavior issue. Individuals are responsible for their own behavior as long as it doesn't harm others. Parents should be allowed to educate their children according to their own standards of behavior and preferences in terms of moral behavior (such as religion).

1. Parents are ultimately responsible for protecting their children.

2. Bullying is a personal behavior issue, and all decisions regarding personal freedom and behavior should be made by parents.

3. Because educating children about bullying is key to preventing it, the content of such training needs to be controlled by parents.

COUNTERPOINT

Schools Must Bear the Responsibility for Protecting Students from Cyberbullying

Cyberbullying affects society because it can severely damage an individual's self-esteem. Cyberbullying is similar to other hate crimes and should enlist public officials (such as educators) in enforcement of the laws.

1. Parents do not supervise their children 24/7 and therefore require help from other responsible adults to protect their children.

2. Parents need to be assured that publicly funded institutions such as schools and libraries are "safe havens" where their children will not be exposed to malicious activities.

3. Educators have better resources than most parents for teaching children about the serious effects of cyberbullying.

FIGURE 12 Cyberbullying involves the use of digital technologies both to bully and to broadcast acts of bullying. *(Rawdon Wyatt/Alamy)*

Using Computers to Support Ethical Conduct

Although there are many opportunities to use computers and the Internet unethically, we can also use technology to support ethical conduct. For example, many charitable organizations use the Internet and other technology tools for fundraising. When tornados struck in Texas in April 2012, the Salvation Army (see Figure 13) and other charities received many pledges via their websites.

And, as we discussed in Chapter 1, the web is also a tool for organizing aid to areas in crisis. When a major earthquake struck Haiti in 2010, Ushahidi allowed organizations and individuals conducting relief efforts to collect and disseminate the latest information on victims and aid efforts.

More recently, after a devastating tornado hit Joplin, Missouri, in May 2011, folks used the Red Cross website and Facebook to locate friends and family members. The level of personal interaction the web supports and the speed at which information can be exchanged are allowing computer technology to support ethical conduct in powerful new ways.

Throughout your life, you'll encounter many ethical challenges relating to information technology. Your personal ethics—combined with the ethical guidelines your company provides and the general ethical environment of society—will guide your decisions.

For further information on ethics, check out the following websites:

- Ethics in Computing (**ethics.csc.ncsu.edu**)
- The Center for Ethics in Science and Technology (**ethicscenter.net**)
- Business Ethics: The Magazine of Corporate Responsibility (**business-ethics.com**)
- Council for Ethical Leadership at Capital University (**businessethics.org**) ■

FIGURE 13 Technology helps charities solicit donations.

check your understanding //

For a quick review of what you've learned, answer the following questions. Visit **pearsonhighered.com/techinaction** to check your answers.

multiple choice

1. Which theory states that there is no universal moral truth?
   a. Relativism
   b. Divine command theory
   c. Utilitarianism
   d. Virtue ethics

2. The ethical theory that states that individual happiness is not important is known as
   a. utilitarianism.
   b. virtue ethics.
   c. deontology.
   d. divine command theory.

3. Which ethical philosophy states that morals are internal?
   a. Deontology
   b. Virtue ethics
   c. Relativism
   d. Divine command theory

4. Which of the following statements is *true*?
   a. Individuals who apply ethics inconsistently exhibit illegal behavior.
   b. Ethical decisions are rarely influenced by personal ethics.
   c. Unethical behavior is always illegal.
   d. Life experience affects an individual's personal ethics.

5. Unethical behavior
   a. is the same as illegal behavior.
   b. is based on civil disobedience.
   c. is different from illegal behavior.
   d. is governed by specific laws passed by legislative bodies.

6. The field of psychology that theorizes that happiness results from ethical living is known as
   a. principled psychology.
   b. positive psychology.
   c. moral psychology.
   d. affirmative psychology.

7. Which system of ethics is most widely agreed on to be the best system?
   a. Utilitarianism
   b. Relativism
   c. Virtue ethics
   d. There is no universally agreed-on best system.

8. What should you do if you spot unethical behavior at your workplace?
   a. Nothing, as long as the behavior is legal.
   b. Report it to the police immediately.
   c. Follow company procedures for reporting unethical behavior.
   d. Start looking for a new job.

9. Which of the following actions would NOT help to identify your personal ethics?
   a. Describe yourself.
   b. Identify the influences of your work environment.
   c. Conduct a genealogic study of your extended family.
   d. Prepare a list of values that are most important to you.

10. Ethical decisions in business affect which of the following?
    a. the employees
    b. the business's clients and customers
    c. the suppliers and financial lenders
    d. all stakeholders

6 Understanding and Assessing Hardware: Evaluating Your System

For all media in this chapter go to **pearsonhighered.com/techinaction** or MyITLab.

(Radius Images/Alamy; nigel james/Alamy; joppo/Fotolia; Cobalt/Fotolia; Scanrail/Fotolia; SSilver/Fotolia; Ivelin Radkov/Alamy)

HOW COOL IS THIS?

Scan here for more info

Just like the car industry has special concept cars, at the 2012 Consumer Electronics Show, Intel showed off a **glimpse** into what your **next computer** may look like, the Nikiski ultrabook. A **transparent track pad** flows across the full length of the machine, so when closed you can still see through to key information like your to-do list, in-box, Facebook, and meeting notes. It also works as a **touchpad interface** so that you can select and respond to important information **without opening the tablet**.

Once you do open the cover, the inside surface of the transparent touchpad acts as a **huge track pad**. It understands the difference between the weight of your wrists or palms and your fingertips and only processes the glide of your fingertips as you scroll or pinch and zoom. Folks were storming the stage after the presentation to get a look at

Evaluating Key Subsystems

It can be tough to know if your computer is the best match for your needs. New technologies emerge so quickly, and it's hard to determine whether these are expensive extras or tools you need. Do you need USB 3.0 instead of USB 2.0? Doesn't it always seem like your friend's computer is faster than yours anyway? Maybe you could get more out of newer technologies, but should you upgrade the system you have or buy a new machine? In this chapter, you'll learn how to measure your system's performance and gauge your needs so that you end up with a system you love.

 your ideal
COMPUTER

When is the best time to buy a new computer? There never seems to be a perfect time to buy. It seems that if you can just wait a year, computers will be faster and cost less. But is this actually true?

As it turns out, it is true. In fact, a rule of thumb often cited in the computer industry called **Moore's Law** describes the pace at which central processing units (CPUs) improve. Named for Gordon Moore, the cofounder of the CPU chip manufacturer Intel, this rule predicts that the number of transistors inside a CPU will increase so fast that CPU capacity will double about every 2 years. (The number of transistors on a CPU chip helps determine how fast it can process data.)

This rule of thumb has held true for over 45 years. Figure 6.1 shows a way to visualize this kind of exponential growth. If CPU capacity were put into terms of population growth, a group of 2,300 people at the start of CPU development would now be a country of over one billion! Moore himself has predicted that around the year 2020, CPU chips will be manufactured in a different way, thus changing or eliminating the effects of Moore's Law altogether.

In addition to the CPU becoming faster, other system components also continue to improve dramatically. For example, the capacity of memory chips such as dynamic random access memory (DRAM)—the most common form of memory found in personal computers—increases about 60% every year. Meanwhile, hard drives have been growing in storage capacity by some 50% each year.

OK, things change fast. How do I know what's best for me? Consider what kind of user you are and what needs you have. For example, are you a power user who wants a machine for doing video editing and high-end gaming? Are you a more casual user, mainly using a device for word processing and Internet access? Are you on the move and need

FIGURE 6.1 Moore's Law illustrates the amazing pace of growth in CPU capabilities.

FIGURE 6.2

What Kind of Computer User Are You?

(llaszlo/Shutterstock; ColorBlind Images/Iconica/Getty Images; olly/Shutterstock)

Casual User
- Uses the computer primarily for Internet access
- Uses some software applications locally, like Microsoft Office
- Uses videos and software but does not create them

Power User
- Needs fast, powerful processing
- Needs fast storage and lots of it
- Creates videos and software programs

Mobile User
- Needs a lightweight computer
- Needs a long battery life
- Is happy to sacrifice some capabilities for less weight

to bring your computer with you everywhere? Figure 6.2 shows a few different types of users—which type (or types) are you?

Now ask yourself, does your current computer match your needs? As we evaluate the pieces of your system, it'll become clear whether you need a few upgrades or perhaps a new machine better matched to you.

How do I pick from all the types of computers available? A huge number of choices are on the market:

- Tablets (like the iPad or Galaxy)
- Ultrabooks (like the MacBook Air)
- Netbooks (which have a screen smaller than 10 inches and a small keyboard)
- Tablet PCs (which have a touch-enabled screen and a full keyboard)
- Laptops (or notebooks)
- Desktops

The main distinction between the available options is based on your need for mobility versus your need for processing power. If you're on the move all the time and have to have the lightest solution possible, an ultrabook may be best for you. At less than 3 pounds, they're great on weight but don't include an optical drive for CDs/DVDs or much storage space. Even lighter are tablets like the iPad, but they also lack optical drives and may not be able to run all the software you need.

Why would I consider buying a desktop? Desktop systems are invariably a better value than lighter, more mobile computers. You'll find you get more computing power for your dollar, and you'll have more opportunity to upgrade parts of your system later. In addition, desktops often ship with a 24-inch or larger monitor, whereas lighter computers offer screens between 10 and 17 inches.

Desktop systems are also more reliable. Because of the vibration that a laptop experiences and the added exposure to dust, water, and temperature fluctuations that portability brings, laptops often have a shorter lifespan than desktop computers. You'll have less worry over theft or loss with a desktop, too. Manufacturers do offer extended warranty plans that cover laptop computers for accidental damage and theft; however, such plans can be costly.

How long should I plan on keeping my computer? You should be able to count on 2 years, and maybe even 4 or 5 years. The answer depends in part on how easy it is to upgrade your system. Take note of the maximum amount of memory you can install in your device. Also, check whether you can upgrade your device's graphics capabilities down the road.

Laptops are often equipped with an **ExpressCard** slot. ExpressCards (shown in Figure 6.3) can add a solid-state drive (SSD), new kinds of ports, and other capabilities to your system. This gives you a way to make sure your laptop doesn't become obsolete before its time. However, note that the lighter ultrabooks and tablets don't have ExpressCard expansion options.

FIGURE 6.3 ExpressCards add functionality to your laptop. *(Editorial Image, LLC/Alamy; Editorial Image, LLC/Alamy)*

How can I tell if my current system is good enough? We'll begin by conducting a **system evaluation**. To do this, we'll look at your computer's subsystems, see what they do, and check how they perform during your typical workday. Then we'll compare that with what is available on the market, and the path forward for you will become clearer. Even if you're not in the market for a new computer, conducting a system evaluation will help you understand what you might want in a new system down the road. ∎

evaluating the
CPU SUBSYSTEM

Let's start by considering your system's processor, or CPU. The CPU is located on the system motherboard and is responsible for processing instructions, performing calculations, and managing the flow of information through your computer. The dominant processors on the market are the Core family from Intel, featuring the i7, i5, and i3 (see Figure 6.4).

How can I find out what CPU my computer has? If you have a PC, System Properties will show you the type of CPU you have installed. For example, the CPU in the computer in Figure 6.5 is an Intel i7 running at 2.2 GHz. Another popular manufacturer of CPUs is the company AMD, so you may have one of its processors, such as the FX-8150 or the Phenom X4. But more detailed information about your CPU, such as its number of cores and amount of cache memory, is not shown on this screen. Let's dive into that.

FIGURE 6.4 The Intel i5 and i7 CPU chips run many of the laptop and desktop offerings on the market today. *(David Caudery/PC Format Magazine/Future/Getty Images)*

FIGURE 6.5 The System Properties window identifies your computer's CPU as well as its speed. This computer has an Intel i7 running at 2.2 GHz.

>*To access your system settings, move your mouse to the lower-left corner of your screen and right-click. From the menu that displays, choose* **System**.

How the CPU Works

How does the CPU actually work? The CPU is composed of two units: the *control unit* and the *arithmetic logic unit (ALU)*. The control unit coordinates the activities of all the other computer components. The ALU is responsible for performing all the arithmetic calculations (addition, subtraction, multiplication, and division). It also makes logic and comparison decisions such as comparing items to determine if one is greater than, less than, or equal to another.

Every time the CPU performs a program instruction, it goes through the same series of steps:

1. It *fetches* the required piece of data or instruction from random access memory (RAM), the temporary storage location for all the data and instructions the computer needs while it's running.
2. It *decodes* the instruction into something the computer can understand.
3. It *executes* the instruction.
4. It *stores* the result to RAM before fetching the next instruction.

This process is called a **machine cycle**. (We discuss the machine cycle in more detail in the Technology in Focus feature "Under the Hood" on page 302.)

CPU Factors

What makes one CPU different from another? You pay more for a computer with an Intel i7 than one with an i5 because of its increased processing power. A CPU's processing power is determined by the following:

- Its *clock speed*
- Whether it has multiple *cores*
- Its amount of *cache memory*

How does a CPU with a higher clock speed help me? The **clock speed** of a CPU dictates how many instructions the CPU can process each second. It is measured in gigahertz (GHz), or billions of steps per second. The faster the clock speed, the more quickly the next instruction is processed. CPUs currently have clock speeds between 2.1 and 4 GHz. There is a huge difference between a computer with a 2.1 GHz CPU and one with a 4 GHz CPU.

Some users push their hardware to perform faster, **overclocking** their processor. Overclocking means that you run the CPU at a faster speed than the manufacturer recommends. It produces more heat, meaning a shorter lifetime for the CPU, and usually voids any warranty, but in gaming systems, you'll see this done quite often.

How does a multi-core CPU help me? A **core** on a CPU contains the parts of the CPU required for processing. As shown in Figure 6.6a, with multiple-core

technology, two or more complete processors live on the same chip, enabling the independent execution of two sets of instructions at the same time. If you had a clone of yourself sitting next to you working, you could get twice as much done, and that is the idea of multi-core processing. With multi-core processing, applications that are always running behind the scenes, such as virus protection software and your operating system (OS), can have their own dedicated processor, freeing the other processors to run other applications more efficiently. This results in faster processing and smoother multitasking.

CPUs began to execute more than one instruction at a time when **hyperthreading** was introduced in 2002. Hyperthreading provides quicker processing of information by enabling a new set of instructions to start executing *before the previous set has finished*. As shown in Figure 6.6b, hyperthreading allows two different programs to be processed at one time, but they're sharing the computing resources of the chip.

All of the Intel Core processors have multiple cores *and* hyperthreading (see Figure 6.6c). The Intel i7-990X has six cores, each one using hyperthreading, so it simulates having 12 processors!

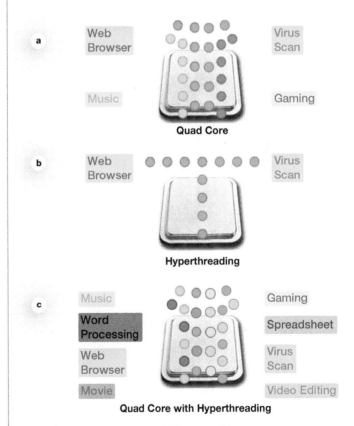

FIGURE 6.6 (a) Intel Quad Core processors have four cores that are able to run four programs simultaneously. (b) Hyperthreading allows work on two processes to happen in one core at the same time. (c) So, a four-core hyperthreaded processor can be working on eight programs at one time.

How does more cache memory help me? The CPU's **cache memory** is a form of RAM that gets data to the CPU for processing much faster than bringing the data in from the computer's RAM. There are three levels of cache memory, defined by their proximity to the CPU:

- *Level 1 cache* is a block of memory built on the CPU chip itself for storage of data or commands that have just been used. That gets the data to the CPU blindingly fast!

- *Level 2 cache* is located on the CPU chip but is slightly farther away and so takes somewhat longer to access than Level 1 cache. It contains more storage area than Level 1 cache.

- *Level 3 cache* is slower for the CPU to reach but is larger in size than Level 2 cache.

The more expensive the CPU, the more cache memory it will have.

So how do I shop for a CPU? You'll often see models of the same computer with just a different CPU varying in cost by $200 or more. Is the price difference worth it? It's hard to know because so many factors influence CPU performance. Picking the best CPU for the kind of work you do is easier if you research some performance benchmarks. **CPU benchmarks** are measurements used to compare performance between processors. Benchmarks are generated by running software programs specifically designed to push the limits of CPU performance. Articles are often published comparing CPUs, or complete systems, based on their benchmark performance. Investigate a few, using sites like **cpubenchmark.net**, before you select the chip that's best for you.

Measuring the CPU

How can I tell whether my current CPU is meeting my needs? One way to determine whether your CPU is right for you is to watch how busy it is as you work. You can do this by checking out your **CPU usage**—the percentage of time your CPU is working.

Your computer's OS has utilities that measure CPU usage. These are incredibly useful, both for considering whether you should upgrade and for investigating if your computer's performance suddenly seems to drop off for no apparent reason.

On Windows systems, Task Manager lets you access this data (see Figure 6.7). The **CPU usage graph** records your CPU usage for the past several seconds. (Note that if you have multiple cores and hyperthreading, you'll see only one physical processor listed, but it

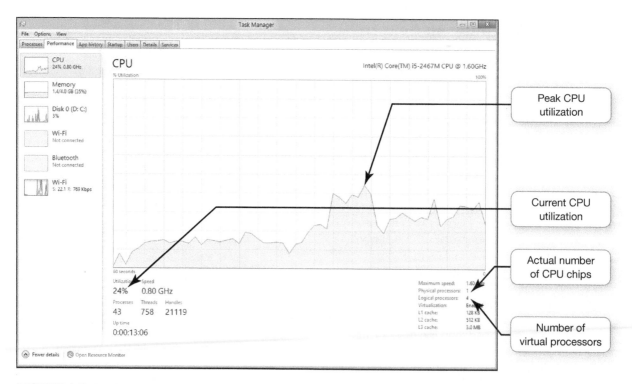

FIGURE 6.7 The Performance tab of the Windows Task Manager utility shows you how busy your CPU is.

>*To access the Performance tab, move your cursor to the lower-left corner and right-click. From the menu, select* **Task Manager***, and then click the* **Performance** *tab.*

BITS&BYTES

Not Much Power at All

The amount of power a CPU requires is very important to designers looking to extend the battery life of an ultrabook or tablet. Intel has created a CPU nicknamed Claremont that can run off only the power of a reading lamp. In fact, the CPU can even be powered by the small solar battery cells used to run solar-powered calculators.

Could these so-called *near threshold voltage (NTV)* CPUs be the beginning of a new series of devices? What kind of design changes are on the horizon once a system can be solar-powered?

SOUND BYTE
Using Windows to Evaluate CPU Performance

In this Sound Byte, you'll learn how to use the utilities provided by Windows to evaluate your CPU's performance. You'll also learn about shareware utilities (software that you can install and try before you purchase it) that expand on the capabilities the Task Manager utility provides.

will show that you have several virtual processors.) Of course, there will be periodic peaks of high CPU usage, but if your CPU usage levels are greater than 90% during most of your work session, a faster CPU will contribute a great deal to your system's performance.

To walk through using the Task Manager, check out the Try This on page 244 and watch the "Using Windows to Evaluate CPU Performance" Sound Byte. Mac OS X has a similar utility named Activity Monitor, which is located in the Utilities folder in the Applications subfolder.

How often do I have to be watching the CPU load? Keep in mind that the workload your CPU experiences depends on how many programs are running at one time. Even though the CPU may meet the specs for each program separately, how you use your machine during a typical day may tax the CPU. If you're having slow response times or decide to measure CPU performance as a check, open the Task Manager and leave it open for a full day. Check in at points when you have a lot of open windows and when you have a lot of networking or disk-usage demand.

So a better CPU means a better performing system? Your CPU affects only the *processing* portion of the system performance, not how quickly data can move to or from the CPU. Your system's *overall* performance depends on many factors, including the amount of RAM installed as well as hard drive speed. Your selection of CPU may not offer significant improvements to your system's performance if there is a bottleneck in processing because of insufficient RAM or hard drive performance, so you need to make sure the system is designed in a balanced way. Figure 6.8 lists factors to consider as you decide which specific CPU is right for you. ■

FIGURE 6.8

How to Evaluate a CPU

- Power users: Clock speed is very important; consider whether overclocking is worth sacrificing CPU longevity
- Casual/Mobile users: Clock speed is not as important

- Power users: Get as many cores as possible
- Casual users: Fewer cores is acceptable
- Mobile users: Low power draw is more critical than number of cores

- Power users: Paying for more cache memory is a good investment
- Casual/Mobile users: Save your money

- Use benchmarks to get an exact measure of the difference between two CPUs

Clock Speed
Multiple Cores
CPU
Cache Memory
CPU Benchmarks

evaluating the
MEMORY SUBSYSTEM

Random access memory (RAM) is your computer's temporary storage space. Although we refer to RAM as a form of storage, it really is the computer's short-term memory. It remembers everything that the computer needs in order to process data into information, such as data that has been entered and software instructions, but only when the computer is on. RAM is an example of **volatile storage**. When the power is off, the data stored in RAM is cleared out. This is why, in addition to RAM, systems always include **nonvolatile storage** devices for permanent storage of instructions and data. Read-only memory (ROM), for example, holds the critical start-up instructions. Hard drives provide the largest nonvolatile storage capacity in the computer system.

Why not use a hard drive to store the data and instructions? It's about one million times faster for the CPU to retrieve a piece of data from RAM than from a mechanical hard drive. The time it takes the CPU to grab data from RAM is measured in nanoseconds (billionths of seconds), whereas pulling data from a fast mechanical hard drive takes an average of 10 milliseconds (ms), or thousandths of seconds.

Figure 6.9 shows the various types of memory and storage distributed throughout your system: memory that is actually part of the CPU (such as CPU registers and cache), RAM, virtual memory, optical drives, and SSD and mechanical hard drives. Each of these has its own tradeoff of speed versus price. Because the fastest memory is so much more expensive, systems are designed with much less of it. This principle is influential in the design of a balanced computer system and can have a tremendous impact on system performance.

The RAM in Your System

Are there different types of RAM? Yes, but in most current systems, the type of RAM used is double data rate 3 (DDR3) memory modules, available in several different speeds (1066 MHz, 1333 MHz, 1600 MHz). The higher the speed, the better the performance. DDR5 (double data rate 5) memory, which has an even

FIGURE 6.9 A computer system's memory has many different levels, ranging from the small amounts in the CPU to the much slower but more plentiful storage of a mechanical hard drive.

FIGURE 6.10 A DIMM memory module holds a series of RAM chips. *(Hugh Threlfall/Alamy)*

faster data transfer rate, is seen in high-performance video graphics cards.

RAM appears in the system on **memory modules** (or **memory cards**), small circuit boards that hold a series of RAM chips and fit into special slots on the motherboard. Most memory modules in today's systems are packaged as a *dual inline memory module (DIMM)*, a small circuit board that holds several memory chips (see Figure 6.10).

How can I tell how much RAM is installed in my computer? The amount of

RAM actually sitting on memory modules in your computer is your computer's **physical memory**. The easiest way to see how much RAM you have is to look in the System Properties window. (On a Mac, choose the Apple menu and then About This Mac.) This is the same tab you looked in to determine your system's CPU type and speed, and is shown in Figure 6.5. RAM capacity is measured in gigabytes (GB), and most machines sold today have at least 4 GB of RAM.

How can I tell how my RAM is being used? To see exactly how your RAM is being used, open the Resource Monitor and click on the Memory tab (see Figure 6.11). The Resource Monitor gives additional details on CPU, disk, network, and memory usage inside your system, and you can use it to see how you're using all the RAM you paid for!

Windows uses a memory-management technique known as **SuperFetch**. SuperFetch monitors that applications you use the most and preloads them into your system memory so that they'll be ready to be used when you want them. For example, if you have Microsoft Word running, Windows stores as much of the information

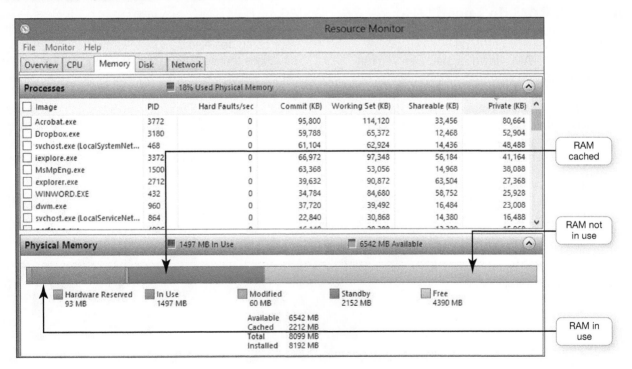

FIGURE 6.11 The Resource Monitor's Memory tab shows a detailed breakdown of how the computer is using memory.

>*To access the Resource Monitor, in the Task Manager, click the **Performance** tab, click **Open Resource Monitor**, and then click the **Memory** tab.*

related to Word in RAM as it can, which speeds up how fast your application responds. This is because pulling information from RAM is much faster than pulling it from the hard drive. You can watch this process at work using the Resource Monitor. Figure 6.11 shows how the 8 GB of installed RAM is being used:

- 1.5 GB is running programs.
- 2.15 GB is holding cached data and files ready for quick access.
- 4.4 GB is currently unused.

How much RAM do I need? At a minimum, your system needs enough RAM to run the OS. Running the 64-bit version of Windows 8 requires a minimum of 2 GB of RAM. However, because you run more applications at one time than just the OS, you'll want to have more RAM than just what's needed for the OS. For example, Figure 6.12 shows how much RAM you'd need to run your OS, a web browser, and some software. In this example, if you have these programs running at the same time, you'll need a minimum of 6 GB of RAM.

It's a good idea to have more than the minimum amount of RAM you need now so you can use more programs in the future. Remember, too, that "required" means these are the *minimum values* recommended by manufacturers; having more RAM often helps programs run more efficiently. New systems today ship with at least 4 GB of RAM, and high-end systems can come with 24 GB. The rule of thumb: When buying a new computer, buy as much RAM as you can afford.

FIGURE 6.12

Sample RAM Allocation

APPLICATION	RAM RECOMMENDED
Windows 8 (64 bit)	2 GB
Microsoft Office Professional 2010	512 MB
Internet Explorer 9	512 MB
iTunes 10	1 GB
Adobe Photoshop Elements 9	2 GB
Total RAM required to run all programs simultaneously	**6 GB**

Adding RAM

Is there a limit to how much RAM I can add to my computer? The motherboard is designed with a specific number of slots into which the memory cards fit, and each slot has a limit on the amount of RAM it can hold. To determine your specific system limits, check the system manufacturer's website.

In addition, the OS running on your machine imposes its own RAM limit. For example, the maximum amount of RAM for the 32-bit version of Windows 8 is 4 GB, whereas the maximum memory you can install using the 64-bit version of Windows 8 Pro is 192 GB.

Is it difficult or expensive to add RAM? Adding RAM is fairly easy (see Figure 6.13). Be sure that you purchase a memory module that's compatible with your computer. Also be sure to follow the installation instructions that come with the RAM module. Typically, you simply line up the notches and gently push the memory module in place.

RAM is a relatively inexpensive system upgrade. The cost of RAM does fluctuate in the marketplace as much as 400% over time, though, so if you're considering adding RAM, you should watch the prices of memory in online and print advertisements. ■

FIGURE 6.13 Adding RAM to a computer is quite simple and relatively inexpensive. On a laptop, you often gain access through a panel on the bottom.
(Editorial Image, LLC/Alamy; Editorial Image, LLC/Alamy)

evaluating the
STORAGE SUBSYSTEM

Remember, there are two ways data is stored on your computer: temporary storage and permanent storage. RAM is a form of temporary (or volatile) storage. The information residing in RAM is not stored permanently. It's critical to have the means to store data and software applications permanently.

Fortunately, several storage options exist. Storage devices include internal hard drives, SSDs, optical drives, and external hard drives. When you turn off your computer, the data that has been written to these devices will be available the next time the machine is powered on. These devices therefore provide *nonvolatile* storage.

Mechanical Hard Drives

What makes the hard drive such a popular storage device? With storage capacities exceeding 4 terabytes (TB), a mechanical **hard drive** has the largest capacity of any storage device. And because it offers the most storage per dollar, the hard drive is also a more economical device than other options.

Today, most desktop system units are designed to support more than one internal hard drive. The Apple Mac Pro has room for four hard drives, and the Thermaltake Level 10 can support six hard drives. Each one simply slides into place when you want to add more storage.

How is data stored on a hard drive? A hard drive is composed of several coated, round, thin plates of metal stacked on a spindle. Each plate is called

a **platter**. When data is saved to a hard drive platter, a pattern of magnetized spots is created on the iron oxide coating of each platter. When the spots are aligned in one direction, they represent a *1*; when they're aligned in the other direction, they represent a *0*. These *0*s and *1*s are *bits* (or *binary digits*) and are the smallest pieces of data that computers can understand. When data stored on the hard drive platter is retrieved (or read), your computer translates these patterns of magnetized spots into the data you have saved.

How quickly does a hard drive find information? The hard drive's **access time**, the time it takes a storage device to locate its stored data and make it available for processing, is faster than optical drives. Mechanical hard drive access times are measured in milliseconds (ms), meaning thousandths of seconds. For large-capacity drives, access times of approximately 12 to 13 milliseconds are typical. That's less than one-hundredth of a second. For comparison, a DVD drive can take over 150 milliseconds to access data.

Solid State Drives

Do mechanical hard drives have the fastest access times? A **solid-state drive (SSD)** uses electronic memory and has no mechanical motors or moving parts. Having no mechanical motors allows SSDs to offer incredibly fast access times, reaching data in only a tenth of a millisecond (0.1 ms). That's about 100 times faster than mechanical hard drives (see Figure 6.14)! SSDs also have a great advantage when booting up since a mechanical hard drive has to wait for motors to bring the plates up to the final rotation speed. The startup time of SSDs is so fast, in fact, that most desktop and laptop systems offer an option to have at least one SSD be used to hold the OS. This "system drive" may only be 20 GB large, but it means the wake-up time for the system will be very fast. In

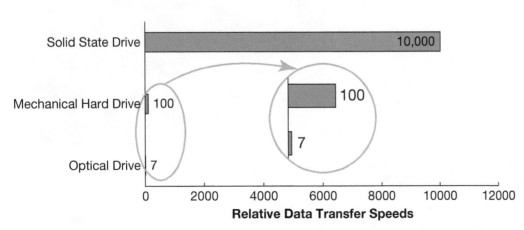

FIGURE 6.14 Relative Data Transfer Speeds for Nonvolatile Storage Options

The thin metal platters that make up a hard drive are covered with a special magnetic coating that enables the data to be recorded onto one or both sides of the platter. Hard drive manufacturers prepare the disks to hold data through a process called *low-level formatting*. In this process, concentric circles, each called a **track**, and pie-shaped wedges, each called a **sector**, are created in the magnetized surface of each platter, setting up a gridlike pattern that identifies file locations on the hard drive. A separate process called *high-level formatting* establishes the catalog that the computer uses to keep track of where each file is located on the hard drive. More detail on this process is presented in the Dig Deeper feature "How Disk Defragmenter Utilities Work" in Chapter 5.

Hard drive platters spin at a high rate of speed, some as fast as 15,000 revolutions per minute (rpm). Sitting between the platters are special "arms" that contain read/write heads (see Figure 6.15). A **read/write head** moves from the outer edge of the spinning platter to the center, as frequently as 50 times per second, to retrieve (read) and record (write) the magnetic data to and from the hard drive platter. As noted earlier, the average total time it takes for the read/write head to locate the data on the platter and return it to the CPU for processing is called its *access time*. A new hard drive should have an average access time of approximately 12 ms.

Access time is mostly the sum of two factors—seek time and latency:

1. The time it takes for the read/write heads to move over the surface of the disk, moving to the correct track, is called the **seek time**. (Sometimes people incorrectly refer to this as access time.)
2. Once the read/write head locates the correct track, it may need to wait for the correct sector to spin to the read/write head. This waiting time is called **latency** (or **rotational delay**).

The faster the platters spin (or the faster the rpm), the less time you'll have to wait for your data to be accessed. Currently, most hard drives for home systems spin at 7,200 rpm.

The read/write heads don't touch the platters of the hard drive; rather, they float above them on a thin cushion of air at a height of 0.5 microinches. As a matter of comparison, a human hair is 2,000 microinches thick and a particle of dust is larger than a human hair. Therefore, it's critical to keep your hard drive free from all dust and dirt because even the smallest particle could find its way between the read/write head and the disk platter, causing a **head crash**—a stoppage of the hard drive that often results in data loss.

SSDs free you from worry about head crashes at all. The memory inside an SSD is constructed with electronic transistors, meaning there are no platters, no motors, and no read/write arms. Instead, a series of cells are constructed in the silicon wafers. If high voltage is applied, electrons move in and you have one state. Reverse the voltage and the electrons flow in another direction, marking the cell as storing a different value. The limiting factor for an SSD's lifespan is how many times data can be written to a cell. But the current generation of SSDs is proving to have very strong performance over time. Intel, one manufacturer of SSDs, says its drives will last five years when being written to heavily (20 GB per day).

Capacities for hard drives in personal computers can exceed 4,000 GB (4 TB). Increasing the amount of data stored in a hard drive is achieved either by adding more platters or by increasing the amount of data stored on each platter. How tightly the tracks are placed next to each other, how tightly spaced the sectors are, and how closely the bits of data are placed affect the measurement of the amount of data that can be stored in a specific area of a hard drive platter. Modern technology continues to increase the standards on all three levels, enabling massive quantities of data to be stored in small places.

FIGURE 6.15 The hard drive is a stack of platters enclosed in a sealed case. Special arms fit between each platter. The read/write heads at the end of each arm read data from and save data to the platters. *(skaljac/Shutterstock)*

addition, SSDs run with no noise, generate very little heat, and require very little power, making them a popular option in ultrabooks.

Storage capacities for SSDs now range up to 2 TB, but such a large SSD is very expensive. Systems now often offer an SSD of 128 GB or 256 GB and then a mechanical hard drive, or two, to provide TBs of inexpensive slower storage space.

Optical Drives

How do optical drives work? Optical drives are disc drives that use a laser to store and read data. Data is saved to a compact disc (CD), digital video disc (DVD), or Blu-ray disc (BD) (called **optical media**) within established tracks and sectors, just like on a hard drive. But optical discs store data as tiny pits that are burned into the disc by a high-speed laser. These pits are extremely small, less than 1 micron (a millionth of a meter).

Figure 6.16 shows how data is read from a disc by a laser beam, with the pits and nonpits (called *lands*) translating into the *1*s and *0*s of the binary code that computers understand. CDs and DVDs use a red laser to read and write data. Blu-ray discs get their name because they are read with a blue laser light, which has

a shorter wavelength and can focus more tightly and pack more information on a disc. Blu-ray drives are the fastest optical devices on the market and deliver the high-definition quality video that larger displays and monitors demand.

Why can I store data on some optical discs but not others? All forms of optical media come in three formats:

1. *Prerecorded* discs are read-only (ROM), meaning you can't save any data onto them.

2. *Recordable* (R) formats allow you to write data to them, but only once.

3. *Rewriteable* (RW) discs let you write and rewrite data to them many times.

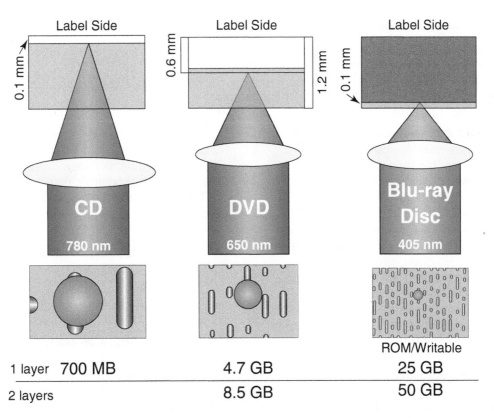

	1 layer	2 layers
CD (780 nm)	700 MB	
DVD (650 nm)	4.7 GB	8.5 GB
Blu-ray Disc (405 nm) ROM/Writable	25 GB	50 GB

FIGURE 6.16 Blu-ray lasers have a shorter wavelength and so can store a much higher density of information than CDs and DVDs.

FIGURE 6.17 In Windows, the free and used capacity of each device in the computer system is shown in the Computer window. The General tab of the Properties dialog box gives you more-detailed information.

>*To view the Computer window, launch File Explorer (previously called Windows Explorer), and then click* **Computer**. *To view the pie chart, right-click the* **C drive***, and select* **Properties**.

Should I bother having an optical disc drive? Traditionally, optical media delivered music and movies, but these are now available through streaming services. Likewise, in the past, software was often installed from a DVD, but now you buy almost all software online. Therefore, many lightweight systems have stopped including optical drives. For example, netbooks and ultrabooks are so thin and lightweight they often leave out an optical drive but may include a slot for an SD memory card to allow you to transfer files. You can buy external optical drives, but if you have a need for optical drives, you're probably better off purchasing a laptop computer; these have optical drives.

Your Storage Capacity and Needs

How do I know how much storage capacity I have? Typically, hard drive capacity is measured in gigabytes (GB) or terabytes (1 TB = 1,000

GB). Windows displays the hard drives, their capacity, and usage information, as shown in Figure 6.17. To get a slightly more detailed view, select a drive and then right-click and choose Properties.

How much storage do I need? You need enough space to store the following:

- The OS
- The software applications you use, such as Microsoft Office, music players, and games
- Your data files
- Your digital music library, photos, videos of television shows and movies, and so on

Figure 6.18 shows an example of storage calculation. If you plan to have a system backup on the same drive, be sure to budget for that room as well. However, note that if you're going to store your data files online instead of on your computer, you may not need much hard drive space. For example, if you stream all the movies you watch from Netflix, keep all your data

FIGURE 6.18

Sample Hard Drive Space Requirements

APPLICATION/DATA	HARD DRIVE SPACE REQUIRED	HEAVY CLOUD STORAGE USER
Windows 8 (64 bit)	20 GB	20 GB
Microsoft Office 2010 Professional	3.5 GB	3.5 GB
Adobe Photoshop Elements 9	2 GB	2 GB
Adobe Premiere Pro CS5.5	10 GB	10 GB
Video library of movies	80 GB (about 40 HD movies)	Streamed through online services
Music library	50 GB (about 7,000 songs)	Stored in cloud (iCloud or Amazon Cloud Drive)
Photographs	5 GB	Stored in iCloud or Dropbox
Total storage in use	**170.5 GB**	**35.5 GB**
Full backup	170.5 GB	Done to cloud using Carbonite
Total required	**341 GB**	**35.5 GB**

files in Microsoft SkyDrive, and use online software like Google Docs to edit, you may need very little hard drive space. Most ultrabooks like the Dell XPS 13 or the Apple MacBook Air are configured with 128-GB drives. In fact, many Chromebooks have only a 16-GB drive.

Also note that you don't need to have an internal hard drive that has all the storage space you need. You can also add an external hard drive to your system, many of which use a USB port to connect. If you're looking to buy an external hard drive, the USB 3.0 standard is about 10 times faster than USB 2.0, so if your system supports USB 3.0, that's the better choice.

Is it better to have one huge drive or several smaller drives? It depends on what's important to you: speed or security. If you purchase two smaller drives, you can combine them using RAID technology. **RAID (redundant array of independent disks)** is a set of strategies for using more than one drive in a system (see

Figure 6.19). RAID 0 and RAID 1 are the most popular options for consumer machines.

• When you run two hard drives in **RAID 0**, the time it takes to write a file is cut in half. If disk performance is very important—for example, when you're doing

FIGURE 6.19 (a) A RAID 0 configuration speeds up file read/write time. (b) A RAID 1 configuration gives you an instant backup. *(World Pictures/Alamy; Ragnarock/Shutterstock)*

BITS&BYTES

Where's the Free TV?

Most major networks are streaming content for free so that you can catch full episodes of most popular TV series on the go. Subscription channels like HBO and Showtime all have free streaming of content. If you have HBO at home, you can watch any show from their HBO GO website on your laptop or tablet. If you're interested in more international viewing, head to Squid TV and select live broadcasts from countries around the world.

If you're looking for homemade shows, sites like Justin.tv and Ustream are filled with live and archived video webcasts. Once you decide to start making television instead of just watching, you can webcast your own television show directly from the Ustream webapp using your webcam or smartphone video camera.

video editing or sound recording—using two files in RAID 0 could be important. RAID 0 is faster because every time data is written to a hard drive, it's spread across the two physical drives (see Figure 6.19a). The write begins on the first drive, and while the system is waiting for that write to be completed, the system jumps ahead and begins to write the next block of data to the second drive. This makes writing

 SOUND BYTE
Installing a Blu-ray Drive
In this Sound Byte, you'll learn how to install a Blu-ray drive in your computer.

information to disk almost twice as fast as using just one hard drive. The downside is that if either of these disks fail, you lose all your data because part of each file is on each drive. So RAID 0 is for those most concerned with performance.

- If you're really paranoid about losing data, you should consider having two drives in RAID 1. In a **RAID 1** configuration, all the data written to one drive is instantly perfectly mirrored and written to a second drive (see Figure 6.19b). This provides you with a perfect, instant-by-instant backup of all your work. It also means that if you buy two 1-TB drives, you only have room to store 1 TB of data because the second 1-TB drive is being used as the "mirror."

RAID 0 and RAID 1 configurations are available on many desktop systems and are even beginning to appear on laptop computers.

So how do my storage devices measure up? Figure 6.20 summarizes the factors you should consider in evaluating your storage subsystem. ■

Before moving on to Part 2:
- Watch Replay Video 6.1 ▶.
- Then check your understanding of what you've learned so far

---

FIGURE 6.20

Evaluating Storage

- How much storage space do you need?
- Do you need a RAID 0 configuration for better performance?
- Do you want a RAID 1 configuration for immediate constant backup?

Mechanical Hard Drive

Storage

Optical Drive

Solid State Drive

- Do you want very fast start-up of the system at boot-up and from sleep mode?
- Are you okay having a second hard disk drive for larger storage space?

- Do you need to read or produce DVD/CDs?
- Do you need to read Blu-ray discs?
- Do you need to produce Blu-ray discs?

(Maxim_Kazmin/Fotolia)

check your understanding //

For a quick review to see what you've learned so far, answer the following questions. Visit **pearsonhighered.com/techinaction** to check your answers.

multiple choice

1. Which statement about ultrabook computers is FALSE?

    a. Ultrabooks have the fastest optical drives.

    b. Ultrabooks are equipped with SSD drives for fast start-up.

    c. Ultrabooks typically weigh less than 3 pounds.

    d. Ultrabooks do not offer an ExpressCard slot for expansion.

2. SSDs are classified as what type of storage?

    a. volatile

    b. nonvolatile

    c. video

    d. cache

3. When would you want to consider RAID 1 technology?

    a. When you need the fastest solution for writing data.

    b. When you need an instant backup of your work.

    c. If you think that SSDs are too expensive.

    d. When you only want to have one hard disk drive.

4. CPUs have several internal components, including

    a. Level 1 cache memory.

    b. ALU.

    c. Level 2 cache memory.

    d. all of the above.

5. SuperFetch is a memory-management technique that

    a. determines the type of RAM your system requires.

    b. makes the boot-up time for the system very quick.

    c. preloads the applications you use most into system memory.

    d. defragments the hard drive to increase performance.

true–false

_____ 1. A quad core CPU with hyperthreading has eight virtual CPUs.

_____ 2. SSD hard drives are a cheaper alternative to RAM.

critical thinking

1. **More and More Storage**

    The amount of storage we have available on hard disk drives has increased again and again. What created our need for such huge amounts of storage? How have our storage habits changed? What is the perfect balance for you in how you use nonvolatile storage?

2. **Emerging Technologies**

    Touch screens are now available in a range of sizes, from smartphones to iPads to larger products like the Microsoft PixelSense. Windows 8 has a redesigned interface for support of touch screens. What other new technologies will become part of our collective experience? How will these technologies and devices change entertainment and how people interact with information? What future technologies would be on your wish list?

Continue ▶

Using the Windows Task Manager and the Resource Monitor can provide you with a lot of useful information about your computer system. Let's make sure you can use these Windows tools to keep an eye on your system performance.

Step 1 Hold the Windows key and hit X. From the pop-up, select **Control Panel** and then **View By Small icons**. Click **Performance Information and Tools**.

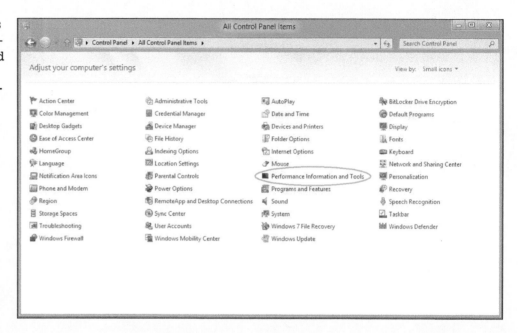

Step 2 You'll now see the Windows Experience Index, a measure of the computer's performance in various subsystems. Click the **View and print detailed performance and system information** link to display a report like the one shown here.

Overall, your system is assigned a base score reflecting the capability of your hardware and software. Base scores range from 1 to 7.9 (this computer has a base score of 5.4). The report also identifies information about the CPU, storage system, memory, and graphics adapter. Each component is assigned a subscore on a scale of 1 to 7.9. This ultrabook actually has a superfast SSD hard drive and achieves a 7.6 subscore in that area but it has a slow built-in Intel graphics card (5.4 subscore). This report gives you a guideline of how you may want to upgrade specific subsystems.

Step 3 To see how your system is running during your workday, select **Advanced tools** from the **Performance Information and Tools** window. Choose **Open Task Manager** and select the **Performance** tab. If you leave this window open while you work, you can pop in and check the history of how your CPU, disk, memory, and network are performing. Let's start by looking at CPU utilization.

This computer is never going over 45%, so the system isn't limited by CPU speed.

Step 4 What about disk usage? Clicking on **Disk** in the left panel shows that we have one disk drive, a 128-GB SanDisk SSD. The lower graph shows the history of data moving back and forth to the disk, the disk transfer rate. The larger upper graph shows how active the disk is—what percentage of time it is reading and writing. If that is consistently high, upgrading to a faster, larger disk will have a big performance impact.

Evaluating Other Subsystems and Making a Decision

The audio and video subsystems of your computer affect much of your enjoyment of the machine. Let's evaluate those subsystems and consider what state-of-the-art audio/video would add to your computing experience. Then let's consider how to make sure your system is reliable—nothing interferes with enjoying technology like a misbehaving computer!

evaluating the
VIDEO SUBSYSTEM

How video is displayed depends on two components: your video card and your monitor. If you're considering using your computer to display complex graphics, edit high-definition videos, or play graphics-rich games with a lot of fast action, you may want to consider upgrading your video subsystem.

Video Cards

What exactly is a video card? A **video card** (or **video adapter**) is an expansion card that's installed inside the system unit to translate binary data into the images you view on your monitor. Modern video cards like the ones shown in Figures 6.21 and 6.22 let you connect video equipment using a number of different ports:

- *DVI ports* for digital LCD monitors
- *HDMI ports* for high-definition TVs, Blu-ray players, or gaming consoles
- *DisplayPort adapters,* a newer style port that can connect to digital monitors or projectors

How much memory does my video card need? All video systems include their own RAM, called **video memory**. Several standards of video memory are available, including graphics double data rate 3 (GDDR3) memory and the newer **graphics double data rate 5 (GDDR5)** memory.

The amount of video memory on your video card makes a big impact on the resolution the system can support and on how smoothly and quickly it can render video. Most new laptop computers come with video cards equipped with a minimum of 1 GB of video memory. For the serious gamer, 2 GB or more is essential, and cards with 3 GB are available. These high-end video cards allow games to generate smoother animations and more-sophisticated shading and texture.

How can I tell how much memory my video card has? You'll find information about your system's video card in the Advanced Settings of

Processor covered by heat sink and fan

Video memory chips

Video memory chip

DisplayPort adapter

HDMI port to digital monitor

Video memory chip

Clips into motherboard

Digital Video Interface (DVI) port to digital monitor

DVI port

FIGURE 6.21 Video cards have grown to be highly specialized subsystems.

FIGURE 6.22 Video card processors produce so much heat that video cards have their own fan—or two.
(nikkytok/Fotolia)

In addition, special lighting effects can be achieved with a modern GPU. Designers can change the type of light, the texture, and the color of objects based on complex interactions. Some GPU designs incorporate dedicated hardware to allow high-definition movies to be decoded or special physics engines to model water, gravity, and rigid body movements.

Why do some people use more than one video card in the same system? For users who are primarily doing text-based work, one video card is certainly enough. Computer gamers and users of high-end visualization software, however, often take advantage of the ability to install more than one video card at a time. Two or even three video cards can be used in one system.

The two major video chip set manufacturers, Nvidia and ATI, have each developed their own standards supporting the combining of multiple video cards. For Nvidia, this standard is named SLI; for ATI, it is called CrossFire. When the system is running at very high video resolutions, such as 1920 x 1200 or higher, multiple video cards working together provide the ultimate in performance. If you're buying a new system and might be interested in employing multiple video cards, be sure to check whether the motherboard supports SLI or CrossFire.

Can I run a few monitors from one video card? Working with multiple monitors is useful if you often have more than one application running

the Screen Resolution dialog box. To get to the Screen Resolution dialog box, right-click on your desktop and select Screen resolution. In the Screen Resolution dialog box, click the Advanced settings link. A window will appear that shows you the type of video card installed in your system, as well as its memory information.

How does the CPU handle intensive video calculations? Because displaying graphics demands a lot of computational work from the CPU, video cards come with their own **graphics processing unit (GPU)**. The GPU is a separate processing chip specialized to handle 3-D graphics and image and video processing with incredible efficiency and speed. When the CPU is asked to process graphics, it redirects those tasks to the GPU, significantly speeding up graphics processing. Figure 6.23 shows how the CPU can run much more efficiently when a GPU does all the graphics computations.

 ACTIVE HELPDESK
Evaluating Computer System Components

In this Active Helpdesk call, you'll play the role of a helpdesk staffer, fielding calls about the computer's storage, video, and audio devices and how to evaluate whether they match your needs, as well as how to improve the reliability of your system.

Without a GPU

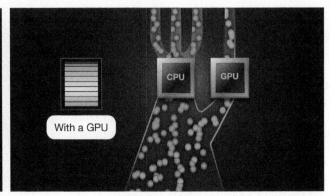

With a GPU

FIGURE 6.23 The GPU is specialized to handle processing of photos, videos, and video game images. It frees up the CPU to work on other system demands.

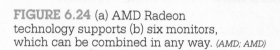

FIGURE 6.24 (a) AMD Radeon technology supports (b) six monitors, which can be combined in any way. *(AMD; AMD)*

at a time (see Figure 6.24) or even if you just want to expand your gaming experience. Some video cards can support up to six monitors from a single card. The AMD Radeon graphics card, for example, lets you merge all six monitors to work as one screen or to combine them into any subset—for example, displaying a movie on two combined screens, Excel on one monitor, Word on another, and a browser spread across the final two.

Can I have a 3-D experience from a computer monitor? 3-D panels are available for desktop monitors and for some laptops. Using the 3-D wireless vision glasses included with the panels, the glasses make existing games or 3-D movies display in stereoscopic 3-D.

How do I know if I'm putting too much demand on my video card? If your monitor takes a while to refresh when you're editing photos or playing a graphics-rich game, then the video card could be short on memory or the GPU is being

taxed beyond its capacity. You can evaluate this precisely using the software that came with your card. For example, AMD Overdrive software monitors the GPU usage level, the current temperature, and the fan speed.

Review the considerations listed in Figure 6.25 to see if it might be time for you to upgrade your video card. On a desktop computer, replacing a video card is fairly simple: Just insert the new video card in the correct expansion slot on the motherboard. The video card in a laptop is more difficult to upgrade since the display and keyboard usually have to be removed to replace the video card. Note that some very basic laptop systems have video adapters integrated into the motherboard, so these video cards can't be upgraded. ■

FIGURE 6.25

Do You Need to Upgrade Your Video Card?

How much total **memory** is on the card?

How many **monitors** can it support?

Does it have the **ports** I need?

Video Card

Is the **GPU** fast enough?

BITS&BYTES

Auto Tech: Can Your Car Do This?

Cool technology isn't just for your laptop. The automotive industry is making its own technological advances as well. For example, the OnStar system distributes sensors around the car that let your car call for help if it detects a crash and you're not responsive. OnStar reports the direction and number of impacts, the car's rollover status, and the car's maximum velocity on impact so medical workers can come better prepared.

Faster is always better, and the newest input/output standard, Thunderbolt, is faster than anything seen before. And speed isn't its only advantage.

Intel used fiber optics—the transmission of digital data through pure glass cable as thin as human hair—to develop the new input/output technology named Thunderbolt. Thunderbolt supports blazingly fast transfer rates of 10 Gb/s, zooming past even the theoretical limit of the new USB 3.0, which is 4.8 Gb/s. How fast is that? Intel says that Thunderbolt could transfer a full-length HD movie in under 30 seconds or copy in just 10 minutes a library of music that would take a solid year to play through. And Thunderbolt can supply much more power to devices than the USB standard allows. It also has a very slim connector design, allowing laptop designers to make their systems even thinner (see Figure 6.26).

But one of the greatest hopes that comes with Thunderbolt is that the technology will be able to replace a number of different ports, cleaning up the cluttered design we see now on the sides of laptops and the backs of desktop units. The first devices using this technology appeared in May 2011 when Apple introduced Thunderbolt ports on the MacBook Pro series. It looks like a single thin port that supports both the video standard DisplayPort and the bus standard PCI Express (see Figure 6.27). So Thunderbolt can connect monitors to computers using VGA, DisplayPort,

Thunderbolt port   USB port

FIGURE 6.26 Thunderbolt ports are very thin, allowing for new design options. *(Kendall Martin)*

DVI, or HDMI and can connect systems to external hard drives that use USB, FireWire, or eSATA. One Thunderbolt port can support several devices because the cables can be daisy-chained (connected one after another in a serial fashion), so having just one Thunderbolt port on a laptop allows you to connect up to six different peripherals to your system.

Thunderbolt technology also gives you a two-for-one deal, because each connector can support two separate channels to send and receive data, each one still operating at the full 10 Gb/s bandwidth.

What will this mean to laptop designers? Some speculate we'll see the heavy, heat-producing video cards currently integrated into gaming laptops become external graphics boxes. An incredibly thin, light laptop design would let you be wonderfully mobile all day, and then when you come home, you'd attach one cable. It would run from your Thunderbolt port to your 60-inch HDTV and then continue on to a separate graphics processor box. That same laptop would then be running a huge high-definition monitor with a high-resolution graphics and physics engine.

Apple is not the only company that will be using the Intel technology. Hard-drive companies like LaCie and Western Digital, as well as audio/video processing companies like Avid and Apogee, have announced Thunderbolt products. And the USB community may need to put up a bit of a fight to keep their standard around. But the allure of incredible speed, great versatility, and small, thin packaging is going to make the Thunderbolt technology a trend to watch.

Could Thunderbolt make USB a thing of the past?

PCI Express →   ← PCI Express →
← Thunderbolt™ Cable →
DisplayPort →   DisplayPort →
Thunderbolt Controller   Thunderbolt Controller

FIGURE 6.27 Thunderbolt can carry two channels of information on the same connector.

evaluating the
AUDIO SUBSYSTEM

For many users, a computer's preinstalled speakers and sound card are adequate. However, if you often use your computer to play games, music, and video, you may want to upgrade your speakers or your sound card.

What does the sound card do? Like a video card, a **sound card** is an expansion card that attaches to the motherboard inside your system unit. A sound card enables the computer to drive the speaker system. Most desktop systems have a separate sound card, although low-end computers often have integrated the job of managing sound onto the motherboard itself. You can upgrade laptop sound cards using an ExpressCard solution, like the Creative Sound Blaster X-Fi.

What does a basic sound card do for me? Many computers ship with a **3-D sound card**. 3-D sound technology is better at convincing the human ear that sound is omnidirectional, meaning that you can't tell from which direction the sound is coming. This tends to produce a fuller, richer sound than stereo sound. However, 3-D sound is not surround sound.

What is surround sound, then? **Surround sound** is a type of audio processing that makes the listener experience sound as if it were coming from all directions by using multiple speakers. The current surround sound standard is from Dolby. There are many formats available, including Dolby Digital EX and Dolby Digital Plus for high-definition audio. Dolby TrueHD is the newest standard. It features high-definition and lossless technology, which means that no information is lost in the compression process.

To create surround sound, another standard, Dolby Digital 7.1, takes digital sound from a medium (such as a Blu-ray disc) and reproduces it in eight channels. Seven channels cover the listening field with placement to the left front, right front, left rear, right rear, and center of the audio stage, as well as two extra speakers to the side, as shown in Figure 6.28. The eighth channel holds extremely low-frequency

sound data and is sent to a subwoofer, which can be placed anywhere in the room.

The name 7.1 surround indicates that there are seven speakers reproducing the full audio spectrum and one speaker handling just lower frequency bass sounds. There is also a 5.1 surround sound standard, which has a total of six speakers—one subwoofer, a center speaker, and four speakers for right/left in the front and the back. If you have a larger space or want precise location of sounds, use the newer 7.1 system.

To set up surround sound on your computer, you need two things:

1. A set of surround-sound speakers and, for the greatest surround-sound experience,

2. A sound card that is Dolby Digital compatible

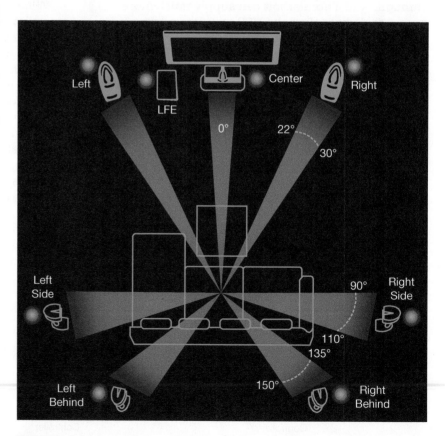

FIGURE 6.28 Dolby Digital 7.1 surround sound gives you better-quality audio output.

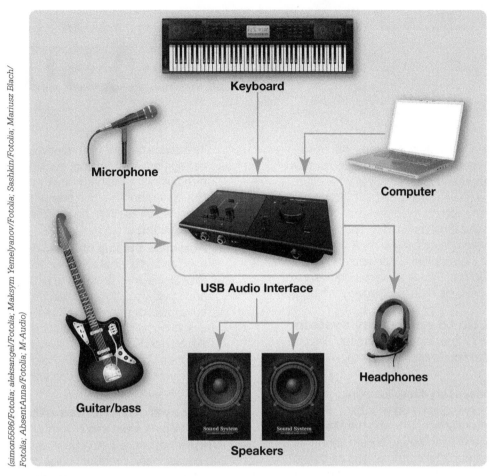

(simon5586/Fotolia; aleksangel/Fotolia; Maksym Yemelyanov/Fotolia; Sashkin/Fotolia; Mariusz Blach/Fotolia; AbsentAnna/Fotolia; M-Audio)

FIGURE 6.29 Sample Home Recording Studio Setup

Does it matter what kind of speakers my laptop has? The limited size for speakers in a laptop and the added weight of circuitry to drive them means most people use headphones or ear buds for great audio instead of speakers. However, some laptops have built-in higher-quality speakers, like the Alienware line featuring Klipsch speakers and the HP series offering Beats speakers.

What setup do I need if I want to use my computer for recording my band? You can connect MIDI instruments, high-quality microphones, and recording equipment to your computer through an **audio MIDI interface** box. MIDI is an electronics standard that allows different kinds of electronic instruments to communicate with each other and with computers. The audio interface box attaches to your computer through a USB port and adds jacks for connecting guitars and microphones. You can edit and mix tracks through many different software packages, like Cakewalk or GarageBand. Figure 6.29 shows a simple home recording studio setup.

Figure 6.30 lists the factors to consider when deciding whether your audio subsystem meets your needs. ■

FIGURE 6.30

Do You Need to Upgrade Your Audio Subsystem?

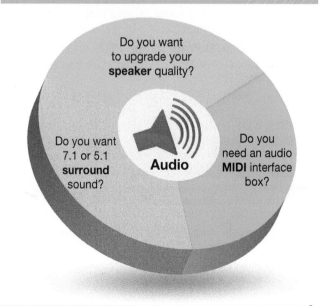

Do you want to upgrade your **speaker** quality?

Do you want 7.1 or 5.1 **surround** sound?

Audio

Do you need an audio **MIDI** interface box?

Trust
Assured relian
confidence or
the truth, wo
dependence
belief in the

evaluating system
RELIABILITY

Many computer users decide to buy a new system because they're experiencing problems such as slow performance, freezes, and crashes. Over time, even normal use can cause your computer to build up excess files and to become internally disorganized. This excess, clutter, and disorganization can lead to deteriorating performance or system failure. If you think your system is unreliable, see if the problem is one you can fix before you buy a new machine. Proper upkeep and maintenance also may postpone an expensive system upgrade or replacement.

What can I do to ensure my system stays reliable? Here are several procedures you can follow to ensure your system performs reliably (see also Figure 6.31):

- **Clear out unnecessary files.** Temporary Internet files can accumulate quickly on your hard drive, taking up unnecessary space. Running the Disk Cleanup utility is a quick and easy way to ensure your temporary Internet files don't take up precious hard drive space. Likewise, you should delete any unnecessary files from your hard drive regularly because they can make your hard drive run more slowly.

- **Install a reliable antivirus package.** Make sure it's set to update itself automatically and to run a full system scan frequently.

- **Run spyware and adware removal programs.** These often detect and remove different pests and should be used in addition to your regular antivirus package.

- **Run the Disk Defragmenter utility on your hard drive.** When your hard drive becomes fragmented,

its storage capacity is negatively affected. When you defragment (defrag) your hard drive, files are reorganized, making the hard drive work more efficiently. But remember that this only makes sense for mechanical drives. With no motors, there is no need to defrag an SSD drive.

- **Automate the key utilities.** The utilities that need to be run more than once, like Disk Cleanup, Disk Defragmenter, and the antivirus, adware, and spyware programs, can be configured to run automatically at any time interval you want. You can use Windows Task Scheduler or third-party programs like Norton Security Suite to set up a sequence of programs to run one after the other every evening while you sleep, so you can wake up each day to a reliable, secure system.

My system crashes often during the day. What can do? Computer systems are complex. It's not unusual to have your system stop responding occasionally. If rebooting the computer doesn't help, you'll need to begin troubleshooting:

1. **Check that you have enough RAM.** You learned how to do this in the "Evaluating the Memory Subsystem" section earlier in this chapter (page 234). Systems with insufficient RAM often crash.

2. **If your system isn't responding, try doing a Refresh on your system.** This Windows 8 utility removes all the changes you've made to the system and brings it back to the state it came to you from the factory. It removes all the applications from third-party vendors, but it won't remove personal files like your music, documents, or videos.

FIGURE 6.31

Utilities to Keep Your System Reliable

TO AVOID THIS PROBLEM	USE THIS TOOL	FOR MORE INFO
Your hard drive is running low on space, making it run slowly	Disk Cleanup utility	Chapter 5
Your system is slowing down, browsers or other programs are behaving strangely	Antivirus software Spyware and adware removal software	Chapter 9
Files are spread across many spots on the hard drive, making the hard drive run slowly	Disk Defragmenter utility	Chapter 5

3. **If a Refresh wasn't enough to fix the problem, consider a full system restore.** Windows 8 automatically creates restore points before any major change to the system takes place, such as when you install a new program or change a device driver. By default, Windows also makes a restore point every 7 days. (You can also manually create a restore point at any time.) You can then select any restore point and bring your system back to the state it was in at that point. Open the Control Panel, click on System, and then select System Protection to learn more about System Restore.

   For Mac systems, the Mac OS X Time Machine, shown in Figure 6.32, provides automatic backup and enables you to look through and restore (if necessary) files, folders, libraries, or the entire system.

4. **If you see an error code in Windows, visit the Microsoft Knowledge Base (support.microsoft.com).** This online resource helps users resolve problems with Microsoft products. For example, it can help you determine what an error code indicates and how you may be able to solve the problem.

5. **Search Google.** If you don't find a satisfactory answer in the Knowledge Base, try copying the entire error message into Google and searching the larger community for solutions.

Can my software affect system reliability? Having the latest version of software makes your system much more reliable. You should upgrade or update your OS, browser software, and application software as often as new patches (or updates) are reported for resolving errors. Sometimes these errors are performance related; sometimes they're potential system security breaches.

If you're having a software problem that can be replicated, use the Steps Recorder to capture the exact steps that lead to it. In Windows 8, display the Charms bar, select Search, then type "ste" in the search box. Now run the Steps Recorder and go through the exact actions that create the problem you're having. At any particular step, you can click the Add Comment button and add a comment about any part of the screen. The Steps Recorder then produces a documented report, complete with images of your screen and descriptions of each mouse movement you made. You can then e-mail this report to customer support to help technicians resolve the problem.

How do I know whether updates are available for my software? You can configure Windows so that it automatically checks for, downloads, and installs any available updates for itself, Internet Explorer, and other Microsoft applications such as Microsoft Office. From the Windows Control Panel, open System and Security and then Windows Update. Click Change Settings.

Many other applications now also include the ability to check for updates. Check under the Help menu of the product, and you'll often find a Check for Updates command.

What if none of this helps? Is buying a new system my only option? If your system is still unreliable after these changes, consider upgrading your OS to the latest version. There are often substantial increases in reliability with a major release of a new OS. However, upgrading the OS may require hardware upgrades such as additional RAM, an updated graphics processor, and even a larger hard drive. When you launch the Windows 8 upgrade from the web, it determines whether your hardware, applications, and devices will work with the new OS. ∎

FIGURE 6.32 Mac's Time Machine keeps copies of files, folders, and libraries and can restore your system back to any previous point in time.

making a final
DECISION

Now that you've evaluated your computer system, you need to shift to questions of *value*. How closely does your system come to meeting your needs? How much would it cost to upgrade your current system to match what you'd ideally like your computer to do, not only today but also a few years from now? How much would it cost to purchase a new system that meets these specifications?

To know whether upgrading or buying a new system would have better value for you, you need to price both scenarios. Conduct a thorough system evaluation (Figure 6.33) to gather the data to help you decide. Purchasing a new system is an important investment of your resources, and you want to make a well-reasoned, well-supported decision.

FIGURE 6.33

Key Items in System Evaluation

CPU
- What is your CPU usage level?

RAM
- Do you have at least 4 GB?

Storage
- Do you need an SSD start-up drive?
- Do you have a fast-access mechanical drive for large storage space?
- Do you need RAID 0 or RAID 1 storage drives for extra-fast performance or mirroring?

Video
- Do you have enough graphics memory?
- Is your GPU powerful enough?
- Do you have HDMI ports?
- How many monitors do you need to run simultaneously?

Audio
- Do you have 7.1 or 5.1 surround sound?

Getting Rid of Your Old Computer

What should I do with my old computer? Before you get rid of your computer, be sure to consider what benefit you might obtain by having two systems. Would you have a use for the older system? Would you be able to donate it?

Also, before you decide to throw it away, consider the environmental impact (Figure 6.34). Mercury in LCD screens, cadmium in batteries and circuit boards, and flame retardants in plastic housings all are toxic. An alarming, emerging trend is that discarded machines are beginning to create an e-waste crisis.

So how can I recycle my old computer? Instead of throwing your computer away, you may be able to donate it to a nonprofit organization. Here are a few ways to do this:

- Many manufacturers, such as Dell, offer recycling programs and have formed alliances with nonprofit organizations to help distribute your old technology to those who need it.
- Sites like Computers with Causes (**computers withcauses.org**) organize donations of both working and nonworking computers, printers, and mice.
- You can also take your computer to an authorized computer-recycling center in your area. The Telecommunications Industry Association provides an e-cycling information site you can use to find a local e-cycling center (**ecyclingcentral.com**).

For companies that need to retire large quantities of computers, the risk of creating an environmental hazard is serious. Firms like GigaBiter (**gigabiter.com**) offer a solution. GigaBiter eliminates security and environmental risks associated with electronic destruction by first delaminating the hard drive and then breaking down the computer e-waste into recyclable products. The result of the final step is a sand-like substance that is 100% recyclable.

Can I donate a computer safely, without worrying about my personal data? Before donating or recycling a computer, make sure you carefully remove all data from your hard drive. Built into Windows 8 is a tool to help with this, Windows 8 Reset. It removes all user-installed applications and all of your personal data, and resets your PC settings back to the default values.

ethics in IT
Free Hardware for All

The open source software movement has flourished over the past decade. In response to increasing prices and the limitations placed on commercially available software, programmers began to donate time to design, develop, and support software systems. These products, like Gimp (a photo-editing tool), were then made freely available.

In the world of hardware, a similar but different approach called the open source hardware movement has flourished. Because hardware projects require materials and tools to assemble, products distributed as open source are not free in terms of cost, but they are free from any restrictions on how you modify them. Sample open source hardware projects include video game systems, audio equipment, and 3-D printers.

Is open hardware good for the world? Does it undermine the intellectual property of others who want to create hardware resources and sell them for a profit? What is the impact on developing countries if they have immediate access to hardware designs instead of being required to purchase these items from a for-profit company? Follow the future of open source hardware by keeping an eye on conferences like the Open Hardware Summit (**openhardwaresummit.org**), developer and supplier sites like littleBits (**littlebits.cc**), and homebrew blogs like Procrastineering (**procrastineering.blogspot.com**).

FIGURE 6.34 An electronics garbage dump can cause environmental concerns like the leaching of lead and mercury into the ground. *(Minnesota Public Radio; Tim Post/AP Photo)*

Becoming a victim of identity theft is a serious risk. Credit card numbers, bank information, Social Security numbers, tax records, passwords, and personal identification numbers (PINs) are just some of the types of sensitive information that we casually record to our computers' hard drives. Just deleting files that contain proprietary personal information is not protection enough. Likewise, reformatting or erasing your hard drive does not totally remove data, as was proved by two MIT graduate students. They bought more than 150 used hard drives from various sources. Although some of the hard drives had been reformatted or damaged so that the data was supposedly nonrecoverable, the two students were able to retrieve medical records, financial information, pornography, personal e-mails, and more than 5,000 credit card numbers!

The U.S. Department of Defense suggests a seven-layer overwrite for a "secure erase." This means that you fill your hard drive seven times over with a random series of 1s and 0s. Fortunately, several programs exist for doing this. For PCs running Windows, look for utility programs like File Shredder or Eraser. Wipe is available for Linux, and ShredIt X can be used for Mac OS X. These programs provide secure hard drive erasures, either of specific files on your hard drive or of the entire hard drive. ∎

Before moving on to the Chapter Review:
- Watch Replay Video 6.2 ▶.
- Then check your understanding of what you've learned so far.

check your understanding//

For a quick review to see what you've learned so far, answer the following questions. Visit **pearsonhighered.com/techinaction** to check your answers.

multiple choice

1. To document a problem you are having, you can use

   a. Disk Cleanup.
   c. PC Decrapifier.

   b. Steps Recorder.
   d. Resource Monitor.

2. Which is NOT a type of video port?

   a. HDMI
   c. USB 3.0

   b. DVI
   d. DisplayPort

3. A sound card that supports 7.1 surround sound will drive

   a. seven speakers.
   c. eight speakers.

   b. one speaker.
   d. Dolby headphones.

4. To improve video performance, modern computers have a _____ in addition to the CPU.

   a. GPU
   c. DPU

   b. VPU
   d. APU

5. The faster data transfer port for computers today is the _____ port

   a. USB 3.0

   b. HDMI

   c. Thunderbolt

   d. DisplayPort

true–false

_____ 1. Donating a computer always puts your personal information at risk.

_____ 2. GDDR5 memory is often used in external hard drives.

critical thinking

1. **The Early Adopter**

   We're all aware of the technology price curve: When first introduced, products have the highest prices and the most instability. As these products settle into the market, they become more reliable and the prices fall, sometimes very quickly. People who make those first-release purchases are called *early adopters*. What are the advantages to being an early adopter? What are the disadvantages? How do you decide at what point you should step into the technology price curve for any given product?

2. **A Green Machine**

   Review the impacts on the environment of your computer during its entire lifecycle. How do the production, transportation, and use of the computer affect the increase of greenhouse gas emissions? How does the selection of materials and packaging impact the environment? What restricted substances (like lead, mercury, cadmium, and PVC) are found in your machine? Could substitute materials be used? How would the ultimate "green machine" be designed?

Continue

6 Chapter Review

Summary //

Your Ideal Computer

1. What kind of computer is best for me?

- Review the types of computer devices available and consider what your needs are for weight, screen size, and processing power.
- Evaluate your computer system so you have clear data on what you currently have. Then you can compare it with what is on the market and make a decision to upgrade or purchase a new device.

Evaluating the CPU Subsystem

2. What does the CPU do, and how can I evaluate its performance?

- You can find out what processor you have using the System Properties window.
- The CPU works by running a series of four steps: fetch, decode, execute, and store.
- CPUs are compared based on their clock speed, the number of cores they have, and their amount of cache memory.
- CPU benchmarks help you compare the overall performance of different CPUs.
- The CPU performance can be measured and recorded using the CPU usage graph of the Resource Monitor.

Evaluating the Memory Subsystem

3. How does memory work in my computer?

- RAM is used to hold instructions and data because the CPU can access RAM much faster than it can access the hard drive.
- Memory modules are small circuit boards that hold a series of RAM chips in your system.

4. How do I evaluate how much memory I need?

- The System Properties window shows how much physical memory you have installed.
- The Resource Monitor shows how the installed RAM is being used by your system.
- You can easily install RAM in your system, though each system has a limit on how much RAM it can hold.

Evaluating the Storage Subsystem

5. What are the computer's storage devices?

- Data is stored on mechanical hard drives, solid state drives, and optical drives.
- There is a wide range of difference in access times and cost between different storage solutions, so most systems have a combination of types.

6. How do I evaluate my storage devices?

- The Properties dialog box in File Explorer (previously called Windows Explorer) displays information on the amount of storage available in your system.
- Compute the amount of storage you need for the software and data files you want to keep locally.
- Decide how many drives you want, what type each should be, and how you will configure them. RAID 0 is an option for combining drives for optimal performance. RAID 1 is an option for combining drives for immediate backup.

Evaluating the Video and Audio Subsystems

7. What components affect the quality of video on my computer?

- The video card is key to video quality. Be aware of how much video memory is installed and what kind of GPU is used on the card.
- Some users install multiple video cards for high-end graphics performance.
- With only one card, you can run multiple monitors.

8. How do I know if I need better video performance?

- If you see long refresh times, you may want an upgraded video card. The software that comes with the card can run performance testing to give you specific data on how the card is doing.

9. What components affect my computer's sound quality?

- The sound card and speakers control the sound quality in your system.
- If you want surround sound, you may want to invest in a new sound card and additional speakers.

Evaluating System Reliability and Making a Final Decision

10. How can I improve the reliability of my system?

- To make sure your system stays reliable, clear out unnecessary files, run antivirus software, run spyware- and adware-removal programs, run the Disk Defragmenter on mechanical hard drives, and use the Task Scheduler to automate these tasks.

- If your system is crashing often, check that you have enough RAM. Then consider doing a system refresh or even a full system restore.
- Keep your software updated. Use the Problem Steps Recorder to capture problems as they happen and report them to the manufacturer.

Be sure to check out the companion website for additional materials to help you review and learn, including a Tech Bytes Weekly newsletter— **pearsonhighered.com/techinaction** And don't forget the Replay Videos .

key terms//

3-D sound card **250**

access time **237**

audio MIDI interface **251**

cache memory **232**

clock speed **231**

core **231**

CPU benchmarks **232**

CPU usage **232**

CPU usage graph **232**

ExpressCard **229**

graphics double data rate 5 (GDDR5) **246**

graphics processing unit (GPU) **247**

hard drive **237**

head crash **238**

hyperthreading **231**

latency (rotational delay) **238**

machine cycle **231**

memory module (memory card) **235**

Moore's Law **228**

nonvolatile storage **234**

optical drive **239**

optical media **239**

overclocking **231**

physical memory **235**

platter **237**

random access memory (RAM) **234**

read/write head **238**

redundant array of independent disks (RAID) **241**

RAID 0 **241**

RAID 1 **242**

sector **238**

seek time **238**

solid-state drive (SSD) **237**

sound card **250**

SuperFetch **235**

surround sound **250**

system evaluation **229**

track **238**

video card (video adapter) **246**

video memory **246**

volatile storage **234**

making the transition to . . . next semester//

1. **Go Small or Stay Home**

   Manufacturers are releasing a number of systems that are trying to capitalize on size—or the lack of size! Explore some of the small form factor (SFF) computers appearing on the market.

   a. Research the Falcon Northwest FragBox (**falcon-nw.com**).

   b. Compare that system with the Apple Mac mini (**apple.com**).

   Why are these SFF computers appearing? What role do you see these systems fulfilling? What kind of performance and hardware would you recommend for such a system?

2. **How Does Your System Measure Up?**

   A number of tools are available to measure your system's performance. Explore the following tools and use one to gather data on your current system's performance.

   a. Windows 8 Resource Monitor: Use the Resource Monitor to collect data on CPU utilization and memory usage over a typical school day.

   b. Benchmarking suites: Examine a sample of consumer benchmarking programs like PassMark's PerformanceTest, Primate Lab's Geekbench, and Maxon's Cinebench. Which subsystems do each of these products evaluate?

making the transition to . . . the workplace//

1. **Video Connections**

   You have a position in a pharmaceutical research firm. Your group does simulations of protein folding to predict if a new drug will be effective. You collaborate daily with a team in India using videoconferencing. Now you've found out you also have the responsibility of creating a series of training videos to teach the Indian team how to use the newest release of software. What video and processing hardware would your workstation need to tackle this? Specify the video card performance and the CPU and memory requirements this project would have.

2. **Let Me Tell You My Problem**

   You may be responsible for helping others solve various computer problems. Test out the Problem Steps Recorder in Windows to see how the program can help you help them. From the charm bar, search for "psr." Run the program and click Start Record. Then just click between different applications, visit the Control Panel, and add a comment. Save the file to your desktop and close the Problem Steps Recorder. View the annotated report. How could you use the Problem Steps Recorder to describe a problem or to gather information?

Many Different Computers for Many Different Needs

Problem

Even within one discipline, there are needs for a variety of types of computing solutions. Consider the Communications department in a large university. Because it's an interdisciplinary area, there are some groups involved in video production, some groups producing digital music, and some groups creating scripts and screenplays. The department as a whole needs to decide on a complete computing strategy.

Process

1. Split the class into teams.

2. Select one segment of the Communications department that your team will represent: video production, digital music, or scripting. The video production team requires its labs to be able to support the recording, editing, and final production and distribution of digital video. The digital music group wants to establish a collegiate recording studio (after the model of the Drexel University recording label, Mad Dragon Records). The scripting group needs to support a collaborative community of writers and voice-over actors.

3. Analyze the computing needs of that segment, with particular focus on how it needs to outfit its computer labs.

4. Price the systems you would recommend and explain how they will be used. What decisions have you made in order to guarantee they will still be useful in three years?

5. Write a report that summarizes your findings. Document the resources you used and generate as much enthusiasm as you can for your recommendations.

Conclusion

The range of available computing solutions has never been so broad. It can be a cause of confusion for those not educated in technology. But with a firm understanding of the basic subsystems of computers, it is precisely this pace of change that is exciting. Being able to evaluate a computer system and match it to the current needs of its users is an important skill.

Benchmarking

In this exercise, you'll research and then role-play a complicated ethical situation. The role you play might not match your own personal beliefs; regardless, your research and use of logic will enable you to represent the view assigned. An arbitrator will watch and comment on both sides of the arguments, and together, the team will agree on an ethical solution.

Problem

We've seen that for complex systems like computers, performance often is determined not by comparing the specifications of individual parts but by using benchmarks, software suites that test a full area of performance. There are benchmarks for battery life, for CPU performance, and for video performance. The results of these tests become a major force in marketing and selling the product.

There have been a number of claims of unethical conduct in the area of benchmarking. Companies have been accused of using out-of-date testing software to skew their results. Some companies have manipulated the settings on the machine to artificially raise their score (for example, turning off the display and wireless network before testing for battery life). Some companies have a pattern of making sure the systems sent out to magazines and other evaluators have better-performing components than you might get off the shelf in your own new system.

Where is the line between gaining a competitive edge and lying when it comes to hardware assessment?

Research Areas to Consider

- SysMark2002
- BAPCo
- MobileMark
- 2009 Nobel Prize for Physics

Process

1. Divide the class into teams.
2. Research the areas cited above from the perspective of either an Intel engineer working on a new CPU, an AMD engineer working on a competing CPU, or a benchmark designer.
3. Team members should write a summary that provides factual documentation for the positions and views their character takes around the issue of equitable testing of hardware. Then, team members should create an outline to use during the role-playing event.
4. Team members should arrange a mutually convenient time to meet for the exchange, using either the collaboration feature of MyITLab or the discussion board feature of your course management software or by meeting in person.
5. Team members should present their case to the class or submit a PowerPoint presentation for review by the rest of the class, along with the summary and resolution they developed.

Conclusion

As technology becomes ever more prevalent and integrated into our lives, more and more ethical dilemmas will present themselves. Being able to understand and evaluate both sides of the argument, while responding in a personally or socially ethical manner, will be an important skill.

How Networks Function

Your Home Network

(Sergej Khackimullin/Fotolia; AKS/Fotolia; ktsimage/iStockphoto; Norebbo/Shutterstock; alengo/iStockphoto)

For all media in this chapter go to **pearsonhighered.com/techinaction** or MyITLab.

(Beboy/Fotolia LLC)

HOW COOL IS THIS?

Scan here for more info

As you know, wireless connectivity isn't always free. You may have **multiple mobile devices**, each requiring Internet access. Some may need a 3G/4G monthly data plan, whereas others may be WiFi only. **Connectify** is software that takes an **existing Internet connection** and turns it into a wireless **hotspot**. So if you're connected to the Internet on your Windows notebook or Android phone or tablet, the Connectify software turns your computing device into a wireless hotspot so that you can **connect all your WiFi-enabled devices**, such as a phone or gaming system, through the **same Internet connection**. The hotspot you create features easy connectivity and encryption of data for solid security.

How Networks Function

You access wired and wireless networks all the time—when you use an ATM, print out a document, or use the Internet (the world's largest network). It's important to understand the fundamentals of networking, such as how networks are set up, what devices are necessary to establish a network, and how you can access a network so that you can share, collaborate, and exchange information between your friends, family, and colleagues.

networking
FUNDAMENTALS

Many of today's homes have more than one computing device capable of connecting to the Internet. A typical family engages in many activities that involve sharing and accessing files over and from the Internet and using a variety of Internet-connected devices (see Figure 7.1). What makes all this technology transfer and sharing possible? A computer network!

A computer **network** is simply two or more computers that are connected via software and hardware so they can communicate with each other. Each device connected to a network is referred to as a **node**. A node can be a computer, a peripheral such as a printer or a game console, or a network device such as a router.

What are the benefits of networks?
There are several benefits to having computers networked:

- *Sharing an Internet connection:* A network lets you share the high-speed Internet connection coming into your home.
- *Sharing printers and other peripherals:* Networks let you share printers and other peripheral devices. For example, say you have a laptop that isn't connected to a printer. To print a document from your laptop without a network, you would need to transfer the file using a flash drive or other device to another computer that's connected to a printer or carry your laptop to the printer and connect your laptop to it. With

Jackie watches a video she took while on vacation

Andy plays PlayStation online and uploads a video he made for school

Mom watches a lecture from her online course while she prepares a snack

Dad watches a streaming movie and checks fantasy football scores on his iPad

Andrea takes pictures of her dog and uploads them directly to Facebook

FIGURE 7.1 With a home network, all family members can connect their computing devices whenever and wherever they want.

a network, you can print directly from your device even if it's not physically connected to the printer.

- *Sharing files:* You can share files between networked computers without having to use portable storage devices such as flash drives to transfer the files. In addition, you can set sharing options in Windows or OS X that let the user of each computer on the network access files stored on any other computer on the network. For example, the Windows network in Figure 7.2 has five computers attached to it. ALAN-DESKTOP, ALAN-NOTEBOOK, and PAT-NOTEBOOK are running Windows. The two MACBOOKs are running OS X. The Public folders enable file sharing because the user of any computer on the network can access the Public folder's contents.

- *Common communications:* As illustrated in Figure 7.2, computers running different operating systems can communicate on the same network.

Are there disadvantages to setting up networks? Fortunately, after most home networks have been set up, there isn't much else that needs to be done to maintain or administer the network; therefore, the benefits of using a network outweigh the disadvantages. However, large networks involve an initial purchase of equipment to set them up. They also need to be administered, which can be costly and time consuming. **Network administration** involves tasks such as:

ACTIVE HELPDESK
Understanding Networking
In this Active Helpdesk call, you'll play the role of a helpdesk staffer, fielding calls about home networks—their advantages, their main components, and the most common types—as well as about wireless networks and how they are created.

- Installing new computers and devices
- Monitoring the network to ensure it's performing efficiently
- Updating and installing new software on the network, and
- Configuring, or setting up, proper security for a network

How fast does data move through networks? Data transfer rate (also called **bandwidth**) is the maximum speed at which data can be transmitted between two nodes on a network. **Throughput** is the actual speed of data transfer that is achieved. Throughput is always less than or equal to the data transfer rate. Data transfer rate and throughput are usually measured in *megabits per second (Mbps)*. A megabit is one million bits. One of the main factors that determines how fast data moves is the type of network, which we'll discuss later in this chapter. ∎

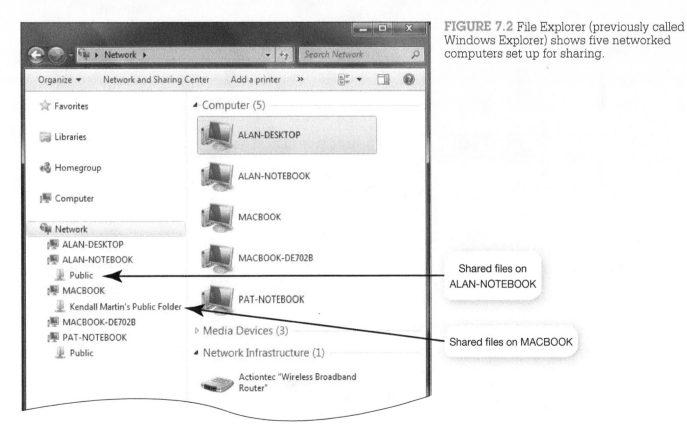

FIGURE 7.2 File Explorer (previously called Windows Explorer) shows five networked computers set up for sharing.

network
ARCHITECTURES

The network you have in your home differs greatly in terms of its size, structure, and cost from the one on your college campus. This difference is based in part on their network architectures. **Network architectures**, or network designs, are classified according to:

- The distance between their nodes
- The way in which they are managed (or administered)
- The set of rules (or *protocol*) used to exchange data between network nodes, and
- The communications medium used to transport the data

Next we'll look at all of these factors plus the hardware that is often used on networks.

Network Architectures Defined by Distance

How does the distance between nodes define a network? The distance between nodes on a network is one way to describe a network. The following are common types of networks (see Figure 7.3):

- A **personal area network (PAN)** is a network used for communication among devices close to one person, such as smartphones, notebooks, and tablets using wireless technologies such as Bluetooth and WiFi.

FIGURE 7.3 Networks can be classified by the distance between their nodes. *(Fenton/Fotolia; redline1980/ Fotolia; SiuWing/Shutterstock; lucadp/Shutterstock)*

WAN
Wide Area
Network

MAN
Metropolitan
Area Network

HAN
Home Area
Network

LAN
Local Area
Network

PAN
Personal Area
Network

- A **local area network (LAN)** is a network in which the nodes are located within a small geographic area. Examples include a network in a computer lab at school or at a fast-food restaurant.
- A **home area network (HAN)** is a specific type of LAN located in a home. HANs are used to connect all of a home's digital devices, such as computers, peripherals, phones, gaming devices, digital video recorders (DVRs), and televisions.
- A **metropolitan area network (MAN)** is a large network designed to provide access to a specific geographic area, such as an entire city. Many U.S. cities are now deploying MANs to provide Internet access to residents and tourists. Some MANs employ WiMAX wireless technology that extends local WiFi networks across greater distances.
- A **wide area network (WAN)** spans a large physical distance. The Internet is the largest WAN, covering the globe. A WAN is also a networked collection of LANs. If a school has multiple campuses located in different towns, each with its own LAN, connecting the LANs of each campus by telecommunications lines allows the users of the LANs to communicate. All the connected LANs would be described as a single WAN.

Network Architectures Defined by Levels of Administration

How does the level of administration define a network?
A network can be administered, or managed, in two main ways—centrally or locally (see Figure 7.4):

- *Central administration:* In a centrally administered network, tasks performed from one computer can affect the other computers on the network. A **client/server network** is an example. In a client/server network, a *client* is a computer on which users accomplish tasks and make requests, whereas the *server* is the computer that provides information or resources to the client computers as well as central administration for network functions such as printing. Most networks that have 10 or more nodes are client/server networks.
- *Local administration:* In a locally administered network, the configuration and maintenance of the network must be performed on each individual computer attached to the network. A **peer-to-peer (P2P) network** is an example. In a P2P network, each node connected on the network can

FIGURE 7.4 Client/Server and P2P Networks *(Scanrail/Fotolia; Scanrail/Fotolia; tuulijumala/Fotolia; Scanrail/Fotolia; Sashkin/Fotolia; Maksym Dykha/Fotolia)*

PAN Clothing: Organization and Power for Portable Gear

Now that people carry so many portable computing devices, clothing designers are starting to offer clothing that facilitates the storage, transportation, charging, and networking of their digital gadgets. The Scottevest is one of a line of vests and jackets designed to hold iPods, smartphones, and even iPads. It also features a built-in PAN to help maintain connectivity of your devices. And because all the devices in your PAN need power, accessories such as the Voltaic Backpack (shown here) help recharge your digital devices using renewable energy sources. So don't forget to consider the perfect fashion accessory for your latest digital acquisition!

The Voltaic Backpack recharges your mobile devices using solar cells. *(Ashley Cooper pics/Global Warming Images/Alamy)*

communicate directly with every other node on the network. Thus, all nodes on this type of network are peers (equals). When printing, for example, a computer on a P2P network doesn't have to go through the computer that's connected to the printer. Instead, it can communicate directly with the printer. Because they're simple to set up, cost less than client/server networks, and are easier to configure and maintain, P2P networks are the most common type of home network. Very small schools and offices may also use P2P networks.

Ethernet Protocols

What network standard is used in my home network? The vast majority of home and corporate networks are Ethernet networks. An **Ethernet network** is so named because it uses the Ethernet protocol as the means (or standard) by which the nodes on the network communicate.

The Ethernet protocol was developed by the Institute of Electrical and Electronics Engineers (IEEE), which develops many standard specifications for electronic data transmission that are adopted throughout the world. Establishing standards for networking is important so that devices from different manufacturers will work well together. The standard for wired Ethernet networks is 802.3. The standard for wireless Ethernet networks, also known as WiFi, is 802.11. The current version of wireless Ethernet is 802.11n. Previous versions included 802.11g, 802.11b, and 802.11a.

How is the 802.11n version different from the previous versions? The current wireless Ethernet standard, 802.11n, is faster and has a better signal range than the earlier 802.11g standard. In addition, the 802.11n standard operates at either a 2.4 GHz or a 5 GHz frequency, whereas most prior standards operated only at the 2.4 GHz frequency. This means the 802.11n standard is more resistant to signal interference from outside sources. 802.11n is now the most desirable wireless option for home networks; however, a newer standard, 802.11ac, is currently being reviewed. 802.11ac is proposed to be twice as fast as 802.11n and will run at a 5-GHz bandwidth.

Will my device that has 802.11g WiFi still work on an 802.11n network? Devices using older standards, such as 802.11g, will still work with 802.11n networks, but they'll operate with slower data transfer rates and may run into some frequency interference. The ability of current devices to use earlier standards in addition to the current standard is known as **backward compatibility**.

Are there different standards for wired Ethernet? The most commonly used wired Ethernet standard for home networks is the **gigabit Ethernet** standard. A data transfer rate of up to 1 gigabit per second (Gbps) is possible using this standard. Computers generally ship with gigabit Ethernet cards installed in them.

For even faster data transfer speeds, *10 gigabit Ethernet* is available. It provides a maximum data transfer rate of 10 Gbps. But 10-gigabit Ethernet networks are primarily used in businesses with large data throughput needs. ■

network
COMPONENTS

To function, all networks must include:

- A means of connecting the nodes on the network (cables or wireless technology)
- Special hardware devices that allow the nodes to communicate with each other and to send data
- Software that allows the network to run (see Figure 7.5)

Transmission Media

How do nodes connect to each other? All network nodes are connected to each other and to the network by transmission media. **Transmission media** can be either wired or wireless; they establish a communications channel between the nodes on a network. The media used depend on the requirements of a network and its users.

What transmission media is used on a wired network? Wired networks use various types of cable (wire) to connect nodes (see Figure 7.6).

The type of network and the distance between nodes determines the type of cable used:

- **Twisted-pair cable** is made up of copper wires that are twisted around each other and surrounded by a plastic jacket. Normal telephone cable is a type of twisted-pair cable, although phone cable won't work for connecting a LAN or HAN. A slightly different type of twisted-pair cable, called **unshielded twisted pair (UTP) cable**, is used for networks. UTP is composed of four pairs of wires twisted around each other to reduce electrical interference.
- **Coaxial cable** consists of a single copper wire surrounded by layers of plastic. If you have cable TV, the cable running into your TV or cable box is most likely coaxial cable.
- **Fiber-optic cable** is made up of plastic or glass fibers that transmit data at extremely fast speeds.

What type of cable is used in most wired home networks? The most popular transmission media option for wired Ethernet networks

FIGURE 7.5 Network Components *(Okea/iStockphoto.com; Sergii Korolko/Shutterstock; Epson; vectorlib-com/Shutterstock; hanibaram/iStockphoto; Norman Chan/Shutterstock)*

FIGURE 7.6

Wired Transmission Media

Twisted-pair cable

Coaxial cable

Fiber-optic cable

(deepspacedave/Shutterstock; zwola fasola/ Shutterstock; zentilia/Shutterstock)

is UTP cable. You can buy UTP cable in varying lengths with Ethernet connectors (called RJ-45 connectors) already attached. Ethernet connectors resemble standard phone connectors (called RJ-11 connectors) but are slightly larger and have contacts for eight wires (four pairs) instead of four wires.

Do all wired Ethernet networks use the same kind of UTP cable? The three main types of UTP cable you would consider using in wired Ethernet home networks and their data transfer rates are as follows (also see Figure 7.7):

1. *Cat 5E:* Although Cat 5E cable is the cheapest of the three types and is sufficient for many home networking tasks, it was designed for 100 Mbps–wired Ethernet networks that were popular before gigabit Ethernet networks became the standard. Therefore, you should probably not install Cat 5E cable even though it's still available in stores.

2. *Cat 6:* Because **Cat 6 cable** is designed to achieve data transfer rates that support a gigabit Ethernet network, it's probably the best choice for home networking cable, though it's more expensive and more difficult to work with than Cat 5E cable.

3. *Cat 6a:* Cat 6a cable is designed for ultra-fast Ethernet networks that run at speeds as fast as 10 Gbps. Installing a 10-gigabit Ethernet network in the home is probably unnecessary because today's home applications (even gaming and streaming media) don't require this rate of data transfer.

What transmission media is used to connect nodes on a wireless network? **Wireless fidelity (WiFi)** is a standard for wireless transmissions using radio waves to connect computing devices to wireless networks and the Internet. With so many portable devices being connected to networks, a network with wireless connectivity is used in businesses as well as in most homes. However, note that wireless networks generally have decreased throughput compared with that of wired networks.

Why are wireless networks slower than wired networks? Some common reasons why wireless signals may have decreased throughput are:

- Wireless signals are more susceptible to interference from magnetic and electrical sources.

- Other wireless networks (such as your neighbor's network) can interfere with the signals on your network.

- Certain building materials (such as concrete and cinderblock) and metal (such as a refrigerator) can decrease throughput.

FIGURE 7.7 The three main UTP cable types used in home networks have different data transfer rates.

- Throughput varies depending on the distance between your networking equipment.
- Wireless networks usually use specially coded signals to protect their data, whereas wired connections don't protect their signals. This process of coding signals can slightly decrease throughput, although once coded, data travels at usual speeds.

Can I have both wired and wireless nodes on the same network? One network can support nodes with both wireless and wired connections. Most people use wireless connections for portable devices such as laptops. However, many of the devices connected to a network, such as printers and TVs, usually stay in one location. Although these devices probably feature wireless connectivity, hooking them up to wired connections lets you take advantage of the faster throughput achieved by wired connectivity. And in situations where you want to achieve the highest possible throughput on your portable device, you may want to use a wired connection temporarily.

Basic Network Hardware

What hardware is needed for different nodes on the network to communicate? For the different nodes on a network to communicate with each other and access the network, each node needs a **network adapter**. All desktop and laptop computers (and many peripherals) sold today contain network adapters installed *inside* the device. This type of integrated network adapter is referred to as a **network interface card (NIC)**. Different NICs are designed to use different types of transmission media. Most NICs included in computing devices today are built to use wireless media, but many can use wired media as well.

What equipment do I need in order to hook up to broadband? A broadband Internet connection requires a modem. Depending on the type of broadband service you have, you'll have either a cable modem or a DSL modem. Often, your Internet service provider will rent the appropriate modem to you or specify what type of modem you have to buy to work properly with the Internet service provider's technology. The modem translates the broadband signal into digital data and back again.

What hardware is necessary to transmit data through a network? Data is sent through a network in bundles called **packets**. For computers to communicate, these packets of data must be able to flow between network nodes. **Network navigation devices**, such as a router or a switch, facilitate and control the flow of data through a network:

- A **router** transfers packets of data between two or more networks. On a home network, you need a router to transfer data between your home network and the Internet, which is considered a separate network. To add WiFi to your home network, you need a router that features wireless capabilities.
- A **switch** acts like a traffic signal on a network (see Figure 7.8). All routers sold for home use have

FIGURE 7.8 A simplified explanation of the function of switches is that, together with NICs, they act like traffic signals or traffic cops. They enforce the rules of the data road on an Ethernet network and help prevent data packets from crashing into each other.

FIGURE 7.9 A small network with a wired/wireless router attached. *(Beboy/Fotolia; Norman Chan/Shutterstock; Arkadiusz Stachowski/ iStockphoto; IKO/Shutterstock; Luca di Filippo/iStockPhoto.com; duckycards/Jill Fromer/iStockphoto)*

integrated switches. Switches receive data packets and send them to their intended nodes on the same network (not between different networks). During the transmission process, data packets can suffer collisions; subsequently, the data in them is damaged or lost and the network doesn't function efficiently. The switch keeps track of the data packets and, in conjunction with NICs, helps the data packets find their destinations without running into each other. The switch also keeps track of all the nodes on the network and sends the data packets directly to the node for which they're headed. This keeps the network running efficiently.

Where should you place the router on your network? Your router should be connected directly to your broadband (cable/DSL) modem (see Figure 7.9). The connection should be an Ethernet cable running from an Ethernet port on your modem to the modem port on your router. Then, all computing devices—such as an HDTV, a tablet, and a laptop—are connected to the router via a wired or wireless connection. Some routers have integrated modems so that you only need one device.

Network Software

What network software do home networks require? Because home networks are P2P networks, they need operating system software that supports P2P networking. Windows, OS X, and Linux all support P2P networking. You can connect computers running any of these operating systems to the same home network.

Is the same network software used in client/server networks? As opposed to P2P networks, the nodes on a client/server network don't communicate directly with each other; rather, they communicate through a centralized server. Communicating through a server is more efficient in a network with a large number of nodes, but it requires more complex software than is necessary for P2P networks. Therefore, the servers on client/server networks have specialized **network operating system (NOS)** software installed. This software handles requests for information, Internet access, and the use of peripherals for the rest of the network nodes. Examples of NOS software include Windows Server and SUSE Linux Enterprise Server. ■

connecting
TO THE INTERNET

One of the main reasons for setting up a network is to share an Internet connection. Some businesses and large organizations have a dedicated connection to the Internet, but other businesses and homeowners purchase Internet access from **Internet service providers (ISPs)**. ISPs may be specialized providers, like Juno, or companies like Comcast that provide additional services, such as phone and cable TV. Broadband is the preferred way to access the Internet, but in some situations, cellular or dial-up access may be necessary.

Wired Broadband Internet Connections

What exactly is broadband Internet access? Broadband, often referred to as "high-speed Internet," refers to a type of connection that offers a faster means to connect to the Internet. Broadband usually has a data transmission rate of 5 Mbps (megabits per second) or greater. This high rate of access is in contrast to dial-up Internet access, which has a maximum transmission speed of 56 Kbps (kilobits per second).

What types of broadband are available? As shown in Figure 7.10, the standard wired broadband technologies in most areas are *cable*, *DSL* (*digital subscriber line*), and *fiber-optic service*. *Satellite broadband* is used mostly in rural or mountain areas that can't get DSL, cable, or fiber-optic service.

There are also wireless broadband options. *Mobile broadband* is offered through many cell-phone service providers through 3G and 4G networks. *Wireless*

Internet (WiFi) is also available via radio waves. We'll discuss these options later in the chapter.

How does cable Internet work? Cable Internet is a broadband service that transmits data over the coaxial cables that also transmit cable television signals; however, cable TV and cable Internet are separate services. Cable TV is a one-way service in which the cable company feeds programming signals to your television. To bring two-way Internet connections to homes, cable companies had to upgrade their networks with two-way data-transmission capabilities.

How does DSL work? DSL (digital subscriber line) uses twisted-pair cable, the same as that used for regular telephones, to connect your computer to the Internet. The bandwidth of the wires is split into three sections, like a three-lane highway. One lane is used to carry voice data. DSL uses the remaining two lanes to send and receive data separately at much higher frequencies than voice data. Although DSL uses a standard phone line, having a traditional phone line in your house doesn't mean you have access to DSL service. Your local phone company must have special DSL technology to offer you the service.

FIGURE 7.10

Comparing Common Wired Broadband Internet Connection Options

BROADBAND TYPE	TRANSMISSION MEDIUM	SPEED CONSIDERATIONS	AVERAGE AND MAXIMUM DOWNLOAD SPEEDS
Cable	Coaxial cable, similar to cable TV wire	Cable connections are shared, so speed can drop during high-usage periods	Average speed of 10 Mbps, with maximum of 30 Mbps
DSL (Digital Subscriber Line)	Copper wire phone line	Speed drops as distance from the main signal source increases	Average speed of 3.7 Mbps, with maximum of 15 Mbps
Fiber-Optic	Strands of optically pure glass or plastic	Transmits data via light signals, which do not degrade over long distances	Average speed of 20 Mbps, with maximum of 150 Mbps

How does fiber-optic service work?
Fiber-optic service uses fiber-optic lines, which are strands of optically pure glass or plastic that are as thin as a human hair. They're arranged in bundles called *optical cables* and transmit data via light signals over long distances. Because light travels so quickly, this technology can transmit an enormous amount of data at superfast speeds. When the data reaches your house, it's converted to electrical pulses that transmit digital signals your computer can "read." Fiber-optic cable is not usually run inside the home. On a fiber-optic network, twisted-pair or coaxial cable is still used inside the home to transport the network signals.

How does satellite Internet work?
To take advantage of **satellite Internet**, you need a satellite dish (see Figure 7.11), which is placed outside your home and connected to your computer with coaxial cable, the same type of cable used for cable TV. Data from your computer is transmitted between your personal satellite dish and the satellite company's receiving satellite dish by a satellite that sits in a geosynchronous orbit thousands of miles above the Earth.

How do I choose which broadband connection option is best for me?
Depending on where you live, you might not have a choice of the broadband connection available. Check with your local cable TV provider, phone company, and satellite TV provider(s) to determine what broadband options are available and what the transfer rates are in your area.

Often, the most difficult decision is choosing between high-speed plans offered by the same company. For instance, at the time of printing, Verizon offered three different fiber-optic plans that featured download speeds of 15, 25, or 50 Mbps. Although 15 Mbps is fine for streaming standard definition video, it may not be fast enough for streaming HD movies, especially if there are two people in the house streaming movies at the same time. Finally, you may also need to consider what other services you want bundled into your payment, such as phone or TV. Consulting with friends and neighbors about the plan they have and whether it's meeting their needs can help you decide on the right plan for you.

Wireless Internet Access

How can I access the Internet wirelessly at home?
To access the Internet wirelessly at home, you need to establish WiFi on your home network by using a router that features wireless capabilities. You also need the right equipment on your mobile device. Virtually all laptops, smartphones, game systems, and personal media players sold today are WiFi enabled and come with wireless capability built in.

How can I access WiFi when I'm away from home?
When you're away from home, you need to find a WiFi hotspot. Many public places, such as libraries, hotels, airports, and fast-food and coffee shops, offer WiFi access. Most locations are free, though a few still charge or require a special password to access the connection. Websites like Wi-Fi-FreeSpot (**wififreespot.com**) and Wi-Fi Planet (**wi-fiplanet.com**) help you locate a free hotspot wherever you're planning to go. When you have to buy WiFi access, you can pay for a single session or a monthly membership through services such as Boingo (**boingo.com**). Boingo has over 400,000 hotspots worldwide, including airports, hotels, and restaurants.

FIGURE 7.11 ISPs that offer satellite Internet can provide Internet access even in remote areas. *(Ilene MacDonald/Alamy)*

BITS&BYTES

Blazingly Fast Wireless Connections on the Horizon

Although most people want wireless connectivity throughout their home, wired connections still provide the best throughput. But the next generation of wireless standards, called WiGig and WirelessHD, will be designed to provide between 7 and 25 Gbps of throughput. This speed will blow away current WiFi standards and wired gigabit connectivity. Whereas WiFi currently operates in the 5 GHz and 2.4 GHz bands, WiGig and WirelessHD will operate in the 60 GHz band, which is currently unlicensed by the FCC. This should prevent many of the interference issues that WiFi users experience. But don't start looking in the stores for this equipment just yet; we're still a few years away from devices using these standards.

Even wireless in-flight Internet service is available! Gogo (**gogoair.com**) is a wireless broadband network that provides coverage on participating airlines across the continental United States. So, when you are cleared to use your portable electronic devices, you can comfortably access wireless Internet from 35,000 feet.

How can I access the Internet when WiFi isn't available? There are often occasions when you're not in a WiFi hotspot but still need to access the Internet. In these instances, you may want to consider signing up for mobile broadband. **Mobile broadband** connects you to the Internet through the same cellular network that cell phones use to get 3G or 4G Internet access.

3G and 4G can be thought of as "WiFi everywhere" in that they provide Internet access to your mobile devices in the same way they provide voice service to your mobile phone. *3G* and *4G* refer to the third and fourth generations, respectively, of cell-phone networks. 4G is the latest service standard and offers the fastest data-access speeds over cell-phone networks. To utilize the 3G or 4G capabilities of a mobile device, you need to sign up for an access plan with a mobile data provider such as Verizon or AT&T.

How does mobile broadband Internet compare with wired Internet access? 3G performs similarly to a standard DSL connection (roughly 3 Mbps). According to the standards set for 4G, the data transfer rate you would get while in a moving vehicle is approximately 100 Mbps; from a fixed location, you can expect up to a 1 Gbps data transfer rate. Some of the early 4G systems released in the market support less than the required 1 Gbit/s rate and are not fully compliant with the 4G standards, and so are being tagged as 4G LTE. They are still faster than 3G, however.

How can I get 3G/4G service if my device doesn't have the right equipment? Many devices such as the iPad, Kindle Fire, Chromebook, and some laptops are available with built-in 3G or 4G capabilities. If your computer doesn't have built-in 3G or 4G equipment, you can buy a *USB modem*. USB modems fit into a USB port on your computer and let you access 3G or 4G networks. Like a smartphone, they also require a service plan.

Alternatively, instead of buying a USB modem that works on one device, you can buy a *mobile hotspot* (see Figure 7.12). These mobile hotspots let you connect

FIGURE 7.12 A MiFi device turns your phone signal into a 4G LTE mobile hotspot for you and four of your friends. *(PRNewsFoto/Verizon Wireless/AP Photos)*

BITS&BYTES

How Do You Find Your WiFi?

Detecting a nearby WiFi signal is important if your device doesn't have 3G/4G connectivity. Here are a few tips:

- Some laptops have a built-in WiFi scanner that displays a row of lights on the case whenever a WiFi signal is available.

- There are also WiFi keychain fobs that light up when they detect WiFi signals.

- If you're running Windows 8, the Networks bar (accessible from the desktop by clicking on the wireless network icon on the taskbar) shows the strength of all wireless networks within range of your computer.

- At ThinkGeek (**thinkgeek.com**), you can find the easiest-to-use WiFi detector ever. The WiFi Detector t-shirt and the WiFi Detector baseball cap have a logo that lights up to indicate the signal strength of a nearby WiFi network (see Figure 7.13). Find your WiFi and look ... well, look geeky while doing it!

FIGURE 7.13 The WiFi Detector T-shirt and cap make a statement—a geeky statement. *(ThinkGeek, Inc.)*

---

more than one device to the Internet with either WiFi or mobile broadband. Mobile hotspots require you to purchase a data plan, but the monthly fee may be less than paying for individual monthly plans on multiple devices. So, if you have several mobile devices that need wireless Internet access, this may be the most economical and functional way to access the Internet while on the road.

Dial-Up Connections

Why would I ever want to consider a dial-up connection to the Internet?
Although about 70% of Internet users in the United States use high-speed Internet connections such as DSL, cable, or fiber-optic, there are still some areas (usually rural) where broadband service isn't available. A dial-up connection needs only a standard phone line and a modem to access the Internet. Therefore, some people choose to use a dial-up connection when there's

no high-speed service in their area. Additionally, a dial-up connection is the least costly way to connect to the Internet, so for those who don't use the Internet frequently, the extra cost of broadband may be unnecessary.

What are the disadvantages of dial-up? The major downside to dial-up is speed. Dial-up modems transfer data about 600 times slower than a fiber-optic broadband connection. Also, dial-up uses a traditional phone line to connect to the Internet; therefore, unless you have a separate phone line just for your dial-up connection, when you're using dial-up, you tie up your phone line. ■

Before moving on to Part 2:
- Watch Replay Video 7.1 ▶.
- Then check your understanding of what you've learned so far.

check your understanding //

For a quick review to see what you've learned so far, answer the following questions. Visit **pearsonhighered.com/techinaction** to check your answers.

multiple choice

1. Each device connected to a network is known as a
   a. peripheral.
   b. network spoke.
   c. node.
   d. computing unit.

2. A small network used for communication between personal computing devices is a
   a. WAN.
   b. PAN.
   c. LAN.
   d. MAN.

3. The fastest broadband Internet service is usually
   a. fiber-optic.
   b. DSL.
   c. cable.
   d. satellite.

4. The part of the network that establishes a communications channel between the nodes of the network is known as
   a. network operating software.
   b. transmission media.
   c. a network navigation device.
   d. a switch.

5. The device used to move data between two networks is called a
   a. gateway.
   b. switch.
   c. wireless range extender.
   d. router.

true–false

_____ 1. Actual data throughput is usually higher on wired networks than on wireless networks.

_____ 2. Home networks are usually configured as a client/server network.

critical thinking

1. **Protecting Yourself on Public Wireless Networks**

   Many people use free public wireless networks to access the Internet. But many public networks don't have adequate security or may be under surveillance by hackers. To protect your sensitive data, there are certain activities you should not engage in while on public networks. What types of activities should you avoid on a public network? What types of information should you only process on your secure home network?

2. **How Networked Are You?**

   You probably use more networks than you realize. List all the networks you access: home, mobile, school, business, etc., and then determine what kind of network each is. What devices do you use when you are accessing each network?

Continue ➡

Testing Your Wired Internet Connection Speed

Your ISP may have promised you certain downloading and uploading data speeds. How can you tell if you're getting what was promised? Numerous sites on the Internet, such as **speedtest.net** and **broadband.gov**, test the speed of your Internet connection. You can then see how your results compare with others, as well as determine whether you're getting the results promised by your ISP.

Step 1 Go to **speedtest.net**, then click **Begin Test**.

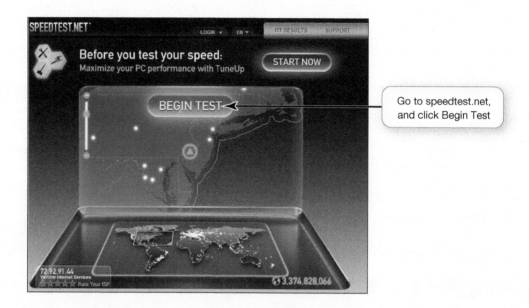

Go to speedtest.net, and click Begin Test

Step 2 The program will display a "signal" being sent as a small data file is downloaded from a remote server to your location. Then, the speed is measured as a data file is uploaded back from your location to the remote server. When the test is done, your results display, along with the location of the server that was used in the test.

Upload Speed: Time taken to move data from your computer to the server

Download Speed: Time taken to move data from the server to your computer

Ping: Measures the time it takes to get a response from the server

Location of the remote server used in the test

Click here to access past test results and how they compare with global averages

Step 3 You can access more information about your results and how they compare with global averages by clicking **View now** in the My Results box at the bottom-right corner of the test screen. Note that many factors can influence your Internet speeds, so be sure to run the test at several different times of the day over the course of a week before complaining to your ISP about not getting your promised speed.

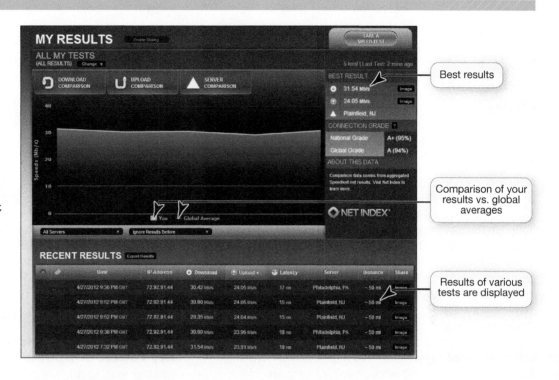

Best results

Comparison of your results vs. global averages

Results of various tests are displayed

Testing Your Wireless Internet Connection Speed

You know wireless Internet speeds are usually slower than wired connections, but what's the actual speed of your wireless connection? You can install various utilities, such as Net Meter (available at **download.com**), on your computer that show the throughput you're achieving on your computer's wireless connection to your network over a period of time. The performance of your WiFi connection depends on several factors, including the quality of the signal strength and which WiFi standard your router and NIC are using (802.11 b/g/n).

Step 1 Go to **download.com**. In the Find Software box on the left, type **Net Meter** and press Enter. Net Meter will display at the top of the list of search results (scroll down if necessary).

Step 2 Select **Net Meter** in the displayed list, then click **Download Now**. Follow the steps in the Net Meter Setup Wizard to install the program on your computer.

Step 3 Once the program is installed, select **Continue Evaluation**. (You can evaluate the program free for 30 days.) Then, run Net Meter. Net Meter shows the maximum connection that is currently being achieved on your wireless network.

Monitor your active wireless connection rate. The rate shown is a maximum connection of 25.7 Mbps on a wireless home network.

You know what a network is and the advantages of having one. In this section, we look at installing or updating a home network and keeping it safe.

installing and configuring
HOME NETWORKS

Now that you understand the basic components of a network and your Internet connection options, you're ready to install a network in your home. If you already have a network in your home, it's useful to examine your network settings and configuration to make sure they're still meeting your needs, especially if you've added new devices.

Only a few years ago, most home networks included just a few computers and a printer. However, a network that can manage those devices is often very different from one that can support the smartphones, gaming consoles, tablets, and smart TVs many homes have added to their networks since. If you're using any of these additional devices and you haven't updated your network equipment or setup in a while, it may be time to do so.

Planning Your Home Network

Where do I start? One of the first things you should do to evaluate your network is list all the devices you're using, as well as any devices you think you may add in the near future. Then, determine whether your network is sufficiently up to date to support all your devices.

What wireless Ethernet standard should my network be using? For a home network to run most efficiently and to provide the fastest experience, it's best that all network nodes—computers, network adapters (NICs), routers, and so on—use the latest Ethernet standard. Devices that support the 802.11n standard have been around for a while, so if you've bought a laptop or other portable device in the past few years, it most likely has an 802.11n NIC.

However, your router may still be supporting the 802.11g standard. If you have the fastest 802.11n NIC in your laptop, but the router is the slower 802.11g standard, then data will be sent at the speeds supported by the lower standard. If you haven't updated your router in a while, you may want to consider getting an 802.11n router (Figure 7.14) to get the fastest connection speeds.

Additionally, the higher standard gives your wireless signal more range, so if you feel that some of your devices aren't connecting properly to the Internet from certain parts of your home, you may want to upgrade to the higher standard.

How can I tell what wireless standard my router supports? You may be able to tell whether your router is supporting the faster 802.11n standard just by looking at it. Many routers have the wireless standard indicated on the device. If you're still not sure, you can search for more information on your router by entering the model number into a search engine. If your router is provided by your ISP and it's an older standard, you should consider having your ISP provide you with a new router.

FIGURE 7.14 802.11n wireless routers offer the fastest connection speeds and a greater wireless signal range. *(Scanrail/Fotolia)*

FIGURE 7.15 The Windows Device Manager shows the wireless and wired network adapters installed on a computer.

>To access the Device Manager, with the cursor in the bottom-left corner of your screen, right-click to display the shortcut menu, and select **Control Panel**. Then click **Hardware and Sound**, and select **Device Manager** from the **Devices and Printers** group.

How can I tell what network adapters are installed in my computer? To see which network adapters are installed in your Windows computer, use the Device Manager utility (see Figure 7.15), which lists all the adapters. If you can't tell which wireless standard the adapter supports from the list, search the Internet for information on your specific adapter to determine its capability. The Device Manager can also alert you if there's a problem with the adapter.

Connecting Devices to a Router

How can I directly connect multiple devices to my router? Most home routers have three or four Ethernet ports on the back to support wired connections. If you have a lot of devices (such as a game console, an HDTV, and a laptop) in your home

that you use at the same time, you might want to connect some of them via a wired connection to increase the bandwidth to each device.

If you need additional ports for plugging in wired connections to your network, you can buy a standalone switch and plug that into one of the ports on your router (see Figure 7.16). This will give you additional ports for making wired connections. However, don't mistakenly buy another router with an embedded switch and try adding that to your network. The two routers will cause conflicts as they fight for control over network navigation.

Router

Switch

FIGURE 7.16 You can add additional ports to your network by connecting a switch to your router.
(Sergey Dashkevich/Fotolia; sergey makarenko/Fotolia; Bart/Fotolia)

FIGURE 7.17 The AirPort Extreme router can be used for home networks with Windows PC and Apple computers. Multiple Ethernet ports enable several devices to access wired Internet connectivity. *(bmcent1/Brian McEntire/iStockphoto; bmcent1/Brian McEntire/iStockphoto)*

How many wireless devices can connect to a router in a home network? Most home wireless routers can support up to 253 wireless connections at the same time, although most home networks have far fewer. Regardless of how many devices your home network has, they all share bandwidth when they're connected to a router. Therefore, the more devices actively transmitting data that you connect to a single router, the smaller the portion of the router's bandwidth each device receives.

To look at this another way, say you have a pizza that represents your router's bandwidth. You can cut the pizza into six or eight pieces (that is, you can connect either six or eight devices to the network). If you cut the pizza into eight pieces, each person who gets a slice receives a smaller portion than if you had cut the pizza into six pieces. Similarly, when you connect eight devices to the network, each device has less bandwidth than it would if only six devices were connected to the network.

Are wireless routers for Windows and OS X networks different? All routers that support the 802.11n standard should work with computers running Windows or OS X. However, Apple has designed routers that are optimized for working with Apple computers. So if you're connecting Apple computers to your network, you may want to use the Apple AirPort Extreme router (see Figure 7.17). Windows machines can also connect to an AirPort router, so it's a great choice for households with both Apples and PCs. It supports up to 50 simultaneous wireless connections and has three gigabit-Ethernet ports for wired connections to hook up all your network-ready devices.

How do I know what's connected to my router? To determine what's connected to your router, you need to log in to an account associated with your router's IP address. You can find your router's IP address on the router manufacturer's website. Once you know it, type it into a web browser. You may need to enter a user name and password, but eventually you'll get to a configuration page that lists what wired and wireless devices are in your network. You may be surprised at all the various devices associated with your network.

Figure 7.18 shows a router network listing with wired (desktop computer) and wireless (TiVo DVR, laptop, iPhone, and iPads) devices connected in a home network. You'll notice that each device also has an IP address. You can think of your network as an apartment building. The router's IP address is the building's street address, while the IP addresses of the individual devices connected to the router are the apartment numbers. Each device needs an IP address so the router knows to which device to send information.

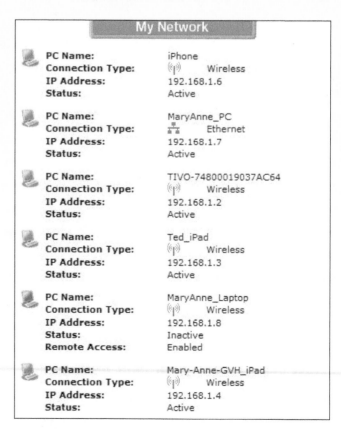

FIGURE 7.18 Wired and wireless connections can use the same router.

BITS&BYTES

Wake Up Your Mac Remotely

Having your computer on a home network with a shared Internet connection makes it possible for you to access your computer and its files even when you aren't at home. But if your computer is asleep, you need some way to "wake it up." Otherwise, you can't access it through the Internet.

Fortunately for Mac users, there's an application called iNet WOL (Wake on LAN) designed to do this (see Figure 7.19). iNet WOL is compatible with the iPhone, iPod Touch, and iPad. The application lets you use your portable device to wake up your computer via the Internet. Once your computer is awake, you can then use your remote access software to access it. Think of iNet WOL as an alarm clock for your computer.

FIGURE 7.19 The application iNet WOL lets you use your iPhone, iPod Touch, or iPad to wake up your Mac from a remote location. *(duckycards/Jill Fromer/iStockphoto.com)*

Network-Attached Storage Devices

What can I attach to my network to facilitate file sharing and backup of data? Network-attached storage (NAS) devices are specialized devices designed to store and manage all network data. Although data can always be stored on individual hard drives in computers on a network, NAS devices provide for centralized data storage and access.

Popular for years on business networks, NAS devices are now being widely marketed for home networks. You can think of them as specialized external hard drives, and many of them actually resemble external hard drives. NAS devices, like the LinkStation series from Buffalo Technology (see Figure 7.20), connect directly to the network through a router or switch. Specialized software is installed on computers attached to the network to ensure that all data saved to an individual computer is also stored on the NAS device as a backup.

For Apple computers, the Time Capsule is a wireless router combined with a hard drive that facilitates the backup of all computers connected to the network. The Time Capsule looks very similar to the AirPort router, and it works in conjunction with the Time Machine backup feature of OS X.

If you buy a Time Capsule, you won't need to buy an AirPort router (or other router) because the Time Capsule also fulfills this function on your network. When the Time Capsule is installed on your network, Macs connected to the network will ask the user if they want to use the Time Capsule as their source for Time Machine backups. The Time Capsule is another type of NAS device.

Ethernet port for easy connection to router

FIGURE 7.20 The LinkStation series from Buffalo Technology features NAS devices that can store 2 TB (terabytes) of data. *(Buffalo Technology)*

trends in IT

Where Should You Store Your Files? The Cloud Is Calling!

You need to store your files where they're backed up regularly and secure. You also need to access your files whenever you need them. So should you store your files on your home network? That might work if your network-attached storage is accessible via the Internet. The latest trend, however, is to store your files in the cloud. Deciding which cloud option to use depends on a number of factors.

For Files Currently Being Used

Having the latest version of a file accessible on any device you use is important. However, constantly saving a file on multiple devices or carrying around a flash drive can be cumbersome and time consuming. When you store your files on the cloud, you avoid the hassle of saving the same file on multiple devices.

A popular web-based application for storing files on the cloud is Dropbox. Dropbox supports computers running Windows, OS X, and Linux, as well as many smartphones and tablets. After installing the Dropbox software on your devices, any files you save in the Dropbox folder are accessible to all your other devices via the Internet. You can also share folders in Dropbox with other Dropbox users, making it ideal for group projects.

Dropbox storage capacity is limited to between 2 GB and 8 GB for free accounts. Other alternatives include Microsoft SkyDrive, which provides 7 GB of free space, and Apple iCloud and Google Drive, which each offer 5 GB of free storage.

For Media on the Go

You might like to view/listen to your media on the go, and storing it out in the cloud and streaming it over the Internet to your device may make a lot of sense. Companies like Apple and Amazon with their iCloud and Cloud Drive offerings let you store all your files on their servers. Both iCloud and Cloud Drive offer limited amounts of space for free, but you can pay a fee for additional storage. However, with limited free storage, these might not be the best options for large media collections.

For Large Media Collections That Need to Be Shared

For large media collections that you want to share with others, sites like ADrive and MediaFire are popular choices. ADrive offers 50 GB of storage for free, but there is no limit to the amount of files you can store on MediaFire (even with its free account). You can easily share files with other people on either site. You can also post links to the files directly to Facebook or Twitter from MediaFire (Figure 7.21). However, with the MediaFire free account, you can't upload files larger than 200 MB. This limit won't impact music or photos, but if you're planning on uploading HD movies, you'll need a pay account. MediaFire does not allow sharing of any copyrighted content.

The advantage of these sites is the amount of free storage and the sharing capabilities. The drawback is that they can't play streaming media (like iCloud and Cloud Drive can), so you need to download files before playing them.

When you choose which option is best for you, make sure to carefully investigate the site's file backup policies. Some free accounts don't feature guaranteed backups of your media, or the site might delete files that you haven't accessed for a certain period of time. The pay accounts generally guarantee that the files are backed up regularly. So don't ignore backup policies—you want your files to be there when you need them!

FIGURE 7.21 MediaFire offers free unlimited storage and file sharing.

Home Network Servers

Besides external hard drives, are there other NAS devices I could use on my network? A more sophisticated type of NAS device is a **home network server**. Home network servers are specialized devices designed to store files, share files across the network, and back up files on computers connected to the network. All computers connected to the network can access the server.

Home network servers (see Figure 7.22) often look like oversized external hard drives. They are configured with operating systems like Windows Server 2012 Essentials and connect directly as a node on your network. Home servers have more sophisticated functionality than NAS devices and often handle the following tasks:

- Automatically back up all computers connected to the network
- Act as a repository for files to be shared across the network
- Function as an access gateway to allow any computer on the network to be accessed from a remote location via the Internet (see Figure 7.23)

Note that even though these devices are servers, they don't convert a home P2P network into a client/server network because these servers don't perform

FIGURE 7.22 Home network servers can perform a variety of tasks that simplify file management on a home network.
(Sashkin/Fotolia)

all the functions performed on client/server networks. Also note that you can access the media stored on your Windows Home Server through your Xbox 360 as long as the Xbox is also connected to your home network.

Digital Entertainment Devices on a Network

What kinds of digital entertainment devices can connect directly to the network? A network-ready device (or Internet-ready device) can be connected directly to a network, either through a wired or wireless connection. Most game consoles, Blu-ray players, and DVRs, as well as many televisions (smart TVs) and home theater systems, are network ready. A device that is not network ready requires that the device be connected directly to another computer via a cable on the network.

Why should I connect digital entertainment devices to my network? One reason for connecting entertainment devices to your network is to access and share digital content between devices on your network. Connecting these devices to your network also gives them access to the Internet so you can access a lot of entertainment content, including movies, videos, and music available online.

You can also use gaming devices to play multiplayer games with players in the next room or all over the world. The content you access is either downloaded or streamed to your devices. Newer smart TVs and other smart devices (such as Blu-ray players, game consoles, and home theater systems) are continually adding apps and video services so that you can play games, view on-demand and online videos, listen to Internet radio,

FIGURE 7.23 Windows Home Server remote access interface.

and access social networking sites (see Figure 7.24). Some smart devices also feature an integrated web browser that lets you access the web directly, without the use of apps.

What if I don't have a smart TV? You can get the same services on your existing television by using a Blu-ray player like the Sony 3-D Blu-ray Disc player. These Blu-ray players feature integrated wireless connectivity to receive streaming media from various ISPs in addition to having high-definition resolution and the capability to display 3-D video. Some set-top boxes, such as the LG Smart TV Upgrader, also provide the same types of connectivity as a Blu-ray player.

Why should I connect my DVR to my network? You may have a digital video recorder (DVR), like the TiVo Premiere, which you use to record high-def TV programs. Connecting your TiVo to your network makes it possible to receive downloads of movies directly to your TiVo from services such as Netflix and Amazon Instant Video. And some home network servers, like the Hewlett Packard MediaSmart servers, now work in conjunction with TiVo devices to provide them with additional storage. The TiVo Desktop software (see Figure 7.25), which you download from **tivo.com**, lets you transfer shows recorded on your TiVo to your computer or portable devices.

Why should I connect my gaming consoles to my home network? Current gaming systems, like the PlayStation 3 (PS3), can function as a

FIGURE 7.24 Smart TVs have their own apps and let you directly access the web so you can play games, connect with your social networking accounts, and view on-demand and online videos. *(Ingo Schulz Image Broker/Newscom)*

total entertainment platform when connected to the Internet through your network. The PS3 has a built-in Blu-ray drive and can play Blu-ray discs, DVDs, and music files. You can download movies, games, and videos from the Internet directly to the PS3. You can also use it to share media across your network and to import photos or video from cameras and phones.

If you have a PS Vita, you can use an application called Remote Play (see Figure 7.26) to access features of your PS3 from your Vita. You can use the Vita to turn your PS3 on and off; access photos, music, and video files; play games; and browse the Internet. Media is transmitted from your PS3 and displayed on the Vita screen.

Specialized Home-Networking Devices

How can I use my home network to share photos?

Digital picture frames that display photos are popular, and some, such as the Kodak Pulse Digital Frame, come with built-in wireless adapters for easy connection to home networks. Featuring a touch-screen interface, this frame can access photos stored on your network or on an online photo-sharing site and display them. You can even set up an e-mail address for the picture

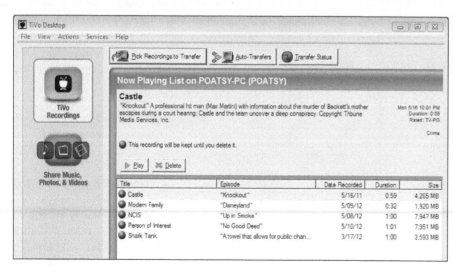

FIGURE 7.25 The TiVo Desktop software facilitates transfer of recorded shows to portable devices so you can enjoy your content on the go.

FIGURE 7.26 The Remote Play feature of the PS Vita and the PS3 lets you access PS3 features, like the PlayStation Store, directly from your Vita. *(Kyodo/AP Images)*

frame so that friends and family can e-mail pictures directly to the frame.

How can I use my home network to enhance my home security? Monitoring cameras, both for indoor and outdoor use, are now available for the home that feature wireless connectivity so you can keep track of your home while you're away. You can connect these cameras to your network and monitor them in real time through software like the Logitech Alert System using portable devices such as an iPhone or Android phone (see Figure 7.27).

The software can be configured to alert you via e-mail or text message when the cameras detect movement, such as a vehicle entering your driveway. Some systems also allow you to receive alerts when there is a lack of movement. This can be useful for monitoring an aging relative or for monitoring the arrival of children coming home from school.

As time goes on, many more types of entertainment devices and home gadgets will be connected to your home network.

Configuring Software for Your Home Network

How do I set up a Windows home network for the first time? In Windows, the process of setting up a network is fairly automated, especially if you're using the same version of Windows on all your computers. The Windows examples in this section assume all computers are running Windows 8. You can launch the Windows network setup wizards from the Network and Sharing Center, which you access via the Network and Internet group in the Control Panel.

FIGURE 7.27 Logitech security systems can help you monitor your home's security from your mobile devices. *(Logitech)*

Before configuring the computers to the network, do the following:

1. Make sure there are network adapters on each node.
2. For any wired connections, plug all the cables into the router, nodes, and so on.
3. Make sure your broadband modem is connected to your router and that the modem is connected to the Internet.
4. Turn on your equipment in the following order (allowing the modem and the router about one minute each to power up) and configure:
   a. Your broadband modem
   b. Your router
   c. All computers and peripherals (printers, scanners, and so on)

You can add other devices, such as TVs, Blu-ray players, and gaming consoles, to the network after you configure the computers.

After you've completed the previous steps, open the Network and Sharing Center from the Control Panel (see Figure 7.28):

- If your computer has a wired connection to the network, you should automatically be connected. You should give the network the same secured name you give to your router (see *Troubleshooting Wireless Network Problems* on page 290). If you're connecting wirelessly, click Connect to a Network in the Network and Internet group of the Control Panel. The Networks panel opens on the right side of your screen, displaying the wired and wireless connection options. You will need to enter your security passphrase to connect to your wireless network initially.

How do I share files with other computers on my network? For ease of file and peripheral sharing, Windows 7 created a feature known as *homegroup* that has carried over to Windows 8. The homegroup is a software device that makes it easier to allow computers on a Windows 8 network to share peripherals and information. To create a homegroup after connecting your first Windows 8 computer to your network, complete the steps outlined in Figure 7.29.

What if I don't have the same version of Windows on all my computers? Computers with various versions of Windows can coexist on the same network. Always set up the computers running the newest version of Windows first. Then consult the Microsoft website for guidance on how to configure computers with previous versions of Windows.

How do Macs connect wirelessly to networks? Connecting Macs to a wireless network is an easy process. When you boot up your Mac, the wireless card should be on by default. The network login screen will appear with a list of available networks that the NIC in your Mac detects. If there is a padlock icon next to the network name, this means that the network is secure and will require a password. Enter the password for the network in the password box, and click the Join button. For unsecure networks, you don't need a password. Checking the "Remember this network" check box will make any network a preferred network, enabling the computer to connect to the network automatically when that network is available. You can have multiple preferred networks, such as your home, school, work, and local coffee shop networks.

FIGURE 7.28 Connecting a Windows 8 computer to a network for the first time is fairly automated.

FIGURE 7.29

Creating a Homegroup in Windows 8

CREATING A HOMEGROUP IN WINDOWS 8

Step 1: Click **Create a homegroup** in the Home-Group window (accessed from the Network and Internet group in the Control Panel).

Step 2: Choose the sharing options for computers that belong to the homegroup. You can choose to share pictures, music, videos, documents, and printers with other Windows computers that belong to the homegroup. Although these are global settings for every computer in the homegroup, you can change these settings on individual computers if you wish.

Step 3: Windows generates a password. All other computers added to the network will need this password to join the homegroup. Once you've created the homegroup on the first computer, it will belong to that homegroup. You can then begin connecting other Windows computers to the network and join them to the homegroup you created.

BITS&BYTES

Want to Use Your Phone as a Remote Control?

Companies are developing apps that let your portable devices act as remote controls. The Media Remote app by Sony for the iPhone, iPod Touch, or iPad lets you control Sony Blu-ray players and TVs. And the Remote app from Apple lets you use your iPhone or iPad to control your iTunes or Apple TV from your handheld device over your WiFi network.

Troubleshooting Wireless Network Problems

What types of problems can I run into when installing wireless networks? The maximum range of 802.11n wireless devices is about 350 feet. But as you go farther away from your router, the throughput you achieve decreases. Obstacles between wireless nodes also decrease throughput. Walls, floors, and large metal objects (such as refrigerators) are the most common sources of interference with wireless signals.

What if a node on the network seems slow? Repositioning the node within the same room (sometimes even just a few inches from the original position) can affect communication between nodes. If this doesn't work, move the device closer to the router or to another room in your house. If these solutions don't work, consider using a dual-band N router or adding a wireless range extender to your network.

What's a dual-band N router? A dual-band N router allows for simultaneous support for both 2.4-GHz and 5-GHz frequency bands for 802.11n and all prior 802.11 standards (a, b, and g). Traditional routers only support one signal band at a time, so they're more likely to experience interference by outside devices (such as cell phones or microwave ovens) using the same bandwidth. Dual-band N routers allow for simultaneous access to both frequencies, and therefore provide maximum flexibility in setting up a home network. For example, data transfers can be set to run on the 2.4-GHz side, without impacting the performance of 802.11n clients that might be streaming video on the 5-GHz band.

What's a wireless range extender? A **wireless range extender** is a device that amplifies your wireless signal to extend to parts of your home that are experiencing poor connectivity. For example, as shown in Figure 7.30, Laptop C on the back porch can't connect to the wireless network even though Computer B in the den can. By placing a range extender in the den, where there is still good connectivity to the wireless network, the wireless signal is amplified and beamed farther out to the back porch. This allows Laptop C to make a good connection to the network. ■

Computer A with wireless network adapter — Computer B with wireless range extender — Laptop C with wireless network adapter

FIGURE 7.30 Because a wireless range extender is installed in the den, Laptop C on the back porch can now connect to the wireless network.

ethics in IT

Sharing Your Internet Connection with Your Neighbors: Legal? Ethical? Safe?

With the advances in wireless equipment, signals can travel well beyond the walls of your home. This makes it possible for a group of neighbors to share a wireless signal and potentially save money by splitting the cost of one Internet connection among them. However, before jumping into this venture, you need to weigh a few issues carefully:

- **State and local laws**: You probably aren't legally prohibited from sharing an Internet connection, but check on state and local laws. Most laws are designed to prohibit piggybacking—using a network without the network owner's consent. However, if you're giving neighbors permission to share your connection, you probably aren't violating any piggybacking laws.

- **ISP restrictions**: The terms of your agreement with your ISP might prohibit you from sharing your connection with people outside your household. If you aren't allowed to share the type of account you have now, your ISP probably offers an account (such as a small business account) that lets you share a connection, but it will most likely be more expensive. You might be able to share a personal account without being detected by your ISP, but that would be unethical because you should be paying for a higher level of access.

- **Range of access**: You also need to consider whether the shared access should be open to all neighbors or just to the neighbors contributing to the cost of the Internet connection (see Figure 7.31). You could leave the connection open, like the connections at your local coffee shop, and let anyone who finds it log on and surf. You could register your free hotspot with a service like JiWire (**jiwire.com**), and then people would be able to find it. However, neighbors who are helping pay for the connection might not want to fund free surfing for everyone. Make sure you work this out before proceeding.

- **Security**: If you're going to host a free and open hotspot, you need to make sure you set it up safely. You want to maintain a secure network for you and your neighbors while still allowing the occasional visiting surfer to use the connection. There are WiFi sharing services such as

Fon (**corp.fon.com**) and Chillifire (**chillifire.net**) that provide hardware and software that let you configure your hotspot so your network remains secure.

Although offering free access to anyone will earn you lots of good karma, additional risks exist because you don't know what mischief or criminal activities someone might engage in while connected to the Internet through your account. Think carefully before you proceed down the sharing path, and make sure you set up your hotspot to protect your internal network.

FIGURE 7.31 You can probably receive many wireless signals from neighbors inside your home (as shown here), but deciding whether to share Internet access requires careful consideration.

securing wireless
NETWORKS

All computers that connect to the Internet, whether or not they're on a network, need to be secured from intruders. This is usually accomplished by using a firewall, which is a hardware or software solution that helps shield your network from prying eyes. (We discuss firewalls at length in Chapter 9.) Wireless networks present special vulnerabilities; therefore, you should take additional steps to keep your wireless network safe. If you're setting up a new network, it's wise to take these precautions *as you set up your network*. If you have a network already installed, check to be sure you've followed the guidelines discussed here.

Why is a wireless network more vulnerable than a wired network? With a wired network, it's fairly easy to tell if a **hacker**, someone who breaks into computer systems to create mischief or steal information, is using your network. However, the newer wireless 802.11 networks have wide ranges that may extend outside your house. This makes it possible for a hacker to access your network without your knowledge.

Also, in some areas where residences are close together, wireless signals can reach a neighbor's residence. Most wireless network adapters are set up to access the strongest wireless network signal detected. **Piggybacking** is connecting to a wireless network without the permission of the owner. This practice is illegal in many jurisdictions but often happens inadvertently between neighbors.

Why should I be worried about someone logging onto my wireless network without my permission? If your neighbor is using your network connection, his or her usage could be slowing down your connection speed. Some neighbors might even be computer savvy enough to penetrate your unprotected wireless network and steal personal information, just as any other hackers would. And any cyberattacks or illegal behavior a hacker

initiates from your wireless network could get you in trouble with the authorities.

How is my wireless network vulnerable? Packets of information on a wireless network are broadcast through the airwaves. Savvy hackers can intercept and decode information from your transmissions that may allow them to bypass standard protections, such as a firewall, that you have set up on your network. Therefore, to secure a wireless network, take the additional precautions described in the Sound Byte "Securing Wireless Networks" and summarized as follows:

1. **Change your network name (SSID).** Each wireless network has its own name to identify it, known as the **service set identifier (SSID)**. Unless you change this name when you set up your router, the router uses a default network name that all routers from that manufacturer use (such as "Wireless" or "Netgear"). Hackers know the default names and access codes for routers. If you haven't changed the SSID, it's advertising the fact that you probably haven't changed any of the other default settings for your router either.

2. **Disable SSID broadcast.** Most routers are set up to broadcast their SSIDs so that other wireless devices can find them. If your router supports disabling SSID broadcasting, turn it off. This makes it more difficult for a hacker to detect your network and nearly impossible for a neighbor to inadvertently connect to your network.

3. **Change the default password on your router.** Routers have default user names and passwords. Hackers can use these to access your router and break into your network. Change the password on your router to something hard to guess. Use at least eight characters that are a combination of letters, symbols, and numbers.

4. **Turn on security protocols.** Most routers ship with security protocols such as Wired Equivalent Privacy (WEP) or Wi-Fi Protected Access (WPA). Both use encryption (a method of translating your data into code) to protect data in your wireless transmissions. WPA is a much stronger protocol than WEP, so enable WPA if you have it; enable WEP if you don't.

5. **Create a passphrase.** When you enable these protocols, you're forced to create a security encryption key (passphrase). When you attempt to connect a node to a security-enabled network for the first time, you're

 SOUND BYTE
Securing Wireless Networks
In this Sound Byte, you'll learn what "war drivers" are and why they could potentially be a threat to your wireless network. You'll also learn some simple steps to secure your wireless network against intruders.

FIGURE 7.32 By accessing your router, you can configure the security protocols available on your router and change the SSID.

required to enter the security key. The security key or passphrase (see Figure 7.32) is the code that computers on your network need to decrypt (decode) data transmissions. Without this key, it's extremely difficult, if not impossible, to decrypt the data transmissions from your network. The Windows 8 Connect to a Network dialog box shows all wireless networks within range. Moving your cursor over the network name will reveal details about the network such as whether it's a secured network. Clicking on a network name allows you to connect to it or prompts you for more information such as the SSID name and security key.

6. **Implement media access control.** Each network adapter on your network has a unique number (like a serial number) assigned to it by the manufacturer. This is called a media access control (MAC) address, and it's a number printed right on the network adapter. Many routers allow you to restrict access to the network to only certain MAC addresses. This helps ensure that only authorized devices can connect to your network.

7. **Limit your signal range.** Many routers allow you to adjust the transmitting power to low, medium,

or high. Cutting down the power to low or medium could prevent your signal from reaching too far away from your home, making it tougher for interlopers to poach your signal.

8. **Apply firmware upgrades.** Your router has read-only memory that has software written to it. This software is known as **firmware**. As bugs are found in the firmware (which hackers might exploit), manufacturers issue patches, just as the makers of operating system software do. Periodically check the manufacturer's website and apply any necessary upgrades to your firmware.

If you follow these steps, you'll greatly improve the security of your wireless network. In Chapter 9, we'll explore many other ways to keep your computer safe from malicious individuals on the Internet and ensure that your digital information is secure. ■

> **Before moving on to the Chapter Review:**
> - Watch Replay Video 7.2 ▶.
> - Then check your understanding of what you've learned so far.

check your understanding//

For a quick review to see what you've learned so far, answer the following questions. Visit **pearsonhighered.com/techinaction** to check your answers.

multiple choice

1. When setting up a home network, the router is attached
   a. directly to the broadband modem.
   b. directly to the NIC in each device.
   c. directly to the Internet.
   d. directly to the Ethernet switch.

2. All of the following are methods to secure your wireless network except
   a. disabling SSID broadcast.
   b. enabling WPA.
   c. changing your network name (SSID).
   d. disabling WEP.

3. Which network-ready device facilitates file sharing and data backup?
   a. Home network server
   b. Time Capsule
   c. Network-attached storage
   d. All of the above

4. To share files between computers on a Windows home network, you must
   a. enable groupsharing.
   b. create a homegroup.
   c. enable Windows sharing.
   d. None of the above

5. Which of the following is not recommended to do when securing a home wireless network?
   a. Change the default password on the router.
   b. Turn on security protocols.
   c. Enable the SSID broadcast.
   d. Change the network SSID name.

true–false

_____ **1.** Network-ready devices contain Ethernet switches.

_____ **2.** Home network servers are a specialized type of NAS device.

critical thinking

1. **Evaluating Your Network Configuration**

   Write down all the devices you believe currently connect to your home network, either wired or wirelessly. Make sure you consider smartphones, tablets, laptops, desktops, gaming consoles, DVRs, smart TVs, and printers. Are there devices (such as printers or TVs) that are not currently able to connect directly to your network that you might want to replace? If so, note those devices, and describe the advantages a network-ready replacement would bring. Are there other devices you might also want to consider adding to your network that you don't currently have, such as a home-monitoring system? If so, why would they be helpful?

2. **Evaluating Your Network Storage Needs**

   You probably have videos, pictures, and music stored on your computer that you may be sharing (or want to share) with others. Research at least three Internet-based media storing/sharing solutions such as Dropbox, MediaFire, and Amazon Cloud Drive. What is the cost of each? Are there individual file-size limitations for storage? What is the total volume of media you can store? Is the media you store on the site easily sharable? Does the service allow storage of all the types of media you need to store? Which solution would you implement? Be sure to justify your choice.

Continue →

summary //

Networking Fundamentals

1. What is a network, and what are a network's advantages and disadvantages?

- A computer network is simply two or more computers that are connected using software and hardware so they can communicate.
- Advantages of networks include allowing users to
  - share an Internet connection,
  - share printers and other peripheral devices,
  - share files, and
  - communicate with computers regardless of their operating system.
- Disadvantages for larger networks are that they require administration and that they may require costly equipment.

Network Architecture and Components

2. What are the different ways to classify networks?

- Networks can be defined by the distance between nodes:
  - A personal area network (PAN) is used for communication among personal mobile devices using Bluetooth or WiFi wireless technologies.
  - A local area network (LAN) connects nodes that are located in a small geographic area.
  - A home area network (HAN) is a specific type of LAN located in a home.
  - A metropolitan area network (MAN) is a large network in a specific geographic area.
  - A wide area network (WAN) spans a large physical distance.
- Networks are classified by administration:
  - Centrally: A client/server network contains two types of computers: a client computer on which users perform specific tasks and a server computer that provides resources to the clients and central control for the network. Most networks that have 10 or more nodes are client/server networks.
  - Locally: Peer-to-peer (P2P) networks enable each node connected to the network to communicate directly with every other node. Most home networks are P2P networks.

3. Which type of network is most commonly found in the home?

- Ethernet networks are the most common networks used in home networking.
- Most Ethernet networks use a combination of wired and wireless connections, depending on the data throughput required. Wired connections usually achieve higher throughput than wireless connections.
- Wired Ethernet home networks use the gigabit Ethernet standard.
- Wireless Ethernet networks are identified by a protocol standard: 802.11 a/b/g/n.
  - 802.11n is the most current standard.

4. What are the main components of every network?

- To function, any network must contain a number of components:
  - A means of connecting the nodes on the network (cables or wireless technology)
  - Special hardware devices that allow the nodes to communicate with each other and to send data
  - Software that allows the network to run

Connecting to the Internet

5. What are my options for connecting to the Internet?

- Wired networks use various types of cable to connect nodes. The type of network and the distance between the nodes determines the type of cable used. Broadband connections include:
  - Cable transmits data over coaxial cable that is also used for cable television.
  - DSL uses twisted-pair wire, similar to that used for telephones.
  - Fiber-optic cable uses glass or plastic strands to transmit data via light signals.
  - Satellite is a connection option for those who do not have access to faster broadband technologies. Data is transmitted between a satellite dish and a satellite that is in a geosynchronous orbit.
  - WiFi allows users to connect to the Internet wirelessly but is not as fast as a wired connection.

- Mobile broadband is a 3G or 4G service delivered by cell-phone networks.
- Dial-up is the cheapest means of accessing the Internet, but it is also the slowest.

Installing and Configuring Home Networks

6. How do I tell if my home network is up to date, and how do I identify the devices on the network?

- Most home network routers should support both wireless and wired access to the Internet.
- For a home network to run efficiently, all nodes such as NICs and routers should use the same Ethernet standard.
- The Device Manager utility in Windows lists all adapters installed on your computer.

7. Besides computers, what other devices can I connect to a home network?

- All devices are connected to your router, either wirelessly or with a wired connection. Wired connections deliver better throughput than wireless.
- To add additional ports to your network, you can connect a switch to your router.
- Network-attached storage (NAS) devices let you store and share data files such as movies and music, as well as provide a central place for file backups. Home network servers can be used instead of an NAS device if your needs require more sophisticated functionality than NAS devices.
- Connecting digital entertainment devices (such as gaming consoles) lets you stream movies and other entertainment directly from the Internet.

8. How do I configure the software on my computer and set up the devices required to get my network up and running?

- The latest versions of Windows make it easy to set up wired and wireless networks.
  - Plug in the modem, the router, and all cables, and then switch on the modem, router, and computers (in that order).
  - Launch the Network and Sharing Center, and select the appropriate links for setup.
  - Make sure each computer has a distinct name, and ensure that all computers are in the same homegroup.

- Devices such as gaming consoles each have their own setup procedures for connecting to wireless networks but usually require the same information as that needed for connecting a computer to a secured wireless network.

9. What problems might I encounter when setting up a wireless network?

- You may not get the throughput you need through a wireless connection. Therefore, you may need to consider a wired connection for certain devices.
- Distance from the router, as well as walls, floors, and large metal objects between a device and the router, can interfere with wireless connectivity.
- To solve connectivity problems, dual-band N routers allow for simultaneous support for devices running on both the 2.4-GHz and 5-GHz frequency bands for 802.11n standards. Wireless range extenders can amplify signals to improve connectivity in areas of poor signal strength.

Securing Wireless Networks

10. Why are wireless networks more vulnerable to security risks than wired networks, and what special precautions are required to ensure my wireless network is secure?

- Wireless networks are even more susceptible to hacking than wired networks because the signals of most wireless networks extend beyond the walls of your home.
- Neighbors may unintentionally (or intentionally) connect to the Internet through your wireless connection, and hackers may try to access it.
- To prevent unwanted intrusions into your network, you should change the default password on your router to make it tougher for hackers to gain access, use a hard-to-guess SSID (network name), disable SSID broadcasting to make it harder for outsiders to detect your network, enable security protocols such as WPA or WEP, create a network passphrase, implement media access control, limit your signal range, and apply firmware upgrades.

Be sure to check out the companion website for additional materials to help you review and learn, including a Tech Bytes Weekly newsletter— **pearsonhighered.com/techinaction**. And don't forget the Replay Videos ▶

key terms//

making the transition to . . . next semester//

1. **Dormitory Networking**

   Often, you and your college suitemates are all on the Internet at the same time downloading movies or other large files, which causes your network's performance to slow down considerably. You realize you need to update your router to the faster 802.11n standard. In addition, you've agreed to buy a printer that you all can share, and someone has suggested also getting shared backup storage.

   a. Research network-ready laser printers on sites such as **hp.com**, **epson.com**, and **brother.com**. What network-ready printer would you recommend? Why?

   b. Research 802.11n wireless routers at sites such as **netgear.com**, **home.cisco.com/en-us/home**, and **dlink.com**. What router do you think will meet your needs? Why?

   c. What would you recommend to address backup needs? Would you recommend individual external devices, an NAS device, a home network server, or cloud storage? What is the rationale for your choice?

2. **Connecting Your Computer to Public Networks**

   You're working for a local coffee shop that offers free wireless access to customers. Your supervisor has asked you to create a flyer for patrons that warns them of the potential dangers of surfing the Internet in public places. Conduct research about using public hotspots to access the Internet. Prepare a flyer that lists specific steps that customers can take to protect their data when surfing on publicly accessible networks.

making the transition to . . . the workplace//

1. **Internet Access for a Small Business in a Remote Area**

   Your uncle owns a combination gas station/coffee shop/general store in a very small town in the Midwest. He currently is using dial-up Internet access to send e-mail and surf the web. Some of his customers have indicated that they would love it if the store had broadband access. No local company supplies broadband service in the town where the business is located. Your uncle has asked you for ideas.

   Investigate three satellite Internet service providers and prepare a summary of features and prices for your uncle. Make sure to find out what the download and upload speeds are for each provider. Also, ensure that the service agreement allows your uncle to use the Internet connection to provide access to his customers. Which service would you recommend to your uncle? Why?

2. **Putting Computers to Work on Research Projects**

   Most computer central processing units (CPUs) use only a fraction of their computing power most of the time. Many medical research companies (such as those seeking cures for cancer and AIDS) could benefit from "borrowing" computer CPU time when computers are not being used or are being underutilized. Virtual supercomputers (which are really networks of computers) can be created using software installed on tens of thousands of computers. This type of computing is also known as *grid* or *distributed computing*. These virtual computing nets can be harnessed to solve complex problems when the individual computer owners are not using their computers. Assume that you are working for a business that has 100 computers and you would like to participate in a grid-computing project. Investigate IBM's World Community Grid (**worldcommunitygrid.org**). Prepare a report for your boss that does the following:

   a. Describes the World Community Grid (WCG) and its objectives

   b. Lists current projects on which the WCG is working

   c. Describes the process for installing the WCG software on the company's computers

   d. Suggests a strategy for publicizing the company's participation in the WCG project that will encourage your employer's customers to participate

Providing Wireless Internet Access to the Needy

Problem

Wireless Internet access in the home is very desirable. However, not everyone is able to afford it, and this can put families, especially ones with school-aged children, at a disadvantage. Providing Internet access to the underprivileged is a way of closing the "digital divide" that exists between those who can afford Internet access and those who cannot.

Task

You're volunteering for a charity that wants to begin installing wireless networks in homes for needy families. The project is funded by charitable grants with the objective of providing basic broadband Internet access and simple networking capabilities homes at no cost to the recipients. The assumption is that each family already has two laptop computers (provided through another charity) that have 802.11n wireless capabilities. You've volunteered to research potential network and Internet solutions.

Process

Break the class into three teams. Each team will be responsible for investigating one of the following issues:

1. **Internet service providers:** Research ISPs that serve the town where your school is located (don't forget to include satellite providers). Compare and contrast their lowest-cost broadband access. Compare maximum upload and download speeds as well as costs. Be sure to consider the cost of the modems—whether they're purchased up front or rented on a monthly basis. Make sure to select what your group considers the best deal.

2. **Networking equipment and network-ready peripherals:** Each home needs to be provided with an 802.11n-capable wireless router (to share the Internet access), a network-ready all-in-one printer, and a Blu-ray player capable of streaming digital video (for educational programs and movies). Research at least three different options for each of these devices. Since this is a grant and money is limited, be sure to consider price as well as functionality.

3. **Security:** The wireless networks need to be secured to keep hackers and piggybackers out. Work in conjunction with the group that is researching routers to determine the best type of router to purchase since it needs to support a strong wireless security protocol such as WPA. Make sure to consider what other types of protection are needed on the network, such as antivirus software, anti-malware software, and firewalls.

Present your findings to your class and come to a consensus about the solution you would propose for the charity. Provide your instructor with a report on your area suitable for presentation to the CEO of the charity.

Conclusion

Providing technology to underserved populations on a cost-effective basis will go a long way toward closing the digital divide and ensuring that disadvantaged youth have the Internet access they need to pursue their education and compete effectively in today's society.

Firing Employees for Expressing Views on Social Media Sites

In this exercise, you'll research and then role-play a complicated ethical situation. The role you play may or may not match your own personal beliefs; regardless, your research and use of logic will enable you to represent the view assigned. An arbitrator will watch and comment on both sides of the arguments, and together, the team will agree on an ethical solution.

Problem

The largest network, the Internet, provides the capability for vast social interaction. Social media sites such as Facebook, YouTube, and Twitter, as well as blogs and wikis, give everyone convenient ways to express their opinions. However, employers often are intolerant of employees who freely express negative opinions or expose inside information about their employers on social media sites. Given that most jurisdictions in the United States use the doctrine of employment at-will (that is, employees can be fired at any time for any reason, or even no reason), many employers are quick to discipline or terminate employees who express opinions with which the company disagrees. When such cases come to court, the courts often find in favor of the employers. It's clear that individuals must exercise extreme care when posting work-related content.

Research Areas to Consider

- Ellen Simonetti and Delta Airlines
- Fired for blogging about work
- Free speech
- Joyce Park or Michael Tunison

Process

1. Divide the class into teams.
2. Research the areas cited above and devise a scenario in which someone has complained about an employee blogging about a sensitive workplace issue such as cleanliness at a food manufacturing facility or employee romances.
3. Team members should write a summary that provides background information for their character—for example: employee, human resources manager, or arbitrator—and that details their character's behaviors to set the stage for the role-playing event. Then, team members should create an outline to use during the role-playing event.
4. Team members should arrange a mutually convenient time to meet for the exchange, using either the collaboration feature of MyITLab or the discussion board feature of your course management software or by meeting in person.
5. Team members should present their case to the class or submit a PowerPoint presentation for review by the rest of the class, along with the summary and resolution they developed.

Conclusion

As technology becomes ever more prevalent and integrated into our lives, more and more ethical dilemmas will present themselves. Being able to understand and evaluate both sides of the argument, while responding in a personally or socially ethical manner, will be an important skill.

Technology in Focus | Under the Hood

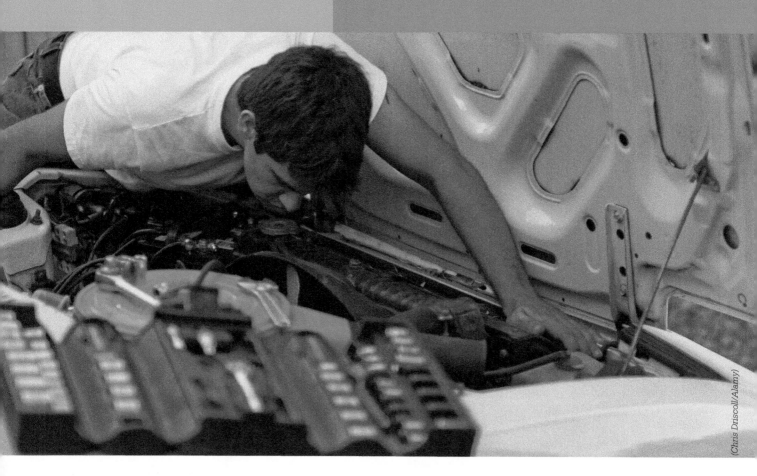

(Chris Driscoll/Alamy)

Some people are drawn to understanding things in detail; others are happy just to have things work. If you use a computer, you may not have been tempted to "look under the hood." However, if you can understand the hardware inside a computer, you'll have some real advantages:

- You won't have to pay a technician to fix or upgrade your computer. You'll be able to fine-tune it yourself, and you'll be able to make your investment in your computer last longer.
- You'll be able to evaluate new advances in technology. For example, what's the impact of a new type of memory or a new processor?
- If you're a programmer, you'll be able to write more efficient and faster programs.

And if you're preparing for a career in information technology, understanding computer hardware is critical for you. In this Technology in Focus feature, we'll build on what you've learned about computer hardware in other chapters and go "under the hood" to look at the components of your system unit in more detail. Let's begin by looking at the building blocks of computers: switches.

Switches

How does a computer process the data you input? A computer system can be viewed as an enormous collection of on/off switches. These simple on/off switches are combined in different ways to perform addition and subtraction and to move data around the system.

Electrical Switches

To process data into information, computers need to work in a language they understand. Computers understand only two states of existence: on and off. Inside a computer, these two possibilities, or states, are defined using the two numbers *1* and *0*; the language represented by these numbers is called **binary language** because just two numbers are used. Everything a computer does, such as processing data or printing a report, is broken down into a series of *0*s and *1*s. **Electrical switches** are the devices inside the computer that are flipped between the two states of *1* and *0*, signifying "on" and "off."

You use various forms of switches every day. The light switch in your kitchen either is ON, allowing current to flow to the light bulb, or OFF. Another switch you use each day is a water faucet. As shown in Figure 1, shutting off the faucet so that no water flows could represent the value 0, whereas turning it on could represent the value 1.

Computers are built from a huge collection of electrical switches. The history of computers is really a story about creating smaller and faster sets of electrical switches so that more data can be stored and manipulated quickly.

Vacuum Tubes. The earliest generation of electronic computers used **vacuum tubes** as switches. Vacuum

FIGURE 2 Early computers were constructed using vacuum tubes (see inset). The difference in size achieved by moving from tubes to transistors allowed computers to become desktop devices instead of room-sized machines. *(CORBIS)*

tubes act as switches by allowing or blocking the flow of electrical current. The problem with vacuum tubes is that they take up a lot of space, as shown in Figure 2. The first high-speed digital computer, the Electronic Numerical Integrator and Computer (ENIAC), was deployed in 1945. It used nearly 18,000 vacuum tubes as switches and was about half the size of a basketball court! In addition to being large, the vacuum tubes produced a lot of heat and burned out frequently.

Since the introduction of ENIAC's vacuum tubes, two major revolutions have occurred in the design of switches, and consequently computers, to make them smaller and faster:

1. The invention of the *transistor*

2. The fabrication of *integrated circuits*

Transistors. Transistors are electrical switches built out of layers of a special type of material called a **semiconductor**. A semiconductor is any material that can be controlled either to conduct electricity or to act as an insulator (to prohibit electricity from passing through). Silicon, which is found in common sand, is the semiconductor material used to make transistors (see Figure 3).

By itself, silicon doesn't conduct electricity particularly well, but if specific chemicals are added in a controlled way to the silicon, it begins to behave like a switch. The silicon allows electrical current to flow easily when a certain voltage is applied; otherwise, it prevents electrical current from flowing, thus behaving as an on/off switch. This kind of behavior is exactly what's needed

FIGURE 1 Water faucets can be used to illustrate binary switches.

FIGURE 3 A silicon wafer like the one shown here holds the transistor circuitry for hundreds of devices. (Justin Sullivan/Staff/Getty Images News)

to store digital information—the 0s (off) and 1s (on) of binary language.

The first transistors were much smaller than vacuum tubes, produced little heat, and could quickly be switched from on to off, thereby allowing or blocking electrical current. They also were less expensive than vacuum tubes.

It wasn't long, however, before transistors reached their limits. Continuing advances in technology began to require more transistors than circuit boards could reasonably handle. Something was needed to pack more transistor capacity into a smaller space. Thus, integrated circuits, the next technical revolution in switches, were developed.

Integrated Circuits. Integrated circuits (or **chips**) are tiny regions of semiconductor material that support a huge number of transistors (see Figure 4). Most integrated circuits are no more than a quarter inch in size yet can hold billions of transistors.

This advancement has enabled computer designers to create small yet powerful **microprocessors**, which are the chips that contain a central processing unit (CPU). The Intel 4004, the first complete microprocessor to be located on a single integrated circuit, was released in 1971, marking the beginning of the true miniaturization of computers. The Intel 4004 contained slightly more than 2,300 transistors. Today, more than 2 billion transistors can be manufactured in a space as tiny as the nail of your little finger!

Number Systems

How can simple switches be organized so that they let you use a computer to pay your bills online or write an essay? How can a set of switches describe a number or a word or give a computer the command to perform addition? Recall that to manipulate the on/off switches, the computer works in binary language, which uses only two digits, *0* and *1*. Let's look at how numbering systems work so that we can begin to understand this more deeply.

The Base-10 Number System

A **number system** is an organized plan for representing a number. Although you may not realize it, you're already familiar with one number system. The **base-10 number system**, also known as **decimal notation**, is the system you use to represent all of the numeric values you use each day. It's called base 10 because it uses 10 digits—0 through 9—to represent any value.

To represent a number in base 10, you break the number down into groups of ones, tens, hundreds, thousands, and so on. Each digit has a place value depending on where it appears in the number. For example, using base 10, in the whole number 6,954 there are 6 sets of thousands, 9 sets of hundreds, 5 sets of tens, and 4 sets of ones. Working from right to left, each

FIGURE 4 An integrated circuit is packaged in a small case but holds billions of transistors. (Gudellaphoto/Fotolia)

place in a number represents an increasing power of 10, as follows:

$$6,954 = (6 * 1,000) + (9 * 100) + (5*10) + (4*1)$$
$$= (6 * 10^3) + (9 * 10^2) + (5 * 10^1) + (4 * 10^0)$$

Note that in this equation, the final digit *4* is represented as $4 * 10^0$ because any number raised to the zero power is equal to 1.

The Base-2 (or Binary) Number System

Anthropologists theorize that humans developed a base-10 number system because we have 10 fingers. However, computer systems are not well suited to thinking about numbers in groups of 10. Instead, computers describe a number in powers of 2 because each switch can be in one of two positions: on or off (see Figure 5). This numbering system is referred to as the **binary number system**.

The binary number system is also referred to as the **base-2 number system**. Even with just two digits, the binary number system can still represent all the values that a base-10 number system can. Instead of breaking the number down into sets of ones, tens, hundreds, and thousands, as is done in base-10 notation, the binary number system describes a number as the sum of powers of 2—ones, twos, fours, eights, and sixteens. Binary numbers are used to represent every piece of data stored in a

THERE ARE
10 KINDS
OF PEOPLE:
THOSE WHO
UNDERSTAND
BINARY AND
THOSE
WHO DON'T

FIGURE 5 Computer humor—the value *2* is written as *10* in binary! (*GroovyGearShop.com/CafePress.com*)

computer: all of the numbers, all of the letters, and all of the instructions that the computer uses to execute work.

Representing Integers. In the base-10 number system, a whole number is represented as the sum of *1*s, *10*s, *100*s, and *1,000*s—that is, sums of powers of 10. The binary system works in the same way, but describes a value as the sum of groups of *1*s, *2*s, *4*s, *8*s, *16*s, *32*s, *64*s, etc.—that is, powers of 2: 1, 2, 4, 8, 16, 32, 64, and so on.

Let's look at the number 67. In base 10, the number 67 would be six sets of *10*s and seven sets of *1*s, as follows:

$$\text{Base 10: } 67 = (6 * 10^1) + (7 * 10^0)$$

One way to figure out how 67 is represented in base 2 is to find the largest possible power of 2 that could be in the number 67. Two to the eighth power is 256, and there are no groups of 256 in the number 67. Two to the seventh power is 128, but that is bigger than 67. Two to the sixth power is 64, and there is a group of 64 inside a group of 67.

67 has	1	group of	64	That leaves 3 and
3 has	0	groups of	32	
	0	groups of	16	
	0	groups of	8	
	0	groups of	4	
	1	group of	2	That leaves 1 and
1 has	1	group of	1	Now nothing is left

So, the binary number for 67 is written as 1000011 in base 2:

$$\text{Base 2: } 67 = 64 + 0 + 0 + 0 + 0 + 2 + 1$$
$$= (1 * 2^6) + (0 * 2^5) + (0 * 2^4) + (0 * 2^3) +$$
$$(0 * 2^2) + (1 * 2^1) + (1 * 2^0)$$
$$= (1000011)_{\text{base 2}}$$

It's easier to have a calculator do this for you! Some calculators have a button labeled DEC (for decimal) and another labeled BIN (for binary). Using Windows 8, you can access the Scientific Calculator that supports conversion between decimal (base 10) and binary (base 2) by accessing Search from the Charms bar and typing "calc" on the Start screen. From the App search results, choose the Calculator. From the Calculator menu, select View and then Programmer. You can enter your calculation in decimal and instantly see the binary representation in 64 bits, as shown in Figure 6.

Hexadecimal Notation. A large integer value becomes a very long string of *1*s and *0*s in binary! For convenience, programmers often use **hexadecimal notation** to make these expressions easier to use. Hexadecimal is

FIGURE 6 The Windows Calculator in Programmer mode instantly converts values from decimal to binary.

FIGURE 7

Sample Hexadecimal Values

DECIMAL NUMBER	BINARY VALUE	HEXADECIMAL VALUE
00	0000	00
01	0001	01
02	0010	02
03	0011	03
04	0100	04
05	0101	05
06	0110	06
07	0111	07
08	1000	08
09	1001	09
10	1010	A
11	1011	B
12	1100	C
13	1101	D
14	1110	E
15	1111	F

a base-16 number system, meaning it uses 16 digits to represent numbers instead of the 10 digits used in base 10 or the 2 digits used in base 2. The 16 digits it uses are the 10 numeric digits, 0 to 9, plus six extra symbols: A, B, C, D, E, and F. Each of the letters A through F corresponds to a numeric value, so that A equals 10, B equals 11, and so on (see Figure 7). Therefore, the value 67 in decimal notation is 1000011 in binary or 43 in hexadecimal notation. It is much easier for computer scientists to use the 2-digit 43 than the 7-digit string 1000011. The Windows Calculator in Programmer view also can perform conversions to hexadecimal notation. (You can watch a video showing you how to perform conversions between bases using the Windows Calculator in the Sound Byte titled, "Where Does Binary Show Up?")

Representing Characters: ASCII. We've just been converting integers from base 10, which *we* understand, to base 2 (binary state), which the computer understands. Similarly, we need a system that converts letters and other symbols that *we* understand to a binary state the computer understands. To provide a consistent means for representing letters and other characters, certain codes

dictate how to represent characters in binary format. Most of today's personal computers use the American National Standards Institute (ANSI, pronounced "An-see") standard code, called the **American Standard Code for Information Interchange** (**ASCII**, pronounced "As-key"), to represent each letter or character as an 8-bit (or 1-byte) binary code.

Each binary digit is called a **bit** for short. Eight binary digits (or bits) combine to create one **byte**. We've been converting base-10 numbers to a binary format. In such cases, the binary format has no standard length. For example, the binary format for the number *2* is two digits (10), whereas the binary format for the number *10* is four digits (1010). Although binary numbers can have more or fewer than 8 bits, each single alphabetic or special character is 1 byte (or 8 bits) of data and consists of a unique combination of a total of eight *0*s and *1*s.

The ASCII code represents the 26 uppercase letters and 26 lowercase letters used in the English language, along with many punctuation symbols and other special characters, using 8 bits. Figure 8 shows several examples of the ASCII code representation of printable letters and characters.

Representing Characters: Unicode. Because it represents letters and characters using only 8 bits, the ASCII code can assign only 256 (or 2^8) different codes for unique characters and letters. Although

SOUND BYTE
Where Does Binary Show Up?

In this Sound Byte, you'll learn how to use tools to work with binary, decimal, and hexadecimal numbers. (These tools come with the Windows operating system.) You'll also learn where you might see binary and hexadecimal values when you use a computer.

FIGURE 8

ASCII Standard Code for a Sample of Letters and Characters

ASCII CODE	REPRESENTS THIS SYMBOL	ASCII CODE	REPRESENTS THIS SYMBOL
01000001	A	01100001	a
01000010	B	01100010	b
01000011	C	01100011	c
01011010	Z	00100011	#
00100001	!	00100100	$
00100010	"	00100101	%

Note: For the full ASCII table, see **ascii-code.com**.

this is enough to represent English and many other characters found in the world's languages, ASCII code can't represent all languages and symbols, because some languages require more than 256 characters and letters. Thus, a new encoding scheme, called **Unicode**, was created. By using 16 bits instead of the 8 bits used in ASCII, Unicode can represent nearly 1,115,000 code

points and currently assigns more than 96,000 unique character symbols (see Figure 9).

The first 128 characters of Unicode are identical to ASCII, but because of its depth, Unicode is also able to represent the alphabets of all modern and historic languages and notational systems, including such languages and writing systems as Tibetan, Tagalog, and Canadian Aboriginal syllabics. As we continue to become a more global society, it's anticipated that Unicode will replace ASCII as the standard character formatting code.

Representing Decimal Numbers. The binary number system can also represent a decimal number. How can a string of 1s and 0s capture the information in a value such as 99.368? Because every computer must store such numbers in the same way, the Institute of Electrical and Electronics Engineers (IEEE) has established a standard called the *floating-point standard* that describes how numbers with fractional parts should be represented in the binary number system. Using a 32-bit system, we can represent an incredibly wide range of numbers.

The method dictated by the IEEE standard works the same for any number with a decimal point, such as the number –0.75. The first digit, or bit (the sign bit), is used to indicate whether the number is positive or negative. The next eight bits store the magnitude of the number, indicating whether the number is in the hundreds or millions, for example. The standard says to use the next 23 bits to store the value of the number.

Interpretation. *All* data inside the computer is stored as bits:

- **Positive and negative integers** can be stored using signed integer notation, with the first bit (the sign bit) indicating the sign and the rest of the bits indicating the value of the number.
- **Decimal** numbers are stored according to the IEEE floating-point standard.
- **Letters and symbols** are stored according to the ASCII code or Unicode.

These number systems and codes exist so that computers can store different types of information in their on/off switches. No matter what kind of data you input in a computer—a color, a musical note, or a street address—that data will be stored as a pattern of 1s and 0s. The important lesson is that the

FIGURE 9 The written languages of the world require thousands of different characters, shown here. The Unicode Code Chart (**unicode.org/charts**) shows how Unicode provides a system allowing digital representation of over 1,100,000 unique characters.

interpretation of *0*s and *1*s is what matters. The same binary pattern could represent a positive number, a negative number, a fraction, or a letter.

How does the computer know which interpretation to use for the *1*s and *0*s? When your mind processes language, it takes the sounds you hear and uses the rules of English, along with other clues, to build an interpretation of the sound as a word. If you're in New York City and hear someone shout, "Hey, Lori!" you expect that someone is saying hello to a friend. If you're in London and hear the same sound—"Hey! Lorry!"—you jump out of the way because a truck is coming at you! You knew which interpretation to apply to the sound because you had some other information—the fact that you were in England.

Likewise, the CPU is designed to understand a specific language or set of instructions. Certain instructions tell the CPU to expect a negative number next or to interpret the following bit pattern as a character. Because of this extra information, the CPU always knows which interpretation to use for a series of bits.

How the CPU Works

Any program you run on your computer is actually a long series of binary code describing a specific set of commands the CPU must perform. These commands may be coming from a user's actions or may be instructions fed from a program while it executes. Each CPU is somewhat different in the exact steps it follows to perform its tasks, but all CPUs must perform a series of similar general steps. These steps, also illustrated in Figure 10, are referred to as a CPU **machine cycle** (or **processing cycle**):

1. **Fetch:** When any program begins to run, the *1*s and *0*s that make up the program's binary code must be "fetched" from their temporary storage location in random access memory (RAM) and moved to the CPU before they can be executed.

2. **Decode:** Once the program's binary code is in the CPU, it is decoded into commands the CPU understands.

3. **Execute:** Next, the CPU actually performs the work described in the commands. Specialized hardware on the CPU performs addition, subtraction, multiplication, division, and other mathematical and logical operations.

4. **Store:** The result is stored in one of the **registers**, special memory storage areas built into the CPU, which are the most expensive, fastest memory in your computer. The CPU is then ready to fetch the next set of bits encoding the next instruction.

No matter what program you're running and no matter how many programs you're using at one time, the CPU performs these four steps over and over at incredibly high speeds. Shortly, we'll look at each stage in more detail. But first, let's examine components that help the CPU perform its tasks.

The Control Unit

The CPU, like any part of the computer system, is designed from a collection of switches. How can the simple on/off switches of the CPU "remember" the fetch-decode-execute-store sequence of the machine cycle?

The **control unit** of the CPU manages the switches inside the CPU. It is programmed by CPU designers to

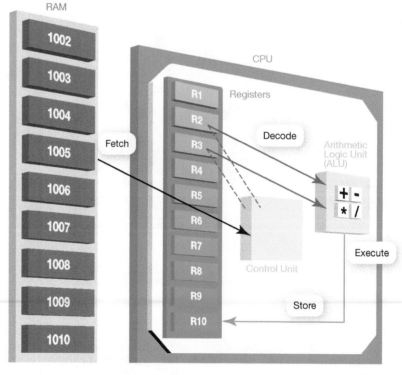

FIGURE 10 The CPU Machine Cycle

remember the sequence of processing stages for that CPU and how each switch in the CPU should be set (i.e., on or off) for each stage. With each beat of the system clock, the control unit moves each switch to the correct on or off setting and then performs the work of that stage.

The System Clock

To move from one stage of the machine cycle to the next, the motherboard uses a built-in **system clock**. This internal clock is actually a special crystal that acts like a metronome, keeping a steady beat and controlling when the CPU moves to the next stage of processing.

These steady beats or "ticks" of the system clock, known as the **clock cycle**, set the pace by which the computer moves from process to process. The pace, known as **clock speed**, is measured in hertz (Hz), which describes how many times something happens per second. Today's system clocks are measured in gigahertz (GHz), or a billion clock ticks per second. Therefore, in a 3 GHz system, there are 3 billion clock ticks each second.

Let's now look at each of the stages in the machine cycle in a bit more depth.

Stage 1: The Fetch Stage

The data and program instructions the CPU needs are stored in different areas in the computer system. Data and program instructions move between these areas as they're needed by the CPU for processing. Programs are permanently stored on the hard drive because it offers nonvolatile storage. However, when you launch a program, the program, or sometimes only its essential parts, is transferred from the hard drive into RAM.

The program moves to RAM because the CPU can access the data and program instructions stored in RAM more than one million times faster than if they're left on the hard drive. In part, this is because RAM is much closer to the CPU than the hard drive is. Another reason for the delay in transmission of data and program instructions from the hard drive to the CPU is the relatively slow speed of mechanical hard drives. The read/write heads have to sweep over the spinning platters, which takes time. Even non-mechanical SSD hard drives have slower access speeds

(Steve Young/Fotolia)

than RAM. RAM is a type of memory that gives very fast, direct access to data.

As specific instructions from the program are needed, they're moved from RAM into registers (the special storage areas located on the CPU itself), where they wait to be executed.

The CPU's storage area isn't big enough to hold everything it needs to process at the same time. If enough memory were located on the CPU chip itself, an entire program could be copied to the CPU from RAM before it was executed. This would add to the computer's speed and efficiency because there would be no delay while the CPU stopped processing operations to fetch instructions from RAM to the CPU. However, including so much memory on a CPU chip would make these chips extremely expensive. In addition, CPU design is so complex that only a limited amount of storage space is available on the CPU itself.

Cache Memory. The CPU doesn't actually need to fetch every instruction from RAM each time it goes through a cycle. Another layer of storage, called **cache memory**, has even faster access to the CPU than RAM. Cache memory consists of small blocks of memory located directly on and next to the CPU chip. These memory blocks are holding places for recently or frequently used instructions or data that the CPU needs the most. When these instructions or data are stored in cache memory, the CPU can retrieve them more quickly than if it had to access them in RAM.

Modern CPU designs include several types of cache memory:

- **Level 1 cache:** If the next instruction to be fetched isn't already located in a CPU register, instead of looking directly to RAM to find it, the CPU first searches Level 1 cache. **Level 1 cache** is a block of memory built onto the CPU chip to store data or commands that have just been used.
  - **Level 2 cache:** If the command is not located in Level 1 cache, the CPU searches Level 2 cache. Depending on the design of the CPU, **Level 2 cache** is either located on the CPU chip but slightly farther away from the CPU than Level 1 or is located on a separate chip next to the CPU and therefore takes somewhat longer to access. Level 2 cache contains more storage area than Level 1 cache. For the Intel Core i7, for example, the Level 1 cache is 64 kilobytes (KB) and the Level 2 cache is 1 megabyte (MB).

Only if the CPU doesn't find the next instruction to be fetched in either Level 1 or Level 2 cache will it make the long journey to RAM to access it.

- **Level 3 cache:** The current direction of processor design is toward increasingly large multilevel CPU cache structures. Today, CPUs such as Intel's Core i7 processors have an additional third level of cache memory storage called **Level 3 cache**. On computers with Level 3 cache, the CPU checks this area for instructions and data after it looks in Level 1 and Level 2 cache but before it makes the longer trip to RAM (see Figure 11). The Level 3 cache holds between 2 and 12 MB of data. With 12 MB of Level 3 cache, there is storage for some entire programs to be transferred to the CPU for execution.

As an end user of computer programs, you do nothing special to use cache memory. The advantage of having more cache memory is that you'll experience better performance because the CPU won't have to make the longer trip to RAM to get data and instructions as often. Unfortunately, because it's built into the CPU chip or motherboard, you can't upgrade cache; it's part of the original design of the CPU. Therefore, as with RAM, when buying a computer it's important to consider buying the one with the most cache memory, everything else being equal.

Stage 2: The Decode Stage

The main goal of the decode stage is for the CPU's control unit to translate (or **decode**) the program's instructions into commands the CPU can understand. The collection of commands a specific CPU can execute is called the

(Andrea Danti/Fotolia)

instruction set for that system. Each CPU has its own unique instruction set. For example, the AMD FX 8150 eight-core processor in a Gamer Mage system has a different instruction set than the Intel Core i5 used in a Dell Inspiron notebook. The control unit interprets the code's bits according to the instruction set the CPU

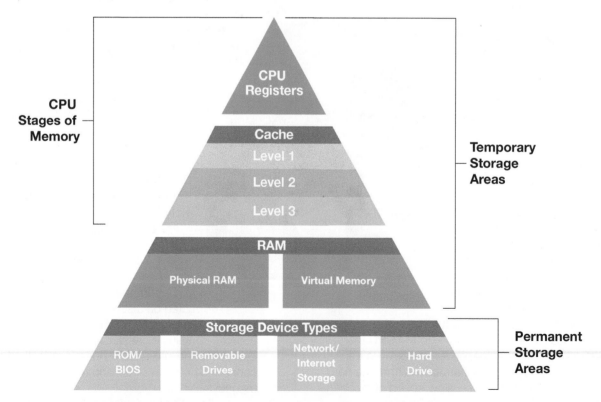

FIGURE 11 The CPU has multiple stages of internal memory, which is just a part of the overall hierarchy of a computer's memory storage.

Using a Little Hideaway

Taking data you think you'll be using soon and storing it nearby is a simple but powerful idea. This strategy shows up in places in your computer system other than cache memory. For example, when you're browsing web pages, it takes longer to download images than text. Your browser software automatically stores images on your hard drive so that you don't have to download them again if you want to go back and view a page you've already visited. Although this cache of files is not related to the cache storage space designed into the CPU chip, the idea is the same. The word *cache* is derived from the French word *cacher*, which means "to hide," and a little bit of memory space used as a hideaway can give performance a big boost.

designers laid out for that particular CPU. The control unit then knows how to set up all the switches on the CPU so that the proper operation will occur.

Because humans are the ones who write the initial instructions, all the commands in an instruction set are written in a language called **assembly language**, which is easier for humans to work with than binary. Many CPUs have similar assembly commands in their instruction sets, including the following commands:

CPU INSTRUCTION	FUNCTION
ADD	Add
SUB	Subtract
MUL	Multiply
DIV	Divide
MOVE	Move data to RAM
STORE	Move data to a CPU register
EQU	Check if equal

CPUs differ in the choice of additional assembly language commands selected for the instruction set. Each CPU design team works to develop an instruction set that is both powerful and speedy.

However, because the CPU knows and recognizes only patterns of 0s and 1s, it can't understand assembly language directly, so these human-readable instructions are translated into binary code. The control unit uses these long strings of binary code called **machine language** to set up the hardware in the CPU for the rest of the operations it needs to perform. Machine language is a binary code for computer instructions, much like the ASCII code is a binary code for letters and characters. Similar to each letter or character having its own unique combination of 0s and 1s assigned to it, a CPU has a table of codes consisting of combinations of 0s and 1s for each of its commands. If the CPU sees a particular pattern of bits arrive, it knows the work it must do. Figure 12 shows a few commands in both assembly language and machine language.

Stage 3: The Execute Stage

(Taras Livyy/Fotolia)

The **arithmetic logic unit (ALU)** is the part of the CPU designed to perform mathematical operations such as addition, subtraction, multiplication, and division and to test the comparison of values such as *greater than, less than,* and *equal to.* For example, in calculating an average, the ALU is where the addition and division operations would take place.

The ALU also performs logical OR, AND, and NOT operations. For example, in determining whether a student can graduate, the ALU would need to ascertain whether the student had taken all required courses AND obtained a passing grade in each of them. The ALU is specially designed to execute such calculations flawlessly and with incredible speed.

FIGURE 12

Representations of Sample CPU Commands

HUMAN LANGUAGE FOR COMMAND	CPU COMMAND IN ASSEMBLY LANGUAGE (LANGUAGE USED BY PROGRAMMERS)	CPU COMMAND IN MACHINE LANGUAGE (LANGUAGE USED IN THE CPU's INSTRUCTION SET)
Add	ADD	1110 1010
Subtract	SUB	0001 0101
Multiply	MUL	1111 0000
Divide	DIV	0000 1111

The ALU is fed data from the CPU's registers. The amount of data a CPU can process at a time is based in part on the amount of data each register can hold. The number of bits a computer can work with at a time is referred to as its **word size**. Therefore, a 64-bit processor can process more information faster than a 32-bit processor.

Stage 4: The Store Stage

In the final stage, the result produced by the ALU is stored back in the registers. The instruction itself will explain which register should be used to store the answer.

(John Takai/Fotolia)

Once the entire instruction has been completed, the next instruction will be fetched, and the fetch-decode-execute-store sequence will begin again.

Making CPUs Even Faster

Knowing how to build a CPU that can run faster than the competition can make a company rich. However, building a faster CPU isn't easy. A new product launch must take into consideration the time it will take to design, manufacture, and test that processor. When the processor finally hits the market, it must be faster than the competition if the manufacturer hopes to make a profit. To create a CPU that will be released 36 months from now, it must be built to perform at least twice as fast as anything currently available.

Processor manufacturers can increase CPU performance in many different ways:

- Using *pipelining*
- Designing the CPU's instruction set so that it contains *specialized instructions for handling multimedia and graphics*, and
- Including *multiple independent processing paths* inside the CPU

Let's explore each of these methods in more detail.

Pipelining

As an instruction is processed, the CPU runs sequentially through the four stages of processing: fetch, decode, execute, and store. **Pipelining** is a technique that allows the CPU to work on more than one instruction (or stage of processing) at the same time, thereby boosting CPU performance.

For example, without pipelining, it may take four clock cycles to complete one instruction (one clock cycle for each of the four processing stages). However, with a four-stage pipeline, the computer can process four instructions at the same time. The ticks of the system clock (the clock cycle) indicate when all instructions move to the next process. Using pipelining, a four-stage processor can potentially run up to four times faster because some instruction is finishing every clock cycle rather than waiting four cycles for each instruction to finish. In Figure 13a, a non-pipelined instruction takes four clock cycles to be completed, whereas in Figure 13b, the four instructions have been completed in the same time using pipelining.

There is a cost to pipelining a CPU, however. The CPU must be designed so that each stage (fetch, decode, execute, and store) is independent. This means that each stage must be able to run at the same time that the other three stages are running. This requires more transistors and a more complicated hardware design.

Specialized Multimedia Instructions

Each design team that develops a new CPU tries to imagine what users' greatest needs will be in four or five years. Currently, several processors on the market reflect this

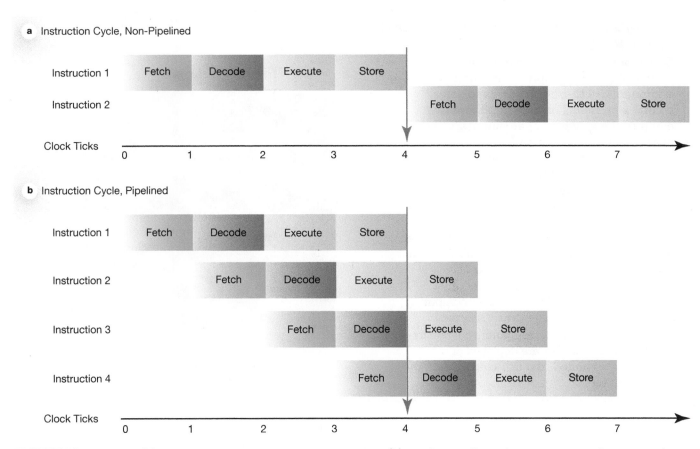

a Instruction Cycle, Non-Pipelined

Instruction 1	Fetch	Decode	Execute	Store

Instruction 2: Fetch | Decode | Execute | Store

Clock Ticks: 0 1 2 3 4 5 6 7

b Instruction Cycle, Pipelined

Instruction 1: Fetch | Decode | Execute | Store

Instruction 2: Fetch | Decode | Execute | Store

Instruction 3: Fetch | Decode | Execute | Store

Instruction 4: Fetch | Decode | Execute | Store

Clock Ticks: 0 1 2 3 4 5 6 7

FIGURE 13 Instead of (a) waiting for each instruction to complete, (b) pipelining allows the system to work on more than one set of instructions at one time.

consideration by incorporating specialized multimedia instructions into the basic instruction set.

Hardware engineers have redesigned the chip so that the instruction set contains new commands customized to speed up the work needed for video and audio processing. For example, Intel has integrated into its second-generation Core processor designs the Advanced Encryption Standard (AES) instruction set. These seven new instructions work to allow the CPU to deliver faster data protection.

Multiple Processing Efforts

Many high-end server systems use a set of completely separate CPU chips on one motherboard. These server systems can later be scaled so that they can accommodate large numbers of processors, like the Cray Jaguar supercomputer, which has over 224,000 independent processors!

In personal computers, Intel uses *multi-core processing* in its Core processor line of chips. Chips with quad-core processing capabilities have four separate parallel processing paths inside them, so they're almost as fast as four separate CPUs. It's not quite four times as fast because the system must do some extra work to decide which processor will work on which part of the problem and to recombine the results each CPU produces.

Six-core processors, like the Intel i7 Extreme Edition, and even eight-core CPUs (like the AMD FX) are available as well, executing six (or eight) separate processing paths. Multiprocessor systems are often used when intensive computational problems need to be solved in such areas as computer simulations, video production, and graphics processing.

Certain types of problems are well suited to a parallel-processing environment. In **parallel processing**, there is a large network of computers, with each computer working on a portion of the same problem simultaneously. To be a good candidate for parallel processing, a problem must be able to be divided into a set of tasks that can be run simultaneously. For example, a problem where millions of faces are being compared with a target image for recognition is easily

Today's Supercomputers: The Fastest of the Fast

Supercomputers are the biggest and most powerful type of computer. Scientists and engineers use these computers to solve complex problems or to perform massive computations. Some supercomputers are single computers with multiple processors, whereas others consist of multiple computers that work together.

The Sequoia BlueGene/Q was recently ranked as the world's fastest supercomputer. It features a whopping 1,572,864 cores and runs the Linux operating system. Sequoia is deployed at the National Nuclear Security Administration and is used primarily to run nuclear weapons simulations, but it's also available for other research projects requiring large-scale computing power, such as human genome research.

The rankings of supercomputers change frequently as new models are deployed or older models are upgraded. You can keep up with the rankings at **top500.org**. *(Yabresse/Fotolia)*

adapted to a parallel setting. The target face can be compared with many hundreds of faces at the same time. But if the next step of an algorithm can be started only after the results of the previous step have been computed, parallel processing will present no advantages.

Thus, what you can continue to expect from CPUs in the future is that they will continue to get smaller and faster and to consume less power. This fits with the current demands of consumers for more powerful portable computing devices.

At the most basic level of binary *1*s and *0*s, computers are systems of switches that can accomplish impressive tasks. By understanding the hardware components that make up your computer system, you can use your system more effectively and make better buying decisions. ■

BITS&BYTES

CPU Wars

Most PCs have an Intel series CPU inside—Intel has dominated the CPU market for years. In fact, even Apple computers now run on Intel CPUs. But the ARM processor, which is used in tablets and smartphones, is emerging as a CPU contender. In fact, Microsoft has released a version of Windows 8 for the ARM processor, which consumes less power and is cheaper than Intel processors. Look for prices on tablets and laptops to begin to drop as the competition between these two processors heats up!

check your understanding //

For a quick review of what you've learned, answer the following questions. Visit **pearsonhighered.com/techinaction** to check your answers.

multiple choice

1. Which is *not* a typical use of parallel-processing systems?
   a. computer simulations
   b. word processing
   c. weather modeling
   d. graphics processing

2. What is another name for the base-10 number system?
   a. decimal notation
   b. binary number system
   c. hexadecimal notation
   d. integer system

3. Which encoding scheme can represent the alphabets of all modern and historic languages?
   a. base-2 number system
   b. Unicode
   c. ASCII
   d. scientific

4. A multi-core processor like the Intel i7 is
   a. one physical chip.
   b. several chips joined together on the motherboard.
   c. two separate cards installed in your system.
   d. a software setting you can use to speed up CPU processing.

5. To regulate the internal timing of a computer system, the motherboard uses
   a. a system clock.
   b. software simulation.
   c. RAM.
   d. a register.

6. Special areas of memory storage built into the CPU are known as
   a. switches.
   b. semiconductors.
   c. registers.
   d. DIMM.

7. Which is the correct set of steps in the machine cycle?
   a. execute, store, fetch, decode
   b. store, fetch, execute, decode
   c. execute first instruction, execute second instruction, execute third instruction
   d. fetch, decode, execute, store

8. All data inside the computer is stored as
   a. words.
   b. numbers.
   c. binary patterns.
   d. cache memory.

9. Which statement about pipelining is FALSE?
   a. Pipelining boosts CPU performance.
   b. Pipeline design is used in many modern CPUs.
   c. Pipelining allows a less complicated hardware design.
   d. Pipelining allows the computer to process multiple instructions simultaneously.

10. From fastest to slowest, which is the fastest sequence of accessing memory?
    a. RAM, Level 1 cache, Level 2 cache, Level 3 cache
    b. registers, Level 1 cache, Level 2 cache, RAM
    c. Level 1 cache, Level 2 cache, RAM, registers
    d. Level 2 cache, Level 1 cache, registers, RAM

8

Digital Devices and Media: Managing a Digital Lifestyle

Mobile Devices

Digital Convergence

OBJECTIVE

1. How is the trend of digital convergence seen in the market? **(p. 318)**

Telephony: Smartphones and Beyond

OBJECTIVES

2. What hardware and software comprise a typical smartphone? **(pp. 319–322)**

3. How do I synchronize information between my phone and my computer, and how do mobile Internet data plans work? **(pp. 322–326)**

4. What do I need to keep my smartphone secure? **(p. 326)**

5. How does digital telephony support VoIP services? **(pp. 326–327)**

🔊 Sound Byte: Smartphones Are Really Smart

🔊 Sound Byte: Connecting with Bluetooth

👤 Active Helpdesk: Keeping Your Data on Hand

Tablets, Netbooks, and Ultrabooks

OBJECTIVE

6. What distinguishes the performance of tablets, netbooks, and ultrabooks? **(pp. 329–330)**

The Digital Information Age

Digital Defined

OBJECTIVE

7. What advantage do digital formats have over analog signals? **(pp. 334–335)**

Digital Media

OBJECTIVES

8. How is the digital format changing the way media is created and distributed? **(pp. 336–342)**

9. How do I work with digital images and videos? **(pp. 342–348)**

👤 Active Helpdesk: Using Portable Media Players

For all media in this chapter go to **pearsonhighered.com/techinaction** or MyITLab.

(kuroji/Fotolia; Scanrail/Fotolia; Frankie Angel/Alamy; Tetra Images/Getty Images; Oleksiy Maksymenko/Getty Images)

(Pebble Technology)

HOW COOL IS THIS?

Scan here for more info

Want a watch that can do more than just tell time? Say hello to the Pebble **e-paper watch**. This customizable watch connects to your smartphone using **Bluetooth, vibrates** when you **get a call**, and can even get **text messages**. It also runs a full set of **apps**. One app turns the Pebble into a rangefinder to help your golf game; another makes it a bicycling computer. The Pebble can also display your **Facebook messages**, weather alerts, and, of course, the time.

As cool as Pebble is, how it was funded is cooler. Its founders used the crowd-funding site **Kickstarter** to ask for $100,000 in pledges. Supporters gave $1 million in the first 28 hours! The Kickstarter crowd-funding session closed out with over **$10 million** in funding.

Mobile Devices

For many of us, our phone is our lifeline to the world, and if not our phone, then our laptop or iPad. We live in a digital world, and our devices have evolved to let us communicate anywhere we go, 24/7. In this section, we'll check out a number of mobile devices and their features. But first, we look at digital convergence.

digital CONVERGENCE

Digital convergence, the use of a single unifying device to handle media, Internet, entertainment, and telephony needs, is exemplified in the range of devices now on the market. You see digital convergence in the

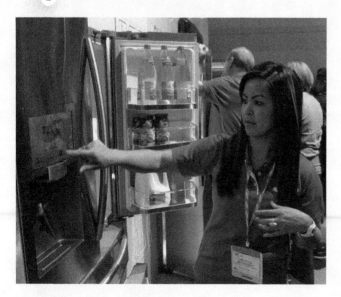

evolution of smartphones, which now let you do just about anything a computer can do. The push to digital convergence is also creating new device combinations like the Padfone, shown in Figure 8.1a, which combines the features of a phone and a tablet into one device. Even some refrigerators, like the one shown in Figure 8.1b, now include LCD touch-screen displays and network adapters so that they can play music and display family photos and recipes from websites such as **epicurious.com**.

In fact, devices are beginning to converge so much that an organization has been created to standardize them. The Digital Living Network Alliance (**dlna.org**) is an organization working to standardize different kinds of appliances and network devices used in our homes. As our appliances, cars, and homes become designed to communicate over a common network, how we manage our media, control our living spaces, and communicate with our families will continue to change.

How have mobile devices converged? As more and more computing power is available in mobile processors, mobile devices have evolved to be able to do multiple tasks. Smartphones can now videoconference like laptops. Tablets such as the iPad are touch sensitive like smartphones. Netbooks and ultrabooks both run traditional desktop operating systems and are lightweight. All these devices have significant overlap in the tasks they can perform, so learning the differences will be important in finding the device that's just right for you. Let's start by taking a look at smartphones. ■

FIGURE 8.1 (a) The Asus Padfone lets you share the processor of the phone with a tablet shell. The phone can function on its own, or you can place it into the tablet shell and run the tablet off the same data plan. (b) Some refrigerators are now equipped with touch screens that connect to the Internet.
(Gustavo Arias R./La Nacion de Costa Rica/Newscom; Steve Marcus/Reuters/Landov)

telephony: smartphones
AND BEYOND

Communication has changed radically in the digital age. Chapter 3 discussed the use of wikis, blogs, and other web-based tools for connecting people and their ideas. All of these software applications are dependent on digital information.

Hardware devices that support communication also have evolved because of digital technologies. **Telephony**, the use of equipment to provide voice communications over a distance, has shifted from an analog science to a digital one. In this section, we examine smartphones and Voice over Internet Protocol (VoIP) devices to see how they're changing to meet modern communication needs.

Smartphone Basics

What makes a smartphone a smartphone? A smartphone does more than let you make and answer phone calls. In fact, smartphones illustrate the power of digital convergence (see Figure 8.2). They incorporate functions and features, such as the following, that used to be available only in separate, dedicated devices:

- Internet access
- Personal information management (PIM) features
- Voice recording features
- The ability to play and organize music files
- GPS services
- Digital image and video capture
- Computing power to run programs like word processors or even video-editing software

Examples of smartphones include the iPhone and the HTC Thunderbolt.

Isn't every phone a smartphone now? All phones that use mobile, cellular technology can be called **cellular (cell) phones**. Although many cell phones on the market are considered smartphones, less powerful cell phones are available. Called **feature phones**, these inexpensive phones have modest processors, simpler interfaces, and often no touch screen. As more features are integrated into every cell phone product, though, it becomes difficult to

distinguish a smartphone from a feature phone. Most providers, like AT&T or Verizon, label a smartphone as one that has sufficient power so that you can use Internet features easily. In addition, you often have to purchase a data plan with a smartphone. In this chapter, we'll use the term *cell phone* to refer to all cellular phones and *smartphones* to refer to the more powerful type of cell phone that can run more complex applications.

Smartphone Components

Are smartphones computers? All cell phones—smartphones and feature phones—have the same components as any computer: a processor

FIGURE 8.2 Digital convergence has brought us single devices like smartphones that play the role of many separate devices. *(Handout/MCT/ Newscom; fsketch/Fotolia; Maksym Yemelyanov/Fotolia; RLG; mrgarry/Fotolia; frank peters/Fotolia; JERMVUT KITCHAICHANK/Fotolia; Leonid Dorfman/Fotolia)*

CPU

LED display

Memory

Camera module

Touch-screen controller

Audio interface

Battery

FIGURE 8.3 Inside your smartphone, you'll find a CPU; a memory chip; input devices such as a microphone, a camera, and a touch screen; and output devices such as a display screen.

(central processing unit, or CPU), memory, and input and output devices, as shown in Figure 8.3. Cell phones require their own operating system (OS) software and have their own application software. So, in effect, all cell phones are computers.

Smartphones use a CPU and an interface so powerful that they can take on many of the same tasks as much more expensive computers: videoconferencing, recording and editing high-definition (HD) video, and broadcasting live-streaming video.

What kind of processor is inside a smartphone? Although the processor in a cell phone is not as fast or as high-powered as a processor in a desktop computer, it's still responsible for a great number of tasks. The processor coordinates sending all of the data among the other electronic components inside the phone. It also runs the cell phone's OS, which provides a user interface so that you can change phone settings, store information, play games, and so on. Popular processors for smartphones include the Qualcomm Snapdragon and the Apple A5. These use dual-core processing technology, which used to be reserved for high-end computer systems.

Is there a standard OS for smartphones? There are a number of operating systems in the smartphone market now. Many smartphones use the Android OS. Apple's iPhone uses iOS, a version of the OS X operating system used in Apple's computers. Microsoft

is also now in the running with the Windows Phone 8 mobile OS. These operating systems are required to translate the user's commands into instructions for the processor. Figure 8.4 illustrates some of the user interfaces featured among smartphone operating systems.

What does the memory inside a smartphone do? Your phone's memory stores all of the phone's information and programs. The OS is stored in read-only memory (ROM), the phone's permanent memory, because the phone would be useless without that key piece of software. Other phone data, such as ring tones and contact lists, is stored in separate internal memory chips.

Many smartphones let you add additional memory through micro SD flash cards, which can store up to 64 GB, as shown in Figure 8.5. Micro SD cards are easy to install inside a phone, and some models have external slots for an SD card. Not all smartphones allow memory upgrades in this way, however. For example, iPhones don't let you add memory.

 SOUND BYTE
Smartphones Are Really Smart
In this Sound Byte, you'll learn how to use a smartphone as a powerful tool to communicate, calculate, and organize your workload.

a

b

c

FIGURE 8.4 (a) Apple iOS, (b) Windows Phone 8, and (c) Android 4 are all mobile operating systems. *(Greg Gard/Alamy; Noah Berger/Reuters/Landov; AnonymousAP Images)*

What input and output devices do smartphones use? The primary input devices for a smartphone are its microphone and touch pad. Some phones, such as the Samsung Impression (see Figure 8.6a), offer both a hidden keyboard and a touch screen. The Apple iPhone provides a software-based keyboard (see Figure 8.6b) that supports more than 40 languages. And a smartphone's digital camera is also an input device, capturing photos and video.

Cell phone output devices include a speaker and a liquid crystal display (LCD). Higher-end models include full-color, high-resolution LCD screens. Newer on the market are OLED (organic light-emitting diode) displays, which allow very bright, sharp imaging and draw less power than LCD screens.

What smartphone software is available? A smartphone OS comes with a standard collection of software, such as a to-do list, contact manager, and calendar. Modified versions of application software such as Microsoft Word, Excel, Outlook, and PowerPoint are

FIGURE 8.5 Micro SD flash cards add memory to some phones. *(Clifford Farrugia/Alamy)*

a

b

FIGURE 8.6 (a) The Samsung Impression includes a touch screen and a built-in keyboard. (b) The Apple iPhone has a touch keyboard that supports more than 40 languages and a range of character sets. *(Jae C. Hong/AP Images)*

FIGURE 8.7 Google Play is one of many online stores delivering software for mobile devices. *(Google Inc./AP Images)*

available for some high-end smartphones. Manufacturers also have web-based software stores, like the App Store for the Apple iPhone and the App World for RIM's BlackBerry devices. Software applications are available for Android through Google Play (Figure 8.7). The Android developer community holds competitions to spur the creation of new software applications for Android-based phones.

How Cell Phone Technology Works

What's "cellular" about a cell phone?

As noted earlier, the term *cell phone* is short for *cellular phone*. A set of connected "cells" makes up a cellular network. Each cell is a geographic area centered on a **base transceiver station**, which is a large communications tower with antennas, amplifiers, receivers, and transmitters. When you place a call on a cell phone, a base station picks up the request for service. The station then passes the request to a central location called a **mobile switching center**. The reverse process occurs when you receive an incoming call. A telecommunications company builds its network by constructing a

BITS&BYTES

How Smart Is Your Phone?

Your smartphone may seem really smart when it can answer your questions! Voice recognition–based apps—Siri for iOS phones and Andy for Android phones—let your phone behave like a digital assistant. These apps translate your oral request into a search through information stored on your phone or into an Internet search request and format the results for you.

For information that needs the human touch, consider using the ChaCha service. You can either call 1-800-2chacha or text 242 242 with any kind of question, and real human "guides" will find the answer for you. So let your smartphone start acting smart!

series of cells that overlap in an attempt to guarantee that its cell phone customers have coverage no matter where they are.

As you move during your phone call, the mobile switching center monitors the strength of the signal between your cell phone and the closest base station. When the signal is no longer strong enough between your cell phone and the base station, the mobile switching center orders the next base station to take charge of your call. When your cell phone "drops out," it may be because the distance between base stations is too great to provide an adequate signal.

How do cell phones use digital signals? When you speak into a cell phone, a series of digital processing steps occur:

1. Sound enters the microphone as a sound wave. Because these sound waves need to be *digitized* (that is, converted into a sequence of *1*s and *0*s that the cell phone's processor can understand), an **analog-to-digital converter chip** converts your voice's sound waves into digital signals.

2. Next, the digital data must be *compressed*, or squeezed, into the smallest possible space so that it will transmit more quickly to another phone. The processor can't perform the mathematical operations required at this stage quickly enough, so there's a specialized chip called the **digital signal processor** included in the cell phone that handles the compression work.

3. Finally, the digital data is *transmitted* as a radio wave through the cellular network to the destination phone.

When you receive an incoming call, the digital signal processor decompresses the incoming message. An amplifier boosts the signal to make it loud enough, and it is then passed on to the speaker.

Synchronizing

What's the best way to synchronize data between my phone and computer?

The process of updating your data so your to-do lists, schedules, and other files on your cell phone and computer are the same is called **synchronizing**, or **syncing**. There are two main ways to transfer information between your phone and computer:

1. *Wired*: Use a micro SD card or a USB cable to directly transfer data.

2. *Wireless*: Use a wireless connection to transfer data.

 SOUND BYTE
Connecting with Bluetooth
In this Sound Byte, you'll learn what freedoms Bluetooth affords you and how to use Bluetooth devices.

How does a wired transfer of data work? Almost all phones are designed with a USB port. Some have a mini–USB connector, while other models require a special cable to connect the phone to a standard USB port. Once connected using a USB data cable, your phone will appear on your computer like an additional flash drive, and you can drag and drop files to it. You can also charge your phone through the USB cable.

If your phone supports a high-density micro SD card, you can easily remove the card and slip it directly into a flash card reader in your computer.

How do I transfer information to and from my phone wirelessly? Most smartphones on the market today are Bluetooth-enabled, meaning they include a small Bluetooth chip that allows them to transfer data wirelessly to any other Bluetooth-enabled device. **Bluetooth** technology uses radio waves to transmit data signals over distances up to approximately 300 feet (for Bluetooth 4). Bluetooth 4 devices are the newest on the market and are almost twice as fast as Bluetooth 3 devices.

Another way to wirelessly transfer data to your phone is to use a wireless connection to a cloud service. A number of web services are now available to synchronize your e-mail, files, contacts, and calendars instantly and wirelessly. SugarSync, for example, wirelessly syncs folders of data and photos on your Android phone to your home computers automatically (see Figure 8.8). These web services follow the model of "cloud computing,"

where Internet-based services and resources are distributed to users instead of being installed as an application on the user's computer. Apple's iOS 5 has cloud support integrated into several of the applications like Calendar, iTunes, PhotoStream, Contacts, and Mail. A photo taken on your iPhone will automatically be transferred to your iPad and your home Windows or Mac computer, for example.

There are other providers of wireless synchronization for mobile devices. Google Sync works with a range of devices. All of your Google e-mail, calendar events, and contacts are automatically backed up online instantly on the Google servers. Even the Amazon Kindle uses wireless synchronization so that if you read a bit further in your e-book on your phone, when you get to your office the Kindle software on your PC will have automatically updated to bookmark the new page you're on.

FIGURE 8.8 A cloud service lets you keep the information on your phone instantly in sync with your other computing devices.

Text Messaging

What does SMS stand for? **Short message service (SMS)**—often just called *text messaging*—is a technology that lets you send short text messages (up to 160 characters) over cellular networks. You can send SMS messages to other mobile devices or to any e-mail address.

Companies now support texting in many ways—for example, your bank may allow you to text commands to request account balances or details about your last transaction and the bank will text the requested information back to you. As shown in Figure 8.9, several companies provide useful services based on text messaging.

How does SMS work? SMS uses the cell phone network to transmit messages. When you send an SMS message, an SMS calling center receives the message and delivers it to the appropriate mobile device using something called *store-and-forward* technology. This technology allows users to send SMS messages to any other SMS device in the world.

Is the same technology used to send and receive photos and videos? SMS technology lets you send only text messages. However, an extension of SMS called **multimedia message service (MMS)** lets you send messages that include text, sound, images, and video clips to other phones or e-mail addresses. MMS messages actually arrive as a series of messages; you view the text, then the image, then the

FIGURE 8.9

Text Messaging Information Services

SMS CODE	SERVICE NAME	WEBSITE	DESCRIPTION
466453 (google)	Google SMS Search	**google.com/mobile/sms**	Obtains information such as addresses, phone numbers, driving directions, sports scores, and movie listings from the Google search engine
44636 (4Info)	4INFO	**alerts.4info.com**	Similar to Google SMS, but also handles flight information and mobile coupons
242 242 (cha cha)	ChaCha	**chacha.com**	Human "guides" answer any question in conversational English
3109043113	411sms	**411sms.com**	Offers address and phone listings, turn-by-turn directions, movie show times, stock quotes, hot spot locations, dictionary definitions, horoscopes, and foreign language translations

sound, and so on. You can then choose to save just one part of the message (such as the image), all of it, or none of it. MMS users can subscribe to financial, sports, and weather services that will "push" information to them, sending it automatically to their phones in MMS format.

Mobile Internet

What's the best way to connect my smartphone to the Internet? There are two ways smartphones (and most mobile devices) can connect to the Internet:

1. Using a WiFi network or
2. Using the cellular phone system (a 3G or 4G connection)

A major advantage of WiFi is that it offers a faster data-transfer speed. However, there may not always be

a WiFi signal available where you are. Cellular networks are much more widely available, whether you're in your car or just walking down the street.

For devices like tablets, manufacturers will offer one model that can only connect to the Internet using WiFi and another model that costs more but can connect with either WiFi or cellular 3G/4G.

Who sells cellular Internet service for my smartphone? Just as you have an Internet service provider (ISP) for Internet access for your desktop or laptop computer, you must have a **wireless Internet service provider** (or **wireless ISP**) to connect your smartphone to the Internet. Phone companies (such as T-Mobile, Verizon, and AT&T) double as wireless ISPs. Most wireless ISPs also offer free login to their network of WiFi hotspots if you're a cellular customer.

How do I purchase Internet time? Providers measure your Internet usage not according to how much time you're on the Internet but according to how much data you download and upload. An Internet connectivity plan is known as a **data plan**. You pay one monthly price and are allowed data transfers up to some fixed limit per month, such as 2 GB or 500 MB. If you exceed your data limit in a month, the fee for the extra data usage is usually very expensive.

Understanding your data usage is complicated. A cellular data plan is for Internet data transfer, not texting. Providers require a separate texting plan. Note that all the data transfer you do using WiFi (instead of the 3G/4G network) do not count as part of your data plan usage.

How big a data plan do I need to buy? Before subscribing to a data plan, you should assess your needs:

- How often will you be able to use WiFi access, and how often will you need to use the cellular network?

BITS&BYTES

Looking for the Perfect Cell Phone Plan? Try Bill Shrink

Cell phone plans are confusing enough before adding the choices for texting plans, data plans, and supporting multiple devices. Before you give up in confusion, let Bill Shrink (**billshrink.com**) help you pick the perfect plan. Bill Shrink is a free service that collects your latest billing information, compares your usage and fees with other plans, and writes a report with specific recommendations for you. It also has options to analyze your credit card choices, television packages, and even your gas usage!

- How often do you download apps, stream music, or play online games?
- Do you use your phone to watch streaming video?
- Do you use your smartphone's Internet access to download files attached to e-mails or from your company website?

Begin by estimating how much data you transfer up and down from the Internet each month. To do so, you can use an online estimator supplied by your provider like the one from AT&T shown in Figure 8.10. Apps such as My Data Usage Pro or 3G Watchdog are also available for any smartphone to keep track of data usage for you.

Be sure you select a plan that provides adequate service at a good price. Remember, each device using cellular Internet needs to be covered by a data plan.

At what speed is digital information transferred to my smartphone? Although broadband speeds of 50 megabits per second (Mbps) are achievable at home using a cable or fiber-optic connection, your smartphone will connect at a much lower speed. The exact speed will depend on which technology you're using: WiFi, 3G cellular, or 4G cellular (see Figure 8.11).

We discussed WiFi networks in depth in Chapter 7. These networks typically run at speeds of 4 to 5 Mbps. Currently, there are two cellular data-transfer standards:

FIGURE 8.11 The range of speeds you achieve when connecting to the Internet with your smartphone or mobile device depends on the type of connection.

1. **3G:** 3G brought mobile device data-transfer rates as high as 3.8 Mbps (or more, under ideal conditions). 3G is more reliable than WiFi and is less susceptible to interference. 3G blankets most major urban areas with connectivity.

2. **4G:** 4G networks are now rolling out across the United States. The promise of 4G is incredible: mobile connection speeds of up to 100 Mbps! Currently, most providers can't deliver true 4G speeds; their 4G networks deliver speeds of 6 Mbps to 11 Mbps. These options, often named "4G LTE," are faster than 3G but don't meet the rate required to be true 4G, so they're referred to as "near 4G" networks. The expansion of 4G will usher in a new generation of mobile devices.

How do I set my phone to use a WiFi connection? It will be slightly different for each mobile OS, but in general, you turn on the setting that allows your phone to look for a network. If a network is found, the phone will try to log in. If the network has security protection, you'll be prompted for a password before joining. Most smartphones then display a special icon to show that you're using a WiFi connection instead of a 3G/4G signal.

Some people choose to leave their phone in the mode where it's looking for a WiFi network so it will always use a WiFi signal if it is available, saving them on data plan usage. This does use more battery life, though, so turn off WiFi detection if you're trying to extend your battery.

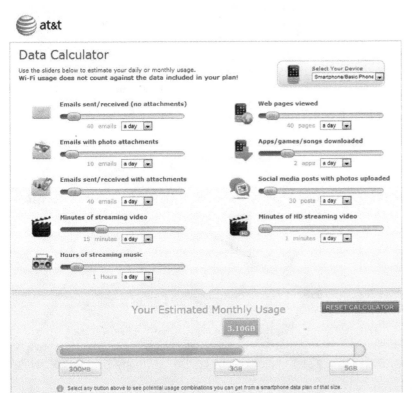

FIGURE 8.10 Online tools can help you estimate your monthly data usage.

Can I use my 3G/4G signal to create a WiFi hotspot for my other devices?

As mentioned in Chapter 7, if a WiFi spot isn't available, there are devices that will instantly create a mobile hot spot for you. Mi-Fi (pronounced "my fy") devices are often available free with a new account from major Internet providers like Verizon and Sprint. These devices connect to the Internet through the 3G/4G wireless phone network and then distribute the WiFi signal over an area of 30 feet. These personal hot spots can then support up to five WiFi–enabled devices.

Another approach is **tethering**, which makes sure that as long as you have a 3G/4G signal, your computer can access the Internet even when it tells you there are no available wireless networks. Several phones offer this capability. For example, an iPhone 4 can connect to your notebook computer through wireless Bluetooth and then provide Internet access through the 3G network signal. Check with your provider, though, because they may charge an extra fee for allowing tethering.

Smartphone Security

Can I get a virus on my smartphone?

Viruses can indeed infect smartphones. Over half of users say they send confidential e-mails using their phones and one-third of users access bank account or credit card information on their phones, so smartphones are the next most likely realm of attack by cybercriminals. Although viruses plaguing smartphones have not yet reached the volume of viruses attacking PC operating systems, with the proliferation of mobile devices, virus attacks are expected to increase.

Kaspersky, McAfee, and F-Secure are among leading companies currently providing antivirus software for mobile devices. Products are designed for specific operating systems; for example, Kaspersky Mobile Security has versions for Android phones and tablets, Windows phones, and BlackBerry devices. Often, businesses will have their information technology department install and configure an antivirus solution like this for all the phones used in the organization.

If no antivirus program is available for your phone's OS, the best precautions are commonsense ones. Check the phone manufacturer's website frequently to see whether your smartphone needs any software upgrades that could patch security holes. In addition, remember that you shouldn't download ring tones, games, or other software from unfamiliar websites.

How do I keep my phone number private?

If you're concerned about widely distributing your phone number and potentially inviting lots of unwanted calls, consider using a virtual phone number. A virtual phone number is a phone number you create that can be assigned to ring on existing phone numbers. Companies such as Telusion (**tossabledigits.com**) will sell you a virtual number. Then, when you're filling out a registration form for some web service, you can input your virtual phone number in the web form instead of giving out your number. When you set up the virtual account, you can restrict the hours that you will receive calls from that number, and if you're receiving many unwanted calls, you can disable the virtual number without affecting your cell/smartphone service.

VoIP

Is the cellular network the only way to place phone calls?

Cell phone service is still not 100% reliable, and dropped calls and poor reception are a problem in some areas. As an alternative, a fully digital phone service called **Voice over Internet Protocol (VoIP)** is available.

How is VoIP different from regular telephone service?

VoIP is a form of voice-based Internet communication that turns a standard Internet connection into a means to place phone calls, including long-distance calls (see Figure 8.12). Traditional telephone communications use analog voice data and telephone connections. In contrast, VoIP uses technology similar to that used in e-mail to transmit your voice data digitally over the Internet.

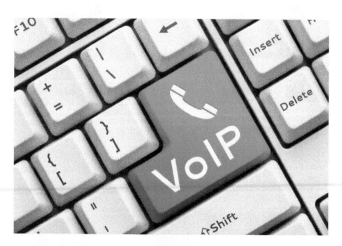

FIGURE 8.12 VoIP technology lets your computing device behave like a phone/video phone, using the Internet instead of the telephone system to transmit data. *(jd-photodesign)*

Who are some VoIP providers? Skype is one very well-known provider. Creating a VoIP account with Skype (**skype.com**) is simple (see the Try This in Chapter 1, pages 12–13). Skype requires that both callers and receivers have the company's free software installed on their device (computer, tablet, or phone). With Skype you can place a phone call, make an HD–video call, and even share screens between users. Calls to other Skype users are free, and you can place low-cost calls to non-Skype users. Other VoIP service providers, such as Vonage (**vonage.com**), are a bit more complicated to set up and are not free. Major ISPs, like Comcast and Verizon, also provide VoIP phone services as an option you can package with your Internet or cable television plan.

What do I need to use VoIP? VoIP calls can be placed from anywhere you have Internet access. Any Android or iOS phone or tablet can also be used as a VoIP device. There are also standalone VoIP phones sold, sometimes called *IP phones*.

What are the advantages and disadvantages of VoIP? For people who make many long-distance phone calls, the advantage of VoIP is that it's free or low cost. Portability is another advantage: As long as you're connected to the Internet, you can sign on to your VoIP service and make your call.

Although VoIP is affordable and convenient, it does have drawbacks:

- Some people regard sound quality and reliability issues as VoIP's primary disadvantages.
- Another drawback when using VoIP at home is the loss of service if power is interrupted.
- Another issue with VoIP is security risks. Having a hacker break in to a VoIP system to make unauthorized calls is a serious but avoidable problem. Encryption services that convert data into a form not easily understood by unauthorized people are being deployed to help protect calls made over the Internet.

VoIP continues to enjoy explosive growth, and the technology will continue to improve.

What new features come with using VoIP? If you set up a VoIP service as your home telephone system, you can have your telephone messages automatically bundled up as e-mails and sent to your account. If you're watching television and a call comes in, it can be displayed on the screen with caller ID information. Some learning management systems also use VoIP. For example, if you're using MyITLab with this course, you can call your professor through VoIP without having his or her personal phone number.

Smartphone GPS

Does my smartphone contain a GPS chip? Today every cell/smartphone has to include a GPS chip. The Federal Communications Commission (FCC) mandated this to enable the complete rollout of the Enhanced 911 (E911) program. E911 automatically gives dispatchers precise location information for any 911 call. It also means your phone records may include this precise tracking information, which indicates where you are when you make a call.

How does GPS work? Built and operated by the U.S. Department of Defense, the **global positioning system (GPS)** is a network of 21 satellites (plus 3 working spares) that constantly orbits the Earth. GPS devices use an antenna to pick up the signals from these satellites and use special software to transform those signals into latitude and longitude. Using the information obtained from the satellites, GPS devices determine geographical location anywhere on the planet to within 3 feet (see Figure 8.13). The exact accuracy depends on such things as

FIGURE 8.13 GPS computes your location anywhere on Earth from a system of orbiting satellites.

trends in IT

Your mobile device performs many tasks, and now, thanks to near field communication (NFC) technology, it will feature yet another form of convergence: the integration of your wallet into your phone. How so? NFC technology allows a device with an NFC chip (such as a smartphone) to communicate with another NFC device (such as a checkout machine) with a single touch. In fact, with NFC, you can forget your wallet: Financial transactions can be processed just by bringing the devices within an inch of each other.

Because NFC has such a short range (up to 1.5 inches), it is being used for secure credit card transactions. Both MasterCard and Visa are piloting programs that would allow cell phones to "tap and go," meaning phone owners would no longer need to carry physical credit cards. Instead, they could simply tap their phone near an NFC checkout device and have it automatically transmit the proper loyalty card information, select and process any coupon offers, and pay all at once (see Figure 8.14).

In countries like Japan, Spain, and Germany, NFC ticketing programs are already in place. The Deutsche Bahn rail system allows users to tap their phones to an NFC tag when they get on the train and to another on departing. The fare is automatically calculated and billed to their credit card monthly. The new "digital wallet" would be a single storage place for all your financial needs.

But you also use your wallet to carry ID information. NFC can handle that as well. The swipe cards that verify your identity for entry into secure areas can be replaced using NFC to exchange stored virtual credentials. The same technology could replace doors protected with PIN numbers or anywhere a user name/password verification is used.

So, opening a door or logging into a computer could all be managed with a tap of your NFC–enabled phone.

Google has already announced a mobile app known as Google Wallet that will conduct NFC transactions as well as collect your loyalty cards, gift cards, receipts, boarding passes, tickets, and keys within your phone. To use Google Wallet to pay in stores, you need to have a phone with an NFC chip.

So imagine a time, soon, when you're out to dinner with friends and need to split the bill. Your NFC phone is already linked to your PayPal account or credit card, and you simply wave your phone next to your friend's phone to transfer him your share of the bill. Some are predicting the worldwide NFC market will grow to be worth $50 billion over the next few years, making this a trend to watch.

FIGURE 8.14 NFC–equipped phones will shift how we handle financial transactions and identify ourselves. *(YOSHIKAZU TSUNO/AFP/Getty Images/Newscom)*

atmospheric conditions and interference from obstacles like mountains or buildings.

Can I track a family member using the GPS chip in his or her phone? Cell phone providers offer plans (for a monthly fee) that allow you to track where a phone is at any given time. For example, AT&T's Family Maps service lets parents track all the phones on their family plan in real time. Locations of all phones are displayed over the web on a map or to an app for your phone, or the service will send an automatic text message alert with the phones' locations at a specific time each day. So a parent could have a text or e-mail sent with his or her daughter's phone location each day at 3 P.M. to be sure she made it home from school. The person being tracked can't turn off the service. ■

tablets, netbooks, and
ULTRABOOKS

The best way to navigate all the mobile devices on the market is to be aware of the boundaries between types of devices. In this section, we'll look at what changes when you move from one type of device to another.

Tablets

How do tablets compare with smartphones?
Tablets are very light, very portable devices. The top-selling tablets include the Apple iPad and the Samsung Galaxy, but there are over 75 tablets on the market (see Figure 8.15). The main difference between any tablet and a smartphone is screen size. Whereas smartphones have displays that are less than 3.5 inches, tablets come with screen sizes between 7 and 10 inches. The larger screen allows for a larger virtual keyboard and higher resolution.

In most other regards, smartphones and tablets are similar. They have the following features:

- Similar operating systems: Whether iOS or Android, common operating systems operate on smartphones and tablets.
- Similar processors: The processing power of smartphones and tablets is often the same.
- Touch-screen interfaces: Smartphones and tablets are both equipped with touch-screen interfaces.
- Long battery life: Most tablets and smartphones run at least 10 hours on a single charge.
- Similar software applications: Most apps available for one device are available for the other.
- Similar Internet connectivity: Both offer 3G/4G as well as WiFi connectivity.
- Bluetooth: Both can be connected over Bluetooth to printers, keyboards, and other peripherals.

Can tablets function as a communication device?
Although tablets are currently not able to make cell phone calls, they can easily place audio or video phone calls if connected to a WiFi network. A VoIP application like Skype is required for that. There are also apps available that allow tablets to handle texting. HeyWire, for example, supports free national and international texting from a range of devices, including tablets as well as phones.

Netbooks

Why would I want a netbook instead of a tablet?
A tablet runs a mobile OS. A *netbook*, on the other hand, uses a full traditional OS, like Windows 8. This means you can't run programs like Microsoft Office on a tablet, but you can on a netbook. In addition, a netbook has a physical keyboard. Netbooks weigh 2 pounds or less and are inexpensive compared with both tablets and ultrabooks, so they are a good option if you're looking for value. Many models are available for under $300.

Why wouldn't I want a netbook?
The processing power and memory on a netbook makes it difficult to run software that does a lot of computation. Netbooks also have very small screens (usually 10 inches or less). The screen resolution and small keyboard may not work for your needs, so be sure to try one out before making a purchase.

FIGURE 8.15 iPad...Xoom...Galaxy? There are over 75 tablets on the market now. Finding the right digital device can be a challenge. *(oliver leedham/Alamy)*

Ultrabooks

How are ultrabooks different from laptops? *Ultrabooks* are a newer category of full-featured computers that focus on offering a very thin, lightweight computing solution. Ultrabooks don't offer optical drives, for example, allowing a very thin profile. Most ultrabooks offer SSD drives and so have very fast response times on boot up and restoring from hibernation. They weigh in at under 3 pounds even though they feature the same operating systems and CPUs as heavier, larger laptops. They also include full-size keyboards and 13- to 15-inch screens. Examples include the Apple Macbook Air and the Asus Zenbook.

How are ultrabooks different from tablets? Whereas tablets share a lot in common with smartphones, ultrabooks are lightweight laptops. They are good choices when you want to run a traditional OS, have a lot of computing power, and aren't concerned with touch-screen features. Figure 8.16 summarizes how tablets and ultrabooks compare.

Making a Choice

With all these choices, how do I know which device is best for me? Use these guidelines to determine what best fits your personal needs for this particular device. Consider the following:

- **Screen size and style of keyboard:** You can adapt these with accessories (add a Bluetooth keyboard or connect to a larger external monitor), but most of the time these will determine how you interact with your device. If you're interested in a touch-based device, you'll want to look into a tablet or smartphone for now. However, touch-screen ultrabooks are set to appear soon because of the support Windows 8 now offers for touch input.

- **Weight:** Does an additional 2 pounds matter? The price of an ultrabook is several hundred dollars more than an equivalent laptop.

- **Number of devices:** Is this your only computing device? As technology prices fall, you may be able to have more than one device. You might find an affordable solution that includes both a very mobile device and a second more powerful one.

Figure 8.17 summarizes several different mobile device categories. ∎

FIGURE 8.16

Tablets versus Ultrabooks

FEATURE	TABLET	ULTRABOOK
Operating System	Mobile OS (iOS, Android, Windows)	Traditional OS (Windows or OS X)
Interface	Touch screen	Non-touch screen and full-size keyboard
Screen Size	7 to 10 inches	13 to 15 inches
Processing Power	Mobile processor	Full quad-core Intel i5, i7
Storage	</= 64 GB	128 to 500 GB
Software	Specialized applications custom designed for touch interface	Standard versions of software for desktop environments (Microsoft Office, etc.)

Laptop
* 5 to 8 lbs
* Traditional OS

Ultrabook
* Less than 3 lbs
* Traditional OS

Netbook
• 1 to 3 lbs
• Traditional OS

Tablet
• Less than 2 lbs
• Mobile OS

Smartphone
• 0.25 lbs
• Mobile OS

FIGURE 8.17 A full spectrum of mobile devices is available.

(Peter Dazeley/Getty Images; Bloomberg/Getty Images; Ethan Miller/Getty Images; Josep Iago/Stringer/Getty Images; Sean Gallup/Getty Images; Sean Gallup/Getty Images; Alan Evans; Alan Evans; Alan Evans)

Before moving on to Part 2:
- Watch Replay Video 8.1 ▶.
- Then check your understanding of what you've learned so far.

check your understanding //

For a quick review to see what you've learned so far, answer the following questions. Visit **pearsonhighered.com/techinaction** to check your answers.

multiple choice

1. The operating system of your cell/smartphone is stored in
   a. read-only memory.
   b. the display.
   c. the digital signal processor.
   d. random access memory.

2. VoIP is phone service that
   a. works even when the electricity goes out.
   b. works over an Internet connection.
   c. is only available for calls within the United States.
   d. has extremely high quality and is very reliable.

3. Which service allows you to use your cell/smartphone to send messages that contain images?
   a. MMS   c. SMS
   b. ISP   d. MiFi

4. Digital convergence means that
   a. all television channels are carried on one digital signal.
   b. analog signals are no longer used.
   c. digital technology will continue to evolve.
   d. one device can perform the jobs of several.

5. There are several categories of mobile devices because
   a. we do not yet have digital convergence.
   b. there is a range of tradeoffs between weight and performance.
   c. everyone wants the fastest processor.
   d. no one has designed a digital device that works well for travel.

true–false

_____ 1. Digital convergence means that all cellular networks will become 4G.

_____ 2. Ultrabooks are a type of notebook computer with the fastest processor and largest screen size.

_____ 3. If you are in a location with free WiFi, it is better to use WiFi than the 3G cellular signal.

critical thinking

1. **The Ultimate Style**

   As mobile devices continue to evolve, they have become lighter and smaller, and we are beginning to see a convergence of computing and clothing.
   a. What would the ultimate convergent mobile clothing be for you? Is there a limit in weight, size, or complexity?
   b. Can you imagine uses for technology in fashion that would support better health? Better social relationships? A richer intellectual life?

2. **The Endpoint**

   We have seen the direction of evolution of portable devices. What will be the final stage of development for mobile devices? What will they weigh? Will they be implanted in the human body?

Continue

You've just taken some fantastic video and photos on a trip to the zoo, and you'd like to organize the media and put it on your Facebook page. What should you do? Try Windows Movie Maker!

Before You Start

a) Before starting, make sure you have several video clips and photos available. If you don't have any of your own, you can use the sample photos and video clips provided with Windows.

b) Windows Movie Maker is part of the Windows Essentials package that is an add-on to Windows (this means it does not come pre-installed in Windows). To install Movie Maker, go to Microsoft's Windows Essentials website (**windows.microsoft.com/en-US/windows-live/essentials-home**) and click the **Download now** link. Once installed, there should be a tile on the Windows 8 Start Screen for Windows Movie Maker. Click (or touch) this tile to launch Movie Maker.

Step 1   The first step is to import your video clips and photos to Movie Maker. On the **Home tab** of the Ribbon, click the **Add Videos and Photos** icon.

Step 2   In the dialog box that appears, browse to where your media files are saved, select the files you wish to import and then click the **Open** button. The files you've added will appear in the Media window.

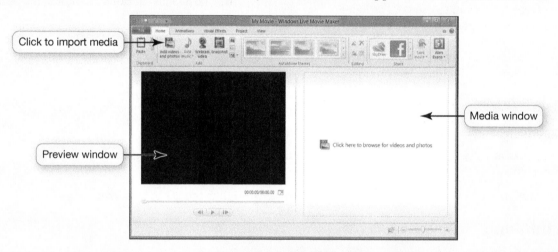

Step 3   In your movie, the video clips and pictures will display in the order shown in the media window (timeline). Click and drag your media to the spot in the timeline where you want it to appear.

Step 4   On the **Home tab** of the Ribbon, click the **Add music** icon and browse to a location on your storage device where you have music files. Select the music file you wish to add as a soundtrack for your movie, and then click the **Open** button.

Step 5 AutoMovie themes will add transitions between clips and title/credit slides based on pre-designed templates. Just click on one of the available themes in the **AutoMovie themes** section on the **Home tab** to apply that theme to your movie.

Step 6 Alternatively, you can manually add a title slide or credit slides by clicking on the appropriate icons on the **Home tab**. Just click on the slide in the preview window to enter a title for your slide.

Step 7 To preview your movie, click the **play** button under the Preview window.

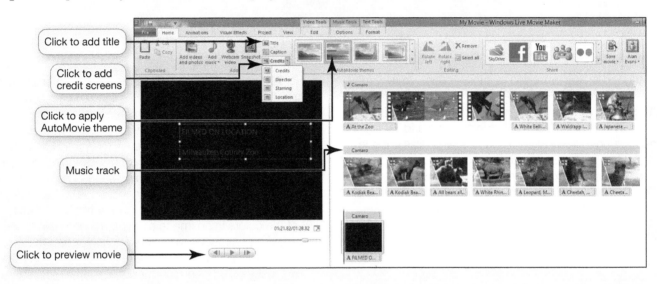

Step 8 When you're satisfied with your movie, go to the **Home tab** and click the **Save movie** icon to save it.

Step 9 To publish your movie on Facebook, go to the **Home tab**, and click the **Facebook** icon. Select an appropriate resolution for your movie, and log on to your Facebook account (if necessary). Movie Maker will add your movie to your Facebook page.

The Digital Information Age

Do you really understand how all the digital technology you use every day actually works? Do you realize how many revolutionary changes are happening in all kinds of media as we continue to use digital formats? Let's take a closer look at what it means to be "digital" and the advantages it brings us.

 digital
DEFINED

Today, no matter what you're interested in—music, movies, TV, radio, stock prices—digital information is the key. All forms of entertainment have migrated to the digital domain (see Figure 8.18). Phone systems and TV signals are now digital streams of data. MP3 files encode digital forms of music, and digital cameras and video cameras are now commonplace. In Hollywood, feature films are being shot entirely with digital equipment, and many movie theaters use digital projection equipment. Satellite radio systems such as SiriusXM satellite radio and HD Radio are broadcast in digital formats.

FIGURE 8.18

Analog versus Digital Entertainment

	ANALOG	DIGITAL
Publishing	Magazines, books	E-books, e-zines
Music	Vinyl record albums and cassette tapes	CDs, MP3 files, and streaming music stations
Photography	35-mm single-lens reflex (SLR) cameras Photos stored on film	Digital cameras, including digital SLRs Photos stored as digital files
Video	8-mm, VHS, and Hi8 camcorders Film stored on tapes	HD digital video (DV) cameras Film stored as digital files; distributed on DVD and Blu-ray discs and streamed
Radio	AM/FM radio	HD Radio, SiriusXM satellite radio
Television	Analog TV broadcast	High-definition digital television (HDTV)

How is digital different from analog?

Any kind of information can be digitized (measured and converted to a stream of numeric values). Consider sound. It's carried to your ears by sound waves, which are actually patterns of pressure changes in the air. Images are our interpretation of the changing intensity of light waves around us. These sound and light waves are called **analog** waves or continuous waves. They illustrate the loudness of a sound or the brightness of the colors in an image at a given moment in time. They're continuous signals because you would never have to lift your pencil off the page to draw them; they are just long, continuous lines.

First-generation recording devices such as vinyl records and analog television broadcasts were designed to reproduce these sound and light waves. A needle in the groove of a vinyl record vibrates in the same pattern as the original sound wave. Analog television signals are actually waves that tell an analog TV how to display the same color and brightness as is seen in the production studio.

However, it's difficult to describe a wave, even mathematically. The simplest sounds, such as that of middle C on a piano, have the simplest shapes, like the one shown in Figure 8.19a. However, something like the word *hello* generates a highly complex pattern, like the one shown in Figure 8.19b.

What advantages do digital formats have over analog ones?

Digital formats describe signals as long strings of numbers. This digital representation gives us a simple way to describe sound and light waves exactly so that sounds and images can be reproduced perfectly any time they're wanted. In addition, we already have easy ways to distribute digital information, such as streaming movies or attaching files to a Facebook message. Thus, digital information can be reproduced exactly and distributed easily; both these reasons give digital huge advantages over an analog format.

a

b

FIGURE 8.19 (a) This is an analog wave showing the simple, pure sound of a piano playing middle C. (b) This is the complex wave produced when a person says "Hello."

How can a sequence of numbers express complicated analog shapes? The
answer is provided by something called *analog-to-digital conversion*. In analog-to-digital conversion, the incoming analog signal is measured many times each second. The strength of the signal at each measurement is recorded

as a simple number. The series of numbers produced by the analog-to-digital conversion process gives us the digital form of the wave. Figure 8.20 shows analog and digital versions of the same wave. In Figure 8.20a, you see the original, continuous analog wave. You could draw that wave without lifting your pencil from the page. In Figure 8.20b, the wave has been digitized and is no longer a single line; instead, it is represented as a series of points or numbers.

How has the change from analog to digital technologies affected our lifestyles? When
the market for communication devices for entertainment media—like photos, music, and video—switched to a digital standard, we began to have products with new and useful capabilities. Small devices can now hold huge collections of a variety of types of information. We can interact with our information any time we like, in ways that, prior to the conversion to digital media, had been too expensive or too difficult to learn. The implications of the shift to digital media are continually evolving. ∎

FIGURE 8.20 (a) A simple analog wave. (b) A digitized version of the same wave.

digital

MEDIA

The entertainment industry has become an all-digital field. The publishing industry, the music recording industry, photography, and film production have all seen radical changes in how content is created and how it is distributed to an audience. Let's look at these forms of entertainment and how they affect you.

Digital Publishing

Are printed books dead? The publishing industry is migrating to digital materials. **Electronic text (e-text)** is textual information captured digitally so that it can be stored, manipulated, and transmitted by electronic devices. With the increasing usage of e-text, the market for printed materials is changing dramatically. In fact, Amazon now sells more Kindle e-books than printed books each year. Several authors, such as Stieg Larsson and James Patterson, have each sold over one million e-books.

What electronic devices are trying to replace books? E-Readers (see Figure 8.21) are devices that can display e-text and have supporting tools, like note taking, bookmarks, and integrated dictionaries. They are selling at a brisk pace with a dizzying range of offerings in the market, including the Amazon Kindle and Fire, Barnes and Noble NOOK, and Sony eReader.

Tablets are also helping to popularize the digitized e-book and electronic versions of major magazines and newspapers. There's evidence that this is increasing all kinds of book buying, not just of digital books. In 2011, Amazon had its greatest growth rate in sales, for all products combined, of the past ten years.

What features make e-readers popular? One big allure of digital publishing is distribution. Ease of access to digital books is very attractive. Even a 1,000-page book can be delivered to your e-reader in under a minute. An incredible array of titles is available—over one million books are available in the Amazon Kindle store alone. In addition, there are millions of texts without copyright that are available for free.

The basic features of e-readers offer many advantages over paper books:

- Integrated dictionaries pull up a definition just by your highlighting a word. The Kindle, for example, can work with both English and German dictionaries—a help in reading foreign works.
- Note taking and highlighting are supported, and you can search the text for your own notes or for specific

terms. You can also easily share the notes you make on the book with others.

- URL links or links to a glossary are often live in the book.
- Bookmarks are immediately pushed through cloud technology so you can read on one device and pick up with the most current bookmark on another device.

Do I need a dedicated device just for reading e-texts? There are free software download versions of the Kindle and the NOOK that run on either PC or Apple computers. You can also download certain texts that have no copyrights and read them directly on a computer either as a PDF file or by using browser add-ons like MagicScroll.

How is digital text displayed? There are two popular technologies used for representing digital text:

1. *Electronic ink:* **Electronic ink** (E Ink) is a very crisp, sharp grayscale representation of text. The "page" is composed of millions of microcapsules with white

FIGURE 8.21 E-Readers are popularizing the digital e-book. *(Kristoffer Tripplaar/Alamy)*

and black particles in a clear fluid. Electronic signals can make each spot appear either white or black. E Ink devices reflect the light that shines on the page, like ordinary paper, and are not backlit. E Ink gives great contrast and is much easier to read in direct sunlight. Examples of devices using E Ink include the Amazon Kindle (see Figure 8.22a) and the Barnes and Noble NOOK.

2. *Backlit monitors:* Another option for presenting e-text is the high-resolution backlit monitors seen in readers like the iPad or the Amazon Fire (see Figure 8.22b). These screens illuminate themselves instead of depending on room lighting conditions. They display color materials, like magazines, with great clarity and full color. The glass does reflect glare, though, which makes them hard to use in bright, direct sunlight. Some people experience more fatigue when reading from a backlit device than when using E Ink. Also note that E Ink readers have a battery life of a month or two on a charge, whereas high-resolution color readers hold a charge for 8 to 10 hours.

Be sure to try both under a variety of conditions before you make a purchasing decision.

What kinds of file formats are used in electronic publishing? Digital formats for publishing vary. Amazon uses a proprietary format (.azw extension), so books purchased for a Kindle are not transportable to a non-Kindle device. An open format also exists, ePub. Some e-readers support the ePub file format. There is an ePub reader plugin available for the browser Firefox and several standalone software ePub readers like Stanza.

Where do I buy e-books? There are a number of vendors associated with e-reader devices:

- Amazon sells the Kindle device, and it connects directly to the Amazon Kindle store.
- The Barnes and Noble NOOK device works with the Barnes and Noble e-bookstore.
- There are many publishers selling e-books online that can be read on any kind of device.
- Textbooks can be purchased in e-book format directly from the publisher; for example, the technology publisher O'Reilly has an online e-bookstore. Another option is a company like CourseSmart, which offers a yearlong subscription to a digital text that times out and disappears from your device after your subscription is up.

What if I just want to borrow a book from a library? Libraries are now including e-book and audio book lending as part of their mission (see Figure 8.23). There is never a late fee; the book just times out and disappears from your device when the borrowing period expires. Products like the Overdrive Media Console (**search.overdrive.com**) let you search to find which area library has the book you want. When you log in to the library website, you can download a text any time of day or night. Libraries have a specific number of copies of each e-book title available, so you may be added to a waiting list if all the copies are checked out, just like with paper books. However, there is a lot of friction between publishers and libraries on how to handle the impact of lending electronically. It's so convenient that some publishers are refusing to allow their e-books to be distributed through libraries.

Can I borrow an e-book from a friend? Lending of e-books is now becoming a popular feature of e-reader systems. The Barnes & Noble NOOK, for example, has a Lend Me feature on certain books. An eligible book can be loaned once for a period of 14 days.

Where can I find free e-books? A great source of free reading is Project Gutenberg (**gutenberg .org**). This repository site is a collection of over 38,000

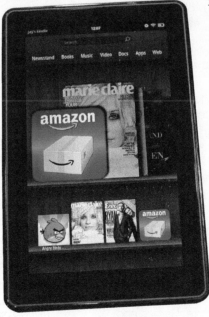

FIGURE 8.22 The two main technologies for e-text display are (a) E Ink grayscale displays, like on the Amazon Kindle, and (b) high-resolution backlit color screens, like on the Amazon Fire. (*EMMANUEL DUNAND/Getty Images*)

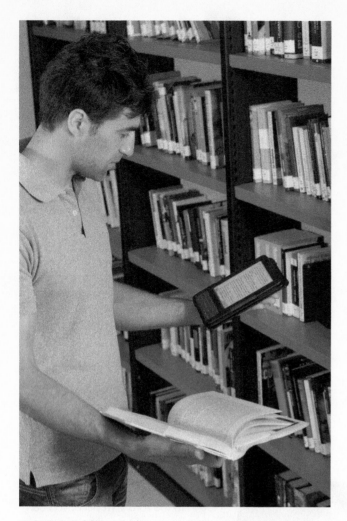

FIGURE 8.23 E-books and audio books can be borrowed for free at most public libraries. *(Olaf Speier/Alamy)*

free books in ePub, Kindle, and PDF formats. It contains books that are free in the United States because their copyrights have expired. The catalog includes many classic titles like *War and Peace* by Leo Tolstoy or mystery novels by Agatha Christie.

How can I publish my own works?
Self-publishing is much easier in the age of digital texts. There are many options available:

- Self-publish into the *Amazon Kindle Store* in a matter of minutes and earn up to a 70% royalty on sales.

- Use a company like *Smashwords* (**smashwords.com**). It accepts a Microsoft Word document from you and then makes your book available through a number of vendors like the Apple iBooks store, Barnes and Noble, and the Sony eReader store. Your book can also be distributed as an app to mobile marketplaces like Google Play or the Apple App Store.

- Use a site like *Lulu* (**lulu.com**) to do social marketing for your book so that you can promote it. In addition, it offers services from editors, designers, and marketers.

Digital Music

How is digital music created? The sound waves created by instruments need to be turned into a string of digital information to record digital music. Figure 8.24 shows the process of digitally recording a song:

1. Playing music creates analog waves.
2. A microphone feeds the sound waves into a chip called an *analog-to-digital converter (ADC)* inside the recording device.
3. The ADC digitizes the waves into a series of numbers.
4. This series of numbers can be recorded onto CDs/DVDs, saved in a file, or sent electronically.
5. On the receiving end, a playback device such as a mobile device or a DVD player is fed that same series of numbers. Inside the playback device is a *digital-to-analog converter (DAC)*, a chip that converts the digital numbers to a continuous analog wave.
6. That analog wave tells the receiver how to move the speaker cones to reproduce the original waves, resulting in the same sound as the original.

More precisely, the digital wave will be *close* to exact. How accurate it is, or how close the digitized wave is in shape to the original analog wave, depends on the sampling rate of the ADC. The **sampling rate** specifies the number of times the analog wave is measured each second. The higher the sampling rate, the more accurately the original wave can be re-created. The improved sound quality higher sampling can afford also depends on the quality of the output device and speakers, of course. However, higher sampling rates also produce much more data, and therefore result in bigger files. For example, sound waves on CDs are sampled at a rate of approximately 44,000 times a second. This produces a huge list of numbers for even a single minute of a song.

What file types store digital music? You're no doubt familiar with the MP3 file format used to store digital music, but many others exist, such as AAC and WMA. If you buy a song from the iTunes Store, for example, you receive an AAC-format file. There are also many formats, such as DivX, MPEG-4 (which usually has an .mp4 extension), WMV, and XviD, which hold both video and audio information. All file formats compete on sound and video quality and *compression*, which relates to how small the file can be and still provide high-quality playback. Be sure to check what kind of files your audio device understands before you store music on it.

How do I know how much digital media my device can hold? The number of songs or hours of video a device like an iPod (see Figure 8.25) can hold depends on how much storage

Singer playing music

Analog wave

ADC

Digital format
28,36,42,
84,120,126,
120,98,98...

MP3 file

MP3 ♪

Speaker

DAC

28,36,42,
84,120,126,
120,98,98...

FIGURE 8.24 During the complete recording process, information changes from analog form to digital data and then back again to analog sound waves. *(Ben Chams/Fotolia)*

space it has. Less expensive mobile devices use built-in flash memory ranging from 1 GB to 32 GB, whereas more expensive models use built-in hard drives, which provide as much as 160 GB of storage.

Another factor that determines how much music a player can hold is the quality of the MP3 music files. The size of an MP3 file depends on the digital sampling of the song. The same song could be sampled at a rate anywhere between 64 kbps and 320 kbps. The size of the song file will be five times larger if it is sampled at 320 kbps rather than the lower sampling rate of 64 kbps. The higher the sampling rate, the better quality the sound—but the larger the file size.

FIGURE 8.25 Apple reports over 1 billion iPods have been sold since they were first introduced. *(Bloomberg/Getty Images)*

How do you control the size of an MP3 file? If you are *ripping*, or converting, a song from a CD to a digital MP3 file, you can select the sampling rate yourself. You decide by considering what quality sound you want, as well as how many songs you want to fit onto your MP3 player. For example, if your player has 1 GB of storage and you have ripped songs at 192 kbps, you could fit about 694 minutes of music onto the player. The same 1 GB could store 2,083 minutes of music if it were sampled at 64 kbps. Whenever you are near your computer, you can connect your player and download a different set of songs, but you always are limited by the amount of storage your player has.

What if I want to access more music than my device has room for? Some of the devices that use flash memory allow you to add storage capacity by purchasing removable flash memory cards. You can also use a service that streams the music to you over WiFi or 3G/4G networks. Companies like Spotify and Rhapsody have subscription plans that let you listen to any of the millions of tracks in their catalog. The music is not yours to own, however—if you cancel your subscription, you no longer have access to the music. But because it's streamed to you, it doesn't take up space on your device drive. Some streaming services offer options that also let you download music so that you can still play the songs on your playlist even if you're not in range of Internet access.

How do I transfer files to my music device? To move large volumes of data between your computer and your music device, you want a high-speed port. Most devices use a USB port, which lets you transfer files quickly. Cloud services are appearing that automatically push music to your mobile device. Apple's iOS 5 operating system supports iCloud technology. This means that as soon as you purchase a new song from iTunes, it's automatically pushed to all your registered iTunes devices—your Mac, your PC, your iPad and iTouch, and your iPhone.

What if I want a lot of people to listen to my digital music? You have a number of options for listening to your music other than with headphones:

- Many audio receivers now come with a port or a dock so that you can connect a mobile device directly to them as another audio input source.

- Networked audio/video receivers have the hardware and software required to connect to your home network and use streaming services like Pandora or Spotify to play music.

- Most new cars are equipped with an auxiliary input to the speaker system to support connecting a mobile device; others have a fully integrated software system that displays and runs your playlists. Many Ford models use the Microsoft Sync system that allows you to navigate through your playlists with just voice commands.

- There are alarm clocks and home speaker docks that can mate, even wirelessly, with a mobile device and that broadcast brilliant sound (see Figure 8.26).

FIGURE 8.26 A wide range of mobile docking stations, like the Bag of Rhythm from The House of Marley, use MP3 players or phones to store music files. *(Ethan Miller/Getty Images)*

The shift to digital music wasn't an easy transition for the recording industry. The initial MP3 craze was fueled by sites such as MP3.com, which originally stored its song files on a public server with the permission of the original artists or recording companies. Therefore, you weren't infringing on a copyright by downloading songs from sites such as MP3.com (which still exists and now provides free music in streaming format).

Napster was a file-exchange site created to correct some of the annoyances found by users of MP3.com (see Figure 8.27). One such annoyance was the limited availability of popular music in MP3 format. Napster differed from MP3.com because songs or locations of songs were not stored in a central public server, but instead were "borrowed" directly from other users' computers. This process of users transferring files between computers is referred to as **peer-to-peer (P2P) sharing**. Napster also provided a search engine dedicated to finding specific MP3 files. This direct search and sharing eliminated the inconvenience of searching links only to find them unavailable.

The problem with Napster was that it was so good at what it did. The rapid acceptance and use of Napster—at one point, it had nearly 60 million users—led the music industry to sue the site for copyright infringement, and Napster was closed in June 2002. Napster has since reopened as a music site that sells music downloads and is now sanctioned by the recording industry.

The music industry has needed to reinvent itself since the demise of Napster. The initial reaction of the recording industry was to continue to enforce its absolute ownership over digital forms of its music. The industry even filed legal actions against individuals who had downloaded large amounts of music from Internet sites. This heavy-handed

FIGURE 8.27 Napster was one of the original P2P music-sharing sites. *(Mike Fanous/Getty Images)*

reaction to the new era of digital music ultimately backfired and left the music industry scrambling. Overall music sales have dropped significantly each year for the last decade. The recording industry is still trying to counter losing CD sales. The approach they took early on did not allow them to adapt quickly enough to the new business models required by the shift to digital technologies.

P2P sharing sites are still operating today. Napster was "easy" to shut down because it used a central index server that queried other Napster computers for requested songs. Current P2P protocols (such as BearShare) differ from Napster in that they don't limit themselves to sharing only MP3 files. Video files are easily obtainable on P2P sites. More importantly, these sites don't have a central computer acting to index all this information. Instead, they operate in a true P2P sharing environment in which computers connect directly to other computers. This makes them a prime source of unwanted viruses and spyware.

The argument these P2P networks make to defend their legality is that they do not run a central server like the original Napster, but only facilitate connections between users. Therefore, they have no control over what the users choose to trade. These legal nuances weren't enough to keep the LimeWire service active, and it was shut down by court order in 2010. Note that not all P2P file sharing is illegal. For example, it is legal to trade photos or movies you've created with other users over a P2P site.

People who oppose such file-sharing sites contend that the sites know their users are distributing files illegally and breaking copyright laws. Be aware that having illegal content on your computer, deliberately or by accident, is a criminal offense in many jurisdictions.

If I don't pay for a music download ... is it illegal? Although you need to pay for most music you download, some artists post songs for free. Business models are still evolving as artists and recording companies try to meet audience needs while also protecting their own intellectual property rights. Several different approaches exist. One is to deliver something called *tethered downloads*, in which you pay for the music and own it, but are subject to restrictions on its use.

Another approach is to offer *DRM–free* music, which is music without any **digital rights management (DRM)**. DRM is a system of access control that allows only limited use of material that's been legally purchased. It may be that the song can only run on certain devices or a movie can only be viewed a certain number of times. A DRM–free song can be placed on as many computers or players as you wish. These song files can be moved freely from system to system.

Will streaming music services eliminate radio stations? The Internet allows artists to release new songs to their fans immediately (on sites such as Facebook) and without relying on radio airtime. This opens up new channels for artists to reach an audience and changes the amount of power radio stations have in the promotion of music. Many radio stations have increased listenership by making their stations available through Internet sites and by broadcasting in high-definition quality.

BITS&BYTES

Need Money for Your Band? Try Indiegogo

What if your band has already built up a fan base but just needs to have the up-front money to go into the studio to record? Indiegogo (**indiegogo. com**) is a crowd-funding website specializing in creative projects and causes. Musicians have a platform to go to their fan base and raise money before a recording session or a tour, or even when tragedy strikes. When cellist Mike Block had a serious accident, he used Indiegogo to raise money to pay off his medical bills. Mike offered copies of an upcoming album or personal lessons as rewards to funders. He raised over $48,000 using Indiegogo and was able to repay years of accumulated medical expenses.

What if I want to publicize my band's music? Digital music has made distributing your own recordings very simple. You can make your own creations available using sites like ReverbNation (**reverbnation.com**). You can quickly create a web page for your band, post your songs, and start building a fan base through Facebook. ReverbNation will send you reports detailing who's listening to your music and what they're saying about it. ReverbNation is also a way to connect with independent recording labels and to find places that want to book your band.

Digital Photography

What is "analog" photography? Before digital cameras hit the market, most people used some form of 35mm single-lens reflex (SLR) camera. When you take a picture using a traditional SLR camera, a shutter opens, creating an aperture (a small window in the camera) that allows light to hit the 35mm film inside. Chemicals coating the film react when exposed to light. Later, additional chemicals develop the image on the film, and the image is printed on special light-sensitive paper. A variety of lenses and processing techniques, special equipment, and filters are needed to create printed photos taken with traditional SLR cameras.

What's different about digital photography? Digital cameras do not use film. Instead, they capture images on electronic sensors called *charge-coupled device (CCD) arrays* and then convert those images to digital data, long series of numbers that represent the color and brightness of millions of points in the image. Unlike traditional cameras, digital cameras allow you to see your images the instant you shoot them. Most camera models can now record digital video as well as digital photos.

How do I select a digital camera? The first question to answer is whether you want a compact "point-and-shoot" camera or a more expensive digital SLR, like the Nikon D3200 in Figure 8.28. If you decide you want a digital SLR, you have a number of options. Some digital SLRs let you switch among different lenses and offer features important to serious amateur and professional photographers. Although having such flexibility in selection of lenses is a great advantage, most of these cameras are also larger, heavier, and use more battery power than the fixed lens models. Think about how you'll be using your camera and decide which model will serve you best in the long run. One great resource to use is Digital Photography Review (**dpreview.com**), a site that compares cameras and provides feedback from owners.

Why not just use the camera on my smartphone? The cameras on smartphones often provide lower resolutions and inferior lenses than stand-alone cameras. In addition, many features that photographers rely on often aren't available in smartphone cameras, such as different types of autofocus, image stabilization algorithms, and smile shutter, which waits to take a shot until your subject is smiling.

What determines the image quality of a digital camera? The overall image quality is determined by many factors:

- The quality of the lenses used
- The file format and compression used
- The color management software included
- The camera's **resolution**, or the number of data points it records for each image captured

A digital camera's resolution is measured in megapixels (MP). The word *pixel* is short for picture element, which is a single dot in a digital image. Point-and-shoot models typically offer resolutions from 10MP to 15MP. Professional digital SLR cameras, such as the Nikon D3200, can take photos at resolutions as high as 24.2MP, but they sell for thousands of dollars.

If you're interested in making only 5" × 7" or 8" × 10" prints, a lower-resolution camera is fine. However, low-resolution images become grainy and pixelated when pushed to larger size. For example, if you tried to print an 11" × 14" enlargement from a 4MP image taken using your smartphone's camera, the image would look grainy; you would see individual dots of color instead of a clear, sharp image. The 10MP to 15MP cameras on the market now have plenty of resolution to guarantee sharp, detailed images even with enlargements as big as 11" × 14".

What file formats are used for digital images? To fit more photos on the same size flash memory card, digital cameras let you choose from several different file types in order to compress the image data into less memory space. When you choose to compress your images, you'll lose some of the detail, but in return, you'll be able to fit more images on your flash card. The most common file types supported by digital cameras are raw uncompressed data (RAW) and Joint Photographic Experts Group (JPEG):

- *RAW files* have different formats and extensions depending on the manufacturer of a particular camera.

FIGURE 8.28 The Nikon D3200 is a digital SLR with 24.2MP resolution. *(Yoshikazu Tsuno/Getty Images)*

The RAW file records all of the original image information, so it's larger than a compressed JPEG file.

- *JPEG files* can be compressed just a bit, keeping most of the details, or compressed a great deal, losing some detail. Most cameras let you select from a few different JPEG compression levels.

Often, cameras also support a very low-resolution storage option that provides images that aren't useful for printing but are so small that they're easy to e-mail. Even people who have slow Internet connections are able to quickly download and view such images on screen.

What's the best way to transfer my photos to my computer? Digital cameras have a built-in USB port you can use to copy the image files to your computer. Another option is to transfer the flash card from your camera directly to a built-in memory card reader on your computer. Some camera models support wireless network connections so that you can transfer the images without the fuss of putting a cable in place. If your model doesn't, you can purchase a memory card with built-in WiFi: the Eye-Fi (see Figure 8.29).

FIGURE 8.29 Eye-Fi combines memory storage and wireless transfer of your photos. *(Handout/MCT/Newscom)*

Eye-Fi wirelessly transfers your photos to Google Picasa, Facebook, or a number of other web destinations. Eye-Fi Mobile X2 uploads images directly from your camera to your tablet or phone, as well. It also backs up the photos and videos you take with your camera to your home computer. And when you're away from home, Eye-Fi comes with hotspot access so you can upload for free from any McDonald's, Starbucks, hotel, or airport.

Can I make my old photos digital?

You can use a scanner to turn your hand-drawn sketches or old photos into digital files. Most scanner software lets you store the converted images as TIFF files or in compressed form as JPEG files. Some scanners include hardware that lets you scan film negatives or slides as well or even insert a stack of photos to be scanned in sequence.

Scanner quality is measured by its resolution, which is given in dots per inch (dpi). Most modern scanners can digitize a document at resolutions as high as 9,600 × 9,600 dpi in either color or grayscale mode. Scanners also typically support optical character recognition (OCR). OCR software converts pages of handwritten or typed text into electronic files. You can then open and edit these converted documents with word processing programs such as Microsoft Word.

How can I share my digital photos?

You've probably shared a number of photos on Facebook already. Other options include creating online albums at sites such as Picasa, which let you share your photos without having to print them. You can also design electronic scrapbooks on a number of digital scrapbooking sites such as **cottagearts.net**.

Of course, you can carry and display your photos on your tablet and smartphone. You can also connect your iPad wirelessly to your TV and deliver slide shows of your photos, complete with musical soundtracks you've selected. If you have networked your home, a TV connected to your network can display all the photos and videos stored on your computer.

What are the best options for printing digital photos?

If you want to print photos, you have two main options:

1. **Use a photo printer:** The most popular and inexpensive ones are inkjet printers. Some inkjet printers can print high-quality color photos, although they vary in speed, quality, and features. Dye-sublimation printers are another option. If you're interested in a printer to use for printing only photos, a dye-sublimation printer is a good choice. However, some models print only specific sizes, such as 4" × 6" prints, so be sure the printer you buy will fit your long-term needs.

2. **Use a photo-printing service:** Most photo-printing labs, including the film-processing departments at stores such as Target, offer digital-printing services.

The paper and ink used at these labs are higher quality than what is available for home use and produce heavier, glossier prints that won't fade. You can send your digital photos directly to local merchants such as CVS and Walgreens for printing using Windows Photo Gallery. Online services, such as Flickr (**flickr.com**) and Shutterfly (**shutterfly.com**), store your images and allow you to create hard-copy prints, albums, mugs, T-shirts, or calendars.

Digital Video

What devices, sites, and other sources provide digital video content?

Digital video surrounds us:

- Television is broadcast in digitally formatted signals.
- The Internet delivers a huge amount of digital video through YouTube, communities like Vimeo (**vimeo.com**), and webcasting sites like Ustream (**ustream.tv**).
- Sites like Hulu (**hulu.com**) rebroadcast many current television shows as well as films and movie trailers.
- Many pay services are available to deliver digital video to you. These include on-demand streaming from cable providers, iTunes, Netflix's Instant Watch films, and Amazon's Instant Video download service.
- And of course, you can create your own digital video. Although you can buy dedicated digital camcorders to record digital video, many smartphones now record HD video. Webcams also work as inexpensive devices for creating digital video.

How do I record my own digital video?

Video equipment for home use stores information in a digital video (DV) format. Such cameras don't require any tapes; they store hours of video on built-in hard drives or flash cards. Some models even record directly to DVD. You can easily transfer video files to your computer and, using video-editing software, edit the video at home. You can save (or write) your final product on a CD or DVD and play it in your home DVD system or on your computer. For true videophiles, cameras and burners are now available for HD video format.

What if I decide to add special effects and a sound track?

Video-editing software presents a storyboard or timeline with which you can manipulate your video file, as shown in Figure 8.30. You can review your clips frame by frame or trim them at any point. You can add titles, audio tracks, and animations; order each segment on the timeline in whichever sequence you like; and correct segments for color balance, brightness, or contrast. Examine online tutorial resources such as Izzy Video podcasts (**izzyvideo.com**) to learn how to make the most impact with the editing and effects you apply to your raw video footage.

FIGURE 8.30 Adobe Premiere Elements allows you to build a movie from video clips and to add sound tracks and special effects.

What kinds of files will I end up with?

Once you're done editing your video file, you can save or export it in a variety of formats. Figure 8.31 shows some of the popular video file formats in use today, along with the file extensions they use.

Your choice of file format for your finished video will depend on what you want to do with the video. For example, the QuickTime streaming file format is a great choice if your file is really large and you plan to post it on the web. The Microsoft AVI format is a good choice if you're sending your file to a wide range of users because it's the standard video format for the Windows Media Player.

Different compression algorithms will have different results on your particular video. Try several to see which

FIGURE 8.31

Typical File Formats for Digital Video

FORMAT	FILE EXTENSION	NOTES
QuickTime	.qt .mov	You can download the QuickTime player without charge from **apple.com/quicktime**. The Pro version allows you to build your own QuickTime files.
Moving Picture Experts Group (MPEG)	.mpg .mpeg .mp4	The MPEG-4 video standard was adopted internationally in 2000; it's recognized by most video player software.
Windows Media Video	.wmv	This is a Microsoft file format recognized by Windows Media Player (included with the Windows OS).
Microsoft Video for Windows	.avi	This is a Microsoft file format recognized by Windows Media Player (included with the Windows OS).
RealMedia	.rm	This format is from RealNetworks and is popular for streaming video. You can download the player for free at **real.com**.
Adobe Flash Video	.flv	This is the Adobe Flash video format, sometimes embedded in Shockwave files (*.swf).

one does a better job of compressing your particular file. A **codec** (*compression/decompression*) is a rule, implemented in either software or hardware, that squeezes the same audio and video information into less space. Some information will be lost using compression, and there are several different codecs to choose from, each claiming better performance than its competitors. Commonly used codecs include MPEG-4, H.264, and DivX. There's no one codec that's always superior—a codec that works well for a simple interview may not do a good job compressing a live-action scene.

What if I want to produce a DVD with a full menuing system? You can use special authoring software such as Pinnacle Studio HD or Adobe Encore. These DVD/Blu-ray software packages often include preset selections for producing video for specific mobile devices. These programs can also create final discs that have animated menu systems and easy navigation controls, allowing the viewer to move quickly from one movie or scene to another. Home DVD and Blu-ray players, as well as gaming systems such as PlayStation and Xbox, can read these discs.

What's the quickest way to get my video out to viewers? The quickest way to get your video content out is to broadcast. Webcasting,

or broadcasting your video live to an audience, is an option that has become simple to do. All you need is a webcam (see Figure 8.32), and sites like **justin.tv** or **ustream.tv** will let you quickly set up to webcast your video as it is captured to a live Internet audience. You can also display an interactive chat next to the video feed. Both the chat and the video are captured and archived for viewers who missed the live broadcast. Most smartphones record video at a quality good enough to directly webcast from your phone, and most laptops have an integrated webcam.

You may want to take time and produce a more polished video. When you have it just right, you can upload it to video-sharing sites like YouTube or Metacafe.

Of course, it's illegal for you to upload videos you don't own. You also can't take a piece of a copyrighted video and post it publicly. The Ethics in IT section in this chapter presents several legal and ethical situations that are important for you to be aware of as a content creator in the digital age.

How is HD different from "plain" digital? *HD* stands for **high definition**. It is a standard of digital television signal that guarantees a specific level of resolution and a specific *aspect ratio*, which

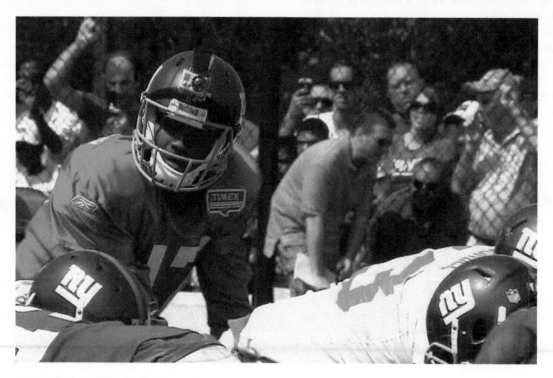

FIGURE 8.32 Webcams are small enough to make them part of any activity (check the quarterback's helmet!). *(AP Photo/New York Giants)*

ethics in IT

You just returned from your trip to the Grand Canyon, and your friends are raving about the photos you took. You decide to put them on Flickr so others can see them. You also think that someone might see your photos and want to use them in a commercial publication such as a magazine. Because you own the copyright to your photos, you control how they can be used—and you want to protect your rights. You add a disclaimer to Flickr indicating that all rights are reserved on your photos. Anyone who wants to use them will need to contact you and request permission.

All of a sudden, you're bombarded by requests for permission to use your photos. A high school student in Illinois wants to feature one on her travel blog. A church in Georgia wants to use a photo for its newsletter. An ad agency in Seattle wants to modify your sunrise photo and use it in an ad. How are you going to manage all these permission requests?

Copyleft, a play on the word copyright, is designed for this situation. *Copyleft* is a term for various licensing plans that enable copyright holders to grant certain rights to the work while retaining other rights. Creative Commons (**creativecommons. org**), a nonprofit organization, has developed various licenses you can use based on the rights you wish to grant. Simply decide which type of license best fits your goals for the work, and Creative Commons provides you with HTML you can use to add the specific licensing information to your site.

The advantage to using Creative Commons licenses is that people won't constantly send you permission requests to use your work. The licenses explain how your work can be used. Also, many advocates of copyleft policies feel that creativity is encouraged when people are free to modify other people's work instead of worrying about infringing on copyright.

Opponents of Creative Commons licenses complain that the licenses have affected their livelihoods. If millions of images are out on Flickr with Creative Commons licenses that permit free commercial use, professional photographers might have a tougher time selling their work. Furthermore, Creative Commons licenses are irrevocable. If you make a mistake and select the wrong license for your work, or you later find out a work is valuable and you've already selected a license that allows commercial use, you're out of luck.

Each of us needs to carefully consider the value of our intellectual property and decide how best to conduct our digital livelihood. Understanding the meaning of copyright, and copyleft, is important both so that you respect the rights of others and so that you can simplify your life in granting permission rights to the works you create.

---

is the rectangular shape of the image. A 1080 HDTV displays 1,920 vertical lines and 1,080 horizontal lines of video on the screen, which is over six times as man pixels as a standard definition TV. The aspect ratio used is 16:9, which makes the screen wider, giving it the same proportions as the rectangular shape of a movie theater screen (see Figure 8.33). This allows televisions to play movies in the widescreen format for which they were created, instead of "letterboxing" the film with black bars on the top and the bottom of the screen.

What types of connectivity are provided on modern TV sets? A typical HDTV set has multiple HDMI connectors, allowing game consoles, Blu-ray players, and cable boxes to be connected and to produce the highest-quality output. HDMI is a single cable that carries all of the video and all of the audio information.

Many TV sets have a built-in SD card reader. This allows users to display slide shows of photographs captured by their digital cameras. A PC VGA port is also included on most sets to allow you to feed your computer's output video signal directly to the television. **What are the advantages to watching digital video on my TV?** Other information services can be integrated with the broadcast; so, for example, if a telephone call came through during the show, a pop-up could appear identifying the caller. Additional content can be delivered in real time with the broadcast, explaining the background of characters or pulling up behind-the-scenes info. In the future, there will be more

Standard television

HDTV

Extra image area

Letterbox

FIGURE 8.33 (a) Standard-definition TV has a more "square" aspect ratio, whereas (b) HDTV matches the 16:9 ratio used in the motion picture industry without resorting to (c) letterboxing. *(Pichugin Dmitry/Shutterstock)*

interactivity integrated so you can participate in live polls or chats on screen as the show is broadcast.

Can I record the digital video that comes over my TV? There are a variety of digital video recorders (DVRs) available that record in HD. Models like TiVo even recommend new shows you might like based on what you've been watching. You can also install PVR (personal video recording) software on your computer. Programs like SnapStream (**snapstream. com**) let you use your computer to view the schedule program guide, select shows to record (without commercials), and then watch them from anywhere you have Internet access.

Can I get digital video to watch on my portable device? Many DVR units, like TiVo, support software that lets you transfer recorded shows to files on your PC and format them for viewing on a mobile device. There are also devices like Slingbox that take the video from your TV and broadcast it to you over the Internet. With Slingbox, you can be in another room, or another country, and control and watch your home TV on your notebook or your smartphone (see Figure 8.34). ■

FIGURE 8.34 Slingbox can send your digital television content to your tablet, notebook, or phone, wherever you may be. *(AP Photo/Paul Sakuma)*

Before moving on to Chapter Review:
- Watch Replay Video 8.2 ▶.
- Then check your understanding of what you've learned so far.

check your understanding //

For a quick review to see what you've learned so far, answer the following questions. Visit **pearsonhighered.com/ techinaction** to check your answers.

multiple choice

1. Which is NOT a factor that determines the quality of images taken with a digital camera?

    a. lens quality   **c.** file format

    b. resolution   **d.** Eye-Fi

2. The quickest way to distribute your band's new song to a lot of listeners is to

    a. use an application to post it on Facebook.

    b. e-mail the song to local radio stations.

    c. hand out CDs that you burned.

    d. You cannot legally distribute music freely.

3. P2P is an acronym for

    a. packet-to-packet networking.

    b. peer-to-peer sharing.

    c. person-to-person texting.

    d. power-to-people delivery.

4. An analog signal is different from a digital signal because

    a. it is continuous.

    b. it has only specific discrete values.

    c. it is easier to duplicate.

    d. it is easier to transmit.

5. Which of the following is NOT true about modern TVs?

    a. They have several HDMI ports.

    b. They allow other services, like caller ID, to be integrated.

    c. You can purchase apps for them.

    d. They run word processing and spreadsheet software.

true–false

_____ **1.** Digital music files must be converted to the MP3 format if they are transferred to a mobile device.

_____ **2.** A codec is the algorithm that compresses and decompresses video files.

_____ **3.** If your digital camera doesn't support wireless connectivity, you can use a memory card with built-in WiFi.

critical thinking

1. **Reinvent Yourself**

    The arrival of digital information has forced major shifts in several industries, such as publishing, music recording, and film. How has each industry reacted? Have they each found ways to reinvent the products and services they deliver to match the challenge of the Digital Age? What other industries have had to realign their business models because of digital information?

2. **Too Much Media?**

    As a manager, what concerns might you have about your employees' use of corporate bandwidth to download and view media files? Do you think it would benefit your business to block certain file transfers or certain sites? As a manager, are there concerns you might have if employees have digital cameras on their smartphones? Would your answers be different in an academic setting?

Continue ➡

8 | Chapter Review

summary //

Digital Convergence

1. How is the trend of digital convergence seen in the market?

- Digital convergence has brought us single devices with the capabilities that used to require four or five separate tools.

Telephony: Smartphones and Beyond

2. What hardware and software comprise a typical smartphone?

- Like a traditional computer, a smartphone has a central processor, memory, and an OS. These components work in the same way as in a computer to process information and support communications, software applications, and other services.

3. How do I synchronize information between my phone and my computer, and how do mobile Internet data plans work?

- Information can be synched between devices using either wired or wireless solutions.
- A wired synch requires either a micro SD card or a USB cable to connect the device directly to the computer.
- A wireless synch can be done using Bluetooth or WiFi or by connecting to a cloud service.
- Mobile data plans allow your device to have access at almost any location.
- Data transfers occur at either 3G or 4G speeds, depending on your device and provider. Fees are tied to the amount of data you transfer each month.

4. What do I need to keep my smartphone secure?

- Viruses can infect smartphones, so using an antivirus software package is important. Check the manufacturer's website frequently for updates and practice safe habits by not downloading or opening files from unknown sources.

5. How does digital telephony support VoIP services?

- VoIP allows inexpensive communication using a computer or a WiFi–enabled phone. Because it's based on a digital format for information, it can support services like automatic delivery of phone messages to an e-mail account or texts to a mobile device.

Tablets, Netbooks, and Ultrabooks

6. What distinguishes the performance of tablets, netbooks, and ultrabooks?

- Mobile devices differ in terms of size and weight, input (physical keyboard, software keyboard on a touch screen), and in terms of OS (mobile OS or traditional OS).
- Netbooks and ultrabooks can run traditional software packages like Microsoft Office, whereas tablets run new versions of productivity software, made to take advantage of the features of the tablet.

Digital Defined

7. What advantage do digital formats have over analog signals?

- Digital media is based on a series of numeric data, number values that were measured from the original analog waveform. As a string of numbers, a digital photo or video file can be easily processed by modern computers.

Digital Media

8. How is the digital format changing the way media is created and distributed?

- The increased use of digital information has led to a period of greater creativity and control of our data. In a digital format, information is easy to carry, manipulate, and exchange. This has led to revolutionary changes in communication, entertainment media, and mobile computing.
- Digital publishing is allowing a variety of new distribution methods into the industry. E-readers and online bookstores are bringing changes to the models of how to sell printed materials.

- Digital music is created by combining pure digital sounds with samples of analog sounds. It has meant changes for the recording industry, for performers, and for music listeners. It's now inexpensive to carry a music library, to create new songs, and to distribute them worldwide.

9. How do I work with digital images and video?

- Digital cameras allow you to instantly capture and transfer images to your devices, computers, and cloud storage sites.
- Using software for video production, you can create polished videos with titles, transitions, a sound track, and special effects and distribute them on DVDs.
- You can also use a webcam to stream live video to sites that will "broadcast" it over the Internet.

Be sure to check out the companion website for additional materials to help you review and learn, including a Tech Bytes Weekly newsletter—**pearsonhighered.com/techinaction**. And don't forget the Replay Videos .

key terms //

making the transition to . . . next semester//

1. **Choosing Mobile Devices to Fit Your Needs**

   As a student, which devices discussed in this chapter would have the most immediate impact on the work you do each day? Which would provide the best value (that is, the greatest increase in productivity and organization per dollar spent)? Consider the full range of devices, from cell/smartphones to laptop systems.

2. **Ready … Set … Act!**

   As a student, you often give presentations or take on student teaching assignments. What steps would you follow to create a digital video recording of one of your presentations? What tools would≈you need to record? What kind of file would you end up producing? How would you distribute the video to a live Internet audience? How would you make a DVD of the performance?

3. **Author, Author**

   As a new author of fantasy stories, you have written a collection of short fiction. You decide to publish the collection yourself. What options are there for you to use? How do they compare/contrast?

making the transition to . . . the workplace//

1. **Subscription versus Ownership**

   With the arrival of reliable, fast, networked digital information, businesses can track the location and status of all kinds of objects, such as cars and bicycles. This is introducing a new business model different from individual ownership—now, using a car can become a "subscription" service.

   What options are there for "subscribing" to a car instead of owning one? How about for a bicycle? Are there other businesses you can identify that would be able to take advantage of digital information and become subscription services instead of vendors of a physical product? What are the advantages to the consumer of subscription over ownership? What are the drawbacks?

2. **Everyone Is a Writer**

   Now that digital publishing is so accessible to everyone, how should a publishing business respond? Are there ways that existing publishing houses can take advantage of the easy access readers have to publish extensions of stories? What about in the fields of video or music—how might a business encourage the involvement of the fan base of a movie or a band by using the media-creation tools available?

3. **Mobile Devices on the Highway**

   Mobile devices used in vehicles are becoming the norm in today's society. Consider the following:

   a. Several car manufacturers provide Bluetooth option packages for their vehicles. What are the advantages to having Bluetooth connectivity in your car? Are there any disadvantages?

   b. Examine the Microsoft Sync software package. List the features and services it provides. If you were a salesperson with a territory that you covered by car, how would Sync help you?

"And one will rule them all"

Problem

Digital convergence posits the dream of one device that can do it all, for everyone. But there are so many different mobile devices saturating the market that many people are left in a state of confusion. Either they are buying too many devices and not using them, or they are paralyzed from buying anything because of the dilemma of too many choices.

Task

For each client scenario described as follows, the group will select the minimum set of devices that would support and enhance the client's life.

Process

1. Consider the following three clients:
    * A retired couple who now travels for pleasure a great deal. They want to be involved in their grandchildren's lives and will need support for their health, finances, and personal care as they age.
    * A young family with two children, two working parents, and a tight budget.
    * A couple in which each individual is a physician and each adores technology.

2. Make two recommendations for your clients in terms of digital technologies that will enhance their business or their lifestyle. Discuss the advantages and disadvantages of each technology. Consider value, reliability, computing needs, training needed, and communication needs, as well as expandability for the future.

3. As a group, prepare a final report that considers the costs, availability, and unique features of the recommendations you have made for your clients.

4. Bring the research materials from the individual team meetings to class. Looking at the clients' needs, make final decisions as to which digital technologies are best suited for each client.

Conclusion

Digital information has allowed the development of a new style of living, both at home and at work. With so many digital solutions on the market today, recommending digital communication, media management, and mobility options needs to focus on converging to the minimum set of tools that will enhance life without adding complication to it.

When Everyone Has a Voice

In this exercise, you'll research and then role-play a complicated ethical situation. The role you play might or might not match your own personal beliefs; in either case, your research and use of logic will enable you to represent the view assigned. An arbitrator will watch and comment on both sides of the arguments, and together, the team will agree on an ethical solution.

Background

Much of the world's population is now equipped with Internet-ready camera phones. Sensors on these phones could measure for viruses or compute pollution indexes, while the cameras could be used to document a range of human behavior. This could create changes in political movements, art, and culture as everyone's experience is documented and shared.

Research Areas to Consider

- Evgeny Morozov RSA Animate
- Mobilebehavior.com
- The Witness Project
- Center for Embedded Networked Sensing

Process

1. Divide the class into teams.
2. Research the areas cited above and devise a scenario in which mobile access could make an impact politically or environmentally, positively or negatively.
3. Team members should write a summary that provides background information for their character—for example: business owner, politician, reporter, or arbitrator—and that details their character's behaviors to set the stage for the role-playing event. Then, team members should create an outline to use during the role-playing event.
4. Team members should arrange a mutually convenient time to meet for the exchange, using either the collaboration feature of MyITLab or the discussion board feature of your course management software or by meeting in person.
5. Team members should present their case to the class or submit a PowerPoint presentation for review by the rest of the class, along with the summary and resolution they developed.

Conclusion

As technology becomes ever more prevalent and integrated into our lives, more and more ethical dilemmas will present themselves. Being able to understand and evaluate both sides of the argument, while responding in a personally or socially ethical manner, will be an important skill.

Major Threats to Your Digital Assets

Cybercrime and Identity Theft

OBJECTIVE

1. What is cybercrime, and who perpetrates it? **(pp. 358–359)**

Protecting Yourself from Computer Viruses

OBJECTIVES

2. What are the types of viruses from which I need to protect my computer? **(pp. 360–363)**

3. What can I do to protect my computer from viruses? **(pp. 364–366)**

🛈 **Active Helpdesk:** Avoiding Computer Viruses

🔊 **Sound Byte:** Protecting Your Computer

Protecting Digital Assets from Hackers

OBJECTIVES

4. How can hackers attack my computing devices, and what harm can they cause? **(pp. 367–370)**

5. What is a firewall, and how does it keep my computer safe from hackers? **(pp. 371–373)**

6. How do I create secure passwords and manage all of my passwords? **(pp. 373–375)**

7. How can I surf the Internet anonymously and use biometric authentication devices to protect my data? **(pp. 375–378)**

🛈 **Active Helpdesk:** Understanding Firewalls

🔊 **Sound Byte:** Installing a Personal Firewall

Protecting Your Digital Property from Yourself

Managing Online Annoyances

OBJECTIVE

8. How do I manage online annoyances such as spyware and spam? **(pp. 382–387)**

Keeping Your Data Safe

OBJECTIVES

9. What data do I need to back up, and what are the best methods for doing so? **(pp. 388–392)**

10. What is social engineering, and how do I avoid falling prey to phishing? **(pp. 393–395)**

🔊 **Sound Byte:** Managing Computer Security with Windows Tools

Protecting Your Physical Computing Assets

OBJECTIVE

11. How do I protect my physical computing assets from environmental hazards, power surges, and theft? **(pp. 396–398)**

🔊 **Sound Byte:** Surge Protectors

For all media in this chapter go to **pearsonhighered.com/techinaction** or MyITLab.

(vege/Fotolia)

HOW COOL IS THIS?

You have a lot of **information** in your **cell phone**. What happens if you **lose your phone**, damage it beyond repair, or want to **switch phones**? Transferring data can be very time consuming, or even impossible if you lose your phone. Apple's iOS devices do a good job of backing up your settings either in iTunes or iCloud. But what about backing up Android devices? Not all settings and apps are backed up on Google's sites. So, apps like **The Missing Sync** provide a solution by allowing you to **back up settings**, contacts, notes, tasks, bookmarks, calendars, music, videos, and photos from your Android phone or tablet to a computer running the Windows operating system. The backups take place automatically **via WiFi or Bluetooth** whenever you are in close proximity to your computer. Then, if your phone is ever lost, stolen, or damaged, or if you are just upgrading to the latest model, you can easily **transfer** your information to a new or replacement phone. So install a backup app on your Android phone today and enjoy some peace of mind!

Scan here for more info

357

Major Threats to Your Digital Assets

The media is full of stories about malicious computer programs damaging computers, criminals stealing people's identities online, and attacks on corporate websites bringing major corporations to a standstill. These are examples of cybercrime. In this part of the chapter, we'll discuss the three most serious types of cybercrime you need to worry about: identity theft, computer viruses, and hackers.

cybercrime and
IDENTITY THEFT

Cybercrime is any criminal action perpetrated primarily through the use of a computer. The existence of cybercrime means that computer users must take precautions to protect themselves. The FBI maintains a website (**fbi.gov/about-us/investigate/cyber/cyber**) specifically to inform the public about types of cybercrimes and methods of protecting yourself.

Who perpetrates computer crimes?
Cybercriminals are individuals who use computers, networks, and the Internet to perpetrate crime. Anyone with a computer and the wherewithal to arm him- or herself with the appropriate knowledge can be a cybercriminal.

What kinds of cybercrimes are conducted over the Internet? The Internet Crime Complaint Center (IC3) is a partnership between the FBI and the National White Collar Crime Center (NW3C). In 2011 (the latest year for which was data available at this book's publication), the IC3 received over 314,000 complaints related to Internet crime. The top four categories of complaints received are shown in Figure 9.1. FBI–related scams involve people pretending

FIGURE 9.1

Top Four Cybercrimes Reported to the IC3 in 2011

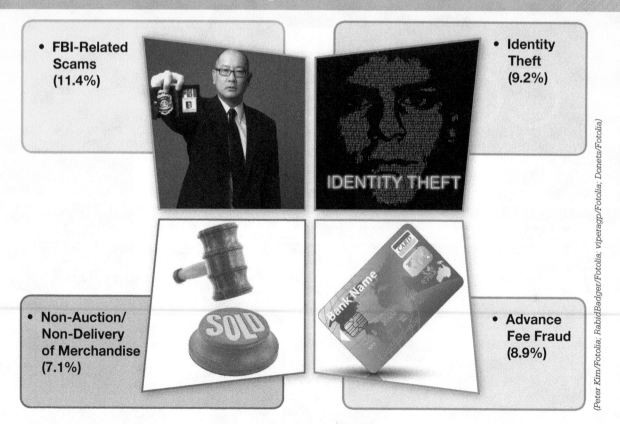

- FBI-Related Scams (11.4%)
- Identity Theft (9.2%)
- Non-Auction/Non-Delivery of Merchandise (7.1%)
- Advance Fee Fraud (8.9%)

IDENTITY THEFT

(Peter Kim/Fotolia; RabidBadger/Fotolia; viperagp/Fotolia; Donets/Fotolia) to represent official organizations, such as the FBI or Homeland Security, to defraud. Non-auction scams involve running auctions of merchandise that does not really exist, wherein the perpetrators just collect funds and disappear without delivering the promised goods. Advance fee fraud involves convincing individuals to send money as a "good faith" gesture to enable them to receive larger payments in return. The scammers then disappear with the advance fees.

Although the top four complaints all relate to some type of fraud, other complaints received involve equally serious matters such as computer intrusions (hacking), child pornography, and blackmail.

What is the most financially damaging cybercrime plaguing individuals? Theft of personal data such as bank account numbers and credit/debit card numbers is of most concern to individuals because this information is usually used for fraudulent purposes. **Identity theft** occurs when a thief steals personal information such as your name, address, Social Security number, birth date, bank account, and credit card information and runs up debts in your name. Many victims of identity theft spend months, or even years, trying to repair their credit and eliminate fraudulent debts.

What types of scams do identity thieves perpetrate? The nefarious acts cover a wide range:

- Counterfeiting your existing credit and debit cards
- Requesting changes of address on your bank and credit card statements, which makes detecting fraudulent charges take longer
- Opening new credit cards and bank accounts in your name and then writing bad checks and not paying off the credit card balances (ruining your credit rating in the process)
- Obtaining medical services under your name (you might lose coverage later if the thief's treatment exceeds the limits of your policy's covered services)
- Buying a home with a mortgage in your name, then reselling the house and absconding with the money (leaving you with the debt)

Many people believe that the only way your identity can be stolen is by a computer. However, the Federal Trade Commission (**ftc.gov**) has identified other methods thieves use to obtain others' personal information:

- Stealing purses and wallets, in which people often keep personal information such as their ATM PIN codes
- Stealing mail or looking through trash for bank statements and credit card bills
- Posing as bank or credit card company representatives and tricking people into revealing sensitive information over the phone
- Installing skimming devices on ATM machines that record information, such as account numbers and passcodes

Although foolproof protection methods don't exist, there are precautions that will help you minimize your risk, which we'll discuss later in this chapter.

With all the news coverage about identity theft and other cybercrimes, aren't people being more cautious? Although most people are aware of spam, a survey by the Messaging Anti-Abuse Working Group (MAAWG) found that half of e-mail users in North America and Europe have opened spam, some of which are designed to trick you into divulging sensitive information. The MAAWG also discovered that 46% of people who opened spam did so intentionally—out of idle curiosity, to follow links to unsubscribe to unwanted e-mails (which only brings more spam), or because they are interested in the product being touted.

Does cybercrime include the theft of computing devices? Although theft of computer equipment is not classified as a cybercrime (it is considered larceny), the theft of tablets, cell phones, notebook computers, and other portable computing devices is on the rise. The resale value for used electronic equipment is high, and the equipment can be easily sold online. ■

computer
VIRUSES

A computer **virus** is a computer program that attaches itself to another computer program (known as the *host* program) and attempts to spread to other computers when files are exchanged. Creating and disseminating computer viruses is one of the most widespread types of cybercrimes. Some viruses cause only minor annoyances, whereas others cause destruction or theft of data. Many viruses are designed to gather sensitive information such as credit card numbers.

Why are viruses such a threat to my security? Computer viruses are threatening because they are engineered to evade detection. Viruses normally attempt to hide within the code of a host program to avoid detection. And viruses are not just limited to computers. Smartphones, tablet computers, and other devices can be infected with viruses. Viruses such as SpyEye Mobile Banking are used to trick users into downloading an infected file to their phones, which then steals their online banking information.

I have an Apple computer, so I don't need to worry about viruses, do I? This is a popular misconception! Everyone, even Apple users, needs to worry about viruses. As the OS X and iOS operating systems have gained market share, the amount of virus attacks against Apple operating systems is on the rise.

What do computer viruses do? A computer virus's main purpose is to replicate itself and copy its code into as many other host files as possible. This gives the virus a greater chance of being copied to another computer system so that it can spread its infection. However, computer viruses require human interaction to spread. Although there might be a virus in a file on your computer, a virus normally can't infect your computer until the infected file is opened or executed.

Although virus replication can slow down networks, it's not usually the main threat. The majority of viruses have secondary objectives or side effects, ranging from displaying annoying messages on the computer screen to destroying files or the contents of entire hard drives.

Catching a Virus

How does my computer catch a virus? If your computer is exposed to a file infected with a virus, the virus will try to copy itself and infect a file on your computer.

Downloading infected audio and video files from peer-to-peer file-sharing sites is a major source of virus infections. Shared flash drives are also a common source of virus infection, as is e-mail. Just opening an e-mail message usually won't infect your computer with a virus, although some new viruses are launched when viewed in the preview pane of your e-mail software. Downloading or running (executing) a file that's attached to the e-mail are common ways that your computer becomes infected. Thus, be extremely wary of e-mail attachments, especially if you don't know the sender. Figure 9.2 illustrates the steps by which computer viruses are often passed from one computer to the next:

1. An individual writes a virus program, attaches it to a music file, and posts the file to a file-sharing site.
2. Unsuspecting Bill downloads the "music file" and infects his computer when he listens to the song.
3. Bill sends his cousin Fred an e-mail with the infected "music file" and contaminates Fred's tablet.
4. Fred syncs his phone with his tablet and infects his phone when he plays the music file.
5. Fred e-mails the file from his phone to Susan, one of his colleagues at work. Everyone who copies files from Susan's infected work computer, or whose computer is networked to Susan's computer, risks spreading the virus.

What types of viruses exist? Although thousands of computer viruses and variants exist, they can be grouped into six broad categories based on their behavior and method of transmission.

Boot-Sector Viruses

What are boot-sector viruses? A **boot-sector virus** replicates itself onto a hard drive's master boot record. The **master boot record** is a program that executes whenever a computer boots up, ensuring that the virus will be loaded into memory immediately, even before some virus protection programs can load. Boot-sector viruses are often transmitted by a flash drive left in a USB port. When the computer boots up with the flash drive

STEP 1: Virus creation

Hacker's computer

File-sharing server

STEP 2: Initial virus infection

Bill's computer

STEP 3: Virus spreads to another computer

Susan's work computer

STEP 5: Other computers susceptible to infection

Fred's smartphone

STEP 4: Fred infects his cell phone

Fred's tablet

FIGURE 9.2 Computer viruses are passed from one unsuspecting user to the next.

connected, the computer tries to launch a master boot record from the flash drive, which is usually the trigger for the virus to infect the hard drive.

Logic Bombs and Time Bombs

What are logic bombs and time bombs?
A **logic bomb** is a virus that is triggered when certain logical conditions are met, such as opening a file or starting a program a certain number of times. A **time bomb** is a virus that is triggered by the passage of time or on a certain date. For example, the Michelangelo virus was a famous time bomb that was set to trigger every year on March 6, Michelangelo's birthday. The effects of logic bombs and time bombs range from the display of annoying messages on the screen to the reformatting of the hard drive, which causes complete data loss.

Worms

What is a worm? Although often called a
virus, a **worm** is subtly different. Viruses require human interaction to spread, whereas worms take advantage of file transport methods, such as e-mail or network connections, to spread on their own. A virus infects a host file and waits until that file is executed to replicate and infect a computer system. A worm, however, works independently of host file execution and is much more active in spreading itself. When the Conficker worm broke out in 2008, it quickly infected up to 15 million computers. It spread through vulnerabilities in the Windows code and compromised computers by disabling certain software services and utility programs, such as Windows Update.

Script and Macro Viruses

What are script and macro viruses?
Some viruses are hidden on websites in the form of scripts. A **script** is a series of commands—actually, a miniprogram—that is executed without your knowledge. Scripts are often used to perform useful, legitimate functions on websites, such as collecting name and address information from customers. However, some scripts are malicious. For example, you might

FIGURE 9.3

Major Categories of Viruses

Boot-sector Viruses
Execute when a computer boots up

Logic Bombs/Time Bombs
Execute when certain conditions or dates are reached

Worms
Spread on their own with no human interaction needed

Script and Macro Viruses
Series of commands with malicious intent

E-mail Viruses
Spread as attachments to e-mail, often using address books

Encryption Viruses
Hold files "hostage" by encrypting them; ask for ransom to unlock them

(tribalium81/Fotolia; LoopAll/Fotolia; dedMazay/Fotolia; Theo Malings/Fotolia; Beboy/Fotolia; Andrea Danti/Fotolia)

click a link to display a video on a website, which causes a script to run that infects your computer with a virus.

A **macro virus** is a virus that attaches itself to a document that uses macros. A *macro* is a short series of commands that usually automates repetitive tasks. However, macro languages are now so sophisticated that viruses can be written with them. In 1999, the Melissa virus became the first major macro virus to cause problems worldwide.

E-Mail Viruses

What is an e-mail virus? The Melissa virus was the first practical example of an e-mail virus. **E-mail viruses** use the address book in the victim's e-mail system to distribute the virus. In the case of the Melissa virus, anyone opening an infected document triggered the virus, which infected other documents on the victim's computer. Once triggered, the Melissa virus sent itself to the first 50 people in the e-mail address book on the infected computer.

Encryption Viruses

What are encryption viruses? When **encryption viruses** infect your computer, they run a program that searches for common types of data files, such as Microsoft Word and Excel files, and compresses them using a complex encryption key that renders your files unusable. You then receive a message that asks you to send money to an account if you want to receive the program to decrypt your files. The flaw with this type of virus, which keeps it from being widespread, is that law enforcement officials can trace the payments to an account and may possibly be able to catch the perpetrators. Figure 9.3 summarizes the major categories of viruses.

Additional Virus Classifications

How else are viruses classified? Viruses can also be classified by the methods they take to avoid detection by antivirus software:

- A **polymorphic virus** changes its own code or periodically rewrites itself to avoid detection. Most

BITS&BYTES

CAPTCHA: Keeping Websites Safe from Bots

Automated programs called *bots* (or web robots) are used to make tasks easier on the Internet. For example, search engines use bots to search and index web pages. Unfortunately, bots can also be used for malicious or illegal purposes because they can perform some computing tasks faster than humans. For example, bots can be used on ticket-ordering sites to buy large blocks of high-demand concert tickets. They are also often used to post spam in the comment sections of blogs. Fortunately, website owners can deploy CAPTCHA software (see Figure 9.4) to prevent such bot activities.

CAPTCHA (Completely Automated Public Turing Test to Tell Computers and Humans Apart) programs generate distorted text and require that it be typed into a box. Because bots can't yet be programmed to read distorted text, which most people can, the CAPTCHA program can verify that a human is performing the task being tested. If you want to try integrating a CAPTCHA program into your website (to protect your e-mail address), go to **google.com/recaptcha**, which offers free CAPTCHA tools to help you protect your data.

FIGURE 9.4 CAPTCHA programs like this one verify that a human, not a bot, is performing the requested task.

polymorphic viruses infect a particular type of file such as .EXE files, for example.

- A **multipartite virus** is designed to infect multiple file types in an effort to fool the antivirus software that is looking for it.
- **Stealth viruses** temporarily erase their code from the files where they reside and then hide in the active memory of the computer. This helps them avoid detection if only the hard drive is being searched for viruses. Fortunately, current antivirus software scans memory as well as the hard drive.

Virus Symptoms

How can I tell if my computer is infected with a virus? Sometimes it can be difficult to definitively tell whether your computer is infected with a virus. However, if your computer displays any of the following symptoms, it may be infected with a virus:

1. Existing program icons or files suddenly disappear. Viruses often delete specific file types or programs.

2. If you start your browser and it takes you to an unusual home page (i.e., one you didn't set) or it has new toolbars.

3. Odd messages, pop-ups, or images are displayed on the screen, or strange music or sounds play.

4. Data files become corrupt. (However, note that files can become corrupt for reasons other than a virus infection.)

5. Programs stop working properly, which could be caused by either a corrupted file or a virus.

6. Your system slows down or takes a long time to boot up. ■

ACTIVE HELPDESK
Avoiding Computer Viruses

In this Active Helpdesk call, you'll play the role of a helpdesk staffer, fielding calls about different types of viruses and what users should do to protect their computer from them.

---

preventing virus
INFECTIONS

Antivirus software is specifically designed to detect viruses and protect your computer and files from harm. Symantec, Kaspersky, AVG, and McAfee are among the companies that offer highly rated antivirus software packages. Antivirus protection is also included in comprehensive Internet security packages such as Norton Internet Security, Kaspersky Internet Security, and McAfee Total Protection. These software packages also help protect you from threats other than computer viruses. For example, Windows 8 includes Windows Defender, which defends against malware as well as viruses.

Antivirus Software

How often do I need to run antivirus software? Although antivirus software is designed to detect suspicious activity on your computer at all times, you should run an active virus scan on your entire system at least once a week. By doing so, all files on your computer will be checked for undetected viruses.

Most modern antivirus programs run scans in the background when your CPU is not being heavily utilized. But you can also configure the software to run scans at times when you aren't using your system—for example, when you're asleep (see Figure 9.5). (However, it's important to note that your computer has to be on and not in sleep mode for these virus scans to take place.) Alternatively, if you suspect a problem, you can launch a scan and have it run immediately.

How does antivirus software work?
The main functions of antivirus software are as follows:

- *Detection:* Antivirus software looks for virus signatures in files. A **virus signature** is a portion of the virus code that's unique to a particular computer virus. Antivirus software scans files for these signatures when

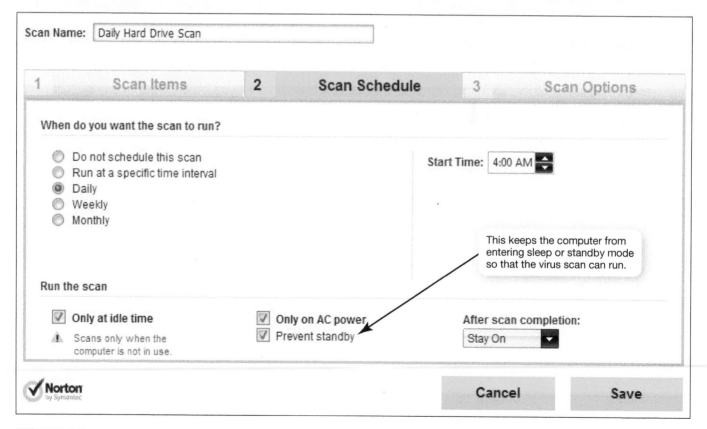

FIGURE 9.5 In Norton Internet Security, you can set up virus scans to run automatically. This computer will be scanned every day at 4 a.m.

they're opened or executed and identifies infected files and the type of virus infecting them.

- *Stopping virus execution:* If the antivirus software detects a virus signature or suspicious activity, such as the launch of an unknown macro, it stops the execution of the file and virus and notifies you that it has detected a virus. It also places the virus in a secure area on your hard drive so that it won't spread to other files; this procedure is known as **quarantining**. Usually, the antivirus software then gives you the choice of deleting or repairing the infected file. Unfortunately, antivirus programs can't always fix infected files to make them usable again. You should keep backup copies of critical files so that you can restore them in case a virus damages them irreparably.

- *Prevention of future infection:* Most antivirus software will also attempt to prevent infection by inoculating key files on your computer. In **inoculation**, the antivirus software records key attributes about your computer files, such as file size and date created, and keeps these statistics in a safe place on your hard drive. When scanning for viruses, the antivirus software compares the attributes of the files with the attributes it previously recorded to help detect attempts by virus programs to modify your files.

Does antivirus software always stop viruses?
Antivirus software catches *known* viruses effectively. However, new viruses are written all the time. To combat unknown viruses, modern antivirus programs search for suspicious virus-like activities as well as virus signatures. To minimize your risk, you should keep your antivirus software up to date.

My new computer came with antivirus software installed, so shouldn't I already be protected?
Most new computers do come with antivirus software preinstalled. However, these are usually trial versions of the software that only provide updates to the software for a limited period of time, usually 90 or 180 days. After that, you have to buy a full version of the software to ensure you remain protected from new viruses.

How do I make sure my antivirus software is up to date?
Most antivirus programs have an automatic update feature that downloads updates for virus signature files every time you go online (see Figure 9.6). Also, the antivirus software usually shows the status of your update subscription so that you can see how much time you have remaining until you need to buy another version of your software.

What should I do if I think my computer is infected with a virus?
Boot up your computer using the antivirus installation disc. This should prevent most virus programs from loading and will allow you to run the antivirus software directly from your disk drive. (*Note:* If you download your antivirus software from the Internet, copy it to a DVD in case you have problems in the future.) If the software does detect viruses, you may want to research them further to determine whether your antivirus software will eradicate them completely or whether you'll need to take additional manual steps to eliminate the viruses. Most antivirus company websites, such as the Symantec site (**symantec.com**), contain archives of information on viruses and provide step-by-step solutions for removing them.

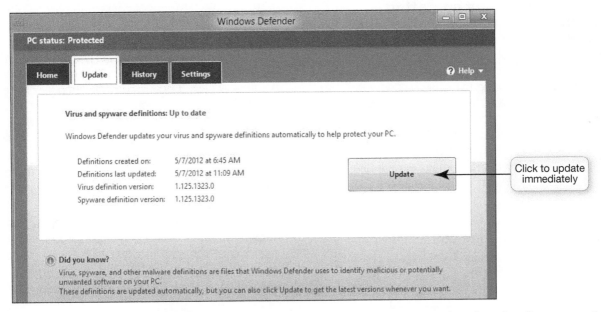

FIGURE 9.6 Antivirus software, such as Windows Defender, provides for automatic updates but also allows manual updates.

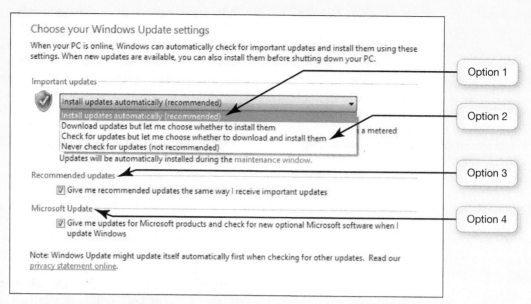

Choose your Windows Update settings

When your PC is online, Windows can automatically check for important updates and install them using these settings. When new updates are available, you can also install them before shutting down your PC.

Important updates

Install updates automatically (recommended)

Install updates automatically (recommended)
Download updates but let me choose whether to install them
Check for updates but let me choose whether to download and install them
Never check for updates (not recommended)

Updates will be automatically installed during the maintenance window.

Recommended updates

☑ Give me recommended updates the same way I receive important updates

Microsoft Update

☑ Give me updates for Microsoft products and check for new optional Microsoft software when I update Windows

Note: Windows Update might update itself automatically first when checking for other updates. Read our privacy statement online.

Option 1
Option 2
Option 3
Option 4

FIGURE 9.7 The Windows Update screen makes it easy for users to configure Windows to update itself.

>*To enable automatic updates, access the Control Panel, select **System and Security**, click the **Windows Update** link, and then click the **Change Settings** link.*

How do I protect my phone from viruses?
Because smartphones and other mobile devices run operating systems and contain files, they are susceptible to infection by viruses. Cybercriminals are now hiding viruses in legitimate-looking apps for download to mobile devices. Many antivirus software companies now offer antivirus software specifically designed for mobile devices, like Trend Micro's Mobile Security for Android.

Software Updates

Why does updating my operating system (OS) software help protect me from viruses?
Many viruses exploit weaknesses in operating systems. Malicious websites can be set up to attack your computer by downloading harmful software onto your computer. According to research conducted by Google, this type of attack, known as a **drive-by download**, affects almost 1 in 1,000 web pages. To combat these threats, make sure your OS is up to date and contains the latest security patches. You can update your Windows OS with an automatic update utility called Windows Update. When you enable automatic

 SOUND BYTE

Protecting Your Computer

In this Sound Byte, you'll learn how to use a variety of tools to protect your computer, including antivirus software and Windows utilities.

updates, your computer searches for updates on the Microsoft website every time it connects to the Internet. Mac OS X has a similar utility for gathering updates.

Do OS updates only happen automatically?
The default option in Windows is to receive updates automatically. There are several other options you can choose from in Windows, as shown in Figure 9.7. The following options are noteworthy:

- *Option 1: Install updates automatically.* Selecting this option will automatically download and install updates at a time you have specified. *We strongly recommend that you select this option.*

- *Option 2: Check for updates but let me choose whether to download and install them.* This is an appropriate choice only if you have low bandwidth Internet access. Because downloads over dial-up can take a long time, you need to control when they will occur. But you need to be extra vigilant with this option because you may forget to install important updates.

- *Option 3: Give me recommended updates.* This option ensures you receive recommended (optional) updates as well as critical (necessary) updates.

- *Option 4: Microsoft Update.* This option ensures you receive updates for other Microsoft products besides Windows, such as Microsoft Office.

If you keep both your antivirus and OS software up to date, you'll help prevent viruses from infecting your computer. ■

understanding
HACKERS

Although there's a great deal of disagreement as to what a hacker actually is, especially among hackers themselves, a **hacker** is most commonly defined as anyone who unlawfully breaks into a computer system—either an individual computer or a network (see Figure 9.8).

Are there different kinds of hackers? Some hackers are offended by being labeled as criminals and therefore attempt to classify different types of hackers as follows:

- **White-hat hackers** (or **ethical hackers**) break in to systems for nonmalicious reasons such as to test system security vulnerabilities or to expose undisclosed weaknesses. They believe in making security vulnerabilities known either to the company that owns the system or software or to the general public, often to embarrass a company into fixing a problem.

- **Black-hat hackers** break into systems to destroy information or for illegal gain. The terms *white hat* and *black hat* are references to old Western movies in which the heroes wore white hats and the outlaws wore black hats.

"Oh, we used to use a crystal ball, but hacking into your credit files is much more informative!"

FIGURE 9.8 Hackers can find lots of personal information about you on the Internet. *(Wildt, Chris/Cartoonstock)*

- **Grey-hat hackers** are a bit of a cross between black and white—they often illegally break into systems merely to flaunt their expertise to the administrator of the system they penetrated or to attempt to sell their services in repairing security breaches.

Regardless of the hackers' opinions, the laws in the United States and in many other countries consider *any* unauthorized access to computer systems a crime.

Problems Hackers Can Cause

Could a hacker steal my debit card or bank account number? Hackers often try to break in to computers or websites that contain credit card information. If you perform financial transactions online, such as banking or buying goods and services, you probably do so using a credit or debit card. Credit card and bank account information can thus reside on your hard drive or an online business's hard drive and may be detectable by a hacker.

Aside from your home computer, you have personal data stored on various websites. For example, many sites require that you provide a login ID and password to gain access. Even if this data isn't stored on your computer, a hacker may be able to capture it when you're online by using a *packet analyzer (sniffer)* or a *keylogger* (a program that captures all keystrokes made on a computer).

What's a packet analyzer? Data travels through the Internet in small pieces called *packets*. The packets are identified with an IP address, in part to help identify the computer to which they are being sent. Once the packets reach their destination, they're reassembled into cohesive messages. A **packet analyzer (sniffer)** is a program deployed by hackers that looks at (or sniffs) each packet as it travels on the Internet—not just those addressed to a particular computer, but all packets coming across a particular network. For example, a hacker might sit in a coffee shop and run a packet sniffer to capture sensitive data (such as debit/credit card numbers) from patrons using the coffee shop's free wireless network. Wireless networks such as these can be particularly vulnerable to this type of exploitation if encryption of data isn't enabled when the networks are set up. (This topic was covered in more detail in Chapter 7.)

What do hackers do with the information they "sniff"?

Once a hacker has your debit/credit card information, he or she can use it to purchase items illegally or can sell the number to someone who will. If a hacker steals the login ID and password to an account where you have your bank card information stored (such as eBay or Amazon), he or she can also use your account to buy items and have them shipped to him- or herself instead of to you. If hackers can gather enough information in conjunction with your credit card information, they may be able to commit identity theft.

Although this sounds scary, you can easily protect yourself from packet sniffing by installing a firewall (which we discuss later in this chapter) and using data encryption on a wireless network (which was covered in Chapter 7).

Trojan Horses and Rootkits

Besides stealing information, what other problems can hackers cause if they break into my computer? Hackers often use individuals' computers as a staging area for mischief. To commit widespread computer attacks, for example, hackers need to control many computers at the same time. To this end, hackers often use Trojan horses to install other programs on computers. A **Trojan horse** is a program that appears to be something useful or desirable, like a game or a screen saver, but while it runs, it does something malicious in the background, without your knowledge (see Figure 9.9).

What damage can Trojan horses do? Often, the malicious activity perpetrated by a Trojan horse program is the installation of a backdoor program or a rootkit. **Backdoor programs** and **rootkits** are programs (or sets of programs) that allow hackers to gain access to your computer and take almost complete control of it without your knowledge. Using a backdoor program, hackers can access and delete all the files on your computer, send e-mail, run programs, and do just about anything else you can do with your computer. A computer that a hacker controls in this manner is referred to as a **zombie**. Zombies are often used to launch *denial-of-service attacks* on other computers.

Denial-of-Service Attacks

What are denial-of-service attacks? In a **denial-of-service (DoS) attack**, legitimate users are denied access to a computer system because a hacker is repeatedly making requests of that computer system through a computer he or she has taken over as a zombie. A computer system can handle only a certain number of requests for information at one time. When it is flooded with requests in a DoS attack, it shuts down and refuses to answer any requests for information, even if the requests are from a legitimate user. Thus, the computer is so busy responding to the bogus requests for information that authorized users can't gain access.

Couldn't a DoS attack be traced back to the computer that launched it? Launching a DoS attack on a computer system from a single computer is easy to trace. Therefore, most savvy hackers use a **distributed denial-of-service (DDoS) attack**, which launches DoS attacks from more than one zombie (sometimes thousands of zombies) at the same time.

Figure 9.10 illustrates how a DDoS attack works. A hacker creates many zombies and coordinates them so that they begin sending bogus requests to the same computer at the same time. Administrators of the victim computer often have a great deal of difficulty stopping the attack because it comes from so many computers. Often, the attacks are coordinated automatically by botnets. A **botnet** is a large group of software programs (called *robots* or *bots*) that runs autonomously on zombie computers. Some botnets have been known to span 1.5 million computers.

Because many commercial websites receive revenue from users, either directly (such as via subscriptions to online games) or indirectly (such as when web surfers click on advertisements), DDoS attacks can be financially distressing for the owners of the affected websites.

FIGURE 9.9 The term *Trojan horse* derives from Greek mythology and refers to the wooden horse that the Greeks used to sneak into the city of Troy and conquer it. Therefore, computer programs that contain a hidden, and usually dreadful, "surprise" are referred to as Trojan horses. *(Ralf Kraft/Fotolia)*

Hacker launches DDoS by activating zombies (red lines)

Hacker's computer

Academic computer (zombie)

Government computer (zombie)

Home computer (zombie)

Corporate computer (zombie)

Internet Service Provider computer (zombie)

Zombie computers attack target system (blue lines)

Victim of DDoS

FIGURE 9.10 Zombie computers are used to facilitate a DDoS attack.

BITS&BYTES

Are Your Photos Helping Criminals Target You?

All cell phones today contain GPS chips. The cameras in phones often use information gathered from the GPS chips to encode information onto photos in the form of geotags. A **geotag** is a piece of data attached to a photo that indicates your latitude and longitude when you took the photo. Geotagging is useful for applications that can take advantage of this information, but problems arise when you share geotagged photos on the web.

If you post a lot of photos, cybercriminals and cyberstalkers can use the information from the geotags on your photos to figure out the patterns of your movements. They may be able to ascertain when you're at work or that you're currently on vacation, which leads them to determine prime times for burglarizing your home. Some sites such as Facebook and Twitter have measures in place to limit the amount of geotagged information that can be seen in photos in order to prevent their users from unwittingly revealing personal information. However, many photo-sharing sites don't have such protections in place.

The safest thing to do is not tag your photos with geotags in the first place. It's usually easy to disable location tracking on your smartphone. For instance, on the iPhone, on the Settings screen, select General, then Location Services, and choose Off. So stop geotagging your photos, and make it tougher for the cybercriminals to figure out your movements.

FIGURE 9.11 Open logical ports are an invitation to hackers.

How Hackers Gain Computer Access

How exactly does a hacker gain access to a computer? Hackers can gain access to computers directly or indirectly:

- Direct access involves sitting down at a computer and installing hacking software. It's unlikely that such an attack would occur in your home, but it's always a wise precaution to set up your computer so that it requires a password for a user to gain access.

- The most likely method a hacker will use to access a computer is to enter indirectly through its Internet connection.

Many people forget that their Internet connection is a two-way street. Not only can you access the Internet, but people on the Internet can access your computer. Think of your computer as a house. Common sense tells you to lock your home's doors and windows to deter theft when you aren't there. Hooking your computer up to the Internet without protection is like leaving the front door to your house wide open. Your computer obviously

doesn't have doors and windows like a house, but it does have logical ports.

What are logical ports? Logical ports are virtual—that is, not physical—communications gateways or paths that allow a computer to organize requests for information, such as web page downloads or e-mail routing, from other networks or computers. Unlike physical ports, such as USB ports, you can't see or touch a logical port; it's part of a computer's internal organization.

Logical ports are numbered and assigned to specific services. For instance, logical port 80 is designated for hypertext transfer protocol (HTTP), the main communications protocol for the web. Thus, all requests for information from your browser to the web flow through logical port 80. Open logical ports, like open windows in a home, invite intruders, as illustrated in Figure 9.11. Unless you take precautions to restrict access to your logical ports, other people on the Internet may be able to access your computer through them.

Fortunately, you can thwart most hacking problems by installing a firewall, which we discuss next. ■

restricting access to your
DIGITAL ASSETS

Keeping hackers at bay is often just a matter of keeping them out. You can achieve this by:

- Preventing hackers from accessing your computer (usually through your Internet connection)
- Protecting your digital information in such a way that it can't be accessed (by using passwords, for example)
- Hiding your activities from prying eyes

In this section, we explore strategies for protecting access to your digital assets and keeping your Internet-surfing activities from being seen by the wrong people.

Firewalls

What is a firewall? A **firewall** is a software program or hardware device designed to protect computers from hackers. It's named after a housing construction feature that slows the spread of fires from house to house. A firewall specifically designed for home networks is called a **personal firewall**. By using a personal firewall, you can close open logical ports to invaders and potentially make your computer invisible to other computers on the Internet.

Which is better, a software firewall or a hardware firewall? Both hardware and software firewalls will protect you from hackers. One type isn't better than the other. Although installing either a software or a hardware firewall on your home network is probably sufficient, you should consider installing both for maximum protection. This will provide you with additional safety, just as wearing multiple layers of clothing helps keep you warmer in the winter than a single layer.

Types of Firewalls

What software firewalls are there? Both Windows and OS X include reliable firewalls. The Windows Action Center is a good source of information about the security settings on your computer (see Figure 9.12), including the status of your firewall. Security suites such as Norton Internet Security, McAfee

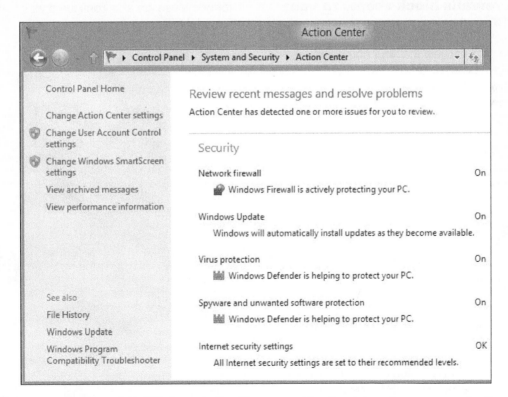

FIGURE 9.12 The security section of the Windows Action Center provides the status of programs protecting your computer. >*To view the Action Center, access the Control Panel, select* **System and Security***, and then click the* **Action Center** *link.*

Internet Security, and ZoneAlarm Internet Security Suite also include firewall software. Although the firewalls that come with Windows and OS X will protect your computer, firewalls included in security suites often come with additional features such as monitoring systems that alert you if your computer is under attack.

If you're using a security suite that includes a firewall, the suite should disable the firewall that came with your OS. Two firewalls running at the same time can conflict with each other and cause your computer to slow down or freeze up.

What are hardware firewalls? You can also buy and configure hardware firewall devices. Many routers sold for home networks include firewall protection. Just like software firewalls, the setup for hardware firewalls is designed for novices, and the default configuration on most routers keeps unused logical ports closed. Documentation accompanying routers can assist more-experienced users in adjusting the settings to allow access to specific ports if needed.

How Firewalls Work

How do firewalls protect you from hackers? Firewalls are designed to restrict access to a network and its computers. Firewalls protect you in two major ways:

1. By blocking access to logical ports and
2. By keeping your computer's network address secure

How do firewalls block access to your logical ports? Certain logical ports are very popular in hacker attacks. To block access to logical ports, firewalls examine data packets that your computer sends and receives. Data packets contain information such as the address of the sending and receiving computers and the logical port the packet will use. Firewalls can be configured so that they filter out packets sent to specific logical ports in a process known as **packet filtering**. Firewalls are also often configured to ignore requests that originate from the Internet asking for access to certain ports. This process is referred to as **logical port blocking**. By using filtering and blocking, firewalls keep hackers from accessing your computer (Figure 9.13).

How do firewalls keep your network address secure? Every computer connected to the Internet has a unique address called an *Internet Protocol address (IP address)*. Data is routed to the correct computer on the Internet based on the IP address. This is similar to how a letter finds its way to your mailbox. You have a unique postal address for your home. If a hacker

finds out the IP address of your computer, he or she can locate it on the Internet and try to break into it. This is similar to how a conventional thief might target your home after finding out you collect antique cars by using your street address to locate your house.

Your IP address for your home network is assigned to your router by your Internet service provider (ISP), but each device on your home network also has an IP address. Firewalls use a process called **network address translation (NAT)** to assign internal IP addresses on a network. The internal IP addresses are used only on the internal network and therefore can't be detected by hackers. For hackers to access your computer, they must know your computer's internal IP address. With a NAT–capable router/firewall installed on your network, hackers are unable to access the internal IP address assigned to your computer, so your computer is safe. You can use NAT in your home by purchasing a hardware firewall with NAT capabilities. Many routers sold for home use are also configured as firewalls, and many feature NAT.

FIGURE 9.13 Firewalls use filtering and blocking to keep out unwanted data and keep your network safe.
(Intelligent Computer Solutions)

Knowing Your Computer Is Secure

How can I tell if my computer is at risk? For peace of mind, you can visit websites that offer free services that test your computer's vulnerability. One popular site is Gibson Research (**grc.com**). The company's ShieldsUP and LeakTest programs are free and easy to run and can pinpoint security vulnerabilities in a system connected to the Internet. If you get a clean report from these programs, your system is probably not vulnerable to attack. See the Try This section in this chapter (page 380) for instructions on how to test your system.

What if I don't get a clean report from the testing program? If the testing program detects potential vulnerabilities and you don't have a firewall, you should install one as soon as possible. If the firewall is already configured and common ports (such as those shown in Figure 9.14) are identified as being vulnerable, consult your firewall documentation for instructions on how to close or restrict access to those ports.

Password Protection and Password Management

How can I best use passwords to protect my computer? You no doubt have many passwords you need to remember to access your digital life. However, creating strong passwords—ones that are difficult for hackers to guess—is an essential piece of security

FIGURE 9.14

Common Logical Ports

PORT NUMBER	PROTOCOL USING THE PORT
21	FTP (File Transfer Protocol) control
23	Telnet (unencrypted text communications)
25	SMTP (Simple Mail Transfer Protocol)
53	DNS (domain name system)
80	HTTP (Hypertext Transfer Protocol)
443	HTTPS (HTTP with Transport Layer Security [TLS] encryption)

that people sometimes overlook. Password-cracking programs have become more sophisticated. In fact, some commonly available programs can test more than one million password combinations per second! Creating a secure password is therefore more important than ever.

Many people use extremely weak passwords. The Imperva Application Defense Center, a computer-security research organization, conducted a review of 32 million passwords that were used at the website **rockyou.com**. More than 345,000 people were using "12345," "123456," or "123456789" as their password. And almost 62,000 people were using "password"! Passwords such as these are easy for hackers to crack.

Websites that need to be very secure, such as those for financial institutions, usually have strong defenses to prevent hackers from cracking passwords. But sites that need less security, such as casual gaming or social networking sites, might have less protection. Hackers attack poorly defended sites for passwords because many people use the same password for every site they use. So if a hacker can get your password from a poorly secured gaming site, they might be able to access your bank account with the same password.

Creating Passwords

What constitutes a strong password? Strong passwords are difficult for someone to guess. Follow these guidelines to create strong passwords (see Figure 9.15):

- Don't use easily deduced components related to your life, such as parts of your name, your pet's name, your street address, or the name of the website or institution for which you are creating the password (i.e., don't use "Citibank" for your online banking password).
- Use a password that is at least 14 characters long. Longer passwords are more difficult to deduce.
- Don't use words found in the dictionary.
- Use a mix of upper- and lowercase letters and symbols (such as # or %).
- Never tell anyone your password or write it down in a place where others might see it, like in your wallet or purse.
- Change your passwords on a regular basis, such as monthly or quarterly. Your school or your employer probably requires you to change your password regularly. This is also a good idea for your personal passwords.
- Don't use the same password for every account you have.

If you have trouble thinking of secure passwords, there are many password generators available for

FIGURE 9.15

Strong and Weak Password Candidates

PASSWORD	RATING	GOOD POINTS	BAD POINTS
Joysmith1022	Poor	• None	• Less than 14 characters • Contains name and birth date
test44drive6car	Mediocre	• 15 characters in length	• Contains three words found in the dictionary • Numbers repeated consecutively
8$RanT%5ydTTtt&	Better	• Good length • Contains upper- and lowercase letters • Contains symbols	• Upper- and lowercase letters repeated consecutively • Still contains one dictionary word (rant)
7R3m3mB3R$5%y38	Best	• All good points from above • Dictionary word (remember) has 3s instead of Es	• None

free, such as the Strong Password Generator (**strongpasswordgenerator.com**).

How can I check the strength of my passwords? You can use online password strength testers, such as the Password Meter (**passwordmeter.com**), to evaluate your passwords. The Password Meter provides guidelines for good passwords and shows you how integrating various elements, such as symbols, affects the strength score of your password.

How do I restrict access to my computer? Windows, OS X, and most other operating systems have built-in password (or passcode) protection for files as well as the entire desktop. After a certain period of idle time, your computer is automatically password locked, and your password must be entered to gain access to the computer. This provides excellent protection from casual snooping if you need to walk away from your computer for a period of time. If someone attempts to log on to your computer without your password, that person won't be able to gain access. It's an especially good idea to use passwords on laptop computers, smartphones, and tablets because this provides additional protection of your data if your device is lost or stolen.

Windows 8 allows you to use picture

passwords. You select a picture and then draw three gestures on it—either straight lines, circles, or taps. This picture then works as an additional method for accessing your computer. You just unlock your computer by repeating the gestures (see Figure 9.16). But if you forget your gestures, you can always access your computer via the conventional password.

Managing Your Passwords

How can I remember all of my complex passwords? Good security practices suggest that you have different passwords for all the different websites that you access and that you change your passwords frequently. The problem with well-constructed passwords is that they can be hard to remember. Fortunately, password-management tools are now available.

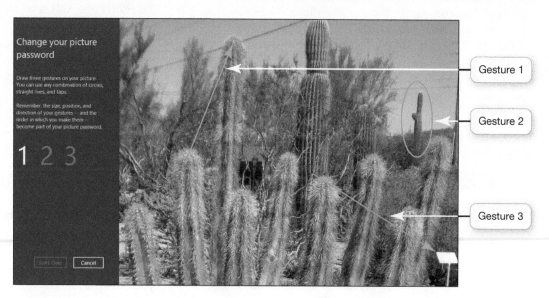

FIGURE 9.16 Drawing three gestures on your picture (and repeating them three times) sets your picture password options in Windows 8.

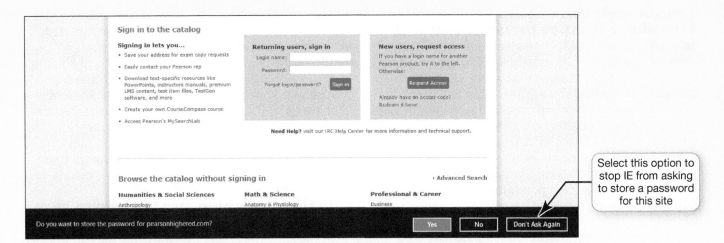

FIGURE 9.17 The password bar in IE 10 displays whenever you type in a password for a website for which IE hasn't yet stored the password.

BITS&BYTES

Connecting to Wireless Networks on the Road? Beware of "Evil Twins"!

Say you're away from campus and need to connect to a wireless network. You switch on your laptop, and the wireless network adapter finds a network called "free wifi" or "airport wireless." You connect, enter your credit card information to buy some books from Amazon. com, and start merrily surfing away. Three days later, your credit card company calls asking about the $2,400 big-screen TV you just bought at the local electronics store. You didn't make this purchase; you probably fell prey to an "evil twin" wireless hotspot.

Hackers know the areas where people are likely to seek access to wireless networks. They'll often set up their own wireless networks in these areas with sound-alike names to lure unsuspecting web surfers. These "evil twins" offer free Internet access, and the hackers monitor traffic looking for sensitive information they can use.

So how can you protect yourself? Check with authorized personnel at places where you'll be connecting to hotspots to determine the names of the legitimate ones. If you run across "free" access to a hotspot that isn't provided by a legitimate merchant, you're better off not connecting at all because you can't be sure your information won't be used against you or that malicious files won't be downloaded to your computer.

They take the worry out of forgetting passwords because the password-management software does the remembering for you.

Where can I obtain password-management software? Most current Internet security suites and web browsers make it easy to keep track of passwords by providing password-management tools. For example, Internet Explorer (IE) 10 will remember passwords for you. When you go to a website that requires a login, IE 10 will display a dialog box prompting you to have IE remember the password for the site (see Figure 9.17). Then, when you return to the site and type in your user name, IE will fill in the password information for you using a process known as auto complete. However, there are some passwords that you shouldn't have your browser remember, such as your online banking password. So be selective when using this feature.

Anonymous Web Surfing: Hiding from Prying Eyes

Should I be concerned about surfing the Internet on shared, public, or work computers? If you use shared computers in public places such as libraries, coffee shops, or student unions, you never know what nefarious tools have been installed by hackers on a public computer. When you browse the Internet, traces of your activity are left behind on that computer, often as temporary files. A wily hacker can glean sensitive information long after you've finished your surfing session. In addition, many employers routinely review the Internet browsing history of employees to ensure that workers are spending their time on the Internet productively.

What tools can I use to keep my browsing activities private when surfing the Internet? The current versions of Google Chrome, Firefox, and Internet Explorer include privacy tools (called Incognito, Private Browsing, and InPrivate, respectively) that help you surf the web anonymously (see Figure 9.18). When you choose to surf anonymously, all three browsers open special versions of their browser windows that are enhanced for privacy. When surfing in these windows, records of websites you visit and files you download don't appear in the web browser's history files. Furthermore, any temporary files generated in that browsing session are deleted when you exit the special window.

Are there any other tools I could use to protect my privacy? Portable privacy devices, such as the Imation Personal Flash Drive (**imation.com**), provide an even higher level of surfing privacy. Simply plug the device into an available USB port on the machine on which you'll be working. All sensitive Internet files, such as cookies, Internet history, and browser caches, will be stored on the privacy device, not on the computer you're using. Privacy devices such as these often come pre-loaded with software designed to shield your IP address from prying eyes, making it difficult (if not impossible) for hackers to tell where you're surfing on the Internet. These privacy devices also have password-management tools that store all of your login information and encrypt it so it will be safe if your privacy device falls into someone else's hands.

Is there anything else I can do to keep my data safe on shared computers? Another free practical solution is to take the Linux OS with you on a flash drive and avoid using the public or work computer's OS. The interfaces of many Linux distros look almost exactly like Windows and are easy to use. There are several

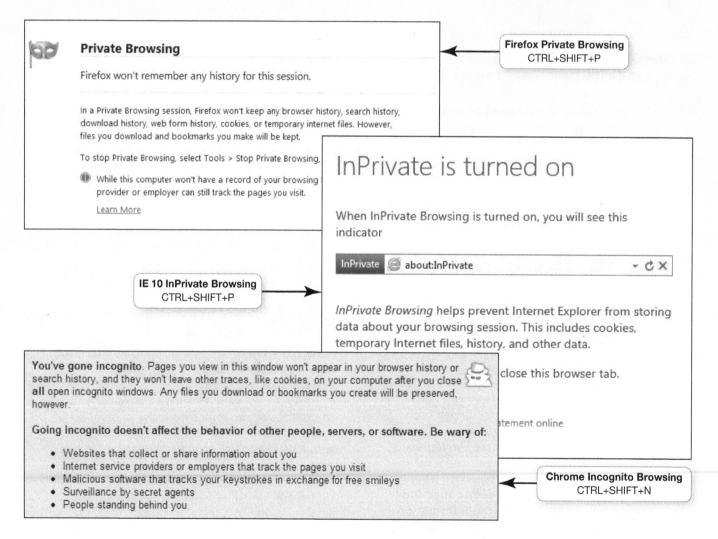

FIGURE 9.18 The current versions of the Firefox, Internet Explorer, and Google Chrome browsers all feature privacy tools for web surfing.

advantages to using a Linux-based OS on a public or work computer:

- Your risk of picking up viruses and other malicious programs is significantly reduced because booting a computer from a flash drive completely eliminates any interaction with the computer's OS. This, in turn, significantly reduces the chance that your flash drive will become infected by any malware running on the computer.

- Virus and hacking attacks against Linux are far less likely than attacks against Windows. Because Windows has about 90% of the OS market, people who write malware tend to target Windows systems.

- When you run software from your own storage medium, such as a flash drive, you avoid reading and writing to the hard disk of the computer. This significantly enhances your privacy because you don't leave traces of your activity behind.

Pendrivelinux (**pendrivelinux.com**) is an excellent resource that offers many different versions of Linux for download and includes step-by-step instructions on how to install them on your flash drive (see Figure 9.19). If you're a Mac user, the gOS version of Linux provides a close approximation of OS X, so you can feel right at home.

Do I need to take special precautions with my tablet devices? Tablets like the iPad run their own proprietary operating systems that differ from the operating systems deployed on laptop and desktop computers. Although tablet operating systems do contain security features, they may not be robust enough to satisfy business users who have a great deal of confidential information on their tablets, especially when the devices are connected to wireless networks. Third-party software developers are now offering many apps to enhance tablet security. Comprehensive suites like IPVanish (**ipvanish.com**) offer features such as government-grade encryption of data, enhanced e-mail security, and anonymous web surfing. So look for security apps that are specifically designed for your tablet device if you often deal with sensitive data on your tablet, such as online banking.

Biometric Authentication Devices

Besides passwords, how else can I restrict the use of my computer? A **biometric authentication device** is a device that reads a unique personal characteristic such as a fingerprint or the iris pattern in your eye and converts its pattern to a digital code. When you use the device, your pattern is read and compared to the one stored on the computer. Only users having an exact fingerprint or iris pattern match are allowed to access the computer.

Because no two people have the same biometric characteristics (fingerprints and iris patterns are

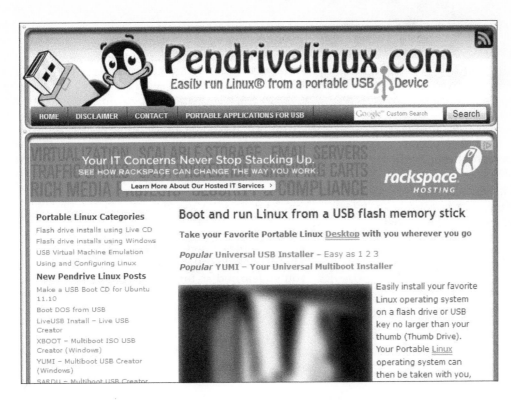

FIGURE 9.19 Pendrivelinux.com can help you load a version of Linux onto a flash drive.

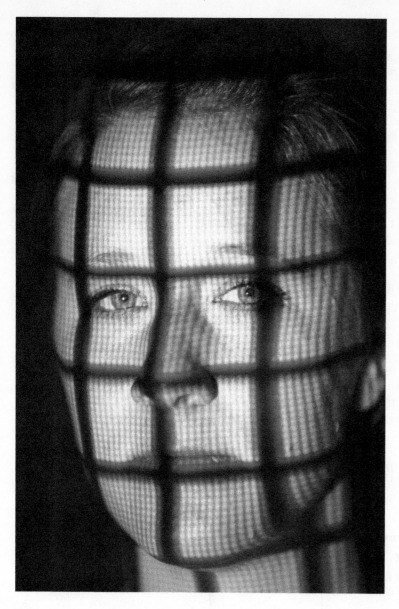

FIGURE 9.20 Face recognition software is now available on laptops. You might forget your password, but you won't forget to bring your face! *(Jochen Tack/Alamy)*

unique), these devices provide a high level of security. They also eliminate the human error that can occur in password protection. You might forget your password, but you won't forget to bring your fingerprint to the computer! Some notebooks, such as Lenovo, feature built-in fingerprint readers, and companies like SecuGen produce computer mice and keyboards that include built-in fingerprint readers. Other biometric devices, including voice authentication and face pattern–recognition systems (see Figure 9.20), are now widely offered in notebook computers.

Make sure to use some (or all) of these methods to keep your activities from prying eyes and to restrict access to your digital information. ■

Before moving on to Part 2:
- Watch Replay Video 9.1 ▶.
- Then check your understanding of what you've learned so far.

check your understanding//

For a quick review to see what you've learned so far, answer the following questions. Visit **pearsonhighered.com/techinaction** to check your answers.

multiple choice

1. When a hacker steals personal information with the intent of impersonating another individual to commit fraud, this is known as

  a. impersonation theft.   **c.** identity theft.

  b. scareware theft.   **d.** malware theft.

2. Viruses that compress files and then demand money to restore them are known as

  a. boot-sector viruses.   **c.** polymorphic viruses.

  b. script viruses.   **d.** encryption viruses.

3. Software designed to close logical ports in your computer is known as a(n)

  a. firewall.   **c.** anti-malware blocker.

  b. packet filter.   **d.** network address translator.

4. Which tool do hackers use to gain access to and take control of your computer?

  a. stealth viruses

  b. backdoor programs

  c. scareware

  d. phishing software

5. A computer that a hacker has gained control of in order to launch DoS attacks is known as a _____ computer.

  a. rootkit

  b. compromised

  c. zombie

  d. breached

true–false

_____ **1.** Password strength is only determined by the length of the password.

_____ **2.** Hackers that break into systems for nonmalicious reasons, such as to test security systems, are known as white-hat hackers.

critical thinking

1. Protecting Your Data from Data Breaches

You most likely have provided personal information to many websites and companies. Consider the following:

a. What information have you provided to companies that you wish you had never disclosed? What types of information have companies asked you that you believe was unnecessary? List specific companies and examples of the extraneous information.

b. If customers' personal information is exposed in a data breach:

- How should customers be informed of the breach (e-mail, snail mail, phone call)? What reassurances should the company provide?

- If information is exposed that might lead to identity theft, should the company be responsible for compensating affected customers? Should the company be required to provide credit report monitoring to affected customers to help detect potential identity theft? For what period of time should the company accept responsibility for any identity theft that occurs?

2. Password Protection

You know from reading this chapter that secure passwords are essential to protecting your digital information. Consider the following:

a. How many online accounts do you have that have passwords? List them. Are the passwords for these accounts secure, based on the suggestions proposed in this chapter? Do you change your passwords on a regular basis?

b. How do you keep track of all of your passwords? Do you use password-management features in your browser? If so, which browser are you using? If you don't use password-management in your browser, what methodology do you use for remembering and tracking your passwords?

Continue

TRY **THIS**

Testing Your
Network Security

A properly installed firewall should keep you relatively safe from wily hackers. But how do you know if your computer system is safe? Many websites help test your security. In this exercise, we'll use tools provided by Gibson Research (**grc.com**) to test the strength of your protection.

Step 1 Open a web browser and navigate to **grc.com**. From the pull-down Services menu at the top of the screen, select **ShieldsUP!**

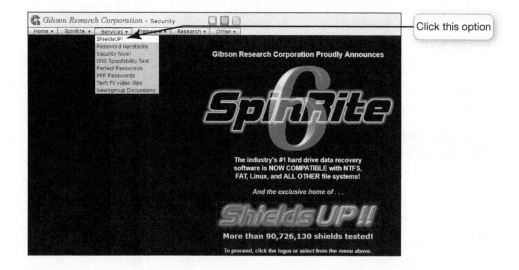

Click this option

Step 2 On the ShieldsUP! welcome screen, click the **Proceed** button.

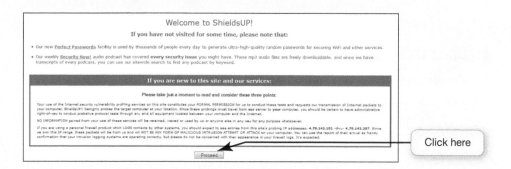

Click here

Step 3 Click the **Common Ports** link to begin the security test. It will take a few moments for the results to appear, depending on the speed of your Internet connection.

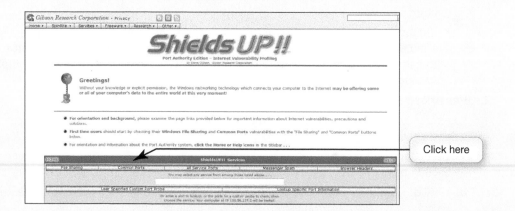

Click here

Step 4 Hopefully, you'll see a report indicating your computer has passed the TruStealth analysis test. This means that your computer is very safe from attack. However, don't panic if your results say **failed for true stealth analysis**. Consider these common issues:

- Ports that only report as being closed will result in a TruStealth analysis failure. As long as all common ports are reporting as stealth or closed, you are well protected. However, if any ports report as being open, this means your computer could be exposed to hackers. Consult your firewall documentation to resolve the problem.

- Another common failure on the TruStealth test is ping reply. This means GRC attempted to contact your computer using a method called ping and it replied to the GRC computer. This is not a serious problem. It just means it's a little easier for a hacker to tell your computer network is there, but that doesn't mean that a hacker can break in. Often your ISP has your home modem configured to reply to ping requests to facilitate remote diagnostics if there is ever a problem with your modem. As long as your ports are closed (or stealthed), your system should still be secure.

Port Authority Edition – Internet Vulnerability Profiling
by Steve Gibson, Gibson Research Corporation.

Checking the Most Common and Troublesome Internet Ports

This Internet Common Ports Probe attempts to establish standard TCP Internet connections with a collection of standard, well-known, and often vulnerable or troublesome Internet ports on **YOUR** computer. Since this is being done from **our** server, successful connections demonstrate which of your ports are "open" or visible and soliciting connections from passing Internet port scanners.

Your computer at IP:

108.36.157.2

Is being profiled. Please stand by. . .

Total elapsed testing time: 4.995 seconds

      TruStealth Analysis

Your system has achieved a **perfect** "TruStealth" rating. **Not a single packet** — solicited or otherwise — was received from your system as a result of our security probing tests. Your system ignored and refused to reply to repeated Pings (ICMP Echo Requests). From the standpoint of the passing probes of any hacker, this machine does not exist on the Internet. Some questionable personal security systems expose their users by attempting to "counter-probe the prober", thus revealing themselves. But your system wisely remained silent in every way. Very nice.

Port	Service	Status	Security Implications
0	<nil>	Stealth	There is NO EVIDENCE WHATSOEVER that a port (or even any computer) exists at this IP address!
21	FTP	Stealth	There is NO EVIDENCE WHATSOEVER that a port (or even any computer) exists at this IP address!
22	SSH	Stealth	There is NO EVIDENCE WHATSOEVER that a port (or even any computer) exists at this IP address!
23	Telnet	Stealth	There is NO EVIDENCE WHATSOEVER that a port (or even any computer) exists at this IP address!

Protecting Your Digital Property from Yourself

Often, we can be our own worst enemies when using computing devices. If you're not careful, you might be taken in by thieves or scam artists who want to steal your digital and physical assets. Being aware of the tricks and traps that criminals use allows you to take steps to avoid being scammed.

 managing online

ANNOYANCES

Surfing the web, sending and receiving e-mail, and chatting online have become common parts of most of our lives. Unfortunately, the web has become fertile ground for people who want to advertise their products, track our browsing behaviors, or even con people into revealing personal information. In this section, we'll look at ways in which you can manage, if not avoid, these and other online headaches.

Malware: Adware and Spyware

What is malware? Malware is software that has a malicious intent (hence the prefix *mal*). There are three primary forms of malware: adware, spyware, and viruses. Adware and spyware are not physically destructive like viruses and worms, which can destroy data. Known collectively as *grayware*, most malware is intrusive, annoying, or objectionable online programs that are downloaded to your computer when you install or use other online content such as a free program, game, or utility.

What is adware? Adware is software that displays sponsored advertisements in a section of your browser window or as a pop-up box. It's considered a legitimate, though sometimes annoying, means of generating revenue for those developers who do not charge for their software or information. Fortunately, because web browsers such as Firefox, Safari, and Internet Explorer

have built-in pop-up blockers, the occurrence of annoying pop-ups has been greatly reduced.

Some pop-ups, however, are legitimate and increase the functionality of the originating site. For example, your account balance may pop up on your bank's website. To control which sites to allow pop-ups on, you can access the pop-up blocker settings in your browser (see Figure 9.21) and add websites

FIGURE 9.21 Firefox's Allowed Sites - Pop-ups dialog box lets you control which sites you'll allow to display pop-ups.

>*To display the pop-up blocker in Firefox, from the Tools menu, select* **Options**, *and then click the* **Content** *tab.*

ethics in IT

Think you aren't being closely watched by your employer? Think again! A recent survey of employers by the American Management Association and the ePolicy Institute revealed that, of the employers surveyed:

- 73% monitored e-mail messages
- 66% monitored web surfing
- 48% monitored activities using video surveillance
- 45% monitored keystrokes and keyboard time
- 43% monitored computer files in some other fashion

As you can see, there is a high probability that you're being monitored while you work and when you access the Internet via your employer's Internet connection.

The two most frequently cited reasons for employee monitoring are to prevent theft and to measure productivity. Monitoring for theft isn't new—monitoring cameras have been around for years, and productivity monitoring has been used for assembly line workers for decades. However, the Internet has led to a new type of productivity drain of concern to employers. **Cyberloafing**, or cyberslacking, means using your computer for nonwork activities while you're being paid to do your job. Examples of cyberloafing activities include playing games and reading personal e-mail. Some employees even do multiple nonwork tasks at the same time, which is known as *multishirking*. Estimates of business productivity losses due to cyberloafing top $50 billion annually.

Do you have a right to privacy in the workplace? Laws such as the 1986 Electronic Communications Privacy Act (ECPA), which prohibits unauthorized monitoring of electronic communications, have been interpreted by the courts in favor of employers. The bottom line is that employers who pay for equipment and software have the *legal* right to monitor their usage (see Figure 9.22).

So, is it *ethical* for employers to monitor their employees? Certainly, it seems fair that employers ensure they're not the victims of theft and that they're getting a fair day's work from their employees, just as employees have an obligation to provide a fair effort for a fair wage. The ethical issue is whether employees are adequately informed of monitoring policies. Employers have an ethical responsibility (and a legal one as well, depending on the jurisdiction) not to place monitoring devices in sensitive locations such as bathrooms and dressing areas. However, in many states, the employer does not legally need to inform employees in advance that they're being monitored. Conscientious employers include monitoring disclosures in published employee policies to avoid confusion and conflict.

The bottom line? Because employers may have a legal right to monitor you in the workplace, operate under the assumption that everything you do on your work computer is subject to scrutiny and behave accordingly. Do your online shopping at home!

FIGURE 9.22 George Orwell was right—at least when you're at work! It's legal for employers to monitor your computer usage. *(SVLuma/Shutterstock)*

FIGURE 9.23 After performing a routine scan of a computer, Malwarebytes returns a log of problems found on the system.

for which you allow pop-ups. Whenever a pop-up is blocked, the browser displays an information bar or plays a sound to alert you. If you feel the pop-up is legitimate, you can choose to accept it.

What is spyware? **Spyware** is an unwanted piggyback program that usually downloads with other software you install from the Internet and that runs in the background of your system. Without your knowledge, spyware transmits information about you, such as your Internet-surfing habits, to the owner of the program so that the information can be used for marketing purposes. Many spyware programs use tracking cookies (small text files stored on your computer) to collect information. One type of spyware program known as a **keystroke logger (key logger)** monitors keystrokes with the intent of stealing passwords, login IDs, or credit card information.

Can I prevent spyware from spying on me? Anti-spyware software detects unwanted programs and allows you to delete the offending software easily. Most Internet security suites now include anti-spyware software. You can also obtain stand-alone anti-spyware software and run it on your computer to delete unwanted spyware. Because so many variants of spyware exist, your Internet security software may not detect all types that attempt to install themselves on your computer. Therefore, it's a good idea to install one or two additional stand-alone anti-spyware programs on your computer.

Because new spyware is created all the time, you should update and run your anti-spyware software regularly. Windows comes with a program called Windows Defender, which scans your system for spyware and other potentially unwanted software. Malwarebytes Anti-Malware, Ad-Aware, and Spybot–Search & Destroy (all available from **download.com**) are other anti-spyware programs that are easy to install and update. Figure 9.23 shows an example of Malwarebytes in action.

Spam

How can I best avoid spam? Companies that send out **spam**—unwanted or junk e-mail—find your e-mail address either from a list they purchase or with software that looks for e-mail addresses on the Internet. Unsolicited instant messages are also a form of spam, called *spim*. If you've used your e-mail address to purchase anything online, open an online account, or participate in a social network such as Facebook, your e-mail address eventually will appear on one of the lists that spammers get.

One way to avoid spam in your primary account is to create a free e-mail address that you use only when you fill out forms or buy items on the web. For example, both Windows Mail and Yahoo! let you set up free e-mail accounts. If your free e-mail account is saturated with spam, you can abandon that account with little inconvenience. It's much less convenient to abandon your primary e-mail address.

Another way to avoid spam is to filter it. A **spam filter** is an option you can select in your e-mail account that places known or suspected spam messages into a

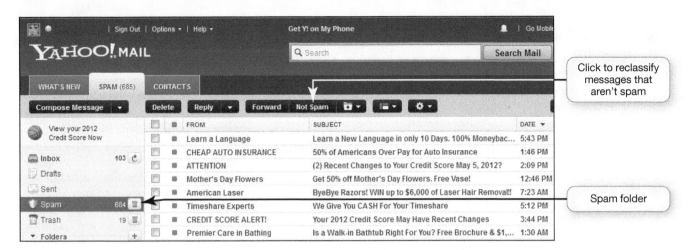

FIGURE 9.24 In Yahoo! Mail, messages identified as spam are directed into a folder called "Spam" for review and deletion. *(SVLuma/shutterstock)*

special folder (called "Spam" or "Junk Mail"). Most web-based e-mail services, such as Hotmail and Yahoo!, offer spam filters (see Figure 9.24). Microsoft Outlook also features a spam filter.

You can also buy third-party programs that provide some control over spam, including SPAMfighter, which you can download at **download.com**.

How do spam filters work? Spam filters and filtering software can catch as much as 95% of spam by checking incoming e-mail subject headers and senders' addresses against databases of known spam. Spam filters also check your e-mail for frequently used spam patterns and keywords, such as "for free" and "over 21." Spam filters aren't perfect, and you should check the spam folder before deleting its contents because legitimate e-mail might end up there by mistake. Most programs let you reclassify e-mails that have been misidentified as spam (see Figure 9.24).

How else can I prevent spam? Here are a few other ways you can prevent spam:

1. Before registering on a website, read its privacy policy to see how it uses your e-mail address. Don't give the site permission to pass on your e-mail address to third parties.

2. Don't reply to spam to remove yourself from the spam list. By replying, you're confirming that your e-mail address is active. Instead of stopping spam, you may receive more.

3. Subscribe to an e-mail forwarding service such as VersaForward (**versaforward.com**) or Sneakemail (**sneakemail.com**). These services screen your e-mail messages, forwarding only those messages you designate as being okay to accept.

Cookies

What are cookies? Cookies are small text files that some websites automatically store on your hard drive when you visit them. When you log on to a website that uses cookies, a cookie file assigns an ID number to your computer. The unique ID is intended to make your return visit to a website more efficient and better geared to your interests. The next time you log on to that site, the site marks your visit and keeps track of it in its database.

What do websites do with cookie information? Cookies can provide websites with information about your browsing habits, such as the ads you've opened, the products you've looked at, and the time and duration of your visits. Companies use this information to determine the traffic flowing through their website and the effectiveness of their marketing strategy and placement on websites. By tracking such information, cookies enable companies to identify different users' preferences.

Can companies get my personal information when I visit their sites? Cookies do not go through your hard drive in search of personal information such as passwords or financial data. The only personal information a cookie obtains is the information you supply when you fill out forms online.

Do privacy risks exist with cookies? Some sites sell the personal information their cookies collect to web advertisers who are building huge databases of consumer preferences and habits, collecting personal and business information such as phone numbers, credit reports, and the like. The main concern is that advertisers will use this information indiscriminately,

On law enforcement TV shows, you often see computer technicians working on suspects' computers to assist detectives in solving crimes. It may look simple, but the science of computer forensics is a complex step-by-step process that ensures evidence is collected within the confines of the law.

Forensic means that something is suitable for use in a court of law. There are many branches of forensic science. For example, forensic pathologists provide evidence about the nature and manner of death in court cases involving deceased individuals. **Computer forensics** involves identifying, extracting, preserving, and documenting computer evidence. Computer forensics is performed by individuals known as *computer forensic scientists*, who rely primarily on specialized software to collect their evidence.

Phase 1: Obtaining and Securing Computer Devices

The first step in a computer forensics investigation is to seize the computer equipment that law enforcement officials believe contains pertinent evidence. Police are required to obtain a warrant to search an individual's home or place of business. Warrants must be very specific by spelling out exactly where detectives can search for evidence and exactly what type of evidence they're seeking. If a warrant indicates that the police may search an individual's home for his laptop computer, they can't then confiscate a tablet computer they notice in his car. It is important to specify in the warrant all types of storage devices where potential evidence might be stored, such as external hard drives, flash drives, and servers.

Once permission to collect the computers and devices containing possible evidence has been obtained, law enforcement officials must exercise great care when collecting the equipment. They need to ensure that no unauthorized persons are able to access or alter the computers or storage devices. The police must make sure the data and equipment are safe; if the equipment is connected to the Internet, the connection must be severed without data loss or damage. It's also important for law enforcement officials to understand that they may not want to power off equipment because potential evidence contained in RAM may be lost. After the devices are collected and secured, the computer forensic scientists take over the next phase of the investigation.

Phase 2: Cataloging and Analyzing the Data

It's critical to preserve the data exactly as it was found, or attorneys may argue that the computer evidence was subject to tampering or altering. Because just opening a file can alter it, the first task is to make a copy of all computer systems and storage devices collected (see Figure 9.25). The investigators then work from the copies to ensure that the original data always remains preserved exactly as it was when it was collected.

After obtaining a copy to work from, forensics professionals attempt to find every file on the system, including deleted files. Files on a computer aren't actually deleted, even if you empty the Recycle Bin, until the section of the hard disk they're stored on is overwritten with new data. Therefore, using special forensic software tools such as SIFT, EnCase, and FTK, the forensic scientists catalog all files found on the system or storage medium and recover as much information from deleted files as they can. Forensic software like FTK can readily detect hidden files and perform

FIGURE 9.25 Portable devices like the RoadMASSter 3 Data Acquisition and Analysis tool make it easy to copy storage devices at crime scenes. *(Intelligent Computer Solutions)*

procedures to crack encrypted files or access protected files and reveal their contents.

The most important part of the process is documenting every step. Forensic scientists must clearly log every procedure performed because they may be required to provide proof in court that their investigations did not alter or damage information contained on the systems they examined. Detailed reports should list all files found, how the files were laid out on the system, which files were protected or encrypted, and the contents of each file. Finally, computer forensic professionals are often called on to present testimony in court during a trial.

Criminals are getting more sophisticated and are now employing anti-forensics techniques to foil computer forensic investigators. Although techniques for hiding or encrypting data are popular, the most insidious anti-forensics techniques are programs designed to erase data if unauthorized persons (i.e., not the criminal) access a computer system or if the system detects forensics software in use. When computer forensic investigators detect these countermeasures, they must often use creative methods and custom-designed software programs to retrieve and preserve the data.

Computer forensics is an invaluable tool to law enforcement in many criminal investigations, but only if the correct procedures are followed and the appropriate documentation is prepared.

FIGURE 9.26 Tools are available, either through your browser (Firefox is shown here) or as separate programs, to distinguish between cookies you want to keep and cookies you don't want on your system.

>On the Firefox menu toolbar, click **Tools**, click **Options**, choose the **Privacy tab**, and then click the **remove individual cookies** link to display the Cookies dialog box.

List of all the cookies on this computer

Click to remove selected cookie

thus invading your privacy. And you may feel your privacy is being violated by cookies that monitor where you go on a website.

Should I delete cookies from my hard drive? Cookies pose no *security* threat because it is virtually impossible to hide a virus or malicious software program in a cookie. Because they take up little room on your hard drive, and offer you small conveniences on return visits to websites, there is no great reason to delete them. Deleting your cookie files could actually cause you the inconvenience of reentering data you have already entered into website forms. However, if you're uncomfortable with the accessibility of your personal information, you can periodically delete cookies (as shown in Figure 9.26) or configure your browser to block certain types of cookies. Software such as Cookie Pal (**kburra.com**) also can help you monitor cookies. ∎

keeping your
DATA SAFE

People are often too trusting or just plain careless when it comes to protecting private information about themselves or their digital data. In this section, we discuss ways to keep your data safe from damage, either accidental or intentional, and to keep unscrupulous individuals from tricking you into revealing sensitive information.

Protecting Your Personal Information

If a complete stranger walked up to you on the street and asked you for your address and phone number, would you give it to him or her? Of course you wouldn't! But many people are much less careful when it comes to sharing sensitive information online. And often people inadvertently share information that they really only intended to share with their friends. With cybercrimes like identify theft rampant, you need to take steps to protect your personal information.

What information should I never share on websites? A good rule of thumb is to reveal as little information as possible, especially if the information would be available to everyone. Figure 9.27 gives you some good guidelines.

Your Social Security number, phone number, date of birth, and street address are four key pieces of information that identity thieves need to steal an identity. This information should never be shared in a public area on any website.

How can I tell who can see my information on a social network? Social networking sites like Facebook make privacy settings available in your profile settings. If you've never changed your default privacy settings in Facebook, you're probably sharing information more widely than you should.

How can I protect my information on Facebook? To begin, you need to change your privacy settings from some of the default options. In general, it's a bad idea to make personal information available to the public, although this is a default setting for some items in Facebook. It's a good idea to set most of the options in your profile's Basic Information section (see Figure 9.28a) to Friends or to Only Me because, presumably, these are personal details you should wish to share only with friends.

In the Contact Information section (see Figure 9.28b), restricting this information only to friends or to yourself is imperative. You don't want scammers contacting you via e-mail or snail mail and trying to trick you into revealing sensitive information.

Backing Up Your Data

How might I damage the data on my computer? The data on your computer faces three major threats:

1. Unauthorized access
2. Tampering
3. Destruction

As noted earlier, a hacker can gain access to your computer and steal or alter your data. However, a more likely scenario is that you'll lose your data unintentionally. You may accidentally delete files. You may drop your laptop on the ground, causing the hard drive to break and resulting in complete data loss. A virus from an e-mail attachment you opened may destroy your original file. Your house may catch fire and destroy your computer. Because many of these possibilities are beyond your control, you should have a strategy for backing up your files

FIGURE 9.27

Internet Information-Sharing Precautions

Information Identity Thieves Crave

- Social Security Number
- Full Date of Birth
- Phone Number
- Street Address

Never make this information visible on websites!

Other Sensitive Information

- Full Legal Name
- E-mail Address
- Zip Code
- Gender
- School or Workplace

Only reveal this information to people you know—don't make it visible to everyone!

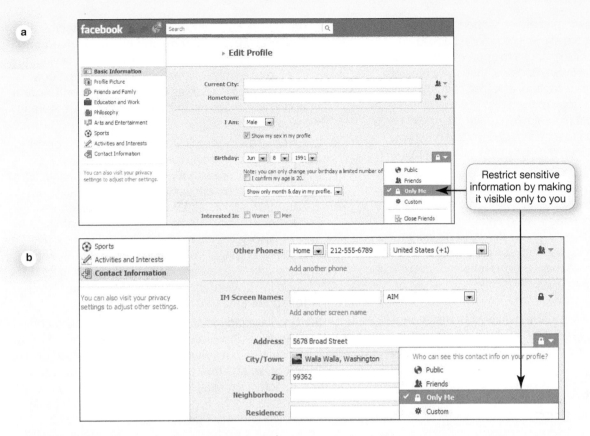

a

b

Restrict sensitive information by making it visible only to you

FIGURE 9.28 You should review the (a) Basic Information and (b) Contact Information privacy settings in Facebook to ensure you aren't sharing too much information.

(see Figure 9.29). **Backups** are copies of files that you can use to replace the originals if they're lost or damaged.

What types of files do I need to back up? Two types of files need backups:

1. **Program files** include files used to install software, usually found on DVDs or downloaded from the Internet. As long as you have the DVDs in a safe place, you shouldn't need to back up these program files. If you've downloaded a program file from the Internet, however, you should make a copy of the program installation files on a removable storage device as a backup.

2. **Data files** include files you've created or purchased, such as research papers, spreadsheets, music and photo files, contact lists, address books, e-mail archives, and your Favorites list from your browser.

What types of backups can I perform? There are two main options for backing up files:

1. An **incremental backup** (or **partial backup**) involves backing up only files that have changed or have been created since the last backup was performed. Using backup software that has an option for incremental backups will save time because backing up files that haven't changed is redundant.

2. An **image backup** (or **system backup**) means that all system, application, and data files are backed up,

FIGURE 9.29

An Effective Backup Strategy

Files to Back Up

- **Program files:** Installation files for productivity software (i.e., Microsoft Office)
- **Data files:** Files you create (term papers, spreadsheets, etc.)

Types of Backups

- **Incremental (partial):** Only backs up files that have changed
- **Image (system):** Snapshot of your entire computer, including system software

Where to Store Backup Files

- Online (in the cloud)
- External hard drives
- Network-attached storage devices or home servers

not just the files that changed. Although incremental backups are more efficient, an image backup ensures you capture changes to application files, such as automatic software updates, that an incremental backup might not capture. The idea of imaging is to make an exact copy of the setup of your computer so that in the event of a total hard drive failure you could copy the image to a new hard drive and have your computer configured exactly the way it was before the crash.

Where should I store my backups? To be truly secure, backups must be stored away from where your computer is located and should be stored in at least two different places. You wouldn't want a fire or a flood destroying the backups along with the original data. You have three main choices for where to back up your files (see Figure 9.30):

1. *Online (in the cloud):* The beauty of online storage is that you don't need to be at your home computer or lug around your external hard drive to access your data. More important, because the information is stored online, it's in a secure, remote location, so data is much less vulnerable to the disasters that could harm data stored in your computer or external

hard drive. Free storage options include Microsoft SkyDrive (**skydrive.com**) and ADrive (**adrive.com**). However, image backups probably won't fit within the storage limits offered by free providers. For a fee, companies such as Carbonite (**carbonite.com**) and IBackup (**ibackup.com**) provide larger storage capacity.

2. *External hard drives:* External hard drives, or even large-capacity flash drives, are popular backup options that are usually connected to a single computer. Although convenient and inexpensive, using external hard drives for backups still presents the dilemma of keeping the hard drive in a safe location. Also, external hard drives can fail, possibly leading to loss of your backed-up data. Therefore, using an external hard drive for backups is best done in conjunction with an online backup strategy for added safety.

3. *Network-attached storage (NAS) devices and home servers:* NAS devices are essentially large hard drives connected to a network of computers instead of one computer, and they can be used to back up multiple computers simultaneously. Home servers also act as high-capacity NAS devices for automatically backing up data and sharing files.

FIGURE 9.30

A Comparison of Typical Data Backup Locations

BACKUP LOCATION	PROS	CONS
Online (in the Cloud)	• Files stored at a secure, remote location • Files/backups accessible anywhere through a browser	• Most free storage sites don't provide enough space for image backups
External Hard Drive	• Inexpensive, one-time cost • Fast backups with USB 3.0 devices connected directly to your computer	• Could be destroyed in one event (fire/flood) with your computer • Can be stolen • Slightly more difficult to back up multiple computers with one device
Network-Attached Storage (NAS) Device and Home Server	• Makes backups much easier for multiple computing devices	• More expensive than a stand-alone external hard drive • Could be destroyed in one event (fire/flood) with your computer • Can be stolen

(mipan//Fotolia; Prapass Wannapinij/Fotolia; darkdesigns/Fotolia)

How often should I back up my data files?

You should back up your data files every time you make changes to them, which can be difficult to remember to do. Fortunately, most backup software can be configured to do backups automatically so you don't forget to perform them. For example, with the Windows 8 File History utility, you can have Windows automatically save your data files from your libraries, desktop, contacts, and favorites to an external hard drive or NAS device. The default setting for File History saves files you changed every hour to the backup location you specify. File History even keeps previous versions of the file on the backup drive so you can revert to a previous version of the file if you need to do so.

To set up File History, you first need to connect an external hard drive to your computer or a NAS device to your network. You can then access File History through the Control Panel (in the System and Security group) and set it up (see Figure 9.31). Once configured, your data files will be backed up as often as you indicate. You can also restore files that you've backed up from the File History utility.

How often should I create an image backup?

Because your program and OS files don't change as often as your data files,

SOUND BYTE

Managing Computer Security with Windows Tools

In this Sound Byte, you'll learn how to monitor and control your computer security using features built into the Windows OS.

you can perform image backups on a less frequent basis. You might consider scheduling an image backup of your entire system on a weekly basis, but you should definitely perform one after installing new software.

How do I perform an image backup?

Windows 8 includes the Windows 7 File Recovery utility, which provides a quick and easy way to schedule regular image backups. You can access this utility from the Windows 7 File Recovery link on the File History screen (see Figure 9.31). Before starting this utility, make sure your external hard drive or NAS device is connected to your computer or network and is powered on. To set it up, follow these steps:

FIGURE 9.31 You can use the Windows 8 File History utility to back up files and restore files from a previous backup. *>Access the Control Panel, select the **System and Security** group, and then click the **File History** link.*

1. When you start the Windows 7 File Recovery utility for the first time, no backups will have ever been configured. Select the Set up backup option to launch the Set up backup dialog box (see Figure 9.32a) and display a list of available backup devices. Select a device, and click Next to proceed.

2. On the next screen (Figure 9.32b), you have the option to let Windows choose what to back up or to choose for yourself what you want to back up. If you let Windows choose, your backup will include your data files as well as a system image backup. Click Next to proceed.

3. On the following screen, you can review your settings and set up a schedule for the backups. When you click the Save settings and exit button, you are returned to the Back up or restore your files screen (see Figure 9.32c), which now shows the scheduled backup. You can also choose to restore backed-up files you have backed up from this screen.

From the Back up or restore your files screen, you can also create a system repair disk by clicking on the appropriate link. A system repair disc is a DVD that you can use to boot your computer in case of a serious Windows error. You also use this disc when you need to restore your computer from an image backup, so it's a good idea to create the repair disc before you begin using your computer heavily.

What about backing up Apple computers? For OS X users, backups are very easy to configure. The Time Machine feature in OS X detects when an external hard drive is connected to the computer or a NAS device is connected to your network. You're then asked if you want this to be your backup drive. If you answer yes, all of your files (including OS files) are automatically backed up to the external drive or NAS device.

Should I back up my files that are stored on my school's network? Most likely, if you're allowed to store files on your school's network, these files are backed up regularly. You should check with your school's network administrators to determine how often they're backed up and how you would request that files be restored from the backup if they're damaged or deleted. But don't rely on these network backups to bail you out if your data files are lost or damaged. It may take days for the network administrators to restore your files. It's better to keep backups of your data files yourself, especially homework and project files, so that you can immediately restore them. ■

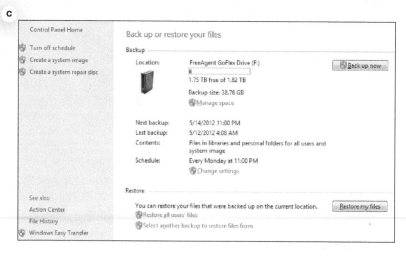

FIGURE 9.32 The Windows 7 File Recovery utility allows you to perform an image backup. (a) Select your backup destination. (b) Choose locations to back up. (c) Review your scheduled backups, restore files, or start the wizard to create a system repair disc.

social
ENGINEERING

Social engineering is any technique that uses social skills to generate human interaction that entices individuals to reveal sensitive information. Social engineering often doesn't involve the use of a computer or face-to-face interaction. For example, telephone scams are a common form of social engineering because it is often easier to manipulate someone when you don't have to look at them.

How does social engineering work?
Most social engineering schemes use a pretext to lure their victims. **Pretexting** involves creating a scenario that sounds legitimate enough that someone will trust you. For example, you might receive a phone call during which the caller says he is from your bank and that someone tried to use your account without authorization. The caller then tells you he needs to confirm a few personal details such as your birth date, Social Security number, bank account number, and whatever other information he can get out of you. The information he obtains can then be used to empty your bank account or commit some other form of fraud. The most common form of pretexting in cyberspace is *phishing*.

BITS&BYTES

Protect Your Credit Card Number Online

Another way to protect yourself is never to use your credit card number when you shop online. Although it sounds impossible, credit card providers such as Citibank are offering services such as virtual account numbers for their customers. Before purchasing a product online, you visit the credit card provider's site, where you're assigned a new virtual account number each time you visit. This number looks like a regular credit card number and is tied to your real credit card account. However, the virtual account number can be used only once. That means that if the number is stolen, it's no good to thieves. They can't use the virtual account number because you've already used it.

Phishing and Pharming

How are phishing schemes conducted?
Phishing (pronounced "fishing") lures Internet users to reveal personal information such as credit card numbers, Social Security numbers, or other sensitive information that could lead to identity theft. The scammers send e-mail messages that look like they're from a legitimate business such as an online bank. The e-mail usually states that the recipient needs to update or confirm his or her account information. When the recipient clicks on the provided link, he or she goes to a website. The site looks like a legitimate site but is really a fraudulent copy the scammer has created. Once the e-mail recipient enters his or her personal information, the scammers capture it and can begin using it.

Is pharming a type of phishing scam?
Pharming is much more insidious than phishing. Phishing requires a positive action by the person being scammed, such as going to a website mentioned in an e-mail and typing in personal information. **Pharming** occurs when malicious code is planted on your computer, either by viruses or by your visiting malicious websites, which then alters your browser's ability to find web addresses. Users are directed to bogus websites even when they enter the correct address of the real website. You end up at a fake website that looks legitimate but is expressly set up for the purpose of gathering information.

How can I avoid being caught by phishing and pharming scams?
Follow these guidelines to avoid falling prey to such schemes:

- Never reply directly to any e-mail asking you for personal information.
- Don't click on a link in an e-mail to go to a website. Instead, type the website address in the browser.
- Check with the company asking for the information and only give the information if you're certain it's needed.
- Never give personal information over the Internet unless you know the site is secure. Look for the closed padlock, *https*, or a certification seal such as Norton Secured to help reassure you that the site is secure.
- Use phishing filters. The latest versions of Firefox, Chrome, and Internet Explorer have phishing filters built in, so each time you access a website, the phishing filter checks for the site's legitimacy and warns you of possible web forgeries.

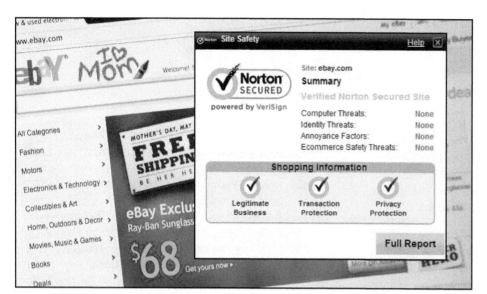

FIGURE 9.33 Not sure whether you're on the eBay website or a cleverly disguised phishing site? Norton Site Safety reassures you that all is well. *(Andrea Zanchi/iStockphoto)*

- Use Internet security software on your computer that's constantly being updated.

Most Internet security packages can detect and prevent pharming attacks. The major Internet security packages—for example, McAfee and Norton (see Figure 9.33)—also offer phishing-protection tools. When you have the Norton Toolbar displayed in your browser, you're constantly informed about the legitimacy of the site you are visiting.

Scareware

What is scareware? Scareware is a type of malware that downloads onto your computer and tries to convince you that your computer is infected with a virus (see Figure 9.34) or other type of malware. Pop-ups, banners, or other annoying types of messages will flash on your screen saying frightening things like, "Your computer is infected with a virus … immediate removal is required." You're then directed to a website where you can buy fake removal or antivirus tools that provide little or no value. Panda Security estimates that scareware scams generate in excess of $34 million a month for cybercriminals. Some scareware even goes so far as to encrypt your files and then demand that you pay to have them unencrypted, which is essentially extortion.

Scareware is a social engineering technique because it uses people's fear of computer viruses to convince them to part with their money. Scareware is often designed to be extremely difficult

to remove from your computer and to interfere with the operation of legitimate security software. Scareware is usually downloaded onto your computer from infected websites or Trojan horse files.

How do I protect myself against scareware? Most Internet security suites, antivirus, and antimalware software packages now detect and prevent the installation of scareware. But make sure you never click on website banners or pop-up boxes that say "Your computer might be infected, click here to scan your files" because these are often the starting points for installing malicious scareware files on your computer. ■

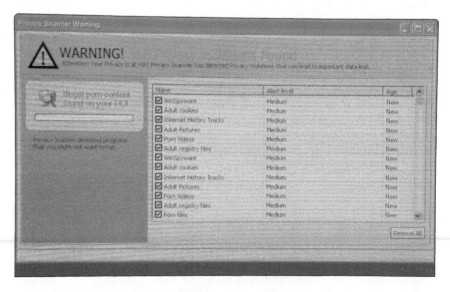

FIGURE 9.34 Preying on people's fears, scareware attempts to convince you that your computer is infected with a virus and you need to purchase a "solution." *(REUTERS/Molly Riley)*

Most people have vast amounts of personal data residing in the databases of the various companies with which they conduct business. Amazon.com has your credit card and address information. Your bank has your Social Security number, birth date, and financial records. Your local supermarket probably has your e-mail address from when you joined its loyalty club to receive grocery discounts. All this data in various places puts you at risk when companies responsible for keeping your data confidential suffer a data breach.

A **data breach** occurs when sensitive or confidential information is copied, transmitted, or viewed by an individual who isn't authorized to handle the data. Data breaches can be intentional or unintentional. Intentional data breaches occur when hackers break into digital systems to steal sensitive data. Unintentional data breaches occur when companies controlling data inadvertently allow it to be seen by unauthorized parties, usually due to some breakdown in security procedures or precautions.

Unfortunately, data breaches appear to be quite common, as there always seems to be another one in the news. In March 2012, Global Payments, a credit card–transaction processor, notified its major credit card customers that its systems had been breached and that credit card data had been taken. Apparently, enough data was accessed so that the cybercriminals would be able to create duplicates of credit cards that could be used to purchase goods and services. Data breaches such as this one pose serious risks to the individuals whose data has been compromised, even if financial data is not involved. The data thieves now have the basis with which to launch targeted social engineering attacks even if they just have contact information, such as e-mail addresses.

With regular phishing techniques, cybercriminals just send out e-mails to a wide list of e-mail addresses, whether they have a relationship with the company or not. For example, a criminal might send out a general phishing e-mail claiming that

a person's Citibank checking account had been breached. People who receive this e-mail that don't have any accounts at Citibank should immediately realize this is a phishing attack and ignore the instructions to divulge sensitive data.

But when cybercriminals obtain data on individuals that includes information about which companies those individuals have a relationship with, they can engage in much more targeted attacks known as **spear phishing**. Spear phishing e-mails are sent to people known to be customers of a company and have a much greater chance of successfully getting individuals to reveal sensitive data. If cybercriminals obtain a list of e-mail addresses of customers from Barclays Bank, for example, they can ensure that the spear phishing e-mails purport to come from Barclays and will include the customer's full name. This type of attack is much more likely to succeed in fooling people than just random e-mails sent out to thousands of people who might not have a relationship with the company mentioned in the phishing letter.

So how can you protect yourself after a data breach? You need to be extra suspicious of any e-mail correspondence from companies involved in the data breach. Companies usually never contact you by e-mail or phone asking you to reveal sensitive information or reactivate your online account by entering confidential information. Usually, these requests come via regular snail mail.

So, if you receive any e-mails or phone calls from companies you deal with purporting to have problems with your accounts, your best course of action is to delete the e-mail or hang up the phone. Then contact the company that supposedly has the problem by a phone number that you look up yourself either in legitimate correspondence from the company (say, the toll-free number on your credit card statement) or in the phone book. The representatives from your company can quickly tell if a real problem exists or if you were about to be the victim of a scam.

protecting your physical
COMPUTING ASSETS

Your computer, tablet, and phone aren't useful to you if they're damaged. Therefore, it's essential to select and ensure a safe environment for these devices. This includes protecting them from environmental factors, power surges, power outages, and theft.

Environmental Factors

Why is the environment critical to the operation of my computer equipment?

Computers are delicate devices and can be damaged by the adverse effects of abuse or a poor environment. Sudden movements, such as a fall, can damage your computing device's internal components. You should make sure that your computer sits on a flat, level surface, and if it's a laptop or a tablet, you should carry it in a protective case.

Electronic components don't like excessive heat or excessive cold. Don't leave computing devices and phones in a car during especially hot or cold weather because components can be damaged by extreme temperatures. Unfortunately, computers generate a lot of heat, which is why they have fans to cool their internal components. Chill mats that contain cooling fans and sit underneath laptop computers are useful accessories for dissipating heat. Make sure that you place your desktop computer where the fan's intake vents, usually found on the rear of the system unit, are unblocked so air can flow inside.

Naturally, a fan drawing air into a computer also draws in dust and other particles, which can wreak havoc on your system. Therefore, keep the room in which your computer is located as clean as possible. Finally, because food crumbs and liquid can damage keyboards and other computer components, consume food and beverages away from your computer.

FIGURE 9.35 Surge protectors such as this one are critical for protecting your electronic devices. *(aberenyi/Fotolia)*

Power Surges

What is a power surge? Power surges occur when electrical current is supplied in excess of normal voltage. Old or faulty wiring, downed power lines, malfunctions at electric company substations, and lightning strikes can all cause power surges. A **surge protector** is a device that protects your computer against power surges (see Figure 9.35).

Note that you should replace your surge protectors every two to three years. Also, after a major surge, the surge protector will no longer function and must be replaced. And it's wise to buy a surge protector that includes indicator lights, which illuminate when the surge protector is no longer functioning properly. Don't be fooled by old surge protectors—although they can still function as multiple-outlet power strips, they deliver power to your equipment without protecting it.

Besides my computer, what other devices need to be connected to a surge protector?

All electronic devices in the home that have solid-state components, such as TVs, stereos, printers, and cell phones (when charging), should be connected to a surge protector. However, it can be inconvenient to use individual surge protectors on everything. A more practical method is to install a **whole-house surge protector** (see Figure 9.36). Whole-house

---

SOUND BYTE

Surge Protectors

In this Sound Byte, you'll learn about the major features of surge protectors and how they work. You'll also learn about the key factors you need to consider before buying a surge protector, and you'll see how easy it is to install one.

surge protectors function like other surge protectors, but they protect *all* electrical devices in the house. Typically, you'll need an electrician to install a whole-house surge protector, which will cost $300 to $400 (installed).

Is my equipment 100% safe when plugged into a surge protector? Lightning strikes can generate such high voltages that they can overwhelm a surge protector. As tedious as it sounds, unplugging computers and peripherals during an electrical storm is the only way to achieve absolute protection.

Deterring Theft

What do I need to worry about if my computing device is stolen? Because they're portable, laptops, tablets, and phones are easy targets for thieves. You have four main security concerns with mobile devices:

1. Keeping them from being stolen
2. Keeping data secure in case they are stolen
3. Finding a device if it is stolen
4. Remotely recovering and wiping data off a stolen device

Keep Them Safe: Alarms

What type of alarm can I install on my mobile device? Motion alarm software is a good inexpensive theft deterrent. Free software such as LAlarm (**lalarm.com**) is effective for laptops. Apps such as SuperAlarm and Alarmomatic help secure your iPad or iPhone. Alarm software either detects motion, like your device being picked up, or sounds near your device and then sets off an ear-piercing alarm until you enter the disable code. Thieves normally don't like it when attention is drawn to their activities, so alarms can be a very effective theft deterrent.

Keeping Mobile Device Data Secure

How can I secure the data on my mobile devices? Encrypting the data on your mobile device can make it extremely difficult, if not impossible, for thieves to obtain sensitive data from your stolen equipment. *Encryption* involves transforming your data using an algorithm that can only be unlocked by a secure code (or key). Encrypted data is impossible to read unless it's decrypted, which

Surge protector →

FIGURE 9.36 A whole-house surge protector usually is installed at the breaker panel or near the electric meter.

requires a secure password, hopefully known only to you.

Safe is an app that provides 256-bit encryption, which is very hard to crack, for data and images on your iPhone and iPad. If your password is not entered, no one can access the data and images on your iPhone or iPad. Data Protection is a similar app for Android devices. ZoneAlarm Data-Lock and SafeHouse are available for laptop computers to provide encryption for files or even entire hard drives.

Software Alerts and Data Wipes

How can my computer help me recover it when it is stolen? You've probably heard of LoJack, the theft-tracking device used in cars. Similar systems now exist for computers. Tracking software such as Computrace LoJack for Laptops (**absolute.com**), PC PhoneHome, and Mac PhoneHome (**brigadoonsoftware.com**) enables your computer to alert authorities to the computer's location if it is stolen. A similar tracking app for Android and iOS devices is iHound.

To enable your mobile device to help with its own recovery, you install the tracking software on your device. The software contacts a server at the software manufacturer's website each time the device connects to the Internet. If your device is stolen, you notify the software manufacturer. The software manufacturer instructs your device to transmit tracking information, such as an IP address, WiFi hotspot, or cell tower location, that will assist authorities in locating and retrieving the mobile device.

What if the thieves find the tracking software and delete it? The files and directories holding the software aren't visible to thieves looking for such software, so they probably won't know the software is there. Furthermore, the tracking software is written in such a way that even if the thieves tried to reformat the hard drive, it would detect the reformat and hide the software code in a safe place in memory or on the hard drive. This works because some sectors of a hard drive are not rewritten during most reformatting. That way, the tracking software can reinstall itself after the reformatting is complete.

What if my device can't be recovered by the authorities? In the event that your laptop can't be recovered, software packages are available that provide for remote recovery and deletion of files. Computrace LoJack for Laptops has these features and allows you to lock your device to keep the thieves from

Find My iPhone

FIGURE 9.37 The Find My iPhone app can help you if your iOS device goes astray.

accessing it or to remotely wipe its contents by deleting all your data from your laptop.

For all iOS devices, Apple offers the Find My iPhone service, which is now part of iCloud. Enabling this service on your device provides you with numerous tools that can assist you in recovering and protecting your mobile devices. Did you forget where you left your iPad? Just sign in with your Apple ID at the iCloud website to see a map showing the location of your iPad (see Figure 9.37). You can also remotely send a message to be displayed on your lost device, such as your phone number and a reward offer, so that someone who finds it will know what to do. If you can't recover the device, you can remotely password lock it so no one can use it or, if necessary, wipe all the data off the device to completely protect your privacy.

How can I ensure that I've covered all aspects of protecting my digital devices? Figure 9.38 provides a guide to ensure you haven't missed critical aspects of security. If you've addressed all of these issues, you can feel reasonably confident that your data and devices are secure. ■

Before moving on to the Chapter Review:
- Watch Replay Video 9.2 ▷.
- Then check your understanding of what you've learned so far.

FIGURE 9.38

Computer Security Checklist

Virus and Spyware Protection

- Is antivirus and anti-spyware software installed on all your devices?
- Is the antivirus and anti-spyware software configured to update itself automatically and regularly?
- Is the software set to scan your device on a regular basis (at least weekly) for viruses and spyware?

Firewall

- Do all your computers and tablets have firewall software installed and activated before connecting to the Internet?
- Is your router also able to function as a hardware firewall?
- Have you tested your firewall security by using the free software available at grc.com?

Software Updates

- Have you configured your operating systems (Windows, OS X, iOS) to install new software patches and updates automatically?
- Is other software installed on your device, such as Microsoft Office or productivity apps, configured for automatic updates?
- Is the web browser you're using the latest version?

Protecting Your Devices

- Are all computing devices protected from electrical surges?
- Do your mobile devices have alarms or tracking software installed on them?

check your understanding //

For a quick review to see what you've learned so far, answer the following questions. Visit **pearsonhighered.com/techinaction** to check your answers.

multiple choice

1. Programs that attempt to trick you into buying software by pretending your computer is infected with a virus fall into the class of malware known as
   a. virusware.
   b. scareware.
   c. spyware.
   d. adware.

2. A backup of all files on your computer, which is essentially a snapshot of exactly how your computer looks at a particular point in time, is known as a(n)
   a. total backup.
   b. incremental backup.
   c. image backup.
   d. global backup.

3. Software that transmits information about you, such as your Internet surfing habits, back to a third party is known as
   a. scareware.
   b. spyware.
   c. adware.
   d. trackingware.

4. Small text files that some websites automatically store on your computer's hard drive are known as
   a. greyware.
   b. spam.
   c. adware.
   d. cookies.

5. A social engineering technique in which you create a scenario to gain someone's trust is known as
   a. pretexting.
   b. phishing.
   c. pharming.
   d. spear phishing.

true–false

_____ **1.** Sending e-mails to lure people into revealing personal information is a technique known as phishing.

_____ **2.** Encrypting data is not an appropriate measure for protecting mobile devices such as tablets.

critical thinking

1. **Restricting Information to Keep You Safe**

   Many countries, such as China, have laws that control the content of the Internet and restrict their citizens' access to information. The United States, with the exception of specific areas such as cyberbullying and child pornography, doesn't currently take steps to restrict its citizens' access to the Internet. Unfortunately, this freedom of information does carry some cost because some information on the web can potentially be dangerous to the general public.

   a. Do you think the U.S. government should censor information on the web, such as instructions for making weapons, to protect the general public? Why or why not? If you think there should be some censorship, do you think such a law would violate the First Amendment right to free speech? Explain your answer.

   b. Would you be willing to live with a lower level of information access to increase your sense of well-being? What topics do you feel would make you feel more secure if they were censored?

Continue ➡

9 Chapter Review

summary //

Cybercrime and Identity Theft

1. What is cybercrime, and who perpetrates it?
- Cybercrime, is any type of crime perpetrated via a computer or a website.
- Major types of cybercrime are identity theft, credit card fraud, computer viruses, illegal access of computer systems, and auction fraud.
- Cybercriminals use computers, the Internet, and computer networks to commit their crimes.

Protecting Yourself from Computer Viruses

2. What are the types of viruses from which I need to protect my computer?
- A computer virus is a program that attaches itself to another program and attempts to spread to other computers when files are exchanged.
- Computer viruses can be grouped into six categories: (1) boot-sector viruses, (2) logic bombs and time bombs, (3) worms, (4) scripts and macro viruses, (5) e-mail viruses, and (6) encryption viruses. Once run, viruses perform their malicious duties in the background and are often invisible to the user.

3. What can I do to protect my computer from viruses?
- The best defense against viruses is to install antivirus software. You should update the software on a regular basis and configure it to examine all e-mail attachments for viruses. You should periodically run a complete virus scan on your computer to ensure that no viruses have made it onto your hard drive.

Protecting Digital Assets from Hackers

4. How can hackers attack my computing devices, and what harm can they cause?
- A hacker is defined as anyone who breaks into a computer system unlawfully. Hackers can use software to break into almost any computer connected to the Internet, unless proper precautions are taken.
- Once hackers gain access to a computer, they can potentially (1) steal personal or other important

information, (2) damage and destroy data, or (3) use the computer to attack other computers.

5. What is a firewall, and how does it keep my computer safe from hackers?
- Firewalls are software programs or hardware devices designed to keep computers safe from hackers. By using a personal firewall, you can close to invaders open logical ports and potentially make your computer invisible to other computers on the Internet.

6. How do I create secure passwords and manage all of my passwords?
- Secure passwords contain a mixture of upper- and lowercase letters, numbers, and symbols and are at least 14 characters long. Passwords should not contain words that are in the dictionary or easy-to-guess personal information, like your pet's name.
- Online password checkers can be used to evaluate the strength of your passwords.
- Utilities built into web browsers and Internet security software can be used to manage your passwords and alleviate the need to remember numerous complex passwords.

7. How can I surf the Internet anonymously and use biometric authentication devices to protect my data?
- The current versions of popular browsers include tools, such as Google Chrome's Incognito feature, that hide your surfing activities by not recording websites that you visit or files that you download in your browser's history files.
- Biometric authentication devices use a physical attribute that is not easily duplicated to control access to data files or computing devices. Some laptops today feature fingerprint readers and facial-recognition software to control access.

Managing Online Annoyances

8. How do I manage online annoyances such as spyware and spam?
- The web is filled with annoyances such as spam, pop-ups, cookies, spyware, and scams such as phishing that make surfing the web frustrating and sometimes dangerous.
- Installing anti-malware software tools helps to prevent, detect, and/or reduce spam, adware, and spyware.

Keeping Your Data Safe

9. What data do I need to back up, and what are the best methods for doing so?

- Data files created by you, such as Word and Excel files, or purchased by you, such as music files, need to be backed up in case they're inadvertently deleted or damaged. Application software, such as Microsoft Office, may need to be reinstalled if files are damaged, so backups, such as the DVDs the application came on, must be maintained.

- An incremental backup means only files that have changed or been created since the last backup was performed will be backed up. Image backups copy all system, application, and data files regardless of whether they changed since the last backup.

- Websites such as ADrive and SkyDrive are great for backing up individual files. External hard drives are popular choices for holding image backups of your entire system, as are online (cloud) storage sites. Windows and OS X contain solid backup tools that help automate backup tasks.

10. What is social engineering, and how do I avoid falling prey to phishing?

- Social engineering schemes use human interaction, deception, and trickery to fool people into revealing sensitive information such as credit card numbers and passwords.

- Phishing schemes usually involve e-mails that direct the unwary to a website that appears to be legitimate, such as a bank site, but that is specifically designed to capture personal information for committing fraud. To avoid phishing scams, you should never reply directly to any e-mail asking you for personal information and never click on a link in an e-mail to go to a website.

- Don't fall for scareware scams that attempt to frighten you by pretending there is something wrong with your computer.

Protecting Your Physical Computing Assets

11. How do I protect my physical computing assets from environmental hazards, power surges, and theft?

- Computing devices should be kept in clean environments free from dust and other particulates and should not be exposed to extreme temperatures (either hot or cold).

- You should protect all electronic devices from power surges by hooking them up through surge protectors, which will protect them from most electrical surges that could damage the devices.

- Mobile devices can be protected from theft by installing software that will (1) set off an alarm if the computer is moved; (2) help recover the computer, if stolen, by reporting the computer's whereabouts when it is connected to the Internet; and/or (3) allow you to lock or wipe the contents of the digital device remotely.

Be sure to check out the companion website for additional materials to help you review and learn, including a Tech Bytes Weekly newsletter—**pearsonhighered.com/techinaction**.

And don't forget the Replay Videos .

key terms//

1. Backup Procedures

You know you should have a good backup strategy in place for your key data. Consider the following:

a. How often do you back up critical data files such as homework files? What type of device do you use for backing up files? Where do you store the backups to ensure they won't be destroyed if a major disaster (such as a fire) destroys your computer? Do you use online sites for file backups?

b. List the applications (such as Microsoft Office) that are currently installed on your computer. Where is the media (DVDs) for your application software stored? For any software you purchased in an Internet download, have you burned a copy of the installation files to DVD/Blu-ray disc in case you need to reinstall the software?

c. Have you ever made an image backup of your entire system? If so, what software do you use for image backups? If not, research image backup software on the Internet and find an appropriate package to use. Suppose you need to purchase an additional backup device to hold your image backup. Find one that is appropriate. What is the total cost of the software and hardware you will need to implement your image backup strategy?

2. Protecting Your Computer for Free

There are many effective, free options for protecting your computer from malware.

a. Research free anti-malware programs using sources such as *PC Magazine* (**pcmag.com**) and *PC World* (**pcworld.com**). What are the highest-rated free software packages available? Are versions available for your OS? Do you have any of these tools installed on your computer already?

b. Many ISPs offer proprietary security software, including major brands such as Norton, free to their subscribers. Research the ISP you use or a local ISP and determine what free software it provides. When selecting an ISP, how important is it to you that it offers free security software?

3. Botnet Awareness

Botnets are serious computer infestations that affect large numbers of computers at one time. Still, many students are unaware of this threat even as botnets strike college campuses. Research botnets and prepare a short flyer for your classmates that explains the threats posed by botnets and the software that can be used to detect botnets.

1. Tracking Employees

Many corporations provide mobile devices to their employees who work outside the office. With apps such as Footprints (from Sollico Software) and GPS tracking (from LOCiMOBILE), it's easy for employers to track the whereabouts of their employees by tracking the location of their mobile devices. Consider the following:

a. How would you feel about your boss tracking your movements during the day? Should employers have to disclose to employees that they're being tracked? Should employers have the right to track employees to ensure they're not slacking off during work hours?

b. Should the tracking software have an option to allow employees to disable the tracking feature temporarily? Under what circumstances should it be permissible for an employee to turn off employer tracking?

2. Computer Security Careers

Computer security professionals are among the highest-paid employees. Using employment sites such as **Monster.com**, **computerjobs.com**, and **dice.com**, research computer security jobs available in the state where your school is located (try searching "computer security"). Select three entry-level computer security jobs from different employers and prepare a document comparing the following: What are the educational requirements? What job skills are required? How much prior work experience are firms looking for? Are programming skills required?

Protecting Senior Citizens from Sharing Too Much Data

Problem

With the proliferation of e-commerce, electronic data capture, and electronic communication such as e-mail, individuals provide numerous companies with sensitive personal data. However, this only encourages hackers to attempt to breach computer systems in order to steal sensitive information or to use social engineering techniques to fool the unwary. Senior citizens are one group often targeted by social engineering attacks because they're perceived to be less computer literate and more easily duped by social engineering tactics.

Task

The residents of a local retirement community, managed by your neighbor, have recently been the victims of e-mail phishing and phone pretexting attacks. In addition, recent examinations of residents' computers by a computer consultant determined that many computers were infected with spyware. Your neighbor has asked you to assist in educating the retirees about the dangers of disclosing too much information or revealing information to unauthorized parties.

Process

1. Break the class into three teams. Each team will be responsible for investigating one of the following issues:

   a **Phishing:** Research popular phishing scams and find examples of phishing e-mails sent to the unwary.

   b **Data breaches:** Research popular e-commerce sites or customer loyalty programs that senior citizens might use. Determine what types of data they collect and which pieces of data are not really needed to participate.

   c **Spyware and scareware:** Research typical examples of these types of malware and free solutions that can be used to protect computers from these threats.

2. Present your findings to the class and discuss methodologies for protecting individuals from cybercrime. Provide your instructor with a report of your findings and suggestions suitable for eventual presentation to the residents of the retirement community.

Conclusion

With the proliferation of electronic data, attempts by cybercrimals to collect sensitive information are inevitable. The best defense is educating individuals about the common types of scams and attacks and clearly explaining steps they can take to prevent themselves from falling prey to nefarious schemes.

Content Control: Censorship to Protect Children

In this exercise, you'll research and then role-play a complicated ethical situation. The role you play might or might not match your own personal beliefs; in either case, your research and use of logic will enable you to represent the view assigned. An arbitrator will watch and comment on both sides of the arguments, and together, the team will agree on an ethical solution.

Problem

Many parents use web-filtering software (also known as content-control software) to protect their children from objectionable content on the Internet. However, the software is also widely used in libraries, schools, and other public places where people other than parents are making decisions about what information to restrict. In 2000, the U.S. federal government began requiring libraries to use content-control software as a condition to receiving federal funds under the provisions of the Children's Internet Protection Act (CIPA). Libraries that don't receive federal funds don't have to install filtering software unless their state (like Virginia) passes laws requiring them to do so to receive state funding. Upon installation of the software, it's up to the library administrators to decide what content is restricted, as guided by the provisions of laws such as CIPA. Therefore, content restriction can vary widely from library to library.

Research Areas to Consider

- U.S. Supreme Court case *United States v. American Library Association* (2003)
- Content-control software and First Amendment rights
- Violation of children's free speech rights
- Children's Internet Protection Act (CIPA)

Process

1. Divide the class into teams.
2. Research the areas cited above and devise a scenario in which someone has complained about objectionable content not being blocked or about innocuous content that was inappropriately blocked.
3. Team members should write a summary that provides background information for their character—for example: library patron, library administrator, or arbitrator—and that details their character's behaviors to set the stage for the role-playing event. Then, team members should create an outline to use during the role-playing event.
4. Team members should arrange a mutually convenient time to meet for the exchange, using either the collaboration feature of MyITLab or the discussion board feature of your course management software or by meeting in person.
5. Team members should present their case to the class or submit a PowerPoint presentation for review by the rest of the class, along with the summary and resolution they developed.

Conclusion

As technology becomes ever more prevalent and integrated into our lives, more and more ethical dilemmas will present themselves. Being able to understand and evaluate both sides of the argument, while responding in a personally or socially ethical manner, will be an important skill.

Technology in Focus

Careers in IT

It's hard to imagine an occupation in which computers aren't used in some fashion. Even such previously low-tech industries as waste disposal and fast food use computers to manage inventories and order commodities. In this Technology in Focus feature, we explore various information technology (IT) career paths open to you.

(Carol and Mike Werner/Alamy)

Rewards of Working in Information Technology

There are many great reasons to work in the exciting, ever-changing field of IT. In this section, we'll explore some reasons why IT fields are so attractive to graduates looking for entry-level positions.

IT Workers Are in Demand

If you're investigating a career with computers, the first question you may have is, "Will I be able to get a job?" Consider the following:

- According to projections by the U.S. Department of Labor's Bureau of Labor Statistics, computer-related jobs are expected to be among the fastest-growing occupations through 2020 (see Figure 1).

- In 2012, *US News and World Report* published a list of the best careers to consider based on growth prospects. Software developers ranked second, and 5 of the top 25 were IT careers.

- According to the National Association of Colleges and Employers (NACE) 2012 Starting Salaries for New College Graduates Survey, the average starting salary for computer science jobs increased by 4.1% in 2011.

The number of students pursuing computer science degrees also has been increasing over the past several years, with slightly over 8,000 computer science degrees awarded in the United States in 2011. Yet, shortages of computing professionals in the United States are still projected over the next 5 to 10 years. What does all this mean? In terms of job outlook, now is a perfect time to consider an IT career.

IT Jobs Pay Well

As you can see from Figure 1, median salaries in IT careers are robust. But what exactly affects your salary in an IT position? Your skill set and your experience level are obvious answers, but the size of an employer and its geographic location are also factors. Large companies tend to pay more, so if you're pursuing a high salary, set your sights on a large corporation. But remember that making a lot of money isn't everything—be sure to consider other quality-of-life issues such as job satisfaction. Of course, choosing a computer career isn't a guarantee you'll get a high-paying job. Just as in any other profession, you'll need appropriate training and on-the-job experience to earn a high salary.

So how much can you expect to start out earning? Although starting salaries for some IT positions (computer desktop support and helpdesk analysts) are in the modest range ($41,000 to $45,000), starting salaries for students with bachelor's degrees in IT are fairly robust. But IT salaries vary widely, depending on experience level, the geographic location of the job, and the size of the employer.

To obtain the most accurate information, you should research salaries yourself in the geographic area where you expect to work. Salary.com provides a free salary wizard to help you determine what IT professionals in your area are making compared with national averages. You can add information such as your degree and the size of the company to your search selection to fine-tune the figures further.

Figure 2 shows that for an entry-level programming position in Chicago, you could expect to earn a salary of between $47,098 and $75,966 at a company of 500 to 1,000 employees. Hundreds of IT job titles are listed in Salary.com, so you can tailor your search to the specific job in which you're interested.

FIGURE 1

High-Growth IT Jobs*

OCCUPATION	MEDIAN PAY ($)	TOP PAY ($)	10-YEAR GROWTH RATE (%)	TOTAL NEW JOBS
Software developers	90,530	143,330	30	270,900
Computer systems analysts	77,740	119,070	22	120,400
Computer support specialists	46,260	76,970	18	110,000
Network and computer systems administrators	69,160	108,090	28	96,600
Information security analysts, web developers, and computer network architects	75,660	119,940	22	65,700
Computer programmers	71,380	114,180	12	43,700
Database administrators	73,490	115,660	31	33,900
Computer and information research scientists	100,660	153,120	19	5,300

*Excerpted from *Occupational Outlook Handbook*, 2012 Edition, Bureau of Labor Statistics

FIGURE 2 The salary wizard at Salary.com is easy to tailor to your location.

IT Jobs Are Not Going "Offshore"

In the global economy in which we now operate, job outlook includes the risk of jobs being outsourced, possibly to other countries. **Outsourcing** is a process whereby a business hires a third-party firm to provide business services (such as customer-support call centers) that were previously handled by in-house employees. **Offshoring** occurs when the outsourcing firm is located (or uses employees) outside the United States.

India, China, Romania, and other former Eastern Bloc countries are major players in providing outsourcing services for U.S. companies. The big lure of outsourcing and offshoring is cost savings: Considering that the standard of living and salaries are much lower in many countries than they are in the United States, offshoring is an attractive option for many U.S. employers.

However, outsourcing and offshoring don't always deliver the cost savings that CEOs envision. Demand for personnel overseas has led to increased costs (primarily due to wage increases) for service providers in foreign markets. Furthermore, other, less-tangible factors can outweigh the cost savings from outsourcing. Communications problems can arise between internal and external employees, for example, and cultural differences between the home country and the country doing the offshoring can result in software code that needs extensive rework by in-house employees. Data also can be less secure in an external environment or during the transfer between the company and an external

vendor. Although outsourcing and offshoring won't be going away, companies are approaching these staffing alternatives with more caution and are looking more to U.S. companies to provide resources.

So, many IT jobs are staying in the United States. According to *InformationWeek* magazine, most jobs in the following three categories (see Figure 3) will stay put:

1. **Customer interaction:** Jobs that require direct input from customers or that involve systems with which customers interface daily

2. **Enablers:** Jobs that involve getting key business projects accomplished, often requiring technical skills beyond the realm of IT, and good people skills

3. **Infrastructure jobs:** Jobs that are fundamental to moving and storing the information that U.S.–based employees need to do their jobs

FIGURE 3

Jobs That Will Likely Remain Onshore

CUSTOMER INTERACTION	ENABLERS	INFRASTRUCTURE JOBS
Web application developers	Business process analysts	Network security
Web interface designers	Application developers (when customer interaction is critical)	Network installation technicians
Database and data warehouse designers/developers	Project managers (for systems with customers and business users who are located predominantly in the United States)	Network administrators (engineers)
Customer relationship management (CRM) analysts		Wireless infrastructure managers and technicians
Enterprise resource planning (ERP) implementation specialists		Disaster recovery planners and responders

In addition, jobs that require specific knowledge of the U.S. marketplace and culture, such as social media managers, are also very likely not to be offshored.

Women Are in High Demand in IT Departments

Currently, women make up about 25% of the IT workforce (per the National Center for Women and Information Technology). This presents a huge opportunity for women who have IT skills, because many IT departments are actively seeking to diversify their workforces. In addition, although a salary gender gap (the difference between what men and women earn for performing the same job) exists in IT careers, it's smaller than in most other professions.

You Have a Choice of Working Location

In this case, location refers to the setting in which you work. IT jobs can be office-based, field-based, project-based, or home-based. Because not every situation is perfect for every individual, you can look for a job that suits your tastes and requirements. Figure 4 summarizes the major job types and their locations.

FIGURE 4

Where Do You Want to Work?

TYPE OF JOB	LOCATION AND HOURS	SPECIAL CONSIDERATIONS
Office-based	Report for work to the same location each day and interact with the same people on a regular basis; requires regular hours of attendance (such as 9 a.m. to 5 p.m.)	May require working beyond "normal" working hours; may also require workers to be on call 24/7
Field-based	Travel from place to place as needed and perform short-term jobs at each location	Involves a great deal of travel and the ability to work independently
Project-based	Work at client sites on specific projects for extended periods of time (weeks or months)	Can be especially attractive to individuals who like workplace situations that vary on a regular basis
Home-based (telecommuting)	Work from home	Involves very little day-to-day supervision and requires an individual who is self-disciplined

You Constantly Meet New Challenges

In IT, the playing field is always changing. New software and hardware are constantly being developed. You'll need to work hard to keep your skills up to date. You'll spend a lot of time in training and self-study trying to learn new systems and techniques. Many individuals thrive in this type of environment because it keeps their jobs from becoming dull or routine.

You Work in Teams

When students are asked to describe their ideal jobs, many describe jobs that involve working in teams. Despite what some people think, IT professionals are not locked in lightless cubicles, basking in the glow of their monitors and working alone on projects. Most IT jobs require constant interaction with other workers, usually in team settings. People skills are highly prized by IT departments. If you have good leadership and team-building skills, you'll have the opportunity to exercise them in an IT job.

You Don't Need to Be a Mathematical Genius

Certain IT careers such as programming involve a fair bit of math. But even if you're not mathematically inclined, you can explore many other IT careers. IT employers also value such attributes as creativity, marketing, and artistic style, especially in jobs that involve working on the Internet or with social media.

IT Skills Are Portable

Most computing skills are portable from industry to industry. A networking job in the clothing manufacturing industry uses the same primary skill set as a networking job for a supermarket chain. Therefore, if something disastrous happens to the industry you're in, you should be able to switch to another industry without having to learn an entirely new skill set. Combining business courses with IT courses will also make you more marketable when changing jobs. For example, as an accounting major, if

you minor in IT, employers may be more willing to hire you because working in accounting today means constantly interfacing with management information systems and manipulating data.

Challenges of IT Careers

Although there are many positive aspects of IT careers, there can be some challenges. The discussions that follow aren't meant to discourage you from pursuing an IT career, but merely to make you aware of exactly what challenges you might face in an IT department.

Stress

Most IT jobs are hectic (see Figure 5). Whereas the average American works 42 hours a week, a survey by *InformationWeek* revealed that the average IT staff person works 45 hours a week and is on call for another 24 hours. On-call time (hours an employee must be available to work in the event of a problem) has been increasing because most IT systems require 24/7 availability.

Women Are in the Minority

A majority of IT jobs are filled by men, so some women view IT departments as *Dilbert*-like microcosms of antisocial geeks and don't feel like they would fit in. Unfortunately, some mostly male IT departments do suffer from varying degrees of gender bias.

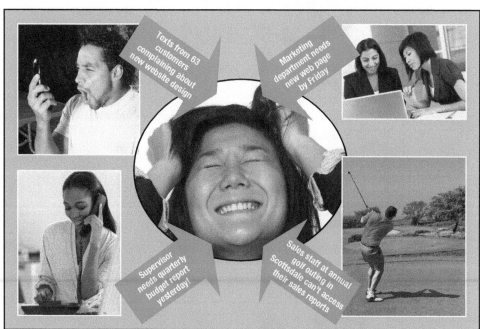

Texts from 63 customers complaining about new website design

Marketing department needs new web page by Friday

Supervisor needs quarterly budget report yesterday!

Sales staff at annual golf outing in Scottsdale can't access their sales reports

FIGURE 5 Stress comes from multiple directions in IT jobs. *(Jenn Mackenzie/Shutterstock; Photobank.ch/Shutterstock; Stephen Coburn/Shutterstock; Wavebreakmedia ltd/Shutterstock; LWPhotography/Shutterstock)*

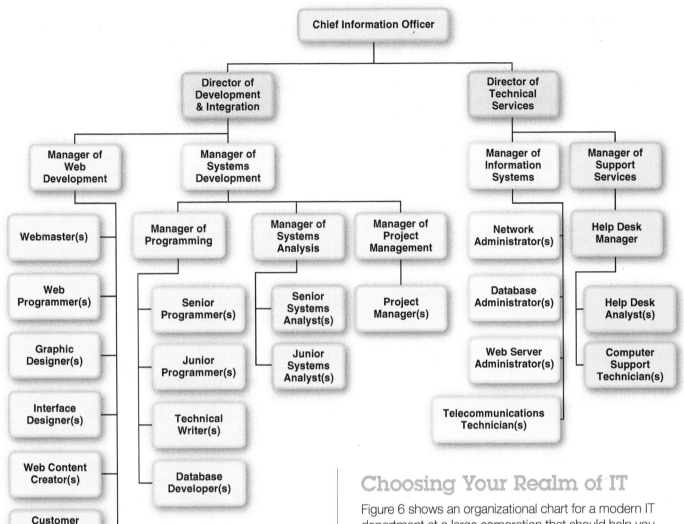

FIGURE 6 This chart represents a typical structure for an IT department at a large corporation.

Although some women may thrive on the challenge of enlightening these male enclaves and bringing them into the twenty-first century, others might find it difficult to work in such environments.

Lifelong Learning Is Required

Although the constantly changing nature of IT can alleviate boredom, keeping up with the changes can also cause some stress. You'll need to take training courses, do self-study, and perhaps take additional college courses, such as getting a graduate degree, to keep up with the vast shifts of technology.

Choosing Your Realm of IT

Figure 6 shows an organizational chart for a modern IT department at a large corporation that should help you understand the variety of careers available and how they interrelate. The chief information officer (CIO) has overall responsibility for the development, implementation, and maintenance of information systems and its infrastructure. Usually, the CIO reports to the chief operating officer (COO).

The responsibilities below the CIO are generally grouped into two units:

1. Development and integration (responsible for the development of systems and websites)
2. Technical services (responsible for the day-to-day operations of the company's information infrastructure and network, including all hardware and software deployed)

In large organizations, responsibilities are distinct and jobs are defined more narrowly. In medium-sized organizations, there can be overlap between position responsibilities. At a small company, you might be the network administrator, database administrator, computer support technician, and social media manager all at the same time. Let's look at the typical jobs found in each department.

Working in Development and Integration

Two distinct paths exist in this division:

1. Web development
2. Systems development

Because everything involves the web today, there's often a great deal of overlap between these paths.

Web Development. When most people think of web development careers, they usually equate them with being a **webmaster**. Webmasters used to be individuals who were solely responsible for all aspects of a company's website. However, today's webmasters usually are supervisors with responsibility for certain aspects of web development. At smaller companies, they may also be responsible for tasks that other individuals in a web development group usually do, such as the following:

- **Web content creators** generate the words and images that appear on the web. Journalists, other writers, editors, and marketing personnel prepare an enormous amount of web content, whereas **video producers**, **graphic designers**, and **animators** create web-based multimedia. Web content creators have a thorough understanding of their own fields as well as HTML, PHP, and JavaScript.
- **Interface designers** work with graphic designers and animators to create a look and feel for the site and make it easy to navigate.
- **Web programmers** build web pages to deploy the materials that the content creators develop. They wield software tools such as Adobe Dreamweaver and Microsoft Expression to develop the web pages. They also create links to databases using products such as Oracle and SQL Server to keep information flowing between users and web pages. They must possess a solid understanding of client- and server-side web languages (HTML, XML, Java, JavaScript, ASP, PHP, Silverlight, and Perl) and of development environments such as the Microsoft .NET Framework.
- **Customer interaction technicians** provide feedback to a website's customers. Major job responsibilities include answering e-mail, sending requested information, funneling questions to appropriate personnel (technical support, sales, and so on), and providing suggestions to web programmers for site improvements. Extensive customer service training is essential to work effectively in this area.
- **Social media directors** are responsible for directing the strategy of the company on all social media sites where the company maintains a presence. Often, supervising customer interaction technicians, social media directors make sure that customers have a quality experience while interacting with company employees and customers on sites such as Facebook, Twitter, and Yelp. Responding to comments left on such sites, developing promotional strategies, and designing functionality of the company's social media sites are common job responsibilities.

As you can see in Figure 7, many different people can work on the same website. Web programming jobs often require a four-year college degree in computer science, whereas graphic designers often are hired with two-year art degrees.

Systems Development. Ask most people what systems developers do and they'll answer, "Programming." However, programming is only one aspect of systems development. Because large projects involve many people, there are many job opportunities in systems development, most of which require four-year college degrees in computer science or management information systems:

- **Systems analysts** gather information from end users about problems and existing information systems. They document systems and propose solutions to problems. Having good people skills is essential to success as a systems analyst. In addition, systems analysts work with programmers during the development phase to design appropriate programs to solve the problem at hand. Therefore, many organizations insist on hiring systems analysts who have solid business backgrounds and programming experience (at least at a basic level).
- **Programmers** attend meetings to document user needs, and they work closely with systems analysts

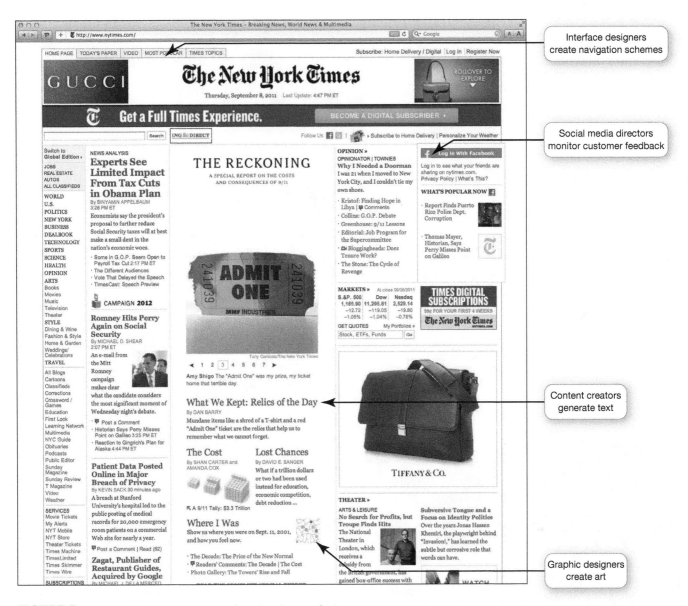

Interface designers create navigation schemes

Social media directors monitor customer feedback

Content creators generate text

Graphic designers create art

FIGURE 7 It takes a team to create and maintain a website. *(Studio 101/Alamy)*

during the design phase of program development. Programmers need excellent written communication skills because they often generate detailed systems documentation for end-user training purposes. Because programming languages are mathematically based, it is essential for programmers to have strong math skills and an ability to think logically.

- **Project managers** manage the overall systems development process: assigning staff, budgeting, reporting to management, coaching team members, and ensuring deadlines are met. Project managers need excellent time management skills because they're often pulled in several directions at once. They usually have prior experience as programmers or systems analysts. Many project managers obtain master's degrees to supplement their undergraduate degrees.

In addition to these key players, the following people are also involved in the systems development process:

- **Technical writers** generate systems documentation for end users and for programmers who may make modifications to the system in the future.
- **Network administrators** help the programmers and analysts design compatible systems, because many systems are required to run in certain environments (UNIX or Windows, for instance) and must work in conjunction with other programs.
- **Database developers** design and build databases to support the software systems being developed.

Large development projects may have all of these team members on the project. Smaller projects

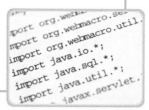

- Programmers build the software that solves problems

- Systems analysts document systems and propose solutions

- Project managers supervise, organize, and coach team members

- Database developers ensure data is accessible when it's needed

FIGURE 8 There are many important team members in systems development. *(Bah69/Fotolia; Rob/Fotolia; FotoLuminate/Fotolia; HaywireMedia/Fotolia)*

may require an overlap of positions, such as a programmer also acting as a systems analyst. As shown in Figure 8, team members work together to build a system.

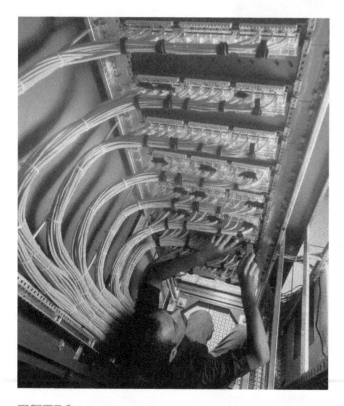

FIGURE 9 At smaller companies, network administrators may be fixing a user's computer in the morning, installing and configuring a new network operating system in the afternoon, and troubleshooting a wiring problem (shown here) in the evening. *(ArtPix/Alamy)*

Working in Technical Services

Technical services jobs are vital to keeping IT systems running. The people in these jobs install and maintain the infrastructure behind the IT systems and work with end users to make sure they can interact with the systems effectively. There are two major categories of technical services careers:

1. Information systems

2. Support services

Note that these also are the *least likely* IT jobs to be outsourced because hands-on work with equipment and users is required on a regular basis.

Information Systems. The information systems department keeps the networks and telecommunications up and running at all times. Within the department, you'll find a variety of positions.

- **Network administrators** (sometimes called *network engineers*) are involved in every stage of network planning and deployment (see Figure 9). They decide what equipment to buy and what media to use, they determine the network's topology, and they help install the network (by supervising contractors or doing it themselves). Network administrators plan disaster-recovery strategies (such as what to do if a fire destroys the server room). When equipment and cables break, network administrators must fix the problem. They also obtain and install updates to network software and evaluate new equipment to determine whether the network should be upgraded. In addition, they monitor the network's performance and often develop policies regarding network usage, security measures, and hardware and software standards.

Get in the Game: Careers in Game Development

The video gaming industry in the United States has surpassed the earning power of the Hollywood movie industry. In 2011, U.S. consumers bought slightly over $17 billion worth of video games and accessories, whereas Hollywood took in just over $10.2 billion. Although some aspects of game development, such as scenery design and certain aspects of programming, are being sent offshore, the majority of game development requires a creative team whose members need to work in close proximity. Therefore, it's anticipated that most game development jobs will stay in the United States.

Consoles such as the Xbox 360 and the PlayStation 3 generate demand for large-scale games. The popularity of mobile devices such as smartphones and tablets is driving demand for lower-end, casual game applications. Casual games are games that can be played relatively quickly, such as puzzle games. Demand for family-friendly games without violence, sex, and profanity is on the rise (see Figure 10). With all this demand, there are many opportunities for careers in game development.

Game development jobs usually are split along two paths: designers and programmers.

- **Game designers** tend to be artistic and are responsible for creating 2-D and 3-D art, game interfaces, video sequences, special effects, game levels, and scenarios. Game designers must master software packages such as Autodesk 3ds Max, Autodesk Maya, NewTek LightWave 3D, Adobe Photoshop, and Adobe Flash.

- **Game programmers** are responsible for coding the scenarios developed by the designers. Using languages and toolsets such as Objective-C, Unity, Apple Xcode, C, C++, Assembly, and Java, programmers build the game and ensure that it plays accurately.

Aside from programmers and designers, play testers and quality assurance professionals play the games with the intent of breaking them or discovering bugs within the game interfaces or worlds. **Play testing** is an essential part of the game development process because it assists designers in determining which aspects of the game are most intriguing to players and which parts of the game need to be repaired or enhanced.

No matter what job you may pursue in the realm of gaming, you'll need to have a two- or four-year college degree. If you're interested in gaming, look for a school with a solid animation or 3-D art program or a computer game–programming curriculum. Programming requires a strong background in math and physics to enable you to realistically program environments that mimic the real world. Proficiency with math (especially geometry) also helps with design careers.

For more information on gaming careers, check out the International Game Developers Association site (**igda.org**) and the Game Career Guide (**gamecareerguide.com**).

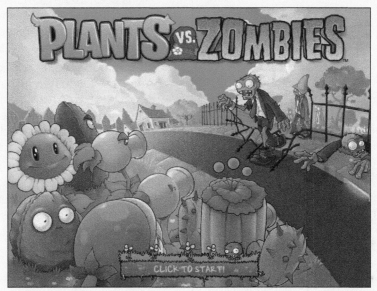

FIGURE 10 Plants vs. Zombies, which has you grow plants to fend off encroaching zombie hordes, is an example of a popular casual game available for many different platforms. *(Vinod Kurien/Alamy)*

- **Database administrators (DBAs)** install and configure database servers and ensure that the servers provide an adequate level of access to all users.
- **Web server administrators** install, configure, and maintain web servers and ensure that the company maintains Internet connectivity at all times.
- **Telecommunications technicians** oversee the communications infrastructure, including training employees to use telecommunications equipment. They are often on call 24 hours a day.

Support Services. As a member of the support services team, you interface with users (external customers or employees) and troubleshoot their computer problems. Support service positions include the following:

- **Helpdesk analysts** staff the phones, respond to Internet live chats, or respond to e-mails and solve problems for customers or employees, either remotely or in person. Often, helpdesk personnel are called on to train users on the latest software and hardware.
- **Computer support technicians** go to a user's location and fix software and hardware problems. They also often have to chase down and repair faults in the network infrastructure.

As important as these people are, they may receive a great deal of abuse by angry users whose computers are not working. When working in support services, you need to be patient and not be overly sensitive to insults!

Technical services jobs often require a two-year college degree or training at a trade school or technical institute. At smaller companies, job duties tend to overlap between the helpdesk and technician jobs. These jobs are in demand and require staffing in local markets, so they are staying onshore. You can't repair a computer's power supply if you are located in another country!

Preparing for a Job in IT

A job in IT requires a robust skill set and formal training and preparation. Most employers today have an entry-level requirement of a college degree, a technical institute diploma, appropriate professional certifications, experience in the field, or a combination of these. How can you prepare for a job in IT?

1. **Get educated.** Two- and four-year colleges and universities normally offer three degrees to prepare students for IT careers: computer science, management information systems, and information technology (although titles vary). Alternatives to colleges and universities are privately licensed technical (or trade) schools. Generally, these programs focus on building skill sets rapidly and qualifying for a job in a specific field. The main advantage of technical schools is that their programs usually take less time to complete than college degrees. However, to have a realistic chance of employment in IT fields other than networking or web development, you should attend a degree-granting college or university.

2. **Investigate professional certifications.** Certifications attempt to provide a consistent method of measuring skill levels in specific areas of IT. Hundreds of IT certifications are available, most of which you get by passing a written exam. Software and hardware vendors (such as Microsoft and Cisco) and professional organizations (such as the Computing Technology Industry Association) often establish certification standards. Visit **microsoft.com**, **cisco.com**, **comptia.org**, and **sun.com** for more information on certifications.

3. **Get experience.** In addition to education, employers want you to have experience, even for entry-level jobs. While you're still completing your education, consider getting an internship or part-time job in your field of study. Many schools will help you find internships and allow you to earn credit toward your degree through internships.

4. **Do research.** Find out as much as you can about the company and the industry it's in before going on an interview. Start with the company's website, and then expand your search to business and trade publications such as *Business Week* and *Inc.* magazines.

Getting Started in an IT Career

Training for a career is not useful unless you can find a job at the end of your training. Here are some tips on getting a job:

Certifications: How Important Are They?

Employees with certifications generally earn more than employees who aren't certified. However, most employers don't view a certification as a substitute for a college degree or a trade school program. You should think of certifications as an extra edge beyond your formal education that will make you more attractive to employers. To ensure you're pursuing the right certifications, ask employers which certifications they respect, or explore online job sites to see which certifications are listed as desirable or required.

FIGURE 11

Professional Organizations

ORGANIZATION NAME	PURPOSE	WEBSITE
Association for Computing Machinery (ACM)	Oldest scientific computing society; maintains a strong focus on programming and systems development	**acm.org**
Association for Information Systems (AIS)	Organization of professionals who work in academia and specialize in information systems	**aisnet.org**
Association of Information Technology Professionals (AITP)	Heavy focus on IT education and development of seminars and learning materials	**aitp.org**
Institute of Electrical and Electronics Engineers (IEEE)	Provides leadership and sets engineering standards for all types of network computing devices and protocols	**ieee.org**
Information Systems Security Association (ISSA)	Not-for-profit, international organization of information security professionals and practitioners	**issa.org**

1. **Use the career resources at your school.** Many employers recruit at schools, and most schools maintain a placement office to help students find jobs. Employees in the placement office can help you with résumé preparation and interviewing skills and can provide you with leads for internships and jobs.

2. **Develop relationships with your instructors.** Many college instructors still work in or previously worked in the IT industry. They can often provide you with valuable advice and industry contacts.

3. **Start networking.** Many jobs are never advertised but instead are filled by word of mouth. Seek out contacts in your field and discuss job prospects with them. Find out what skills you need, and ask them to recommend others in the industry with whom you can speak. Professional organizations such as the Association for Computing Machinery (ACM) offer one way to network. These organizations often have chapters on college campuses and offer reduced membership rates for students. Figure 11 lists major professional organizations you should consider investigating.

   If you're a woman and are thinking about pursuing an IT career, many resources and groups cater to female IT professionals and students (see Figure 12).

FIGURE 12

Resources for Women in IT

ORGANIZATION NAME	PURPOSE	WEBSITE
Anita Borg Institute for Women and Technology	Organization whose aim is to "increase the impact of women on all aspects of technology"	**anitaborg.org**
Association for Women in Computing (AWC)	A not-for-profit organization dedicated to promoting the advancement of women in computing professions	**awc-hq.org**
The Center for Women in Technology (CWIT)	An organization dedicated to providing global leadership in achieving women's full participation in all aspects of IT	**cwit.umbc.edu**
Diversity/Careers in Engineering & Information Technology	An online magazine whose articles cover career issues of technical professionals who are members of minority groups, women, or people with disabilities	**diversitycareers.com**
Women in Technology International (WITI)	A global trade association for tech-savvy, professional women	**witi.com**

The oldest and best-known organization is the Association for Women in Computing, founded in 1978.

4. Check corporate websites for jobs. Many corporate websites list current job opportunities. For example, Google provides searchable job listings by geographic location. Check the sites of companies in which you are interested and then do a search on the sites for job openings or, if provided, click their employment links.

5. Visit online employment sites. Most of these sites allow you to store your résumé online, and many sites allow employers to browse résumés to find qualified employees. Begin looking at job postings on these sites early in your education, because these job postings detail the skill sets employers require. Focusing on coursework that will provide you with desirable skill sets will make you more marketable. Figure 13 lists employment sites as well as sites that offer other career resources.

The outlook for IT jobs should continue to be positive in the future. We wish you luck with your education and job search.

FIGURE 13

Resources for IT Employment

SITE NAME	URL
CareerBuilder	careerbuilder.com
ComputerJobs.com	computerjobs.com
ComputerWork.com	computerwork.com
Dice	dice.com
Gamasutra	gamasutra.com
JustTechJobs	justtechjobs.com
LinkedIn	linkedin.com
Monster	monster.com
TechCareers	techcareers.com

For a quick review of what you've learned, answer the following questions. Visit **pearsonhighered.com/techinaction** to check your answers.

multiple choice

1. The individuals responsible for generating images for websites are referred to as

    a. network administrators.

    b. graphic designers.

    c. web programmers.

    d. interface designers.

2. What type of job involves working at client locations and the ability to work with little direct supervision?

    a. field-based

    b. project-based

    c. office-based

    d. home-based

3. Which position is NOT typically a part of the information systems department?

    a. helpdesk analyst

    b. telecommunications technician

    c. network administrator

    d. web server administrator

4. Outsourcing is thought to be an attractive option for many companies because of

    a. the emphasis on employee training.

    b. the cost savings that can be realized.

    c. increased data security.

    d. decreased travel and entertainment costs.

5. Which role best describes those employees who implement solutions designed by systems analysts?

    a. project managers

    b. network administrator

    c. programmers

    d. database administrators

6. Which of the following statements about IT careers is FALSE?

    a. IT employers typically prefer experience to certification.

    b. Women who have IT skills have ample opportunities for securing IT employment.

    c. Many IT jobs are staying in the United States.

    d. Most IT jobs require little interaction with other people.

7. Which task is NOT typically performed by a network administrator?

    a. developing network usage policies

    b. installing networks

    c. planning for disaster recovery

    d. web programming

8. Interface designers are the people responsible for

    a. orchestrating the company strategy in online venues.

    b. providing feedback to website customers.

    c. creating the look and feel of a website.

    d. deploying the materials prepared by content creators.

9. The oldest scientific computing organization is the

    a. Institute of Electrical and Electronics Engineers.

    b. Association for Computing Machinery.

    c. Information Systems Security Association.

    d. Association for Women in Computing.

10. Which position is NOT a part of the Systems Development department?

    a. systems analyst   c. programmer

    b. project manager   d. database administrator

Database Basics

Database Building Blocks

OBJECTIVES

1. What is a database, and why is using one beneficial? **(pp. 466–470)**

2. What do database management systems do? **(p. 470)**

3. What components make up a database? **(pp. 470–474)**

👤 **Active Helpdesk:** Using Databases

Database Types

OBJECTIVE

4. What types of databases are there? **(pp. 475–476)**

👤 **Active Helpdesk:** Understanding Database Management Systems

Database Functions

OBJECTIVE

5. How do relational databases organize and manipulate data? **(pp. 478–484)**

🔊 **Sound Byte:** Creating an Access 2010 Database

🔊 **Sound Byte:** Improving an Access 2010 Database

How Businesses Use Databases

Database Warehousing and Storage

OBJECTIVE

6. What are data warehouses and data marts, and how are they used? **(pp. 488–490)**

👤 **Active Helpdesk:** Data Warehouses, Data Marts, and Information Systems

Business Intelligence Systems

OBJECTIVE

7. What is a business intelligence system, and what types of business intelligence systems are used by decision makers? **(pp. 492–496)**

Data Mining

OBJECTIVE

8. What is data mining, and how does it work? **(pp. 497–499)**

For all media in this chapter go to **pearsonhighered.com/techinaction** or MyITLab.

(Marek Uliasz/Alamy; Kheng Ho Toh/Alamy; Juri Samsonov/Fotolia; Mira/Alamy; S.John/Fotolia; S.John/Fotolia)

HOW COOL IS THIS?

You've just **lost your wallet**. You have to cancel all your **credit cards** and notify your bank. You never wrote down your credit card information, so now you're stuck going through bills trying to piece together the details. Moreover, you've used some of the credit cards for automatic payments on other bills, so you have to remember what card was used to pay which account. Wouldn't it be great if you had this information securely stored in a database on your phone or computer? With **Tap Forms Database** installed on your computer, iPhone, or iPad, you could have had all this data at your fingertips. Tap Forms Database **organizes** different types of information so that you can keep track of your **important information** such as membership accounts, bank accounts, passwords, combinations, homework, and frequent flyer numbers, as well as your favorite movies, music, or recipes. The application is **secured** with tight encryption, and it integrates with Dropbox. So, get your life organized today with Tap Forms Database.

465

Database Basics

You interact with databases every day—when you retrieve a friend's phone number from your contacts, post to your Facebook page, or add a song to your iTunes playlist. In this part of the chapter, we'll look at the basics of databases and how databases can be used to provide relevant information quickly and easily.

 ## database building
BLOCKS

A **database** is a collection of related data that can be stored, sorted, organized, and queried. Many actions we do every day (use an ATM, shop online, make an airplane reservation) generate data that needs to be stored, managed, and used by others. Most likely, a database has been created that receives and stores our generated data and that enables that data to be processed and used by others. By creating an organized structure for data, databases make data more meaningful and therefore more useful. Databases effectively turn data into information.

Why do I need to know about databases? Since you interact with databases every day, understanding how databases work and what you can do with databases will help you use the ones you

interact with more effectively. For example, *categorizing, sorting,* and *filtering* are key attributes of most databases. If a database isn't set up correctly or if you don't know how to use the database, you may not get the type of information you're looking for.

StubHub, the online ticket-exchange platform (see Figure 11.1), is an example of a database. Sellers list tickets on StubHub. They specify the categories the tickets fall into (sports, concerts, theater) and other details, such as day, time, and seat location of the event, and set a price. Buyers then access the website, using its filters to narrow down to the type of ticket they're looking to purchase. If the database doesn't have the right categories for sellers to choose from, buyers won't be able to locate the tickets they want.

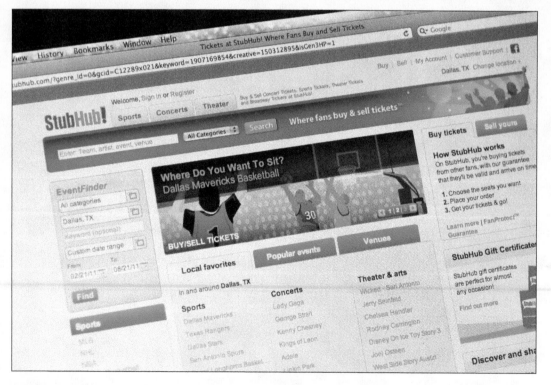

FIGURE 11.1 StubHub is a database that provides for the exchange of tickets between sellers and buyers. *(NetPhotos/Alamy)*

BITS&BYTES

Music Database Helps You Find New Music

Having good music at hand is easy thanks to music databases such as Pandora and Spotify. The *Music Genome Project* makes it possible for these applications to provide music based on specific preferences. Using almost 400 attributes such as "female lead vocalist" or "club rap roots," the Music Genome Project analyzes, categorizes, and organizes songs into a database that Pandora and Spotify access.

With Pandora (**pandora.com**), you create radio stations that play music with attributes similar to those you provide. For example, if you enjoy music from The Black Eyed Peas or you like the song "Rolling in the Deep," you would enter these as "seeds." Pandora then plays randomly selected songs with attributes similar to the seeds you provided.

Spotify (**spotify.com**) offers music, but in a less random way. With Spotify, you can search to find the songs or artists you want to listen to (see Figure 11.2). Moreover, Spotify incorporates a social networking aspect by informing you what songs your friends are listening to and by sharing playlists from users who choose to make their lists public. Spotify also offers Artist Radio, which acts similarly to Pandora's random music generator.

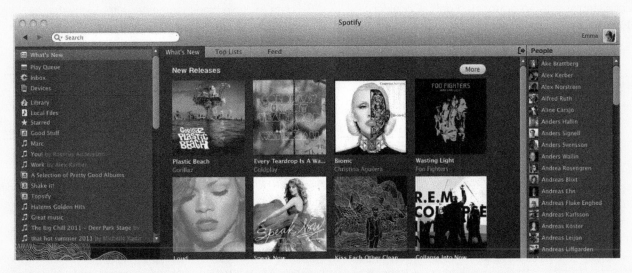

FIGURE 11.2 Spotify lets you create and share your playlists or listen to those created by your friends or others. *(Handout/MCT/Newscom)*

Databases versus Lists

Do I need databases for managing all types of data? Not every situation in which related data needs to be turned into organized information demands the complexity of a database. For simple tasks, lists are adequate. Most word processing and spreadsheet applications have tools to help you create simple lists. A table you create in Microsoft Word can serve as a list, as can a spreadsheet you create in Microsoft Excel.

Figure 11.3 shows a simple "Books to Buy" list you might create in Excel before beginning college. This list works well because it's simple and suited to just one purpose: to provide you with a list of books you need to buy for a particular semester. If all the information that needs to be tracked were as simple as the information in Figure 11.3, there would be little need for databases.

When is a list not sufficient for organizing data? If complex information needs to be organized or more than one person needs to access it, a list isn't an efficient solution. For example, when you enrolled in college, you provided to a number of people basic information about yourself, including your name and address as well as the classes you wished to take. Your school also tracks other information about you, such as your residence hall assignment and meal plan

	A	B	C	D
2	**Books To Buy**			
3				
4	Class	Title	Author	Bought
5	American Literature 1	Anthology of American Literature, Volume 1	McMichael et al.	
6	American Literature 1	Moby Dick	Melville	Yes
7	American Literature 1	The Last of the Mohicans	Cooper	Yes
8	English Composition 1	The Academic Writer's Handbook	Rosen	
9	English Composition 1	The Write Stuff: Thinking Through Essays	Sims	Yes
10	Intro to Business	Better Business	Solomon, Poatsy, Martin	Yes

FIGURE 11.3 A basic list created as a spreadsheet in Microsoft Excel or as a table in Microsoft Word is often sufficient to organize simple data.

preferences. Consider the lists shown in Figure 11.4. Figure 11.4a is a list the registrar's office might use to keep track of students and the classes they're taking. Figure 11.4b is a list the Housing and Dining manager might use to track a student's assigned housing and his or her selected meal plan.

What's the problem with lists? Lists can lead to inefficiencies due to repetition of data and errors from inconsistently entered or updated data. Consider Figure 11.4 again:

1. There is a great deal of duplicated data in the two lists. For example, each time Julio Garza registers for a class, his name and address are entered. He also provides the same data to the Housing and Dining manager when he makes his residence hall and meal plan selections. This **data redundancy** can be problematic, especially when a school has thousands of students. Imagine the time wasted by entering data multiple times, semester after semester, as well as the time required for the database to search

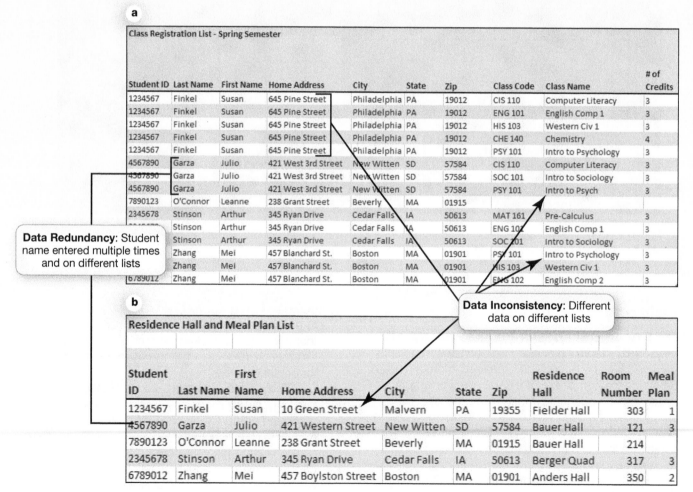

FIGURE 11.4 (a) A class registration list and (b) a list of residence hall assignments are two lists a college might create to keep track of student information.

through the duplicated information. Consider, too, the increased likelihood that someone will make a data-entry mistake. Additionally, if data is entered multiple times, as is Arthur Stinson's in the list in Figure 11.4a, any reports (such as student bills) generated based on this list will be inaccurate because of the duplicate data. In this case, Arthur could be sent multiple bills for his classes.

2. Each time the information in the list changes, multiple lists must be updated. If a student moves, his or her data will need to be updated in all the lists that contain his or her address. It would be easy to overlook one or more lists or even one or more rows in the same list. This would lead to a state of **data inconsistency**. It wouldn't be possible to easily tell which data is correct. Notice in Figure 11.4 that Susan Finkel's address on the Registrar's list differs from that on the Housing and Dining list. It's impossible to tell which address is correct, resulting in data inconsistency.

3. Correct data can be entered into a list but in an inconsistent format. Look at students Julio Garza and Mei Zhang in Figure 11.4a. Both are registered for PSY 101, but two different course names appear: *Intro to Psychology* and *Intro to Psych*. Are these the same course? Which name is correct? Confusion arises when data is inconsistently entered. Establishing data consistency is difficult to do with a list.

Aside from data redundancy and inconsistency, are there any other problems with using lists instead of databases? Other problems that occur when using simple lists to organize data are as follows:

- *Inappropriate data:* In Figure 11.4b, each student has selected one of the college's three meal plans. What if someone enters a nonexistent meal plan? This is not only wrong, it can also be confusing to anyone viewing the list. With a list, there are few checks to make sure that data entered is valid.

- *Incomplete data:* In Figure 11.4, Leanne O'Connor has enrolled in the college but hasn't yet registered for courses or chosen a meal plan. It's difficult to tell by looking at her record whether data relating to her course registration and meal plan is available and just wasn't entered or is truly missing.

Can't I just exercise caution and set rules for creating and updating lists? Carefully following the rules when you create and update a list like the ones in Figure 11.4 can address many of the problems mentioned, but there's still room for error. Being careful doesn't avoid the problems of data redundancy and inconsistency. And even if you could surmount these problems, it's difficult to share

a list with other users and have the data remain consistent. Therefore, for any complex data that needs to be organized or shared, using a database is the most practical and efficient way to avoid the pitfalls associated with using lists.

Advantages of Using Databases

How do databases make our lives easier? Databases provide several main advantages: They manage large amounts of data efficiently, they enable information sharing, and they promote data integrity.

How can databases manage large amounts of data efficiently? Often, large amounts of data are complex and need to be organized in specific ways in order to be used most efficiently. Figure 11.4 illustrates some issues that can occur when complex data is put in list format. The more data you have, the more likely you are to store that data in multiple lists or tables in a database. A database has mechanisms to manage large amounts of data and to keep it accurate as it's updated and manipulated.

How do databases make information sharing possible? With a database, only one file is maintained. Because of this, databases provide **data centralization**. There is no need for multiple lists, as there was when the individual college offices each maintained their own independent lists. A centralized database becomes a shared source of information that everyone can access (see Figure 11.5). Each department that needs to use student information accesses it from the same set of data. A centralized database also increases efficiency because there are no files to reconcile with each other. In addition, many databases also provide the ability to control who has access to the data, so security of data isn't diminished because it's centralized.

How do databases promote data integrity? **Data integrity** means that the data contained in the database is accurate and reliable. Data centralization goes a long way toward ensuring data integrity. Instead of information being stored in multiple lists that have to be maintained, data is stored in only one place. When multiple lists are kept, information may become inconsistent because each list is

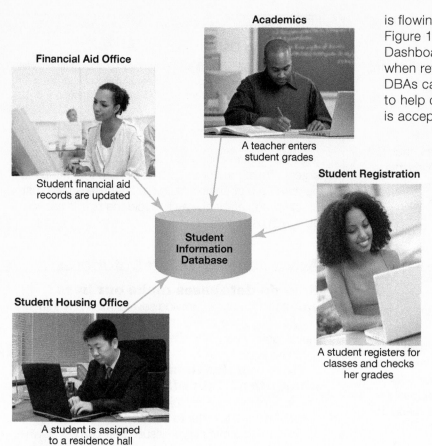

Financial Aid Office

Student financial aid records are updated

Academics

A teacher enters student grades

Student Housing Office

A student is assigned to a residence hall

Student Information Database

Student Registration

A student registers for classes and checks her grades

FIGURE 11.5 A database centralizes data so that only one copy of relevant data must be maintained. All database users therefore access the same up-to-date information. *(wavebreakmedia/Shutterstock; AVAVA/ Shutterstock; Monkey Business Images/Shutterstock; Tan Kian Khoon/Shutterstock)*

is flowing smoothly into and out of the database. Figure 11.6 shows a view of the MySQL Enterprise Dashboard screen, a tool used primarily by DBAs when reviewing the performance of a database. DBAs can monitor table usage and CPU utilization to help determine whether database performance is acceptable.

Database Management Systems

How are databases created? Databases are created and managed using a **database management system (DBMS)**.

A DBMS is specially designed application software (such as Oracle Database or Microsoft Access) that interacts with the user, other applications, and the database to capture and analyze data. The four main operations of a DBMS are as follows:

1. Creating databases and entering data
2. Viewing (or browsing) and sorting data
3. Querying (extracting) data
4. Outputting data

In this section we look at the considerations required in creating and maintaining a database. But first, you need to understand some basic database terminology.

maintained separately. If an address changes, it needs to be changed in only one place in a database, whereas with multiple lists, it's quite possible that information will be updated in one list and not in another, as was illustrated with a change in address for Susan Finkel in Figure 11.4.

Are there any disadvantages associated with databases?

Databases can be more time consuming and expensive to set up and administer than lists. Great care must be exercised in the design of databases to ensure they'll function as intended. Although average individuals can design small databases, it's helpful to have an experienced **database administrator** (or **database designer**)— an IT professional who is responsible for designing, constructing, and maintaining databases—for larger databases. Database administrators (DBAs) review and manage data on an ongoing basis to ensure the data

FIGURE 11.6 The Enterprise Dashboard in MySQL helps DBAs review database performance.

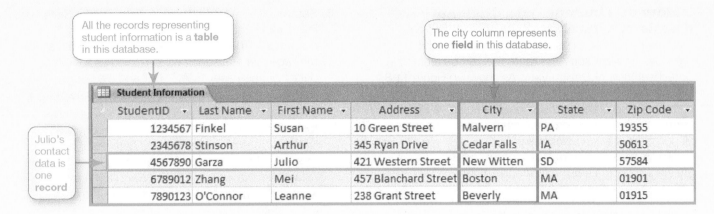

All the records representing student information is a **table** in this database.

The city column represents one **field** in this database.

Julio's contact data is one record

StudentID	Last Name	First Name	Address	City	State	Zip Code
1234567	Finkel	Susan	10 Green Street	Malvern	PA	19355
2345678	Stinson	Arthur	345 Ryan Drive	Cedar Falls	IA	50613
4567890	Garza	Julio	421 Western Street	New Witten	SD	57584
6789012	Zhang	Mei	457 Blanchard Street	Boston	MA	01901
7890123	O'Connor	Leanne	238 Grant Street	Beverly	MA	01915

FIGURE 11.7 In a database, a category of information is stored in a field. A group of related fields is called a record, and a group of related records is called a table.

Database Terminology

How is data stored in a database? Understanding how databases store information requires knowing the unique terminology developed to describe databases. As shown in Figure 11.7, databases have three main components:

1. *Fields:* A database stores each category of information in a **field**. Fields are displayed in columns. Each field is identified by a field name, which is a way of describing the information in the field. In Figure 11.7, there are seven different fields (Student ID, Last Name, First Name, Address, City, State, and Zip Code).

2. *Records:* A group of related fields is called a **record**. For example, in Figure 11.7, a student's ID, name, and complete address comprise a record.

3. *Tables (Files):* A group of related records is called a **table** (or **file**). Tables are usually organized by a common subject. Figure 11.7 shows a table (called "Student Information") that contains records representing contact information for students.

Planning and Creating the Database

How do I create a database with a DBMS? To create a database with a DBMS, you must first describe the data to be captured. This description is contained in the database's files and is referred to as

ACTIVE HELPDESK
Understanding Database Management Systems

In this Active Helpdesk call, you'll play the role of a helpdesk staffer, fielding calls about database management systems, what they do, and how people can use them.

SOUND BYTE
Creating an Access 2010 Database

In this Sound Byte, you'll learn how to create an Access database to catalog a collection of CDs and DVDs. The Sound Byte will take you through a systematic process that will result in a fully functional small database.

the **data dictionary** (or the **database schema**). The data dictionary is like a map of the database and defines the features of the fields in the database. You need to build a data dictionary entry for each field you'll use in a database before you enter data into the database. This forces you to consider up front the data you need to capture.

The attributes that define the data in the data dictionary include the following:

- The field name
- The *data type* (type of data in the field, such as text, numeric, date/time, etc.)
- The description of the field (optional)
- Any properties (decimals, formatting, etc.) of that particular type of data, and
- The *field size* (the expected length of data for each field)

These attributes are **metadata**: data that describes other data. Metadata is an integral part of the data dictionary. Describing the data in this way helps to categorize it and sets parameters for entering valid data into the database (such as a 10-digit number in a phone number field). In addition to describing the specific features of the data to be entered in the database, the data dictionary describes relationships between the data, how the data will be indexed (which speeds up access to the data), and what kind of output may be required of the database.

How do I include data dictionary details in a database? The information from the data dictionary is used to create the tables in the database. In Microsoft Access, tables can be created in Datasheet View or Design View. As shown in Figure 11.8, Design View gives you a detailed view of the field name, data type, and other data elements—known as **Field Properties** in an Access database table—which were all defined in the data dictionary.

How are data tables created? Data tables are simple to create using four basic steps:

1. Input field names. Field names must be unique within a table. For example, in the table in Figure 11.8a, the field name "StateAbbreviation" is used to store the abbreviation for the state where the student lives. Sometimes the field name used to create the table may not be the best to display on forms and reports. The Caption property in Microsoft Access lets you display a name of your choice. In Figure 11.8a, the caption "State" is used.

2. Define the data type for each field. For the "State" field in Figure 11.8a, you use a Text data type because state names are expressed using text characters.

3. Set a maximum field size for the field. For the State field in Figure 11.8a, the Field Size property is set to "2" (two characters). Therefore, the data would be restricted to the two-letter state abbreviations such as "OR" (the default, in this case), "MA," "TX," and the like.

4. Set a **default value** for a field, if necessary. A default value is the value the database automatically uses for the field unless the user enters another value. Default values are useful for field data that's frequently the same. For example, setting a default value for a "State" field saves users from having to enter that value for each student if most students live in the same state.

You need to repeat these steps for each field in the table. When completed, the resulting table, shown in Datasheet View in Figure 11.8b, is ready for data entry.

How do I know what fields are needed in my database? Careful planning is required to identify each distinct piece of data you need to capture. Each field should describe a unique piece of data and should not combine two separate pieces of data. For example, first and last names are

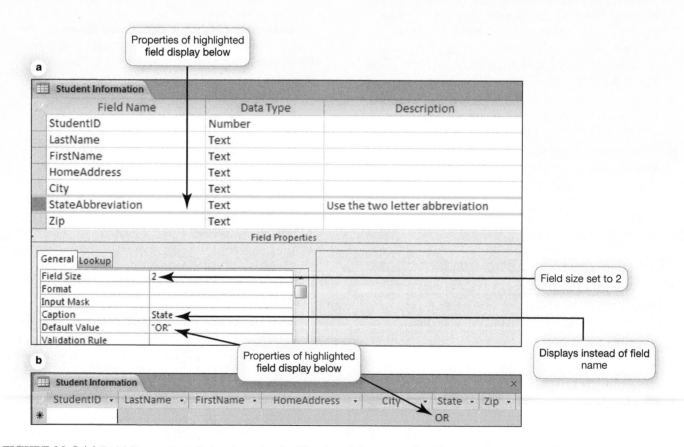

FIGURE 11.8 (a) Field Properties, shown here for the "Student Information" table in an Access database, represent the database's data dictionary. The Field Properties pane is displayed when a table is shown in Design View. (b) The "Student Information" table is ready for data input in Datasheet View.

separate pieces of data, and you'd want to create a separate field for each rather than having one field for "Name." For instance, suppose you want to send an e-mail message to students addressing all of them by their first name (such as "Dear Geri"). If Geri's first and last names are in the same field in the database, extracting just her first name for the salutation will be difficult. Similarly, if the name data are combined, it will be difficult to sort by last name (unless the data are inputted with last name first). Separating the data into individual fields allows for better filtering and sorting of all data.

What happens if I need to add or delete fields from the database? The purpose of planning the database ahead of time is to avoid having to change the structure of the database. Once relationships between the data are established and data is entered in the database, it's difficult to add and delete fields. It's often best to add sample or limited amounts of data to test your database before you fully populate (enter data into) it.

Are there specific rules for establishing field names? The following are some guidelines in establishing field names:

- Field names must be unique within a table. For example, you can't have two fields labeled "Name" in one table; they must be different, such as "First Name" and "Last Name."

- It's helpful to distinguish similarly named fields on different tables to avoid confusion if those fields appear together in other components of the database. For example, in a college database, there may be separate tables for Student and Faculty. In each table, there will be fields for "First Name" and "Last Name." Those fields may be used together in the same report that details a student's schedule. To avoid confusion, it would be better to use field names with some notation that distinguishes the table that the field is from, such as "S LastName" and "S FirstName" in the Student table and "F LastName" and "F FirstName" in the Faculty table.

Creating a data dictionary will help you plan for these types of naming arrangements.

Can any type of data be entered in any field? As noted earlier, when fields are created in the database, the user assigns each field a **data type** (or **field type**). The data type indicates what type of data can be stored in the field and prevents the wrong type of data from being entered into the field. Data types for Microsoft Access include text, numbers, and hyperlinks. Figure 11.9 lists the most common data types, with examples of each.

How much data can be entered into a field? As noted above, **field size** defines the maximum number of characters that a field can hold. As a rule, you should tailor the field size to match the maximum length of the data it contains. If a numeric field has a size of 5, it can hold a number that has up to 5 digits (from 1 to 99999). It is important to ensure that the selected field length is long enough to enable storage of the longest possible piece of data that might be entered into the field. Otherwise,

FIGURE 11.9

Common Data Types

DATA TYPE	USED TO STORE	EXAMPLES
Text	Letters, symbols, or combinations of letters, symbols, and numbers (up to 255 characters). Text also contains numbers that can't be used in calculations, such as in phone numbers and zip codes.	Cecilia PSY 101 (610) 555-1212
Memo	Long blocks of text (up to 65,535 characters).	Four score and seven years ago our fathers brought forth on this continent, a new nation, conceived in Liberty, and dedicated to the proposition that all men are created equal.
Numeric	Numeric data that can be used in calculations or that is represented as currency.	512 1.789 $1,230
Date/Time	Dates and times in standard notation. Data may be used in calculations, such as calculating the number of days between today and your next birthday.	2/21/2016 10:48:01
Calculated	Results of a calculation; often involves numeric or date/time data from other fields in the database.	Price × Quantity × .06
Object	Pictures, charts, or files from another Windows-based application.	JPG file Word document
Hyperlink	Alphanumeric data stored as a hyperlink address to a web page, an e-mail address, or an existing file.	pearsonhighered.com/ techinactionname@email.com

data may be truncated (a portion of it chopped off and lost) during data entry.

Using Primary Keys

Can fields have the same values in the same table? It's possible that two students live in the same town or have the same last name, so it's possible for different fields to have the same values. However, to keep records distinct, each record must have one field that has a value unique to that record. This unique field is called a **primary key field**. For example, as shown in Figure 11.10, in the "Student Information" table, the primary key field is "Student ID." Establishing a primary key and ensuring that it's unique makes it impossible to duplicate records.

What makes a good primary key? The most important constraint is that the primary key be unique, though there are other considerations. Social Security numbers, although unique to individuals, aren't a good choice because people often don't want them used for fear of identity theft if the data were misused. Other common numbers that might be used to identify data within a specific organization (such as a credit card number or driver's license number) also have their own flaws as universal unique identifiers.

In practice, primary keys don't have to be numbers that already represent something. In most instances, the number used to represent a record is some form of serial number that begins with the first record and increases serially as each new record is generated. For example, when you place an order with Amazon.com, your transaction gets a unique order number. This number is a primary key in Amazon's database. It's essential to have a unique number for each order because it would be difficult to keep track of the order without one. Many database programs have a means of automatically generating a unique identifier that has no meaning outside of the database system. In Microsoft Access, for example, this unique identifier is the AutoNumber data type.

Is there a way to ensure data is organized efficiently? You create database tables for two reasons: to hold unique data about a subject and to describe unique events or transactions. In databases, the goal is to reduce data redundancy by recording data only once. The process to ensure data is organized most efficiently is called data **normalization**. For example, normalization would remove issues such as the data redundancy shown in Figure 11.3 by separating data into two distinct student information and course information tables. ■

Student Information						
StudentID	LastName	FirstName	HomeAddress	City	State	Zip
1234567	Finkel	Susan	645 Pine Street	Philadelphia	PA	19012
3456789	Finkel	Susan	25 Maywood Road	Darien	CT	06820
6789012	Zhang	Mei	457 Blanchard St.	Boston	MA	01901
2345678	Stinson	Arthur	345 Ryan Drive	Cedar Falls	IA	50613
4567890	Garza	Julio	421 West 3rd Street	New Witten	SD	57584

Same name, different StudentID

FIGURE 11.10 The "StudentID" field makes an ideal primary key field because even students with the same name won't have the same ID number.

database
TYPES

Many different types of electronic databases have been used since the invention of the computer. The three major types of databases currently in use are *relational, object-oriented,* and *multidimensional*. Of these three, relational databases have the largest market share, but the market share of multidimensional databases is growing at a fast pace. Microsoft Access is the most popular relational database software.

Relational Databases

What is a relational database? Relational **databases** operate by organizing data into various tables based on logical groupings. For example, all student address and contact information would be grouped into one table, while the housing and dining information is grouped into a separate table. It would be redundant to have the same student contact information also included in the housing and dining table, so there needs to be some way in which the student contact information can be linked to the housing and dining information. In relational databases, a link between tables that defines how the data is related is referred to as a **relationship**. A common field between the two tables is used to create the link. "StudentID" is the common field in the "Residence Assignments" and "Student Information" tables, and "ResidenceID" is the common field in the "Residence Halls" and "Residence Assignments" tables. The common field in one table is that table's *primary key,* and the common field in the related table is called a **foreign key** (see Figure 11.11).

Because data is changed continually in a database, it's important to ensure that the data in related tables is synchronized and that a record isn't added or modified in one table and not the other. To prevent orphan records and to keep related data synchronized, you have the option of enforcing **referential integrity** for each relationship. Referential integrity means that for each value in the foreign key table there is a corresponding value in the primary key table.

For instance, if you attempt to enter a student's record in the "Residence Assignments" table with a StudentID number that doesn't exist in the "Student Information" table (the primary key table) and referential integrity is being

enforced, an error message will display. You would first need to add the student to the "Student Information" table and then enter the student in the "Residence Assignments" table.

Are there different types of relationships in relational databases? A relationship in relational databases can take one of three forms:

1. A **one-to-many relationship** is characterized by a record appearing only once in one table while having the capability of appearing many times in a related table. For example, as shown in Figure 11.11, the "1" next to ResidenceID in the "Residence Halls" table indicates there is only one instance of each ResidenceID in the "Residence Halls" table, and the "∞" next to ResidenceID in the "Residence Assignments" table indicates that many records can have the same ResidenceID in the "Residence Assignments" table. There is only one of each residence hall, but each residence hall will be listed for each student who will be living there. One-to-many relationships are the most common type of relationship in relational databases.

2. A **one-to-one relationship** indicates that for each record in a table there is only one corresponding record in a related table. For example, each student is assigned a room. Because a student can only live in one residence hall at a time, a one-to-one relationship is established, as shown in Figure 11.11 by the "1" next

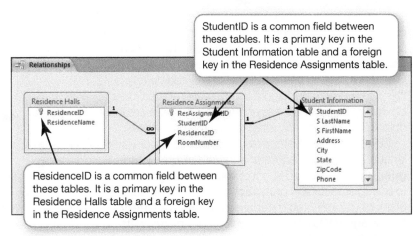

StudentID is a common field between these tables. It is a primary key in the Student Information table and a foreign key in the Residence Assignments table.

ResidenceID is a common field between these tables. It is a primary key in the Residence Halls table and a foreign key in the Residence Assignments table.

FIGURE 11.11 The foreign key field is the same as the primary key field in a related table.

to the StudentID field in both the "Residence Assignments" table and the "Student Information" table.

3. A **many-to-many relationship** is characterized by records in one table being related to multiple records in a second table and vice versa. For instance, a table of students could be related to a table of student employers. The employers could employ many students, and students could work for more than one employer.

Relational databases are great for data that can fit into tables and be organized into fields and records. But some data, such as graphics, video, or audio files, are handled better in an object-oriented database.

Object-Oriented Databases

What is an object-oriented database?

An **object-oriented database** stores data in objects rather than in tables. Objects contain not only data but also methods for processing or manipulating that data. This allows object-oriented databases to store more types of data than relational databases and to access that data faster.

For example, a "student" object that contains data about the courses a student is taking might also store the instructions for generating a bill for the student based on his or her course load. Because object-oriented databases store the instructions for doing computations in the same place as they store the data, they can usually process requests for information faster than can relational databases (which would only store the student information).

Why would I use an object-oriented database?

Object-oriented databases are more adept at handling **unstructured data** such as audio clips (including MP3 files), video clips, pictures, and extremely large documents. Data of this type is known as a **binary large object (BLOB)** because it's encoded in binary form. In comparison, relational databases are best for the storage of **structured (analytical) data** (such as "Bill" or "345").

Because businesses today need to store a greater variety of data, object-oriented databases are becoming more popular. Many relational database systems have been expanded to include object-oriented components. For a business to use its data in an object-oriented database, the data needs to undergo a costly conversion process. However, the faster access and reusability of the database objects can provide advantages for large businesses.

Object-oriented databases also need to use a query language to access and manage data. A **query language** is a specially designed computer language used to manipulate data in or extract data from a database. Many object-oriented databases use **Object Query Language (OQL)**, which is similar in many respects to **SQL (Structured Query Language)**, a standard language used to construct queries to extract data from relational databases.

Multidimensional Databases

What is a multidimensional database? A
multidimensional database stores data that can be analyzed from different perspectives, called dimensions. This distinguishes it from a relational database, which stores data in tables that have only two dimensions (fields and records). Multidimensional databases organize data in a cube format. Each data cube has a *measure attribute,* which is the main type of data that the cube is tracking. Other elements of the cube are known as *feature attributes,* which describe the measure attribute in some meaningful way.

For example, sales of automobiles (measure attribute) could be categorized by various dimensions such as region, automobile model, or sales month—all feature attributes (see Figure 11.12). In addition, the database could be constructed to define different levels within a particular feature attribute (such as state and town within a region).

What are the advantages of multidimensional databases? The two main advantages of multidimensional databases are as follows:

1. They can be customized to provide information to a variety of users (based on their needs).

2. They can process data much faster than pure relational databases can.

The need for processing speed is critical when deploying a large database accessed via the Internet. Therefore, large databases such as eBay are usually designed as multidimensional databases. Oracle Corporation has morphed its relational database into a multidimensional database. This was primarily in response to customers who were using an Oracle database for applications deployed on the web and who needed better ways of storing and accessing image, audio, and video files. ■

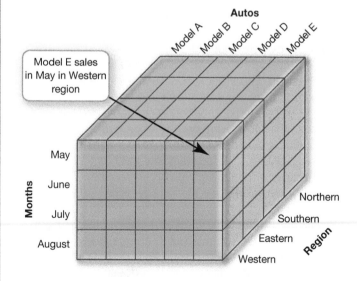

FIGURE 11.12 Multidimensional databases store data in at least three dimensions.

trends in IT

Computers in Society: User-Populated Databases

Web 2.0 applications are about making it easy for users to create and disseminate their own content. So if you have a database that needs populating, why not seek help from the web community to populate it, especially if it's designed as a resource for the masses?

Yelp (**yelp.com**) is conceived as the "yellow pages" for the twenty-first century. Yelp is free to use, and anyone can write a review of a business and post it to the site. Users can easily search the site, find service providers in their area, and see what ratings consumers have given them. Thinking about going to a Mexican restaurant in the San Jose area that you've never visited (see Figure 11.13)? A quick search on Yelp will lead to more than 500 restaurants that fit this criteria. Surely you'll be able to find one that fits your budget and that other people enjoyed visiting.

However, Yelp is not without its critics. Because it allows anonymous posting, some people argue that businesses may try to increase their ratings by posting their own positive reviews. And Yelp actively markets to businesses to pay for placement of ads on its site that some users may mistake for unsponsored reviews. (To avoid this kind of consumer misinterpretation, the Federal Communications Commission [FCC] now requires commercial websites to clearly identify reviews that are sponsored, but some consumers remain oblivious.)

An alternative to Yelp that addresses these concerns is Angie's List. Angie's List (**angieslist.com**) focuses primarily on service companies and health care professionals, not entertainment and food service businesses. Members pay a monthly fee to access the reviews on Angie's List.

What do you get for your fee? Angie's List doesn't permit anonymous reviews. This is a big benefit for business owners because it makes it easier to contact dissatisfied customers and try to resolve issues. Angie's List also has a verification process with reviewers to ensure that businesses don't report on themselves. And businesses don't pay to advertise on Angie's List; they make it on the site only when they're reviewed by a consumer.

Both Yelp and Angie's List are searchable databases, but whereas most companies usually populate databases themselves, these websites rely on users to create their content. The databases still need to be well designed to capture this content, and processes need to be in place to review the data entered for appropriateness. By harnessing the power of large groups of users to populate a database, the database owners can reap the rewards of saving time, effort, and money.

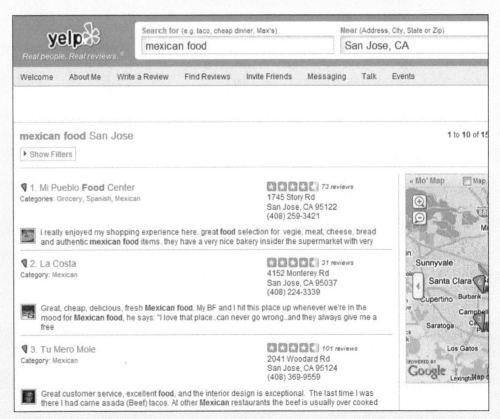

FIGURE 11.13 Yelp's database is populated with reviews created by users.

database
FUNCTIONS

Once you've designed and tested your database to ensure that it works properly, you can begin creating individual records in (or populating) the database. After the database has been populated with data, users can employ certain methods to extract subsets of data from the database and then output the data in a meaningful and presentable format. In this section, we look at these database functions.

Inputting Data

How do I get data into the database? You can key data directly into the database. However, because a great deal of data already exists in some type of electronic format, such as word processing documents, spreadsheets, and web-based sources, most databases can import data electronically from other files, which can save an enormous amount of keying and reduces the amount of data entry errors.

When importing data, the data must exactly match the format of the database. Most databases usually apply filters to the data to determine whether it's in the correct format as defined by the data dictionary. Nonconforming data is flagged (either on-screen or in a report) so that you can modify the data to fit the database's format.

How can I make manual entry into a database more efficient? Input forms are used to control how new data is entered into a shared database. Figure 11.14 shows an example of an input form for the "Student Information" table. Each field has a label that indicates the data to be placed in the field. The data is inputted into the blank boxes. Notes have been added to the form to guide the users. In addition to being used to input new data, input forms are used to make changes to existing data in the database. Because a form can be configured to display individual records, making changes to data by using a form ensures that the change is made to the right record.

Data Validation

How can I ensure that only valid data is entered into a field? Validation is the process of ensuring that data entered into a field meets specified guidelines. A **validation rule** is generally defined as part of the data dictionary and is specified in the field properties for each field. Violations of validation rules usually result in an error message displayed on the screen with a suggested action so that the error can be addressed. Common validation rules include the following:

- *Range check:* A **range check** ensures that the data entered into the field falls within a certain range of values. For instance, you could set a **field constraint** (a property that must be satisfied for an entry to be accepted into the field) to restrict the rate of pay to fall within a certain range. Figure 11.15 shows a range check in the Field Properties pane for an Access database. A validation rule restricts the entries for a student's rate of pay for his or her campus job to amounts between $7.25 and $15.50. If users tried to enter a rate of pay less than $7.25 or greater than

---

Student Information Form

Student Information Input Form

Student ID		Enter a 7 digit Student ID number
Last Name		
First Name		
Address		Student's permanent home address
City		
State		Use the 2 letter state abbreviation
Zip Code		

NOTE: All fields must be completed!

FIGURE 11.14 Input forms are used to enter data into tables.

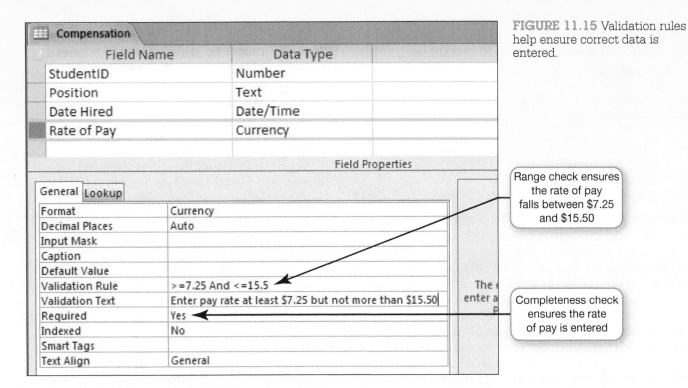

FIGURE 11.15 Validation rules help ensure correct data is entered.

Range check ensures the rate of pay falls between $7.25 and $15.50

Completeness check ensures the rate of pay is entered

$15.50, they would be notified of a range error and the input would not be accepted, as shown in Figure 11.16.

- *Completeness:* A **completeness check** ensures that all required fields have been completed. For example, Figure 11.15 shows the "Required" property set to "Yes," so when data is not entered in the field, as is the case in Figure 11.17, the database performs a completeness check, notices the blank "Rate of Pay" field, and displays an error message to alert the user of the omission.
- *Consistency check:* A **consistency check** compares the values of data in two or more fields to see if those values are reasonable. For example, your birth date and the date you enrolled in school are often in a

college's database. It's not possible for you to have enrolled in college before you were born. Furthermore, most college students are at least 16 years old. Therefore, a consistency check on these fields might ensure that your birth date is at least 16 or more years before the date when you enrolled in college.

- *Alphabetic and numeric checks:* An **alphabetic check** confirms that only textual characters (such as "Robin") are entered in a field. A **numeric check** confirms that only numbers are entered in the field. With these checks in place, "$J2.5n" would not be accepted as the price of a product or as a first name. Setting the data type as "Number" (or "Currency") will help ensure that numeric information is entered.

FIGURE 11.16 Access users see this pop-up when they enter a value that falls outside the stated range of acceptable values. The displayed message is generated from the text typed in the "Validation Text" property.

FIGURE 11.17 Access users see this pop-up when they do not enter a value in a field that has been indicated as being required.

Viewing and Sorting Data

How can I view the data in a database?

Displaying the tables on-screen and browsing through all the data is an option with most databases. In many instances, you'll only want to view the data one record at a time and not display all the data in an entire table. Forms are used to display individual records, either alone or in conjunction with other related data.

How can I reorder records in a database?

You can easily sort data into ascending or descending order. Figure 11.18a shows an Access data table in which the records were inputted in no particular order. By highlighting a column (in this case "Last Name") and then clicking Ascending on the Ribbon, the database displays the records in alphabetical order by last name, as shown in Figure 11.18b.

Extracting or Querying Data

What if I want to display only a certain subset of data in a database?

There are two ways to display only those records that match particular criteria:

1. *Use a filter:* A **filter** temporarily displays records that match certain criteria. When you apply a filter, you can't save the results, so filters are useful if you don't need to view the results frequently. Filters can only be applied to fields in one table, so if you need to combine fields from multiple tables to achieve your subset of data, queries would be a better option.

2. *Create a query:* A database **query** is a way of retrieving information that defines a particular subset of data. However, unlike a filter, a query can be used to extract data from one or multiple tables. When you create a query, you choose the fields that should be included in the results and specify the criteria for selecting records. For example, as shown in Figure 11.19a, if you wanted to create a list of students living in the Boyer 1 dorm and their room numbers, you would need to pull information from the "Student Information" table (S First Name and S Last Name), "Residence Halls" table (Residence Name), and "Residence Assignments" table (RoomNumber). Then, you'd need to specify to see only those records

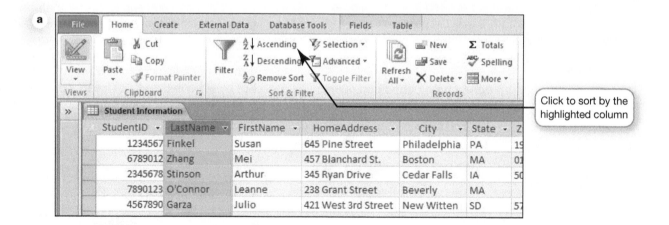

FIGURE 11.18 (a) Shown is an unsorted table. Notice that the "Last Name" column is selected (highlighted) for sorting. Selecting the sorting option "Ascending" produces the sorted output (b) with the records sorted in ascending alphabetical order by last name.

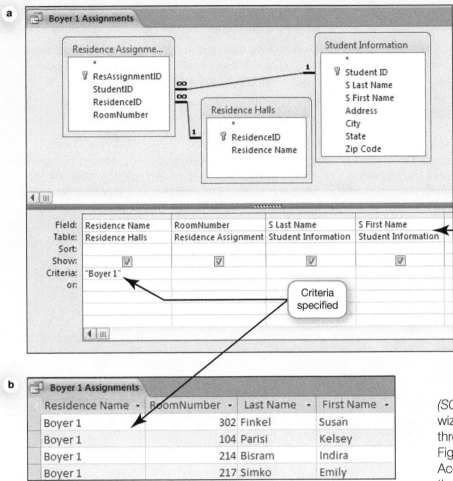

Boyer 1 Assignments

Residence Assignme...

*
- ResAssignmentID
  StudentID
  ResidenceID
  RoomNumber

Residence Halls

*
- ResidenceID
  Residence Name

Student Information

*
- Student ID
  S Last Name
  S First Name
  Address
  City
  State
  Zip Code

Field:	Residence Name	RoomNumber	S Last Name	S First Name
Table:	Residence Halls	Residence Assignment	Student Information	Student Information
Sort:				
Show:	☑	☑	☑	☑
Criteria:	"Boyer 1"			
or:				

Fields pulled from multiple tables

Criteria specified

FIGURE 11.19 (a) When creating a query, you can specify fields from multiple tables as well as specific criteria within a field. (b) The outcome reflects those records meeting the specified criteria.

Boyer 1 Assignments

Residence Name ▾	RoomNumber ▾	Last Name ▾	First Name ▾
Boyer 1	302	Finkel	Susan
Boyer 1	104	Parisi	Kelsey
Boyer 1	214	Bisram	Indira
Boyer 1	217	Simko	Emily

full-blown programming languages but are usually much easier to learn. The most popular query language used today is *Structured Query Language (SQL)*. Modern database systems provide wizards or other mechanisms to guide you through the process of creating queries. Figure 11.19a shows an example of an Access query being created in Design View that allows you to easily select query elements. You can also create a query using a Simple Query Wizard in Microsoft Access. When you use the Simple Query Wizard or Design View, you're actually using SQL commands without realizing it.

However, you may want to create your own SQL queries in Access, modify existing queries at the SQL language level, or view the SQL code that the wizard created. Figure 11.20 shows the SQL code that the query in Figure 11.19 created.

pertaining to a specific dorm, in this case Boyer 1. Figure 11.19b displays the results for this query.

Do I have to learn a query language to develop queries for my database? All modern DBMSs contain a query language that the software uses to retrieve and display records. A query language consists of its own vocabulary and sentence structure that you use to frame the requests. Query languages are similar to

Boyer 1 Assignments

```
SELECT [Residence Halls].[Residence Name], [Residence Assignments].RoomNumber, [Student Information].[S Last Name], [Student Information].[S First Name]
FROM [Student Information] INNER JOIN ([Residence Halls] INNER JOIN [Residence Assignments] ON [Residence Halls].ResidenceID = [Residence Assignments].ResidenceID) ON [Student Information].[Student ID] = [Residence Assignments].StudentID
WHERE ((([Residence Halls].[Residence Name])="Boyer 1"));
```

FIGURE 11.20 The SQL View window in Access shows the SQL code for the query in Figure 11.19. Although it's a relatively simple SELECT statement, it's much easier to create the query using the Access tools provided.

>To display SQL code for a query, open a query and select **SQL View** from the View drop-down list on the Home tab of the Ribbon.

To extract records from a database, you use a query language. Almost all relational and object-oriented databases today use Structured Query Language, or SQL. Oracle, Microsoft SQL Server, Microsoft Access, IBM DB2, and MySQL are examples of popular databases that use SQL.

SQL uses relational algebra to extract data from databases. **Relational algebra** is the use of English-like expressions that have variables and operations, much like algebraic equations. Variables include table names, field names, or selection criteria for the data you wish to display. Operations include directions such as *select* (which enables you to pick variable names), *from* (which tells the database which table to use), and *where* (which enables you to specify selection criteria). The two most common queries used to extract data using relational algebra are select queries and join queries.

A **select query** displays a subset of data from a table (or tables) based on the criteria you specify. A typical select query has the following format:

SELECT (Field Name 1, Field Name 2, ...)
FROM (Table Name)
WHERE (Selection Criteria)

The first line of the query contains variables for the field names you want to display. The FROM statement enables you to specify the table name from which the data will be retrieved. The last line (the WHERE statement) is used only when you wish to specify which records need to be displayed (such as all students with GPAs greater than 3.3). If you wish to display all the rows (records) in the table, then you don't use the WHERE statement (see Figure 11.21).

Suppose you want to create a phone list that includes all students from the Student Information

Student Information

StudentID	LastName	FirstName	HomeAddress	City	State	Zip	CellPhone
1234567	Finkel	Susan	645 Pine Street	Philadelphia	PA	19012	(610) 555-2367
4567890	Garza	Julio	421 West 3rd Street	New Witten	SD	57584	(454) 555-6512
7890123	O'Connor	Leanne	238 Grant Street	Beverly	MA		(303) 555-8723
2345678	Stinson	Arthur	345 Ryan Drive	Cedar Falls	IA	50613	(427) 555-2398
6789012	Zhang	Mei	457 Blanchard St.	Boston	MA	01901	(302) 555-4976

Query applied to this table

SELECT (FirstName, LastName, CellPhone)
FROM (Student Information Table)

Query applied to this table

SELECT (FirstName, LastName, CellPhone)
FROM (Student Information Table)
WHERE (State = MA)

Produces this output

b

FirstName	LastName	CellPhone
Susan	Finkel	(610) 555-2367
Julio	Garza	(454) 555-6512
Leanne	O'Connor	(303) 555-8723
Arthur	Stinson	(427) 555-2398
Mei	Zhang	(302) 555-4976

Produces this output

c

FirstName	LastName	CellPhone
Leanne	O'Connor	(303) 555-8723
Mei	Zhang	(302) 555-4976

FIGURE 11.21 When the query on the left is applied to the (a) "Student Information" table, it restricts the output to (b) only a phone list. The query on the right, which uses a WHERE statement, further restricts the phone list to (c) only students from Massachusetts.

table in Figure 11.21a. The SQL query you would send to the database would look like this:

SELECT (FirstName, LastName, CellPhone)
FROM (Student Information Table)

Figure 11.21b shows the output from this query.

What if you want a phone list that shows only students from Massachusetts? In that case, you would add a WHERE statement to the query, as follows:

SELECT (FirstName, LastName, CellPhone)
FROM (Student Information Table)
WHERE (State = MA)

This query restricts the output to students who live in Massachusetts, as shown in Figure 11.21c. Notice that the "State" field in the "Student Information" table can be used by the query (in this case, as a limiting criterion) but that the contents of the "State" field aren't required to be displayed in the query results. This explains why the output shown in Figure 11.21c doesn't show the "State" field.

When you want to extract data that is in two or more tables, you use a **join query**. The query actually links (or joins) the two tables using the common field in both tables and extracts the relevant data from each. The format for a simple join query for two tables is as follows:

SELECT (Field Name 1, Field Name 2)
FROM (Table 1 Name, Table 2 Name)
WHERE (Table 1 Name.Common Field Name = Table 2 Name.Common Field Name)
AND (Selection Criteria)

Notice how similar this is to a select query, although the FROM statement must now contain two table names. In a join query, the WHERE statement is split into two parts. In the first part (right after WHERE), the relation between the two tables is defined by identifying the common fields between the tables. The second part of the statement (after AND) is where the selection criteria are defined.

The AND means that both parts of the statement must be true for the query to produce results (i.e., the two related fields must exist and the selection criteria must be valid). Figure 11.22 illustrates using a join query for the "Student Information" and "Roster Master" tables to produce a class roster for students.

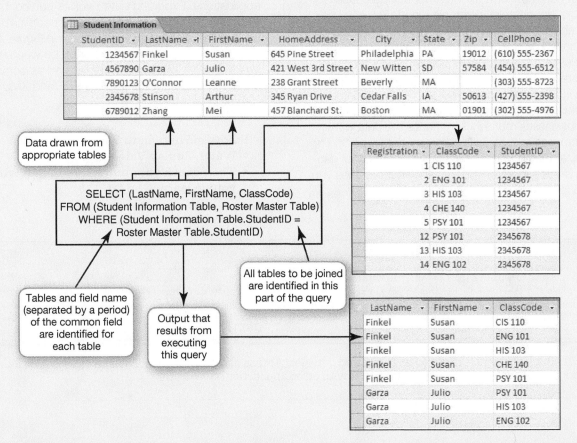

FIGURE 11.22 This join query will display a student roster for each student in the "Student Information" table. Notice that the WHERE statement creates the join by defining the common field (in this case, StudentID) in each table.

BITS&BYTES

iTunes Smart Playlists—They're Just Queries!

Ever built a smart playlist in iTunes? If so, you've created a database query. iTunes is just a relational database that manages your media. A smart playlist (see Figure 11.23) allows you to define multiple criteria to create a playlist. Say you want all songs in the genre Rock, except for the artist Pink and the album *Monkey Business*. When you define these criteria as "match all" in the Smart Playlist dialog box, you'll get a smart playlist that contains the music you want. You have built a query that tells iTunes exactly what music to extract from the database and to include in your playlist.

FIGURE 11.23 The iTunes Smart Playlist dialog box creates a database query.

Outputting Data

How do I get data out of a database?
The most common form of output for any database is a viewable (or printable) electronic report. You can use data in tables to create reports, or you can generate reports based on queries you create. Although you can print tables and the results of queries directly, when you create a report, you can make other adjustments to how the information is displayed, such as grouping like information and including aggregate information such as totals. Businesses routinely summarize the data within their databases and compile summary data reports. For instance, at the end of each semester, your school generates a grade report for you that shows the grades you received for the classes you took.

Can I transfer data from a database to another software application? Database systems also can be used to export data to other applications. Exporting data involves putting it into an electronic file in a format that another application can understand. For example, as shown in Figure 11.24, data can be imported and exported between Access and Microsoft Word and Excel, as well as converted to and from other formats such as PDF and XML for use with other applications. ■

> Before moving on to Part 2:
> • Watch Replay Video 11.1 ▶.
> • **Then check your understanding of what you've learned so far.**

FIGURE 11.24 Data can be imported and exported between Access and other Microsoft Office applications as well as converted to PDF, XML, and other formats for use with other applications.

check your understanding //

For a quick review to see what you've learned so far, answer the following questions. Visit **pearsonhighered.com/techinaction** to check your answers.

multiple choice

1. Two lists showing the same data about the same person is an example of

    a. data redundancy.
    b. data inconsistency.
    c. data disparity.
    d. data irregularity.

2. Which of the following is NOT an advantage of using databases instead of lists?

    a. Data can be easily shared among users.
    b. Data-entry errors can be minimized with databases.
    c. Data integrity can be ensured with a database.
    d. Databases are easier to build and maintain than lists.

3. A field that has a unique entry for each record in a database table is called the

    a. logical key.
    b. master field.
    c. crucial field.
    d. primary key.

4. A(n) _____ database organizes data in two-dimensional tables.

    a. relational
    b. object-oriented
    c. rectangular
    d. multidimensional

5. Ensuring that a field must contain a number that is between two values is an example of a(n)

    a. alphabetic check.
    b. completeness check.
    c. range check.
    d. consistency check.

true–false

_____ 1. A query is used to extract information from a database.

_____ 2. Validation checks ensure that required fields in a database are filled in completely.

critical thinking

1. **Databases Are Everywhere**

    Think about specific examples of databases you interact with. Try to list at least 10 different ones. Discuss the specific advantages these databases have in your daily life, as well as some of the precautions you may need to take to ensure your privacy.

2. **Facebook as a Database**

    If you have a Facebook page or some other social networking page, information from your page is often shared with other databases when you participate in various games and other applications that require access to your personal data as a condition of participation. How many games and other applications do you estimate have access to your information? Check your privacy settings for your Facebook page and look in the Apps and Games section to see how many apps you're actually using. Were you surprised at the difference in the actual number of apps and your estimate? What apps do you think you should disable to prevent them from accessing your information? Give reasons for the ones you will disable (don't trust them, don't use them, etc.).

Continue ➤

Using Excel's Database Functions

Databases are great for organizing lots of data, but they can be difficult to understand and to learn how to use. If your data is "flat"—that is, if it doesn't need to be divided into multiple tables—you can use Excel's database functions to organize your data. Excel is able to work with an enormous amount of data. Using Excel 2010, you're allowed 1,048,576 rows and 16,384 columns on one worksheet, with a theoretical limit of 255 worksheets. If your computer had enough memory, you could process a lot of data!

Excel includes several useful database functions: sorting one or multiple columns, applying filters, and applying data validation. All the database commands in Excel 2010 are on the Data tab.

Sorting in Alphabetical Order

Excel lets you sort one column of data in alphabetical or numerical order.

Step 1 Place your cursor anywhere in the column you want to sort.

Step 2 In the Sort & Filter group, click **Sort A to Z** or **Sort Z to A**, depending on whether you want to sort in ascending or descending order.

Applying Filters

When you want to isolate a subset of data, you should apply a filter.

Step 1 Click anywhere in the table, then click **Filter** in the Sort & Filter group. Filter arrows will display next to each column heading.

Step 2 Click the filter arrow beside the column heading for the column you want to filter.

Step 3 Remove the checkmark from Select All, and then click the filter value you'd like to apply. Click **OK**.

Step 4 Review the data to ensure the filter has been applied correctly. (Note: To remove the filter, click **Filter** in the Sort & Filter group to unselect the option.)

	A	B	C	D	E	F
	First Name ▾	Last Name ▾	Team # ▾	T-Shirt Si ▾	Quanti ▾	Payme ▾
	Kassie	Schultz	1	M	2	$30
	Joseph	Harper	2	M	1	$15
	Quang	Tran	2	M	1	$15
	Samantha	O'Connell	3	M	2	$30

Applying Data Validation

Using Data Validation, you can apply rules to data so that you can assure the proper data is being entered.

Step 1   Click **Data Validation** in the Data Tools group to display the Data Validation dialog box.

Step 2   On the **Settings** tab in the Data Validation dialog box, choose the type of data value to be allowed and the value limits in the **Data** and **Maximum** boxes. (Note: Depending on the criteria selected in the Allow field, the criteria in the Data box and other limits will vary.)

Set type of data to be allowed.

Set value limits in Data box.

Other limits (such as Maximum) will vary depending on criteria selected in Allow box.

Step 3   On the **Error Alert** tab, select the style of error message you want displayed (Stop, Warning, or Information), and then type the title of the error message and the error message text. Click **OK**.

Step 4   Test the data validation by entering an unacceptable value. When an unacceptable value is entered, an error message like the one shown here displays.

Last Name	Team #	T-Shirt Size	Quantity	Payment
Schultz	1	M	3	$30
Kuyper	1	L	2	$30
Gormley	1	XL		
Shakh	1	XL		
Kim	2	S		
Parrish	2	S		
Harper	2	M		
Tran	2	M		
Patel	3	S		
O'Connell	3	M	2	$30
Robinson	3	L	1	$15

Quantity Ordered

Quantities ordered above 2 are paid for by the player.

Continue?

Yes   No   Cancel   Help

Was this information helpful?

Large organizations accumulate massive amounts of data—both internal and external. By using *data warehousing*, *data marts*, and *data mining*, these organizations can use databases to tap into this wealth of information, improving their internal operations as well as their customer relationships. In this section, we'll look at how they do just that.

data warehousing
AND STORAGE

At the simplest level, data is stored in a single database on a database server, and you retrieve the data as needed. This works fine for small databases and simple enterprises where all the data you're interested in is in a single database. Problems can arise, however, when the organization gets much larger and department-specific data is stored in separate databases. Traditionally, the individual databases are used by different areas of the business and kept separate; however, the benefits of accessing data from all databases are being recognized. The problem with most databases is that they aren't designed to be accessed together to retrieve this type of data. Large storage repositories called *data warehouses* and *data marts* help solve this problem.

Data Warehouses

What is a data warehouse? A **data warehouse** is a large-scale collection of data that contains and organizes in one place all the data from an organization's multiple databases. Individual databases contain a wealth of information, but each database's information usually pertains to one area in the organization. For instance, the order database at Amazon.com contains information about book orders, such as the buyer's name, address, and payment information and the book's name. However, the order database doesn't contain information on inventory levels of books, nor does it list suppliers from which out-of-stock books can be obtained. Data warehouses, therefore, consolidate information from various operational systems to present an enterprise-wide view of business operations.

Is data in a data warehouse organized the same way as in a normal database? Data in the data warehouse is organized by *subject*. Most databases focus on one specific operational aspect

of business operations. For example, a large electronics retailer sells many types of electronics, such as TVs and cell phones. Different departments in the retailer are responsible for each type of product and track the products they sell in different databases (one database for TV sales and one for cell phone sales, for example), as shown in Figure 11.25.

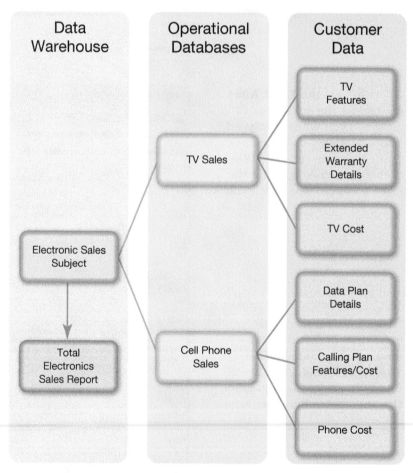

FIGURE 11.25 Data from individual databases is drawn together in a data warehouse. Managers can then produce comprehensive reports that would be impossible to create from the individual databases.

These databases capture specific information about each type of electronics. The "TV Sales" database captures information such as TV features, extended warranty details (and costs), and the cost of the TV because this information is pertinent to determining the ultimate value of TV sales. The "Cell Phone Sales" database captures information such as data plan details, calling plan features (and costs), and phone costs.

However, data on total electronic devices sold (and the resulting revenue generated) is critical to the management of the electronics retailer no matter what types of products are involved. Therefore, an electronics retailer's data warehouse would have a subject called "Electronics Sales Subject" (see Figure 11.25) that would contain information about *all* electronic devices sold throughout the company. "Electronics Sales Subject" is a database that contains information from the other databases the company maintains. However, all data in the "Electronics Sales Subject" database is specifically related to electronics sales (as opposed to, say, appliances, which the retailer also carries).

From the "Electronics Sales Subject" database, it's easy for managers to produce comprehensive reports, such as the "Total Electronics Sales Report," as shown in Figure 11.25, which can contain information pertaining to all types of electronics sales.

Do data warehouses capture data from only one time period? Data warehouse data is **time-variant data**, meaning it doesn't all pertain to one period in time. The warehouse contains current values, such as amounts due from customers, as well as historical data. If you want to examine the buying habits of a certain type of customer, you need data about both current and prior purchases. Having time-variant data in the warehouse enables you to analyze the past, examine the present in light of historical data, and make projections about the future.

Populating Data Warehouses

How are data warehouses populated with data? Source data for data warehouses can come from three places:

1. *Internal sources*: Sales, billing, inventory, and customer databases all provide a wealth of information. Spreadsheets and other ad hoc analysis tools may contain data that can be loaded into the data warehouse.

2. *External sources*: Vendors and suppliers often provide data regarding product specifications, shipment methods and dates, billing information, and so on.

3. *Clickstream data:* Software used on company websites to capture information about each click that users make as they navigate through the site is referred to as **clickstream data**. Using clickstream data-capture tools, a company can determine which pages users visit most often, how long users stay on each page, which sites directed users to the company site, and the user demographics. Such data can provide valuable clues as to what a company needs to improve on its site to stimulate sales.

Data Staging

Does all source data fit into the warehouse? Although two source databases might contain similar information (such as customer names and addresses), the format of the data is most likely different in each database. Therefore, source data must be "staged" before entering the data warehouse. **Data staging** consists of three steps:

1. Extraction of the data from source databases
2. Transformation (reformatting) of the data
3. Storage of the data in the data warehouse

Many different software programs and procedures may have to be created to extract the data from varied sources and reformat it for storage in the data warehouse. The nature and complexity of the source data determine the complexity of the data-staging process.

How can data stored in the data warehouse be extracted and used? Managers can query the data warehouse in much the same way you would query an Access database. However, because there is more data in the data warehouse, special software is needed to perform such queries. **Online analytical processing (OLAP)** software provides standardized tools for viewing and manipulating data in a data warehouse. The key feature of OLAP tools is that they enable flexible views of the data, which the software user can easily change.

Data Marts

What if a smaller amount of data is needed? Small slices of the data warehouse, each called a **data mart**, are often created so that

 ACTIVE HELPDESK
Data Warehouses, Data Marts, and Information Systems

In this Active Helpdesk call, you'll play the role of a helpdesk staffer, fielding calls about data warehouses, data marts, and information systems.

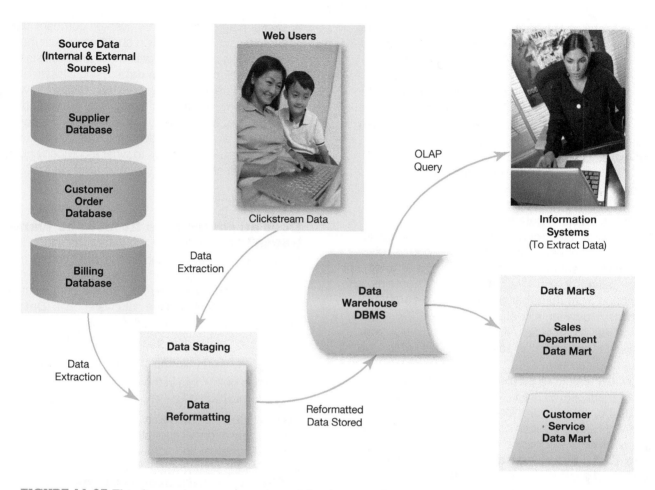

FIGURE 11.27 This figure shows an overview of the data warehouse process. *(Bikeriderlondon/Shutterstock; REDAV/Shutterstock)*

companies can analyze a related set of data that are grouped together and separated out from the main body of data in the data warehouse. Whereas data warehouses have an enterprise-wide depth, the information in data marts pertains to a single component of the business.

For instance, if you need accurate sales-related information and you don't want to wade through customer service data, accounts payable data, and product shipping data to get it, a data mart that contains information relevant only to the sales department can be created to make the task of finding this data easier. An overview

of the data-warehousing process is illustrated in Figure 11.27. Data staging is vital because different data must be extracted and then reformatted to fit the data structure defined in the data warehouse's DBMS. Data can be extracted using powerful OLAP query tools, or it can be stored in specialized data marts for use by specific employee groups.

Now that you understand how databases are created and how data is stored in large-scale repositories, we'll explore in the next section the types of information systems that utilize databases to provide business intelligence to managers. ■

trends *in IT*

Emerging Technologies: Can Your Business Partner Deliver the Goods? Enhanced Databases Can Help You Decide!

Suppose you manufacture T-shirts, and to keep costs low, you'd like to explore Vietnamese T-shirt manufacturers. You could use the terms "Vietnamese t-shirt manufacturers" in a search engine and you'd probably find many leads. The information in the leads available online may be factually correct, but how do you determine how reliable these suppliers are? Alibaba and Panjiva are two online business-to-business databases that help to navigate these transactions.

Developed to respond to business needs, Alibaba (**alibaba.com**) is one of the world's largest online business-to-business databases (see Figure 11.26). Alibaba.com specializes in matching suppliers with buyers for all types of manufactured goods and raw materials. With the global nature of business, databases such as those maintained by Alibaba are essential tools that assist businesspeople in managing their global businesses.

Panjiva (**panjiva.com**) is a website that also has a searchable database, this one of over 1.5 million suppliers. The founders of Panjiva decided to make their database different. They gather data that indicates the reliability of suppliers from sources such as government agencies, independent certification companies, nonprofit organizations, and customers. Using the reliability information, Panjiva then creates ratings for companies (on a scale of 1 to 100) based on specific business performance criteria such as number of shipments to the U.S. market, the company's environmental record, and their capability to deliver shipments within promised time frames. Companies such as The Home Depot that subscribe to Panjiva's database can feel more comfortable about doing business with suppliers that Panjiva has rated for reliability.

Databases with enhanced information are the wave of the future in the business world. So, before you make that next crucial business decision, ask yourself how much you really know about your prospective business partner. If you don't know enough, then find a database that can make you feel more at ease.

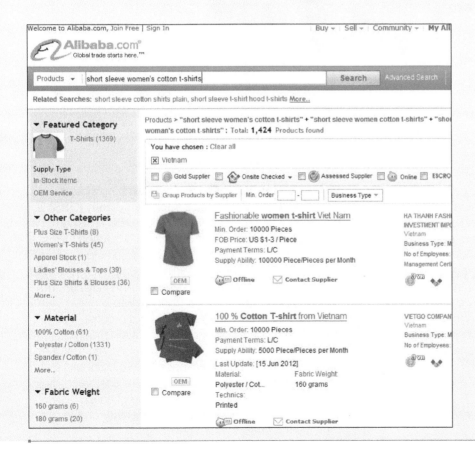

FIGURE 11.26 Using the Alibaba database, a search for short-sleeved women's cotton T-shirts in Vietnam results in over 1,400 links to vendors selling some type of women's T-shirt.

business intelligence

SYSTEMS

Making intelligent decisions about developing new products, creating marketing strategies, and buying raw materials requires timely, accurate information. An **information system** is a software-based solution used to gather and analyze information. A system that delivers up-to-the-minute sales data on shoes to the computer of Zappos's president is one example of an information system. Databases, data warehouses, and data marts are integral parts of information systems because they store the information that makes information systems functional.

Are all information systems the same? All information systems perform similar functions, including acquiring data, processing that data into information, storing the data, and providing the user with a number of output options with which to make the information meaningful and useful (see Figure 11.28).

What information systems are used by business managers? Most information systems fall into one of five categories:

1. *Office support systems*
2. *Transaction-processing systems*
3. *Management information systems*
4. *Decision support systems*, and
5. *Enterprise resource planning (ERP) systems*

Each type of system almost always involves the use of one or more databases. Management information systems, decision support systems, and enterprise resource planning systems are often classified as business intelligence systems. **Business intelligence systems** are used to analyze and interpret data in order to enable managers to make informed decisions about how best to run a business. Data warehouses and data marts are key components of business intelligence systems because they enable access to information gathered from multiple sources. Increased access to information usually enables business intelligence systems to provide better information to managers in a timely fashion, which can lead to enhanced decision making.

In the following sections, we'll examine each of the five types of systems in greater detail.

FIGURE 11.28 Information systems acquire data, process that data into information, store the data, and provide the user with a number of output options to make the information useful. *(wavebreakmedia/Shutterstock; wavebreakmedia/Shutterstock; Michaeljung/Shutterstock; Raisa Kanareva/Shutterstock)*

Office Support Systems

What does an office support system accomplish? An **office support system (OSS)** is designed to improve communications and assist employees in accomplishing their daily tasks. Microsoft Office is an example of an OSS because it assists employees with routine tasks such as maintaining an employee phone list in Excel, designing a sales presentation in PowerPoint, and writing customer letters using Word.

Modern OSSs include e-mail, word processing, spreadsheet, database, and presentation programs. Office support systems have their roots in manual, paper-based systems developed before computers. A paper listing of employee phone extensions typed by an administrative assistant is an example of an early OSS. A modern OSS might publish this directory on the company's intranet (its internal network).

Transaction-Processing Systems

What is a transaction-processing system? A transaction-processing system (**TPS**) keeps track of everyday business activities. For example, colleges have TPSs in place to track transactions that occur frequently, such as registering students for classes, accepting tuition payments, and printing course catalogs. When computers were introduced to the business world, they often were first put to work hosting TPSs.

How are transactions entered into a TPS? Transactions can be entered manually or electronically. When you buy gas at a pay-at-the-pump terminal, the pump captures your credit card data and transmits it to a TPS, which records a sale (gallons of gas and dollar value). Transactions are processed either in batches or in real time. Various departments in an organization then access the TPSs to extract the information they need to process additional transactions, as shown in Figure 11.29.

What is batch processing? **Batch processing** means that transaction data is accumulated until a certain point is reached and then several transactions are processed at once. Batch processing is appropriate for activities that aren't time sensitive. For example, you may not receive a bill for each charge you make at the bookstore. Instead, the college may collect your charges and batch them together into one monthly billing. It's more efficient to batch and process all requests periodically.

When are TPS transactions processed? For most activities, processing and recording transactions in a TPS occur in real time. **Real-time processing** means that the database is updated while the transaction is taking place. For instance, when you register for classes online, if spots are still available for the classes you want, the database immediately records your registration in the class to ensure you have a spot. This **online transaction processing (OLTP)** ensures that the data in the TPS is current.

Management Information Systems

What is a management information system? A management information system (**MIS**) provides timely and accurate information that enables managers to make critical business decisions. MISs were a direct outgrowth of TPSs. Managers quickly realized that the data contained in TPSs could be an extremely powerful tool only if the information could be organized and outputted in a useful form. Today's MISs are often included as a feature of TPSs.

FIGURE 11.29 Transaction-processing systems help capture and track critical business information needed for successful completion of business transactions such as selling merchandise over the Internet. *(Bikeriderlondon/Shutterstock; Penka Todorova Vitkova/Shutterstock; Chuck Rausin/Shutterstock; Nataliia Natykach/Shutterstock)*

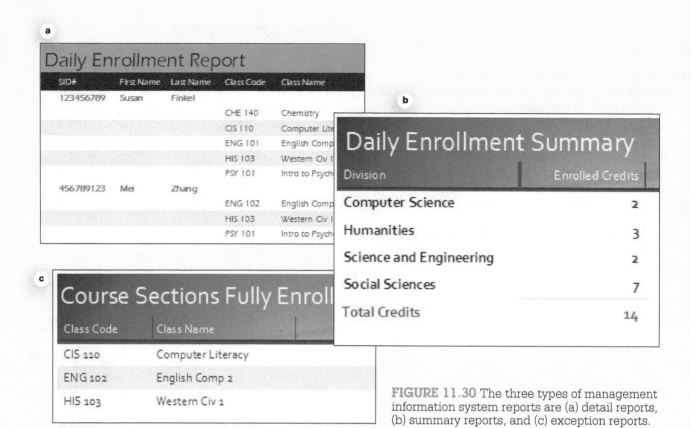

a

Daily Enrollment Report

SID#	First Name	Last Name	Class Code	Class Name
123456789	Susan	Finkel		
			CHE 140	Chemistry
			CIS 110	Computer Lite...
			ENG 101	English Comp...
			HIS 103	Western Civ 1
			PSY 101	Intro to Psych...
456789123	Mei	Zhang		
			ENG 102	English Comp...
			HIS 103	Western Civ 1
			PSY 101	Intro to Psych...

b

Daily Enrollment Summary

Division	Enrolled Credits
Computer Science	2
Humanities	3
Science and Engineering	2
Social Sciences	7
Total Credits	14

c

Course Sections Fully Enroll...

Class Code	Class Name
CIS 110	Computer Literacy
ENG 102	English Comp 2
HIS 103	Western Civ 1

FIGURE 11.30 The three types of management information system reports are (a) detail reports, (b) summary reports, and (c) exception reports.

What types of reports are generated by MISs?
MISs generate three types of reports:

1. A **detail report** provides a list of the transactions that occurred during a certain time period. For example, during registration at your school, the registrar might receive a detail report that lists the students who registered for classes each day. Figure 11.30a shows an example of a detail report on daily enrollment.

2. A **summary report** provides a consolidated picture of detailed data. These reports usually include some calculation (totals) or visual displays of information (such as charts and graphs). Figure 11.30b shows an example of a summary report displaying total daily credits enrolled by division.

3. An **exception report** shows conditions that are unusual or that need attention by system users. The registrar at your college may get an exception report when all sections of a course are full, indicating that it may be time to schedule additional sections. Figure 11.30c shows an example of such an exception report.

Decision Support Systems

What is a decision support system?
A **decision support system (DSS)** is another type of business intelligence system designed to help managers develop solutions for specific problems. A DSS for a marketing department might provide statistical information on customer attributes, such as income levels or buying patterns, that would assist managers in making advertising strategy decisions. A DSS not only uses data from databases and data warehouses, it also enables users to add their own insights and experiences and apply them to the solution.

What does a DSS look like?
DBMSs, while playing an integral part of a DSS, are supplemented by additional software systems in a DSS. In a DSS, the user interface provides the means of interaction between the user and the system. An effective user interface must be easy to learn. The other major components of a DSS are internal and external data sources, model management systems, and knowledge-based systems. As shown in Figure 11.31, these systems work together to provide the user of the DSS with a broad base of information on which to base decisions.

How do DSSs get data?
Internal and external data sources provide a stream of data that is integrated into the DSS for analysis. Internal data sources are maintained by the same company that operates the DSS. For example, internal TPSs can provide a wealth of statistical data about customers, ordering patterns, inventory levels, and so on. An external data source is any source not owned by the company that owns the DSS, such as customer demographic data purchased from third parties, mailing lists, or statistics compiled by the government.

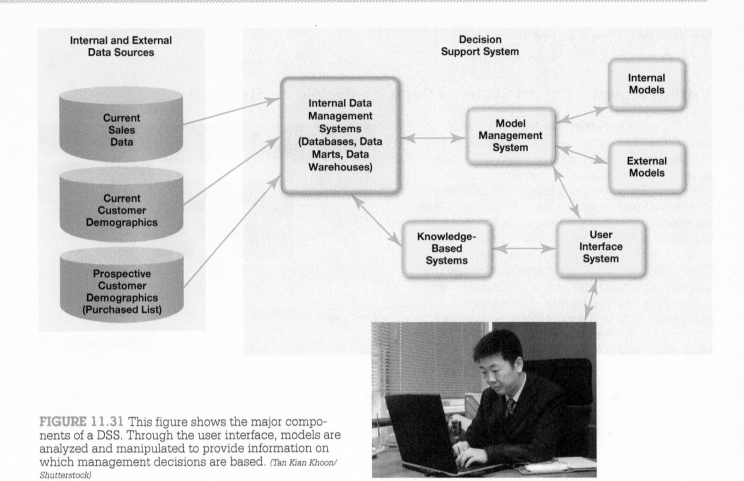

FIGURE 11.31 This figure shows the major components of a DSS. Through the user interface, models are analyzed and manipulated to provide information on which management decisions are based. *(Tan Kian Khoon/Shutterstock)*

What function does a model management system perform? A **model management system** is software that assists in building management models in DSSs. A management model is an analysis tool that, through the use of internal and external data, provides a view of a particular business situation for the purposes of decision making. Models can be built to describe any business situation, such as the classroom space requirements for next semester or a listing of alternative sales outlet locations. Model management systems typically contain financial and statistical analysis tools that are used to analyze the data provided by models or to create additional models.

What is a knowledge-based system, and how is it used in DSSs? A **knowledge-based system** provides intelligence that supplements the user's own intellect and makes the DSS more effective. It could be an **expert system** that tries to replicate the decision-making processes of human experts in order to solve specific problems. For example, an expert system might be designed to take the place of a physician in a remote location. A physician expert system would ask the patient about symptoms just as a live physician would, and the system would make a diagnosis based on the algorithms programmed into it.

Another type of knowledge-based system is a **natural language processing (NLP) system**. NLP systems enable users to communicate with computer systems using a natural spoken or written language instead of using a computer programming language. Individuals just speak to the computer and it understands what they're saying, without users needing to use specific computer commands. Siri, the personal assistant application currently on Apple's iPhone 5, is an NLP system.

All knowledge-based systems fall under the science of artificial intelligence. **Artificial intelligence (AI)** is the branch of computer science that deals with the attempt to create computers that think like humans. To date, no computers have been constructed that can replicate the thinking patterns of a human brain, because scientists still do not fully understand how humans store and integrate knowledge and experiences to form human intelligence.

How does a knowledge-based system help in the decision-making process? Databases and the models provided by model management systems tend to be extremely analytical and mathematical in nature. If we relied solely on databases and models to make decisions, answers would be derived with a "yes or no" mentality, allowing no room for human thought. Fortunately, human users are involved in these

BITS&BYTES

Virtual Agents: Expert Systems Replace People on the Web

An offshoot of expert systems are the virtual agents that you encounter on the web or on the phone. Virtual agents are frequently used to interface with a database to answer customers' questions. For example, a typical virtual agent on the web features a picture, a name, and a box for entering questions, as shown in Figure 11.32. No virtual agent can be programmed to contain all the possible questions a human might ask. Therefore, the virtual agent software breaks the question down into key words and phrases, which it compares to a database containing question responses. It picks the most likely response and provides the answer. Customers provide feedback as to whether the response adequately answered their question. Usually, if results from the virtual agent aren't satisfactory or if customers need more information, they can connect to a live customer service agent. Virtual agents, although not perfect, save companies money by answering common questions without using expensive human labor.

FIGURE 11.32 Spike, Gonzaga University's sports team mascot, has been transformed into a virtual agent to direct people to the appropriate page of the school's website. *(Courtesy of Gonzaga University.)*

systems, providing an opportunity to inject human judgment into the decision-making process.

The knowledge-based system also provides an opportunity to introduce experience into the mix. Knowledge-based systems support the concept of fuzzy logic. Normal logic is highly rigid: If "x" happens, then "y" will happen. **Fuzzy logic** enables the interjection of experiential learning into the equation by considering probabilities. Whereas an algorithm in a database has to be specific, an algorithm in a knowledge-based system could state that if "x" happens, 70% of the time "y" will happen.

For instance, managers at Best Buy would find it extremely helpful if their DSSs informed them that 45% of customers who bought an iPad also bought a Smart Cover for it. This could suggest that designing a discount program for Smart Covers bought with iPads might spur sales. Fuzzy logic enables a system to be more flexible and to consider a wider range of possibilities than would conventional algorithmic thinking.

Enterprise Resource Planning Systems

What does an enterprise resource planning system do? An *enterprise* is any business entity, large or small. All businesses have data and information to manage, and large, complex organizations can benefit from managing that information with a central piece of software. An **enterprise resource planning (ERP) system** is a software system that accumulates in a central location all information relevant to running a business and makes it readily available to whoever needs it to make decisions. ERP systems use a common database to store and integrate information. This enables the information to be used across multiple areas of an enterprise.

Human resource functions (such as the management of hiring, firing, promotions, and benefits) and accounting functions (such as payroll) are often the first processes integrated into an ERP system. Historically, human resource records and accounting records were kept in separate databases, but having the information reside in one database makes the management and compensation of employees more streamlined. If manufacturing operations were then integrated into the ERP system, the data that was already in place regarding the employees and payroll could be easily used for determining the cost of running an assembly line or for scheduling workers to run the assembly line. ▪

data
MINING

Just because you have captured data in an organized fashion and have stored it in a format that seems to make sense doesn't mean that an analysis of the data will automatically reveal everything you need to know. Trends can sometimes be hard to spot if the data isn't organized or analyzed in a particular way. To make data work harder, companies employ data-mining techniques.

Data mining is the process by which great amounts of data are analyzed and investigated. The objective is to spot significant patterns or trends within the data that would otherwise not be obvious. For instance, by mining student enrollment data, a school may discover that there's been a consistent increase in new engineering-degree students who are women.

Why do businesses mine their data?

The main reason businesses mine data is to understand their customers better. If a company can better understand the types of customers who buy its products and can learn what motivates its customers to do so, it can market effectively by concentrating its efforts on the populations most likely to buy. You may have noticed that products are frequently moved around in supermarkets. This is usually the result of data mining. With electronic scanning of bar codes, each customer's purchase is recorded in a database. By classifying the data and using *cluster analysis,* supermarket managers can determine which products people usually purchase with other products. The store then places these products close to each other so that shoppers can find them easily. For instance, if analysis shows that people often buy potato chips with soft drinks, it makes sense to place these items in the same aisle.

How do businesses mine their data?

Data mining enables managers to sift through data in several ways. Each technique produces different information on which managers can then base their decisions.

Managers make their data meaningful through the following techniques (see Figure 11.33):

- *Classification:* Before mining, managers define data classes they think will be helpful in spotting trends. They then apply these class definitions to all unclassified data to prepare it for analysis. For example, "good credit risk" and "bad credit risk" are two data classes managers could establish to determine whether to grant car loans to applicants. Managers would then identify factors, such as credit history and yearly income, that they could use to classify applicants as good or bad credit risks.

FIGURE 11.33

Data-Mining Techniques

Classification
Define data classes to help spot trends, then apply the class definitions to all unclassified data.

Estimation
Assign a value to data based on some criterion.

Affinity Grouping (or Association Rules)
Determine which data goes together.

Clustering
Organize data into similar subgroups, or clusters, without using predefined classes.

Description and Visualization
Describe data so that managers can interpret it in new and different ways.

ethics in IT

Data, Data Everywhere—But Is It Protected?

As databases have become commonplace, an ever-increasing amount of information about you and your habits has been placed into various databases. Consider the following:

- Every credit card purchase generates a record of that transaction, and both the merchant from whom you purchased the item and the credit card company have gathered information about your buying habits (see Figure 11.34). In March 2012, private customer information was improperly exposed from all the major credit card brands, potentially affecting millions of credit card holders.

- Automated highway toll records are routinely subpoenaed in court cases. For example, toll records were used in an Illinois court by a husband in a 2007 divorce case to prove his wife was rarely home and therefore unfit to have custody of their son.

- Many companies such as Target collect e-mail addresses so they can correspond with customers, but the e-mails don't come directly from those companies. Large marketing companies such as Epsilon are hired to manage customer e-mail programs. Unfortunately, in March 2011 Epsilon's database servers suffered an attack that exposed millions of individuals' e-mail addresses to hackers.

FIGURE 11.34 Think about all the data about you that is stored in databases. Do you feel your privacy is protected? *(UK Stock Images Ltd/Alamy)*

Inadvertently exposing information to inappropriate or unauthorized individuals is known as a *data breach*. What responsibility do companies have in safeguarding your data? Should they inform you that your data might be shared with other corporations and obtain your permission before sharing it? How should consumers be compensated (and by whom) if their data is misused?

What Can You Do?

Providing information and having it recorded in databases are part of our way of life now. Because refusing to give information out at all is bound to be impractical, ask the following questions related to data you're providing:

- **For what purpose is the data being gathered?** When the clerk at the electronics superstore asks for your zip code, ask why he or she wants it.

- **Are the reasons for gathering the data legitimate or important to you?** You might not want to share your information for marketing purposes, but might want to in order to initiate a product warranty. Similarly, disclosing personal information to your pharmacist may be important for receiving good care and therefore is important to you. If you don't see the advantage, then ask more questions or don't reveal the information.

- **How will the collected information be protected?** Ask about data protection policies before you give information. Most websites provide access to their data protection policies when they ask you for information.

If an organization doesn't have a data protection policy, be wary of giving them sensitive information. Data protection doesn't just refer to keeping data secure, it also means restricting access to the data to employees of the organization that need to use that data. A shipping clerk might need to see your address, for example, but doesn't need to see your credit card information.

- **Will the collected information be used for purposes other than the purpose for which it was originally collected?** This might be covered in a data protection policy. If it isn't, ask about it. Will your information be sold to or shared with other companies? Will it be used for marketing other products to you?

- **Could the information asked for be used for identity theft?** Identity thieves usually need your Social Security number and your birth date to open credit card accounts in your name. Be especially wary when asked for this information, and make sure there is a legitimate need for it. Most organizations and businesses are shying away from using Social Security numbers to track customers because of the risk of identity theft. And do you really need an e-mail from someone on your birthday advertising a product? It really isn't worth exposing your birth date to potential misuse.

- **Are organizations safeguarding your data?** Don't just consider new requests for information. Think about organizations, such as banks, that already have your information. Have they been in the news lately because of a major data breach? (Is your bank a customer of Epsilon, for instance?) You might want to consider switching institutions if yours has a poor record of data security.

Think carefully before providing information and be vigilant about monitoring your data when you can. It may make the difference between invasion of privacy and peace of mind.

- *Estimation:* When managers classify data, the record either fits the classification criteria or it doesn't. Estimation enables managers to assign a value to data based on some criterion. For example, assume a bank wants to send out credit card offers to people who are likely to be granted a credit card. The bank may run the customers' data through a program that assigns a score based on where they live, their household income, and their average bank balance. This provides managers with an estimate of the most likely credit card prospects to target.

- *Affinity grouping (or association rules):* When mining data, managers can determine which data goes together. In other words, they can apply affinity grouping or association rules to the data. For example, suppose analysis of a sales database indicates that two items are bought together 60% of the time. Based on this data, managers might decide that these items should be pictured on the same page of their website.

- *Clustering:* Clustering involves organizing data into similar subgroups, or clusters. It's different from classification in that there are no predefined classes. The data-mining software makes the decision about what to group, and it's up to managers to determine whether the clusters are meaningful. For example, the data-mining software may identify clusters of customers with similar buying patterns. Further analysis of the clusters may reveal that certain socioeconomic groups have similar buying patterns.

- *Description and visualization:* Often, the purpose of data mining is to describe data so that managers can interpret it in new and different ways. For example, if large amounts of data revealed that right-handed women who live in rural environments never take philosophy courses, it would most likely spark a heated discussion about the reasons why. It would certainly provide plenty of opportunities for additional study on the part of psychologists, sociologists, and college administrators!

As we continue to accumulate data, the development of faster and bigger databases will be a necessity. You can expect to interact with more and more databases every year, even if you don't realize you're doing so. While you may never have to create a database, understanding how databases work will enable you to interact with them more effectively. ∎

> Before moving on to the Chapter Review:
> - Watch Replay Video 11.2 ▶.
> - Then check your understanding of what you've learned so far.

check your understanding //

For a quick review to see what you've learned so far, answer the following questions. Visit **pearsonhighered.com/ techinaction** to check your answers.

multiple choice

1. Which best describes a data warehouse?

    a. a building that stores computer servers

    b. a software program that assists with file management

    c. a collection of data that organizes all of an organization's data

    d. a database that organizes data from multiple organizations

2. Which of the following is a component of data staging?

    a. extraction of data from source databases

    b. transformation of the data

    c. storage of the data in the data warehouse

    d. all of the above

3. A system that's designed to help perform routine daily tasks is known as (a)n

    a. data mart.

    b. office support system.

    c. data warehouse.

    d. decision support system.

4. A system that tries to mimic human decision making processes is an example of a(n)

    a. transaction-processing system.

    b. decision support system.

    c. expert system.

    d. model management system.

5. The process of analyzing and investigating large amounts of data to spot trends is called

    a. data mining.

    b. batch processing.

    c. transaction processing.

    d. data marting.

true–false

_____ 1. A transaction-processing system (TPS) is an example of a business intelligence system.

_____ 2. Customer demographic data purchased from a third party is an example of an internal data source.

critical thinking

1. **Database Privacy Policies**

    Most likely, you've provided personal information to various companies when you became their customer. Companies have an ethical responsibility to protect sensitive data obtained from customers. Think about a retailer that you've done business with recently. What personal information did you provide to that retailer? What personal information should a company not be allowed to disclose to others? What information does the company have of yours that you don't care if they share with (or sell to) other companies?

2. **Social Security Database**

    The U.S. Social Security Administration (SSA) maintains a large database containing a great deal of information on the personal income of individuals that would be of value to marketing professionals for targeted marketing. Currently, the SSA is prohibited from selling this information to third parties. However, the SSA and other government agencies face increasing pressure to find ways to generate revenue or decrease expenses.

    a. Do you favor a change in the laws that would permit the SSA to sell names and addresses with household income information to third parties? Why or why not?

    b. Would it be acceptable for the SSA to sell income information to marketing firms if it did not include personal information but only included income statistics for certain geographic areas? How is this better (or worse) than selling personal information?

    Continue ➡

11 Chapter Review

summary

Database Building Blocks

1. What is a database, and why is using one beneficial?

- Databases are electronic collections of related data that can be organized so that data is more easily accessed and manipulated. Properly designed databases cut down on data redundancy and duplicate data by ensuring relevant data is recorded in only one place. This also helps eliminate data inconsistency, which comes from having different data about the same transaction recorded in different places.
- When databases are used, multiple users can share and access information at the same time.
- Databases are used any time complex information needs to be organized or when more than one person needs to access the information. In these cases, lists (which are used to keep track of simple information) are no longer efficient.

2. What do database management systems do?

- Database management systems (DBMSs) are specially designed applications (such as Microsoft Access) that interact with the user, other applications, and the database itself to capture and analyze data.
- The main operations of a DBMS are creating databases, entering data, viewing (or browsing) data, sorting (or indexing) data, extracting (or querying) data, and outputting data.
- A query language is used to extract records from a database. Almost all relational databases today use structured query language, or SQL. However, most DBMSs include wizards that enable you to query the database without learning a query language.
- The most common form of output for any database is a printed report.

3. What components make up a database?

- The three main components of a database are fields, records, and tables.
- A category of information in a database is stored in a field. Each field is identified by a field name, which is a way of describing the field. Fields are assigned a data type that indicates what type of data can be stored in the field. Common data types include text, numeric, computational, date, memo, object, and hyperlink.
- A group of related fields is a record.

- A group of related records is a table or file.
- To keep records distinct, each record must have one field that has a value unique to that record. This unique field is a primary key (or a key field).

Database Types

4. What types of databases are there?

- The three major types of databases currently in use are relational, object-oriented, and multidimensional.
- Relational databases are characterized by two-dimensional tables of data in which a common field is maintained in each of two tables and the information in the tables is linked by this field.
- Object-oriented databases store data in objects, not in tables. The objects also contain instructions about how the data is to be manipulated or processed.
- Multidimensional databases represent data in three-dimensional cubes to enable faster retrieval of information from the database.

Database Functions

5. How do relational databases organize and manipulate data?

- Relational databases operate by organizing data into various tables based on logical groupings. Because not all of the data in a relational database is stored in the same table, a methodology must be implemented to link data between tables. In relational databases, the links between tables that define how the data is related are referred to as relationships.
- To establish a relationship between two tables, both tables must have a common field (or column). Once linked, information can be drawn from multiple tables through the use of queries (for on-screen viewing of data) or report generators (used to produce printed reports).

Database Warehousing and Storage

6. What are data warehouses and data marts, and how are they used?

- A data warehouse is a large-scale collection of data that contains and organizes in one place all the relevant data for an organization. Data warehouses often contain information from multiple databases.

- Because it can be difficult to find information in a large data warehouse, small slices of the data warehouse, called data marts, are often created. The information in data marts pertains to a single department within the organization, for example.
- Data warehouses and data marts consolidate information from a wide variety of sources to provide comprehensive pictures of operations or transactions within a business.

Business Intelligence Systems

7. What is a business intelligence system, and what types of business intelligence systems are used by decision makers?

- Business intelligence systems are used to analyze and interpret data in order to enable managers to make informed decisions about how best to run a business.
- An office support system (OSS) is designed to assist employees in accomplishing their day-to-day tasks and improve communications.
- A transaction-processing system (TPS) is used to keep track of everyday business activities.
- A management information system (MIS) provides timely and accurate information that enables managers to make critical business decisions.
- A decision support system (DSS) is designed to help managers develop solutions for specific problems.
  - A model management system is software that assists in building analysis tools for DSSs.
  - A knowledge-based system provides intelligence to make the DSS more effective. There are several kinds of knowledge-based systems. An expert system tries to replicate the decision-making process of human experts to solve specific problems. A natural language processing (NLP) system uses natural spoken or written language rather than a computer programming language to communicate with a computer. Lastly, artificial intelligence (AI) attempts to create computers that think like humans.
- An enterprise resource planning (ERP) system is a large software system that gathers information from all parts of a business and integrates it to make it readily available for decision making.

Data Mining

8. What is data mining, and how does it work?

- Data mining is the process by which large amounts of data are analyzed to spot otherwise hidden trends. Through processes such as classification, estimation, affinity grouping, clustering, and description (visualization), data is organized so that it provides meaningful information that can be used by managers to identify business trends.

Be sure to check out the companion website for additional materials to help you review and learn, including a Tech Bytes Weekly newsletter—**pearsonhighered.com/techinaction**. And don't forget the Replay Videos .

key terms//

alphabetic check **479**

artificial intelligence (AI) **495**

batch processing **493**

binary large object (BLOB) **476**

business intelligence systems **492**

clickstream data **489**

completeness check **479**

consistency check **479**

database **466**

database administrator (database designer) **470**

database management system (DBMS) **470**

data centralization **469**

data dictionary (database schema) **471**

data inconsistency **469**

data integrity **469**

data mart **489**

data mining **497**

data redundancy **468**

data staging **489**

data type (field type) **473**

data warehouse **488**

decision support system (DSS) **494**

default value **472**

detail report **494**

enterprise resource planning (ERP) system **496**

exception report **494**

expert system **495**

field **471**

field constraint **478**

field properties **472**

field size **473**

filter **480**

foreign key **475**

fuzzy logic **496**

information system **492**

input form **478**

join query **483**

knowledge-based system **495**

management information system (MIS) **493**

many-to-many relationship **476**

metadata **471**

model management system **495**

multidimensional database **476**

natural language processing (NLP) system **495**

normalization **474**

numeric check **479**

object-oriented database **476**

Object Query Language (OQL) **476**

office support system (OSS) **492**

one-to-many relationship **475**

one-to-one relationship **475**

online analytical processing (OLAP) **479**

online transaction processing (OLTP) **493**

primary key field **474**

query **480**

query language **476**

range check **478**

real-time processing **493**

record **471**

referential integrity **475**

relational algebra **482**

relational database **475**

relationship **475**

select query **482**

structured (analytical) data **476**

Structured Query Language (SQL) **476**

summary report **494**

table (file) **471**

time-variant data **489**

transaction-processing system (TPS) **493**

unstructured data **476**

validation **478**

validation rule **478**

making the transition to . . . next semester //

1. **Designing Your Own Database**

   Students at your school want to collect and refurbish used computer equipment and donate it to underprivileged individuals. You offer to create a database to facilitate the tracking of the donated equipment. Determine the following:

   a. What fields do you need in your database to capture information about the clients donating the computing equipment? What would be the primary key of the "client" table? Explain your choice.

   b. What fields do you need to identify and categorize equipment? What would be a good primary key to use for the "computer inventory" table? Explain your choice.

   c. Design a table that tracks the donations. What fields from the other tables should be included in the "donation transaction" table? Justify your answer.

2. **Comparing Databases**

   Amazon.com and eCampus.com are two sites used to buy books. On both sites, you interact with a database to search for and purchase books. Visit both sites and without using specific book information (title, author, or ISBN), search for several of your textbooks. Compare your experiences on both sites.

   a. Which site is easier to use? Why?

   b. What fields did you search on to find your books? Would searching on another field have produced more-accurate results?

   c. What would you change in both sites to improve your time shopping?

making the transition to . . . the workplace //

1. **Data Marts**

   You work in the IT group of a chain of sporting goods stores, which has 40 locations in seven states. The 40 locations are organized into four regions (north, south, east, and west) with 10 stores in each. Regional managers are responsible for inventory, sales, and marketing for their region. The company has been processing all transactions electronically, and it has captured all the data in a large data warehouse. Unfortunately, there is so much information in the data warehouse that extracting meaningful data has become difficult. You've just been placed on the team that will design a new data strategy for the company.

   a. What type of data marts would you suggest setting up? Who will benefit from the data marts you suggest?

   b. For the data marts you identified, what data should be stored in each data mart? Explain how the regional managers could make use of that information to manage their group of stores.

2. **Recovering from a Data Breach**

   You work in the marketing department of XYZ Drugs that has an established buyer loyalty program. XYZ Drugs collects customer e-mail addresses and has engaged ABC Marketing to routinely send out marketing e-mails. ABC has just informed XYZ that its servers suffered a data breach and that all the names and e-mail addresses of XYZ's customers in ABC's database were compromised. You're working to inform XYZ's customers of the possible consequences of the data breach.

   a. What are the risks that XYZ's customers face from the data breach?

   b. What steps should the customers take to mitigate these risks? You need to be tactful and careful in your suggestions to customers because you want them to continue to trust XYZ with their personal information.

   c. Prepare a list of precautions customers can take with their personal data to avoid being victims of these types of data breaches. Try searching on the Internet for ideas using search terms such as "data breach protection" or "e-mail breach safeguards."

Redesigning Facebook

Problem

Facebook is the most popular social media site—it's also a database. But as with any product, there is always room for improvement. Facebook management has made decisions about what data they require from users who create Facebook accounts. They also have set up specific areas to display what management considers to be pertinent information on a user's main Facebook page. But perhaps you as a user would have designed Facebook differently.

Task

Your class has volunteered to work as a focus group for Facebook as part of a nationwide project to assess the usefulness of the information it gathers. Users often provide unique perspectives, and they should be consulted whenever possible during the design, implementation, and updates of websites. As heavy users of Facebook, management feels that student input is invaluable to ensuring currency and usability of its features.

Process

1. Divide the class into small groups.

2. Your group members should examine their individual Facebook accounts. Pay particular attention to the profile area of your account. What fields in the profile do you consider to be most useful? Which fields do you think are unnecessary and could be eliminated? What fields are missing from the profile that you think would be useful to you and your friends?

3. Investigate your account settings and application settings, paying particular attention to items that are displayed on the main page of your account. What changes would you make to these settings? Are options missing that you would find helpful to configuring your Facebook page?

4. Present your group's findings to the class. Compare your suggestions to those of other groups. Be sure to think about the needs of other groups of users (such as your parents, grandparents, or teenagers).

5. Prepare a list of recommendations for improvements to the current Facebook home page and settings pages. Clearly indicate how the proposed changes will benefit both users and the management of Facebook (retaining users, being able to better target advertising to users, and so on).

Conclusion

Facebook will most likely experience competition in the future from other social networking sites that will want to poach its huge base of users. To remain competitive, Facebook needs to consider the input of users like you to ensure that it delivers a cutting-edge product with features its customers want and need.

Private Information on Public Databases

In this exercise, you'll research and then role-play a complicated ethical situation. The role you play might not match your own personal beliefs, but your research and use of logic will enable you to represent the view assigned. An arbitrator will watch and comment on both sides of the arguments, and together, the team will agree on an ethical solution.

Problem

As more tasks in our lives are conducted online, there is a tremendous amount of data accumulated about us in online databases. Unfortunately, much of this material is accessible in databases that are searchable by anyone with Internet access or to anyone willing to pay a small fee. Websites such as **spokeo.com** and **411.com** comb through publicly accessible databases to compile information on individuals. These databases include social networking sites (Facebook or LinkedIn), online phone books, business sites where you have accounts, and government (federal, state, and local) websites. There is probably a lot of information about you available on sites such that could expose you to risks such as identify theft.

Research Areas to Consider

- Electronic information privacy
- Electronic Privacy Information Center (**epic.org**)
- Protecting your online privacy
- Protecting yourself on Facebook
- Protecting yourself from data breaches

Process

1. Divide the class into teams.
2. Research the areas cited above and devise a scenario in which someone has complained about a website (such as **spokeo.com**) providing information that led to his or her identity being stolen.
3. Team members should write a summary that provides background information for their character—for example: victim of identity theft, website owner, or arbitrator—and that details their character's behaviors to set the stage for the role-playing event. Then, team members should create an outline to use during the role-playing event.
4. Team members should arrange a mutually convenient time to meet for the exchange, using either the collaboration feature of MyITLab or the discussion board feature of your course management software or by meeting in person.
5. Team members should present their case to the class or submit a PowerPoint presentation for review by the rest of the class, along with the summary and resolution they developed.

Conclusion

As technology becomes ever more prevalent and integrated into our lives, ethical dilemmas will present themselves to an increasing extent. Being able to understand and evaluate both sides of the argument, while responding in a personally or socially ethical manner, will be an important skill.

Glossary

3-D sound card An expansion card that enables a computer to produce omnidirectional or three-dimensional sounds.

A

access card reader A device that reads information from a magnetic strip on the back of a credit card–like access card.

access method A method to control which computer is allowed to use transmission media at a certain time.

access time The time it takes a storage device to locate its stored data.

accounting software An application program that helps business owners manage their finances more efficiently by providing tools for tracking accounting transactions such as sales, accounts receivable, inventory purchases, and accounts payable.

ActionScript The programming language used by Adobe Flash; similar to JavaScript.

Active Server Pages (ASP) Programming language used to build websites with interactive capabilities; adapts an HTML page to the user's selections.

active topology In a network, a type of topology where the nodes participate in moving data through the network.

Adobe Flash A software product for developing web-based multimedia.

adware A program that downloads on your computer when a user installs a freeware program, game, or utility. Generally, adware enables sponsored advertisements to appear in a section of a browser window or as a pop-up ad.

affective computing A type of computing that relates to emotion or that deliberately tries to influence emotion.

aggregator A software program that finds and retrieves the latest update of web material (usually podcasts) according to your specifications.

AJAX (Asynchronous JavaScript and XML) A collection of technologies that allow the creation of web applications that can update information on a page without requiring the user to refresh or leave the page.

algorithm A set of specific, sequential steps that describe exactly what the computer program must do to complete the required work.

all-in-one computer A desktop system unit that houses the computer's processor, memory, and monitor in a single unit.

all-in-one printer Combines the functions of a printer, scanner, copier, and fax into one machine.

alphabetic check In a database, confirms that only textual characters are entered in a field.

analog Waves that illustrate the loudness of a sound or the brightness of the colors in an image at a given moment in time.

analog-to-digital converter chip Converts analog signals into digital signals.

antivirus software Software specifically designed to detect viruses and protect a computer and files from harm.

app bars Bars that float above the screen and that contain applications such as the Tabs bar and the Address bar; a new feature of Internet Explorer 10.

applet A small application located on a server; when requested, the applet is downloaded to the client.

application programming interface (API) A set of software routines that allows one software system to work with another.

application server A server that acts as a repository for application software.

application software The set of programs on a computer that helps a user carry out tasks such as word processing, sending e-mail, balancing a budget, creating presentations, editing photos, taking an online course, and playing games.

architecture neutral A feature of Java whereby code needs to be compiled only once, after which the code can be run on many different CPUs.

artificial intelligence The branch of computer science that deals with the attempt to create computers that think like humans.

aspect ratio The width-to-height proportion of a monitor.

assembly language See *second-generation language (2GL)*.

audio-editing software Programs that perform basic editing tasks on audio files such as cutting dead air space from the beginning or end of a song or cutting a portion from the middle.

audio MIDI interface Interface technology that allows a user to connect guitars and microphones to their computer.

augmented reality A combination of our normal sense of the objects around us with an overlay of information displayed.

authentication The process of identifying a computer user, based on a login or username and password. The computer system determines whether the computer user is authorized and what level of access is to be granted on the network.

authentication server A server that keeps track of who's logging on to the network and which services on the network are available to each user.

B

backdoor program Program that enables a hacker to take complete control of a computer without the legitimate user's knowledge or permission.

backup A copy of a computer file that can be used to replace the original if it's lost or damaged.

backward compatibility The accommodation of current devices being able to use previously issued software standards in addition to the current standards.

bandwidth The maximum speed at which data can be transmitted between two nodes on a network; usually measured in megabits per second (Mbps). See also *data transfer rate*.

base class In object-oriented analysis, the original class.

base transceiver station A large communications tower with antennas, amplifiers, and receivers/transmitters.

basic input/output system (BIOS) A program that manages the data between a computer's operating system and all the input and output devices attached to the computer; also responsible for loading the operating system (OS) from its permanent location on the hard drive to random access memory (RAM).

bastion host A heavily secured server located on a special perimeter network between the company's secure internal network and its firewall.

batch processing The accumulation of transaction data until a certain point is reached, at which time several transactions are processed at once.

beta version A version of the software that's still under development. Many beta versions are available for a limited trial period and are used to help the developers correct any errors before they launch the software on the market.

binary decision A type of decision point in an algorithm that can be answered in one of only two ways: yes (true) or no (false).

binary digit (bit) A digit that corresponds to the on and off states of a computer's switches. A bit contains a value of either 0 or 1.

binary language The language computers use to process data into information, consisting of only the values 0 and 1.

biometric authentication device A device that uses some unique characteristic of human biology to identify authorized users.

black-hat hacker A hacker who uses his or her knowledge to destroy information or for illegal gain.

binary large object (BLOB) See *unstructured data.*

blog A personal log or journal posted on the web; short for *web log.*

Bluetooth (technology) A type of wireless technology that uses radio waves to transmit data over short distances (approximately 3-300 feet depending on power); often used to connect peripherals such as printers and keyboards to computers or headsets to cell phones.

Blu-ray disc (BD) A method of optical storage for digital data, developed for storing high-definition media. It has the largest storage capacity of all optical storage options.

bookmarks Features in some browsers that place markers of websites' Uniform Resource Locators (URLs) in an easily retrievable list.

Boolean operator A word used to refine logical searches. For Internet searches, the words AND, NOT, and OR describe the relationships between keywords in the search.

boot process The process for loading the operating system (OS) into random access memory (RAM) when the computer is turned on.

boot-sector virus A virus that replicates itself into the master boot record of a flash drive or hard drive.

botnet A large group of software applications (called *robots* or *bots*) that run without user intervention on a large number of computers.

breadcrumb trail A navigation aid that shows users the path they have taken to get to a web page or where the page is located within the website; it usually appears at the top of a page.

bridge A device that's used to send data between different collision domains in a network, depending on where the recipient device is located.

broadband A high-speed Internet connection such as cable, satellite, or digital subscriber line (DSL).

brute force attack An attempt to access an account by repeatedly trying different passwords.

bus (linear bus) topology A system of networking connections in which all devices are connected in sequence on a single cable.

business intelligence systems Systems used to analyze and interpret data in order to enable managers to make informed decisions about how best to run a business.

business-to-business (B2B) E-commerce transactions between businesses.

business-to-consumer (B2C) E-commerce transactions between businesses and consumers.

byte Eight binary digits (bits).

C

C A programming language originally developed for system programmers.

C++ A programming language; takes C to an object-oriented level.

C# A Microsoft programming language developed to compete with Java.

cable Internet A broadband service that transmits data over coaxial cables.

cache memory Small blocks of memory, located directly on and next to the central processing unit (CPU) chip, that act as holding places for recently or frequently used instructions or data that the CPU accesses the most. When these instructions or data are stored in cache memory, the CPU can more quickly retrieve them than if it had to access the instructions or data from random access memory (RAM).

cascading style sheet A list of rules that defines in one single location how to display HTML elements.

Cat 6 cable A UTP cable type that provides more than 1 Gb/s of throughput.

cellular (cell) phone A telephone that operates over a mobile network. Cell phones can also offer Internet access, text messaging, personal information management (PIM) features, and more.

central processing unit (CPU, or processor) The part of the system unit of a computer that is responsible for data processing; it is the largest and most important chip in the computer. The CPU controls all the functions performed by the computer's other components and processes all the commands issued to it by software instructions.

centralized A characteristic of client/server networks where the server, not the individual user, coordinates data security.

cgi-bin On a web server, a directory created by the network administrator who configures the web server.

CGI script A CGI program file.

charms Special shortcuts for performing common tasks, such as searching or sharing information, created for Windows 8.

circuit switching Where a dedicated connection is formed between two points (such as two people on telephones) and the connection remains active for the duration of the transmission.

class A category of input identified in object-oriented analysis; classes are defined by information and actions.

classless interdomain routing (CIDR) An Internet addressing scheme that allows a single Internet protocol (IP) address to represent several unique IP addresses by adding a *network prefix* to the last octet.

clickstream data Software used on company websites to capture information about each click that users make as they navigate through the site.

client A computer that requests information from a server in a client/server network (such as your computer when you are connected to the Internet).

client/server model A model of network communications where a client device such as a computer, tablet, or smartphone uses browsers to request services from networks that make up the Internet.

client/server network (server-based network) A type of network that uses servers to deliver services to computers that are requesting them (clients).

client-side program A program that runs on the client computer and that requires no interaction with a web server.

clock speed The steady and constant pace at which a computer goes through machine cycles, measured in hertz (Hz).

cloud computing The process of storing data, files, and applications on the web, which allows access to and manipulation of these files and applications from any Internet-connected device.

cloud server A server that is maintained by a hosting company and that is connected to networks via the Internet.

cluster The smallest increment in which data is stored on hard disks; hard disks are divided into *tracks*, then *wedges*, then *sectors*, then clusters.

coaxial cable A single copper wire surrounded by layers of plastic insulation, metal sheathing, and a plastic jacket; used mainly in cable television and cable Internet service.

code editing The step of programming in which a programmer types the code to be executed.

codec A rule, implemented in either software or hardware, which squeezes a given amount of audio and video information into less space.

coding Translating an algorithm into a programming language.

cognitive surplus The combination of leisure time and the tools needed to be creative.

cold boot The process of starting a computer from a powered-down or off state.

collaborative consumption Joining together as a group to use a specific product more efficiently.

command-driven interface Interface between user and computer in which the user enters commands to communicate with the computer system.

comment A note left by a programmer in the program code to explain the purpose of a section of code, to indicate the date the program was written, or to include other important information about the code so that other programmers can more easily understand and update it.

commerce server Computers that host software that enables users to buy goods and services over the web.

Common Gateway Interface (CGI) A method of designing programs that provides a methodology by which a browser can request a program file be executed instead of just being delivered to the browser.

communications server A server that handles all communications between the network and other networks, including managing Internet connectivity.

compact disc (CD) A method of optical storage for digital data; originally developed for storing digital audio.

compilation The process by which code is converted into machine language—the language the central processing unit can understand.

compiler A program that understands both the syntax of the programming language and the exact structure of the central processing unit and its machine language.

completeness check In a database, ensures that all required fields have been completed.

computer A data-processing device that gathers, processes, outputs, and stores data and information.

computer-aided design (CAD) A 3-D modeling program used to create automated designs, technical drawings, and model visualizations.

computer forensics The application of computer systems and techniques to gather potential legal evidence; a law enforcement specialty used to fight high-tech crime.

computer literate Being familiar enough with computers that a user knows how to use them and understands their capabilities and limitations.

computer protocol A set of rules for exchanging electronic information.

connection-oriented protocol A protocol for exchanging information that requires two computers to exchange control packets, thereby setting up the parameters of the data-exchange session, before sending packets that contain data.

connectionless protocol A protocol that a host computer can use to send data over the network without establishing a direct connection with any specific recipient computer.

connectivity port A port that enables a computing device to be connected to other devices or systems such as networks, modems, and the Internet.

consistency check In a database, compares the values of data in two or more fields to see if those values are reasonable.

consumer-to-consumer (C2C) E-commerce transactions between consumers through online sites such as eBay.com.

control structure General term used for a keyword in a programming language that allows the programmer to direct the flow of the program based on a decision.

cookie A small text file that some websites automatically store on a client computer's hard drive when a user visits the site.

copyleft A simplified licensing scheme that enables copyright holders to grant certain rights to a work while retaining other rights.

core A complete processing section from a central processing unit, embedded into one physical chip.

course management software A program that provides traditional classroom tools, such as calendars and grade books, over the Internet, as well as areas for students to exchange ideas and information in chat rooms, discussion forums, and e-mail.

CPU benchmarks Measurements used to compare performance between processors.

CPU usage The percentage of time the central processing unit (CPU) is working.

CPU usage graph Records your central processing unit (CPU) usage for the past several seconds.

crisis-mapping tool A tool that collects information from e-mails, text messages, blog posts, and Twitter tweets and maps them, making the information instantly publicly available.

crowdfunding Asking for small donations from a large number of people, often using the Internet; a style of generating capital to start a business through social media.

crowdsourcing The phenomenon of consumers checking in with the voice of the crowd before making purchases.

CSMA/CD The method used on Ethernet networks to avoid data collisions; short for *carrier sense multiple access with collision detection*. A node connected to the network uses carrier sense to verify that no other nodes are currently transmitting data signals.

custom installation The process of installing only those features of a software program that a user wants on the hard drive.

cybercrime Any criminal action perpetrated primarily through the use of a computer.

cybercriminal An individual who uses computers, networks, and the Internet to perpetrate crime.

cyberloafing Doing anything with a computer that's unrelated to a job (such as playing video games) while one's supposed to be working. Also called *cyberslacking*.

D

data Numbers, words, pictures, or sounds that represent facts, figures, or ideas; the raw input that users have at the start of a job.

data breach When sensitive or confidential information is copied, transmitted, or viewed by an individual who is not authorized to handle the data.

data centralization When data is maintained in only one file.

data collision When two computers send data at the same time and the sets of data collide somewhere in the connection media.

data dictionary (database schema) A map of a database that defines the features of the fields in the database.

data file A file that contains stored data.

data-flow diagrams Diagrams that trace all data in an information system from the point at which data enters the system to its final resting place (storage or output).

data inconsistency Data for a record being different in two different lists.

data integrity When the data in a database is accurate and reliable.

data mart Small slices of a data warehouse grouped together and separated from the main body of data in the data warehouse so that related sets of data can be analyzed.

data mining The process by which great amounts of data are analyzed and investigated. The objective is to spot significant patterns or trends within the data that would otherwise not be obvious.

data plan A connectivity plan or text messaging plan in which data charges are separate from cell phone calling charges and are provided at rates different from those for voice calls.

data redundancy Duplicated data in a list.

data staging The act of formatting data from source databases before fitting it into a data warehouse; it consists of three steps: extraction, transformation, and storage.

data transfer rate The maximum speed at which data can be transmitted between two nodes on a network; measured in megabits per second (Mbps) or gigabits per second (Gbps).

data type (field type) (1) Describes the kind of data being stored at the memory location; each programming language has its own data types (although there is some degree of overlap). (2) In a database, indicates what type of data can be stored in a field and prevents the wrong type of data from being entered into the field.

data warehouse A large-scale collection of data that contains and organizes in one place all the data from an organization's multiple databases.

database A digital collection of related data that can be stored, sorted, organized, and queried.

database administrator (database designer) An information technology professional responsible for designing, constructing, and maintaining databases.

database management system (DBMS) A specially designed application software used to create and mage databases.

database server A server that provides client computers with access to information stored in databases.

database software An electronic filing system best used for larger and more complicated groups of data that require more than one table and the ability to group, sort, and retrieve data and generate reports.

debugger A tool in an integrated development environment that helps programmers analyze a program as it runs.

debugging The process of running a program over and over to find and repair errors and to make sure the program behaves in the way it should.

decentralized A characteristic of peer-to-peer networks where the individual user coordinates data security.

decision point A place where a program must choose from a list of actions based on the value of a certain input.

decision support system (DSS) A type of business intelligence system designed to help managers develop solutions for specific problems.

dedicated server A server used to fulfill one specific function, such as handling e-mail.

default value The value a database automatically uses for a field unless the user enters another value.

denial-of-service (DoS) attack An attack that occurs when legitimate users are denied access to a computer system because a hacker is repeatedly making requests of that computer system that tie up its resources and deny legitimate users access.

derived class In object-oriented analysis, the modified class.

desktop computer A computer that's intended for use at a single location. A desktop computer consists of a case that houses the main components of the computer, plus peripheral devices.

desktop publishing (DTP) software Programs for incorporating and arranging graphics and text to produce creative documents.

detail report A report generated by a management information system that provides a list of the transactions that occurred during a certain time period.

device driver Software that facilitates the communication between a device and its operating system or between a network adapter and a server's operating system and the operating system of the computer in which the adapter is installed.

digital convergence The use of a single unifying device to handle media, Internet, entertainment, and telephony needs; expressed in the range of devices now on the market.

digital divide The discrepancy between those who have access to the opportunities and knowledge that computers and the Internet offer and those who do not.

digital rights management (DRM) A system of access control that allows only

limited use of material that has been legally purchased.

digital signal processor A specialized chip that processes digital information and transmits signals very quickly.

digital subscriber line (DSL) A type of connection that uses telephone lines to connect to the Internet and that allows both phone and data transmissions to share the same line.

digital video (or versatile) disc (DVD) A method of optical storage for digital data that has greater storage capacity than compact discs.

digital video–editing software A program for editing digital video.

digital video interface (DVI) port Video interface technology that newer LCD monitors, as well as other multimedia devices such as televisions, DVD players, and projectors, use to connect to a PC.

directory A hierarchical structure that include files, folders, and drives used to create a more organized and efficient computer.

Disk Cleanup A Windows utility that removes unnecessary files from the hard drive.

disk defragmenting A utility that regroups related pieces of files on the hard drive, enabling faster retrieval of the data.

distributed denial of service (DDoS) attack An automated attack that's launched from more than one zombie computer at the same time.

Distributions (distros) Linux download packages.

Document Object Model (DOM) Used by JavaScript to organize objects and page elements.

documentation Description of the technical details of the software, how the code works, and how the user interacts with the program; in addition, all the necessary user documentation that will be distributed to the program's users.

domain name A part of a Uniform Resource Locator (URL). Domain names consist of two parts: the site's host and a suffix that indicates the type of organization (example:

popsci.com, where *popsci* is the domain name and *com* is the suffix).

domain name system (DNS) server A server that maintains a database of domain names and converts domain names to Internet protocol addresses.

dotted decimal number (dotted quad) The form of an Internet protocol address, where sets of numerals are separated by decimals, i.e., 197.169.73.63.

drawing software (illustration software) Programs for creating or editing two-dimensional line-based drawings.

drive bay A special shelf inside a computer that is designed to hold storage devices.

drive-by download The use of malicious software to attack a computer by downloading harmful programs onto a computer, without the user's knowledge, while they are surfing a website.

dynamic addressing A way of assigning Internet protocol addresses where a computer is assigned a temporary address from an available pool of addresses.

dynamic decision making The ability of a web page to decide how to display itself based on the choices the reader makes.

Dynamic Host Configuration Protocol (DHCP) A protocol for assigning dynamic internet protocol addresses.

Dynamic HTML (DHTML) A combination of technologies—HTML, cascading style sheets, and JavaScript—used to create lively and interactive websites.

E

e-commerce (electronic commerce) The process of conducting business online for purposes ranging from fund-raising to advertising to selling products.

editor A special tool in an integrated development environment (IDE) that helps programmers as they enter code.

electronic data interchange (EDI) The exchange of large amounts of data in a standardized electronic format.

electronic ink (E ink) A very crisp, sharp grayscale representation of text achieved by using millions of microcapsules with white and black particles in a clear fluid.

electronic text (e-text) Textual information stored as digital information so that it can be stored, manipulated, and transmitted by electronic devices.

element In HTML, a pair of tags and the text between them.

e-mail (electronic mail) Internet-based communication in which senders and recipients correspond.

e-mail client A software program that runs on a computer and is used to send and receive e-mail through an Internet service provider's server.

e-mail server A server whose sole function is to process and deliver incoming and outgoing e-mail.

e-mail virus A virus transmitted by e-mail that often uses the address book in the victim's e-mail system to distribute itself.

embedded computer A specially designed computer chip that resides inside another device, such as a car. These self-contained computer devices have their own programming and typically neither receive input from users nor interact with other systems.

encryption The process of coding e-mail so that only the person with the key to the code (the intended recipient) can decode the message.

encryption virus A malicious program that searches for common data files and compresses them into a file using a complex encryption key, thereby rendering the files unusable.

End User License Agreement (EULA) See *software license*.

enterprise resource planning (ERP) system A business intelligence system that accumulates in a central location all information relevant to running a business and makes it readily available to whoever needs it to make decisions.

e-reader A device that can display e-text and that has supporting tools, like note taking, bookmarks, and integrated dictionaries.

ergonomics How a user sets up his or her computer and other equipment to minimize risk of injury or discomfort.

error-checking A Windows utility that checks for lost files and fragments as well as physical errors on a hard drive.

error handling The part of a problem statement where programmers describe what the program should do if the input data is invalid or just gibberish.

Ethernet network A network that uses the Ethernet protocol as the means (or standard) by which the nodes on the network communicate.

Ethernet port A port that's slightly larger than a standard phone jack and that transfers data at speeds of up to 10,000 Mbps; used to connect a computer to a DSL or cable modem or to a network.

event The result of an action, such as a keystroke, mouse click, or signal to the printer, in the respective device (keyboard, mouse, or printer) to which the operating system responds.

exception report A report generated by a management information system that shows conditions that are unusual or that need attention by system users.

executable program The binary sequence that instructs the central processing unit to run the programmer's code.

expansion card (adapter card) A circuit board with specific functions that augment the computer's basic functions and provide connections to other devices; examples include the sound card and the video card.

expert system A system that tries to replicate the decision-making processes of human experts in order to solve specific problems.

ExpressCard Laptops are often equipped with an ExpressCard slot. The ExpressCard can add a solid-state drive (SSD), new kinds of ports, and other capabilities to a system.

eXtensible Markup Language (XML) A markup language that enables designers to define their own data-based tags, making it much easier for a website to transfer the key information on its page to another site; it defines what data is being described rather than how it's to be displayed.

extension (file type) In a file name, the three letters that follow the user-supplied file name after the dot (.); the extension identifies what kind of family of files the file belongs to, or which application should be used to read the file.

external hard drive A hard drive that is enclosed in a protective case to make it portable; the drive is connected to the computer with a data transfer cable and is often used to back up data.

extranet An area of an intranet that only certain corporations or individuals can access; the owner of the extranet decides who will be permitted to access it.

F

Favorites A feature in Microsoft Internet Explorer that places a marker of a website's Uniform Resource Locator (URL) in an easily retrievable list in the browser's toolbar. (Called Bookmarks in some browsers.)

feature phones Inexpensive cell phones with modest processors, simple interfaces, and, often, no touch screens.

fiber-optic cable A cable that transmits data at close to the speed of light along glass or plastic fibers.

fiber-optic service Internet access that is enabled by transmitting data at the speed of light through glass or plastic fibers.

field The component of a database in which the database stores each category of information.

field constraint A property that must be satisfied for an entry to be accepted into the field.

Field Properties In an Access database table, the field name, data type, and other data elements.

field size Defines the maximum number of characters that a field can hold in a database.

fifth-generation language (5GL) A computer language in which a problem is presented as a series of facts or constraints instead of as a specific algorithm; the system of facts can then be queried; considered the most "natural" of languages.

file A collection of related pieces of information stored together for easy reference.

file allocation table (FAT) An index of all sector numbers that the hard drive stores in a table to keep track of which sectors hold which files.

file compression utility A program that takes out redundancies in a file in order to reduce the file size.

File Explorer The main tool for finding, viewing, and managing the contents of your computer by showing the location and contents of every drive, folder, and file; called Windows Explorer prior to Windows 8.

File History A Windows utility that automatically creates a duplicate of your libraries, desktop, contacts, and favorites and copies it to another storage device, such as an external hard drive.

file management The process by which humans or computer software provide organizational structure to a computer's contents.

file name The first part of the label applied to a file; generally the name a user assigns to the file when saving it.

file path The exact location of a file, starting with the drive in which the file is located and including all folders, subfolders (if any), the file name, and the extension (example: C:\Users\username\Documents\Illustrations\EBronte.jpg).

file server A server that stores and manages files for network users or that acts as a storehouse for files that users can download.

File Transfer Protocol (FTP) A protocol used to upload and download files from one computer to another over the Internet.

filter In a database, temporarily displays records that match certain criteria.

financial planning software Programs for managing finances, such as Intuit's Quicken, which include electronic checkbook registers and automatic bill-payment tools.

firewall A software program or hardware device designed to prevent unauthorized access to computers or networks.

FireWire 400 An interface port that transfers data at 400 Mbps.

FireWire 800 An interface port that transfers data at 800 Mbps.

firmware System software that controls hardware devices.

first-generation language (1GL) The machine language of a central processing unit (CPU); the sequence of bits that the CPU understands.

flash drive A drive that plugs into a universal serial bus (USB) port on a computer and that stores data digitally. Also called a USB drive, jump drive, or thumb drive.

flash memory card A form of portable storage; this removable memory card is often used in digital cameras, smartphones, video cameras, and printers.

flowchart Visual diagram of a process, including the decisions that need to be made along the way.

folder A collection of files stored on a computer.

For In Visual Basic, programmers use the keyword For to implement a loop; after the keyword For, an input or output item is given a starting value, and then the statements in the body of the loop are executed.

foreign key In a relational database, the common field between tables that's not the primary key.

fourth-generation language (4GL) A computer language type that includes database query languages and report generators.

frame Groups of data packets that are sent together in a package.

freeware Any copyrighted software that can be used for free.

full installation The process of installing all the files and programs from the distribution media to the computer's hard drive.

fuzzy logic Enables the interjection of experiential learning into knowledge-based systems by allowing the consideration of probabilities.

G

general availability (GA) The point in the release cycle, where, after release to manufacturers, software is available for purchase by the public.

geotag Data attached to a photograph that indicates the latitude and longitude where you were standing when you took the photo.

gigabit Ethernet The most commonly used wired Ethernet standard deployed in devices designed for home networks; provides bandwidth of up to 1 Gbps.

gigabyte (GB) About a billion bytes.

gigahertz (GHz) One billion hertz.

global positioning system (GPS) A system of 21 satellites (plus 3 working spares), built and operated by the U.S. military, that constantly orbit the earth. The satellites provide information to GPS–capable devices to pinpoint locations on the earth.

graphical user interface (GUI) Unlike the command- and menu-driven interfaces used in earlier software, GUIs display graphics and use the point-and-click technology of the mouse and cursor, making them much more user-friendly.

graphics double data rate 5 (GDDR5) A standard of video memory.

graphics processing unit (GPU) A specialized logic chip that's dedicated to quickly displaying and calculating visual data such as shadows, textures, and luminosity.

grey-hat hacker A cross between black and white—a hacker who will often illegally break into systems merely to flaunt his or her expertise to the administrator of the system he or she penetrated or to attempt to sell his or her services in repairing security breaches.

H

hacker Anyone who unlawfully breaks into a computer system (whether an individual computer or a network).

handshaking In a connection-oriented protocol, the process of exchanging control packets before exchanging data packets.

hard disk drive (HDD) The computer's nonvolatile, primary storage device for permanent storage of software and documents.

hardware Any part of a computer or computer system you can physically touch.

head crash Impact of the read/write head against the magnetic platter of the hard drive; often results in data loss.

hexadecimal digit A digit with 16 possible values: 0–9 and A–F.

hibernate A power-management mode that saves the current state of the current system to the computer's hard drive.

high definition A standard of digital TV signal that guarantees a specific level of resolution and a specific *aspect ratio*, which is the rectangular shape of the image.

high-definition multimedia interface (HDMI) A compact audio–video interface standard that carries both high-definition video and uncompressed digital audio.

home area network (HAN) A network located in a home that's used to connect all of its digital devices.

home network server A device designed to store media, share media across the network, and back up files on computers connected to a home network.

honey pot A computer system that's set up to attract unauthorized users by appearing to be a key part of a network or a system that contains something of great value.

host The portion of a domain name that identifies who maintains a given website. For example, berkeley.edu is the domain name for the University of California at Berkeley, which maintains that site.

HTML embedded scripting language A programming language that tucks programming code directly within the HTML of a web page; the most popular example is JavaScript.

HTML tags Tags that surround and define HTML content (such as <b> and </b>, which indicate bolding).

hybrid topology Combining multiple topologies into one network.

hyperlink A type of specially coded text that, when clicked, enables a user to jump from one location, or web page, to another within a website or to another website altogether.

Hypertext Markup Language (HTML) A series of tags that define how elements on a website should be displayed in a browser.

Hypertext Transfer Protocol (HTTP) The protocol that allows files to be transferred from a web server so that you can see them on your computer by using a browser.

Hypertext Transfer Protocol Secure (HTTPS) The Internet protocol that ensures data is sent securely over the web.

hyperthreading A technology that permits quicker processing of information by enabling a new set of instructions to start executing before the previous set has finished.

I

identity theft The process by which someone uses personal information about someone else (such as the victim's name, address, and Social Security number) to assume the victim's identity for the purpose of defrauding another.

if else In C++, a binary decision in the code where the program can follow one of two paths: If the decision is made one way, the program follows one path; if made the other way (else), the program follows another path.

image backup (system backup) A copy of an entire computer system, created for restoration purposes.

image-editing software Programs for editing photographs and other images.

impact printer A printer that has tiny hammer-like keys that strike the paper through an inked ribbon, thus making a mark on the paper. The most common impact printer is the dot-matrix printer.

incremental backup (partial backup) A type of backup that only backs up files that have changed since the last time files were backed up.

information Data that has been organized or presented in a meaningful fashion; the result, or output that users require at the end of a job.

information assurance Ensuring that information systems contain accurate information and are adequately secured against tampering.

information system A system that includes data, people, procedures, hardware, and software that help in planning and decision making; a software-based solution used to gather and analyze information.

information technology (IT) The set of techniques used in processing and retrieving information.

inheritance In object-oriented analysis, the ability of a new class to automatically pick up all the data and methods of an existing class and then extend and customize those to fit its specific needs.

initial value A beginning point.

inkjet printer A nonimpact printer that sprays tiny drops of ink onto paper.

inoculation A process used by antivirus software; compares old and current qualities of files to detect viral activity.

input device A hardware device used to enter, or input, data (text, images, and sounds) and instructions (user responses and commands) into a computer. Some input devices are keyboards and mice.

input form Used to control how new data is entered into a shared database.

instant messaging (IM) A program that enables users to communicate online in real time with others who are also online.

integrated development environment (IDE) A developmental tool that helps programmers write and test their programs; one IDE can be configured to support many different languages.

internal hard drive A hard drive that resides within the computer's system unit and that usually holds all permanently stored programs and data.

Internet A network of networks that's the largest network in the world, connecting billions of computers globally.

Internet backbone The main pathway of high-speed communications lines over which all Internet traffic flows.

Internet cache A section of the hard drive that stores information that may be needed again, such as Internet protocol addresses and frequently accessed web pages.

Internet Corporation for Assigned Names and Numbers (ICANN) The organization that registers Internet protocol addresses to ensure they're unique and haven't been assigned to other users.

Internet exchange point (IXP) A way of connecting Internet service providers (ISPs) that's made up of one or more network switches to which the ISPs connect.

Internet Protocol (IP) One of the original two protocols developed for the Internet.

Internet Protocol (IP) address The means by which all computers connected to the Internet identify each other. It consists of a unique set of four numbers separated by dots, such as 123.45.178.91.

Internet Protocol version 4 (IPv4) The original Internet protocol addressing scheme, created in 1981.

Internet Protocol version 6 (IPv6) An Internet protocol (IP) addressing scheme that makes IP addresses longer, thereby providing more available addresses.

Internet service provider (ISP) A company that specializes in providing Internet access. ISPs may be specialized providers, like Juno, or companies that provide other services in addition to Internet access (such as phone and cable television).

interpreter For a programming language, translates the source code into an intermediate form, line by line; each line is then executed as it's translated.

interrupt A signal that tells the operating system that it's in need of immediate attention.

interrupt handler A special numerical code that prioritizes requests from various devices. These requests then are placed in the interrupt table in the computer's primary memory.

intranet A private network set up by a business or an organization that's used exclusively by a select group of employees, customers, suppliers, volunteers, or supporters.

IP address See *Internet Protocol (IP) address.*

J

jam signal A special signal sent to network nodes alerting them that a data collision has occurred.

Java An object-oriented programming language that has a large set of existing classes.

Java applet A small Java-based program.

JavaScript A scripting language that's often used to add interactivity to web pages; often used for creating Dynamic HTML effects.

JavaServer Pages (JSP) Programming language used to build websites with interactive capabilities; adapts the HTML page to the user's selections.

join query A query used to extract data that's in two or more tables in a database.

K

kernel (supervisor program) The essential component of the operating system that's responsible for managing the processor and all other components of the computer system. Because it stays in random access memory (RAM) the entire time the computer is powered on, the kernel is called memory resident.

key pair The two keys used in public-key encryption.

keyboard A hardware device used to enter typed data and commands into a computer.

keystroke logger (keylogger) A type of spyware program that monitors keystrokes with the intent of stealing passwords, login IDs, or credit card information.

keyword (1) A specific word a user wishes to query (or look for) in an Internet search. (2) A specific word that has a predefined meaning in a particular programming language.

kilobyte (KB) A unit of computer storage equal to approximately 1,000 bytes.

knowledge-based system A business intelligence system that provides intelligence that supplements the user's own intellect and makes the decision support system more effective.

L

laptop (or notebook) computer A portable computer with a keyboard, a monitor, and other devices integrated into a single compact case.

laser printer A nonimpact printer known for quick and quiet production and high-quality printouts.

latency (rotational delay) The process that occurs after the read/write head of the hard drive locates the correct track and then waits for the correct sector to spin to the read/write head.

legacy technology Comprises computing devices, software, or peripherals that use techniques, parts, and methods from an earlier time that are no longer popular.

library Introduced with Windows 7, a folder that's used to display files from different locations as if they were all saved in a single folder, regardless of where they are actually stored in the file hierarchy.

light-emitting diode (LED) A newer, more energy-efficient technology used in monitors. It may result in better color accuracy and thinner panels than traditional LCD monitors.

Linux An open-source operating system based on UNIX. Because of the stable nature of this operating system, it's often used on web servers.

liquid crystal display (LCD) The technology used in flat-panel computer monitors.

live bookmark A bookmark that delivers updates as soon as they become available, using Really Simple Syndication (RSS).

local area network (LAN) A network in which the nodes are located within a small geographic area.

logic bomb A computer virus that runs when a certain set of conditions is met, such as when a program is launched a specific number of times.

logical error An error in a program that produces unintended or undesired output, where the syntax is correct but some other human error has occurred.

logical port A virtual communications gateway or path that enables a computer to organize requests for information (such as web page downloads and e-mail routing) from other networks or computers.

logical port blocking A condition in which a firewall is configured to ignore all incoming packets that request access to a certain port so that no unwanted requests will get through to the computer.

loop A type of decision point in an algorithm. In a loop, a question is asked, and if the answer is *yes*, a set of actions is performed. Once the set of actions has finished, the question is asked again, creating a loop. If the answer to the question is *no*, the algorithm breaks free of the loop and moves on to the first step that follows the loop.

M

Mac OS The first commercially available operating system to incorporate a graphical user interface (GUI) with user-friendly point-and-click technology.

machine cycle The series of steps a central processing unit goes through when it performs a program instruction.

machine language See *first-generation language (1GL)*.

macro A small program that groups a series of commands to run as a single command.

macro virus A virus that's distributed by hiding it inside a macro.

mainframe A large, expensive computer that supports hundreds or thousands of users simultaneously and executes many different programs at the same time.

malware Software that's intended to render a system temporarily or permanently useless or to penetrate a computer system completely for purposes of information gathering. Examples include spyware, viruses, worms, and Trojan horses.

management information system (MIS) A type of business intelligence system that provides timely and accurate information that enables managers to make critical business decisions.

many-to-many relationship In a relational database, records in one table are related to multiple records in a second table, and vice versa.

master boot record A small program that runs whenever a computer boots up.

media access control (MAC) address The physical address, similar to a serial number, of each network adapter.

megabyte (MB) A unit of computer storage equal to approximately 1 million bytes.

memory module (memory card) A small circuit board that holds a series of random access memory (RAM) chips.

menu-driven interface A user interface in which the user chooses a command from menus displayed on the screen.

metadata Data that describes other data.

metasearch engine A search engine, such as Dogpile, that searches other search engines rather than individual websites.

method The process of how a program converts inputs into the correct outputs.

metropolitan area network (MAN) A wide area network (WAN) that links users in a specific geographic area (such as within a city or county).

microphone (mic) A device that allows you to capture sound waves, such as those created by your voice, and to transfer them to digital format on your computer.

mobile broadband Connection to the Internet through the same cellular network that cell phones use to get 3G or 4G Internet access.

mobile switching center A central location that receives cell phone requests for service from a base station.

model management system Software that assists in building management models in decision support systems; an analysis tool that, through the use of internal and external data, provides a view of a particular business situation for the purposes of decision-making.

modem port A port that uses a traditional telephone signal to connect a computer to the Internet.

monitor (display screen) A common output device that displays text, graphics, and video as soft copies (copies that can be seen only on screen).

Moore's Law A prediction, named after Gordon Moore, the co-founder of Intel; states that the number of transistors on a central processing unit chip will double every two years.

motherboard A special circuit board in the system unit that contains the central processing unit, the memory (RAM) chips, and the slots available for expansion cards;

all of the other boards (video cards, sound cards, and so on) connect to it to receive power and to communicate.

mouse A hardware device used to enter user responses and commands into a computer.

multidimensional database A database that stores data from different perspectives, called dimensions, and organizes data in cube format.

multimedia Anything that involves one or more forms of media plus text.

multimedia software Programs that include image-, video-, and audio-editing software, animation software, and other specialty software required to produce computer games, animations, and movies.

multipartite virus Literally meaning "multipart" virus; a type of computer virus that attempts to infect computers using more than one method.

Multipurpose Internet Mail Extensions (MIME) Specification for sending files as attachments to e-mail.

multitask The ability of an operating system to perform more than one process at a time.

multiuser operating system (network operating system) An operating system that enables more than one user to access the computer system at one time by efficiently juggling all the requests from multiple users.

N

natural language processing (NLP) system A knowledge-based business intelligence system that enables users to communicate with computer systems using a natural spoken or written language instead of a computer programming language.

negative acknowledgment (NAK) In data exchange, the communication sent from one computer or system to another stating that it did not receive a data packet in readable form.

netbook A computing device that runs a full-featured operating system but that weighs two pounds or less.

network A group of two or more computers (or nodes) that are configured to share information and resources such as printers, files, and databases.

network adapter A device that enables the computer (or peripheral) to communicate with the network using a common data communication language, or protocol.

network address translation (NAT) A process that firewalls use to assign internal Internet protocol addresses on a network.

network administration Involves tasks such as (1) installing new computers and devices, (2) monitoring the network to ensure it's performing efficiently, (3) updating and installing new software on the network, and (4) configuring, or setting up, proper security for a network.

network administrator Person who maintains networks for businesses.

network architecture The design of a computer network; includes both physical and logical design.

network-attached storage (NAS) device A specialized computing device designed to store and manage network data.

network interface card (NIC) An expansion card that enables a computer to connect other computers or to a cable modem to facilitate a high-speed Internet connection.

network navigation device A device on a network such as a router or switch that moves data signals around the network.

network operating system (NOS) Software that handles requests for information, Internet access, and the use of peripherals for the rest of the network node, providing the services necessary for the computers on the network to communicate.

network prefix The slash and number added to the end of an internet protocol (IP) address that allows a single IP address to represent several unique IP addresses in *classless interdomain routing*.

network-ready device A device (such as a printer or an external hard drive) that can be attached directly to a network instead of needing to attach to a computer on the network.

network topology The physical or logical arrangement of computers, transmission

media (cable), and other network components.

Next In Visual Basic, programmers use the keyword Next to implement a loop; when the Next command is run, the program returns to the For statement and increments the value of the input or output item by 1 and then runs a test cycle.

node A device connected to a network such as a computer, a peripheral (such as a printer), or a communications device (such as a modem).

nonimpact printer A printer that sprays ink or uses laser beams to make marks on the paper. The most common nonimpact printers are inkjet and laser printers.

nonvolatile storage Permanent storage, as in read-only memory (ROM).

normalization A process to ensure data is organized most efficiently in a database.

numeric check In a database, confirms that only numbers are entered in a field.

O

object An example of a class in object-oriented analysis.

object-oriented analysis A type of analysis in which programmers first identify all the categories of inputs that are part of the problem the program is meant to solve.

object-oriented database A database that stores data in objects rather than in tables.

Object Query Language (OQL) A query language used by many object-oriented databases.

Objective C The programming language most often used to program applications to run under OS X.

octet A reference to each of the four numbers in a dotted decimal number internet protocol address, so called because each number would have eight numerals in binary form.

office support system (OSS) A system designed to improve communications and assist employees in accomplishing their daily tasks.

one-to-many relationship In a relational database, a record appears only once in one table while having the capability of appearing many times in a related table.

one-to-one relationship In a relational database, for each record in a table there's only one corresponding record in a related table.

online analytical processing (OLAP) Software that provides standardized tools for viewing and manipulating data in a data warehouse.

online transaction processing (OLTP) The real-time processing of database transactions online.

open source software Program code made publicly available for free; it can be copied, distributed, or changed without the stringent copyright protections of proprietary software products.

open system A system having the characteristic of being public for access by any interested party; as opposed to a *proprietary system*.

Open Systems Interconnection (OSI) A networking protocol established by the Institute of Electrical and Electronics Engineers (IEEE) that provides guidelines for modern networks.

operating system (OS) The system software that controls the way in which a computer system functions, including the management of hardware, peripherals, and software.

operator A coding symbol that represents a fundamental action of the programming language.

optical carrier (OC) line A high-speed fiber-optic line.

optical drive A hardware device that uses lasers or light to read from, and even write to, CDs, DVDs, or Blu-ray discs.

optical media Portable storage devices, such as CDs, DVDs, and Blu-ray discs, that use a laser to read and write data.

optical mouse A mouse that uses an internal sensor or laser to control the mouse's movement. The sensor sends signals to the computer, telling it where to move the pointer on the screen.

organic light-emitting diode (OLED) displays Displays that use organic compounds to produce light when exposed to an electric current. Unlike LCDs, OLEDs do not require a backlight to function and therefore draw less power and have a much thinner display, sometimes as thin as 3 mm.

output device A device that sends processed data and information out of a computer in the form of text, pictures (graphics), sounds (audio), or video.

overclocking Running the central processing unit at a speed faster than the manufacturer recommends.

P

packet (data packet) A small segment of data that's bundled for sending over transmission media. Each packet contains the address of the computer or peripheral device to which it's being sent.

packet analyzer (sniffer) A computer hardware device or software program designed to detect and record digital information being transmitted over a network.

packet screening Having an external screening router examine incoming data packets to ensure they originated from or are authorized by valid users on the internal network.

packet switching A communications methodology that makes computer communication efficient; in packet switching, data is broken into smaller chunks called *packets*.

paging The process of swapping data or instructions that have been placed in the swap file for later use back into active random access memory (RAM). The contents of the hard drive's swap file then become less active data or instructions.

Pascal A programming language; the only modern language that was specifically designed as a teaching language.

passive topology In a network, a type of topology where the nodes do nothing to move data along the network.

path (subdirectory) The information after the slash that indicates a particular file or path (or subdirectory) within the website.

path separator The backslash mark (\) used by Microsoft Windows and DOS in file

names. Mac files use a colon (:), and UNIX and Linux use the forward slash (/) as the path separator.

peer-to-peer (P2P) network A network in which each node connected to the network can communicate directly with every other node on the network.

peer-to-peer (P2P) sharing The process of users transferring files between computers.

peripheral device A device such as a monitor, printer, or keyboard that connects to the system unit through a data port.

personal area network (PAN) A network used for communication among devices close to one person, such as smartphones, laptops, and tablets, using wireless technologies such as Bluetooth.

personal firewall A firewall specifically designed for home networks.

personal information manager (PIM) software Programs such as Microsoft Outlook or Lotus Organizer that strive to replace the various management tools found on a traditional desk such as a calendar, address book, notepad, and to-do lists.

pharming Planting malicious code on a computer that alters the browser's ability to find web addresses and that directs users to bogus websites.

phishing The process of sending e-mail messages to lure Internet users into revealing personal information such as credit card or Social Security numbers or other sensitive information that could lead to identity theft.

PHP (Hypertext Preprocessor) Programming language used to build websites with interactive capabilities; adapts the HTML page to the user's selections.

physical memory The amount of random access memory (RAM) that's installed in a computer.

piggybacking The process of connecting to a wireless network without the permission of the owner of the network.

pinning The process through which you choose which applications are visible on the Windows Start screen.

pixel A single point that creates the images on a computer monitor. Pixels are illuminated by an electron beam that passes rapidly back and forth across the back of the screen so that the pixels appear to glow continuously.

platform The combination of a computer's operating system and processor. The two most common platform types are the PC and the Apple.

platter A thin, round, metallic storage plate stacked onto the hard drive spindle.

plotter A large printer that uses a computer-controlled pen to produce oversize pictures that require precise continuous lines to be drawn, such as maps and architectural plans.

Plug and Play (PnP) The technology that enables the operating system, once it is booted up, to recognize automatically any new peripherals and to configure them to work with the system.

plug-in (player) A small software program that "plugs in" to a web browser to enable a specific function—for example, to view and hear certain multimedia files on the web.

podcast A clip of audio or video content that's broadcast over the Internet using compressed audio or video files in formats such as MP3.

point of presence (POP) A bank of modems, servers, routers, and switches through which Internet users connect to an Internet service provider.

polymorphic virus A virus that changes its virus signature (the binary pattern that makes the virus identifiable) every time it infects a new file. This makes it more difficult for antivirus programs to detect the virus.

port An interface through which external devices are connected to the computer.

portability The capability to move a completed solution easily from one type of computer to another.

positive acknowledgement (ACK) In data exchange, the confirmation sent from one computer or system to another saying that the computer has received a data packet that it can read.

possessed object Any object that users carry to identify themselves and that grants them access to a computer system or facility.

power-on self-test (POST) The first job the basic input/output system (BIOS) performs, ensuring that essential peripheral devices are attached and operational. This process consists of a test on the video card and video memory, a BIOS identification process (during which the BIOS version, manufacturer, and data are displayed on the monitor), and a memory test to ensure memory chips are working properly.

power supply A power supply regulates the wall voltage to the voltages required by computer chips; it's housed inside the system unit.

preemptive multitasking When the operating system processes the task assigned a higher priority before processing a task that has been assigned a lower priority.

presentation software An application program for creating dynamic slide shows, such as Microsoft PowerPoint or Apple Keynote.

pretexting The act of creating an invented scenario (the pretext) to convince someone to divulge information.

Pretty Good Privacy (PGP) A public-key package for encryption available for download on the Internet.

primary key field In a database, a field that has a value unique to a record.

print queue A software holding area for print jobs. Also called a print spooler.

print server A server that manages all client-requested printing jobs for all printers on a network.

printer A common output device that creates tangible or hard copies of text and graphics.

private key The key for decoding retained as private in public-key encryption.

private-key encryption A type of encryption where only the two parties involved in sending the message have the code.

problem statement The starting point of programming work; a clear description of what tasks the computer program must accomplish and how the program will execute those tasks and respond to unusual situations.

processing Manipulating or organizing data into information.

productivity software Programs that enable a user to perform various tasks generally required in home, school, and business. Examples include word processing, spreadsheet, presentation, personal information management, and database programs.

program A series of instructions to be followed by a computer to accomplish a task.

program development life cycle (PDLC) The process of performing a programming project, which consists of five stages: describing the problem, making a plan, coding, debugging, and testing and documentation.

program files Files that are used in the running of software programs and that do not store data.

program specification A clear statement of the goals and objectives of the project.

programming The process of translating a task into a series of commands a computer will use to perform that task.

programming language A kind of "code" for the set of instructions the central processing unit knows how to perform.

projector A device that can project images from your computer onto a wall or viewing screen.

proprietary software Custom software application that's owned and controlled by the company that created it.

proprietary system A system having the characteristic of being closed to public access (private), as opposed to an *open system*.

protocol A set of rules for exchanging communications.

prototype A small model of a program built at the beginning of a large project.

proxy server A server that acts as a go-between, connecting computers on the internal network with those on the external network (the Internet).

pseudocode A text-based approach to documenting an algorithm.

public key The key for coding distributed to the public in public-key encryption.

public-key encryption A type of encryption where two keys, known as a *key pair*, are created. One key is used for coding and the other for decoding. The key for coding is distributed as a public key, while the private key is retained for decoding.

Q

quarantining The placement (by antivirus software) of a computer virus in a secure area on the hard drive so that it won't spread infection to other files.

query In a database, a way of retrieving information that defines a particular subset of data; can be used to extract data from one or more tables.

query language A specially designed computer language used to manipulate data in or extract data from a database.

QR (quick response) codes Technology that lets any piece of print in the real world host a live link to online information and video content.

QWERTY keyboard A keyboard that gets its name from the first six letters on the top-left row of alphabetic keys on the keyboard.

R

RAID 0 The strategy of running two hard drives in one system, cutting in half the time it takes to write a file.

RAID 1 The strategy of mirroring all the data written on one hard drive to a second hard drive, providing an instant backup of all data.

random access memory (RAM) The computer's temporary storage space or short-term memory. It's located in a set of chips on the system unit's motherboard, and its capacity is measured in megabytes or gigabytes.

range check Ensures that the data entered into the field of a database falls within a certain range of values.

rapid application development (RAD) An alternative program-development method; instead of developing detailed system documents before they produce the system, developers first create a prototype, then generate system documents as they use and remodel the product.

read-only memory (ROM) A set of memory chips, located on the motherboard, which stores data and instructions that cannot be changed or erased; it holds all the instructions the computer needs to start up.

read/write head The mechanism that retrieves (reads) and records (writes) the magnetic data to and from a data disk.

real-time operating system (RTOS) A program with a specific purpose that must guarantee certain response times for particular computing tasks or else the machine's application is useless. Real-time operating systems are found in many types of robotic equipment.

real-time processing The processing of database transactions in which the database is updated while the transaction is taking place.

Really Simple Syndication (RSS) An XML–based format that allows frequent updates of content on the World Wide Web.

record A group of related fields in a database.

Recycle Bin A folder on a Windows desktop in which deleted files from the hard drive are held until permanently purged from the system.

redundant array of independent disks (RAID) A set of strategies for using more than one drive in a system.

referential integrity In a relational database, a condition where, for each value in the foreign key table, there's a corresponding value in the primary key table.

Refresh your PC A new utility program in Windows 8 that attempts to diagnose and fix errors in your Windows system files that are causing your computer to behave improperly.

registry A portion of the hard drive containing all the different configurations (settings) used by the Windows operating system as well as by other applications.

relational algebra The use of English-like expressions that have variables and operations, much like algebraic equations, to extract data from databases using Structured Query Language.

relational database A database type that organizes data into related tables based on logical groupings.

relationship In a relational database, a link between tables that defines how the data is related.

release to manufacturers (RTM) The point in the release cycle, where, after beta testing, a manufacturer makes changes to the software and releases it to other manufacturers, for installation on new machines, for example.

resolution The clearness or sharpness of an image, which is controlled by the number of pixels displayed on the screen.

reusability In object-oriented analysis, the ability to reuse existing classes from one project for another project.

ring (loop) topology A type of network topology where computers and peripherals are laid out in a configuration resembling a circle.

root directory The top level of the filing structure in a computer system. In Windows computers, the root directory of the hard drive is represented as C:\.

root DNS server A domain name system (DNS) server that contains the master listings for an entire top-level domain.

rootkits Programs that allow hackers to gain access to your computer and take almost complete control of it without your knowledge. These programs are designed to subvert normal login procedures to a computer and to hide their operations from normal detection methods.

router A device that routes packets of data between two or more networks.

runtime error An error in a program that occurs when a programmer accidentally writes code that divides by zero, a mathematical error.

S

sampling rate The number of times per second a signal is measured and converted to a digital value. Sampling rates are measured in kilobits per second.

satellite Internet A way to connect to the Internet using a small satellite dish, which is placed outside the home and is connected to a computer with coaxial cable. The satellite company then sends the data to a satellite orbiting the Earth. The satellite, in turn, sends the data back to the satellite dish and to the computer.

scalability A characteristic of client/server networks where more users can be easily added without affecting the performance of other network nodes.

scanner A type of input device that inputs images into computers.

scareware A type of malware that's downloaded onto your computer and that tries to convince you that your computer is infected with a virus or other type of malware.

scope creep An ever-changing set of requests from clients for additional features as they wait longer and longer to see a working prototype.

script A list of commands (mini-programs or macros) that can be executed on a computer without user interaction.

scripting language A simple programming language that's limited to performing a set of specialized tasks.

search engine A set of programs that searches the web for specific words (or keywords) you wish to query (or look for) and that then returns a list of the websites on which those keywords are found.

second-generation language (2GL) A computer language that allows programmers to write programs using a set of short, English-like commands that speak directly to the central processing unit and that give the programmer direct control of hardware resources; also called *assembly language*.

second-level domain A domain that's directly below a top-level domain.

sector A section of a hard drive platter, wedge-shaped from the center of the platter to the edge.

Secure Sockets Layer (SSL) A network security protocol that provides for the encryption of data transmitted using the Internet. The current versions of all major web browsers support SSL.

seek time The time it takes for the hard drive's read/write heads to move over the surface of the disk to the correct track.

select query In Structured Query Language, displays a subset of data from a table (or tables) based on the criteria specified.

semantic web (Web 3.0) An evolving extension of the World Wide Web in which information is defined in such a way as to make it more easily readable by computers.

server A computer that provides resources to other computers on a network.

server-side program A type of program that runs on a web server rather than on a computer.

service pack A software update.

service set identifier (SSID) A network name that wireless routers use to identify themselves.

shielded twisted-pair (STP) cable Twisted-pair cable that contains a layer of foil shielded to reduce interference.

short message service (SMS) Technology that enables short text messages (up to 160 characters) to be sent over mobile networks.

Simple Mail Transfer Protocol (SMTP) The protocol responsible for sending e-mail along the Internet to its destination; part of the Internet Protocol suite.

simulation program Software, often used for training purposes, which allows the user to experience or control an event as if it's reality.

sleep mode A low-power mode for electronic devices such as computers that saves electric power consumption and saves the last-used settings. When the device is "woken up," work is resumed more quickly than when cold booting the computer.

social bookmark (tagging) A keyword or term that Internet users assign to a web resource such as a web page, digital image, or video.

social commerce A subset of e-commerce that uses social networks to assist in marketing and purchasing products.

social engineering Any technique that uses social skills to generate human interaction for the purpose of enticing individuals to reveal sensitive information.

social networking A means by which people use the Internet to communicate and share information among their immediate friends and to meet and connect with others through common interests, experiences, and friends.

software The set of computer programs or instructions that tells the computer what to do and that enables it to perform different tasks.

Software as a Service (SaaS) Software that's delivered on demand over the Internet.

software license An agreement between the user and the software developer that must be accepted before installing the software on a computer.

software piracy Violating a software license agreement by copying an application onto more computers than the license agreement permits.

software suite A collection of software programs that have been bundled together as a package.

solid-state drive (SSD) A storage device that uses the same kind of memory that flash drives use but that can reach data in only a tenth of the time a flash drive requires.

sound card An expansion card that attaches to the motherboard inside the system unit and that enables the computer to produce sounds by providing a connection for the speakers and microphone.

source code The instructions programmers write in a higher-level language.

spam Unwanted or junk e-mail.

spam filter An option you can select in your e-mail account that places known or suspected spam messages into a folder other than your inbox.

speakers Output devices for sound.

spear phishing A targeted phishing attack that sends e-mails to people known to be customers of a company. Such attacks have a much greater chance of successfully getting individuals to reveal sensitive data.

spooler A program that helps coordinate all print jobs being sent to the printer at the same time.

spreadsheet software An application program such as Microsoft Excel or Lotus 1-2-3 that enables a user to do calculations and numerical analyses easily.

spyware An unwanted piggyback program that downloads with the software you want to install from the Internet and then runs in the background of your system.

star topology The most widely deployed client/server network topology, where the nodes connect to a central communications device called a switch in a pattern resembling a star.

Start screen The first interaction you have with the Windows operating system and the pace where you begin your computing activities.

statement A sentence in a code.

static addressing A way of assigning internet protocol addresses where the address for a computer never changes and is most likely assigned manually by a network administrator or an Internet service provider.

stealth virus A virus that temporarily erases its code from the files where it resides and hides in the active memory of the computer.

streaming audio Technology that enables audio files to be fed to a browser continuously. This lets users avoid having to download an entire file before listening.

streaming video Technology that enables video files to be fed to a browser continuously. This lets users avoid having to download the entire file before viewing.

structured (analytical) data Data such as "Bill" or "345," as opposed to *unstructured data*.

Structured Query Language (SQL) A database programming language used to construct queries to extract data from relational databases; one example of a fourth-generation language.

stylus A pen-shaped device used to tap or write on touch-sensitive screens.

subject directory A structured outline of websites organized by topics and subtopics.

summary report A report generated by a management information system that provides a consolidated picture of detailed data; these reports usually include some calculation or visual displays of information.

supercomputer A specially designed computer that can perform complex calculations extremely rapidly; used in situations in which complex models requiring intensive mathematical calculations are needed (such as weather forecasting or atomic energy research).

SuperFetch A memory-management technique used by Windows 7. Monitors the applications you use the most and preloads them into your system memory so that they'll be ready to go.

surge protector A device that protects computers and other electronic devices from power surges.

surround sound A type of audio processing that makes the listener experience sound as if it were coming from all directions.

surround-sound speaker A system of speakers set up in such a way that it surrounds an entire area (and the people in it) with sound.

swap file (page file) A temporary storage area on the hard drive where the operating system "swaps out" or moves the data or instructions from random access memory (RAM) that haven't recently been used. This process takes place when more RAM space is needed.

switch A device for transmitting data on a network. A switch makes decisions, based on the media access control address of the data, as to where the data is to be sent.

synchronizing (or syncing) The process of updating data on portable devices (such as a cell phone or iPod) and a computer so that they contain the same data.

syntax An agreed-on set of rules defining how a language must be structured.

syntax error A violation of the strict set of rules that define the programming language.

system development life cycle (SDLC) A process used to develop information systems; it consists of the following six steps: problem and opportunity identification, analysis, design, development, testing and installation, and maintenance and evaluation.

system evaluation The process of looking at a computer's subsystems, what they do, and how they perform to determine whether the computer system has the right hardware components to do what the user ultimately wants it to do.

system files The main files of an operating system.

system requirements The set of minimum storage, memory capacity, and processing standards recommended by the software manufacturer to ensure proper operation of a software application.

System Restore A utility in Windows that restores system settings to a specific previous date when everything was working properly.

system restore point In Windows, a snapshot of your entire system's settings used for restoring your system to a prior point in time.

system software The set of programs that enables a computer's hardware devices and application software to work together; it includes the operating system and utility programs.

system unit The metal or plastic case that holds all the physical parts of the computer together, including the computer's processor (its brains), its memory, and the many circuit boards that help the computer function.

T

T line A communications line that carries digital data over twisted-pair wires.

table (file) A group of related records in a database.

tablet computer A mobile computer, such as the Apple iPad or Samsung Galaxy Tab, integrated into a flat multitouch-sensitive screen. It uses an onscreen virtual keyboard, but separate keyboards can be connected via Bluetooth or wires.

tablet PC A laptop computer designed specifically to work with handwriting-recognition technology.

Task Manager A Windows utility that shows programs currently running and permits you to exit nonresponsive programs when you click End Task.

taskbar In later versions of Windows operating systems, a feature that displays open and favorite applications for easy access.

tax preparation software An application program, such as Intuit's TurboTax or H&R Block's At Home, for preparing state and federal taxes. Each program offers a complete set of tax forms and instructions as well as expert advice on how to complete each form.

TCP/IP The main suite of protocols used for transmitting data over the Internet. Named after Transmission Control Protocol (TCP) and the Internet Protocol (IP).

telephony The use of equipment to provide voice communications over a distance.

template A form included in many productivity applications that provides the basic structure for a particular kind of document, spreadsheet, or presentation.

Terabyte (TB) 1,099,511,627,776 bytes or 2^{40} bytes.

terminator A device that absorbs a signal so that it's not reflected back onto parts of the network that have already received it.

test condition A check to see whether the loop in an algorithm is completed.

testing plan The part of the problem statement that lists specific input numbers the programmers would typically expect the user to enter; the plan then lists the precise output values that a perfect program would return for those input values.

tethering Approach which makes sure that as long as you have a 3G signal, your computer can access the Internet even when it tells you there are no available wireless networks. Several smartphones offer this capability.

thermal printer A printer that works either by melting wax-based ink onto ordinary paper (in a process called *thermal wax transfer printing*) or by burning dots onto specially coated paper (in a process called *direct thermal printing*).

third-generation language (3GL) A computer language that uses symbols and commands to help programmers tell the computer what to do, making 3GL languages easier for humans to read and remember; examples of 3GL languages include BASIC, FORTRAN, COBOL, C/C++, and JAVA.

thrashing A condition of excessive paging in which the operating system becomes sluggish.

three-way handshake In Transmission Control Protocol, the process used to establish a connection between two computers before exchanging data. The steps in a three-way handshake are as follows: One computer establishes a connection to the Internet service provider (ISP) and announces it has e-mail to send, the ISP server responds that it's ready to receive, and the computer acknowledges the ready state of the server and begins to transmit the e-mail.

throughput The actual speed of data transfer that's achieved. It's usually less than the data transfer rate and is measured in megabits per second (Mbps).

time bomb A virus that's triggered by the passage of time or on a certain date.

time-variant data Data that doesn't pertain to one period in time.

token A special data packet used to pass data in a ring topology network.

token method The access method used by ring networks to avoid data collisions.

top-down design A systematic approach in which a problem is broken into a series of high-level tasks.

top-level domain The suffix, often of three letters (such as .com or .edu), in the domain name that indicates the kind of organization the host is.

touch pad (trackpad) A small, touch-sensitive screen at the base of a laptop keyboard that's used to direct the cursor.

touch screen A type of monitor (or display in a smartphone or tablet computer) that accepts input from a user touching the screen.

track A concentric circle that serves as a storage area on a hard drive platter.

trackpoint device A small, joystick-like nub that enables you to move the cursor with the tip of your finger.

transaction-processing system (TPS) A type of business intelligence system for keeping track of everyday business activities.

Transmission Control Protocol (TCP) One of the original two protocols developed for the Internet.

transmission media The radio waves or the physical system (cable) that transports data on a network.

Transport Layer Security (TLS) An updated extension of *Secure Sockets Layer*.

Trojan horse A computer program that appears to be something useful or desirable (such as a game or a screen saver), but at the same time does something malicious in the background without the user's knowledge.

tunneling The main technology for achieving a virtual private network; the placement of data packets inside other data packets.

twisted-pair cable Cables made of copper wires that are twisted around each other and are surrounded by a plastic jacket (such as traditional home phone wire).

U

ultrabook A full-featured but lightweight laptop computer that features a low-power processor and a solid-state drive; it tries to reduce its size and weight to extend battery life without sacrificing performance.

Uniform Resource Locator (URL) A website's unique address; an example is microsoft.com.

uninterruptible power supply (UPS) A device designed to power a computer from large batteries for a brief period during a loss of electrical power.

universal serial bus (USB) port A port that can connect a wide variety of peripheral devices to the computer, including keyboards, printers, mice, smartphones, external hard drives, flash drives, and digital cameras.

UNIX An operating system originally conceived in 1969 by Ken Thompson and Dennis Ritchie of AT&T's Bell Labs. In 1974, the UNIX code was rewritten in the standard programming language C. Today there are various commercial versions of UNIX.

unshielded twisted-pair (UTP) cable The most popular transmission media option for Ethernet networks. UTP cable is composed of four pairs of wires that are twisted around each other to reduce electrical interference.

unstructured data Audio clips, video clips, pictures, and extremely large documents. Also called *binary large object (BLOB)*.

User Datagram Protocol (UDP) An Internet Protocol that creates data packets across the Internet.

user interface Part of the operating system that enables individuals to interact with the computer.

utility program A small program that performs many of the general housekeeping tasks for the computer, such as system maintenance and file compression.

V

validation The process of ensuring that data entered into a field of a database meets specified guidelines.

validation rule In a database, generally defined as part of the data dictionary and specified in the field properties for each field; violations result in an error message and a suggested action.

variable Each input and output item the program manipulates.

variable declaration Tells the operating system that the program needs to allocate storage space in RAM.

VBScript A subset of Visual Basic, used to introduce dynamic decision making into web pages.

vertical market software Software that's developed for and customized to a specific industry's needs (such as a wood inventory system for a sawmill) as opposed to software that's useful across a range of industries (such as word processing software).

video card (video adapter) An expansion card that's installed inside a system unit to translate binary data (the *1*s and *0*s the computer uses) into the images viewed on the monitor.

video graphics array (VGA) port A port to which a cathode ray tube monitor connects.

video log (vlog or video blog) A personal online journal that uses video as the primary content in addition to text, images, and audio.

video memory Random access memory that's included as part of a video card.

virtual memory The space on the hard drive where the operating system stores data if there isn't enough random access memory to hold all of the programs you're currently trying to run.

virtual private network (VPN) A network that uses the public Internet communications infrastructure to build a secure, private network among various locations.

virtualization Using specialized software to make individual physical servers behave as though they are more than one physical device.

virus A computer program that attaches itself to another computer program (known as the host program) and attempts to spread itself to other computers when files are exchanged.

virus signature A portion of the virus code that's unique to a particular computer virus and that makes it identifiable by antivirus software.

Visual Basic (VB) A programming language used to build a wide range of Windows applications.

visual programming In programming languages that support Windows programming, programmers can use the mouse to lay out on the screen where the scroll bars and buttons will be in the application; the code needed to explain this to the computer is then written automatically.

Voice over Internet Protocol (VoIP) A technology that facilitates making telephone calls across the Internet instead of using conventional telephone lines.

volatile storage Temporary storage, such as in random access memory. When the power is off, the data in volatile storage is cleared out.

W

warm boot The process of restarting the system while it's powered on.

Web 2.0 Tools and web-based services that emphasize online collaboration and sharing among users.

web-based application A program that's hosted on a website and that doesn't require installation on the computer.

web-based e-mail A type of e-mail system that's managed by a web browser and that allows access to e-mail from the web.

web browser (browser) Software installed on a computer system that allows individuals to locate, view, and navigate the web.

web page–authoring software Programs you can use to design interactive web pages without knowing any HyperText Markup Language (HTML) code.

web server A computer running a specialized operating system that enables it to host web pages (and other information) and to provide requested web pages to clients.

web services Part of the Microsoft .NET Framework, programs that a website uses to make information available to other websites.

webcam A small camera that sits on top of a computer monitor (connected to the computer by a cable) or that's built into a laptop computer and is usually used to transfer live video.

webcast The broadcast of audio or video content over the Internet. Unlike a podcast, a webcast is not updated automatically.

website A location on the web.

white-hat hacker (ethical hacker) A hacker who breaks into systems just for the challenge of it (and who doesn't wish to steal or wreak havoc on the systems). Such hackers tout themselves as experts who are performing a needed service for society by helping companies realize the vulnerabilities that exist in their systems.

whole-house surge protector A surge protector that's installed on (or near) the breaker panel of a home and that protects all electronic devices in the home from power surges.

wide area network (WAN) A network made up of local area networks (LANs) connected over long distances.

wiki A type of website that allows anyone visiting the site to change its content by adding, removing, or editing the content.

Windows An operating system by Microsoft that incorporates a user-friendly, graphical interface.

Windows 8 Newest release of Microsoft's operating system that provides, a new interface optimized for touch-screen devices.

Windows 8 apps Applications specifically designed to run in the Windows 8 interface; these apps are displayed full screen, without borders or controls.

Windows 8 interface New interface designed for Windows 8; features large type with clean, readable block images inspired by metropolitan service signs such as those found on bus stations and subways.

Windows Explorer The main tool for finding, viewing, and managing the contents of your computer by showing the location and contents of every drive, folder, and file; called File Explorer in Windows 8.

Windows account A tool for allowing multiple people to share a Windows 8 computer while maintaining individual settings and preferences.

wireless access point (WAP) Gives wireless devices a sending and receiving connection point to the network.

wireless fidelity (WiFi) The 802.11 standard for wireless data transmissions established by the Institute of Electrical and Electronics Engineers (IEEE).

wireless Internet service provider (wireless ISP) An ISP that provides service to wireless devices such as smartphones.

wireless network interface card (wireless NIC) A special network adapter card that allows a computing device to connect to a network using wireless access.

wireless range extender A device that amplifies your wireless signal to get it out to parts of your home that are experiencing poor connectivity.

wizard A step-by-step guide that walks a user through the necessary steps to complete a complicated task.

word processing software Programs used to create and edit written documents such as papers, letters, and résumés.

World Wide Web (WWW or the web) The part of the Internet used the most. What distinguishes the web from the rest of the Internet are (1) its use of common communication protocols (such as Transmission Control Protocol/Internet Protocol, or TCP/IP) and special languages (such as the HyperText Markup Language, or HTML) that enable different computers to talk to each other and display information in compatible formats and (2) its use of special links (called hyperlinks) that enable users to jump from one place to another in the web.

worm A program that attempts to travel between systems through network connections to spread infections. Worms can run independently of host file execution and are active in spreading themselves.

Z

zombie A computer that's controlled by a hacker who uses it to launch attacks on other computer systems.

Index